For Protection and Promotion

THE DESIGN AND IMPLEMENTATION
OF EFFECTIVE SAFETY NETS

For Protection and Promotion

THE DESIGN AND IMPLEMENTATION OF EFFECTIVE SAFETY NETS

Margaret Grosh, Carlo del Ninno, Emil Tesliuc, and Azedine Ouerghi

with the assistance of
Annamaria Milazzo and Christine Weigand

THE WORLD BANK
Washington, D.C.

IISBN-13: 978-0-8213-7581-5
eISBN: 13: 978-0-8213-7582-2
DOI: 10.1596/978-0-8213/7581-5

Library of Congress Cataloging-in-Publication Data

For protection and promotion: the design and implementation of effective safety nets / Margaret Grosh, Carlo del Ninno, Emil Tesliuc, Azedine Ouerghi
        p. cm.
    ISBN 978-0-8213-7581-5 (alk. paper) — ISBN 978-0-8213-7582-2
        1. Economic assistance, Domestic. 2. Poverty—Prevention. 3. Social policy. 4. Social planning.
    5. Poor—Services for. I. Grosh, Margaret E.
    HC79.P63F67 2008
    362.5'6—dc22

                                                                    2008032155

Cover design by Drew Fasick.

Contents

Appendixes

Glossary

References

Index

Boxes

Figures

Acknowledgments

In writing this book we benefited from the forbearance of our director, Robert Holzmann, and from the contributions of many colleagues. The Safety Net Primer steering committee provided useful input into the concept note and early outline of the study. Helpful comments were received from a quality enhancement review panel chaired by John Hoddinott and consisting of Van Adams, Harold Alderman, Tamar Manueylan Atinc, Kathy Lindert, Michael Lipton, Mamta Murti, Sandor Sipos, and Kalanidhi Subbarao. Jehan Arulpragasam, Tamar Manuelyan Atinc, Francisco Ferreira, John Hoddinott, and Kathy Lindert provided indispensable comments in their role as official peer reviewers. Comments on various chapters or sections were received from Harold Alderman, Francisco Ayala, Jeanine Braithwaite, Bénédicte de la Briere, David Coady, Aline Couduel, Indermit Gill, Markus Goldstein, Theresa Jones, Valerie Kozel, Maureen Lewis, Jennie Litvack, Daniel Mont, Demetra Nigthingale, Harry Patrinos, Robert Prouty, Carolina Sanchez-Paramo, Kalanidhi Subbarao, Cornelia Tesliuc, Steven Webb, and William Wiseman. John Blomquist was an important member of the team in the early years of work regarding the related suite of safety net primer papers and training, which helped to cement the knowledge that underlies the whole work, especially chapter 7. Emanuele Baldacci wrote a background note for a section of chapter 3; material from it is incorporated in table 3.2, and boxes 3.2, 3.3 and 3.4. Jane Hoddinott did much of the research for and first drafting of chapter 5, section 4. Lucian Pop contributed the analysis of the World Values Survey data. Asmara Achcar, Deni Sanchez, and Kaleb Tamiru helped locate background materials for chapters 9 and 10. Manorama Rani was in charge of document processing. Alice Faintich edited the document, Nita Congress laid it out, and Bob Elwood did the indexing. Paola Scalabrin arranged translations into Russian, Spanish, and Vietnamese and oversaw the production process along with Elizabeth Kline.

Preface

This book is part of a larger Safety Net Primer work program supported by the Social Protection Unit of the Human Development Network. The full work program comprises a variety of activities all designed to share information on the design and implementation of safety net programs around the world.

Safety Nets Primer Papers are good starting points to learn about an important aspect of safety nets. Some summarize international "good practices" on which there is a great deal of consensus. This is especially the case for papers on the most common types of interventions. Some primers present new research, such as the work commissioned on targeting. Other primers represent the views of individual thinkers, moving forward the international debate on themes where there is not yet firm consensus—for example, on issues of institutions, political economy or the role of safety nets in development policy. Still other primers offer case studies, such as the work on social safety net assessments in Latin America. Most Safety Nets Primer Papers are commissioned by the team, often with the support of the World Bank Institute or regional partners, to fill gaps in knowledge or as teaching tools. Other papers are the results of jointly sponsored work or work done by others that provides useful information to the primer's audience.

Primer Notes are brief pamphlets that distill the main messages of the underlying primer papers. They serve as a briefing for those who do not have time to read comprehensively on all aspects of safety nets, and as an introduction to those who will want to read more on the specific theme. A list of primer papers and notes is provided at the back of this book.

The team offers a variety of **training, workshops, and conferences** either based on primer materials or contributing to them. Together with the World Bank Institute, the team jointly offers an annual two-week, Washington, D.C.-based course, "For Protection and Promotion: The Design and Implementation of Effective Safety Nets," and periodically offers distance versions in English, French, Russian, and Spanish. A second week-long course, "How the Rich Protect Their Poor: Social Safety Nets in the Organisation for Economic Co-operation and Development," is offered on demand for small groups of countries. Occasional multiday workshops are organized on themes of importance. These have included three international conferences on conditional cash transfer programs, two workshops on protection for orphans and vulnerable children, and one workshop on food aid. Also, there are periodic internal training events and a brown-bag-lunch seminar series for World Bank staff.

The Web site of the Safety Nets team, **www.worldbank.org/safetynets**, is a comprehensive guide to its knowledge on safety nets. It contains primer papers and notes, often in several languages. It archives agendas, presentations, and papers from all the training events, workshops, and brown-bag seminars for the last several years. The Web site also contains a catalogue of World Bank projects and analytic work on safety nets. And it provides references to much other work—abstracts of, links to, and copies of hundreds of other papers on safety net programs or themes.

Abbreviations

AFDC	Aid for Families with Dependent Children (United States)
ATM	automated teller machine
BULOG	National Food Logistics Agency (Indonesia)
CCT	conditional cash transfer
EFC	error, fraud, and corruption
GDP	gross domestic product
GMI	guaranteed minimum income
JPS	Jaringan Pengaman Sosial (Social Safety Net) (Indonesia)
JRY	Jawahar Rozgar Yojana (Jawahar Employment Program) (India)
M&E	monitoring and evaluation
MDS	Ministry for Social Development and the Fight against Hunger (Brazil)
MEGS	Maharashtra Employment Guarantee Scheme (India)
MIS	management information system
MISSOC	Mutual Information System on Social Protection
MPCT	marginal propensity to consume out of the transfer
NGO	nongovernmental organization
OECD	Organisation for Economic Co-operation and Development
PDS	public distribution system
POS	point of service
PROGRESA	Programa de Educación, Salud y Alimentación (Education, Health, and Nutrition Program) (Mexico)
PSNP	Productive Safety Net Program (Ethiopia)
VAT	value added tax
WFP	World Food Programme

## CHAPTER 1

Introduction

All countries fund safety net programs for the protection of their people. Though an increasing number of safety net programs are extremely well thought out, adroitly implemented, and demonstrably effective, many others are not. This book aims to assist those concerned with social policy to understand why countries need social assistance, what kind of safety programs will serve them best and how to develop such programs for maximum effectiveness.

1.1 How Do Safety Nets Contribute to Development Policy?

Safety nets are part of a broader poverty reduction strategy—interacting with and working alongside of social insurance; health, education, and financial services; the provision of utilities and roads; and other policies aimed at reducing poverty and managing risk. Safety net programs can play four roles in development policy:

- **Safety nets redistribute income to the poorest and most vulnerable, with an immediate impact on poverty and inequality.** Most societies hold strong convictions that adequate provision for the poor is required, though they may differ in how this should be achieved.

- **Safety nets can enable households to make better investments in their future.** In this role, safety nets basically act to remedy credit market failures, allowing households to take up investment opportunities that they would otherwise miss—both in the human capital of their children and in the livelihoods of the earners.

- **Safety nets help households manage risk.** At minimum, safety net programs help households facing hard times avoid irreversible losses, allowing them to maintain the household and business assets on which their livelihoods are based, and to adequately nourish and school their children. At best, they can provide an insurance element that lets households make choices about livelihoods that yield higher earnings. Safety nets thus both protect households and promote their independence.

- **Safety nets allow governments to make choices that support efficiency and growth.** An adequate permanent social assistance system can fulfill whatever redistributive goals the society has, freeing other sectors from the role and letting them concentrate on efficient provision of services. Thus, for example, energy sectors can price for efficiency, and trade policy can focus on growth rather than job protection. Short-term safety net programs can compensate those negatively affected by needed reforms or who may oppose and stall these reforms.

Though useful, safety nets are not a panacea, and there are real concerns over whether they are affordable and administratively feasible or desirable in light of the various negative incentives they might create. In most settings where there is political will to do so, such concerns can be managed through a number of prudent design and implementation features. Much information and innovation exist on these topics; this book summarizes, references, and builds on this knowledge base to promote well-crafted safety nets and safety net policy.

1.2 What Is a Good Safety Net?

Safety net systems are usually woven of several programs, ideally complementing each other as well as complementing other public or social policies. A good safety net system is more than a collection of well-designed and well-implemented programs, however; it also exhibits the following attributes.

- **Appropriate.** The range of programs used and the balance between them and with the other elements of public policy should respond to the particular needs of the country. Each program should be customized for best fit with the circumstances.

- **Adequate.** The safety net system overall covers the various groups in need of assistance—the chronic poor, the transient poor, those affected by reforms, and all the various subsets of these groups. Individual programs should provide full coverage and meaningful benefits to whichever subset of the population they are meant to assist.

- **Equitable.** The safety net should treat beneficiaries in a fair and equitable way. In particular, it should aim to provide the same benefits to individuals or households that are equal in all important respects (horizontal equity) and may provide more generous benefits to the poorest beneficiaries (vertical equity).

- **Cost-effective.** Cost-effective programs channel most program resources to their intended target group. They also economize the administrative resources required to implement the program in two ways. First, at the level of the whole safety net system, they avoid fragmentation and the subsequent need to develop administrative systems without realizing economies of scale. Second, they run efficiently with the minimum resources required to achieve the desired impact, but with sufficient resources to carry out all program functions well.

- **Incentive compatible.** Safety nets can change households' behavior, for better or worse. To ensure that the balance of changes is positive, the role of safety nets should be kept to the minimum consistent with adequacy. The safety net system often may include programs that explicitly help build assets or incomes of their individual clients or communities by linking transfers to required or voluntary program elements. Public works programs can provide physical assets to communities. Conditional cash transfer programs build the human capital of households. Links to financial, job search, training, or social care services may help households raise their incomes.

- **Sustainable.** Prudent safety net systems are financially sustainable, in that they are pursued in a balanced manner with other aspects of government expenditure. Individual programs should be both financially and politically sustainable so that stop/start cycles of programs are avoided, as these result in enormous lost opportunities for efficient administration and the achievement of programs' promotive aspects. In low-income countries, programs started with donor support are gradually incorporated into the public sector.

- **Dynamic.** A good safety net system will evolve over time. The appropriate balance of programs will change as the economy grows and changes, as other elements of policy develop, or when shocks occur. The management of specific programs should also evolve as problems are solved and new standards set.

Much of the quality of a safety net is in the details of its implementation (figure 1.1). An adequate transfer program involves at the least a system to register clients, pay them, and eventually take them off the rolls. An exceptional program can entail much more—the minimal registry of clients is supplemented with strong outreach campaigns to ensure that errors of exclusion are low, a strong screening mechanism to ensure that ineligible people do not register, a mechanism to handle grievances, periodic monitoring of targeting

FIGURE 1.1 **Processes and Stakeholders Involved in a Safety Net**

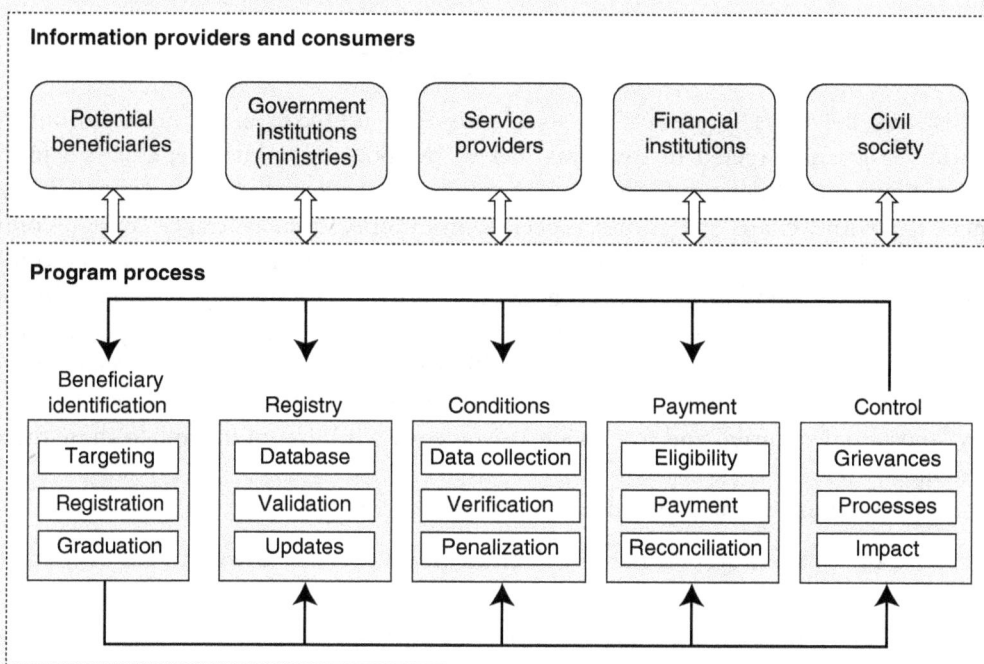

SOURCE: Adapted from Arribas-Baños and Baldeón 2007.

outcomes, and so on. The payment process may become more complex with differentiated payments, more convenient or sophisticated payment mechanisms, more attention to fraud and error control, and the like. A range of noncash benefits or requirements may be added to the program to help households improve their earnings. Monitoring and evaluation functions will take on increased importance the more complex the program becomes or the larger and more long lasting. Each of these functions requires systems, data, and interactions among different agencies or groups. Figure 1.1 shows some of these interactions.

In recent years, there has been a great deal of innovation and learning in safety nets and allied programs. This book focuses on these program "how to" aspects in their myriad details. Two overarching and linked lessons are stressed:

- **The quality of implementation is vital.** Good intentions are not sufficient; real working systems need to be developed. A badly implemented program is not worth doing. While numerous good examples exist to show that worthwhile programs are possible in many settings, there are still more programs that do not deliver all they could, and some do not deliver enough to be worth the money spent.

- **Good safety net programs require investments in their administrative systems.** Excessively high overheads are obviously undesirable—but so too are insufficient systems. Developing systems that allow programs to become their most effective and deliver the most value for the money will require some investment. An important part of that investment is development over time by self-critical and proactive managers.

1.3 What Is a Safety Net?

In this book, the terms "safety nets" or "social assistance" is used to refer to noncontributory transfer programs targeted in some manner to the poor or vulnerable; this is a fairly commonly accepted definition (box 1.1). Some writers, especially in the United States, equate this with welfare. Sometimes, especially in Europe, social assistance connotes only means-tested cash transfer programs, but we use the term much more broadly and often substitute the term safety nets to recognize the varied forms the programs take in the developing world. We recognize that safety net is not a particularly apt metaphor. In the circus, a safety net catches those who are falling from a height; in social policy, safety net programs are meant both to help catch those falling downward economically before they land into destitution and to provide assistance or a minimum income to those more permanently poor.

The programs we here include as common elements in a safety net follow:

- Cash transfers or food stamps, whether means tested or categorical as in child allowances or social pensions

- In-kind transfers, with food via school feeding programs or mother/child supplement programs being the most common, but also of take-home food rations, school supplies and uniforms, and so on

> **BOX 1.1 Definitions of Safety Nets and Social Assistance**
>
> - The **Asian Development Bank** defines social assistance as programs designed to assist the most vulnerable individuals, households, and communities meet a subsistence floor and improve living standards (Howell 2001).
> - The U.K. **Department for International Development** defines social assistance as noncontributory transfers to those deemed eligible by society on the basis of their vulnerability or poverty. Examples include social transfers and initiatives such as fee waivers for education and health, and school meals (DFID 2005).
> - **The International Labour Organization** defines social assistance as tax-financed benefits to those with low incomes (ILO 2000).
> - The **International Monetary Fund** defines safety nets as instruments aimed at mitigating possible adverse effects of reform measures on the poor (Chu and Gupta 1998a).
> - The **Organisation for Economic Co-operation and Development** defines social assistance as support targeted to households that are clustered within the lower segment of the income distribution and provided to prevent extreme hardship among those with no other resources, reduce social exclusion, minimize disincentives to paid employment, and promote self-sufficiency (Adema 2006).
> - The **Food and Agriculture Organization** defines social safety nets as cash or in-kind transfer programs that seek to reduce poverty by redistributing wealth and/or protect households against income shocks. Social safety nets seek to ensure a minimum level of well-being, a minimum level of nutrition, or help households manage risk (FAO 2003).

- Price subsidies meant to benefit households, often for food or energy
- Jobs on labor-intensive public works schemes, sometimes called workfare
- In-cash or in-kind transfers to poor households, subject to compliance to specific conditionalities on education or health
- Fee waivers for essential services, health care, schooling, utilities, or transport

The following further clarifies what this book does and does not consider under the rubric of safety nets.

- **Social protection.** As used here, safety nets do not include the rest of social protection—that is, social insurance programs such as pensions and unemployment insurance. To the extent that these schemes deliver benefits based on contributions of their own members, they are not safety nets; rather, they might be thought of as deferred compensation packages for affiliated employees.
- **Labor.** The extensive regulatory aspects of labor are separate from safety nets. Active labor market policies and income support to the unemployed are closely related to—and, indeed, sometimes directly overlap with—safety nets, but most of the programs used to these purposes are well covered elsewhere and are not discussed here.

- **Social policy.** In our nomenclature, safety nets are complemented by social insurance contributory programs such as pensions and unemployment insurance, and more broadly by the rest of social policy, especially in health and education, sometimes with important elements of housing or utility policy.

Because we define safety nets rather narrowly, their costs are lower than some people associate with safety nets. In Uruguay, for example, total social sector expenditure (social assistance, social insurance, health, education, and other) is quite high—accounting for between 20 and 25 percent of gross domestic product (GDP) between 2000 and 2005—but expenditures on safety nets per se are only 0.5 percent of GDP (World Bank 2007g). On average, expenditures on safety nets as we define them account for 1 to 2 percent of GDP, though sometimes much less or much more.

Finally, note that our definition concentrates on *publicly* financed safety nets—that is, those funded by national or local government or by official international aid. Most often, such safety nets are delivered by the state, although nongovernmental organizations may be used as well and certain functions contracted to the private sector. Even though private action via interhousehold transfers, community support arrangements, private religious contributions, private contributions to nongovernmental organizations, and other forms of charity may involve substantial flows of resources (indeed, sometimes exceeding public funds), and while the policy maker must understand the scope and shape of these privately financed safety nets, the main realm of public action is via publicly financed programs. Thus, this book focuses on the public sector.

A last point on terminology: Throughout the book, it is presumed that readers are familiar with policy areas such as social protection, social risk management, or poverty reduction, and the distinct but related concepts of poverty, vulnerability to poverty, vulnerable groups; social risk management instruments or arrangements; safety nets, social protection or social policy. For those who are not, a briefing is provided in appendix A.

1.4 How Is This Book Organized?

In designing and implementing effective safety nets, the big picture and the details have to fit together and so must both be kept in mind simultaneously. The traditional metaphor for this is to look at the big picture and then to zoom in on some detail within it. In the case of safety nets, the more appropriate metaphor might be a "picture in a picture" computer display where the big picture is kept crisp while the display with the finer detail is equally crisp as well. This presents something of a dilemma in writing a book which must be presented, if not necessarily read, linearly.

We have chosen to present the big picture at the beginning and end of the book, in chapters 2, 3, 9, and 10. Chapters 2 and 3 make the case for safety nets and their financing. Chapters 4 through 6 are the "how to" key processes of all safety nets; chapters 7 and 8 summarize design features and choices of specific interventions. Thus chapters 4 through 8 supply information that can help in assessing choices, culminating in a treatment in chapter 9 of principals to be used in "weaving" the safety net and fitting it into broader social policy. Chapter 10 illustrates how those principals lead to different variations of safety net systems and programs in different country circumstances. While this structure may make it seem that the big picture is initially left incomplete, the big decisions cannot be made wisely without a good understanding of the details involved.

We recognize that some readers will approach the material sequentially while others may sample different chapters or subchapters according to their interests. To assist both sets of readers, key messages for each chapter are presented at its beginning, and the following describes the main themes of each:

Chapter 2: The Case for Safety Nets. This chapter describes and illustrates the reasons for having safety nets—how they provide immediate redistribution and poverty reduction, how they allow households to invest in their children and their livelihoods, how they help households manage risk, and how the provision of safety nets can handle redistributive concerns thoroughly, thereby enabling governments to make more efficient policy choices in other sectors. The chapter then describes how safety nets fit within the broader policy agendas for poverty reduction, risk management, and social sectors. It also describes the principal challenges to the acceptance and use of safety nets, especially in low-income countries, and provides cross-references to other parts of the book where the details of overcoming these challenges are elaborated. The chapter emphasizes that safety nets are never the whole or sufficient answer to poverty reduction or risk management, but must be fitted appropriately into the existing policy context.

Chapter 3: Financing of and Spending on Safety Nets. Financing safety net programs is not theoretically different from financing any other government program and is therefore seldom discussed in the safety net literature, yet policy makers concerned with implementing or reforming safety nets face a constant stream of challenges regarding their finance. This chapter is targeted to this audience, providing a brief synopsis of some of the pertinent public finance literature with illustrations from safety net programs. The first section focuses on the theory of how much governments should spend on safety nets. This is followed by a review of special considerations about each of the possible sources of funds for safety nets—reallocations from other expenditures, increased tax revenues, grants, and loans. The chapter also discusses how to secure countercyclical finance, findings from the literature on whether expenditures on the welfare state impede economic growth, and new data on how much developing countries spend in order to allow benchmarking. The chapter concludes with a discussion of how to share finance among levels of government.

Chapter 4: Enrolling the Client: Targeting, Eligibility, and Intake. This chapter is the first of three on the processes common to all safety net programs. It briefly reviews the benefits and costs of targeting and the choice of targeting method. It then details how to implement four important steps that determine who is actually in the beneficiary group: precisely defining the eligibility criteria, conducting outreach to ensure low errors of exclusion, screening to ensure low errors of inclusion, and rescreening or exit policies to ensure that people move out of the program as appropriate. It concludes with a discussion of the administrative requirements to carry out these tasks. The chapter is a summary of a much wider body of literature and refers the reader to several other pertinent comparative studies.

Chapter 5: Benefit Levels and Delivery Mechanisms. This chapter brings together a dispersed body of knowledge on the conceptual and practical details of program benefits and payments. It covers how to determine what benefit levels might be and how to structure them, reviews issues of labor disincentives and how they can be handled via the benefit structure, describes program elements designed to move households toward independence through required or optional linkages to actions or services that are likely to help in that effort, and discusses how to handle payment mechanisms.

Chapter 6: Using Monitoring and Evaluation to Improve Programs. This chapter discusses the value added by and the know-how involved in developing and using monitoring and evaluation systems for safety net programs. A monitoring system is an essential management tool that regularly supplies information about how well a program is working so that program managers can take action to improve the program's implementation. Program evaluation refers to an external assessment of program effectiveness that uses specialized methods to ascertain whether a program meets some standards, to estimate its net results or impact, and/or to identify whether the benefits the program generates outweigh its costs to society. The chapter focuses on the most frequent types of evaluation used for safety net programs: process evaluation, assessment of targeting accuracy, and impact evaluation. For each type, guidance is given regarding the value of such an evaluation and how it should be conducted.

Chapter 7: Understanding Common Interventions. Because there is no single recipe for a safety net, policy makers must clearly understand the range of options they face. This chapter presents that menu of options: cash transfers of various sorts, food transfers, general price subsidies, public works, conditional cash transfers, and fee waivers for access to critical services. For each option, it describes key design features, outcomes, advantages, disadvantages, and lessons. The chapter emphasizes that even within a given type of program, there are many variations in detail and that how these are handled can modify the program for different circumstances and determine its degree of success. The chapter summarizes a vast literature and provides references to it. Many of the basic messages are not new, but many examples are fresh and the synthesis mature and useful.

Chapter 8: Assisting Traditionally Vulnerable Groups. This chapter outlines the issues concerned with assisting people with disabilities, the elderly, and orphans and vulnerable children. While the specifics vary somewhat, there are common themes in thinking about how to serve these groups via safety nets. A key issue is whether to have special programs for these groups or to serve them within the social assistance programs designed for the wider population. This is problematic, since the members of the groups are not all poor, yet the group as a whole is poorer than average and the members have some specific vulnerabilities. If they are to be helped by general social assistance programs, these programs may need to be modified somewhat. Moreover, income support is not the only public action needed to support these groups, and often it is not even the most important. Thus, the *coordination* of policy—or, in some cases, the integration of transfers and services—is even more important for these groups than social policy broadly speaking.

Chapter 9: Weaving the Safety Net. The objective of this chapter is to help policy makers and sector specialists choose the right mix of safety net policies and programs to meet national goals. The weaving of the safety net consists of two interrelated components: fitting individual programs into a congruent whole and ensuring that the safety net sector complements the country's other social policies. The chapter presents a four-step process to assess the safety net sector: (1) diagnosing the sources of poverty and vulnerability, (2) evaluating the effectiveness and efficiency of individual safety net interventions, (3) determining how to improve the safety net program mix, and (4) devising a concrete plan to implement the chosen strategy.

Chapter 10: Customizing Safety Nets for Different Contexts. This chapter discusses different country contexts and what they may imply for sensible safety net design and implementation. Six settings are covered—low income, middle income, in or following an economic crisis, following natural disasters, using safety nets to facilitate reform, and for rising food prices. For each setting, the chapter discusses how the safety net might be composed in terms of both the mix of programs and their specific tailoring to the situation at hand. Actual program examples are provided throughout.

The book also features two appendixes and a glossary. **Appendix A: Basic Concepts of Poverty and Social Risk Management** reviews social policy concepts used throughout the book to ensure a common understanding of key terminology and ideas. **Appendix B: Main Features of Selected Safety Net Programs** describes salient features of many of the programs from around the world discussed and used as illustrations throughout the book. It is intended as a selective reference on individual safety net programs.

With regard to these programs, a word of explanation is in order as to how we are referring to them throughout the book. In general, we here use the names by which the programs are most commonly known in the literature, regardless of whether that term is English, non-English, or an acronym. Thus, we refer to Argentina's Trabajar program, Indonesia's various JPS (Jaringan Pengaman Sosial, or Social Safety Net) programs, Jamaica's PATH initiative, and Mexico's PROGRESA, generally without translation or explication beyond an indication of their relevance to the discussion at hand. All of these programs are fully described, and their names and acronyms translated as necessary, in appendix B.

## CHAPTER 2

The Case for Safety Nets

KEY MESSAGES

Safety nets deserve a role in development policy in all countries. They mitigate extreme poverty through redistribution of resources; they help households invest in their future and manage risks; and they help governments make sound policy decisions in macro-economic, trade, labor, and many other sectors.

Safety nets face—and create—challenges to the implementing government. They compete for fiscal resources, require competent administration, and can result in negative incentives. These challenges demand prudent choices by program designers about the role, design, and implementation of safety nets. Fortunately, there are many options available to help manage the challenges.

Safety nets are never the whole or sufficient answer to poverty reduction or risk management. They must operate within the existing policy context and be balanced with existing or planned safety nets, social insurance, and other social or poverty alleviation policies. No single prescription fits all circumstances. The mix of support to the chronic poor, the transient poor, and vulnerable groups will be complex, and, until the safety net is adequate for all, the subject of difficult and controversial triage decisions.

> *"Nobody likes welfare—not the taxpayers who foot the bill, not the politicians who represent them, and not the poor who find welfare inadequate and personally degrading."*
> —*David Ellwood,* Poor Support: Poverty in the American Family

Safety nets contribute to poverty reduction and social risk management.[1] Yet their appropriate scope is a fraught subject, revealing deep ambivalence and controversy among policy makers, analysts, and the general public in many countries. The wide variation in attitudes toward safety nets can be seen in the following paraphrasings of commonly held views: *"We must provide for our poor—we can't let our children starve or the elderly beg." "Transfers discourage work among recipients and among those taxed to support them." "We don't need to give people fish, we need to give them fishhooks."*

This chapter shows how to reconcile these apparently contradictory and yet partially accurate views. It outlines the various arguments for having safety nets, describes the complementary role safety nets play in the broader set of poverty reduction policies and in providing adequate risk management options for the poor and the vulnerable, and outlines some of the challenges to safety nets' being an integral and permanent part of social policy in developing countries and how these can be managed.

2.1 Why Should Countries Have Safety Nets?

Safety nets can help achieve four objectives that are in turn part of larger poverty reduction and risk management goals.

- Safety nets and transfers have an immediate impact on inequality and extreme poverty.
- Safety nets enable households to make better investments in their future.
- Safety nets help households manage risk.
- Safety nets help governments make beneficial reforms.

As shown in figure 2.1, safety nets fit into the wider array of policies involved in poverty reduction, social risk management, and social protection. Safety nets are part, but not the whole, of each, and poverty reduction and risk management strategies overlap substantially but not entirely. Safety nets are not the only or even the principal tool for achieving any of the ends they serve, yet they can make a significant contribution. When situations are dire, they can help save lives. When situations are less dire—and programs are especially good—they can save or help build livelihoods as well.

FIGURE 2.1 **Where Safety Nets Fit in Larger Development Policy**

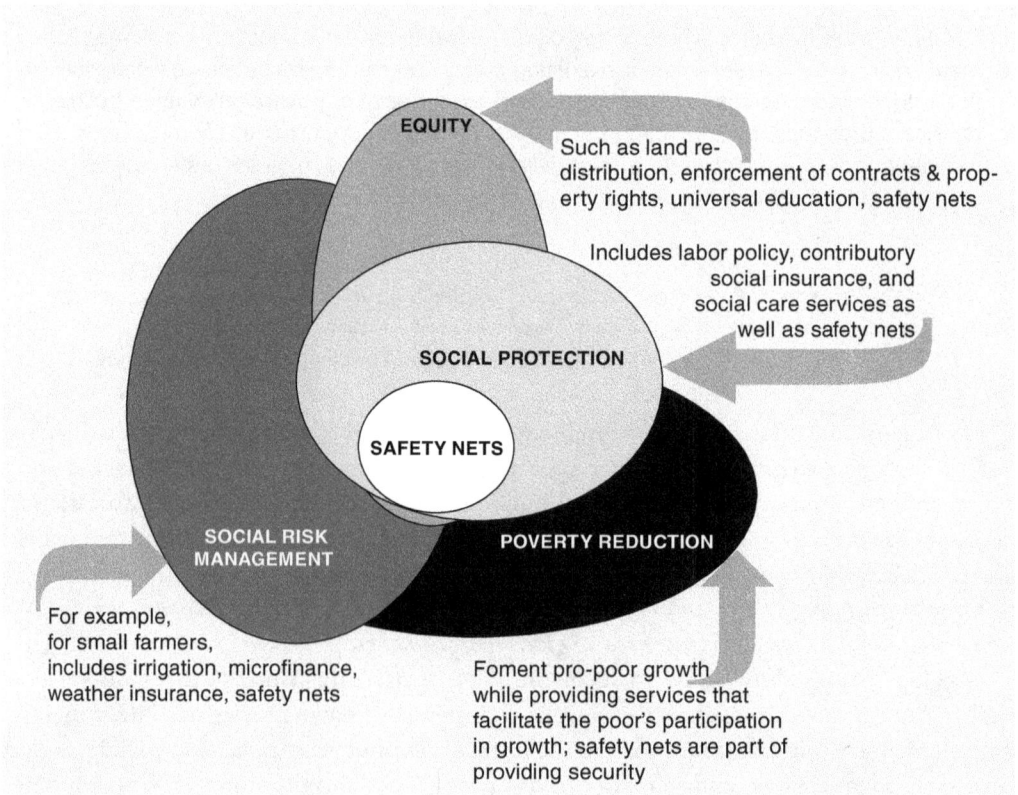

SOURCE: Authors.

NOTE: See appendix A for further explication of these concepts.

SAFETY NETS HAVE AN IMMEDIATE IMPACT ON REDUCING INEQUALITY AND EXTREME POVERTY

Safety nets can make poverty survivable or more bearable; this is their minimal function, accomplished simply by getting the transfers to the poorest.

Societies have understood and valued this function for centuries, often finding support for it in major religious teachings. For example, many of the rules set out in Deuteronomy concern social justice; chapter 15, verse 11, says, "There will always be poor people in the land. Therefore I command you to be openhanded toward your brothers and toward the poor and needy in your land." The New Testament contains similar teachings. Luke 3:11 says, "He who has two coats, let him share with him who has none; and he who has food, let him do likewise." The Koran enjoins (2:177) that " righteousness is that…and give away wealth out of love for Him to the near of kin and the orphans and the needy and the wayfarer and the beggars and for (the emancipation of) the captives, and keep up prayer and pay the poor-rate."

More secular, and technical, versions of the arguments that destitution and/or inequality are to be remedied are presented by modern liberal theories of economics, which posit a social welfare function that weights the welfare of the poorer more than the welfare of the less poor. These theories say, in essence, that society benefits more if a poor person receives an extra unit of income than if a rich person does. There are many variations on the theme and numerous ways of weighting among individuals and income levels (see Barr 2004 for a discussion), but the basic notion is the moral judgment that welfare gains for the poorer are more important to society than those for the less poor.

Popular support for such views is shown in opinion polls of private citizens and in summit documents signed by their governments. For example, the 2001 Latinobarómetro public opinion survey found that in all but 1 of the 18 countries surveyed, over 80 percent of the population believes the current distribution of country income to be unfair or very unfair (figure 2.2) This public attitude is also manifest in the international decrees signed by national governments. The Universal Declaration of Human Rights (UN 1948) implies social protection and safety net policies in article 25, stating, "Everyone has the right to a standard of living adequate for the health and well-being of himself and of his family, including food, clothing, housing and medical care and necessary social services, and the right to security in the event of unemployment, sickness, disability, widowhood, old age or other lack of livelihood in circumstances beyond his control." Article 23.3 goes further, saying, "Everyone who works has the right to just and favourable remuneration ensuring for himself and his family an existence worthy of human dignity, and supplemented, if necessary, by other means of social protection." (For a good discussion on right-based approaches to social protection, see Piron 2004.)

SAFETY NETS ENABLE HOUSEHOLDS TO MAKE BETTER INVESTMENTS IN THEIR FUTURE

Safety nets allow households to take up investment opportunities that they would otherwise miss—both with regard to the human capital of their children and the livelihoods of household earners—despite credit market failures. Specifically, safety net programs can contribute to capital accumulation among the poor by preventing the negative outcomes

FIGURE 2.2 Perceptions of Fairness of Country Income Distribution in Latin America

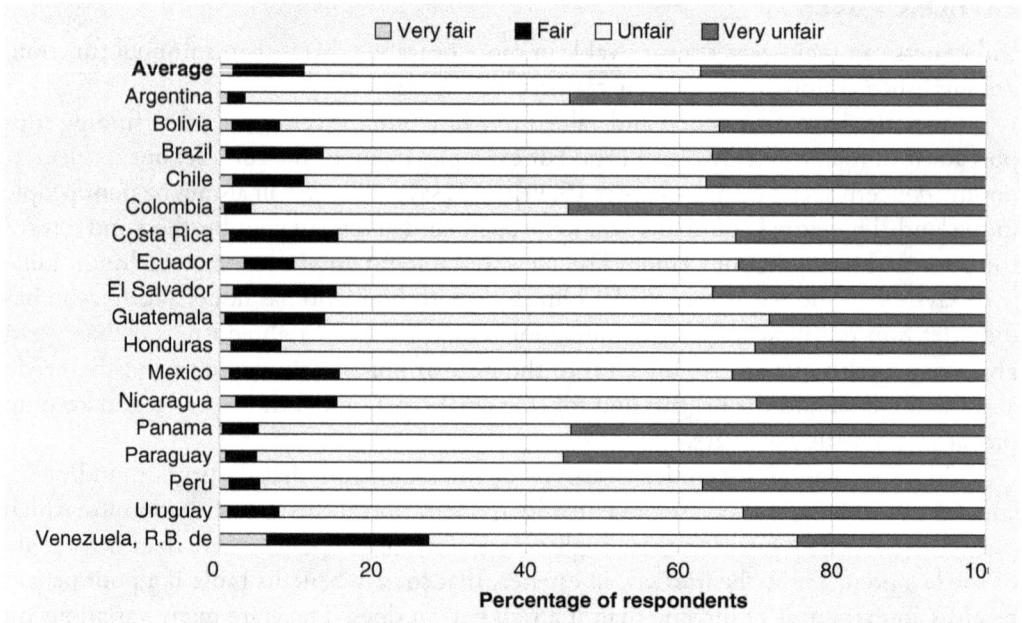

SOURCE: Lindert, Skoufias, and Shapiro 2006, p. 24. Responses to question: "Do you think that the income distribution is...?" posed in the 2001 Latinobarómetro.

of malnutrition and underinvestment in education, and by enabling investment in productive assets.

Preventing Malnutrition

Many children in developing countries are affected by malnutrition. In low-income countries, 43 percent of children aged 0–5 are underweight, compared to 11 percent of their peers in middle-income countries (World Bank 2006m). Within each country, the poor are disproportionately affected by malnutrition; in fact, the prevalence of malnutrition is often two to three times higher among the poorest income quintile than among the wealthiest (Wagstaff and Watanabe 2000). Malnutrition accounts for about half of the 10 million deaths each year among children aged 0–5 in developing countries (Wagstaff and Watanabe 2000). Moreover, there is strong scientific evidence that malnourished survivors are sicker, more disabled, weaker, less educated, and have a lower cognitive ability than better nourished counterparts.[2]

These outcomes are individually unacceptable and, in aggregate, reduce economic growth. The Food and Agriculture Organization has estimated that at least US$120 billion per year of benefits would be generated through the longer, healthier, and more productive lives of the 400 million people freed from food insecurity if the first Millennium Development Goal of halving hunger by 2015 were met (FAO 2002). The same report cites studies on India, Pakistan, and Vietnam that show that the combined effect of stunting and iodine and iron deficiencies reduced gross domestic product (GDP) by 2 to 4 percent per year. Not surprisingly, investments in reducing malnutrition are cost-effective. Behrman and

Rosenzweig (2001) estimate that every US$1 invested in an early childhood nutrition program in a developing country could potentially return at least US$3 worth of gains in academic achievement alone, without even considering the other benefits that would accrue.

Inadequate income can contribute to malnutrition by curtailing diets in quantity and quality; reducing access to services such as health, education, water, and sanitation; and affecting the knowledge and time available for and dedicated to adequate feeding of young children. The transfers inherent in safety net programs can allow households to increase the quantity and quality of food they consume. They can also help provide complementary inputs to good nutrition and alleviate constraints to adopting the behavioral changes promoted by nutritionists. They can, for example, enable households to purchase containers for transporting, storing, and treating water or to purchase water itself and soap so that promoted hygiene practices can be followed. In some cases, additional income may allow households to rearrange responsibilities so that children have more adequate caretakers, which would in turn facilitate the multiple active feeding sessions needed each day for very young and already malnourished children.

Many safety net programs have spillover effects beyond the direct transfer. The construction or maintenance of roads, markets, irrigation, drainage, domestic water supplies, schools, clinics, and the like accomplished through labor-intensive public works jobs can help improve livelihoods, food availability, and/or services for the poor. Prepared meals, take-home food rations, food stamps, and cash can all be (and often have been) linked to the use of health services, which usually include prenatal care, nutrition education, and growth monitoring; or to schools where children are then more accessible for nutrition education, deworming, vitamin supplements, or fortified school feeding.

Preventing Underinvestment in Education

There is ample and systematic evidence that chronically poor families are less likely to obtain adequate schooling for their children (World Bank 2005n). Children who do not have the opportunity to attend, or who are withdrawn early from school, face a lifetime of lower earnings (Hoddinott and Quisumbing 2003). Basic transfers can help households bear the direct costs of schooling—tuition and fees, transport, school supplies, uniforms. These costs can be quite substantial; a study of Bangladesh, Kenya, Nepal, Sri Lanka, Uganda, and Zambia undertaken by the United Kingdom's Department for International Development found that education spending was second only to food expenditures (DFID 1999). School fees alone can range from 5 to 20 percent of total household consumption (World Bank 2006c). And of course on top of the direct fees, the opportunity cost of the child's time for paid and unpaid labor must be taken into account.

Good safety net programs have been effective in helping households build human capital. The largest body of evaluation evidence comes from the new wave of conditional cash transfer (CCT) programs that condition receipt of benefits on meeting prescribed (often quite substantial) levels of service use. Evidence is very strong that these programs raise school enrollment rates (box 2.1), especially among the most disadvantaged groups, and can raise the use of health services. Social pension programs too, even though explicitly designed to protect the elderly poor, have had demonstrated effects on increasing the human capital of both children and the elderly in households (Carvalho 2000a; Case 2001; Duflo 2003).

BOX 2.1 The Motivating Force of Educational Stipends: The Bangladesh Female Secondary School Assistance Program

Selina is 18 years old. She hails from Daragaon Village under Chunarughat Upazila of Habiganj district. Selina comes from a poor family. There are seven brothers and sisters in her family, and Selina is the third oldest. Her father, Abdur Razzak, is a retired guard of the Daragaon Tea Estate. He has a piece of land that he cultivates, but this land is too small to support his family. Abdur Razzak has always been eager to educate his children, but he has not been able to afford to educate his first two children up to secondary school certificate level. The new Female Secondary School Assistance Program renewed his optimism that he will be able to provide Selina with such an education.

Selina was enrolled in Mirpur Girls High School in 1995, which is about five kilometers from her home. She received a regular stipend while attending grades 6–10. She used a part of the stipend money to pay for her commute to school; she had to walk about 1.7 kilometers to the Kamaichauri police box, from where she would catch a bus to the school. The commute was hard for Selina, but she knew that she had to maintain 75 percent attendance in school to continue getting the stipend, so she was seldom absent. Because of her regular attendance, she was able to improve her results every year; when she was first enrolled in grade 6 she was 72nd in her class, in grade 7 she was 6th, and in grade 8 she was 5th. In 2000, Selina passed the secondary school certificate exam in humanities with a B average.

SOURCE: Ahmed 2004a.

Investing in Productive Assets

Growing evidence indicates that cash assistance can help households not only subsist but actually improve livelihoods by investing a portion of the transfers they receive. Gertler, Martinez, and Rubio-Codino (2006) report that beneficiaries of Mexico's Oportunidades CCT program invested about 12 percent of their transfers, allowing them to raise their consumption by about a third after five and half years in the program. Earlier, Bezuneh, Deaton, and Norton (1988) found that food-for-work programs in northern Kenya during the lean season allowed households to purchase additional agricultural inputs and increase net returns from their farms by 52 percent. Sadoulet, de Janvry, and Davis (2001) note similar findings for PROCAMPO, Mexico's Program for Direct Assistance in Agriculture, which involves a transfer to farming households meant to compensate for income losses expected from the adoption of the North American Free Trade Agreement. Households invest the funds to purchase inputs and serve as collateral for borrowing, resulting in a positive multiplier effect in the range of 1.5 to 2.6 for the program.

This investment effect was found in social pension schemes as well in Bolivia, Brazil, and South Africa. The schemes studied are pure transfers targeted to the elderly for consumption purposes—a classic case of programs geared exclusively at avoiding destitution. Yet they have had important welfare impacts well beyond that goal. They have reduced poverty (Case and Deaton 1998); improved access to credit, thanks to the regularity of pension payments (Ardington and Lund 1995); and resulted in higher levels of investment in households' physical capital (Delgado and Cardoso 2000). More recent evidence from Bolivia's Bono Solidario program suggests that, in rural areas, pension recipients are investing their transfers in smallholder agriculture; as a result, their food consumption has gone up by twice the amount of the transfer received (Martinez 2005).

To allow households to invest, programs should offer benefits for a reasonably long period, and not withdraw them if the income or assets of the households increase slightly. It is not quite clear whether all safety net programs stimulate investment among their typically poor beneficiaries with the effect proportionate on the size of the benefit. Some (see Carter and Barrett 2006, for example) argue that there are "threshold effects"—that is, until households reach a certain minimum threshold of welfare, they cannot invest effectively. The literature on this is incipient, and the evidence is not clear (see Lentz and Barrett 2005). The idea of such a minimum is consonant with the fact that the programs for which clear investment impacts have been shown have benefit levels higher than average in developing countries. Of course this may also be, at least in part, because the measurement of such effects is difficult and effects are easier to observe if they are large.

Public works programs can help achieve the longer run welfare of households or communities through a different investment channel—the construction or maintenance of infrastructure that yields services to households. Access to roads can help households get their products to market; journey to work outside their villages; or obtain health, education, or other government services. In Bangladesh, Khandker, Bakht, and Koolwal (2006) found that certain road improvement projects led to a 27 percent increase in agricultural wages and an 11 percent increase in per capita consumption. Road improvement also led to an increase in schooling of both boys and girls.

SAFETY NETS HELP HOUSEHOLDS MANAGE RISKS

When families, especially poor families, face reductions in income or assets, they may resort to costly coping strategies that perpetuate poverty, such as selling their most productive assets. Moreover, when risk becomes too threatening, households may try to reduce it, thereby making livelihood choices that reduce their earnings. A good safety net can reduce the need for either of these strategies which can trap households in poverty.

Reducing the Incidence of Negative Coping Strategies

There is clear evidence that families that suffer from short-term shocks may be forced to cut back on the feeding or schooling of their children; deterioration in nutritional or health status is found more often than withdrawals from school. Thus, Peruvian children suffered higher infant mortality during the country's 1988–92 economic crisis (Paxson and Schady 2004). Enrollment rates dropped during the Indonesian financial crisis, especially for the poor and those in rural areas (Frankenberg, Thomas, and Beegle 1999). Hoddinott and Kinsey (2001) trace a whole series of effects on Zimbabwean children who were 12–24 months old when affected by a drought. They show that stunted preschoolers will have lower height during adolescence, will delay school enrollment, and will reduce grade completion. The magnitudes of these impacts are quite large: the 1982–4 drought shock resulted in a loss of stature of 2.3 centimeters, 0.4 grades of schooling, and a school start delay of 3.7 months for this age group. Using estimates of the values for the returns to education and age/job experience in the Zimbabwean manufacturing sector, the researchers calculate the shock impact as translating to a 7 percent loss in lifetime earnings for the affected children. Safety net programs can help prevent such losses.

In the absence of safety nets, shocks may force poor households with low coping capacity to sell their productive assets. Families that have to disinvest in their livelihoods—eating their seed grain; selling their draft animals or the tools of their small enterprise; or defaulting on rent or mortgage payments and consequently losing their homes, farms, or workshops—will find it very difficult to rebuild their earning capacities. The effect will be all the more marked if there are inadequate credit markets,[3] and, as discussed in boxes 2.2 and 2.3, the assets required to rebuild livelihoods are relatively large or lumpy so that a family must make a big purchase before it can return to its full earnings potential (Carter and others 2004; Fafchamps, Udry, and Czukas 1998; Jalan and Ravallion 2002; Lokshin and Ravallion 2000). In the wake of Hurricane Mitch in Honduras, for example, Carter and others (2007) calculate that a loss of 10 percent of a poor household's assets would result in a rate of growth in household income over the following 2.5 years 18 percent lower than if the assets had not been lost; a similar loss of assets would lower the growth rate of richer households by only 9 percent.

> BOX 2.2 **The Loss of an Ox**
>
> The long-run effects of asset loss are powerfully illustrated in this case study:
>
> > Ato Mohammed, 55 and illiterate, resides in the Bati district of South Wollo Zone (Ethiopia) and heads a household of nine. He has [sic] been chronically food insecure for more than 10 years when he lost his only oxen due to drought. He sold the animal to buy food at the time and has not been able to acquire another. Currently, Mohammed holds one hectare of farm land and he has no grazing land. Since he owns no oxen, he has been leasing out the land for share-cropping on a 50/50 sharing arrangement. Mohammed and his family members are engaged in various types of daily labor activities for cash and food, and the household is a regular recipient of food aid.
> >
> > Mohammed asserts "oxen are the crucial productive asset that would liberate me from this insecurity trap." On the other hand, however, he does not want to take credit from a regional credit organization to buy an ox as he does not want to be indebted and fears that the debt may be passed on to his children if he fails to repay. He fears that the ox may die due to lack of adequate feed or animal diseases for which there is no dependable animal health service in the community. He also fears that he may not be able to pay back since crop failure is frequent due to insects and droughts. (Carter and others 2007, pp. 835–36).

When available, safety nets have reduced the incidence of negative coping strategies. For example, in response to the financial crisis of 1998, the Indonesian government put in place a system of targeted fee waivers for public health care and scholarships for poor schoolchildren. Both programs have been evaluated to show that service use fell less among recipient households than they would have in the absence of the programs (Cameron 2002; Saadah, Pradhan, and Sparrow 2001). Children benefiting from the pilot cash transfer scheme in Kalomo District, Zambia, are eating better and are less underweight (MCDSS and GTZ 2007). CCT programs targeted to the chronic poor have helped beneficiaries affected by shocks withstand them (see de Janvry, Sadoulet, and others 2006 for a review). In Nicaragua and Honduras, beneficiary households hit by the coffee crisis were able to

BOX 2.3 **A Poverty Trap in Shinyanga**

In Shinyanga, cattle are a high-return investment (25 to 30 percent annually). Cattle are also a liquid asset that can be used for consumption smoothing, which makes cattle ownership attractive. But they are also a lumpy investment. Wealthier rural households have been found to specialize in cattle rearing, while poorer households derive a larger share of their income from off-farm activities. Differences in comparative advantage do not offer a convincing explanation for this phenomenon. Households specializing in off-farm activities have much lower incomes but are unlikely not to have the skills required because cattle rearing is a traditional activity in the area.

The lack of credit markets and the indivisibility of cattle imply that households must be able to put up relatively large amounts of money to invest in cattle rearing. However, poor households with low initial endowments from which only low incomes are earned find it hard to save enough to invest in cattle. That problem is exacerbated by the fact that, because of low endowments, the poor have limited ability to cope with shocks. Consequently, such households enter into safe, lower-return activities, making saving even harder. That combination of factors explains why poorer households specialize in off-farm activities (such as weeding or casual labor) that require few skills or investments but are safe. That pattern effectively traps poor households in poverty, despite the attractive investment opportunities that exist in the area.

SOURCE: Dercon 1997.

maintain their children's schooling and not increase child labor. In Nicaragua's case, consumption did not fall as much as for nonbeneficiary families; in Honduras, adults were able to increase their labor. In Mexico, beneficiary children in households that were hit by shocks were able to maintain their school enrollments, in contrast to similarly affected nonbeneficiary families.

Managing Risks Ex Ante

Families that are so poor they cannot afford a bad year may minimize the variance of their incomes in ways that also lower the means. They may plant low-risk, low-return crops; abstain from investments in fertilizer; diversify activities rather than specialize in those with highest return; and keep savings in liquid but low-return forms. The evidence of the cost of such ex ante risk management mechanisms is hard to compile, and mostly comes from very poor rain-fed smallholder agriculture or pastoralism; intuition suggests that the issue could apply equally well to poor urban households. The calculated impact in studies to date is quite substantial (see Dercon 2006 for a review), indicating that the poor sacrifice as much as a quarter of their income in return for greater security.

The underlying problem faced by the poor in addressing risk management is a lack of insurance against risk. Some safety net programs can provide an insurance function to help households avoid taking ex ante risk management decisions that lower their incomes.[4] If households could know that in the event of a bad year they would have reliable access to a safety net program, they could make their income and investment decisions based more on return and less on security. Walker, Singh, and Asokan (1986) quantified this effect to some extent when looking at the income streams for landless agricultural laborers in two

Indian villages, one in which the statewide Maharashtra Employment Guarantee Scheme operated and one in which it did not. Households in program villages had 50 percent less variable income streams than did their nonprogram counterparts. Ravallion (1991) contrasts the high correlation of distress land sales with famines in Bangladeshi villages and the lack of such correlation in India, where public works programs were operating.

For safety net programs to deliver this insurance effect, they must provide a credible ex ante guarantee of quick assistance in time of need—something that few programs to date have done. For example, a program could, like the Maharashtra Employment Guarantee Scheme, provide a minimum number of days of employment on a guaranteed public works initiative. India's new National Employment Guarantee Scheme is meant to deliver such an insurance benefit, but evidence of its impact is not yet available. Another approach could be a cash transfer with a means test or other entry criterion sufficiently agile to permit new entrants to be assessed and granted benefits promptly when their incomes decline. A few Eastern European programs have managed this. Regardless of approach, the program must have an adequate budget, since the guarantee of an adequate income floor is critical to the change in risk-taking behavior sought. Because this guarantee has rarely been available to households in practice and over long enough periods for them to gain confidence in it, the role of safety nets in ex ante risk management has been largely unrealized to date.

SAFETY NETS HELP GOVERNMENTS MAKE BENEFICIAL REFORMS

Safety nets can support good social policy with varying degrees of directness. A strong social assistance program can directly replace inefficient redistributive elements in other programs. Less directly, safety nets play a role in helping governments adopt or sustain sound macroeconomic, trade, and other policies. Least directly, safety nets may reduce inequality over the short term, thus tempering the high inequality harmful to the development of sound institutions that underlie good policy and governance.

Replacing Inefficient Redistributive Elements in Other Programs

Many sectors and programs historically have intertwined equity and efficiency goals; the general thrust of recent policy has been to focus on efficiency. Recognition of the need to think explicitly about the distributional impact of these policy reforms has been manifest in the call in the development community for "poverty and social impact analysis" to be part of the policy decision process (see World Bank 2003i). The goal is to design reforms with fewer losses to the poor or that compensate them, sometimes through sector-specific compensatory mechanisms, but often through a more general safety net program as discussed below. Indeed, Kanbur (2005) and the World Bank (2005n) suggest that the use of a specialized redistributive mechanism such as a permanent transfer program is preferable to designing specific compensatory packages for each reform option.

Take the example of labor markets. The growing consensus is that for them to be efficient and play their role in an investment climate conducive to growth and poverty reduction, they must be relatively flexible. Further, they must aim to protect workers, who will likely change jobs at least once and possibly several times over the course of their lives, rather than protect jobs per se. This focus implies a lessening of the role of labor market regulation in worker protection and an improvement of income support to the unemployed. Safety nets, especially in the form of workfare schemes, may be a sensible means of providing such income support. They can be used to complement unemployment insurance, as they were in Argentina and the Republic of Korea; or as substitutes for it, which was done in Bolivia and Peru (Vodopivec 2004; World Bank 2004e).

Eastern Europe and Central Asia's experience with utility pricing provides another example of how the provision of social assistance can enable efficient policies in other sectors (Lampietti 2004; Lovei and others 2000; Saghir 2005; Shopov forthcoming; World Bank 2000b). Gas, electricity, and heat prices were set very low during the socialist era. With the transition to the market, this practice became unsustainable and by the mid-1990s could no longer go unaddressed. Utility companies could not continue to shoulder the losses, and governments lacked the resources to cover the costs of the price subsidies. Domestic utility prices had to rise, and countries experimented with ways to reform the sector for greater efficiency while protecting consumers at least partially.

Some countries chose to ensure a minimum provision of utility services explicitly via social assistance rather than implicitly through utility pricing. This approach has much to recommend it. It makes both the subsidy budget and the efficiency of the utility company more explicit and transparent. It allows for greater targeting, if that is desired, and can take advantage of eligibility and payment systems common to other social assistance programs. The approach also provides appropriate economic incentives to consumers, as they will save by reducing usage. In Bulgaria, for example, the same staff administers the heating allowances system and the Guaranteed Minimum Income Scheme, using broadly the same methods, instruments, and budget level—0.23 percent of GDP for each program. However, eligibility thresholds are higher for the heating allowance, and the benefit is paid only during the cold months of the year. Where a social assistance program exists or can feasibly be created, such as Brazil's Auxilio Gás (Cooking Gas Grant) program, it can take the burden of social guarantees off utility companies and allow them to focus on efficient service provision.[5]

Facilitating Changes in the Economy Aimed at Supporting Growth

There will be less opposition to reform when there are mechanisms to compensate losers or to assist the poor who often become poorer during a downturn; less opposition to reform allows for better macroeconomic policy and growth. Rodrik (1998) provides supporting empirics for this premise, looking at the presence of mechanisms for societal conflict resolution (safety nets and social insurance among them), macroeconomic policies, and robust growth. See box 2.4 for how the U.S. Federal Reserve Board chairman recently explained the issue in a business context and box 2.5 for an account of how the British Poor Laws helped fuel the agricultural revolution which in turn fueled the industrial revolution.

Following the Latin American debt crisis of the 1970s and 1980s, many governments in the region implemented structural adjustment policies—macroeconomic and sectoral policies designed to downsize ailing branches of the economies that generated losses or that were kept afloat via costly fiscal or quasi-fiscal subsidies. These policies would allow a more efficient use of resources over the medium term. However, over the short term, workers in the affected industries would lose their jobs, suppliers to these industries would lose business, and so on. Governments soon recognized that safety nets could facilitate these reforms with immediate costs and delayed benefits. Chile, for example, instituted a

---

BOX 2.4 A Policy Maker's Take on Growth, Equality, and Policy

Steven Pearlstein (2007, p. D1) of the *Washington Post* discusses U.S. Federal Reserve Board Chairman Bernanke's speech to the Omaha Chamber of Commerce:

> Perhaps the best part of Bernanke's speech yesterday was the graceful way he framed the tradeoff between growth and equality.
>
> One reason the U.S. economy is the most productive, the most dynamic, the most innovative in the world, Bernanke explained, is that we offer the biggest rewards to skill, effort and ingenuity. We also have an economic framework that not only allows companies and individuals the flexibility to adapt to changes in technology or consumer tastes or competition, but rewards them handsomely when they do. Bernanke says the flip side of this dynamism has been to generate not only a higher level of inequality, but also a higher level of economic insecurity. Now, he says, the only way to make these politically acceptable is to "put some limits on the downside risks to individuals affected by economic change."
>
> One way to limit those risks, of course, would be to restrict trade, impose new regulations on labor and product markets, or use the tax code to massively redistribute incomes. For Bernanke, the costs in terms of slower growth and higher unemployment would be too high. The better alternative, he argued, is to preserve the political consensus for open and flexible markets by offering Americans a stronger economic safety net.

---

large public employment program in 1975 which continued for several years to accompany deep reforms of its economy (Raczynski and Romaguera 1995). Bolivia instituted an Emergency Social Fund in 1987; the World Bank's loan in support of it was the first project by the agency specifically designed to protect the poor during a macroeconomic adjustment initiative (Jorgensen, Grosh, and Schacter 1992). Such support has become widely accepted over the years. For example, Chu and Gupta (1998b, p. v) summarize the International Monetary Fund's position on the issue, noting that "the only realistic alternative is to proceed with the necessary adjustment policies but complement them with the adoption of social safety nets."

This logic might suggest that a safety net is a temporary solution to be implemented in the wake of a crisis. However, experience has shown that it is difficult to start a program from scratch and get it up and running during a crisis. One of the features of safety net policy most agreed on after the East Asian financial crisis was that safety net programs should be built during good times and expanded during bad; the Asian Pacific Economic Consortium's lessons and guidelines paper notes:

> Social safety nets should be in place before a crisis occurs. Permanent, rather than ad hoc, social safety nets can more effectively protect the poor from the adverse effects of crises without compromising longer-term goals. During good economic times, social safety net instruments help to alleviate poverty among the chronically poor and those suffering from the effects of non-economic shocks (APEC 2001, p. 6).

Fostering More Inclusive Growth

Transfers play both direct and indirect roles in reducing inequality. Reducing inequality should help create a "virtuous circle," leading to more inclusive institutions and thus indirectly to better policy and higher growth.

BOX 2.5 **The Developmental Effects of the Elizabethan Poor Laws**

The famous British Poor Laws were written in 1598 and 1601. They provided a system of social security—relief in kind for the "helpless" poor (the ill, the elderly, children), workfare or wage subsidies to the able-bodied, apprenticeships to children, and foster care for orphans. The poor laws were centrally mandated, but wholly financed by local property taxes and implemented at the parish level. Of course, their application varied from place to place and over the centuries. The World Bank provides an interesting view of their impacts on economic development:

> The comprehensive social security system provided by the Poor Laws had a number of highly significant economic consequences. In combination with laws (dating from the thirteenth century) granting complete alienability of land, it encouraged labor mobility and reduced the attachment to land holding as the only form of security for peasants. Individuals had a relative certainty of being provided for, wherever they moved to work in the economy, no matter what their property-ownership status. Landlords and farmers could reap the economic gains to be had from increased farm sizes, from enclosure, and from laying off workers or changing their labor contracts to more efficient weekly or day labor, without provoking the same degree of peasant protest as occurred on the continent. But equally, employers in England had a strong incentive only to do this if it made economic sense because, through the Poor Law, they would also have to reckon with their liability to pay for the families of the laid-off workers (World Bank 2005n, p. 120).

New evidence is emerging that high levels of inequality can be costly to growth and poverty reduction (see De Ferranti and others 2004 and World Bank 2005n for extensive literature reviews). High inequality slows economic growth and development itself. When political and economic inequalities are great, they can lead to the development of institutions and policy choices that favor the generation of profits to particular groups rather than a broader base of growth. This narrowing of benefits is in turn bad for the investment, innovation, and risk taking that underpin long-term growth.

As an example, Haber (2001) attributes the large economic gap that opened between the United States and Mexico during the 19th century to the difference in the competitiveness of their banking industries, which reflected the differences in political institutions in the two countries at that time. In the United States, political institutions allocated power to a broad base of people who wanted access to credit and loans, which led governments to allow free entry into banking sectors—which in turn resulted in a highly competitive market, low interest rates, and high investment rates. In contrast, Mexican political institutions granted banking monopoly rights to a cabal of political supporters, which resulted in an oligopolistic market structure and lower levels of credit and investment, but generated high profits for the select few. Initial differences reinforced themselves, resolving in the United States into a virtuous circle and in Mexico, a vicious one.

High levels of inequality can also hamper the ability to manage economic volatility and worsen the quality of macroeconomic response to shocks. With higher inequality, the institutions responsible for sharing the burdens of adjustment work less well, and definitive policies are harder to establish. The sluggish growth performance in Latin America following the oil shock of 1973 is explained, in a cross-country regression setting, by the higher income and land inequality and higher murder rate during that period (Rodrik

1999). High levels of inequality may make violent crime more pervasive, and crime is bad for growth. In Jamaica, a 1 percent increase in youth violence was estimated to decrease tourism revenue by 4 percent (World Bank 2003e).

The direct role of transfers in redistribution is obvious and can be effective. Brazil's Bolsa Familia (Family Grant) and Mexico's Oportunidades programs each reach about a quarter of the national population with benefits of about a quarter of household base income. They lower the respective countries' Gini coefficients by 2.7 points, or about 5 percent. These unusually large impacts are due to the size and relative generosity of the programs involved. In Latin America as a whole, the full tax and transfer system reduces the Gini for incomes by only 2 points; in Europe, the Gini for disposable incomes is 15 points lower than that for market incomes (Perry and others 2006). This finding suggests that there is more room for tax and transfer policies in reducing high inequality in Latin America, and likely in many countries outside the region with similarly high levels of inequality.

Additional Empowerment Effects

Indications—albeit tending more toward anecdotal than econometric evidence—that safety nets may have empowerment effects that go beyond the transfer of income are beginning to emerge. These effects seem to stem from the way programs can pull their participants into new roles. CCTs, for example, have been shown to increase enrollments, especially in secondary school. In the long run, the increase in education achieved should lower inequalities in education, thereby lowering inequality in autonomous incomes. It should also ensure nation-building benefits of shared education and, if schools offer a sense of connectedness, help youth steer clear of costly risky behaviors. The impacts on enrollment are greatest for the most disadvantaged beneficiaries—the poor, females, and ethnic minorities—which should imply that the empowerment effects will be greatest for them too (World Bank forthcoming).

There are intriguing, if not yet well-documented, indications that some CCT programs may have even farther-reaching subtle and qualitative effects. In Colombia, mothers have to go to their children's schools regularly to handle the associated paperwork. Program officials report that this increased frequency of contact is breaking down traditional status-based barriers to teacher-parent communication (Combariza 2006). Levy (2006) reports that in Mexico, communities are now putting greater pressure on teachers to reduce their absenteeism. Participation in community groups is giving poor women new experiences in leadership and community action. In Turkey, women are registering marriages and children who would otherwise have been undocumented and are thus gaining protection under family law; they are also going to government offices, banks, and town centers to handle program-related paperwork—a type of errand many of the Kurdish mothers have never performed (Ahmed and others 2007). Voter turnout among the poor was higher in Brazil's 2006 presidential run-off than expected, which some analysts attribute to the workings of Bolsa Familia (Hunter and Power 2007), indicating that political power is being shifted along with economic power. These indirect effects of safety net programs seem to work toward increasing the inclusion or voice of the poor in ways that complement and reinforce the increase in income and may contribute to the formation of a virtuous circle.

SAFETY NETS FOR PROTECTION AND PROMOTION

The role of safety nets and their objectives show that they can have a protection and promotion function. They protect the poor from the worst of destitution and from falling deeper into poverty when faced with an economic shock. They also promote independence, allowing households to invest and thereby improve their livelihoods, and allowing governments to choose more efficient policies, which result in stronger growth and possibly higher levels of consumption for all households.

To meet these various roles, objectives, and functions, safety nets must incorporate specific design features (table 2.1). For a safety net to be able to protect the extreme or chronic poor from the full burden of their poverty, the net transfer (excluding the taxes that finance the transfer) must be redistributive, and its effects will be greater for more marked degrees of redistribution. Individual households facing shocks can be protected from irreversible losses if they gain access to the program in time; thus, program entry criteria and processes must be sufficiently open. Benefits will be proportional to the number of needy served—even if some cannot be accommodated, protection will be effective for those who are. The requirements are more demanding for safety nets to help households manage risk ex ante, since households must have a credible guarantee that assistance will be available when needed. Thus, both the intake processes and budget must be flexible and sufficiently demonstrated for households to trust the program. Promotion via assistance to sound government policy choices will be best achieved through a safety net that is permanent, but that can expand or add elements as needed to deal with specific shocks or reforms.

TABLE 2.1 **Safety Nets for Protection and Promotion**

Safety net role/objective	Nature of benefit		Design elements required to deliver benefit
	Protection	Promotion	
Provide transfers that can accomplish redistribution	X		Progressive redistribution at least, often narrow targeting is chosen
Enable households to make better investment in their future		X	May be inherent; evidence unclear whether any size transfer is enough for a promotive effect or whether transfers must move a household above a certain threshold to realize this effect
Help households manage risks			
• Avoid irreversible losses	X		• Easy access once need is felt
• Allow higher risk/return activities		X	• Credible guarantee that help will be available when needed
Help government make sound choices	X	X	Base safety net would be permanent; may be supplemented in times of covariate shock or with temporary compensatory programs to accompany some reforms

SOURCE: Authors.

Various arguments suggest that good safety nets should contribute to growth. This is, however, a difficult claim to substantiate with robust empirical evidence. Where effects should be direct—for example, safety nets allowing households to overcome credit market deficiencies and make productive investments—there is evidence at the household level but not at the community or macroeconomic level. Even if household effects are large, the weight of these households in total production is small, so the macroeconomic effects may not be large in aggregate, although clearly important in poverty reduction. A more substantial aggregate effect on efficiency or growth might be expected where social assistance enables sectoral, trade, or macroeconomic reforms. However, because the causal chain is rather long and indirect, it remains impossible to quantify the full benefits of safety net policy.

It must also be acknowledged that many safety net programs and systems operated today do not meet all the requirements to deliver their potential benefits. Few programs operate with credible guarantees and so are unlikely to change household ex ante risk management decisions. Many offer insufficient coverage or benefits to yield large protection or promotion effects. And a few are admittedly outright failures of administration. Nonetheless, the general trend is toward more substantial safety nets, more sophisticated understandings of how to run them, and more credible estimates of their impacts. In 10 years, both safety net practices and the evidence of their worth will likely be much stronger than is the case today.

In the interim, it is probably safe to say that relatively few policy makers or voters fully perceive the efficiency-enhancing role of safety nets, and base their support primarily on the redistributive rationale. This undervaluation of safety nets probably leads to their underprovision.

2.2 How Do Safety Nets Fit in Wider Development Policy?

Safety nets, while extremely useful, are never the only or wholly sufficient solution to poverty and risk. Rather, they are part of a country's development policy. To determine the parameters of their role and see how safety nets fit in with the other instruments a government uses to address poverty and risk, it is useful to examine which groups of households can and should benefit from safety net programs.

Safety nets may serve one or a combination of the following groups:

- **Chronic poor.** Members of this group lack the assets (broadly defined) to earn sufficient income, even in "good" years. The Chronic Poverty Research Centre (2004) estimates that between 300 and 420 million people are chronically poor. This is a substantial subset of the 1 billion people—18 percent of the world's population—who live on less than US$1 per day (Chen and Ravallion 2007).[6]

- **Transitory poor.** Members of this group earn sufficient income in good years but fall into poverty, at least temporarily, as a result of idiosyncratic or covariate shocks ranging from an illness in the household or the loss of a job to drought or macroeconomic crisis. Transient poverty is apparently very substantial. Baulch and Hoddinott (2000) review a number of studies that show that, in a typical year, anything up to half of the US$1 per day poor may be "transient" poor, meaning that their stay in poverty will be relatively short—less than one, two, or five years, depending on the study.

- **Vulnerable groups.** Membership in these groups overlaps with the chronic and transient poor since these same individuals may also have low assets or face shocks. However, some individuals within these groups will not be poor, especially where the vulnerability is an individual one and the individual is part of a nonpoor family or community. Some large vulnerable groups commonly served by safety nets are listed below; there will be others that are locally pertinent, such as minority ethnic groups.
  - **People with disabilities.** Statistics are problematic, but 10 to 15 percent of the world's population may be disabled, with 2 to 3 percent with severe disabilities that put them in need of income support (Mont 2007; WHO 2008).
  - **Elderly.** People aged 60 and above account for about 10 percent of the global population at present; this proportion is projected to reach about 21 percent by 2050. About 12 percent of this elderly population is older than 80; this proportion is expected to increase to about 19 percent by 2050 (UN 2002).
  - **Orphans.** There are 143 million orphans (children who have lost one or both parents) in Asia, Sub-Saharan Africa, and Latin America and the Caribbean; of these, 16 million are double orphans who have lost both parents. In some countries, as many as 15 percent of all children are orphans (UNAIDS/UNICEF/USAID 2004)
  - **Refugees.** There are 20.5 million international and internal refugees, returned refugees, internally displaced people, asylum seekers, and stateless people (UNHCR 2003).
- **Losers in reforms.** The number of losers, and the extent of their loss, is very reform specific. Global numbers for this category are thus unavailable, and analysis must be conducted for each case. Policy makers can then determine how broadly or narrowly to focus compensation and how much is required.

Because transitory poverty can be as high as half of total poverty, most societies will feel the need for safety nets both to help households cope with shocks and to provide some sort of assistance for the chronically poor. These two groups overlap incompletely with those with specific vulnerabilities, making the triage process yet more complex. Transfer policy also is often motivated by a desire to compensate losers in the reform of other schemes that have affected patterns of income or welfare. The losers may not be poor, but transfers may be called upon to compensate them.

The challenge is to strike the right balance among groups to serve, the reasons for doing so, and the instruments to use. Table 2.2 carries through the logic of the chapter, showing different goals that safety nets can help to achieve, the groups that can be reached, the specific roles/objectives of safety nets and some of the complementary policies for that group.

The role of safety nets within the overall development policy mix has grown over the last 20 or more years, for two reasons. First, the move to markets and liberalization—not only in the centrally planned economies of Eastern Europe, the former Soviet Union, and

TABLE 2.2 **Possible Target Groups, the Role of Safety Nets, and Complementary Policies**

Motivation/goal	Group	Role/objective of safety net	Design element required	Complementary policy
Mitigation of poverty	Chronic poor/ extreme poor	Provide transfers and support to reduce inequality and unacceptable deprivation	Progressive, possibly narrowly targeted, redistribution	Labor-intensive growth; access to adequate health, education, water, electricity and transportation services, microfinance and agricultural extension, and so on
	Vulnerable groups, including the elderly, orphans, disabled, displaced, groups suffering from discrimination			Interventions to encourage inclusion in society and work opportunities; family law may help protect widows, divorcees, and orphans; social care services
Increase household human capital and livelihoods	Chronic poor/ extreme poor	Foment investments in human capital and livelihoods	Some level is automatic, possible threshold effects	Same as above; also health and education policies (such as community health project)
Help households manage risks	Those vulnerable to shocks (often the poorer among them)	Prevent losses to livelihoods or human capital	Timely entry required to avoid losses after shock	Stable economies, well-functioning labor markets, and social insurance programs to mitigate risks of sickness, disability, unemployment, or retirement to reduce number and severity of episodes of transitory poverty, especially for workers in the formal sector
	Chronic poor or chronically exposed to high risks	Allow adoption of higher risk–higher return livelihood strategies	Guarantee required to promote ex ante changes	For those engaged in agriculture, especially smallholder or rain-fed agriculture, irrigation, microfinance weather insurance, or well-developed markets and access to supplemental nonfarm income
Help governments make sound choices	Lower quarter or half of income distribution	Provide compensation for reforms or provide alternative vehicle for redistributional objectives	Targeting either to specific losers, or lower portion of income distribution	

SOURCE: Authors.

China but also in Latin America and India—has meant that the basic distributional or protection role has been increasingly allocated to safety nets as prices are freed, employment less protected, and services less guaranteed. Second, the understanding that safety nets assist in promotion as well as protection is increasing, if still not universal. Safety nets thus enter more in the discourse everywhere, perhaps most notably in lower-income countries and in Sub-Saharan Africa.

Instead of grouping populations by degree of poverty, policy makers and the public may use other ways to classify those who may need support. A common alternative categorization is to look at the population along the life cycle. Table 2.3 provides examples of programs serving segments of the population based on age groups from infancy to old age. Regardless of how the population is disaggregated, it remains evident that safety nets are only part of the policies needed to support each group.

TABLE 2.3 **Examples of Social Protection Programs by Life Cycle**

Group served	Complementary policy or service	Regulation	Social protection policy	
			Social insurance	Safety net
Nonworking young	• Health care • Education • Family law	• Child labor laws	• Universal child allowances • Maternity benefits	• Means-tested child allowances • Transfers linked to maternal and child health programs • School feeding • CCTs
Working poor or unemployed	• Labor-intensive growth • Economic stability	• Minimum wage laws • Job security regulations • Severance pay	• Unemployment insurance	• Transfers • Workfare • General subsidies for food, utilities, or housing
Nonworking elderly	• Financial system to facilitate savings	• Retirement age	• Contributory pensions	• Transfers • Social pensions
Special groups	• Health care and traffic safety to prevent disability • Education inclusive of minorities, the disabled, and so on	• Affirmative action or compensatory investments for minorities, worker safety laws to prevent disability, family law to protect assets of widows and orphans	• Disability insurance for people with disabilities	• Transfers

SOURCE: Authors.

2.3 What Are the Challenges to Safety Nets?

Despite the many arguments in favor of publicly provided safety nets, there are still some reservations in the development community about their feasibility and desirability. This section summarizes these concerns and briefly explains how various program design and implementation features can be used to help address these issues so that, on balance, good programs will be beneficial in most settings.

The qualifiers in that sentence are important. Much safety net practice around the world over the last 20 years has not been particularly good, and what works in one setting may not succeed in another. Fortunately, a recent explosion of innovations in safety net programs makes for many highly promising options, and there are numerous successful programs from which future initiatives can learn.

Managing the challenges is complex, often requiring actions on multiple dimensions of design and implementation. The following discussion offers only brief summaries of these issues, with more detailed information provided as indicated throughout the rest of the book.

CAN DEVELOPING COUNTRIES AFFORD SAFETY NETS?

The premier reason safety nets are not a headline social policy on the development agenda is concern over whether countries—especially poor countries—can afford to transfer meaningful resources to their poor. This is a complex issue, which involves many nuances and trade-offs; chapter 3 provides a comprehensive treatment of the financing of safety nets.

In the poorest countries, the sheer magnitude of spending that would be required to provide an adequate safety net is quite daunting when viewed relative to the size of the economy as a whole. This discussion focuses on long-term safety net programs to aid the chronic poor and those households facing idiosyncratic shocks because these needs are permanent, the expenditures ongoing, and the related budget constraints most apparent. But safety nets are also needed to handle large covariate shocks such as an economic recession or natural disaster. Because such requirements are temporary and consequently less onerous, national governments and international agencies readily agree that safety nets are needed in these cases; indeed, humanitarian assistance usually is offered to countries in times of need.

For example, consider the extreme case of Ethiopia, where annual per capita income is about US$100 (World Bank 2004a). To provide adequate food for all the inhabitants whose consumption is below the food poverty line would require an annual expenditure of about US$810 million—12 percent of GDP, or about one-third of all public spending. This expenditure would obviously compete for resources against many other unmet needs, since only 52 percent of appropriately aged Ethiopian children are in primary school, infant mortality is 117 per 1,000 live births (one of the highest rates in the world), and water supply coverage is only 24 percent (the lowest in Sub-Saharan Africa). It would be difficult to say that safety nets should be funded, or fully funded, when the opportunity cost is primary education, primary health care, or water supply systems.

High Cost of Inaction

The flip side of the high cost of providing adequate safety nets in poor countries is the high cost of inaction. How much will an economy lose by not providing safety nets? Malnutrition, for example, can cost (based on lost productivity) at least 2 to 3 percent of GDP (Horton 1999 on low-income Asian countries), and lock affected children in a cycle of impaired cognitive development and physical growth, lower productivity, less education, lower earnings, and higher health care needs—in short, the intergenerational transmission of poverty. In Ethiopia, stunting affects 46.5 percent of children under the age of five (World Bank 2007r). To not address the issue essentially condemns the nation as a whole to poverty for at least the next generation.

Malnutrition per se may not be a concern in less poor countries, but there may be issues of low or late school enrollment, repetition, high dropout rates, and child labor or issues of social inclusion and cohesion in general. Each of these problems is more prevalent among the poor than the nonpoor, and to ignore them ensures impoverishment of the children over their lifetime and perpetuates the causes of social division.

Trade-offs and Balances

The stark apparent trade-off between, say, vaccinations or schools and safety nets may be something of an exaggeration, or at least a mislabeling of the choice. Safety nets are often (and can usually be) composed in ways that complement traditional development spending for human capital or infrastructure. So the issue is not so much one of transfers versus human capital or productive investments, but of balancing the use of tools to achieve these. How much should be spent to get teachers and classrooms ready for students versus on getting students fit for and in school? Should some of infrastructure construction and maintenance be organized in ways that provide safety net services in addition to infrastructure? These issues of fitting safety nets into other antipoverty and social policy are discussed in chapter 9. It is also worth noting that the large welfare states in Europe do not fund social protection instead of education or infrastructure but in addition to them. They thus have larger government sectors and apparently with no big cost to growth, a theme taken up in chapter 3.

In this regard, the stunning poverty of Ethiopia represents an extreme case. More typical is a country like Brazil. In Brazil, the income gap constitutes 1.6 percent of GDP, less than 5 percent of the income of the wealthiest 10 percent of Brazilians, and is small in comparison with total social spending in the country. Thus, theoretically and in the aggregate, Brazil has the resources necessary for solving its poverty problems through redistributive transfers alone, without raising taxes (World Bank 2001b). Similar situations exist for other high-inequality countries—Argentina, the Philippines, the Russian Federation, and South Africa, among others—though of course such calculations abstract from the very real issues of targeting, administration, incentives, and political economy within safety nets, and from the issues of the opportunity costs of other uses of the funds.

Recent years have seen a growing consensus among scholars regarding the productive role that safety nets can play in low-income countries both on their own terms and in complementing other efforts to achieve growth and human capital formation (Devereux 2002a; Lipton 1997; Sinha and Lipton 1999; Smith and Subbarao 2003). For example:

> An astonishing feature of the developing consensus about poverty, given the strong tide of anti-State sentiment in the 1980s, has been the widespread agreement that even very low-income countries can and should "afford" some types of public provision for

poor people whose health or age prevents work, or who are made unemployed by the vagaries of climate or market demand (Lipton 1997, p. 1006).

Safety Net Spending May Replace Other Less Effective Spending

Safety nets may serve as more efficient ways of redistributing income than alternative policies. For example, when Sri Lanka began its Food Stamp Program in the 1980s, it was not additional to existing policy, but a more cost-efficient replacement of the general food price subsidies previously in place. Similarly, Indonesia's new cash transfer program is not an additional burden on the budget but a lower-cost substitute for energy subsidies.

The discussion of whether countries can afford safety nets has been implicitly couched in terms of pitting one set of high priority, pro-poor or pro-growth expenditures against another. This orientation puts the matter in the harshest possible light, since few governments spend so efficiently. All governments make a certain number of idiosyncratic funding decisions, and all exhibit patterns of sometimes large and unproductive expenditures. Subsidies to manufacturing are not uncommon; these are of limited value in producing growth or jobs and can sometimes be costly. Brazil, for example, gave tax incentives to auto manufacturers that cost over US$200,000 per job created; India did the same with a cost of over US$400,000 per job created. In the Philippines, the effective corporate tax rate declines from the nominal 47 percent to 21 percent once fiscal incentives to firms are considered; in Thailand, the effect is even larger, a decline from 46 percent to 7 percent (World Bank 2004e). Military expenditures represent another large use of funds that is never linked to development. Vietnam spends 7.1 percent of its GDP on defense, Cape Verde 3.2 percent, and Mali 2.3 percent (Chamberlin 2004); yet each country is poor with underdeveloped safety nets.

Redistribution to the Rich versus Redistribution to the Poor

The idea that governments cannot afford to redistribute income to the poor must be contrasted with the evidence that they regularly redistribute income to the nonpoor. Energy subsidies are highly regressive and often more costly than safety nets. The Arab Republic of Egypt spent 8 percent of its GDP on several energy subsidies in 2004 (World Bank 2005c), and Indonesia spent up to 4 percent of GDP between 2001 and 2005 on fuel subsidies (World Bank 2007r). Similarly, countries dedicate resources to bailouts of insolvent contributory pension funds by transferring general revenues to support them. The expansion of Brazil's well-targeted CCT program Bolsa Familia to cover the bottom quintile of the population is raising some questions as to whether the country can afford to redistribute so much. The program cost 0.4 percent of GDP in 2006. In contrast, the deficit in the main federal pension program covered from general revenues is 3.7 percent of GDP and delivers over 50 percent of its benefits to the country's richest quintile (Lindert, Skoufias, and Shapiro 2006). This pattern is not unusual, at least in Latin America. Figure 2.3 shows the distribution of general revenue–financed transfers for several countries in absolute terms. Safety nets are progressive, but their cost is small compared to that of the general revenue used to finance the deficits in nominally contributory pension systems.

Another example of where governments have found money to assist the rich but not the poor is the bailouts made to financial sectors. In the East Asian financial crisis, Indonesia's bank bailout cost 50 percent of GDP (Honohan and Klingebiel 2000); spending

FIGURE 2.3 **Distribution of General Revenue–Financed Transfers for Selected Countries by Population Quintile**

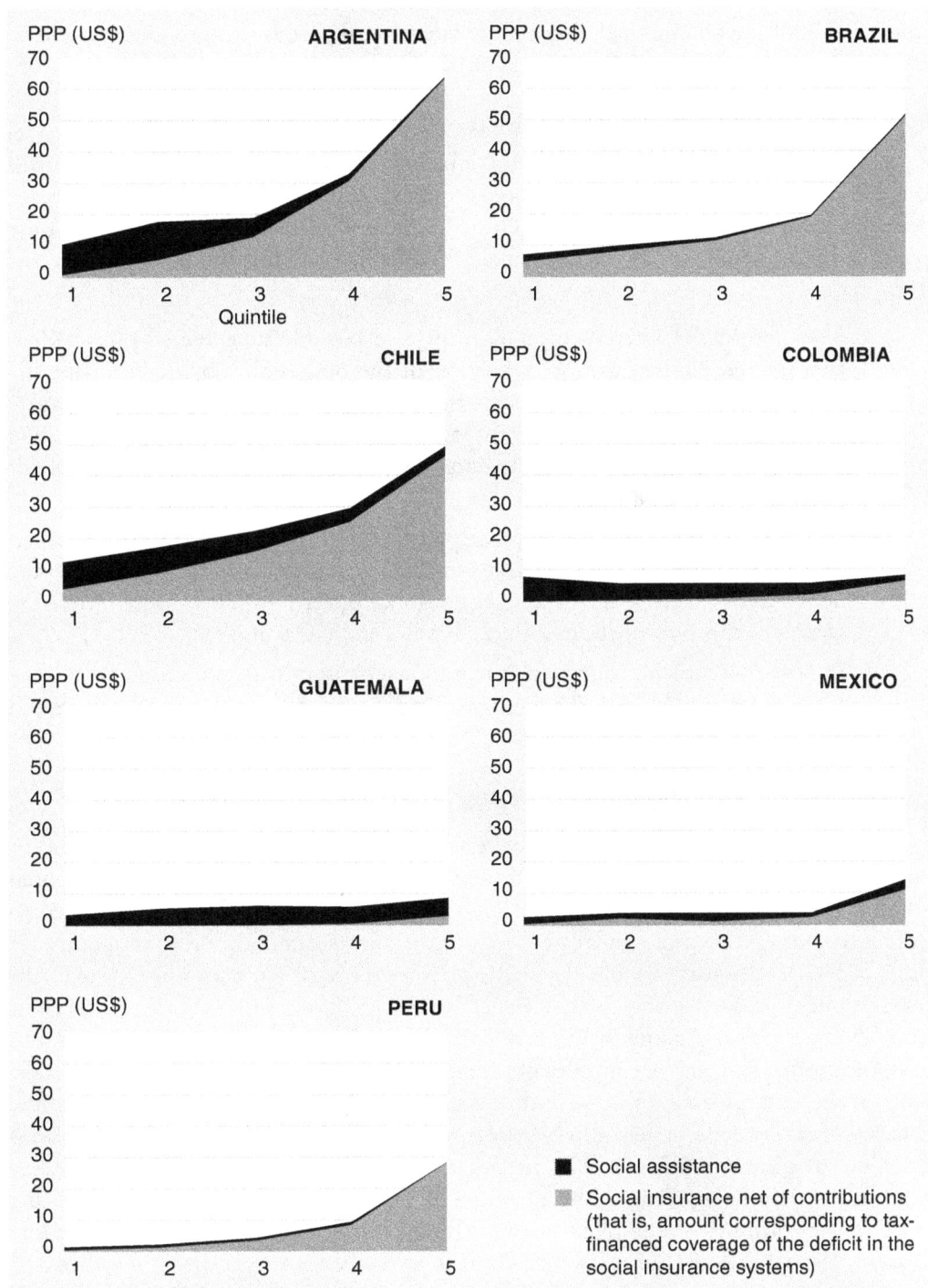

SOURCE: Lindert, Skoufias, and Shapiro 2006.

NOTE: PPP = purchasing power parity. Quintile 1 is poorest; quintile 5 richest.

on the accompanying safety net for the poor was about 2.4 percent of GDP in 1998/99, including food subsidies, public works, targeted scholarships, and fee waivers for health care (APEC 2001). In Korea, the bank bailout cost 27 percent of GDP (Honohan and Klingebiel 2000), while the spending on the safety net tripled from about 0.6 percent in 1997 to nearly 2 percent in 1999 (APEC 2001).

Bottom Line on Finding Budget for Safety Nets

Even where safety nets have a place at the table when resources are allocated, they will face budget constraints so tight that policy makers will have to make difficult triage decisions about how to allocate money insufficient to meet reasonable needs. There are typically three approaches that may be taken in different combinations in response to the dilemma.

- Keep the role of safety nets small relative to possible statements of need. Benefits may be limited to only a portion of the poor, either by defining specific subcategories of individuals (usually those in the traditional especially vulnerable groups); using an eligibility threshold well below the poverty line; or providing only seasonal benefits (during the hungry season in agricultural economies or the heating season in cold climates).

- Insofar as possible, ensure complementarities with building physical and human capital. This approach will provide twice the "bang for the buck" by helping the poor survive today and by reducing causes of poverty in future years. Prime examples of this type of approach are workfare and CCT programs.

- In very low-income countries, international assistance may be used to finance social assistance. Indeed, there is increasing willingness on the part of donors and countries to use aid in such ways.

CONCERN OVER REDUCING WORK EFFORT

One of the most common stumbling blocks for political support of safety nets is concern over the labor disincentives of welfare dependency (box 2.6). The fear is that potential beneficiaries will either work less after receiving the benefits or, if eligibility is tied to earned incomes or unemployment, will reduce their work efforts in order to qualify for the transfer. Both arguments and the evidence differ substantially across groups of countries, classes of programs, and types of beneficiaries.

The theoretical arguments are intuitive.[7] Transfers provide unearned income and thus inherently will lower the incentives for recipients to work, as beneficiaries may trade some of the extra income for more leisure. This outcome is sometimes referred to as the "income effect." Transfers may also change a recipient's effective wage rate if their size is based on the recipient's income. This situation arises for verified means-tested programs, where the benefit level is reduced by a fraction of a currency unit for each additional currency unit in earnings; the implicit tax on earnings is called the marginal tax rate of the program. This outcome is sometimes referred to as the "price effect." In the hypothetical perfectly means-tested guaranteed minimum income program where the size of the benefit is adequate to a decent minimum living standard and is reduced as income rises, the recipient whose initial income is below the guaranteed income has no incentive to work.

BOX 2.6 **Is Dependency Always Bad?**

Concerns over "dependency" have long been cited by skeptics of safety nets. But dependency is an emotionally charged term, so it is worth pausing to consider what lies behind it and how robust the empirical evidence about it is. Lentz, Barrett, and Hoddinott (2005) provide a model of how to do this, writing about food aid in response to emergencies and reviewing a largely African literature.

Lentz, Barrett, and Hoddinott (p. 10) consider that "a household or community exhibits dependency when it cannot meet its immediate basic needs without external assistance." They point out that dependence is not always bad, since the alternative to external assistance may be destitution. They use the term "positive dependency" to refer to such welfare-enhancing assistance and "negative dependency" to refer to situations in which external assistance helps meet current needs but is achieved at the cost of reducing recipients' capacity to meet their own basic needs in the future without external assistance.

In reviewing the many avenues through which such negative dependency may occur at the household level, the authors find little evidence that food aid discourages the labor supply of households that receive aid, crowds out remittances, or encourages moral hazard (the assumption of unwarranted risk).

They point to an alternative definition of dependency, when rather than households it is governments that come to rely on relief resources. But they show evidence that because aid is quite irregular—multilateral aid flows via the World Food Programme respond only weakly but at least predictably to shocks, bilateral aid flows from the United States do not respond to shocks at all—governments cannot become dependent on it. The authors also find that food aid has no persistent negative effects on national food production.

Concerns over dependency in other settings are usually less precisely defined, often concerning issues about the opportunity costs of funds devoted to transfers and one or more of the negative disincentives possible at the household level. In this book, we have therefore found it appropriate to discuss each issue separately rather than taking on "dependency" in the generic.

Developed Countries

Concerns about labor disincentives have traditionally been strongest in wealthy countries with generous safety nets and high unemployment rates. However, the evidence shows that participation in safety net programs has only small or moderate effects on employment or hours worked. In Ontario, Canada, in the 1990s, beneficiaries of a rather generous safety net program reduced their work effort by 3 to 5 percent when benefits tripled from Can$185 to Can$507 (Lemieux and Milligan 2008). The bulk of the evidence comes from only one country, the United States. Here, for the numerous initiatives providing small benefits, such as food stamp, nutrition, and child care subsidy programs, most studies have found no evidence of reduced work effort. Similar results were obtained for in-kind programs, such as housing programs or Medicaid (health insurance coverage for the poor) (Moffitt 2003). More generous pilot programs, such as the negative income tax experiments, did moderately reduce the work effort of participants. Male earners benefiting from the negative income tax experiments reduced employment and earnings by 7 percent on average; for wives, only 17 percent of whom were employed, employment and earnings dropped by 17 percent (Burtless 1986). Among nonexperimental U.S. programs, only one—Aid for Families with Dependent Children—was shown to be associated with large reductions in work effort. Moffitt (2002b) found evidence that single mothers benefiting from the program had reduced their work effort by 10 to 50 percent; however, he also found that the program contained specific features that would make it especially susceptible to labor disincentives. (See box 5.3.) Consequently, extrapolating results from the Aid for Families with Dependent Children program to other safety net programs in developed countries would not be advisable.

Developing Countries

The theoretical model predicts that reduction in work efforts will be proportional to the size of the benefit (income effect) and the implicit marginal tax rate on earnings of the program (price effect). The theory thus supports the view that the impact of safety net programs on work disincentives should be smaller in developing countries, for four reasons:

- Programs are less generous in developing countries; most safety net programs complement, rather than substitute for, the earnings of able-bodied beneficiaries.
- Very few programs in developing countries use and are able to enforce effectively benefit formulas with marginal tax rates and frequent recertification of household income.
- Many developing countries target their programs only to households without able-bodied adults (for example, Zambia's Kalomo scheme and Ethiopia's Direct Support program) or require able-bodied beneficiaries to work in return for benefits (all workfare programs, but also some cash transfer programs).
- The static model does not take into account the fact that transfers help households make productive investments in their future.

The evidence supports the view that, in developing countries, safety net programs do not often reduce labor effort substantially. In Mexico, adult earners benefiting from the CCT initiative PROGRESA (now known as Oportunidades) worked as much as those in a randomized control group; at the same time, the program achieved its objective of increasing schooling and reduced child labor by 15 percent (Parker and Skoufias 2000; Skoufias and di Maro 2006). In Brazil, Leite (2006a) simulated the potential impact of Bolsa Familia on adult work effort and found that the transfer amounts would have very little impact. In Armenia, the employment rate and hours worked by adults in the Family Poverty Benefits Program were similar to those for a matched sample of nonparticipants (Posarac, Tesliuc, and Urdinola forthcoming). In Romania, a qualitative review of the Guaranteed Minimum Income Program found little evidence of an adverse impact on labor force participation; conversely, "because there is a small bonus for employment, there may be a small positive impact on participation compared with more traditional systems of aid" (Birks Sinclair & Associates Ltd. 2004). On the other hand, in Sri Lanka, Sahn and Alderman (1995) studied a rice subsidy program that induces labor disincentives through income effects; they found labor reductions on the order of 10 percent.

Measures to Foment Work Effort

There is increasing evidence, especially from developed countries, that measures to counteract welfare dependency exist and can be effective. In the United States, a number of welfare-to-work experiments reviewed by Hamilton (2002) and Greenberg and others (2002) found that a combination of work requirements, financial incentives for work, and/or services supporting welfare recipients increased earnings and employment on average from 6 to 10 percent. Grogger and Karoly (2006) showed that welfare recipients (single mothers) respond to financial incentives and workfare tests in the way predicted by the static labor supply decision model. In Canada, beneficiaries of the Self-Sufficiency Project increased their full-time employment and earnings by 15 percentage points. In the United Kingdom, the welfare-to-work measures introduced under the New Deal for adults reduced the unemployment rate by 6 to 10 percent.

Policy makers and administrators have a variety of tools at their disposal to manage labor disincentives, including the following:

- Limit programs to those who traditionally are not expected to work anyway—the very young, the very old, those with disabilities, and so on, often referred to as the "deserving" poor. Although this limitation is a fairly common one, it results in only a partial safety net. (See chapters 8 and 9.)

- Choose a targeting mechanism not directly tied to earnings—this leaves the rewards to working intact. Few developing countries use a means test or minimum income guarantee, though many transition countries do. Infrequent recertification will also mute the labor disincentives. Most programs outside of Europe recertify only once every two or three years; some even less frequently. (See chapter 4.)

- Set benefit levels to maintain work incentives. Most programs in developing countries have very low benefits, often equivalent in amount to only a few percentage points of the poverty line. Thus they inherently leave plenty of incentive to work. The low benefits proffered are usually due more to fiscal constraints than concern over work disincentives, but the result is the same. In countries with a full suite of social protection programs, social assistance payments should be less than unemployment insurance and the minimum pension provided by the contributory pension system. (See chapter 5, section 1.)

- When benefit levels are customized to earnings, ensure that there is still incentive to work—set exit thresholds higher than entrance thresholds, use sliding withdrawals of benefits as incomes rise or earned income tax credits to help make work pay. Alternatively or additionally, provide lump sum graduation benefits, or pay for allied benefits such as child care or transportation allowances for a period after work starts. Admittedly, these options are administratively demanding and will result in those above the poverty line receiving some program benefits. (See chapter 5, section 1.)

- Link transfers to program elements, such as job training or placement, education, microcredit, social support services, meant to help households move out of assistance and toward independence. Such links also may be administratively demanding, but they are fully consistent with broad social policy objectives. (See chapter 5, section 2.)

Concerns over reduction in work effort will be strongest when programs are most generous and eligibility or benefit levels depend more on recent or current earnings. Since generous programs with customized benefit levels are becoming more common, features to manage work effort may be needed more often as well. But it is usually the middle- and upper-middle-income countries where program generosity is sufficiently great to make work effort a concern, and these are the countries most likely to manage the sophisticated program elements to mitigate the problem. Concern over work effort should thus lead the policy maker to consider various features of program design and of the balance across social assistance of last resort, unemployment insurance, and contributory pension programs carefully, but should rarely imply abandoning social assistance as a policy tool.

CROWDING OUT PRIVATE TRANSFERS

Private transfers are important to the informal safety nets that arise when official public action is limited or nonexistent. If public safety nets are put in place, these private transfers might be diminished—a consideration that must be weighed in determining how and whether to implement the public program.

To make this determination, policy makers must understand the adequacy of private social protection systems in a particular setting. In some countries or among some groups, they can be quite substantial and appear to exhibit the same features as a good public social protection system—they go from richer to poorer households and to those facing shocks such as illness or unemployment. For example, Cox and Jimenez (1997) found that 40 percent of black South Africans reported either receiving or giving cash transfers. Though undoubtedly helpful, informal insurance and interhousehold transfers are not sufficient safety nets. Many people are left out of such networks, and even for those who receive some assistance, it may not be enough to avoid poverty traps and the intergenerational transmission of poverty. Moreover, the entire support network may be affected by widespread shocks and thus unable to provide support to all members when it is most needed. Finally, private support can sometimes be part of a larger set of patron-client relationships that are not conducive to the client's long-term income growth (Glewwe and Hall 1998; Morduch 1999; Skoufias 2003).

Next, policy makers must understand the extent to which the introduction of public transfers might affect private ones. One of the most credible investigations of this question is Jensen's 1998 examination of the effects of the expansion of the South African old-age pension program to Africans. Though means tested, the eligibility threshold and benefit levels in this program are quite generous. Jensen estimates that for those households receiving private transfers, every publicly provided rand led to a reduction of 0.2 to 0.4 rands in private transfers to the elderly. This reduction in the burden of private support indirectly raises the income of poor donors. The South African social pension program is quite unusual in the generosity of its benefit—more than twice the median per capita monthly household income of Africans. The Nicaraguan and Mexican CCT programs are also relatively generous, though their benefits are only about 15 to 25 percent of household income. In the Nicaragua program, the probability that program households will receive interhousehold food transfers is lowered by about 10 percent. In Honduras, where the CCT program benefit is only about 4 percent of annual household expenditures, no such crowding out of private transfers is found. In none of the three countries did remittance to the households fall (Nielsen and Olinto 2006; Teruel and Davis 2000). Program generosity would appear to affect the degree of crowding out, but the results may be rather context specific. Lentz and Barrett (2005) find no evidence that food aid receipt crowds out private transfers in pastoralist households in southern Ethiopia and northern Kenya. Gibson, Olivia, and Rozzelle (2006) found little evidence of crowding-out effects in China, Indonesia, Papua New Guinea, and Vietnam, concluding that crowding-out problems are, in fact, not a significant policy concern.

To address issues associated with the crowding out of private transfers, public transfer programs should be designed as follows.

- Programs should be of sufficient scope to cover people missed in the private system. They should be permanent and reliable programs so as to not undermine private systems without providing a better alternative.

- If eligibility is determined through a means test, the income from private transfers may be excluded in whole or part from the calculation of income, or the income of the full household or even of nonresident parents or children may be considered in the calculation. Such adaptations help preserve incentives for the continued transfer of income within families, but they can be administratively complex and lead to errors of inclusion.

- If possible, consider how to use public systems to reinforce private systems. In Zimbabwe, the traditional chief sets aside community land to be farmed by community/volunteer labor so the resultant crops can be distributed to the needy in the village. Public subsidies to nonlabor inputs for the scheme should improve the yield and assist the private safety net system.

POSSIBLE EFFECTS ON FERTILITY

Economic theory holds that the demand for children is a function of individual preference and the cost of children, under an income constraint. Social assistance alters the income constraint and, depending on how benefits are set, may lower the direct costs of raising children. This theory raises the possibility that social assistance programs might result in higher fertility.

Empirical evidence that social assistance increases fertility is scant. Gauthier and Hatzius (1997) look at family benefits and fertility among Organisation for Economic Co-operation and Development (OECD) countries and conclude that, while there is an effect on fertility, it is of a small magnitude: a 25 percent increase in family benefits would increase fertility on the order of 0.07 children per woman. Stecklov and others (2006) provide estimates of impacts on fertility of the Honduran and Nicaraguan CCT programs. They find significant though small positive effects in the former, but not in the latter. In Turkey, Ahmed and others (2007) show that the CCT program reduces fertility by 2 to 3 percent. Box 2.7 reports the reactions of this program's beneficiaries when evaluators held discussion groups aimed at understanding the impact of the program's pregnancy benefit.

BOX 2.7 **Women's Reactions to Questions about Transfers and Fertility**

The Turkish CCT program includes a small cash benefit for pregnant women. Both quantitative and qualitative studies were done to understand how the program might affect fertility. The quantitative study showed the small decrease already cited. A complementary survey found that 97 percent of respondents said that women would not get pregnant because of the benefit. In fact, many thought such a question to be strange, humorous, absurd, or offensive. One woman (Illyaskoy, Sengul G.) said, "Allah, were there women that got pregnant just for this money, really? Ha ha ha!…of course you have to ask these questions, this is your duty! But mothers have to think about their children's futures as well" (Ahmed and others 2007, p. 61).

Adato and others (2007, p. 135) report that women understand that bearing children has many costs and that these go far beyond what a small cash transfer can alleviate. They also document the reasons that many children are desired, including powerful cultural factors in favor of large family size. One woman (Nafia S. Beyüzümü, Van) summed it up this way: "I don't think a woman can give birth to get money…If a woman gives birth it is because first God, second her husband, and third her husband's mother want her to."

There are several actions programs can take to contain any possible side effects related to fertility; some may have unintended side effects of their own:

- Keep benefits reasonably low or temporary. Given the total psychic, time, and monetary investment implicit in child bearing and rearing, low-level benefits from safety nets are unlikely to have much impact on fertility decisions. Public opinion surveys in OECD countries, which feature relatively more stable and generous assistance programs than others worldwide, revealed that this support might help families achieve desired family size, but would not increase it (Gauthier and Hatzius 1997).

- Keep benefits flat per household, or, if given on a per capita or per child basis, cap the total benefit or number of children. While this approach will minimize the incentives for fertility, it will also reduce the poverty targeting of the benefit as larger families are often poorer (even with appropriate treatment of economies of scale). Also, where there are marked differences in family size across ethnic groups, such caps may carry a political dimension far more important than the possible effect on fertility.

- Introduce elements in the program that would tend to reduce fertility. The welfare-to-work reforms in OECD countries increase women's labor force participation, which usually discourages fertility. CCT programs require women to get minimal preventive health care and health education, which usually includes opportunities to deliver messages about the health benefits of breastfeeding and birth spacing, as well as family planning services. The availability of this information may reduce unwanted fertility among adults. Also, the increased educational level of the female children in these programs will likely serve to lower their family size when they become adults.

DOUBTS ABOUT ADMINISTRATIVE FEASIBILITY AND PROGRAM MANAGEMENT

While concerns over administrative capacity are not trivial, there are often ways to deliver some sort of safety net program if due creativity is brought to bear on the issue. Taking advantage of existing public systems outside the welfare agency, contracting out to private firms, simplifying design, and prudently guarding against the perfect becoming the enemy of the adequate will usually result in a feasible program. Chapter 7 contains many examples of acceptably administered programs in a wide range of countries and circumstances. Chapters 4 to 6 go into much more detail about different facets of program implementation and administration, outlining requirements and different ways of fulfilling them, again with examples from a broad range of countries.

Two politically charged concerns may hide under the more neutral term "administrative feasibility." Both have to do with who really benefits from programs carried out in the name of the poor or vulnerable.

The first concern has to do with targeting and doubts about whether it can really be accomplished well, especially in low-income or low-capacity settings. (This theme is taken up in detail in chapter 4.) On average, targeting results are better for middle-income than low-income developing countries, but there have been successful cases of the use of all sorts of targeting instruments in low-income settings (Coady, Grosh, and Hoddinott 2004). The overall poor results are at least partially due to the nature of the programs chosen (general food subsidies) and to the stop-and-go nature of many other interventions, which makes it difficult to develop good systems.

A second concern has to do with the potential for misuse of funds. Some believe that safety net programs should not be funded on the grounds that resources will leak away from intended beneficiaries. A number of safety net programs have famously suffered from graft and corruption, and, in some countries, the track record is rather poor. But a blanket abandonment of safety net policy would be akin to forsaking infrastructure projects because of reports of occasional contractor kickbacks and rakeoffs. The solution instead lies in determining how to minimize such problems, about which much is already known.

In addition to the broad government-wide governance agenda of due process, transparency, and accountability which is being increasingly explored and applied, there are a number of design and administrative features specific to social assistance programs that can help prevent fraud, error, and corruption. Key measures are summarized below.

- Use program design to minimize incentives and opportunities for misuse of funds.
  - Ensure that program budgets are consistent with eligibility criteria. If funding is adequate to serve all those eligible, applicants will have little reason to offer bribes to get into the program. If program slots are rationed so that only a small portion of eligible applicants can be admitted, there is ample motivation for bribery and kickbacks.
  - Consider carefully the eligibility criteria. The simpler they are, and the less discretion they offer to eligibility intake officers, the less opportunity there will be for corruption. Where complex criteria are needed, reinforce mechanisms of control. (See chapter 3, section 6, and chapter 4.)

     — Consider the benefit level for a participant with respect to the salary of intake officers. Ineligible applicants may offer a cut of their benefits in return for entry into the program. If such an offer is low relative to officers' base earnings, it will be less attractive.

     — Conditionalities such as requirements for recipients to obtain health care, attend school, or work may help guard against "ghost" beneficiaries. In programs with no conditionality, an intake worker can easily register ghost beneficiaries. With conditionality, another official in the health clinic, school, or worksite would have to collude with the officer by providing certification of attendance. Public posting of the list of beneficiaries is another means of exposing invented beneficiaries.

     — Use payment mechanisms that move benefits from the treasury to the individual recipient with as few intermediaries as possible, as each additional link in the chain increases the potential for diversion of funds. (See chapter 5, section 4.)

- Set up adequate administrative procedures.
  - Ensure that administrative processes are clearly defined, and that staff and other resources are adequate to carry them out. A culture of compliance can only be created where rules are clear and reasonable. (See chapters 4 and 5.)
  - Institute a range of quality control procedures to ensure that eligibility criteria are respected, payments are audited, information systems have appropriate safeguards, and so on. (See chapter 6.)
  - Establish sensible tolerances in quality control procedures. For example, given the difficulty in measuring income, an initial eligibility evaluation and subsequent recheck might arrive at slightly varying estimates of income. Only if the difference is substantial and larger than the expected measurement error should this variation be considered fraud. Such an approach also facilitates respect for rules and makes efforts to enforce them more cost-effective. (See chapter 6.)
  - Set up adequate grievance, appeal, and "whistle-blowing" procedures for applicants who believe they are eligible but were denied entry, for beneficiaries who are receiving incorrect payments or are requested to pay kickbacks, for program workers who suspect fraud by their coworkers, and for the general public that suspects irregularities of any sort. (See chapter 4, section 4.)
  - Take action against miscreants with meaningful penalties.
- Use transparency and communications well.
  - Ensure that the eligibility criteria, benefit levels, and rules are clear to both the public and beneficiaries. People can only seek redress when they understand what is due. Conversely, clarity can help eliminate unwarranted appeals or claims of malfeasance.
  - Publicize cases of detected fraud and the penalties imposed.

Some of these techniques involve trade-offs with other desirable features of safety net policy. For example, although the stratagem of fully funding safety nets should eliminate a source of corruption, it is not always feasible to do so given budget constraints. Keeping eligibility criteria and payment structures simple will reduce the probabilities of fraud, error, and corruption, but it will make programs less precise in their targeting and lower the impact on poverty per currency unit spent on legitimate beneficiaries. Policy makers may need to forego some of the design options for minimizing fraud, error, and corruption, but will need to develop correspondingly more sophisticated administrative procedures as an alternative means of keeping problems in check. Because such systems take time to develop, they are more feasible or effective in permanent programs.

SUMMARY

Table 2.4 summarizes how the various challenges posed by safety nets discussed in this section may be handled.

TABLE 2.4 **Summary of How to Handle Challenges to Safety Nets**

Challenge to safety net	Management strategy
Affordability	• Consider the costs of inaction • Keep safety nets lean • Leverage improvements in physical or human capital if possible
Reduction in work effort	• Craft eligibility criteria, benefit levels and structures, countervailing conditionalities appropriately
Crowding out of private transfers	• Some is inevitable and not necessarily bad • Some mitigating measures may be feasible
Incentives for fertility	• Craft benefit structure to minimize • Build in elements to shift preference for family size
Administrative feasibility and accountability	• Employ design elements that minimize opportunities for corruption • Develop administrative systems • Use communications and transparency

SOURCE: Authors.

Notes

1. Social risk management refers to how society manages risks (not to how to manage social risks), a conceptual framework introduced by Holzmann and Jorgensen (2000). See appendix A for a brief exposition.

2. Low birthweight and malnutrition among young children are well established as being linked with higher child mortality and higher risk of illness (with attendant costs for medical care and time requirements for caregiving) and, later in the life cycle, with lower cognitive development, lower schooling, and lower physical productivity. Iodine deficiency hinders cognitive development and increases child mortality. Vitamin A deficiency can increase morbidity and mortality and, in severe cases, cause blindness. In children, iron deficiency can reduce cognitive capacity and affect schooling and future productivity; in adults, it can impede hard work. Zinc has an appreciable impact on growth in children (Behrman, Alderman, and Hoddinott 2004; Webb and Rogers 2003; World Bank 2005n).

3. Adequate access to credit can help families avoid negative coping strategies, but the poor often lack access to credit or have access only on particularly onerous terms (for example, from

moneylenders). Where credit is available, it can lead to large indebtedness, which can have repercussions on family welfare for years to come.

4. The underlying problem is uninsured risk. One means of addressing it is to improve insurance against the risk being directly faced. For example, weather insurance is being considered as a new option for reducing the income risks to small farmers of too much or too little rainfall, thus freeing them to adopt income-maximizing rather than risk-minimizing choices of crops and inputs. Though theoretically attractive, weather insurance has not yet been implemented anywhere at a large scale or long enough to see how much of the problem it solves.

5. Other sector-specific policies have been tried in various places, beginning with lax collections or "no disconnection" policies; these provided little predictability to the consumer, greater benefits to the nonpoor than the poor, and erratic revenue flows to the utility. Across-the-board subsidies, life-line or block pricing, and burden limit programs were also introduced; these too had efficiency drawbacks and, except for the across-the-board subsidies, not inconsiderable administrative requirements.

6. The US$1/day rate was found by Chen and Ravallion to be representative of the poverty lines found among low-income countries in the first years such calculations of global poverty were done. These calculations attempt to express in a common currency the purchasing power of varied domestic currencies; such purchasing power parity comparisons, while useful, are inexact. US$2/day is more representative of poverty in middle-income countries.

7. The predictions that increased transfers will reduce the labor supply of beneficiary households are based on the static labor supply model (Moffitt 2002b).

## CHAPTER 3

Financing of and Spending on Safety Nets

KEY MESSAGES

The economic theory underlying the question of how much to spend on safety nets is the same as for other forms of government expenditure—that is, the marginal benefits of different types of expenditure should be equal to each other and to the marginal costs of raising public funds. Increases in spending are more likely to be justified the more the following conditions hold: the proposed safety net programs are "good," the programs are small, alternative uses for the funds are of low priority, taxes can be raised efficiently, and the combined package of expenditure and financing is redistributive.

If countries wish to increase their spending on safety nets, they can reallocate expenditures, raise taxes, obtain aid grants, or borrow. Reallocation of funds from less important items is preferable when possible. If taxes are to be raised, the government must pay attention to the economic and political costs. If international grant (donor) finance is to be used, the government and donors should try to ensure that funding flows are stable and that procedures are conducive to building long-term implementation capacity. Debt finance is appropriate for safety nets when they benefit future generations in ways that will raise their productivity, and consequently future tax revenues, or when temporarily increased expenditures are needed as during a recession.

Safety nets should be financed in a countercyclical manner, yet few governments manage this. Developing countries' prospects for solving this problem seem slim until safety nets are fully financed in stable times and volatility is lower than has recently been the case. Expenditure reallocation in favor of safety nets during economic downturns along with generally prudent fiscal policy will help and have been put into effect, but to a degree insufficient to yield countercyclical funding for safety nets.

The literature on the costs of the welfare state from countries of the Organisation for Economic Co-operation and Development (OECD) suggests that they have spent substantial sums on their social protection systems, but have financed them prudently and reaped benefits from them such that they have not suffered the reduced growth that economists often predict will accompany such high redistributive expenditures.

Most developing countries spend in the range of 1 to 2 percent of their gross domestic product (GDP) on safety nets. Analysis of new data shows that spending on safety nets as a percentage of GDP is weakly but positively correlated with income and democracy. The analysis does not find any relationship between spending on safety nets and several other plausible variables, including governance, ethnic fragmentation, and public attitudes about inequality. When spending is broadened to include all social spending (safety nets, social protection, and the social sectors), we find more of the expected relationships.

Conventional wisdom in the public finance literature suggests that redistribution is a role most appropriate for higher levels of government because of interregional equality considerations, but that subnational jurisdictions may be well placed to administer safety nets, because they may have greater knowledge of or contact with programs' client base. Thus many programs will involve multiple levels of government and shared responsibilities. Consequently, designing appropriate systems of intergovernmental transfers, managing the incentives contained in them, and developing and implementing shared administrative responsibilities can present challenges.

Financing safety net programs is not theoretically different from financing any other government program. The safety net literature thus seldom provides information about this topic,[1] yet policy makers concerned with implementing or reforming safety nets face a constant stream of demands competing for limited funds. This chapter is targeted to such policy makers. It provides a synopsis of some of the pertinent public finance literature with illustrations from safety net programs and new data on spending on safety nets in developing countries.

3.1 The Theory on Expenditure Allocation

The economic theory to help address how much to spend on safety nets is the same as for other forms of government expenditure: the marginal benefits of different types of expenditure should be equal to each other and to the marginal costs of raising public funds.

While the specifics depend on the type of program, the benefits tend to include improved equity, increased household welfare via investments or improved risk management, and such economywide effects as higher growth associated with successful reforms facilitated by safety net programs (see chapter 2). Typically, improvements in equity are measured by changes in indexes of inequality such as the Gini coefficient or by the reduction in the extent of poverty among beneficiaries. Welfare improvements are gauged by the increase in recipient earnings; the improvement in their children's welfare in terms of nutrition, schooling, or child labor; or by the level of recipient savings and investments. The marginal costs associated with safety net programs include the cost of the transfers, administrative costs, and efficiency costs. The latter are of two sorts: they are either due to behavioral change by beneficiaries, such as reduced work effort, or to the economic costs of collecting taxes to finance the program. Box 3.1 illustrates these costs.

Compared with other public interventions, such as building roads and dams and providing education and health, quantifying both the benefits and costs of safety net programs in monetary terms is more difficult for two reasons. First, other types of programs are primarily or exclusively judged using efficiency criteria—that is, whether they generate a high economic rate of return—whereas safety net programs are primarily judged by their contribution to improved equity. However, translating improvements in equity into monetary terms is an academic exercise dependent on subjective assumptions that cannot be tested.[2] Second, safety net programs tend to have a diverse set of impacts, and quantifying their benefits and costs is only partially possible, a complexity less apparent for some other public actions. For example, in the case of a direct public road between two cities, an analyst can estimate the project's economic rate of return as the funds private operators

BOX 3.1 **Okun's Leaky Bucket**

In his classic treatise, Okun (1975) provides an intuitive explanation of what he refers to as the leaky bucket used to transfer money from better-off taxpayers to poorer ones. He enumerates the leaks as administrative costs, reduced or misplaced work effort, distorted saving and investment behavior, and possible changes in socioeconomic attitudes. Okun's idea of a leaky bucket is often cited by those who characterize transfers as costly and appropriate for only a small policy role, but Okun's comments on the size of the leaks in the bucket suggest that their magnitude is fairly modest, which recent research on safety nets in developing countries largely confirms.

Administrative costs. These are the costs to the government of tax administration and to taxpayers of such items as recordkeeping. Okun deems that these are easily measured, are subject to policy control, and amount to only a few percentage points of overall costs at most. Experience in developing countries confirms that safety net programs can be run well for modest administrative costs: a useful rule of thumb is roughly 10 percent of overall program costs (see chapter 9 for more on the topic).

Work effort. Okun (1975, p. 99) notes that the literature shows "virtually no effects on the amount of work effort of the affluent," a limited effect of transfers on the work effort of secondary earners in low-income households, and virtually no effect on low-income households' primary earners. A much greater effect can be found in tax avoidance behavior by corporations shifting remuneration and benefit packages in ways that reduce their tax liabilities. As the synopsis of labor disincentive effects in chapter 5, section 2, indicates, recent experience with safety nets shows that well-designed programs have modest and manageable labor disincentives.

Savings and investment. These are important for programs that tax one generation to support another, as in pay-as-you-go pension systems, and presumably less so for safety net spending. Okun notes that in the United States, savings rates were 16 percent of GDP in both 1929, when taxes were low and flat and the social protection system was small, and in 1973, when taxes were higher and more progressive and the social protection system was much larger. He infers that a massive increase in the tax and transfer system had not lowered savings. We note that some safety nets actually help recipient households invest in their livelihoods, if not in financial markets.

Socioeconomic attitudes. These are a less tangible concern and relate to the effort to balance the benefits of social inclusion against possible harm to the work ethic. Socioeconomic attitudes are a recurring theme in social assistance policy for all countries.

Modern aggregate estimates of the cost of funds. The economic literature on the cost of funds uses general equilibrium models that essentially try to measure the leaks in Okun's bucket. Estimates of the cost of raising US$1.00 for developed countries mostly range from US$1.00 to about US$1.50; about US$1.25 is common, although there are a few much higher estimates. Fewer estimates are available for developing countries, but they fall in the same range, perhaps tending to be a bit lower (Devarajan, Theirfelder, and Suthiwart-Narueput 2001; Martin and Anderson 2005). Warlters and Auriol (2005) estimate the average in 38 African countries as US$1.17.

save when transporting goods and people compared with alternative but longer routes. By contrast, a child welfare safety net program will generate a host of impacts, some of which are hard to quantify: the children may benefit from a more nurturing climate at home, better education, and improved health and subsequently stay in school longer and be more likely to avoid risky or illegal behaviors in their youth; as adults, they may be more likely to be employed and earn good wages.

Nonetheless, a partial estimation of the ratio of marginal benefits and cost can be undertaken. So far, such evaluations have been done for only a handful of programs, mostly in the United States, but also in Mexico for PROGRESA (now known as Oportunidades). The evaluation of the opportunity cost of a given safety net program is best determined through a cost-benefit analysis (see chapter 6, section 5), which compares the program's net impact on its ultimate outcomes (as determined, ideally, from an impact evaluation) with the extra costs associated with implementing the program. Consider the following three examples.

Beecroft, Lee, and Long (2003) examine the effects of the 1996 U.S. welfare reform on the first cohort of beneficiaries affected in Indiana. The welfare reform focused on a "welfare to work" transition. Support became conditional on recipients pursuing a job search or education activities, and support for these activities was provided along with child care and transportation subsidies. Time limits on the benefits were set, with each family allowed only five years of benefits over a lifetime. The analysts consider two perspectives: that of the families receiving the support and that of taxpayers as reflected in the costs to the U.S. and Indiana budgets not only of the Temporary Assistance for Needy Families (TANF) welfare program, but also for food stamps and medical assistance, which have linked application procedures. According to Beecroft, Lee, and Long (2003, p. 104):

> The economic benefits of welfare reform to families—resulting mainly from increased employment—slightly outweighed the losses in welfare payments and other income. While changes in income varied across families, the typical family's economic position was very modestly improved. Welfare reform benefited taxpayers because savings more than offset welfare reform expenditures. Savings occurred primarily because clients spent less time on cash assistance, reducing benefit payments for the TANF, Food Stamp, and Medicaid programs. These reductions more than offset increased spending on employment and training services and child care subsidies. The budget savings were shared by Indiana and the federal government.

The impact evaluation of Ecuador's Bono de Desarrollo Humano (Human Development Bond) program shows that it increased school enrollment by 10 percent and reduced child labor by 17 percent, with the effects concentrated among older children (Schady and Araujo 2006). Nominally a conditional cash transfer (CCT) initiative, the program aims to ensure that beneficiary households have their children attend school and obtain certain preventive health care services. The cost-benefit analysis focused on the program's education benefits and effects on increased consumption, because evaluation data are available for these impacts; possible impacts on nutrition and empowerment had not yet been studied. The cost-benefit analysis used a national household survey to compare earnings among adults with different levels of schooling, estimate the increased years of schooling each child would receive as a result of the program, predict future earnings for beneficiary and nonbeneficiary children, discount these earnings over their lifetimes, and compare them with estimates of program costs, employing sensitivity analysis for key parameters (World Bank 2006l). The result varies depending on the economy's growth rate and whether the program becomes more effective at implementing the conditions that children enroll in and attend school (its "conditionality"). As shown in table 3.1, the cost-benefit analysis suggests that, under most scenarios, the program is justified on the grounds of its education benefits alone; it is expected to produce parallel improvements in health and nutrition as well. For example, with a growth rate of 5 percent and effective conditionality, the program's education benefits would be more than twice its total costs. Education benefits would exceed total costs even with only a 1 percent growth rate and conditionality, or without effective conditions and a 5 percent growth rate.

TABLE 3.1 **Cost-Benefit Estimates of the Education Effects of the Bono de Desarrollo Humano Program, Ecuador**

Item	1% growth	3% growth	5% growth
Without conditionality	0.62	0.82	1.13
With conditionality	1.15	1.50	2.05

SOURCE: World Bank 2006l.

The economic analysis also simulates the impact of the program's transfer element on consumption poverty and predicts that poverty falls by about 2.5 percent using a poverty line of either US$1 or US$2 per day. This is an upper bound of the short-run effect. If households save and invest any of the transfer, or if they reduce the number of hours they work, the immediate poverty impact will be lower. If the investments yield a return, the long-run effects on poverty reduction may be higher (World Bank 2006a).

Note that neither of the foregoing examples explicitly values the welfare of the poor more than that of the nonpoor, although economists often think this should be done and that redistribution is one of the fundamental motivations of transfer programs. Alderman and del Ninno (1999) provide a relatively rare example of such an analysis. They introduce explicit distributional weights into the analysis of potential reforms to the value added tax (VAT) in South Africa. They construct a cost-benefit measure of a tax change with losses in personal consumption in the numerator, with distributional weights in the aggregation, and with revenue gains in the denominator. The higher the ratio, the greater the social cost compared with the revenue gained. Alderman and del Ninno find that when the welfare of all households is weighted equally, the VAT on maize, beans, and sugar is the most socially costly—or, conversely, that these are the best candidates for exemptions from the VAT. When higher weights are given to the welfare of the poor, maize remains the commodity most important to exempt, but kerosene becomes a better choice for exemption than sugar or beans.

The difficulties in quantifying all the impacts of safety net spending and the competing ways in which funds may be spent in different sectors and programs and putting them in a common metric are significant. Thus most economists recognize that, in practice, rigorously quantifying the marginal benefits from different forms of spending with each other and with marginal costs is generally not feasible (Besley, Burgess, and Rasul 2003; Devarajan, Theirfelder, and Suthiwart-Narueput 2001; Gupta and others 2001). Nonetheless, budget planners are deeply imbued with the principal that they should be equated and will do what they can to respect it, even if they can only base their decisions on qualitative judgments.

We can consider in a qualitative way when the marginal benefits of additional safety net spending would be most likely to outweigh the alternative uses of funds or marginal costs (see Coady and Harris 2004 for the theory and for an application to the Mexican reform that replaced general food subsidies with the PROGRESA CCT program in 1997). Benefits from additional safety net spending are more likely to be justified under the following circumstances:

- **When the program is "good."** As chapter 2 shows, safety nets can alleviate some of the misery of destitution, may help households invest in their livelihoods or their children's futures and manage risks, and can facilitate reform of government policies. Some programs will do better at producing some of these effects than others depending on their scale, consistency, flexibility, features, and the like. Chapters 2 and 9 provide criteria by which to judge programs in more detail, and the remainder of the book provides advice on how to achieve good outcomes. Funding proposals can be judged against this information when rigorous impact evaluations are unavailable.

- **When the net expenditure and/or tax package is progressive.** One of the goals of safety nets is redistribution; thus, expenditures will be more justified if they are distributed progressively. Moreover, the productive effects will be more likely to be greatest for the poorest. Redistribution per currency unit transferred will be heightened if the expenditures are concentrated at the bottom end of the welfare distribution and if taxes are progressive rather than regressive.

- **When base spending on safety nets is low.** When expenditures are low, more spending may well be justified, but as the program achieves something approaching adequate financing, the value of additional spending will decline. Higher funding would allow the program to expand from the poorest to the less poor, which implies a lower redistributive impact, and/or the larger budget could increase the level of benefits given to each beneficiary. This again implies less social value, as an additional currency unit of transfer will be less important for a less poor household than for a poorer one.

- **When alternative uses of funds are less important.** Increasing spending on safety nets is certainly more socially valuable than buying another palace for a dictator or his mistress. It is extremely likely to be more socially valuable than spending on a regressive gasoline subsidy that encourages pollution, but may or may not be more valuable than financing vaccinations or bednets to prevent malaria for the poor.

- **When the extra taxes to finance the expenditures have the lowest efficiency costs.** Different tax instruments vary in the extent of distortions they introduce. Broadly based tax instruments—especially a VAT, and occasionally an income tax—will be less distortionary than choices such as trade taxes.

Achieving the first three conditions will increase a program's marginal benefits, while achieving the last two will result in lower marginal costs.

3.2 Sources of Financing for Safety Nets

Money is fungible from one use to another, so the issue is whether an expenditure is justified in relation to the alternatives. Governments basically have four choices for how to finance a specific expenditure: reallocate expenditures from something else, increase taxes, find international grant financing, or borrow.[3] Each of the four financing sources has advantages and disadvantages (table 3.2). Which option or combination of options is preferable depends on a country's situation: some have no possibility of increasing aid financing, some are so heavily indebted that further debt financing is unwise, and some have tax rates well above the average; but at the same time, some do have some flexibility on one or more dimensions (World Bank 2007e).

TABLE 3.2 **Options for Increasing Safety Net Budgets: Advantages and Disadvantages**

Financing source	Advantages	Disadvantages
Expenditure reallocation	• Finances programs within budget constraints • Increases overall productivity of government outlays	• No additional funds relative to the budget • Many countries have low levels of discretionary spending
Increased taxation	• More sustainable than other options	• Economic costs • Politically unpopular
International grants	• Increases availability of funds	• Inflexibility in use of funds • Instability of funding • Donor coordination issues • Government autonomy issues
Borrowing	• Finances investment in productive activities in countries with low public savings • Finances temporary expansion of programs during crises	• Currency mismatch in balance sheets • High debt service burden • Debt overhang impact on growth • Vulnerability to a solvency crisis

SOURCE: Authors.

REALLOCATING EXPENDITURES

It is often possible to reallocate expenditures from other programs to safety nets. The advantage of expenditure reallocation is, obviously, that it does not require new resources and thus leaves the spending envelope unchanged. If the resources are reallocated from less effective or important programs to good safety nets, the overall productivity of government outlays may increase. A disadvantage of expenditure reallocation is that the room for it may be limited. Government spending may be low, may be confined to equally important activities, or may have limited flexibility. Reallocation can also be politically difficult. Even where economists may see areas where the redeployment of funds could increase efficiency, politicians may see no realistic possibility of accomplishing the change.

Reallocations to finance safety nets are most visible when the government reduces or eliminates an across-the-board subsidy and replaces it with a targeted transfer program.

Jamaica, for example, eliminated general food subsidies in 1984 and used some of the savings to fund its Food Stamp Program (Grosh 1992). Brazil reduced the subsidy on cooking gas in 2001 and funded the Auxílio Gás (Cooking Gas Grant) cash transfer program as compensation (Lindert, Skoufias, and Shapiro 2006). In 2005, Indonesia instituted a massive reduction in petroleum subsidies and reallocated half the funds implicitly saved to spending on health, education, and a new cash transfer program (Indrawati 2005). More subtle reallocations can also occur, as when other sectors are made more efficient and the savings reallocated.

If reallocation within a given budget is impossible, the budget may need to be increased to accommodate the desired spending on safety nets.

INCREASING TAXES

Governments never take the option of increasing taxes lightly because it can have real economic costs, as well as the obvious political ones (see box 3.2 for a discussion of tax instruments). However, taxes in some developing countries are sufficiently below those of comparable countries that increased revenue collection seems economically feasible, even wise. Uganda, for example, raises the equivalent of about 11 to 12 percent of GDP in domestic revenues; this is much less than the 20 percent raised in Ethiopia, a country with otherwise similar fiscal characteristics, or the 25 percent average for low-income countries. Uganda might consider revenue enhancement seriously, and such enhancement is even a feature of policy dialogue in Ethiopia. Higher up the income scale, Chile and South Africa, which raise the equivalent of 24 and 25 percent of GDP in taxes, respectively, have much more potential to consider revenue enhancement than Brazil (45 percent of GDP) or Turkey (31 percent of GDP) (World Bank 2007e). Note that Chile and South Africa have managed to provide comprehensive safety net systems despite their relatively low expenditures.

If taxes are to be raised to finance safety nets, they must not take more away from those who will benefit from safety nets than they give back. At a minimum, they should be neutral in their incidence. Chu, Davoodi, and Gupta (2000) provide a comprehensive overview of the tax incidence literature in developing countries. They note that 36 studies of 19 countries find that their overall tax systems are progressive in 13 cases, neutral in 7, and regressive in 7. The other studies have mixed findings or show insignificant effects. This indicates that, in most cases, progressively targeted safety net spending will be redistributive, but that this will not be true for a number of cases—underscoring the need to be cautious about financing increased safety net expenditures via increased taxation.

OBTAINING GRANT FINANCING

Grant financing from donor agencies does not solve the trade-offs issue: the use of funds still has opportunity costs. Grant aid and tax revenues should be considered as if they were part of one big budget that is allocated according to the merits of different uses of funds, with the grants increasing the size of the total pie, but not necessarily earmarking the size of the slice that goes to safety nets. The consensus around agreements and meetings such as the Monterrey Accords, the Millennium Development Goals, the Gleneagles Summit of the Group of Eight, and the African Action Plan is for increased donor support for low-income countries, which may indirectly increase the volume of resources available for

BOX 3.2 **What Tax Instruments Should Governments Use to Support Safety Nets?**

Governments can chose from several different types of tax instruments (see table). Public finance experts regard general revenues, that is, the pool of all government revenues, as the most appropriate source of financing for safety nets. Because safety nets are noncontributory benefits targeted to the poor, financing them through the broadest available base would ensure the largest degree of redistribution through the tax system. Financing them with progressive taxes would enhance the redistribution.

Tax instrument	Advantages	Disadvantages
General revenues (income taxes, VAT, sales taxes)	• Large and stable tax base • Progressive incidence (income tax)	• Distortions of labor supply, saving, and consumption behaviors • Regressive (VAT) • Procyclical (income tax)
Payroll taxes	• Protected in the budget • Linked to benefits	• Regressive incidence • Labor market segmentation • Procyclical
Earmarked sin taxes	• Politically viable • Tax may be desirable in its own right	• Usually yields limited revenues
Cross-subsidization	• Redistributive effect within a program	• Incentives for overconsumption • Lack of fiscal transparency • Potential for contingent fiscal liabilities

SOURCE: Authors.

Payroll taxes are the classic instrument used to finance social insurance programs, so the question often arises whether they should be used to finance safety nets. In general, the answer is no for the following reasons:

- If the proposal implies that, as with social insurance, the benefit is limited to those who have contributed, such an arrangement would exclude those most in need of a safety net. With high levels of informal and self-employment (up to half the economy in Latin America and much higher shares in Africa and South Asia), those outside the formal sector would be ineligible, but usually have lower incomes and no access to the risk mitigation conveyed by the social insurance.

- Payroll taxes contribute to the segmentation of the labor market into formal and informal sectors. Keeping payroll taxes as low as is consistent with their use in affiliation-based social insurance is thus desirable.

- Payroll taxes are often less progressive than income taxes. The net impact is higher the more progressive the financing that supports expenditure on safety nets.

- Earmarking of payroll taxes introduces rigidities in the budget and can favor inefficiencies. Some safety net programs in Colombia receive earmarked funds; critics believe this has induced an inefficient mix of programs (World Bank 2002d).

safety nets.[4] Some donors are increasingly supportive of aid for safety nets specifically and so may label their support as being intended for safety nets. For example, a U.K. white paper on international development (DFID 2006) pledges to increase such spending in at least 10 African or South Asian low-income countries and double to 16 million the number of families moved from emergency relief to long-term social protection programs.

Three major problems arise with the way grant financing is usually delivered (see World Bank 2005e, chapter 3, for a cogent analysis of the issues powerfully illustrated with evidence from the health and education sectors). First, grants are often inflexible, covering only some parts of program costs. Second, aid flows can be volatile, and most donors operate on the basis of one- or two-year commitment cycles. At worst, this can result in programs that start up and disappear during short time horizons and thus never get past the initial start-up or troubleshooting phase. Even an attenuated version of the problem can result in a reluctance to undertake administrative improvements that require a number of years to accomplish or to achieve their payoff. Third, development assistance can carry high transaction costs. Many donors may be present in a single country, and frequently each donor funds separate, often similar, programs, which precludes the realization of economies of scale. Donors also often insist on their own sets of procedures for accounting or procurement, so a country must run parallel administrative systems and devote effort to managing donors rather than to service delivery. As grant aid is meant for lower-income countries, such inefficiencies are especially regrettable.

Ethiopia's experience with support for its safety net program prior to its 2005 reform illustrates some of the problems common to grant aid. The funding was significant, averaging about US$265 million per year from 1997 to 2002, but it was generated on a system of annual emergency appeals and thus was volatile in amount, varying from US$152 million in 1998 to US$449 million in 2000. Based on policy, 80 percent of the aid was dedicated to public works programs, but the programs encountered problems that were exacerbated by the aid arrangements. The World Bank (2004a, p. 135) summarizes these problems:

> Food comes too late, the amount of food distributed is so diluted that each household receives too little to materially affect their welfare. In the case of works programs, the stop-start nature of programs prevents them having a sustained impact on the incomes of the poor; and the absence of counterpart funds and integration with local capital plans means they often do not result in creation of lasting, productive assets.

Ethiopia's 2005 reforms of the productive safety net are intended to overcome several of these problems by establishing a government-driven system for aid to feed into, requesting multiyear pledges, and changing administrative arrangements to pave the way to greater impact. The reform effort required significant political will to begin and will need to be sustained over subsequent years to achieve its full effect.

BORROWING OR USING DEFICIT FINANCING

The general wisdom in public finance is that debt financing is advisable only when the extra spending financed by borrowing raises the country's ability to repay the debt in the future—for example, spending on infrastructure or education. Borrowing to finance current expenditure with no impact on future income-generation capacity and productivity can lead to a debt overhang, a lack of fiscal sustainability, and a greater likelihood of financial crises (Ter Rele and Westerhout 2003). Safety nets traditionally have been considered unproductive and merely redistributive. As argued in chapter 2, this may be an unduly harsh view, at least when safety nets are effectively run and targeted.

Debt financing may be particularly applicable for safety nets when they benefit future generations in ways that will raise their productivity, and consequently future tax revenues, or when a temporary increase in expenditures is needed, as after an economic crisis or a natural disaster. Both these conditions pertained in 2001 when Colombia and Turkey borrowed money from the International Bank from Reconstruction and Development to found CCT programs to ensure that the economic crises in their countries did not impair the poor's ability to build human capital for their children. At the same time, such programs do not always scale back automatically after a crisis.

Governments may borrow from international development banks in part to obtain the technical assistance and oversight that is often bundled with international development lending or to signal a multiyear commitment of funds to stakeholders, indicate a likelihood of technical quality, or the like. Borrowing from international development banks can entail some of the same problems as grant financing, although sometimes to a lesser extent, as the funding is more often multiyear and integrated into the government budget and the programs are executed by government agencies.

3.3 In Search of Countercyclical Financing for Safety Nets

A special concern in financing safety nets is how to guarantee adequate resources during macroeconomic crises or following disasters. This is particularly important in developing countries. Ferreira, Prennushi, and Ravallion (1999) point out that crises in which gross national product declines over a 12-month period and/or inflation doubles to a monthly rate above 40 percent per year are rare in OECD economies, but relatively common in the developing world. In such crises, the living standards of many people—almost invariably including the poorest—will fall for some period of time. If safety nets are to protect the poor in times of economic downturn, they obviously will need larger budgets than in times of growth to grant benefits to the increased number of poor and to grant higher benefits to those who were already poor and become poorer.

When funding increases in such times of need, it is called countercyclical (see Alderman and Haque 2006 for a thorough discussion of what it takes to provide a countercyclical safety net, including not only financing, but adequate targeting rules and ability to scale up quickly). The term is perhaps a bit pallid for the developing country context. It originated in the public finance jargon of the industrial countries, where the ups and downs are mild and are associated with the business cycle rather than the enormously greater volatility in developing countries.

Unfortunately, in practice, safety net spending has tended to be procyclical rather than countercyclical (Braun and Di Gresia 2003). De Ferranti and others (2000), for example, find that even though seven Latin American countries did a good job of maintaining the share of targeted and social spending in the budget during a crisis, for every 1 percent decline in GDP, spending per poor person fell by 2 percent.

Governments often try to protect budgets for safety net programs by increasing their share of the budget and reducing the shares of other items, but such reallocation is unlikely to fully protect spending per poor person during crises. Even when governments give safety net spending high priority, spending itself will fall. Crises involve declines in real wages and employment, which lower revenues. Moreover, the stabilization packages adopted to try to pull the economy out of the crisis often involve reducing fiscal deficits, with expenditure reduction usually an important means of doing so. Simultaneously, the number of poor people rises, as does the level of need among the chronically poor. Thus just when needs are rising, means are falling.

The apparent solution to this problem is to prefund safety net program budgets. Some unemployment insurance funds work on this principal, collecting contributions in a special fund while workers are employed and paying out during recessions. Such arrangements do have their limits. In the early 1990s, several Eastern European countries reduced the replacement rate and duration of unemployment benefits, at least in part because of fiscal pressures associated with the transition (Vodopivec, Wörgötter, and Raju 2003). Some countries have tried to hold reserve stocks of grain, with less than desired outcomes (World Bank 2005h).

Some countries, such as India, Mexico, and the Philippines, hold reserve funds for relief programs (Gurenko and Lester 2004). The state of Maharashtra in India has earmarked a specific tax to fund countercyclical public works. While such funding may be adequate for localized emergencies, the needs imposed by large covariate shocks, such as the flood in Bangladesh in 1998 or the 2004 Asian tsunami, cannot be met without external support and/or macroeconomic consequences (Alderman and Haque 2006). Prefunding is quite rare for social assistance programs. Instead, countercyclical finance may be achieved through prudently low overall spending during stable times and increased spending or borrowing in times of increased need. Chile and Colombia are among the countries that have taken this route.

Pressures on governments to spend revenues as they are collected have hampered the accumulation of fiscal savings to be used in the case of need. A typical example is the procyclical accumulation of oil revenues (Alesina and Tabellini 2005; Davis, Ossowsky, and Fedelino 2003). The tendency is general, but pertains fully in the case of safety nets.

Governments have used fiscal responsibility laws as a way to enforce broad countercyclical fiscal policy. These rules are intended to aid in maintaining fiscal discipline and, perhaps equally important, to signal to creditors and other concerned parties that deficits during times of recession are not to be seen as a sign of irresponsibility but as part of a planned countercyclical policy. The overall performance of fiscal rules has been mixed. They are apparently neither necessary nor sufficient for overall fiscal discipline, much less do the results pass through directly to a single rubric of spending, such as safety nets (box 3.3).

The desire for countercyclical funding for safety nets stems from the aim of serving those who need help. But it is pertinent to note that even in good times very few safety net programs in developing countries are fully funded. In industrial countries, most safety net programs are operated as "entitlement" programs—that is, all households meeting the eligibility criteria are guaranteed entry, with administrative processes and budgets (or budget flexibility) to back that promise. In developing countries, the vast majority of programs have some sort of a rationing mechanism to ensure that budgets are kept to an allowed

---

BOX 3.3 Fiscal Responsibility Laws

Fiscal responsibility laws can be of two different types:

- Laws that mostly establish quantitative fiscal targets (Kopits and Symansky 1998), such as the government's overall deficit or a ceiling on certain high-priority spending levels, for example, the fiscal responsibility legislation in India
- Laws that focus on enhanced fiscal transparency and public expenditure management, for example, as in New Zealand

Countries' experiences show that unless important preconditions in term of fiscal transparency, budget accounts, political consensus, and enforcement mechanisms are met, fiscal responsibility legislation in itself is insufficient to ensure that fiscal policy is sound. Also, fiscal rules tend to be less effective if they only cover the central government, are too specific, and do not foster a reallocation of government spending among programs.

Countries that have successful fiscal rules include Brazil, where the law has fostered the credibility of the government's policies, and Chile, where fiscal rules had a role in protecting social spending in 2004. Automatic stabilizers tend to be most effective in industrial countries. Failures of fiscal rules in Argentina and elsewhere in Latin America are among the factors that contributed to macroeconomic instability (Singh and others 2005). An example of a fiscal rule that has not been fully enforced is the European Union's Stability and Growth Pact.

---

amount: sometimes beneficiary rosters are opened once only and then closed for years, or they are opened annually to a number of beneficiaries who exhaust the fixed budget and then closed. There are several programs in Eastern Europe that have entry rules and administrative processes sufficient for an entitlement program but that have sometimes lacked the fiscal support and thus had to run in arrears. It is sobering to note that even these upper-middle income European Union accession countries cannot deliver an entitlement system. The larger magnitudes and greater frequency of downturns in developing economies implies that the fiscal risk that would be incurred by moving to an entitlement design would be greater than borne in the OECD countries where entitlement is commonplace.

With entitlement programs, the number of beneficiaries and program budget naturally fall once the general economy recovers. People get jobs, their earnings increase and place them over the threshold for a means test, or they become too well-off to choose to participate in self-targeting programs. When programs are not operated as entitlements, this decline in expenditures will be less automatic. Some households will leave the program as a result of their greater prosperity, but other eligible households that have been rationed out will be waiting to take their place. Reducing program expenditures may mean introducing tighter rationing, which may be politically difficult to do. Program managers and advocates for the poor will point to unmet needs and available resources and wonder why they cannot be matched up. In this way, the desirable goal of assisting the needy in good times comes into partial conflict with achieving the countercyclical husbanding of resources to help them during hard times.

Prospects for achieving countercyclical financing for safety nets in developing countries seem slim until safety nets are fully financed in stable times and volatility is lower than has recently been the case. Expenditure reallocation in favor of safety nets during downturns and generally prudent fiscal policy will help and have been put into effect, but to a degree insufficient to yield countercyclical funding for safety nets.

3.4 The Cost of the Welfare State in Developed Countries

One of the implications of the basic theory of optimal spending is that a country that spends too much on safety nets will pay a price: it will fail to invest in other, more important things and/or it will struggle under unduly burdensome taxes. So another way to think about how much effort countries might be able to devote to safety nets comes from looking at the empirical literature on the cost of safety nets.

The literature on the costs of the welfare state predominately concerns OECD countries, because that is where such expenditures are dramatically the highest and the issues most pressing. Atkinson (1999), Barr (2004), and Lindert (2004) critique older literature in ways that largely discount the concern that high expenditures on well-designed social protection systems will slow growth. They put forward the following arguments for how countries can afford substantial transfer systems, which are traditionally viewed as unproductive and are expected to lower growth through the burden of the taxes to support them and the labor disincentives effects among recipients:

- The simplistic models used to describe the labor-reducing effects of tax and transfer policies are too simple and extreme, and are therefore misleading.

- The assessments of the cost of the welfare state have focused on the costs in terms of growth but have not tried to calculate the benefits that derive from the programs, and as such are erroneously specified.

- The empirical evidence shows that in practice, growth and welfare state spending are weakly correlated. Lindert (2004, p. 234) notes: "Within the range of true historical experience, there is no clear net GDP cost of higher social transfers."[5]

All three authors provide examples of how real-life social protection policies have design features to limit their potential distortions. Blank (2002) joins the chorus. She categorizes the ways in which program design can minimize the leaks in Okun's bucket by supporting those unlikely to work (the elderly, children, people with disabilities); imposing job search, work, or study requirements on those who can work (often labeled as activation or welfare-to-work reforms) in industrial countries, CCT programs in middle-income countries, or public works jobs in low-income countries; or by investing, as in many programs for young children, certainly including those linked to their health or education, and possibly even general child allowances. Though not precisely quantified, a substantial share of safety net spending actually goes to such programs.

The implications of the OECD literature for developing countries are as follows:

- The literature is concerned with the whole package of social protection or of social protection and health insurance, so that the transfers considered average 21 percent of GDP for the OECD countries and range up to 30 percent for the highest spenders, an order of magnitude more than the range of spending on safety nets in developing countries. This implies that developing countries spending little on safety nets may be able to spend a bit more without unduly harming their economies.

- The OECD countries have essentially added their social protection systems to the list of other social service and infrastructure duties of government. Social protection has not come directly as a trade-off between, for instance, establishing universal education or good road systems, but in addition to them. In the low-income country setting, debates on safety nets are often couched as transfers versus development. Perhaps the issue should be rephrased in terms of whether safety nets are an important (additional) component of development policy.

- The highest-spending countries have chosen a relatively efficient pattern of taxation, more so than some of the lower spenders (Lindert 2004). The impact of social protection on growth depends not only on the magnitude of spending, but on how the spending is financed.

- Because the OECD literature covers long-standing systems, their benefits are perhaps being realized and captured in effects on growth as a counterbalance to their costs. This suggests that the findings could easily apply to developing countries that have well-designed safety nets and less so to those whose programs are ineffective.

The issue of how much a country can "afford" to spend on safety nets is dictated by more than the technical issues of economics. It involves choices between things society values, and is thus deeply political as well. The literature on the political economy of support for social spending or safety nets shows that public attitudes on the topic vary within any given country and that the predominant view also differs among countries.

The World Values Survey and the similar Latinobarómetro provide evidence on the strength of beliefs that poverty is largely due to individual behavior, such as laziness, or to forces outside the individual's control, such as bad luck, lack of family connections, or the fault of society.[6] This evidence can be tied to facts about the welfare programs in the pertinent polities, as illustrated in figure 3.1 typifies the finding. The figure shows that social welfare spending is much higher as a percentage of GDP in countries where public attitudes reflect a

FIGURE 3.1 **Societal Attitudes about Poverty and Spending on Social Welfare**

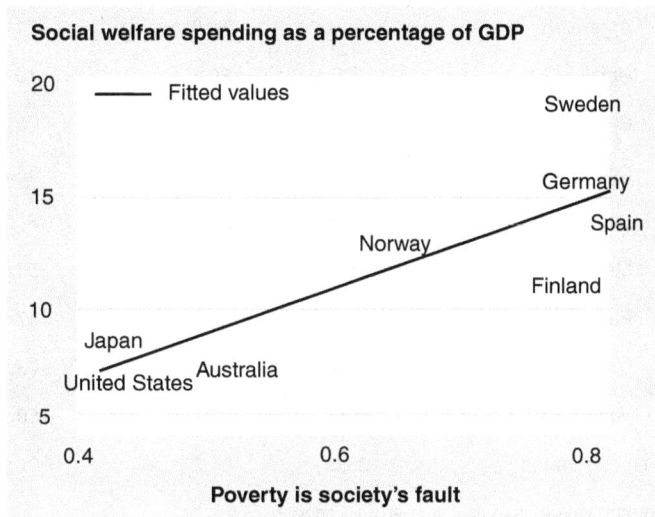

SOURCE: Alesina and Glaeser 2004.

view that poverty is caused by forces outside of an individual's control. Alesina and Glaeser (2004) show that among U.S. states, a similar correlation is apparent between beliefs about the cause of poverty and maximum benefit levels in the Aid to Families with Dependent Children program, the former principal welfare program in the United States. Lindert, Skoufias, and Shapiro (2006) report that, in general, Latin American attitudes about the causes of poverty, redistribution, and intergenerational mobility follow the European pattern and thus provide substantial support for safety nets (table 3.3).

Other political factors are important as well. Substantial work has been devoted to the role of ethnic homogeneity and its effects on support for safety nets. Most analysts agree that homogeneity is supportive of safety nets and heterogeneity is harmful (Alesina and Glaeser 2004; Lee and Roemer 2004; Lindert 2004). The extent of democracy (Lindert 2004) and the form of its institutions—for instance, proportional versus majoritarian representation—seem to matter as well (Alesina and Glaeser 2004).

Societal attitudes about the causes of poverty define who the "deserving" poor are. In turn, the view of deservedness influences the choice of transfer programs and their design. The deserving poor are usually a subset of the poor who are poor through no fault of their own. The view of who among the poor is perceived as deserving of public transfers differs from country to country and in the same country over time.

TABLE 3.3 **Perceptions of Poverty in the United States, Europe, and Latin America, 1995–7 (percentage of respondents)**

Region and country	The poor are poor because		The poor have little chance of escaping from poverty	The government's response to poverty is inadequate
	Society is unjust	They are lazy		
Continental Europe	63.3	17.1	60.2	64.5
Latin America and the Caribbean (average)	65.8	28.3	62.0	67.7
Argentina	74.0	26.0	74.5	81.7
Brazil	75.7	20.5	70.5	—
Chile	55.6	36.9	58.5	58.7
Colombia	—	—	55.8	—
Dominican Republic	68.6	24.5	61.2	89.0
Mexico	65.8	24.6	56.9	71.1
Peru	56.5	34.2	47.1	44.8
Uruguay	77.2	12.4	73.5	80.8
Venezuela, R. B. de	52.9	47.1	59.6	79.9
United States	38.8	61.2	29.5	41.8

SOURCE: Lindert, Skoufias, and Shapiro 2006, table 3.

NOTE: — = not available.

Consider the example of Bulgaria. In 1996 and 1997, Bulgaria experienced a deep economic crisis. GDP fell by 15 percentage points over two years, and unemployment rose from 10 percent in 1995 to 14 percent in 1997. The view that the whole country had suffered from the transition to a market economy was pervasive. To arrest the negative consequences of the crisis on the poorest, the government increased the threshold of its Guaranteed Minimum Income Program, a cash transfer program designed to support everyone whose income fell below a certain threshold, by topping up their actual incomes to bring them to a standard minimum. This topping-up procedure meant that every beneficiary household received only the minimum it needed and spread the scheme's resources as thinly as possible. Such a program would, at least in theory, provide huge labor disincentives. Why would people earning below the threshold work at all if their income were raised to the threshold level regardless of whether they worked? Given the sharp rise in unemployment at that time, such concerns were not central to the policy debate. Unemployment did not carry the stigma of laziness; rather, people were sorry for those down on their luck.

Five years after the crisis, the circumstances were quite different: Bulgaria had registered its fifth consecutive year of robust growth of 5 to –6 percent per person per year, but at 18 percent, unemployment was both persistent and high. Concerns about the negative impact of the Guaranteed Minimum Income Program on work incentives took center stage in the policy debate. In 2002, the government implemented a public works program targeted to the long-term unemployed receiving transfers from the program, who accounted for half of all beneficiaries. The public works jobs paid the minimum wage plus benefits. The program's coverage and spending fell by one-third while substantially improving its targeting performance. The shift in political attitudes about who was considered to be the deserving poor brought about the 2002 reforms, influenced the mix of safety net programs, and altered program features to reduce labor disincentives.

3.5 Levels and Patterns of Safety Net Spending in Developing and Transition Countries

Because indicating precisely what countries should spend on safety nets based on theory is so difficult, analysts often seek guidance based on benchmarks. Benchmarking is, of course, imperfect, as there is nothing to indicate whether the countries used in the benchmarks are spending the "right" amount. In addition, choosing benchmarks is an art. Countries are often compared with their neighbors, which may share the same historical and institutional forces—and may therefore share the same tendencies to "wrong" expenditure. More thoughtful selection of benchmarks considers a wider set of countries at the same economic level and with comparable demographic characteristics, or ones that the country in question hopes to emulate in the future.

To assist in benchmarking, we have developed a new dataset on spending in developing and transition countries and have tried to understand some of the factors that may be associated with relatively high or low spending on safety nets. These factors include level of income, extent of inequality, governance, democracy, presence of different ethnic groups, and variation in public attitudes. We present our findings and provide the raw data in Weigand and Grosh (2008) so that analysts may use them for their own benchmarking exercises.

Quantifying spending on safety nets is difficult. The conceptual definition used in this book does not fit within a single ministry's mandate, so the most easily and regularly obtainable sets of numbers on government spending are not useful for tracking spending on safety nets. In Peru, for example, the main safety net programs fall under half a dozen ministries and three different levels of government. And Peru only has about 20 major safety net programs, many fewer than commonly found elsewhere: Bulgaria has 34 programs; Mexico over 100, spread through dozens of agencies and three levels of government.

The International Monetary Fund's (IMF's) *Government Finance Statistics* is accessible, published frequently, and takes care to establish comparability, but does not have a category that closely matches the concept of safety nets as used in this book (IMF 2001). It lumps much social assistance in with social insurance to come up with a single figure for "social security and welfare"; other social assistance may fall under the "transfers to households and other organizations" category;[7] and more will be reported in the accounts of the ministries that house or serve as umbrella organizations for the various programs, especially if these are in-kind programs. Despite their shortcomings, the IMF numbers have been the basis of a literature on safety net spending summarized in box 3.4.

To fill the gap in knowledge about safety net spending in developing countries, we rely here on information provided by Weigand and Grosh (2008) that more closely follows the conceptual definition of safety nets used in this book. We supplement this information with data for a handful of OECD countries from the OECD Social Expenditure Database (OECD 2004b) and with data from the World Bank (2007c). Weigand and Grosh (2008) compile data from World Bank public expenditure reviews and other similar analytical work. These studies, performed as one-time or periodic reviews of social policy, try to sort through countries' budgets and programmatic structures to assemble comprehensive numbers, an exercise inherently different from that usually carried out for a given country as part of its annual budgetary process.

The following three caveats to these data are in order:

- **Incomplete coverage.** Weigand and Grosh provide data for 87 countries between 1996 and 2006.[8] Coverage varies by region. It is high for Europe and Central Asia, with 25 of the 29 countries covered (and 96 percent of the population). Coverage is much less for Sub-Saharan Africa, with 9 of the 47 countries covered (and 18 percent of the population).

- **Comparability.** Because the expenditure numbers compiled by Weigand and Grosh were calculated by the various authors of the many country reports, the precise definition of what to include in the safety net or social protection sector as a whole varies. Weigand and Grosh report the composites largely as they occur in the reports, trusting to the judgments of the authors of the individual reports to include what was pertinent and available in a given country. For health and education expenditures, Weigand and Grosh use World Bank (2007c), which has less serious comparability issues.

- **Interpretation.** What countries do spend is not necessarily what they should spend. The reports underlying the data reported here were undertaken because the level of spending was a policy issue at the time the individual country studies

BOX 3.4 **Literature on Safety Net Spending Levels Based on the IMF's** *Government Finance Statistics*

Safety net programs typically represent about 1 to 2 percent or less of GDP in developing countries. This compares with spending levels of 2 to 4 percent of GDP in industrial countries (Atkinson 1995). Average spending levels tend to be higher in middle-income countries than in low-income countries, reflecting the low revenue base in the latter countries, but variability is large (Fox 2003). Spending levels also vary by region, with South Asian and Sub-Saharan African countries spending less than Latin American and Caribbean countries and countries in Eastern and Central Europe and the Middle East spending more (Besley, Burgess, and Rasul 2003).

Various authors have tested for and found different factors that may affect the level of safety net spending or of social spending more broadly. Higher per capita incomes tend to be associated with higher spending on social assistance programs, while the incidence of poverty and inequality are not necessarily good predictors of the level of spending on safety nets. This is because in many regions—for example, Latin America and the Caribbean—the system of social protection is split between social insurance for the (wealthier) formal sector worker and meager social assistance for the (poorer) worker in the informal sector (Fiszbein 2004). Schwabish, Smeeding, and Osberg (2004) find that inequality between the middle class and the poor (as measured by the ratio of welfare between those at the 50th percentile and those at the 10th percentile) has a small, positive impact on social spending, but that inequality between the ends of the distribution and the middle class (as measured by the ratio of welfare between those at the 90th percentile and those at the 50th percentile) has a large and negative impact. Also, spending levels tend to be higher for countries with better governance indicators (Baldacci, Hillman, and Kojo 2004), but are not necessarily different in decentralized and centralized economies (Ter-Minassian 1997). Spending on safety nets tends to be correlated with government size, but is generally negatively correlated with fiscal deficits and inflation. This is because countries with unstable macroeconomic conditions are more likely to have insufficient resources to finance the safety net (de Ferranti and others 2000).

were done. This suggests that at least some parties thought the spending level was inappropriate.

Spending on safety nets as a percentage of GDP provides a summary measure of a government's efforts to provide safety nets. We also broaden our view to consider wider concepts of spending. We define social protection as the sum of safety nets (social assistance) and social insurance (pensions, unemployment insurance). We define the social sectors as the sum of spending on social protection, health, and education.

The data show the following:

- Mean spending on safety nets is 1.9 percent of GDP, and median spending is 1.4 percent of GDP. For about half of the countries, spending falls between 1 and 2 percent of GDP (figure 3.2).[9] Some variation is apparent. For example, Bosnia and Herzegovina, Pakistan, and Tajikistan spend considerably less than 1 percent of GDP. At the other extreme, spending on safety nets in Ethiopia and

FIGURE 3.2 **Safety Net Expenditures as a Percentage of GDP, Selected Countries and Years**

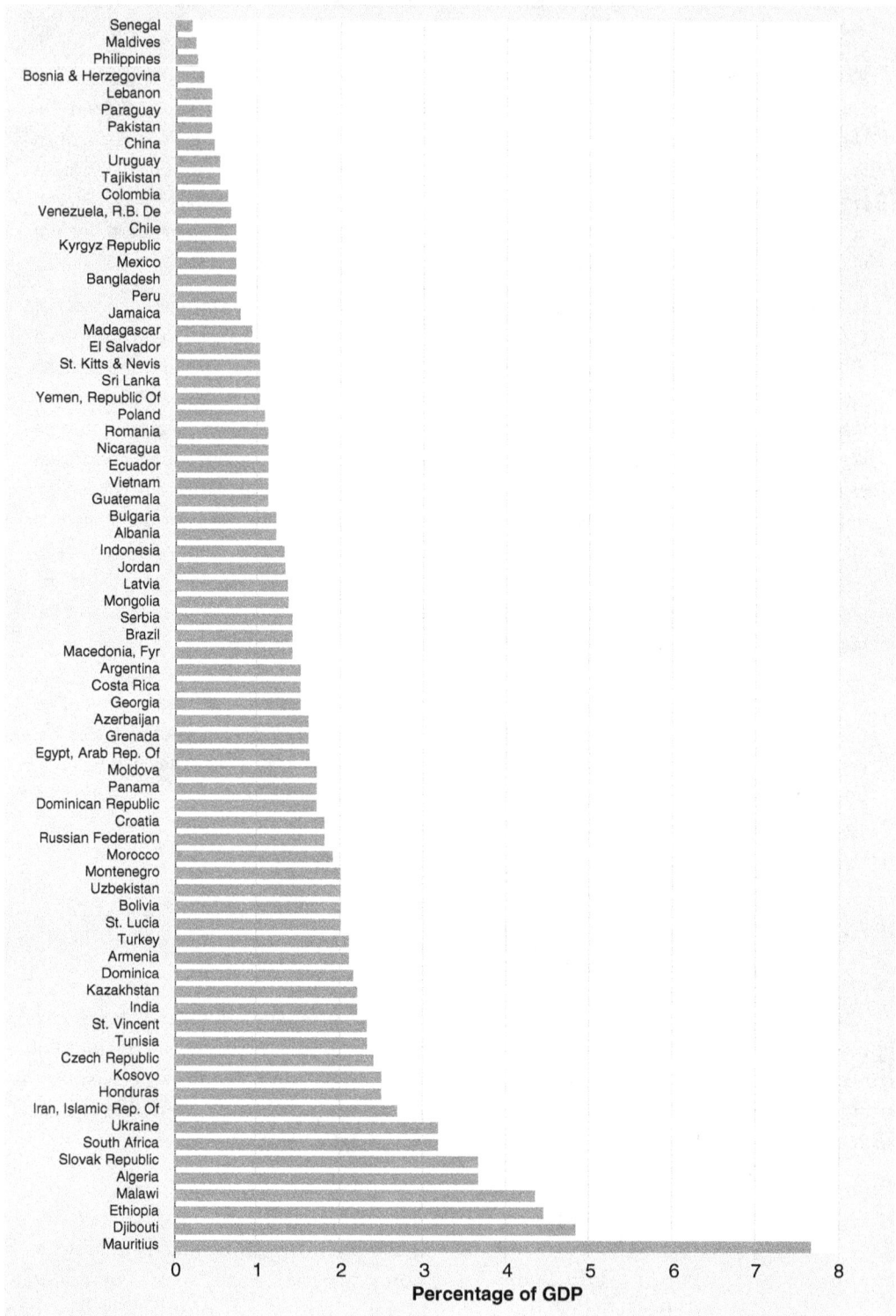

SOURCE: Weigand and Grosh 2008.
NOTE: Kosovo data are for 2003.

Malawi is nearly 4.5 percent of GDP because international aid is counted; these shares would be closer to 0.5 percent if only domestically financed spending were counted. Other high-spending countries—Mauritius, South Africa, and the Slovak Republic—finance their safety nets domestically.

- Regional patterns are about as might be expected, with the Middle East and North Africa spending the most (2.2 percent on average), followed by Europe and Central Asia (1.7 percent on average), and Latin America and the Caribbean (1.3 percent on average). The smaller number of observations makes the averages less robust for the other regions. For instance, the average of 3.5 percent for Sub-Saharan Africa is based on only six observations and includes external financing.

- Spending on safety nets is less variable than spending on social protection or the social sectors (figures 3.3 and 3.4).

To try to understand the sources of variation in spending patterns, we look at these patterns and their relationship to the following variables typically discussed in the literature on developed countries:

- **Country income** as measured by GDP per capita with purchasing power parity adjustments. The hypothesis is that richer countries will spend more.

- **Inequality** as measured by the Gini coefficient. The hypothesis varies with the model of power assumed. A one-person, one-vote economy with higher inequality will face more pressure for redistribution, because the number of people with incomes below the mean will be higher. In a model with elite capture of government, the elite may use private providers of social services and give little support to public ones, so higher inequality may lead to lower spending.

- **Voice** as measured by the Kaufmann, Kraay, and Mastruzzi (2005) index for voice. We hypothesize is that greater voice will be positively related to spending on safety nets, social protection, and/or the social sectors.

- **Ethnic fragmentation** as measured by Alesina and others (2002). The hypothesis is that greater fragmentation will lead to lower spending on safety nets, social protection, and/or the social sectors.

- **Democracy** as measured by the Polity IV Project (2008). The hypothesis is that greater democracy will lead to higher spending on safety nets, social protection, and/or the social sectors.

- **Attitudes about inequality** as based on a question from the 1990–2004 questionnaires of the World Values Survey, which asks respondents to score their attitudes on a scale with "incomes should be made more equal" at one end and "we need larger income differences as incentives for individual efforts" at the other. We hypothesize that spending will be higher when more people believe in the need for greater equality.

In simple correlations, most of the factors have the expected sign, but the strength of the correlation is generally higher the broader the concept of spending used (table 3.4). For spending on safety nets alone, none of the factors examined correlate significantly.

FIGURE 3.3 **Social Assistance and Social Insurance as a Percentage of GDP by Region, Selected Years**

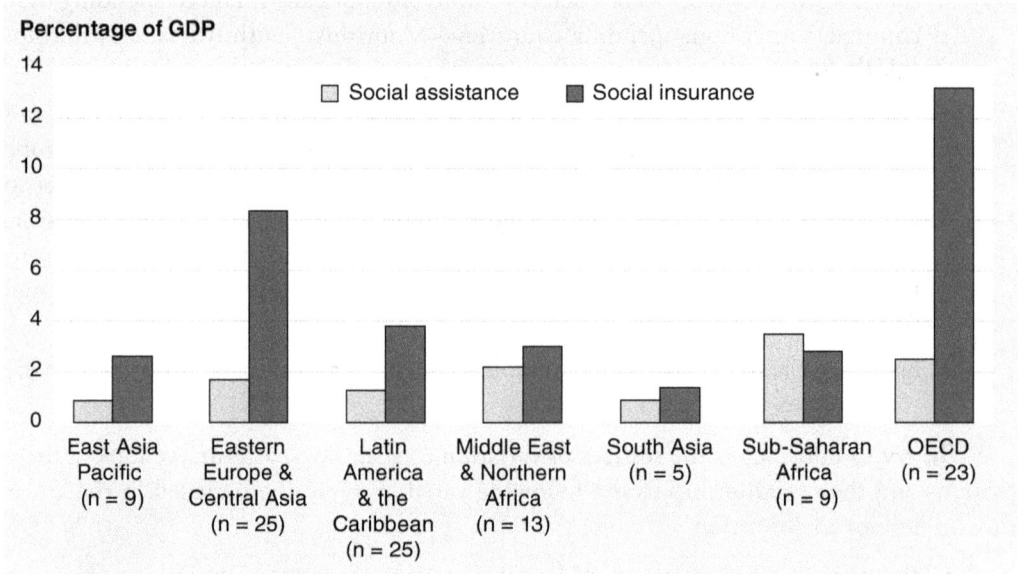

SOURCES: Weigand and Grosh 2008; OECD 2004b.

NOTE: Not all the reports Weigand and Grosh use offer data on all categories of spending. For the OECD, we used 23 countries, as such countries as Mexico and Poland are already accounted for in the regional averages.

FIGURE 3.4 **Social Assistance, Social Insurance, and Social Sector Spending by Region, Selected Years**

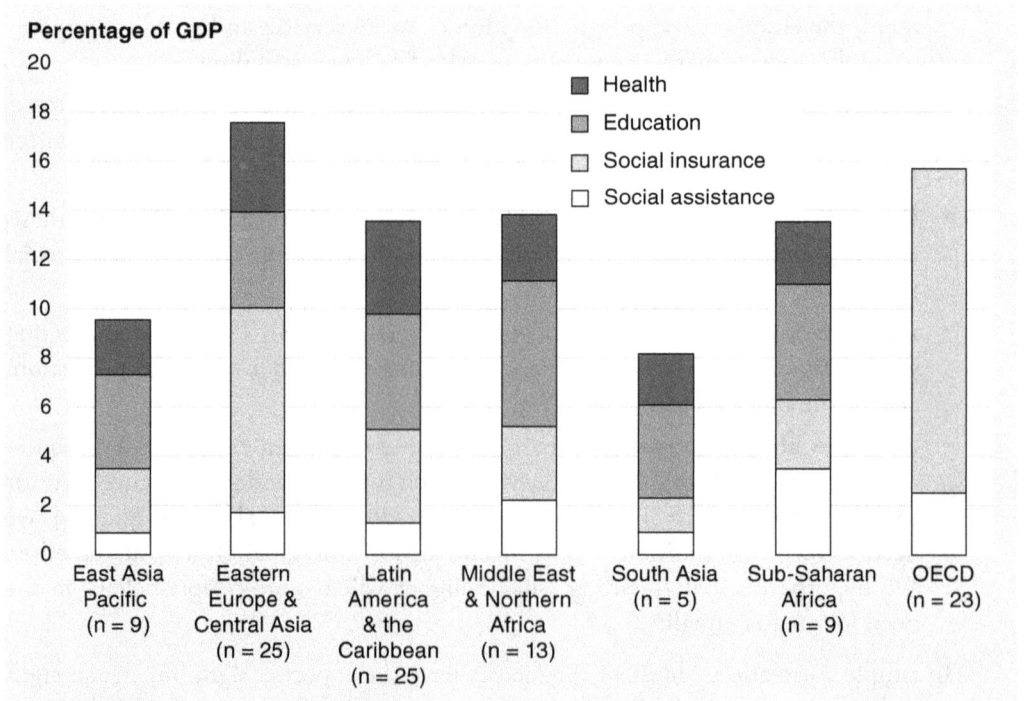

SOURCES: Weigand and Grosh 2008; OECD 2004b.

NOTE: See note to figure 3.3.

However, spending on social protection and the social sectors is significantly higher where income or voice are higher and lower where inequality is higher.

TABLE 3.4 **Correlations between Spending on Social Sectors and Other Factors**

Factor	Safety net spending as % of GDP	Social protection spending as % of GDP	Social sector spending as % of GDP
Per capita GDP (PPP)	0.0768	0.5045**	0.5460**
Gini coefficient	−0.1104	−0.3410**	−0.2686*
Voice	0.0678	0.2294**	0.2607**
Ethnic fragmentation	0.1628	−0.0204	−0.0972
Democracy	0.1733	−0.0533	0.1907
Attitudes about inequality	0.1234	−0.1694	−0.1559

SOURCE: Authors' calculations.

NOTE: PPP = purchasing power parity. Factors are measured as described in the text. * indicates that coefficients are significant at the 10 percent level or better. ** indicates that coefficients are significant at the 5 percent level or better.

The results on measured inequality are worth noting: the correlations are all negative, that is, higher Ginis associated with lower spending on safety nets, social protection, and the social sectors as a whole. In examining the data in detail, most of the low Gini countries are in Europe and Central Asia, which historically has large social protection sectors; the high Gini countries are in Latin America and the Caribbean, which has a history of truncated welfare states. Because these two regions dominate the dataset, the inequality variable used may be capturing a historical legacy more than the real workings of inequality in relation to decision making.

Figure 3.5 shows the more robust correlations for broader concepts of spending. The relationship with GDP is much more marked for the social sectors than for safety nets alone. In looking at attitudes to inequality, the finding for the social sectors echoes Alesina and Glaeser's (2004) findings for OECD economies presented in section 3.4; in contrast, the pattern for safety nets is not statistically significant and is of the opposite slope as would be expected.

We interpret the pattern of results—that the correlates of social spending viewed broadly are more definitive than the determinants of spending on safety nets—to mean that societies agree that a certain floor of safety nets is required, but that they also have reservations about making the safety net too large. Thus, when support for social policy is higher, it tends not to be expressed through more spending on safety nets, but through more spending on allied social policies pertaining to social insurance, health, and/or education. This interpretation is consistent with the patterns of spending shown in figure 3.5.

In sum, safety net spending as a share of GDP is not too diverse, with most countries concentrated in the 1 to 2 percent range. There may be a case for those much below this range to move into it and for higher spending in low-income countries, but clearly for many countries, the most pressing issue will not be changing the size of the budget

FIGURE 3.5 **Spending, Income, and Public Attitudes**

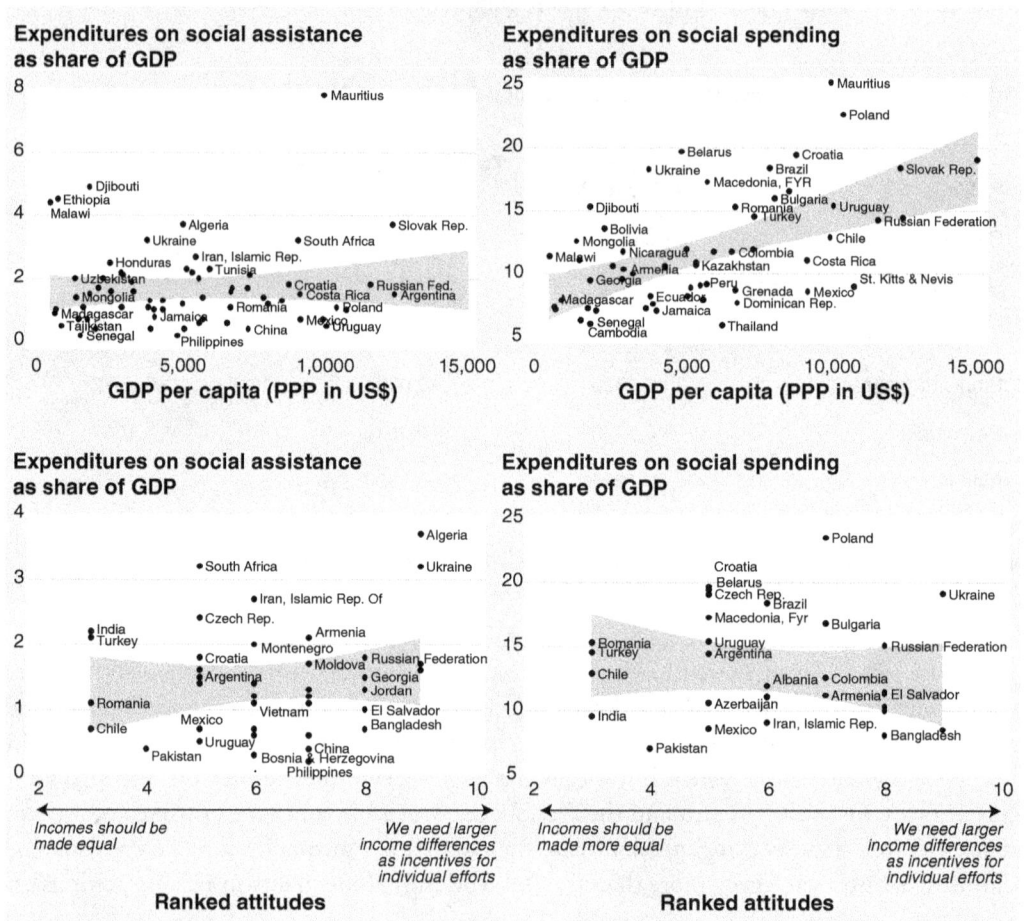

SOURCE: Weigand and Grosh (2008).

NOTE: PPP = purchasing power parity. In the interest of legibility, not all data points are labeled. Gray shading indicates the 95 percent confidence interval around the regression.

envelope devoted to safety nets, but making the most of that spending. That is the theme of the remainder of this book.

3.6 Delivering Safety Nets in a Decentralized World

Conventional wisdom in the public finance literature suggests that redistribution is a role most appropriately handled by central governments, because they are inherently in the best position to handle interregional inequalities and risk pooling, but that subnational jurisdictions may be well placed to administer safety nets, because they may have greater knowledge of or contact with the client base for the programs (Musgrave 1959; Oates 1972). The idea that people of similar circumstances should be treated alike underlies the call for national financing for safety net programs. It also implies a role for national standard setting, not only in relation to eligibility criteria and benefit levels, but to features of service delivery as well.

Decentralization has swept the developing world. In the last 25 years, governments of more than 75 countries have shifted more responsibilities to lower tiers of government. Most of these lower-level governments are elected, so the decentralization is political as well as administrative. The motivations for this vary. In Eastern Europe and the former Soviet Union, decentralization was part of the reaction to the former system of central planning; in Latin America, it was part of the transition to democracy; in countries such as Indonesia and Sri Lanka, it was a way to deal with regional and ethnic conflicts; and elsewhere, such as in Chile and Uganda, the goals were more explicitly related to the quality of service delivery.

The reality today is that a large share of safety net programs involve multiple tiers of government, which invokes what economists call the principal-agent problem. The national government is the financier, or the principal, and wants the programs it funds to operate in certain ways. It must rely on local governments—the agents—to carry out program-related functions, but cannot observe and control every action that these agents take. The solution lies in creating a mix of incentives and oversight mechanisms that bring the agents' actions in line with the principal's goals at an acceptable cost.

THE CENTRAL GOVERNMENT AS PRINCIPAL FINANCIER OF SAFETY NETS

Interregional inequalities can be significant and can present a conundrum: The poorest regions will have the highest poverty rates and the greatest need for social assistance for the chronically poor, but, at the same time, have the least capacity to tax their residents to raise revenues for distribution. For example, poverty rates in the regions of the Russian Federation vary from 3 to 56 percent. People with the same education levels and family composition are three times more likely to be poor in Dagestan Oblast or the Tuva Republic than those in the rich Tumen Oblast or in the city of Moscow (World Bank 2005l). This is not surprising in such a large, federal country; the situation is much the same in Brazil, China, India, and Nigeria. But such disparity also exists in much smaller, unitary countries. In Latvia, poverty estimates in 2004 ranged from 4 percent in Riga to 12 percent in Latgale (World Bank 2007i). Because local governments both finance and implement Latvia's Guaranteed Minimum Income Program, the relatively richer regions have considerably more funds available to spend than the poorer regions. This results in a perverse outcome whereby more than 40 percent of total social assistance transfers in Latvia go to people living in Riga, even though they are, on average, considerably better off than those residing in other parts of the country (World Bank 2007o).

Experience from Bosnia and Herzegovina, Bulgaria, and Romania demonstrates even more acutely the problem of assuming that local governments can reasonably finance safety nets. In 1995, Romania introduced Social Aid, a last-resort social assistance program. During its first year of implementation, the central government's budget financed the program, while implementation was decentralized to local governments. The program covered about 10 percent of the population, a figure close to the estimated number of extreme poor. During 1996–2001, the responsibility for program financing was transferred to local governments, with no extra resources transferred from the central government budget. The program's caseload plummeted to 6 percent of the population in 1996 and 2 percent in 2001, with the highest reductions in number of beneficiaries occurring in the poorest municipalities (World Bank 2003h). Two key factors behind the program's collapse were the inability of the poorest municipalities to pay eligible applicants and unclear legal provisions about the nature of the program. The central government altered and clarified program rules, but the finance problem and poor performance persisted until the program was recentralized in 2003. In Bosnia and Herzegovina, decentralized financing mechanisms have resulted in substantial interregional disparities in coverage, with poorer localities providing the fewest services. In the face of resource constraints, eligibility criteria for most benefits are ad hoc, as local welfare offices use discretion when rationing available resources. These sorts of regional inequalities in social assistance can be particularly troubling when they are linked, as they so often are, to ethnic or other social divisions.

Programs to protect those who have suffered shocks should be based on the largest possible risk pool, and should therefore be nationally financed. Thus most pension and unemployment insurance programs are centrally funded. The central government should also finance transfers related to natural disasters. Mexico's Natural Disaster Fund provides funding to local governments in areas hit by natural disasters to provide for temporary employment programs to help recipients replace lost income, help poor households rebuild their housing, and assist local governments in reestablishing public services and infrastructure (Government of Mexico 2003). The weakness of subnational risk pooling is seen in an example from the United States. Until 1988, the federal government paid for unemployment benefits for workers unemployed as the result of a natural disaster; the states have since been made responsible for this function. To manage the implied fiscal risk, many states have adopted systems in which if the reserve fund falls below a certain threshold, benefit cuts and tax increases are automatic. Louisiana hit this threshold following Hurricanes Katrina and Rita in 2005, when the single-state risk pool was too small given the dimensions of the disaster. Consequently, just when workers and businesses needed assistance, the system became less generous (*Washington Post* 2005).

A number of observers see welfare migration as another reason why national governments should play a central role in safety net finance and standard setting, though the case is not nearly as persuasive as for interregional equity and risk pooling. The economics literature and much political discourse in countries with federal social assistance systems are concerned with the idea that poor people will migrate from one region to another based on differences in the generosity of the regions' welfare programs. If this happens, or is even perceived as happening by policy makers and voters, it can lead each region to legislate a less generous program than it would otherwise have done. In the presence of welfare migration, the cost of an increase in a benefit would be not only the amount of the benefit increase multiplied by the number of current beneficiaries, but also the cost of the full amount of the benefit multiplied by the number of welfare migrants who would be attracted to the region. Similarly, a reduction in a benefit would both lower the cost per welfare recipient and reduce their number by inducing some of them to move away. Voters or legislators trying to balance costs with perceived satisfaction in providing for the poor will face a biased calculation. This issue is often referred to as "the race to the bottom," a catchy, though possibly exaggerated, term.

The issue has been little studied in developing countries. For the United States, Brueckner (2000) reviews studies of the Aid to Families with Dependent Children program, the main decentralized federal welfare program prior to the 1996 reforms. The studies reviewed provide mixed evidence on whether or not the system induced significant welfare migration, although the author shows that states tended to set their policy taking the policy of neighboring states into account, which may indicate that policy makers were concerned about the issue. Harrison (2006) reviews the issue in Canada and finds little evidence of a race to the bottom. Dahlberg and Eadmark (2004) study asylum seekers in Sweden and conclude that they migrate from the locations to which they are initially assigned to the three largest cities, which have more generous social assistance. Of course, these cities will also have more jobs and a more cosmopolitan atmosphere, which may be desirable to these immigrants.

As concerns implications for other countries, Canada and the United States are thoroughly integrated economically, and for individuals to move several times over the course of a lifetime is completely normal, both economically and culturally. Even in such countries, evidence on welfare migration is mild. The Swedish study is interesting, but considers a rather specialized subset of social assistance beneficiaries. We suspect that in many developing countries, the economic and social costs of moving will be much greater than in Canada and the United States, and thus welfare migration is less of a concern.

Three options are available for reducing the downward bias in program generosity that may result from concern about welfare migration: (1) make funding a fully national responsibility; (2) set national standards for program generosity; and (3) use a matching grant system of joint finance, with the national share being sufficiently high to offset the downward bias in local decisions about program generosity.

LOCAL GOVERNMENTS AS IMPLEMENTERS OF SAFETY NETS

The public finance literature notes that subnational jurisdictions may be well placed to administer safety nets. In particular, local government officials are expected to have greater knowledge of or contact with programs' client base and thus be able to reach the needy and exclude the non-needy. Local governments can also adjust policies to reflect local preferences, such as by serving locally preferred foods in school lunch programs. Further, decentralizing social assistance may make it easier for municipalities to establish links between social services and social assistance programs or achieve desirable moves toward service integration. This will be more important for some programs than others. For CCTs, this can be important if local governments are responsible for education and/ or health service delivery. For public works, the municipality or district may be the most sensible agency to determine what works should be carried out.

At the same time, the extent of administrative decentralization is limited because of the desirability of national standard setting, the existence of economies of scale, and the likelihood of low capacity at local levels.

PRINCIPLES AND MECHANISMS FOR SHARING FINANCIAL SUPPORT

Good practices for managing nationally financed but locally implemented safety net programs are in the process of being devised. Experience with the decentralization of social assistance has intensified in the last decade concurrent with trends in program management emphasizing monitoring for performance management and results-based financing and technology changes that have increased the ability to generate and analyze data on needs, clients, and service providers at a reasonable cost.

As table 3.5 shows, the various mechanisms for providing funds raised at the national level to local governments to run their safety net programs have specific advantages and disadvantages.[10] In most countries with multilevel safety net programs, the financing is passed from the national level to subnational units using some form of earmarking. This ensures that the subnational units provide a minimum safety net, which is consistent with the reasons for financing safety nets at the national level.

A common mechanism used by central governments to provide financing is open-ended capitation grants that cover all expenditures at the local level for the specified program. In one popular form of the model, the reimbursement formula is calculated as the

TABLE 3.5 **Advantages and Disadvantages of Financing Sources for Subnational Governments**

Financing source	Advantages	Disadvantages
Assigning unconditional resources to subnational level for general use		
Unfunded mandate	• Conveys full discretion to the local level	• May result in insufficient spending
Rights to raise revenues locally (for example, from property taxes, surcharges, and user fees)	• Provides a link between taxpayers and beneficiaries • Gives incentive for fiscal responsibility	• Increases the tax burden • May lead to duplication of taxes between the central and subnational governments • May yield small revenues • Local tax revenues often do not grow as quickly as income overall
Borrowing	• Finances investment projects to increase future productivity	• May induce fiscal vulnerability, high debt service, and debt overhang and thereby contribute to macroeconomic instability
Shared taxes	• Provide a predictable source of income with technical criteria and transparency of allocation • Do not incur local tax administration costs	• Local governments lack control over tax compliance and the tax base • Yields are procyclical
Transferring earmarked resources to subnational level for safety nets		
Capitation grants	• Ensure that funding is fair	• Local governments have incentives for lenience in determining eligibility
Block grants	• Can be redistributive • Ensure vertical balance • Provide funds based on a formula	• No incentive to raise own revenues • Formula may be complex and lack transparency
Matching grants	• Provide an incentive to cofinance programs	• Limited by available funds
Specific grants	• Help redistribute assets among regions • Avoid the need for counterpart funds	• Identification of programs may suffer from political capture • No incentive to raise own revenues • Subject to political discretion

SOURCE: de Neubourg 2002; authors.

average benefit per beneficiary, which is determined by the central government, plus a sum for administration. These schemes result in local providers having an incentive to maximize the number of social assistance recipients without regard to the fiscal costs of the benefits. The outcome will depend on the level of discretion allowed with respect to eligibility and on countervailing supervisory tools. The art is to balance these appropriately (table 3.6).

TABLE 3.6 Options for Managing Local Governments' Incentives to Use Lax Entry Criteria for Centrally Financed Safety Net Programs

Eligibility criteria	Management tool	Example
Simple, little role for local discretion	• Little supervision required	• Universal child allowances
Complex, such as a means test or certification of disability	• Extensive quality control procedures • Local performance incentives	• U.S. Food Stamp Program • Brazil's Bolsa Familia program
Locally defined procedures	• Hard budget constraint or cap on the number of beneficiaries assigned to each jurisdiction	• Indonesian JPS Scholarship and Grant Program
Any	• Require local contribution, with higher contribution required where more discretion is given	• Romania Guaranteed Minimum Income Program

SOURCE: Authors.

The simplest case with regard to eligibility determination is a universal categorical benefit program, such as a child benefit that is disbursed to the parents or guardians of all children in the country. The benefit is allocated based on a single, simple criterion that is easy to administer and monitor. Local providers will have an incentive to ensure that all residents in their jurisdiction benefit, but they cannot inflate the number of beneficiaries unduly, because the eligibility criteria are simple and the benefit is universal.

In the case of a means-tested program, benefit allocation decisions are based on relatively complex criteria that require providers to make judgments, and they may have a tendency to be lenient with respect to these. Benefit providers do not have a financial incentive to limit program expenses, and may therefore allocate benefits in borderline cases to increase output and case numbers. Individual social workers usually find it more gratifying to help than to deny assistance to applicants, and local communities will welcome the extra infusion of cash. This is not a case of corruption, but of providers reacting rationally to the incentives designed into the program. Box 3.5 provides an example.

When local governments have significant discretion in determining eligibility, the central government will need to closely monitor the processes or control the outcomes. It has three ways to do this: extensive quality control, incentive-based performance mechanisms, and budget caps. The U.S. Food Stamp Program involves a complex means test and is locally implemented but federally funded through an open-ended capitation grant. It is

BOX 3.5 **Financing Arrangements and Incentives in the Netherlands**

The Netherlands' Alegemene Bijstandswet (National Assistance), the cash transfer of last resort, is provided through social service departments in local municipalities. Prior to 2001, 90 percent of the funding for the activities of these departments came from an open-ended capitation grant from the national government. The remaining 10 percent came from a block grant from the National Fund for Municipalities.

A working group that assessed the system determined that the financial incentives given to the municipalities did not adequately encourage them to lower the number of beneficiaries either by reducing the number of new enrollees or by encouraging recipients to leave the safety net. This was because municipalities did not bear the costs of providing services and were not rewarded if costs were contained and if program effectiveness were improved.

A new funding arrangement was initiated in January 2001 that reduced the national government's contribution to 75 percent, still in the form of an open-ended capitation grant; the remaining 25 percent was still provided in the form of a block grant. However, the budgeting rules were changed so that a municipality that spent less than the full amount of the block grant could use the remainder for other local policy initiatives. Early indications were that municipalities were more actively pursuing policies to help beneficiaries leave welfare rolls and find employment.

The funding arrangements were changed again in 2004 to give municipalities even more incentives to reduce participation. Municipalities now receive an annual budget divided into two parts, one for paying cash assistance benefits and one for providing labor activation services. If municipalities exceed the assistance budget, they can only request additional funds in exceptional circumstances and only for amounts in excess of 110 percent of the original budget. If they underspend the budget, they may use the savings for any purpose. This has had three effects on how municipalities run programs: they devote their activation efforts to those who are most likely to find jobs easily, in general, the young unemployed; they use a stronger "work first" policy, whereby the unemployed are obliged to take any generally acceptable job rather than one that matches their experience or training; and they pay more attention to their gatekeeping role (van Berkel 2006).

SOURCES: de Neubourg 2002 and van Berkel 2006.

thus a candidate for excessive expenditures. The federal government manages this risk with a heavy set of quality control measures (box 3.6).

Brazil's Bolsa Familia (Family Grant) program faces similar risks which it manages by using performance-based incentives. The central government monitors municipalities' performance using an index based on four elements: the quality of data collected for determining eligibility, the timeliness of recertification, children's compliance with the use of health services, and children's compliance with the use of education services. The municipalities have an incentive to perform well, because the share of the program's administrative costs paid for by the federal government depends on the municipalities' performance scores.

BOX 3.6 Quality Assurance of Eligibility Determination in the U.S. Food Stamp Program

As the benefits provided by the U.S. Food Stamp Program are entirely federally funded but eligibility determination is handled at the local level, the federal government mandates a thorough system of quality control that it has developed to monitor and reduce errors in eligibility.

Quality control measures the accuracy of states' eligibility decisions and benefit calculations. Each month, the states randomly select a specified number of cases from two sample frames. The first is a sample of all those who were provided benefits in a given month ("active cases"). The second is a sample of those who were denied benefits or whose benefits were terminated in a given month ("negative cases"). The states review random samples of a total of some 50,000 active cases and 30,000 negative cases each year. The federal government conducts a random re-review of about 30 percent of the cases to verify that the states' quality control review was conducted appropriately.

The active case review is to determine whether households were eligible for benefits and whether they received the correct amount of food stamps during the month. State quality control reviewers conduct detailed examinations of case files and in-depth field reviews, including interviews with adult members of each sample household and with others familiar with the households' circumstances. If a reviewer determines that a household received an incorrect allotment, the case is cited as a payment error. Reviewers calculate two types of payment errors: (1) overpayment errors, which include benefits issued to ineligible households and benefits paid to eligible households in excess of the appropriate benefit level (which varies with household size and income); and (2) underpayment errors, which measure errors in which eligible households received fewer benefits than they were eligible to receive (they do not include the value of benefits that should have been paid to households that were denied or terminated from the program). These errors are then added (not netted) to yield the combined error rate, cited as a share of total benefits paid that month.

Negative case reviews determine the share of households wrongly classified as ineligible or wrongly terminated in the total caseload. These reviews are less rigorous and usually consist of desk reviews of eligibility caseworker records.

The Food Stamp Program attaches financial incentives to targeting accuracy. States are subject to financial sanctions if their combined error rate (overpayment + underpayment) is higher than the national average. Conversely, they can receive enhanced administrative funding if their combined error rate is less than 6 percent and they do not have a high negative case error rate. This means that even if all states make progress in reducing their error rates, roughly half of all states can expect financial penalties if their rates are higher than the national average. In 2002, the average national combined error rate was 9.9 percent, and the states paid federal penalties of about US$46 million.

SOURCE: Lindert 2005a.

The problem of excessive enrollment numbers would become acute if local jurisdictions were allowed to determine their own criteria for poverty or eligibility and receive funding for everyone who met those criteria, as this would give them incentives to set criteria that many people would meet. Thus, where local jurisdictions have full autonomy over entry criteria, the total number of permissible beneficiaries should be rationed so that jurisdictions face a hard budget constraint. This rationing should be done based on estimations of the poverty rate in each jurisdiction. This is the design used, for example, in the Indonesian JPS Scholarship and Grant Program that was put in place as part of the safety net response to the Asian financial crisis. Each school was told how many scholarships it could award, and a local committee determined which students would receive them.

Another way of giving local jurisdictions the incentive to be strict in their decisions on eligibility is to require them to contribute some financing to the program. A contribution of 10 to 20 percent is most common, but local contributions sometimes go as high as 50 percent. Extremely low local contributions provide correspondingly weak discipline, and so may be appropriate for programs with little local discretion or with budgetary caps. Higher contributions are appropriate when local governments have more discretion or an open-ended commitment from the central government. Matching grants are only applicable when local governments have independent spending and revenue authority and do not address the issue of interregional inequalities.[11]

In sharing financial responsibilities among levels of government irrespective of which financing option is used, it is important that programs receive adequate funding. In practice, most of the programs discussed in this book are nationally financed; this is true, for example, of all the CCT programs and general food subsidies. In other cases, local governments cover a minor share of programs, often about 20 percent; examples include Ethiopia's Productive Safety Net Program and Romania's Guaranteed Minimum Income Program. Programs funded largely by localities are found primarily in large federal countries; exemplifying such programs are the Maharashtra Employment Guarantee Scheme in India and cash transfer programs in several Brazilian states. Large-scale municipal programs that operate in addition to national programs are also found in some megacities, for example, Mexico City's social pension.

Funds should be assigned fairly and predictably; this can be ensured through the use of an appropriate formula to determine the level of transfers from the national to subnational levels. In the best cases, the formula takes population size, level of poverty, or sometimes a measure of tax capacity into account. Colombia's constitution, for example, stipulates substantial transfers to municipalities based on a formula that gives 60 percent weight to the number of poor people and 40 percent to population, fiscal and administrative efficiency, and progress in improving the quality of life (Ahmad and Baer 1997). In less optimal cases, the amount of central financing is not so clearly assigned. In China's urban *di bao* (minimum living guarantee) cash transfer program, for example, the allocation of central budgetary resources to provinces is neither transparent nor stable, but is determined in an ad hoc manner each year on the basis of a negotiated mixture of factors whose relative importance varies over time. The allocations from provinces to municipalities are similarly characterized by a lack of transparency and predictability. To date, the results are roughly in line with equity considerations: a number of better-off provinces received no central allocation in recent years and poorer provinces received much more—as much as 88 percent of financing in Ningxia and 100 percent in Tibet. However, the uncertainty makes planning by service delivery units difficult (World Bank 2007q).

Transfers from national to subnational governments may be provided to support a wide set of local activities for which these governments are accountable, in which case they are unconditional. Alternatively, transfers may be tied to specific programs, in which case they are referred to as conditional or earmarked. Some commentators view conditional central grants as constraining local autonomy; others welcome them as a way to ensure a minimum provision of public goods, especially of safety nets.

Note that the effects of grants on local spending decisions may not be a one-for-one increase in spending on the item nominally financed. Where subnational governments complement funding for centrally subsidized programs with local revenues, an increase or decrease in central funding may not be fully passed through to the target program, but tempered by changes in the allocation of locally raised funds. Theoretically, giving an unconditional grant to a region would allow some fraction of the income to be spent on current goods and services and some on other items such as investment and tax relief. In practice, governments tend to spend a large fraction of grants on goods and services. For example, many U.S. studies of the actual effect of various types of federal grants on state and local government spending suggest that nearly all grant funds are spent on public goods and services (Hines and Thaler 1995). This phenomenon is known as the "flypaper effect," a concept introduced by the economist Arthur Okun and captured by the phrase "money sticks where it hits." Numerous hypotheses have been put forward for this finding, including the explanation that politicians gain more politically from higher spending than from offering minor tax cuts to citizens. As a result, grants from the central government may have a greater positive effect on local spending than theory predicts.

ALLOCATION OF ADMINISTRATIVE FUNCTIONS BETWEEN CENTRAL AND SUBNATIONAL GOVERNMENTS

Even though funding may be largely central, actual delivery may be done through central agencies, through subnational entities, or through a combination of the two. Practices vary widely, and two of the most positively evaluated programs in recent years have taken opposite approaches. Mexico's Oportunidades CCT program is highly centralized, is well targeted, and has improved the use of health and education services. In Argentina's Trabajar workfare program, municipalities played a large role, the program was even better targeted, and it delivered useful infrastructure.

Decisions about which level of government should be responsible for what function are often not "all or none." This section therefore discusses various factors to consider in determining, on a case-by-case basis, which level of government should be responsible for how much of which function.

Economies of Scale

The idea of economies of scale is that costs may not be fully proportional to the number of beneficiaries. Evaluation is a classic example, because the costs of designing an evaluation, writing data collection instruments, and analyzing datasets do not vary by the size of the dataset; moreover, through sampling, data collection costs increase far less than proportionately with an increase in the size of the population being studied. Thus, evaluating a program with 10 million beneficiaries costs little more than evaluating one with 10,000.

An initial rule of thumb is to keep functions that are subject to significant economies of scale at the national level. Table 3.7 shows how the World Bank (2006f) allocates functions for wage employment programs in India. The example presented is an analysis of the decentralized Village Full Employment Program, which is one of India's largest wage

TABLE 3.7 **An Example of a Functional Analysis of a Program and Responsible Levels of Government: The Village Full Employment Program, India**

Function	Activity	Responsibility					
		Central	State	District	Block	Village council	Village meeting
Policy design, standards	Implementation rules	X	X				
	Targeting	X	X				
	Budgeting	X	X				
	Standards	X	X				
Planning	Activity prioritization, action plan					X	X
	Activity selection					X	X
Asset creation	Human capital						
	Skill development		X	X			
	Social capital						
	Information dissemination					X	
	Physical capital						
	Public works					X	
	Beneficiary selection						
	Identification of beneficiaries					X	X
	Awareness raising			X	X	X	
Operations	Recurring activities						
	Provision of wages, food grains					X	
	Supervision & quality control					X	
	Personnel						
	Hiring and firing					X	
	Maintenance						
	Accounting and financial management					X	
	Repairs					X	X
Monitoring and evaluation	Assets						
	Recording of assets			X	X	X	
	Physical verification of assets created			X			X
	Audits						
	Financial audits		X				
	Social audits			X			X

SOURCE: World Bank 2006e.

employment programs. The table makes explicit what is often obscured in theoretical writing on decentralization: (1) multiple tiers of government may be involved, not just two; and (2) any analysis of how functions should be or are being performed needs to include all pertinent levels.

Functions should be broken down into specific actions and then allocated to a specific level of government. Consider eligibility determination, which is typically used as an example of a function that can be performed locally and is the most commonly given reason for having local governments administer safety nets. Determining eligibility requires person-to-person contact for each beneficiary; thus, a large part of the cost is proportional to the size of the program. Some aspects of the development of household targeting systems are subject to economies of scale, however, such as developing the formulas and supporting software or running cross-checks against national data registries to verify information. Thus, some aspects of eligibility determination may be carried out more effectively at the national level and some more effectively at the subnational level (table 3.8).

TABLE 3.8 **Advantages of Alternative Allocations of Institutional Responsibilities for Household Targeting Systems**

Responsibility	Decentralized	Centralized
Design	• More involvement of local authorities in social policy • System can reflect local preferences and circumstances	• More transparent with federal guidelines for eligibility criteria, other design factors • Common framework for monitoring and evaluation • Common software facilitates national database • Standard questionnaires more efficient and transparent • Less costly (economies of scale)
Data collection	• Empowerment of local authorities • Can be more efficient • Interviewers familiar with local cultures and languages • Infrastructure network with local offices more likely to be in place	• Better quality control, consistency of data collection practices • Lower risk of manipulation by local authorities • Better when local capacities are limited
Database management	• Databases can be tailored for use with other local programs	• Facilitates assignment of single identification number • Better quality control and auditing of databases • Facilitates building a national, consolidated database • Lower costs (economies of scale) • Facilitates cross-checks with other automated systems • Lower risk of corruption at local levels • Better when local capacities are limited

SOURCE: Castañeda and others 2005.

Decentralizing to the point of losing economies of scale is possible. In the United States, for example, administration of the TANF program is almost wholly decentralized to states, and often to counties within the states. Because the supporting information systems and payment contracts are designed and purchased at the state rather than the national level, the program's administrative costs are higher and it suffers from substantive information deficiencies: it cannot easily verify that households are not receiving benefits in multiple states or enforce the five-year time limit for participating in the program. The much more centralized Food Stamp Program has fewer such problems and greater economies of scale in payment systems.

Administrative Capacity

Local governments may have limited administrative capacity, either generally or with regard to a particular program. Examples of general administrative capacity are the presence of electricity and the full complement of office equipment, such as telephones, photocopiers, facsimile machines, and computers. Program-specific capacity refers to the availability of sufficient staff who are adequately trained with respect to their roles. Both of these may be built up over time if the decision is taken to decentralize an existing program or to create a new one using a decentralized structure. The usual teething problems will arise while capacity is developed to match responsibility. This process can be aided by the provision of adequate funding and training and proactive management, but may still be a multiyear effort. Sometimes, however, a program may face constraints that are not just transitional, but structural. In Mexico, for example, municipal civil service rules are weak and mayors are allowed to serve only a single term. Because each election is followed by a high turnover of municipal staff, the ability to train or build local capacity is limited—which in turn limits the tasks that can be assigned to municipal staff.

Clarity and Consistency

However responsibilities are assigned, they must be clearly specified and understood by all pertinent parties, otherwise some tasks will not be done or will be duplicated in wasteful and often contradictory ways. Roles should also be consistent with funding mechanisms and capacities. Diagnoses of poorly performing programs are replete with examples of lack of clarity as to who does what and the ensuing problems. Table 3.7 illustrates an analysis done in an effort to sort out issues of clear and inconsistent allocation of responsibilities across actors.

Management of Heterogeneity in Program Administration

Whenever a program is carried out in many different places, its implementation will vary. Managing this heterogeneity in program administration is inherent in all large programs. The issue is especially salient for decentralized programs, as heterogeneity is likely to be greater when the acting units are different municipalities with their particular preferences and capacities rather than local offices of a national agency.

There are essentially two facets to managing heterogeneity. The first is to ensure a minimum standard of service delivery. This can be accomplished either through imposing strict rules and monitoring compliance with them (as in the U.S. Food Stamp Program), or by establishing incentives for programs to meet those standards (as with Brazil's Bolsa Familia municipal performance index and central payment of administrative costs based on the index).

The other aspect of managing heterogeneity is to learn from the variability by ascertaining who the good performers are and what makes what them do work better than average. The United States accomplishes this by having a large evaluation industry involved in its decentralized programs. Brazil's Bolsa Familia program has instituted a competition for innovations or good practices whereby municipalities submit ideas that are then shared with other municipalities. The United Kingdom's Job Centre Plus program has a small team of roving staff members who both help poor performers troubleshoot their problems and identify high performers and share their approaches.

A MULTIFACETED APPROACH TO MANAGING A SAFETY NET IN A DECENTRALIZED SETTING

In closing, we present a thumbnail sketch of how Brazil manages the issues pertaining to the involvement of multiple layers of government in Bolsa Familia to show how multiple tools can be used simultaneously to address the various challenges.[12] Bolsa Familia is a CCT program, and so is relatively complex. In addition, Brazil is a federal country with 5,564 autonomous municipalities with a great deal of heterogeneity in capacity levels among them. Moreover, a number of municipalities also operate their own cash transfer programs.

The basic assignment of roles for the Bolsa Familia program is as follows. Eligibility is determined through self-reported incomes which are verified through a combination of multidimensional proxy indicators and internal and external cross-checks. Municipalities are responsible for data collection for registering potential beneficiaries; Caixa Econômica Federal (a federal savings and credit organization) consolidates the national registry database; and the Ministry of Social Development makes final eligibility decisions. Payments are channeled through the banking system under a contract with Caixa. Municipalities play the lead role in registering potential beneficiaries, monitoring compliance with health and education conditions, and establishing social oversight councils. Brazil's three supreme audit agencies provide additional oversight.

Given the level of complexity of the program and actors, extra thought and well-developed tools are needed to manage coordination and address principal-agent problems. The main approaches used are summarized in table 3.9.

Different countries might choose a different set of tools, but the idea of thinking critically about what is needed and formulating a comprehensive approach to managing the challenges of decentralization is transferable. This particular set of tools seems to be balanced and appropriate for Brazil's context. The quality of service delivery seems to have improved since the introduction of the index of decentralized management, although definitive studies have not yet been done (Lindert and others 2007). Challenges remain, especially with respect to aspects of service delivery not covered by the index, and heterogeneity will never be eradicated in such a large and diverse country.

TABLE 3.9 **Management Solutions to Implementation Challenges in a Decentralized Context, Bolsa Familia Program, Brazil**

Challenge	Solution
Principal-agent dilemma inherent in executing federal programs via autonomous municipalities	• Requiring municipalities to sign joint management agreements with the Ministry of Social Development (which specify the roles and responsibilities of each agency involved and establish minimum service standards) before receiving subsidies to cover the program's administrative costs • Ensuring that oversight and control audits include the activities undertaken by municipalities
Heterogeneity in the quality of municipal implementation resulting from capacity differences	• Assessing the quality of implementation by municipalities via a quantifiable index of decentralized management based on four key aspects of quality • Providing performance-based financial incentives (administrative cost subsidies) based on municipalities' scores on the index • Targeting training and capacity building to municipalities with low scores on the index
Principal-agent dilemma caused by contracting out payments and the registry database	• Using a performance-based contract for Caixa with enforceable sanctions for inadequate quality standards • Ensuring that oversight and control audits also cover Caixa activities
Potential duplication with subnational CCTs	• Providing for vertical integration of subnational programs with Bolsa Familia via joint cooperation agreements
Need for mechanisms to promote the sharing of experiences and innovations across municipalities	• Introducing the Bolsa Familia Innovations Award in 2006, which is intended to promote the sharing of municipal experiences and includes field visits as part of the awards process • Publishing descriptions of innovative experiences in the form of case studies

SOURCE: Lindert and others 2007.

Notes

1. A few exceptions to the general lack of information are Bose, Holman, and Neanidis (2004) and Coady and Harris (2004). Chu and Gupta (1998b) report the example of safety net implementation accompanied by tax reform to finance it.

2. Welfare economics formalizes a moral philosophy that values a currency unit transferred to the poor more than a currency unit transferred to the middle class and substantially more than a currency unit transferred to the rich. The benefits of programs that improve equity via redistribution are estimated empirically by assigning different distributional weights to currency units received by households with different welfare levels. Essentially, the weights represent a way to translate a value judgment (how much a society values equity, and thus redistribution, as a means to achieve equity) into mathematical terms. However, there is no clear-cut empirical way to estimate the set of distributional weights of a society. Absent this, some researchers assume a certain function form (Squire and van der Tak 1975) and run sensitivity analyses with different values for the propensity for redistribution.

3. Technically, a fifth option is to create money to cover deficits. However, experiences like those of Latin America in the 1970s and early 1980s have shown printing money to be such an inflationary, inefficient, and inequitable source of financing that all prudent governments have discarded it as an option.

4. The Monterrey Accords were agreed on at the International Conference for Financing and Development held in Monterrey, Mexico, in March 2002; the Millennium Development Goals were agreed on at the United Nations Millennium Development Summit held in New York in September 2000; the Gleneagles Summit of the Group of Eight was held in Gleneagles, Scotland, in 2005; and the African Action Plan was agreed on at the Kananaskis, Canada, Group of Eight Summit in 2002.

5. Lindert (2004) suggests a number of explanations for this "free-lunch puzzle," concluding that countries that spend more have more pro-growth tax packages; welfare states have minimized the work disincentives of young adults; early retirement subsidies have little effect on GDP, in part because they are skewed toward less productive workers; unemployment programs raise unemployment, but raise productivity among those employed, and so have little effect on GDP; and many social transfer programs raise GDP per person even after accounting for the effects of taxes to support the spending.

6. The World Values Survey is a worldwide investigation of sociocultural and political change conducted by a nonprofit association funded by scientific foundations from around the world. Interviews have been carried out with nationally representative samples of the publics of more than 80 societies on all six inhabited continents. For more information, see www.worldvaluessurvey.org/. Latinobarómetro is an annual public opinion survey conducted by Latinobarómetro Corporation, a nonprofit nongovernmental organization based in Santiago, Chile, that involves some 19,000 interviews in 18 Latin American countries, representing more than 400 million inhabitants. For more information, see www.latinobarometro.org/.

7. "Social assistance and welfare" includes transfer payments (including in kind) to compensate recipients for reduction or loss of income or for inadequate earning capacity; sickness, maternity, disability, old-age, and survivors' benefits; government employee pension schemes; unemployment compensation; family and child allowances; other social assistance for individuals; and payments to residential institutions for children and the elderly. "Transfers to households and other organizations" includes transfer payments to private social institutions such as hospitals and schools, learned societies, associations, and sports clubs that are not operated as enterprises and current payments in cash to households that add to their disposable income without any simultaneous, equivalent counterpart provided in exchange by the beneficiary and that does not generate or eliminate a financial claim, and is usually intended to cover charges incurred by households because of certain risks or needs.

8. For the analysis and discussion in this section, the dataset used excludes Iraq, an outlier that has, because of its unique circumstances, been spending 15 percent of GDP on social assistance.

9. Country expenditures are rounded to the nearest half percent for this calculation.

10. This section draws on de Neubourg (2002).

11. Matching grants can actually exacerbate horizontal differences. Consider a 90-10 matching scheme. The local government that can put up 10 units of finance will end up with a total budget for the program of 100. The local government that can afford 5 units of finance will end up with a total budget of 50. Thus an initial budget difference of 5 becomes a final difference of 50 in absolute terms, even though in relative terms the difference is still 2 to 1.

12. This section is drawn from Lindert and others (2007).

## CHAPTER 4

Enrolling the Client: Targeting, Eligibility, and Intake

KEY MESSAGES

Concentrating resources on the poor or vulnerable can increase the benefits that they can achieve within a given budget or can achieve a given impact at the lowest cost. The theoretical gain from targeting can appear to be large. For example, if all the benefits provided by a transfer program were targeted to the poorest quintile of the population rather than uniformly distributed across the whole population, the budget savings or the difference in impact for a fixed budget would be five to one. In practice, the full theoretical gain is not realized, because targeting is never completely accurate, and because costs are associated with targeting. These costs include administrative costs borne by the program, transaction and social costs borne by program applicants, incentive costs that may affect the overall benefit to society, and political costs that may affect support for the program. The size of targeting errors and costs will differ according to the setting and the types of targeting methods used and must be assessed carefully in any policy proposal.

Good evidence indicates that, for the most part, programs can focus resources on the poor to a moderate or high degree without incurring unacceptably high errors of exclusion and administrative, private costs, and/or incentive costs, although not all do so. Factoring in judgments on social and political costs is harder, partly because their metrics are so different, and partly because discussions about them are often more polemical than quantitative, but the widespread and increasing interest in targeting from policy makers suggests that these costs are not preclusive.

A few methods of targeting and types of programs go hand-in-hand, for example, self-selection and commodity price subsidies. However, several different methods can often be used for a particular type of program; for instance, cash and food transfers can be targeted by means tests, proxy means tests, nutritional status or risk factors, geographic area, demographic characteristic, or self-selection. For a single program to use a number of methods is common and usually yields better targeting than a single method. Means tests and proxy means tests have the highest costs, but tend to produce the lowest errors of inclusion and are often good investments. Self-selection via a low wage rate and geographic targeting are also powerful and proven targeting tools.

The details and quality of implementation will have a significant effect on targeting outcomes. Programs need extensive outreach to keep errors of exclusion low. Reducing errors of inclusion requires a definition of eligibility that sorts the poor from the nonpoor well and can be implemented at a tolerable cost. Targeting systems should be dynamic, allowing new or newly poor households to access the program and moving out households that are no longer eligible. The inputs to good targeting outcomes include adequate staffing; well-defined rules of the game; clearly assigned and sensible institutional roles;

and adequate information systems, material inputs, monitoring, and evaluation. Systems also need time and effort to develop.

A good household targeting system may be complex to develop, but can be used for many programs, not only for direct transfers in cash or in kind, but for entry into programs that provide free or subsidized health care, schooling, training, housing, utilities, and the like. The shared overhead is not only efficient, but can lead to a more coherent overall social policy.

Funds for safety net programs are scarce, and competing demands on the public budget are many. Thus policy makers always face pressure to use funds as effectively as possible and usually have to make significant trade-offs. Should a program serve many people but limit the level or the duration of benefits? Alternatively, should a program be more selective but more generous to those it does serve? The answers to those questions are part of the larger diagnostic process described in chapter 9 and have links to targeting (discussed in this chapter), benefit levels (chapter 5, section 1), and repercussions in relation to the choice of programs (chapters 7 and 8).

4.1 Basic Concepts of Targeting

Targeting is a tool policy makers sometimes employ to make a program efficient. It is not an end in itself. How much to target and how to do so depend on program-specific answers as to whether the gains outweigh the costs.

POSSIBLE GAINS FROM TARGETING

Targeting can increase the benefits that the poor can realize with a given budget (maximizing impact) or can achieve a given impact at least budgetary cost (minimizing costs). This is accomplished by channeling resources to a target group, typically the poor or a subset of the poor. Targeting is an attractive option for many kinds of poverty reduction programs and expenditures. It is particularly important for safety nets, because in contrast to, say, education, the transfers confer a benefit that is largely a private good for the recipient household and because there is no natural limit to the amount a household might like to receive.

The basic case for targeting is simple. Consider a country with 100 million people of whom 20 million are poor. The country's budget for a transfer program is US$200 million. With no targeting, the program could give everyone US$2. If the program could be targeted only to the poor, it could give each poor person US$10 and spend the full budget, thereby maximizing the impact using the given budget. Alternatively, it could give each poor person US$2 for a budget of US$40 million, thereby minimizing costs for a given impact.

The theoretical gain from targeting can appear to be large. In practice it is less than indicated here, because targeting is never completely accurate and because it has costs, including administrative, private, incentive or indirect, social, and political costs.

COSTS OF TARGETING

Accurately distinguishing between who is and who is not needy incurs costs. The different types of costs are defined here, while evidence on their magnitudes is reviewed in the next section.

- **Administrative costs** are the costs to the program of gathering information to help make the decision about who should be admitted to the program.

- **Private costs** are the costs to an applicant of applying for a program, including the time or cash costs of gathering the necessary information, traveling to the registration site and lining up for registration, complying with any preconditions, and so on. Private costs always reduce a program's net benefit to the recipient. If they are sufficiently large, they may discourage eligible people from participating altogether.

- **Incentive (or indirect) costs** arise when eligibility criteria induce households to change their behavior in an attempt to become beneficiaries. They can be negative, for example, when a program open only to those below a minimum income causes some households to work less so that they fall below that minimum income. Sometimes they can be positive, for example, a food ration or daily meal supplied only to those children who attend school may encourage some families to enroll more of their children or ensure that they attend school every day.

- **Social costs** may arise when participation in a program carries with it some sort of stigma. Stigmatization may affect households' decisions about participating. For those that do participate, stigmatization may lower households' psychological welfare, if not their incomes.

- **Political costs** can arise if the degree of targeting negatively affects the program's budget.

TARGETING ERRORS

In practice, program officials do not have perfect information about who is poor, because collecting such information is time consuming and costly. When program eligibility is based on imperfect information, program officials or the targeting rules they use may mistakenly identify nonpoor people as poor, and therefore admit them to the program (referred to as an error of inclusion), or do the opposite, that is, mistakenly identify poor people as nonpoor, and thus deny them access to the program (referred to as an error of exclusion). Consider the matrix in table 4.1. Of 100 households, 20 are classified as poor (eligible) based on the poverty line (eligibility threshold). Now consider a program that gives benefits to 20 households selected according to imperfect targeting criteria. Of these, 15 are poor (have incomes below the poverty line) and 5 are nonpoor (have incomes above the poverty line). Both the 15 poor households included in the program and the 75 nonpoor

TABLE 4.1 **Errors of Inclusion and Exclusion**

	Welfare status		
Households	**Poor**	**Nonpoor**	**Total**
Included in program	15 successful targeting	5 inclusion error	20
Excluded from program	5 exclusion error	75 successful targeting	80
Total	20	80	100

SOURCE: Authors.

households excluded are successful targeting. The 5 poor households excluded are errors of exclusion, while the 5 nonpoor households are errors of inclusion.

An easy and preferable extension of this approach is to present similar information over the entire welfare distribution, showing by means of graphs or tables how many people fall in each decile or quintile and how many in each receive benefits.[1] This shows whether funds are going to the very poor or to the moderately poor, if leakage is to the near poor or to the wealthy, and so on. It also permits differentiating the size of the benefit received. Presenting information on the entire distribution facilitates comparative work and benchmarking, as different programs have different eligibility thresholds. Figures 4.1 and 4.2 illustrate the presentation of information across the full welfare distribution and how programs can be compared to one another.

A further extension of the basic framework is to take differentiated benefits into account. Most programs still offer a uniform transfer to participants, but a sizable number now tailor the benefit to the degree of need or to the size or structure of the recipient household (for more details, see chapter 5, section 1). Customized benefits somewhat complicate the ex post evaluation of targeting performance, but not intractably so.

In relation to the measurement of targeting errors, information on targeting is usually shown as the percentage of program benefits reaching the poor or a given decile or group of deciles. This information comes from a household survey that has some sort of welfare measure, some measure of whether the household or its members benefit from a program, and ideally an indication of the level of

FIGURE 4.1 **Share of Population by Quintile That Received Benefits in Selected Safety Net Programs, India, Fiscal 2004/05**

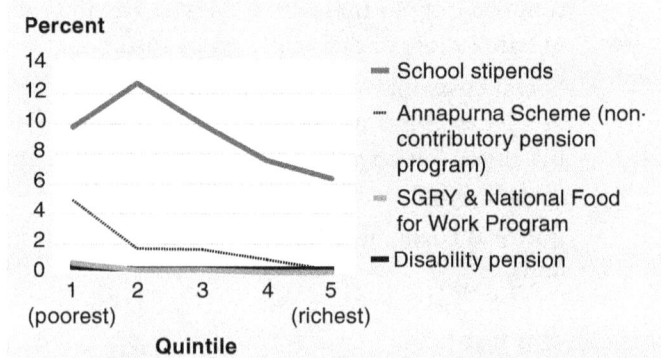

SOURCE: Based on data from World Bank 2007a.

NOTE: SGRY = Sampoorna Grameen Rozgar Yojana (Village Full Employment Program).

FIGURE 4.2 **Share of Benefits Accruing to Each Quintile for Selected Safety Net Programs, India, Fiscal 2004/05**

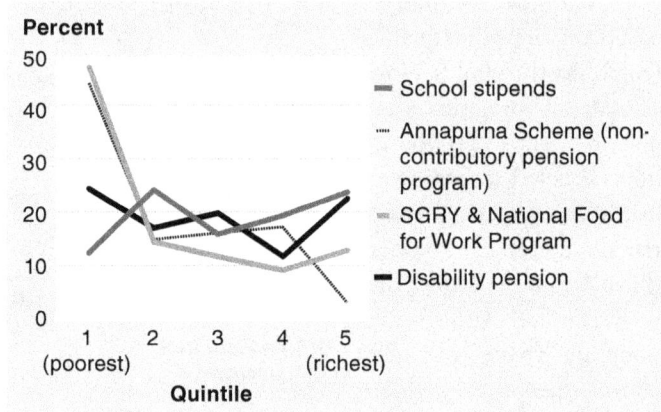

SOURCE: Based on data from World Bank 2007a.

NOTE: SGRY = Sampoorna Grameen Rozgar Yojana (Village Full Employment Program).

the benefit (for methodological information see chapter 6, section 5). The welfare measure used may not, however, correspond closely to the welfare measure used to define the program's eligibility criteria or the definition of the household in the survey to the definition of the assistance unit for the program. Thus while the usual survey-based information will show whether the funds are going to the poorer groups in society, it will not reveal whether the program's criteria are being followed well. For that, an internal quality control procedure will be needed as described in box 3.6. If the survey uses the same definitions of welfare and the social assistance unit used for the program's eligibility criteria, a modeling exercise can be undertaken to establish who would be eligible to examine whether the rules, if properly followed, are well designed.

4.2 Results of Targeting

Good evidence indicates that, on balance, programs can focus resources on the poor to a moderate degree without incurring unacceptably high rates of exclusion or of administrative, private, and/or incentive costs, although not all do so. Factoring in judgments on social and political costs is harder, partly because their metrics are so different, and partly because discussions about them are often more polemical than quantitative, but the widespread and increasing interest in targeting from policy makers suggests that these costs are not preclusive.

ERRORS OF INCLUSION

Coady, Grosh, and Hoddinott (2004) summarize targeting outcomes from 122 targeted social assistance programs in 48 countries. The median program in their sample provides a quarter more resources to the poor than would random allocations. The best programs were able to concentrate a high level of resources on poor individuals and households. Argentina's Trabajar workfare program, the best program in this regard, was able to transfer 80 percent of program benefits to the poorest quintile, or four times the share they would have received in a random allocation. The 10 programs with the best incidence delivered two to four times the share of benefits to the poor that they would have got with random allocations. Progressive allocations were possible in all country settings, in countries at markedly different income levels, and in most types of programs.

A more recent and selective comparison of evidence (figure 4.3) confirms that in middle-income countries at least, programs can, but are not guaranteed to, have errors of inclusion as low as those found in some programs in countries such as the United States. Box 4.1 discusses targeting goals in much poorer countries.

Targeting does not always work. The state-of-the-art as practiced around the world is highly variable. According to Coady, Grosh, and Hoddinott (2004), while median performance was good, in a quarter of the cases targeting was regressive, and thus a random allocation of resources would have provided a greater share of benefits to the poor. For every method of targeting considered except targeting based on a work requirement, the sample of programs included at least one example of a regressive program. Given that good incidence is achievable in many settings and that poor performance is also found in many, where poor performance is found, it may not be inherent, but can be improved upon.

FIGURE 4.3 **Errors of Inclusion, Selected Programs and Countries**

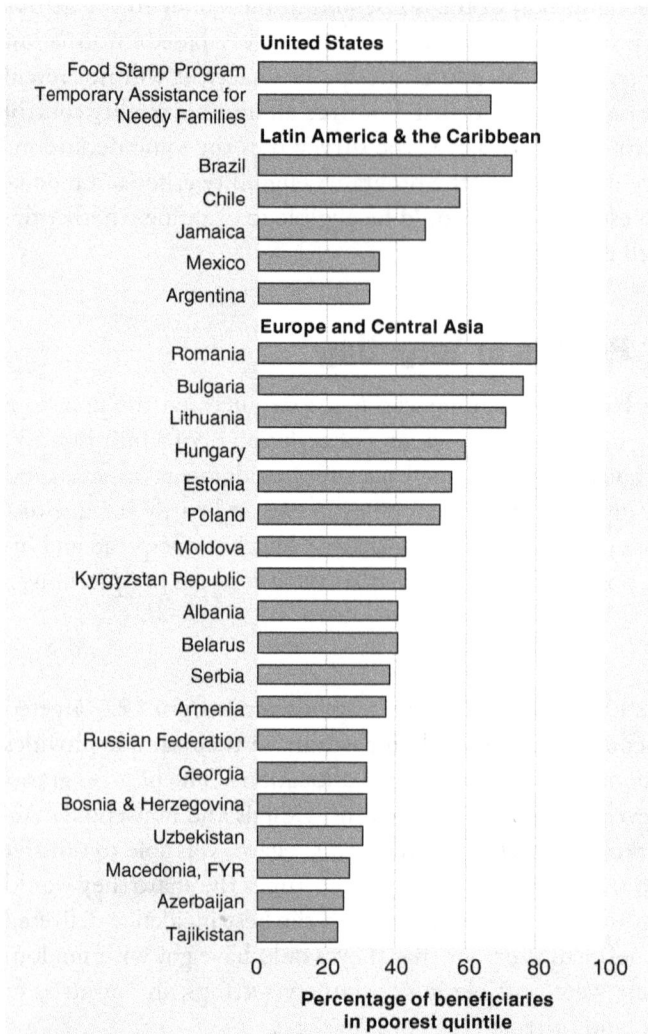

United States

Food Stamp Program	
Temporary Assistance for Needy Families	

Latin America & the Caribbean

Brazil
Chile
Jamaica
Mexico
Argentina

Europe and Central Asia

Romania
Bulgaria
Lithuania
Hungary
Estonia
Poland
Moldova
Kyrgyzstan Republic
Albania
Belarus
Serbia
Armenia
Russian Federation
Georgia
Bosnia & Herzegovina
Uzbekistan
Macedonia, FYR
Azerbaijan
Tajikistan

0   20   40   60   80   100

Percentage of beneficiaries in poorest quintile

SOURCES: United States: Lindert 2005a; Latin America and the Caribbean: Lindert, Skoufias and Shapiro 2006; Europe and Central Asia: Tesliuc and others forthcoming.

NOTE: For Europe and Central Asia, the programs referenced are each country's means-tested or proxy means-tested social assistance of last resort. The programs in Latin America and the Caribbean refer to each country's conditional cash transfer program, except for Argentina, which references the Jefes de Hogar workfare program.

ERRORS OF EXCLUSION

Participation rates as reported in household surveys are the most common source of information on errors of exclusion; however, they only report the outcome, not its cause, and errors of exclusion have multiple sources. Where social assistance programs are not fully funded, as is the case for the vast majority of programs, errors of exclusion will occur because of the caps put on enrollment to keep programs within budget allocations. For example, Argentina's Trabajar program covered only 7.5 percent of the unemployed. Even though it had the lowest errors of inclusion in the global Coady, Grosh, and Hoddinott (2004) review, it had high errors of exclusion.

Errors of exclusion include the influence of self-targeting. This includes both the desirable aspect of the better-off choosing not to participate and the less desirable aspect of the needy being discouraged as well. Uzbekistan's social assistance program uses community-based targeting via traditional groups of neighborhood elders. Micklewright, Coudouel, and Marnie (2004) break down the final outcomes into different factors: households' awareness of the program; of those households that are aware of the program, the decision on whether or not to apply for a benefit; and for those that apply for the benefit, the percentage that are awarded the benefit and the amount of that benefit. The scheme fared quite well with respect to knowledge, with 85 percent of the

BOX 4.1 **How Narrow Should Targeting Be?**

The question often arises as to how narrow targeting should be, especially when poverty rates are high. Is ensuring that benefits go primarily to the large number of poor satisfactory, or should benefits go to the poorest subgroup, say the bottom 10 percent of the distribution?

Trying to concentrate benefits as far down the distribution as possible, even when overall poverty is high, is advisable for two reasons. The first reason is cost. Especially where many people are poor, the budget derived from taxes will be limited, because the pool of people who can pay taxes will be small. International assistance may provide a good deal of the social assistance budget in such cases, but it is still always insufficient to provide for all the basic priorities in a country. Thus safety net budgets tend to be low relative to needs, and the more so the poorer the country.

The second reason to try to concentrate benefits as far down the distribution as possible is that most moral philosophy values the welfare of the poorest more than the welfare of the less poor. We illustrate the difference in welfare among the poor empirically with an example from Burkina Faso. When looking at the full distribution of welfare as shown in figure a, poverty is high and the distribution looks fairly flat, but when we zoom in on the poor end of the spectrum as shown in figure b, we see that the bottom 10 percent of the distribution has consumption levels of half or less than those who are just poor. Thus this group is much needier and will benefit much more from a transfer.

a. All households	b. Poor households

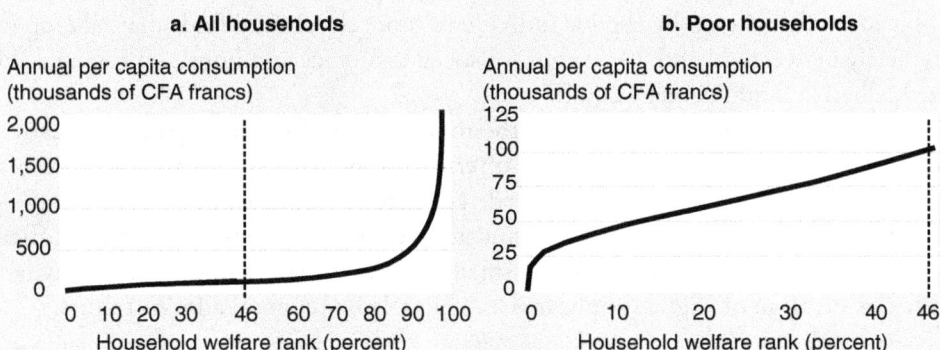

SOURCE: Based on data from the 3rd Priority Survey, National Institute of Statistics and Economic Studies, Ouagadougou, Burkina Faso.

NOTE: The dotted vertical line is the poverty line. The richest 0.5 percent of households were omitted.

Targeting the poorest households and not all the poor is conceptually appropriate when poverty rates are high. However, poorer countries may face capacity constraints that make setting up systems to target narrowly relatively difficult. This practical issue, rather than the conceptual one, may be important in determining the targeting choices made.

poorest quintile being aware of the program. Claims were self-targeted, with those in the poorest quintile applying for a benefit more than twice as often as those in the top three quintiles. Nevertheless, only half the households in the poorest quintile that knew about the program applied for it.

Errors of exclusion are often measured only approximately, as many household surveys do not contain sufficiently detailed information to calculate exactly whether households meet program eligibility criteria. What is most commonly reported is participation by members of the poorest quintile of the population, but many of these may not have met any criteria for the program not related to poverty. A study of housing allowances in the Russian Federation (Struyk, Petrova, and Lykova 2006) makes this distinction and finds that when coverage was estimated as a percentage of eligible households rather than of all households, coverage rates increased by 40 percent or more. For example, participation rates in the city of Omsk were 5.3 percent overall, but 9.4 percent of eligible households.

Even given a measure of participation rates, what their causes are and what should be done about the rates is unclear. It is perhaps for these reasons that errors of exclusion are not reported as often as errors of inclusion. Two recent studies in Latin America (Lindert, Skoufias, and Shapiro 2006) and in Eastern Europe and Central Asia (Tesliuc and others forthcoming) report coverage rates for the lowest quintile. In the Latin American study of 40 targeted programs, the mean coverage rate of the poorest quintile is 19 percent. It is higher but far from complete even for the large, well-known programs that anchor countries' social assistance strategy—for example, 32 percent for Mexico's PROGRESA (now known as Oportunidades) initiative. In the second study, the mean coverage rate for the poorest quintile is 42 percent. A study that reviewed experience in a small number of countries in the Organisation for Economic Co-operation and Development (OECD) was able to model take-up by eligible individuals more closely and finds that take-up rates are typically between 40 and 80 percent for social assistance and housing programs (Hernanz, Malherbet, and Pellizzari 2004).

While few studies can disentangle the root causes of low participation robustly, we believe that the main and largest source of errors of exclusion is budgets that are insufficient to serve all those meant to be served. The second largest cause may be insufficient policy attention paid to outreach and administrative budgets too small to permit sufficient outreach efforts. The third, and possibly smallest, cause of errors of exclusion may be incorrect classification of eligible applicants as ineligible by program administrators.[2]

ADMINISTRATIVE COSTS

Data on the administrative costs of targeting are scarce and their interpretation is problematic. Measurement issues abound, because staff and systems are usually shared among the various functions of a single program, and often among several programs. For example, a social worker might determine eligibility, provide case counseling advice, make payments, and handle appeals issues for one or more programs. Thus determining the administrative costs of targeting requires detailed budget data and often a lot of imputations, assumptions, or special data collection exercises to decide how to allocate the costs of systems and staff who work on more than one function and/or program. Moreover, what is a cost of targeting is not well defined. Time spent verifying reported levels of income is clearly a targeting cost, but registration procedures and databases of participants will be needed even for universal programs. Intake interviews and supporting databases are more complicated and costly for programs with complex targeting criteria, but not all of the costs are due to targeting.

Care must be taken when interpreting administrative costs. A large program that puts little effort into targeting will have lower administrative costs as a share of total program expenditures than a more narrowly targeted, and therefore smaller, program, because the administrative effort devoted to targeting is low and the total program expenditures are high. That does not imply that the investment in targeting was not worthwhile for the overall efficiency of the program. Consider figure 4.4, which illustrates the cost structure for a universal child allowance and for a targeted child allowance. For the targeted program, the ratio of total administrative costs to total costs (BDEG/ADEH) is higher than for the universal program (BCIJ/ACIK), but the extra administrative costs of targeting (CDEF) are small in relation to the savings in benefits paid to the nonpoor children (HGJK). This simple illustration probably underestimates the value that extra administrative costs can have on targeting outcomes. First, it does not capture the value that extra effort of the appropriate sort can have in lowering errors of exclusion. Second, this illustration is for child allowances, a program that is often universal rather than targeted. The desire to limit benefits to the poorest is often stronger for other programs.

FIGURE 4.4 **Conceptualizing Administrative Costs**

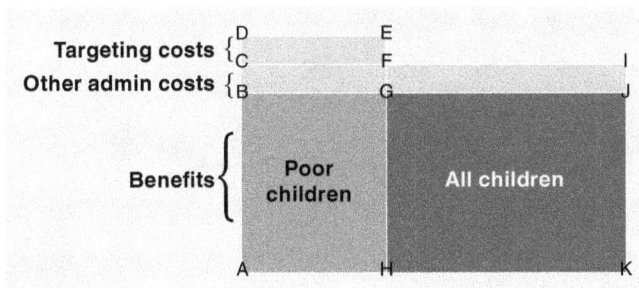

SOURCE: Authors.

For those programs for which they have been measured, the administrative costs of targeting are usually reasonably low. Tables 4.2 and 4.3 provide data from the handful of recent studies that try to document these for some well-established means-tested and proxy means-tested programs. In table 4.2, specific programs are the unit of observation. Targeting costs average about 4 percent of total program costs, range from about 25 to 75 percent of total administrative costs, and in absolute terms cost US$8 or less per beneficiary in all but one case. The share of total costs is slighter higher than Grosh (1994) indicates for some older and less well-targeted Latin American programs that use similar targeting mechanisms, but is still hardly prohibitive. In table 4.3, household targeting systems used for multiple programs in five Latin American countries are the unit of observation. Costs per interview cluster in the range of about US$3 to US$8 per beneficiary and the share of targeting costs in benefits transferred is less than 1.5 percent. The costs cited are for the most complex mechanisms: means and proxy means tests. Costs for other targeting mechanisms are almost by definition substantially lower, but are usually not well measured.

In thinking about whether household targeting systems such as those in table 4.3 would be affordable in a new setting, three factors should be taken into account. First, some adjustments in pricing may be sensible, as labor usually accounts for the largest share of costs and its price is quite variable. To solve this problem in extrapolating lessons from U.S. eligibility processes for Latin America, Castañeda and Lindert (2005) approximate

TABLE 4.2 **Administrative Costs of Targeting for Selected Means-Tested and Proxy Means-Tested Programs, Various Years**

Country, program, and year	Targeting costs as share of total...		
	Administrative costs	Program costs	US$/ beneficiary
Albania: Ndihme Ekonomika, 2004	88	6.3	7
Armenia: Family Poverty Benefits Program, 2005	26	0.6	3
Bulgaria: Guaranteed Minimum Income Program, 2004	64	6.3	7
Kyrgyz Republic: Unified Monthly Benefit Program, 2005	24	2.3	1
Lithuania: Social Benefit Program, 2004	41	2.7	8
Romania: Guaranteed Minimum Income Program, 2005	71	5.5	25
Colombia: Familias en Acción, 2004	34	3.6	—
Mexico: PROGRESA, 1997–2000	40	2.4	—

SOURCES: Colombia: Lindert, Skoufias, and Shapiro 2006; Mexico: Caldés, Coady, and Maluccio 2004; other countries: authors' calculations.

NOTE: — = not available. Targeting costs include those related to outreach to beneficiaries, determination of eligibility, home visits, verification of information, and maintenance of databases.

the number of hours of staff time required, valued at US$86 in the United States, and then reprice them with salary levels more typical of middle-income Latin American countries, thereby deriving a value of US$25.

Second, looking at the size of the transfer to be targeted is important. Administrative costs accrue in absolute terms, not as a proportion of benefits. For example, spending US$10 per beneficiary in targeting costs to target a benefit of US$10 would be inefficient, but spending US$10 to target a benefit worth US$40 might make sense; it would certainly make sense for one worth US$100. This explains the low percentage of administrative costs in total costs for Argentina's Jefes de Hogar (Heads of Household) program or the large conditional cash transfer (CCT) programs in Brazil and Mexico, where the transfers are large. Another way to achieve good cost-effectiveness is to use the same targeting system for multiple programs. Colombia, for example, first developed its proxy means test to target subsidized health insurance, and later used it for targeting hospital fee waivers and its CCT, public works, youth training, and social pension programs. Armenia, Chile, and Jamaica also use their proxy means test for several programs. This can not only yield economies of scale in the targeting system, but can also lead to a more integrated package of support for households that may provide better risk management and more effective assistance for moving them out of poverty.

Third, overall administrative costs, especially as a percentage of a program's overall budget, tend to be higher during the program's start-up phase. During the first seven years of implementation of Mexico's PROGRESA program, its administrative costs fell from 51 percent of the program's total budget to 6 percent. This was because of large up-front expenditures for systems (purchase of equipment, design of systems, definitions of proce-

TABLE 4.3 **Estimated Total and Annual Costs of Household Targeting Systems, Selected Countries, 2002**

Country, targeting system	No. registered (millions)	No. of beneficiaries (millions)	Interview cost per person (US$)	Annual cost per person registered (US$)	Annual cost per beneficiary (US$)	Benefits targeted (US$ millions)[a]	Cost per benefits targeted (%)[b]
Brazil, Cadastro Único	29.0	19.1	3.90[c]	0.40	0.60	877	1.4
Chile, Ficha CAS	5.6	1.9	8.40[d]	1.20	3.60	526	1.3
Colombia, SISBEN	27.0	12.9	1.80 urban; 2.90 rural[e]	0.20	0.40	941	0.5
Costa Rica, SIPO	1.0	0.21	4.20 urban; 7.00 rural[e]	1.00	4.80	116	0.9
Mexico, Oportunidades registry	36.9	21.0	4.90 urban; 6.80 rural[e]	0.40	0.70	2,300	0.7
United States, TANF registries	—	—	86.00[f,g]	—	86.00[g]	—	—

SOURCE: Castañeda and Lindert 2005.

NOTE: — = not available; CAS = Comité de Acción Social (Social Action Committee); SISBEN = Sistema de Selección de Beneficiarios (System for Selecting Beneficiaries); SIPO = Sistema de Información de la Población Objetivo (Information System for the Targeted Population); TANF = Temporary Assistance for Needy Families. Data presented here exclude costs of equipment and information systems. Not all of those registered will receive benefits, as some will be above the beneficiary threshold.

a. Total amount of benefits for all programs using this targeting system/registry to select beneficiaries.

b. Cost of the targeting system as a share of total program(s) budget.

c. Recertification period has not been established.

d. Recertification every two years (new interview required).

e. Recertification every three years (new interview required).

f. Recertification is annual.

g. This is approximately equal to US$25.00 when referenced to salary levels typical of middle-income Latin American countries.

dures, and the like) that yield benefits for multiple years, coupled with a gradual rollout of the program with successively larger numbers of clients served by those systems (Lindert, Skoufias, and Shapiro 2006).

PRIVATE COSTS

Private costs always reduce a program's net benefit to the recipient. If they are sufficiently large, they may discourage eligible people from participating altogether. Evidence on private costs is rarely quantified systematically and reported in internationally comparable ways, but assessments of such costs often give program managers some sense of the size of the problem and the factors that contribute to it. A 1998 assessment in Armenia undertaken to lay the basis for some of the reforms then on the drawing board found that among the poorest people, the causes for not registering for benefits included having insufficient information about the safety net system; being unable to pay the bus fares, fees, and sometimes the under-the-table payments required to get all the required documentation in order; and having difficulty standing in lines for long periods because of disability, pregnancy, or child care needs (World Bank 1999d). The costs were particularly high for those who needed to get a medical certification of disability. In addition, people were confused about whether those who needed to update the documents testifying to their place of residence first had to pay in full any back taxes or utility bills. Such barriers are common, indeed almost inherent in, social assistance programs, but the Armenian program subsequently took a number of steps to reduce them.

The highest private costs are for programs with a work requirement. Many of those who participate in public works programs would earn at least something, usually from intermittent work or self-employment, if they were not working on the public works jobs. Thus the amount they are paid (the gross wage) is more than the additional income they gain from the public works job (the net wage). The cost of the income foregone through not being able to pick up odd jobs or work in self-employment while on the public workfare job is the private cost of participation in this kind of program, and is often high, on the order of a quarter to half of the benefit (see chapter 7, section 4).

INCENTIVE COSTS

The basic issue of incentive costs is outlined in chapter 2, section 3, and evidence on the topic is treated more thoroughly in chapter 5, section 2. Note that incentive costs pertain most directly to only two targeting methods: means testing that is based on current income and self-targeting through public works, because the work requirement may reduce the time available for work outside the program.

SOCIAL COSTS

Receiving public assistance can generate a feeling of shame about receiving it or being publicly seen to be receiving it. How important the issue is appears to be highly variable. One factor seems to concern general public attitudes about the receipt of public programs. Rainwater (1982) shows that stigmatization seemed to be a larger factor in program nonparticipation in the United Kingdom than in Italy, for example.

Programs can do much to foment or minimize stigmatization. One way they do this is through the public portrayal of the program. In Jamaica, the government used publicity to minimize stigmatization of participants in the maternal and child health portion of its former Food Stamp Program. The program was open to all pregnant or lactating women and to children under the age of five using public health clinics (the use of which was in itself a source of self-targeting). However, when the program was initiated, the stress was on its universality. Publicity spots were run on television showing the pregnant wife of a cabinet minister signing up for her food stamps with the explicit goal of removing stigmatization (Grosh 1992). In contrast, in Armenia during reforms to the Family Poverty Benefits Program, the publicity campaign focused on the targeted nature of the benefits, stressing that they were meant for, and only for, the poor. The hope was that this would encourage more self-selection among applicants, that is, that stigmatization would keep the nonpoor from applying.

Programs also adopt quite different strategies about whether or not nonparticipants can identify participants. The assumption is that when nonparticipants cannot identify participants, the latter will be less likely to be stigmatized. In some cases, the entire beneficiary roster is confidential or the information system may incorporate safeguards so that social workers or program administrators can only access the subset of cases under their own jurisdiction. In other cases, the beneficiary roster is made public as part of the mechanism to ensure transparency and fairness. In the latter case, the nonpoor may be embarrassed to be seen on the roster and therefore not apply. If they do apply, they may be subject to social pressure or denouncement to the authorities and removed from the roster. Program participants may be identifiable in other ways. In Bulgaria's public works program, participants wear reflective safety vests when working outdoors. Though intended for their safety, some say they are stigmatizing. The increasing trend of paying benefits in cash rather than in kind and via banking systems, post office accounts, or checks is probably making benefit receipt less stigmatizing than for the previous generation of programs. The debit card used in the Brazilian Bolsa Família (Family Grant) program, for example, looks similar to any other credit or debit card carried by the middle class. This approach stands in sharp contrast to what poor Bolivians participating in the 1980s food programs experienced when they lugged home sacks of grain and tins of oil bearing the U.S. PL480 food assistance logo.

POLITICAL COSTS

As noted earlier, the technical justification for budgeting is that, for a given budget, narrow targeting can maximize the program's impact on the poor, or for a given impact, can minimize the budget. But this does not take into account how a budget is actually determined, which involves political processes. Targeting choices and outcomes will play into those processes.

The evidence on the political response to the degree or method of targeting is scant and debate is ongoing (box 4.2). Most of the modeling work focuses on models in which voters determine the program budget, and voters' interest in funding a program relates to their likely direct benefits from the program (Gelbach and Pritchett 2002; Pritchett 2005). In such models, more universal programs are predicted to have larger sustaining budgets, and under many constructions narrowly targeted programs would end up with no allocation at all. Some of the more interpretive literature (Esping-Anderson 1990) follows a similar chain of logic.

Other interpretive literature points out that sources of political support may be more varied. Voters may support a program because they value social justice or perceive indirect benefits to assisting the poor, such as being hassled by fewer beggars, facing lower risks of property theft or political instability, or feeling that they have met their social obligations without having to respond to myriad personal or nongovernmental solicitations for support. Such voters will appreciate deriving these indirect benefits at as low a tax burden as possible, which may call for some narrow targeting. To the extent that social assistance programs are externally financed, most development agencies also have this bias in seeking the maximum impact on social indicators for the minimum budget, and thus will also favor narrow targeting.

BOX 4.2 **Universalism versus Targeting**

Targeting is a hugely controversial topic, considered anathema by some and panacea by others when, as with many divisive topics, the most sensible view is probably somewhere in between.

In relation to social protection, the universalist approach proposes that all citizens of a nation receive the same state-provided benefits. Targeting proposes that state-provided benefits differ depending on individuals' circumstances. Proponents of both approaches understand that in most developing countries, current budgets do not allow a meaningful provision of transfers to all citizens, and also that targeting experience is far from uniformly excellent. There are two glasses of milk, each of them half empty and half full; the "camps" differ about which they perceive can be filled.

Universalists are optimistic that the social unity resulting from a uniform provision of benefits will garner a sufficient budget (nationally financed in middle-income countries and donor assisted in low-income countries) to provide meaningful protection. Universalists believe that experience with targeting as a way to increase the efficiency of redistributive spending has been unsatisfactory to date, uninspiring in relation to hope for the future, and detrimental to efforts to increase the budget.

In contrast, targeters have a more optimistic assessment of targeting experience and are hopeful that bad experiences can be replaced by good experiences and that perhaps the good experiences can be improved. Targeters' pessimism concerns budgets, seeing both political and technical obstacles to budgets becoming sufficient to provide meaningful universal benefits.

In reality, the distinction between the approaches is not absolute. Even the European welfare states that have gone the furthest in universal provision of child allowances, education, and health insurance and have extensive minimum wage laws, labor market activation and the like have last resort needs-based programs that are tightly targeted. Thus even though they may choose wider or narrower ranges of programs to target or different mixes of programs, all countries need to understand how to target.

Political support may also come from interest groups that are suppliers to the program or advocates for its beneficiaries. Farmers and teachers' unions may support school lunch programs on these grounds. Political support can also be garnered from adroit mixes of interest. The recent upswing in social assistance budgets in Latin America seems to have been greatly assisted by the advent of the CCT program. Because they tie social assistance to more broadly supported goals of universal health care and education, and because they demand "good behavior" on the part of recipients, CCT programs have garnered much greater political support than their predecessor programs, despite being much more effectively and often narrowly targeted.

An intriguing piece of empirical evidence comes from an analysis of municipal elections in northeastern Brazil. De Janvry and others (2005) find that mayors were more likely to be reelected when their implementation of the Bolsa Familia program had the following characteristics: good coverage, low errors of inclusion, functioning social control councils, and higher impacts. The voters valued several of the same features that contribute to a program's technical efficiency.

4.3 Targeting Options

A number of different targeting methods are available for directing resources to a particular group. Some demand some sort of assessment of eligibility for each applicant (individual or household). Others grant eligibility to broad categories of people, for instance, all those residing in certain areas or all those of a certain age. Others are designed to discourage the non-needy from entering the program, but do not actually prohibit them from doing so. This section defines a number of the common methods and summarizes some of the main advantages and disadvantages of each. A great deal of detailed implementation know-how is available for many of these methods, and box 4.3 provides references.

BOX 4.3 **Resources on Different Targeting Methods**

The World Bank has contributed to the large body of material available on targeting. Some key readings by methods are listed below.

Overview. Coady, Grosh, and Hoddinott (2004) provide a comprehensive overview of targeting issues and methods and international comparisons based on a review of 122 programs in 48 countries.

Individual or Household Assessment. Castañeda and Lindert (2005) provide an in-depth treatment of the implementation details of household targeting systems based on case studies of Brazil's unverified means test; Chile's, Colombia's, Costa Rica's, and Mexico's proxy means tests; and the verified means tests used in the United States. It is especially rich in dealing with the details of data collection, database management, and the like.

Tesliuc and others (forthcoming) provide an in-depth treatment of the implementation of means-tested systems based on case studies in Albania, Bulgaria, the Kyrgyz Republic, Lithuania, and Romania and on Armenia's proxy means test.

Conning and Kevane (2001) summarize the little that is known about community-based targeting systems.

Geographic Targeting. Hentschel and others (2000) provide one of the early descriptions of how to construct poverty maps with small area estimation techniques with illustrations for Ecuador.

Information on the World Bank methodology and experience with small area estimation poverty maps is available at the World Bank poverty Web site: worldbank.org/poverty.

Henninger and Snel (2002) review the policy uses of poverty mapping in 14 countries and how institutional details can affect its use.

Self-Targeting. Given the relative simplicity of self-targeting, fewer implementation details need to be considered. Subbarao's (2003) primer paper on public works reviews design features and experiences pertaining to self-targeting through wage selection, and Alderman's (2002) paper on food subsidies reviews self-selection through the choice of commodities.

MEANS TESTS

A verified means test is usually regarded as the gold standard of targeting. It seeks to collect (nearly) complete information on households' income and/or wealth and verifies the information collected against independent sources. Where suitable databases exist and interagency cooperation can be obtained, information may be verified by cross-linking the registries of, say, the welfare agency, property registrars, tax authorities, social security agencies, and the like. When this is not possible, households may be asked to submit copies of records of transactions, such as pay stubs, utility bills, or tax payments.

Simple means tests with no independent verification of income are not uncommon. Sometimes verification is completely nonexistent in that a program intake worker simply records what an applicant says. Sometimes a social worker will visit the household to verify in a qualitative way that visible standards of living (which reflect income or wealth) are more or less consistent with the figures reported. Alternatively, the social worker's assessment may be wholly qualitative, taking into account many factors about the household's needs and means, but not having to quantify them. These types of simple means tests are used for both direct transfer programs and for fee waiver programs, with or without household visits.

In the best of cases, means testing can be extremely accurate. However, means tests work best in situations of high levels of literacy and documentation of economic transactions. They are administratively demanding when combined with meaningful attempts at verification. Means testing is also the form of targeting most like to discourage work effort, because eligibility is linked directly to current income. Means testing is most appropriate where declared income is verifiable, where some form of self-selection limits applications by nontarget groups, where administrative capacity is high, and/or where benefit levels are large enough to justify the costs of administering a means test. Some countries have started with rudimentary systems and refined them over time.

PROXY MEANS TESTS

Proxy means tests generate a score for applicant households based on fairly easy-to-observe household characteristics, such as the location and quality of the household's dwelling, its ownership of durable goods, its demographic structure, and the education and possibly the occupations of its adult members. The indicators used to calculate this score and their weights are derived from statistical analysis (usually regression analysis or principal components analysis) of data from detailed household surveys of a sort too costly to be carried out for all applicants to large programs. The information provided by the applicant is usually partially verified either by a program official collecting information on a visit to the home or by having the applicant bring written verification of some of the information to the program office. Eligibility is determined by comparing the household's score against a predetermined cutoff.

The advantage of proxy means testing is that it requires less information than true means testing, and yet is objective. Moreover, because it does not actually measure income, it may discourage work effort less than a means test would. Proxy means testing also has some drawbacks. Administering it requires a large body of literate and probably computer-trained staff and moderate to high levels of information and technology. It also implies an inherent inaccuracy at the household level, as the formula is only a prediction, although on average, good results have been observed. The formulas used usually rely on indicators that are fairly stable, and may distinguish chronic poverty well, but can be insensitive to quick changes in household welfare or disposable income, which may be frequent and large when an economy is suffering from a large downturn. Moreover, the formula and results may seem mysterious or arbitrary to some households and communities.

Proxy means tests are most appropriately used where a country has reasonably high administrative capacity, for programs meant to address chronic poverty in stable situations, and where they are used to target a single program with large benefits or to target several programs so as to maximize the return for a fixed overhead.

COMMUNITY-BASED TARGETING

Community-based targeting uses a group of community members or leaders whose principal functions in the community are not related to the transfer program to decide who in the community should benefit. School officials or the parent-teacher association may determine entry to a school-linked program, a group of village elders may determine who receives grain provided for drought relief, or special committees composed of community members or a mix of community members and local officials may be specially formed to determine eligibility for a cash transfer program.

The advantage of community-based targeting is that it relies on local information on individual circumstances, which may be more accurate and less costly to collect than using other methods. In addition, it can permit local definitions of need and welfare. At the same time, community targeting may encounter several possible problems. Local actors may have other incentives besides good targeting of the program. For example, the granting or denial of benefits to different members of the community may lower the authority or cohesion of local actors involved in the decision. Also such a system may continue or exacerbate any existing patterns of social exclusion. In addition, if local definitions of welfare are used, evaluating how well community-based targeting works becomes more difficult and ambiguous.

Community-based targeting may be most appropriate where local communities are clearly defined and cohesive, for programs that plan to include just a small portion of the population, and for temporary or low-benefit programs that cannot support administrative structures of their own.

GEOGRAPHIC TARGETING

With geographic targeting, location determines eligibility for benefits: people who live in the designated areas are eligible and those who live elsewhere are not. Few programs target only on the basis of geography, but many programs use geographic targeting in conjunction with other targeting methods, especially when programs are not fully funded. In such cases poverty maps can be used to focus the program in only some areas of the country or to allocate spaces in the program among subnational jurisdictions.

The advantage of geographic targeting is that it is administratively simple, requiring none of the machinery for individual assessment programs described earlier. It will have no direct labor disincentive and is unlikely to result in stigmatization, as poor and nonpoor neighbors alike will benefit. Geographic targeting will perform poorly when poverty is not spatially concentrated. It also depends on the accuracy of the poverty map, a concern that is diminishing in importance as small area estimation techniques improve and are widely applied.[3] Political compromises may be required, as politicians from each jurisdiction will lobby to have their districts included. This may mean that a fixed portion of districts within each province may benefit, rather than the poorest districts overall.

The most appropriate circumstances for geographic targeting are when living standards across regions vary significantly, when administrative capacity is too limited or transfer amounts too low to make individual assessment methods sensible, and/or when additional self-targeting can be induced through the use of some public service used mainly by the poor.

DEMOGRAPHIC TARGETING

The usual and simple forms of demographic targeting are based on age, with child allowances and social pensions being the most common. Part of the rationale is that individuals may be particularly vulnerable in childhood and old age. The logic is somewhat clouded by the reality that most individuals, certainly children, and in most countries the large majority of the elderly as well, live in households with several individuals and generally one or more income earners. Because households tend to pool their resources, at least in part, many children and elderly do not live in poverty even though they do not generate income for themselves.

Demographic targeting is obviously administratively simple. Moreover, it carries the appeal of universality, and is thus often politically popular, plus those participating in programs targeted in this way are not stigmatized. The limitation of demographic targeting is that age may be only weakly correlated with poverty. Current research shows that observed correlations are sensitive to assumptions made about economies of scale and equivalence used in constructing measures of welfare, an area where economists agree that some corrections are useful, but do not agree on exactly how to do them (see box 8.2 for a discussion).[4]

Demographic targeting is a low-cost targeting method and is particularly useful when age and welfare are highly correlated or for programs that include an element of self-targeting to complement the demographic targeting. For example, food supplements may be given to children who use public health services in locations where private health providers siphon off much of the demand from the upper part of the income distribution, or a social pension may serve those elderly who are excluded from the contributory program, which usually serves the top end of the wealth distribution.

SELF-TARGETING

Self-targeted programs are technically open to everyone, but are designed in such a way that take-up is expected to be much higher among the poor than the nonpoor or the level of benefits is expected to be higher among the poor.

One of the most common applications of self-targeting in social assistance is the use of low wages in public works programs to induce participation only by the poor. The less poor will be able to command higher wages elsewhere. The administrative costs of the targeting are quite low, although administering public works programs is not simple. As, by definition, such programs put people to work, they may be politically supportable. However, the net benefits are usually substantially lower than the gross benefits. In addition, the associated stigmatization can be considerable.

The other common application of self-targeting in social assistance is in the subsidization of staple foods that are more heavily consumed by the poor than by the nonpoor. In practice, few goods may be consumed more in absolute terms by the poor, because the poor consume less in total, and thus the benefits are often regressive, or mildly progressive at best. Errors of exclusion and stigmatization are concomitantly low.

GUIDANCE ON CHOICE OF METHOD

Most targeting methods are applicable to most programs, but a few programs and methods go hand-in-hand. As just noted, self-targeting through the use of a low wage is only applicable to public works programs and is used by most of them. Similarly, food subsidy programs require the choice of appropriate commodities. Aside from such examples, choices must be made. Cash transfers, for example, have been targeted using virtually all methods and many combinations of methods.

Coady, Grosh, and Hoddinott (2004) assess which methods deliver the best results in relation to errors of inclusion. In the sample of programs they review, 80 percent of the variability in targeting performance as measured by errors of inclusion was due to differences within targeting methods, and only 20 percent was due to differences across methods. Interventions that used means testing, geographic targeting, and self-selection based on a work requirement were all associated with an increased share of benefits going to the bottom two quintiles compared with targeting that used self-selection based on consumption. Proxy means testing,[5] community-based selection of individuals, and demographic targeting of children showed good results on average, but with considerable variation. Demographic targeting of the elderly and self-selection based on consumption showed limited potential for good targeting. Figure 4.5 provides simple comparisons of the range of benefits for each method. The use of multiple targeting methods within a single program generally produced better targeting than the use of a single method.

The ranking by Coady, Grosh, and Hoddinott (2004) cannot be

FIGURE 4.5 **Targeting Performance by Targeting Method**

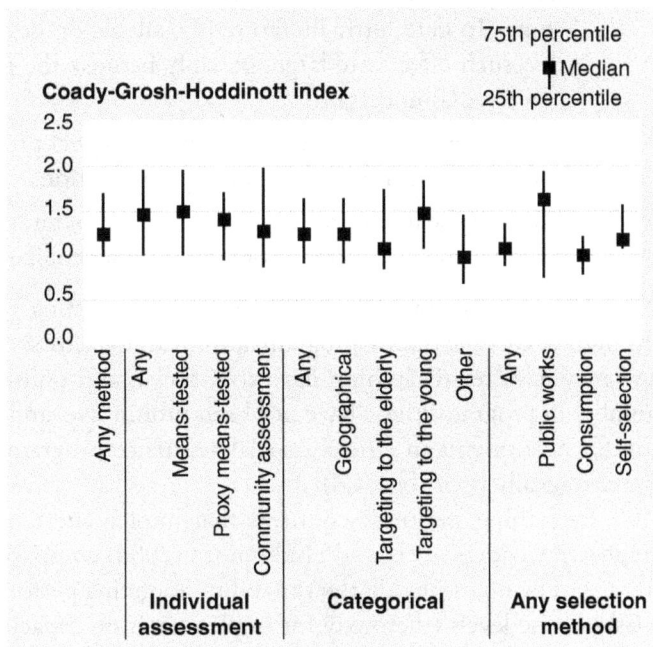

SOURCE: Coady, Grosh, and Hoddinott 2004, table 3.4.

NOTE: The Coady-Grosh-Hoddinott index reports the share of benefits accruing to the group observed divided by the share of the group observed in the total population—for example, the share of benefits going to the poorest 40 percent of the population divided by 40. For most observations, it reflects the distribution of benefits to the poorest two quintiles, or to the poorest quintile or fraction of the poor.

taken as a blanket preference for one method over another. It does not consider errors of exclusion, different elements of cost, or feasibility constraints. We have less good information with which to differentiate between methods in relation to these elements, but the following observations are probably true:

- Methods may be ranked differently when errors of exclusion are factored in. Self-targeting through wages in public works programs, for example, may have among the lowest errors of inclusion, but tends to have high errors of exclusion, because programs are small relative to needs and are inappropriate for labor-poor households. Given a sufficient budget, errors of exclusion will, by definition, be lowest for demographically targeted programs or for those that subsidize a commodity or service used universally.

- Means and proxy means tests seemingly demand the highest administrative costs, but these costs may not be a large marginal addition to the costs of registering beneficiaries, and systems have certainly been set up for large programs or for combinations of programs that incur low costs as a fraction of benefits. Grosh (1994) shows that the extra costs are generally balanced by the more accurate targeting achieved. Private transaction costs are probably also higher for such programs, but again, need not be prohibitive.

- All transfers could reduce work effort because they supply unearned income to households. Means-tested transfers will have a somewhat stronger influence on work, because they link eligibility, and sometimes benefit levels, directly to income. To date, little literature is available on developing countries that indicates that such effects are large, possibly because the transfers are small and are often perceived as uncertain.

- Stigmatization can occur in any nonuniversal programs, but can be greatly influenced by program design and implementation.

- Much of the literature voices the concern that nonpolitical costs may be higher for more narrowly targeted programs, but generalizing about such costs is difficult.

As concerns costs, means and proxy means testing systems will clearly have many of the highest costs, certainly program administrative costs; transaction costs to beneficiaries; and may have relatively high incentive, social, and political costs as well. Yet for a large number of programs these have not been prohibitive, and indeed, they seem to have been fruitful investments in efficient social assistance programs, especially for those geared to the chronically poor (box 4.4).

Everything we know confirms that implementation matters tremendously to outcomes. In Coady, Grosh, and Hoddinott's (2004) comparisons, country context explained some, but by no means all, the variability. Targeting performance improved with the countries' income levels (the proxy for implementation capacity), the extent to which governments were held accountable for their actions, and the degree of inequality. Unobserved factors, however, explained many of the differences in targeting success. Improvements in the design and implementation of targeting methods thus have great potential. If programs with poor targeting success were brought up to the median level of success, the share of program benefits going to the poor would increase by 10 percentage points.

BOX 4.4 **How Do the Reasons for Adopting a Program Affect Targeting Choices?**

Much of the targeting literature, and this chapter, is geared toward targeting the chronically poor. A good deal of experience with targeting this group has been accumulated, and several good options are usually available in most settings.

When programs are designed to assist those who have experienced some sort of shock, the range of most applicable options and implementation issues for each change slightly. Proxy means testing, one of the workhorse options for targeting the chronically poor, is usually ruled out, as the proxies used usually change slowly. Means testing can theoretically be used, but would entail both open registration procedures and recertification as frequent as every few months. This is somewhat daunting. Thus self-targeting will be even more desirable than usual as the targeting method. Categorical methods may also be applicable. Hurricanes, tornados, and landslides may have defined geographical effects, and assisting all those in affected areas may be sensible. Even a more general phenomenon such as a drought or flood may have broad primary and secondary effects that geographic targeting alone, or geographic targeting plus some sort of simple take on long-term welfare or risk, may be sufficient. Widespread crop loss in a region, for example, would directly affect most farmers, and would also probably have significant second-round effects on the demand for labor by landless laborers and on products from small-scale services in the area.

When the motive of a program is to compensate losers in a reform process, distinguishing how specifically identifiable the losers and the extent of their losses are is important. If fully identifying these is possible, specific compensation may be offered. For example, when public enterprises are scaled back, fired workers are easily identified and can be offered severance pay, training, access to credit, and so on. Targeting such specific compensation is not an issue, although designing the package of compensation may be. When reforms are more general, for example a reduction of food or utility subsidies, the goal of a safety net program is not to compensate each loser for his or her loss individually and separately, but more generally to assist the poor, and possibly the middle class, and to make the reforms politically sustainable. In such cases, the eligibility threshold may be higher than for programs meant for the chronically poor and/or the program's time horizon may be relatively short. Usually such reforms are aimed at moving from untargeted programs to more targeted ones, so some sort of household targeting mechanism may be devised. Sometimes these are a bit rough in the first instance so as to allow the reform to move ahead quickly and the targeting system is improved over time.

4.4 Implementation Matters for Targeting

Because outcomes depend greatly on implementation, and because even a single method can be implemented in a variety of ways, discussing implementation in detail is important. This section summarizes some of the key lessons derived from the literature introduced in box 4.1 with a focus on issues common across methods. Program managers are advised to read the reference materials on the specific methods in which they are interested.

Figure 4.6 presents a generic outline of the successive steps involved in targeting from the general population to program beneficiaries.

FIGURE 4.6 **From Population to Beneficiary: The Stages of Targeting**

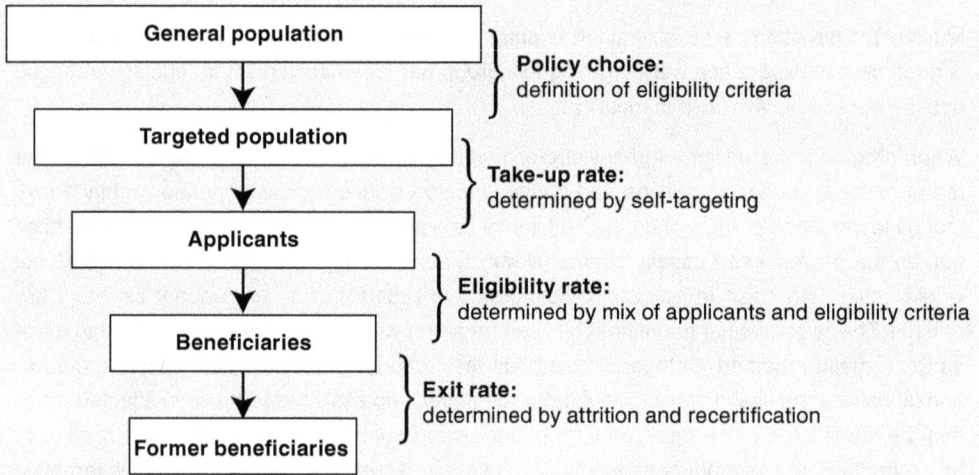

SOURCE: Adapted from de Neubourg, Castonguay, and Roelen 2007.

FROM THE GENERAL POPULATION TO THE TARGETED POPULATION

One of the first steps in social assistance policy making is to define what benefit a program will offer: how much, under what conditions, for how long, and to whom. This step is complex and based on many factors that are discussed in detail throughout the book and brought together in chapter 9.

The next step is to define the specifics of eligibility, translating from intuitive notions to specifics amenable to actual administration. The details of this can be quite complex. Suppose the decision is to target the elderly. How old is elderly? Is it everyone above age 60? Age 70? Age 80? Should the same threshold apply for men and women? Is the age to be used determined only by the needs of this program or in coordination with retirement ages in contributory pension schemes? Similarly, for a program targeted to the needy, how poor is poor? Should the threshold vary by family size or composition or by cost of living differences for different areas of the country? Or consider a program to assist single working mothers. The intuitive understanding of who is to be served may be clear, but a precise definition can be technically difficult to come up with. How much work is enough to count as working? Does working seasonally or at home count? At what age does a child become an adult, and thus a mother become just an adult woman? When is a mother single? When she is unmarried? What if she gets formal alimony or substantial transfers from the child's father? What if she is legally married but her husband has abandoned her or migrated elsewhere? How would a program official verify the hours of seasonal or at home work or support from absent fathers?

Because the range of different sorts of programs and of various country contexts are both great, providing a list of criteria that might be used for all such definitions is hard. Instead, the following subsections deal with some general factors that may help program managers arrive at specifics for their situation.

Budgetary Implications

The more generous the definition of eligibility, the larger the applicant pool and the greater the cost of the program (of course the size and duration of the benefit are important cost variables as well). For its universal social pension, Nepal defines the elderly as those aged 75 and over. This is high relative to most definitions of old age, but allows all those who meet the criterion to be served within the available budget. Similarly, in countries with a high poverty headcount, assisting all the poor is infeasible, and so a program eligibility threshold might be set that is significantly lower than the poverty line. The Kalomo District Pilot Social Cash Transfer Scheme in Zambia, for example, targets only the poorest 10 percent in each village even though a third of the Zambian population is chronically poor, and the proportion is probably even higher in Kalomo.

Policy Coordination

Especially in a country with a fairly full set of social protection policies, having some coordination among them can be helpful. Thus the definition of old age used for a social pension might be the same as that used for a contributory pension scheme. Similarly, the definition of unemployment in a social assistance program might be the same as for unemployment insurance or verified by registration with the labor bureau.

Administrative Feasibility and Accuracy

Simple criteria are likely to be the easiest to administer and may be appealing for this reason, but they can also be inaccurate. A balance must be found. Consider, for example, a national eligibility threshold for a means-tested program. This is a simple criterion, but if the cost of living is much higher in urban areas than in rural areas, the program would be inherently biased against the urban population. Thus having a spatially differentiated eligibility threshold would be fairer. The ability to accomplish this will depend on the country's general administrative capacity and on having at least periodic access to data on how costs of living differ across the country.

Transparency and Political Feasibility

For transparency, simplicity may again be valuable, but transparency is partly a way to allow the public to perceive that a program is fair. If a program is simple to the point that it seems unfair, it may garner more criticism than approval. In the end, programs must pass the test of political supportability, and targeting criteria can be critical in this regard.

FROM THE TARGETED POPULATION TO THE POOL OF APPLICANTS

Bureaucrats may define who is in the target population, but households will determine who is in the applicant pool as they make their individual decisions about whether or not to apply. To be able to apply, households first need to know about and understand the program, and then they must make individual calculations about whether the program's potential benefits outweigh its transaction and social costs. Programs may wish to induce a significant level of self-targeting, and thus hope that the better-off among the eligible population will not apply, but at the same time, if errors of exclusion are to be kept acceptably low, measures need to be taken to ensure that the neediest will apply. Such measures are needed no matter what targeting mechanism is used.

In determining whether to apply, participants estimate the entire range of costs and benefits to them of the program. They take into account the benefit level and the transaction costs of not just the application process, but also of collecting the benefit and complying with any requirements, such as a work requirement. Thus many parts of program design and implementation are intended to address errors of exclusion. Here we focus on those related to the process of applying to the program.

Have a Sufficient Budget for Adequate Outreach and Intake

One of the principal reasons why households may fail to apply for programs for which they are eligible is that the program has an inadequate administrative budget to employ the various strategies described in the following subsections. To do so requires sufficient staff; enough offices and travel funds to get the staff to the offices; and adequate spending on literature, media campaigns, the targeted dissemination of information to other intermediaries who may help reach clients, and so on.

Ensure Adequate Dissemination of Information about the Program

All those potentially eligible need to know about the program and who might be eligible, what sort of benefit they might get, and how to apply to or find out more about the program. Reaching the candidate pool can take diligence and creativity. Social assistance programs target those who may face significant barriers to information: they are likely to be less educated, less likely to speak the official language, less likely to own the televisions or radios or read the newspapers that are used for mass media campaigns, more likely to live in areas that are remote or underserved by government services, and more likely to belong to socially excluded groups.

Governments can use various avenues to get the messages out. Brochures and posters in appropriate languages that are simply worded or rely largely on illustrations are usually part of a good effort. These can be disseminated through multiple channels, not only through the social assistance offices, but also through other service providers such as schools, health clinics, post offices, and municipal offices; through other authority figures such as those at local places of worship, community structures, and nongovernmental organizations; or through commercial agents such as local shops, bars, and marketplaces.

Mass media campaigns can help, and so can training and/or information sessions for workers in the places that distribute information or for community groups in the poorest areas. Strong evidence from OECD countries indicates that information costs are a significant barrier to participation and that removing them results in higher take-up rates (Hernanz, Malherbet, and Pellizzari 2004).

Ensure Low Transaction Costs for Beneficiaries

To apply for a program, applicants must usually go to a specified place with some set of documentation. To keep costs for applicants low, getting to the point of entry into the program must be convenient. Usually that means putting registration offices within easy reach of households, which can be achieved in various ways. If the government's district offices are in market towns that most potential applicants visit regularly, that may be sufficient. Alternatively, the network of offices can be made more extensive. That is usually expensive, so an intermediate approach of using periodic service delivery points can be helpful. In this system program staff are available on a regular schedule, say once a week or once a month, at some temporary location, perhaps in the village office, school, or health clinic. The extreme of convenience can be a door-to-door sweep of poor areas to notify potential applicants of a new program and assess their eligibility. A number of large, new, proxy means-tested programs in Latin America have taken this approach, at least in poorer districts for initial registration. The different approaches have various advantages (table 4.4). Convenience requires that time costs be kept tolerable as well, so lines should be kept short and the offices open at hours that allow the working population access without loss of work time.

Keeping the required documentation to the minimum necessary is also important, as getting each piece of paperwork is likely to involve a whole new round of logistical and cost issues for applicants. Programs can do various other things to help keep the burden for applicants low. They can allow more easily available substitutes for formal documents when these are not readily available. Nepal's social pension program, for example, accepts

TABLE 4.4 Approaches to Household Registration

	Survey sweep approach	Application approach
Definition	• All households in a particular area are interviewed and registered in a nearly exhaustive system	• Relies on households to come to a local welfare office or designated site to apply for benefits
Advantages	• Better chance of reaching the poorest, who are likely to be less informed than others • Lower marginal unit registration costs because of economies of scale for travel costs	• Lower total costs because of self-selection of the nonpoor out of the registration process (fewer nonpoor households are interviewed) • Dynamic, ongoing access • More democratic: anyone has the right to be interviewed at any time • Permanent process helps build and maintain institutional structures
Best suited for	• High poverty areas (more than 70 percent of the population is poor) • Homogeneous poverty areas (rural areas, urban slums) • New programs, when there is a need for speed	• Moderate or low poverty areas • Heterogeneous areas • The program is well known and publicized
Examples of targeting systems using approach	• Brazil: Cadastro Único • Chile: Ficha CAS until the 1990s • Colombia: SISBEN • Costa Rica: SIPO in poor areas • Mexico: registry for Oportunidades in rural areas	• Chile: Ficha CAS since the early 1990s • Colombia: SISBEN • Costa Rica: SIPO • Mexico: registry for Oportunidades in urban areas

SOURCE: Castañeda and Lindert 2005.

NOTE: CAS = Comité de Acción Social (Social Action Committee); SISBEN = Sistema de Selección de Beneficiarios (System for Selecting Beneficiaries); SIPO = Sistema de Información de la Población Objetivo (Information System for the Targeted Population)

horoscopes as proof of age when applicants do not have birth certificates. Programs can also help applicants obtain their formal documents. The CCT programs in the Dominican Republic and El Salvador have components that help families obtain birth certificates for their children. Programs can arrange to supply documents at no fee as Armenia's Family Poverty Benefits Program does, or they can get information directly from other government offices, a change made recently in Albania.

Physical accessibility for people with disabilities, the elderly, and mothers with small children should be considered, especially as these groups are likely to be more numerous in the target population than in the general population. Allowing designated proxies to carry out transactions on behalf of individuals in these groups may help. Or intake workers may need to do home visits to reach the homebound. In Albania, the Ndihme Ekonomika (Economic Assistance) program can arrange for village leaders to collect payments for distribution to the homebound.

Have an Open Application Process

The best arrangement is to ensure that people can apply for a program at any time. The social assistance ideal is an entitlement program that admits anyone who meets the eligibility criteria as soon as they apply and grants benefits immediately. If limitations on the budget ration the number who may be served, the preferred option is to recalibrate the eligibility criteria, for example, by lowering the eligibility threshold for a means-tested or proxy means-tested benefit, adjusting the age of eligibility for a social pension upward so that fewer people are eligible, or limiting the program to only certain areas based on a poverty map. However, programs often do not take this route. Program rosters are kept open until the beneficiary cap imposed by the budget is reached and then closed. This will obviously create errors of exclusion. New households are formed, some households move, others fall newly into poverty, and still others find out about programs belatedly. All these groups will be excluded with a closed registry system. Allowing households to register, even if they cannot benefit immediately may be useful, especially for programs that expect a relatively large turnover.

FROM APPLICANTS TO BENEFICIARIES

In self-targeting programs, or those targeted only by demographic or geographic criteria, application and acceptance into the program are essentially synonymous. Targeting methods that use individual assessment have a further stage of targeting that demands significant information. Twenty years ago such methods were rare in developing countries, but today they are common, especially in middle-income and transition countries.

The first element of an individual assessment mechanism is a set of criteria that does well at distinguishing welfare, is feasible to assess for each applicant, and creates few or tolerable disincentive effects. The next elements of household targeting systems concern the means of gathering, and usually of verifying, information about applicants, and then reaching a decision.

Individual assessment mechanisms will produce the most accurate targeting if the information on which the eligibility determination is made is accurate. There are various ways of trying to achieve this.

No Verification

The simplest option is not to verify any information, but households have an obvious incentive to convey wrong information to become eligible. Moreover, concepts such as total income are complex. People with multiple or seasonal jobs and those with earnings from self-employment where household and business accounts are intertwined may honestly not know how much their income is, or at least not as a program official would have calculated it. Household surveys that make serious efforts to build comprehensive income aggregates can include hundreds of questions for multiple time periods, enterprises, jobs, and miscellaneous sources of income (McKay 2000a).

The utility of verification is supported by experience in the state of Maryland and in Brazil. In Maryland, for a brief period in the 1970s, the state experimented with self-declared income and the threat of audit (as does the U.S. income tax system). Case error rates increased rapidly to 53 percent and payment error rates to 23 percent (modern payment error rates are 13 percent) (Lindert 2005). In Brazil, the means testing system used for several programs, most notably Bolsa Familia and its predecessors, did not verify income.[6] It reported more poor households, more very poor households, and more households reporting zero income than general household surveys would predict or than a small survey of registered households showed (Castañeda and Lindert 2005). Nonetheless, no verification may be done in some situations. This will be most appropriate when the main information collected is not monetary, as it is less likely to be distorted; when the benefit is small or one-time; or when speed of response is of the essence, as in a hospital emergency room when determining how to charge a patient.

Applicants Provide Paper Documentation

Applicants may be asked to supply paperwork that testifies to their income, expenditures, assets, or at least to those parts of these that are amenable to documentation and reveal something about their economic welfare. They may be asked for pay stubs, records of utility bills, tax bills, certificates that confirm that they do not benefit from other social programs in the country, or other similar documents. The Unified Monthly Benefit Program in the Kyrgyz Republic may require up to 25 such documents, depending on households' specific circumstances, but analysts calculate that on average, about 5 are required.

Having applicants provide documentation may put a significant burden on households. Thus the usefulness of verification in reducing errors of inclusion must be weighed against the increase in transaction costs for applicants and possible increase in errors of exclusion. Moreover, the provision of some of the documents may generate administrative costs for the bureaus that supply them. Because these costs do not usually accrue to the social assistance agency itself, they are not usually counted. Such extra costs will not accrue for documents issued regularly anyway, such as utility bills, but if a household needs certification that it does not own land or automobiles or does not receive a pension, the appropriate bureau must produce such documentation only for use in targeting the social assistance program. Albania's Ndihme Ekonomika program switched to electronic third party verification to eliminate the need for such extra documents.

Applicant-provided documentation of welfare works best when a program's client base regularly participates in a substantial range of documented transactions. It may work less well where sources of income are largely informal and undocumented; where assets are so small that they are not taxable; where the real and property tax systems are undeveloped; or where the poor may not have utilities, or even if they do have access, the utility services may not bill consistently. In middle-income and transition countries, by contrast, building a useful, if partial, picture of household welfare with such documentation may be possible.

Program Intake Workers Make Home Visits

Proxy means tests are built largely around variables that are easy to verify with a home visit, such as the location and quality of the dwelling, the presence of utility services, and the ownership of durable goods. The problem with home visits is that they require additional staff time, and possibly laptop computers or other portable equipment. The benefits in reducing errors of exclusion must be weighed against the extra administrative costs. The additional staff time required can be somewhat reduced with the survey sweep approach described in table 4.4, because home visits are grouped geographically, thereby reducing travel time. Unfortunately, little experience is available to verify whether systematic use of spot checks or random sample home visits induce sufficient accuracy in reporting to completely substitute for 100 percent home visits.

A Third Party Verifies Welfare: The Community Option

Community-based targeting is predicated on the notion that community members will know who is poor in their communities because of routine transactions. They see on a daily basis who spends what, who owns what, and what livelihood strategies households resort to. Thus placing the eligibility decision in the hands of a suitably constituted community group or agent implies verification at no cost either to the program or the applicant. However, the community group may incur costs that are not counted. Sometimes such groups carry out interviews or home visits and incur substantial unrecorded and unreimbursed administrative costs. Certainly they spend some time in the decision-making process. Whether they bear any social costs in terms of resentment by others for decisions made or with respect to their main social roles is not well studied and presumably varies by situation, but may be significant for the accuracy, costs, and sustainability of such systems.

A Third Party Verifies Welfare: The Electronic Option

An alternative to having households amass documentation verifying their economic conditions and bringing it to welfare offices is for the social assistance agency to obtain the information directly from other agencies' records. Third party verification is becoming more common in middle-income and transition economies where the data systems of individual ministries are fairly well developed. To use them for third party verification, legal issues regarding the confidentiality of records must be addressed and a technical means of cross-checking databases must be established via personal identification numbers, addresses, or names. The usual approach is electronic verification by merging databases, either periodically or continuously. The solution does not, however, have to be high-tech. In Albania, the social welfare office receives a quarterly printout of who is registered with the unemployment office and consults it as it processes applications for the Ndihme Ekonomika.

Irrespective of the means of verification, the quality of the application interview is important. The information should be gathered in an accurate, complete, efficient, and polite manner. During the interview, the eligibility worker should not only elicit information from applicants, but should also supply information to them (box 4.5).

BOX 4.5 Communications and Transparency in Program Intake

Adequate face-to-face communications with program applicants and beneficiaries are important for several reasons: they are respectful to the client and thus lower social costs, they can help achieve the outcomes for targeting and for the household behavior sought and thereby increase the program's efficiency, and they can help a program to be judged as fair and thereby increase its political sustainability. Program staff should

- explain the confidentiality policy with respect to information relating to the household's application or benefits;
- use respectful, culturally appropriate manners;
- provide multilingual staff or translation services as needed;
- give all applicants information on clients' rights and responsibilities in relation to recertification, continued eligibility, and so on, as well as on who to contact and how if applicants have questions and how to file an appeal;
- allow clients to ask questions.

SOURCE: Castañeda and Lindert 2005.

FROM BENEFICIARIES TO FORMER BENEFICIARIES

Safety net programs are rarely designed to provide permanent support for individuals or households (although some social insurance programs may be). Thus programs need to have a way to move beneficiaries off the rosters. Note that this is a somewhat different issue than helping households achieve economic independence, which is discussed in chapter 5, section 3.

Beneficiaries may move out of a program through natural attrition. Each year a cohort of children will exceed the age limit set for the child allowance and some of the elderly receiving social pensions will die. This attrition leaves space in the program for the next group of children born or those elderly just reaching the age threshold to be admitted. While the concept is simple and parallel in these two cases, the administrative implication is not. The child allowance program needs only to establish the child's age on entry and then stop payment an appropriate number of years later. This can be built directly into a data system or noticed easily in pencil and paper systems. The removal of deceased elderly from the roles of a social pension program is harder, as it requires that the program administrator learn of the death of the beneficiary. Even though families are usually required to make such notification, unless there is a significant lump sum death benefit, they have little incentive to notify the program administrator of the death and may not do so, or may not do so promptly. Moreover, some elderly will not have families and neighbors may not wish to take on the public service of notifying the program. Social pension programs may try to obtain information from official death registries, but these are often incomplete. As a third strategy, social pension programs may build in a system to suspend benefits for persons who do not collect them for two or three consecutive months, hoping in this way to learn of deaths. Of course, the payments might go uncollected for other reasons, such as a nonfatal illness or disability or higher than average transaction costs for individual participants, and there are circumstances when aid is most needed.

Beneficiaries may move out of a program on their own initiative as their circumstances improve. One of the attractions of a public works program targeted through low wages is that as the economy improves, either seasonally or after a severe downturn, the number of workers willing to work for low wages declines and the program shrinks of its own accord. Similarly, some beneficiaries of other programs may withdraw or cease to collect benefits regularly if the benefit is small relative to the transaction costs of obtaining it. Again, given little incentive to formally notify a welfare office and withdraw, programs often build in the suspension of benefits to those who do not collect them regularly. This allows them to recognize an available slot and enroll another needy family. Again, however, noncollection may occur for reasons other than withdrawal.

Individual assessment mechanisms need to build in recertification requirements. Usually these come in two forms. First, households are required to notify the social assistance program of any material change in their welfare, such as changes in income, household composition, or address, whenever such changes occur. Second, households are required to go through a rescreening process periodically. This rescreening process has been a particularly weak point of many household targeting systems. Often the systems are set up for new programs, and often these programs are implemented in a hurry because of economic or political imperatives and the focus is on getting people in. Only a few years later once the system is running does attention turn to how long people have received benefits. Ideally, rules pertinent to recertification are clearly defined from the beginning of a program, rules are explained to clients as they enroll, and systems are built to handle recertification interviews as a routine part of the workload.

How often recertification ought to take place should be informed by an empirical look at how rapidly households move in and out of poverty, how sensitive the targeting systems are to that, and the costs of recertification. In practice, such studies have not generally fed into policy decisions about recertification, but the requirements are fairly sensible. In Europe and Central Asia's means tests, recertification is quite frequent, at least annually, and frequently more often. In Latin American countries' proxy means tests, recertification tends to occur every two or three years. Recertifying more often for means tests than proxy means tests makes sense, as the variables measured in means tests are more sensitive to changes in short-term welfare. Proxy means test measure longer-term correlates, so what is measured is likely to change little even if short-run welfare has changed.

To reduce the administrative burden and transaction costs of recertification for clients, programs may vary the frequency depending on the type of household. In the Kyrgyz Republic's Unified Monthly Benefit Program, for example, families in urban areas are usually granted benefits for only three months, whereas in rural areas benefits are granted for a year in the expectation that rural residents have less access to new jobs, and that if their welfare were to change, in small villages the change would be noticed and the social worker would be able to detect any lapse in the required notification of change in circumstances. In Albania, the main provision is for monthly recertification, but when frequent changes in welfare are not expected, recertification can be required only annually, for instance, where the household head is disabled, over 70, or a single mother with multiple children. In both countries, social assistance workers have some discretion in assigning the recertification period for specific households.

Programs may also build in explicit time limits. Time limits can serve two functions. Most obviously and importantly, time limits serve as a way to spread resources among more people. This will be especially important when program funding is much less than what is needed to support those eligible. This, for example, is the predominant motivation for the 18-month time limit for Bangladesh's Vulnerable Group Development Program. Even in more generously funded programs such as Mexico's Oportunidades, time limits are used in addition to the slow attrition resulting from the demographic criteria and the medium-term attrition that might happen through recertification via the proxy means test every three years. Families receive full benefits for four years in urban areas and six years in rural and semi-urban areas, with reduced benefits for a further three years. Even in fully funded programs where rationing is not an issue, time limits are sometimes used to ensure that the recipients of social assistance have incentives to become self-sufficient. That is the logic behind the five-year lifetime limit in the U.S. Temporary Assistance for Needy Families Program and the two-year limit for intensive psychosocial support in Chile Solidario.

The administration of time limits has implications for the program's data management system. A national database will be required, or at least local databases will need to be organized in a way that makes cross-checking feasible. The Temporary Assistance for Needy Families Program, for example, has no national database, so the five-year time limit cannot realistically be enforced.[7] Residents can move from one state to another and essentially restart their time in the program. Some cross-checking takes place, but it is far from complete. Where time limits are for life, this implies that databases include information not just on current recipients, but on past recipients.

The administration of time limits also poses challenges in defining recipients. If a family unit consisting of a mother, a father, and one child receives assistance for two years and then the couple is divorced and each remarries, do the new family units each count as having been on welfare for two years? Does the one with the child? Do neither? What if a mother and her children are on welfare and then the mother dies or relinquishes the care of the children to a grandmother. Does the grandmother start a new entitlement allotment? The variations on the theme are nearly endless, but they are not only of academic interest, as family and household structures are fluid in many societies and often more so in low-income strata.

MECHANISMS FOR HANDLING APPEALS AND GRIEVANCES

In every program's transactions, mistakes occur. Even more often people may believe a mistake has occurred when it has not. Having mechanisms for handling these issues is important both for correcting the mistakes and for perceived fairness. A program without a way to address such issues runs the risk of wrecking its reputation.

The concerns to be resolved via appeals can occur at any point in a program, but the largest share is usually concentrated around eligibility, as this is clients' first encounter with the program and often the most complicated. Thus this chapter discusses this issue, though the same mechanisms will be useful for resolving complaints about payments, compliance with any conditions, and the like.

Systematic, professional, rules-based procedures for handling grievances and appeals are a hallmark of modernity, accountability, and democracy in a social protection program. These are lacking in all too many safety net programs in developing countries, with the more common recourse being either that concerned clients grumble to friends and neighbors without taking any action to redress the problem with the program, or that they appeal in person or via a better connected intermediary to the highest level of official possible. Such personal rather than rules-based appeals systems open the door to governance and accountability problems. They can also consume a great deal of time when managers are working on individual cases when they should be working on managing processes that affect everyone. Some programs are working diligently to modernize their appeals systems, but so far few case studies or overviews on the subject have been undertaken to help countries learn from one another (for an example of a case study, see Planning and Development Collaborative International 2001). The information in this section is therefore much less well grounded than in the rest of the chapter.

Mechanisms to handle appeals and grievances have the following three goals:

- To resolve concerns according to the program's rules
- To minimize costs to both clients and the program
- To be, and to be perceived as being, accessible, simple, transparent, fair, and prompt

Appeals and grievance processes involve multiple levels. Each higher level is more costly to both the client and the program and should be used only when the prior level has not resolved the issue.

The Frontline Service Provider

The bulk of complaints should be resolved easily. The file may contain a clerical error that can readily be corrected. Information may be missing that can be obtained from the client or from a government unit, for example, to cross-check information on eligibility or to verify compliance with a condition of the program. Misunderstandings about rules can be cleared up. A frontline service provider can often handle such issues promptly and easily in a face-to-face contact. Handling them at the lowest level of service delivery has several advantages, namely: it is most accessible to the client; it is often cheapest for the program; and it usually means that the social worker or service delivery unit that made an error or did a poor job of communications sees the consequences of that and can not only fix the specific case appealed, but can understand what went wrong to prevent the same problem from arising in the future. Enacting this piece of the appeals system is quite simple: it requires only that the schedules of program intake workers be set in a way that allows a repeat interview with any applicant who wants one and that the workers have access to client files.

In cases where more than one agency may be involved in providing frontline service, working out which will have the information and ability to solve which problems and making that known to participants is important. For example, in a CCT program the municipality might handle the determination of eligibility and complaints about that aspect of the program, but schools might verify attendance and contracted banks might make payments. Applicants who did not get admitted to the program will clearly go first to the municipality to verify if that was correct, but to whom should participants go if they think the size of a payment was incorrect? They may discover the problem upon collecting the payment, but the bank teller would usually not be the person to whom to address complaints, as he or she would usually only have information on the amount to be paid, not on the reasons why. Thus where particular complaints are handled needs to be decided, adequate rules must be established for one agency correcting or acting on data from another, data systems must be built, and rules for who does what need to be communicated clearly to staff and to the public.

The Higher or Independent Level of Appeal

A second line of appeal needs to be available for parties not satisfied at the first level. This may be within the same agency at a higher level; for example, appeals may be handled by the district rather than the subdistrict office. It may be a specialized branch within the same agency, for example, an office of appeals (often for appeals across a range of programs) within the same ministry or municipality. Alternatively, it may be an independent committee or an ombudsman's office.

A second line of appeal will be particularly important when the cause of the problem is some sort of incompetence, negligence, or malfeasance in the frontline office, but will also be useful in other cases. If complaints are arising because of some sort of systematic flaw in the program's design or implementation, the authorities who handle the second line of appeal often have more clout with program management than frontline eligibility workers and may be able to help get troublesome policies or procedures changed. A second line of appeal may also give a sense of recourse to complainants who are not happy with the outcome of the first-line appeal, even if it was correct according to the program's rules. This can be particularly important for eligibility decisions, as the targeting rules are only approximations of the kind of justice a program seeks. Thus in some cases applicants may not be eligible according to the rules, but many people would agree that they should be.

Administrative appeals should have clear service standards, that is, that cases will be resolved within a given time period and that complainants will receive a full explanation of the rationale for the decision.

Judicial Appeals

When all else fails, complainants may have access to the legal system. This is obviously the most expensive way to solve cases and therefore should not be used as a matter of course. Judicial appeals can be particularly powerful in setting or altering rules or their interpretation. In South Africa, for example, a constitutional court case has been brought against the social pensions program, claiming that granting the pension at age 60 for women but age 65 for men is unfair. The program is therefore lowering the eligibility age for men to match that for women.[8]

Examples of Promising Practice

We close with some examples of promising practice. The cases have not been fully evaluated, but thumbnail sketches of them help illustrate the range of tools available for addressing complaints.

Communications and Clerical Accuracy. A great deal of the art of handling complaints is preventing them. Making clear what the program's rules are will help clients know whether they have been treated according to them and whether or not an appeal is needed. Having good pamphlets and posters available, holding group information sessions to explain the rules, giving eligibility officers enough time to be thorough in their conversations with applicants, having applicants review and sign their completed applications, and using double blind entry of data from applications can all help.

Community Committees to Validate Eligibility Decisions. Several programs, for instance, Mexico's Oportunidades program, have formal consultation mechanisms where draft beneficiary lists are presented at formal community meetings. This gives communities a chance to point out both errors of exclusion and of inclusion. In practice, few changes are made as a result and consist mostly of adding households. This is perhaps not surprising: helping a needy household missed in the original outreach campaign is a benevolent act that all in the community will value. In contrast, suggesting that a household is wrongly included is divisive and can carry social costs for the person who makes the observation. If the household is only a little too well-off to qualify for the program, probably no one would want to take their benefit away, and if the household is glaringly among the well-off and powerful in the community, few may dare to suggest such a thing. To lessen that problem, in El Salvador's CCT program, nongovernmental organizations are allowed to challenge the inclusion of non-needy households and program officials then investigate, a technique designed to address the imbalance of power between intended participants and the powerful.

Community Agents. Several CCT programs have so-called mother leaders. These are beneficiaries who are usually elected by groups of beneficiaries. They receive some training in the program's rules and help convey information back and forth between clients and program officials. They do not have the power to make decisions on eligibility and payments, but can be useful in helping clients understand the rules and verifying that complete and correct information is being used.

Call Centers. Providing information by phone (or even online) can be efficient when the telecommunications infrastructure is well developed and cheap. Clients may find placing a call much easier than traveling to an office and lining up. For a large program to run such a back office function may also be safer for its employees and cheaper. However, carefully determining access to information and the authority to make changes that call center staff should have is important. One variant allows them only to explain program rules. Another gives them full access to the files on all clients, which allows them to fix missing or incorrect information. Call center staff may even be able to seek information from other government agencies if necessary. Good call centers can be helpful, although they are never sufficient by themselves, as some part of the client base may find using them impossible or uncomfortable. Moreover, they have to be adequately staffed and equipped and well monitored. Calls that are never answered, or worse, answered incorrectly, only harm a program's reputation.

Community Appeals Committees. Armenia uses local social protection councils composed of five representatives of local government social sector offices and five representatives of nongovernmental organizations. Among other functions, the councils hear appeals from those deemed ineligible by the proxy means test, but who consider themselves in need. The councils have the right to grant entry to up to 5 percent of the roster. This allows the Family Poverty Benefits Program to address cases where the rules and fairness do not quite match up, but in a transparent way.

ADMINISTRATIVE CAPACITY TO SUPPORT TARGETING SYSTEMS

Effective selection and intake of applicants into a safety net program requires sufficient administrative capacity. The specific requirements will depend on the targeting method selected and the myriad details of its implementation. Moreover, the systems for intake, payment, and provision of other services may be intertwined, so capacity is required for more than just targeting. This section therefore cannot be comprehensive, but it does illustrate some of the issues pertaining to administrative capacity with respect to eligibility for programs and how they influence costs and performance.

Staffing

Obviously adequate staff time and general skills are required. Surprisingly little documentation about program staffing is available, therefore saying exactly what defines "adequate" in a quantitative sense is difficult. Documentation of even such basic facts as caseloads is uncommon, and moreover is hard to compare, because the range of tasks may not be comparable. In the city of Arzamas in Russia, each staff member in the one-stop shops that integrate the means tests and application procedures for several previously separate benefits can process 127 benefit claims per month (Institute for Urban Economics, Independent Institute for Social Policy, and Urban Institute 2006). Castañeda and Lindert (2005) report that proxy means test interviews take about 15 to 20 minutes in Chile, Colombia, and Costa Rica. These interviews are done in applicants' homes. Staff can undertake interviews in about 15 homes per day (or about 300 per month) in urban areas using the survey sweep approach, where the outreach is scheduled ahead of time and concentrated in areas of high poverty. When interviews are on an on demand basis, staff can undertake only about 8 or 9 a day (160 to 180 per month) in urban areas because of the greater travel times between households. The Latin American systems can probably handle more applicants per month than elsewhere, partly because proxy means tests forms can be short, but probably also because, for example, the case workers in Arzamas also perform other tasks such as data entry. Where staff also provide significant counseling services, caseloads will be lower.

The formal levels of education of program intake workers tend to vary with the country. In most countries, program workers have completed high school, or at least have had some secondary education. In higher-income countries, some workers may have an undergraduate degree, or at least have taken some university-level courses. In OECD countries, many workers have undergraduate degrees in social work.

The minimum skills required relate to the targeting method used and how data collection is organized. For proxy means tests, much of the work required for data collection using massive survey drives is contracted out to professional survey teams that will understand the questionnaire and survey techniques, but may know little about the program or social policy. Their job is basically to collect the data that determine eligibility.

For community-based methods, the essential requirement is that the community members involved know the poverty situation of their fellow community members. They will need some understanding of the program to make effective decisions and to help get those selected signed up. Such knowledge is usually rudimentary, as the community members are not, by definition, full-time program workers. In the more classic case of eligibility workers conducting means or proxy means tests, they should fully understand all the ins and outs of the program's rules in at least a mechanical sense.

A desirable, but less common, feature of programs is that program intake workers understand some of the goals and concepts behind the rules. When they do, they can make more effective decisions in borderline cases and they can be better ambassadors of the program to applicants. This is important. If intake workers make inappropriate decisions about eligibility, the program's effectiveness is directly impaired, and the lack of credibility that the program does what it says it does may impair its political sustainability. Clients' understanding of the criteria for eligibility is important in terms of their compliance with them, and again in terms of public perceptions about whether the program is operating fairly.

A need commonly expressed, but not usually incorporated in hiring criteria or formal training for intake workers, is that they be trained in communications so that they can deal with conflict. An inherent part of their job is to say no to rejected applicants, which is never pleasant news to deliver or receive. Moreover, a subset of applicants may have mental illnesses or substance abuse problems, as these conditions often lead to poverty. Being able to handle such potentially difficult conversations skillfully is important for good community relations. It will also lower job stress, which can cause burnout and staff turnover.

As the main knowledge that eligibility staff need is highly specific to the program, they acquire that knowledge through some sort of training provided by the program. Training is one of the areas of capacity building that often needs attention. Often on-the-job training consists only of watching workers with longer tenure do their jobs. Some programs have formal training courses provided by the appropriate agency, but a high portion of these is likely externally financed, and thus may train specific cohorts of workers, but not be fully adequate for handling the ongoing training needed to deal with attrition and replacement of program workers.

Rules of the Game

Program rules and regulations must be clear and well defined. Certainly a trade-off exists between too much and too little elaboration of the rules. Programs with little elaboration of their rules may have problems making decisions that are consistent from one case to the next, especially for cases that are not clear-cut. At the same time, excessive detail may mean that workers are unlikely to know or understand them all or that they can be adequately conveyed to the public.

Rules should also be defined in such a way that they incorporate reasonable, but not excessive, flexibility in legal terms. A few programs are defined in countries' constitutions, and are thus extremely inflexible, almost certainly too inflexible for good economic management. Rules contained in laws can be changed periodically, but still require significant political will and time to adjust. Those rules contained in operational manuals issued by the executive branch of government are the most flexible. Some regional variation is apparent, with programs in Eastern Europe and Central Asia being supported by laws, and programs in Latin American more commonly being supported by executive decrees and operational manuals.[9] This partly reflects the relative roles of the branches of government in the different systems, but it may also contribute to the Latin American tendency for programs to come and go with new administrations.

Information Systems and Technology

Programs can be reasonably well targeted with little more than pencil and paper records kept in local offices as, for example, done by Cambodia's Japan Fund for Poverty Reduction Girls Scholarship Program or, until fairly recently, the Unified Monthly Benefit Program in the Kyrgyz Republic. However, computerization can allow programs to incorporate more sophisticated designs, services, and monitoring. A consolidated national database can help avoid duplication and track beneficiaries. Computerization is an essential prerequisite for cross-checking eligibility information with other databases, such as other program rosters, social security registries, and tax registries. Computerization of records can help track what services households have received and what other services they might be eligible to receive.

Castañeda and Lindert (2005) consider experience with information systems for several Latin American means and proxy means testing systems. They identify the following lessons:

- Proper identification of individuals is crucial. A unique social identification number should be used, ideally one that is used on a countrywide basis to link registry information and beneficiaries with other systems and programs. Such cross-checks can reduce both errors of inclusion and fraud.

- Software and coding systems need to be designed so that individuals are linked to their families or other assistance units. Such identification features have been stumbling blocks in many developing countries. They are not insurmountable, however. While countries would ideally assign individuals unique numbers at birth, in the absence of a single national identification number, registry questionnaires often collect information on multiple identification numbers and then assign a new social identification number upon registration (and codes to link individuals to families). This is a feasible solution, provided that (1) data are consolidated and cross-checked in a single database system, and (2) the system has the capacity to be updated to reflect changes and can store and reference historical data.

- Updates and recertification are important for tracking fraud and avoiding situations such as "ghost" beneficiaries, which can emerge as registries become dated. They also allow for turnover in beneficiaries to make space for other poor families to gain entry into programs.

- Database management should be designed so that it can respond flexibly to changing policies and updates and can rely on common software (even if data entry is decentralized), with pretesting of systems, well-designed manuals, and adequate training for users.

Material Inputs

Just like schools and health clinics, social assistance programs need a suitable share of variable inputs to function effectively. In far too many cases, errors of exclusion are high because of a lack of brochures, application forms, transport budgets for staff, and the like. Similarly, client services and monitoring are often deficient because of the absence of computerization.

Institutional Roles

As discussed in chapter 3, section 6, social assistance programs are often a joint effort by national and local governments. This leads to the question of who should perform which functions. Most important, roles should be clearly assigned. No clear blueprint of how that should be done is available. Table 3.8 shows the advantages of different arrangements for various aspects of household targeting systems. The case for local management is strongest for data collection, although it can certainly be organized centrally as well. The central level has a greater comparative advantage for database management, but that conclusion is partly based on the idea of optimal management of individual vertical programs. If local actors run many different programs, and especially if locally financed programs are an important part of the overall policy package, the overall coordination or integration of services for clients might be better achieved with more decentralized database management arrangements.

Monitoring and Oversight

Strong mechanisms for monitoring and oversight are crucial for all systems, but especially with decentralized data collection. While no system is completely immune to fraud or leakages, a variety of tools should be used to minimize them. A number of mechanisms are available, including supervising interviews, verifying information, comparing targeting registries with other data, carrying out random sample quality control reviews, and encouraging citizen oversight (or social controls). Using multiple instruments strengthens the system.

Time

Details of design and implementation have a major impact on distributive outcomes. Too often, however, governments want to launch programs quickly, and they—and the consultants they hire to help them—do not pay enough attention to the necessary details that go into designing and implementing effective household targeting systems. Such systems take time to design, pilot, and implement on a large scale, usually at least 18 months. To get the best out of a system probably takes 5 to 10 years or successive rounds of critique (internal and external), adjustment, and critique.

POLICY REFORM AND TARGETING SYSTEMS: AN ILLUSTRATION FROM ARMENIA

As this chapter has shown, targeting outcomes depend on the big picture of policy choices about who the intended target group for a specific program is, the factors that will affect households' decisions about whether to apply for the benefit, and a host of details concerning how the selected targeting mechanism is implemented. This chapter concludes with a discussion of the reform of social assistance in Armenia, which shows how targeting systems are built.

In 1991, Armenia, a country of 3 million people located in the Caucasus, inherited a generous and regressive cash benefit system plus a system of parastatals obliged to provide subsidized goods and services to "privileged" citizens such as veterans, members of the armed forces, mothers of many children, and persons with disabilities, through quasi-fiscal means from the former Soviet Union. The period following independence was difficult, with the disruption of trading patterns resulting from the dissolution of the Soviet Union, a major earthquake that wiped out a great deal of the nation's industrial capacity, and a conflict with Azerbaijan which resulted in a trade blockade. By 1993, Armenia's gross domestic product had fallen to half of its pre-independence value. By 1998, the social assistance system consisted of 26 small, uncoordinated cash programs covering 15 percent of the population and providing small benefits to different categories of individuals (orphans, single mothers, large families, pensioners living alone, and the like). The entire social assistance system channeled fewer resources to beneficiaries than the regressive electricity subsidy scheme.

In 1999, the government reformed the system by consolidating most programs into a single program, the Family Poverty Benefits Program. The program's design conformed to international best practice. It was implemented via a tightly run administration. The program targeted low-income households instead of categories of poor and not poor individuals. Eligibility was determined using a proxy means test tailored to Armenian conditions, where a large informal economy made income or means testing infeasible. Initially, the program covered 27 percent of the population, roughly similar to the share of the population living below the extreme poverty line, and provided more generous benefits than the programs it had replaced. At the same time, the government discontinued the inefficient electricity subsidy. The new design paid off. An assessment of its targeting showed that the share of benefits going to the poorest 20 percent of the population had risen from 16 percent in 1998 under the old system to 32 percent by 1999 (figure 4.7).

FIGURE 4.7 **Fraction of the Social Assistance Budget Captured by Each Quintile, Armenia, 1998 and 1999**

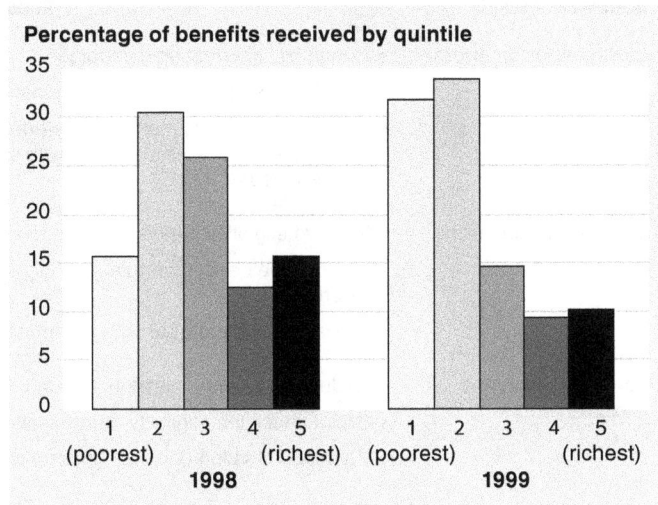

SOURCES: Tesliuc and others forthcoming; World Bank 2002a.

The early success of the program, quite singular in the Caucasus at the time, captured donors' interest, and the U.S. Agency for International Development funded a multiyear program of technical assistance supplied by Planning and Development Collaborative International. Since 1999, the program has received a large amount of technical assistance for capacity building, especially for staff training and process evaluation. According to Planning and Development Collaborative International, the most effective assistance was (1) the recommendations for improved auditing in field offices; (2) the preparation of operational and staff manuals covering customer service, claims processing, human rights, social legislation, and office administration; (3) the evaluation of the implementation of child-focused social policies; (4) the annual survey of the public's use, knowledge, and perceptions of social services; (5) the design and evaluation of two one-stop shops; and (6) the comprehensive outreach campaign using multiple media channels (press, television, radio, posters, and leaflets informing people of their rights).

The institutional consolidation of the program (table 4.5) triggered better service and greater reductions in fraud and error rates. According to an Armenia Social Transition Program survey, public awareness of the program increased from 50 percent in 2001 to 78 percent in 2004, and the service quality of the 55 frontline regional centers rose 25 percent between 2000 and 2004. Better trained staff and the introduction of an integrated database for determining eligibility helped reduce fraud and error rates. The share of benefits going to the poorest increased from 2004 to 2006.

Thanks to economic growth, extreme poverty fell from 23 to 14 percent between 1999 and 2003, while 40 percent of the original caseload graduated out of the program. Thus the fiscal cost of the program went down by 30 percent, despite an increase in its benefits and the eligibility threshold. Had the prior system of categorical targeting remained in place, such a reduction in caseload would not have been possible.

TABLE 4.5 Institutional Consolidation, Family Poverty Benefits Program, Armenia, 1999–2004

Improvement sought	Action
Lower exclusion errors	• Run public information campaigns
	• Place points of service close to beneficiaries
	• Institute an appeals mechanism—here the Social Assistance Board, a community-based institution—with an important role in selecting beneficiaries
Lower inclusion errors	• Improve eligibility criteria (give more weight to children and the elderly)
	• Improve the benefit formula (give higher benefits to children and the elderly)
	• Cross-check databases with information about assets or expenditures
Lower inclusion and exclusion errors	• Reduce data entry mistakes through double entry of household records
	• Cross-check the eligibility determination process
	• Have coordinating unit staff undertake regular audits and other controls
Lower private costs	• Provide the documents required to determine eligibility free of charge
	• Locate the offices or points where applications are collected close to the beneficiaries
	• Implement a one-stop shop system
Improved administration	• Provide training
	• Provide adequate documentation for program staff
	• Implement a strong monitoring and evaluation system
Greater economies of scale	• Use the targeting instruments for other poverty-focused programs

SOURCE: Authors.

Notes

1. A number of indexes are available that summarize the full distributional information into a single summary statistic and are sometimes useful. Ravallion (2007) reviews these.

2. In geographic targeting, when some areas, districts, or states are excluded from a program, obviously poor residents of these localities are excluded from the program. As few social assistance programs are targeted using only a geographic criterion (usually explicit elements of self-selection or individual assessment are used as well), geographic targeting and the exclusion errors it induces are usually symptoms of insufficient budgets.

3. Small area estimation techniques combine data from censuses and detailed household surveys to create poverty maps representative of small areas. An inherent challenge of poverty mapping is data. Censuses have data on every household, and thus are representative of small areas, but the details they contain are limited and are not sensitive predictors of household welfare. More detailed surveys, such as household expenditure surveys or living standard measurement study surveys, do a much better job of measuring household welfare, but have small samples representative of only very aggregated areas. In small area estimation, the welfare measure observed in the detailed dataset is regressed on a subset of variables that also appear in the census. Then using the formula so derived, household welfare is predicted for every household in the census and the predictions are aggregated into poverty maps with a finer level of detail than the use of survey data alone will permit and with greater accuracy than using census data alone will permit.

4. Economies of scale refer to the idea that two can live more cheaply than one, for example, heating needs do not increase because an apartment has two residents rather than one. Similarly, some durable goods may be shared. Economies of equivalence refer to the fact that among goods that are less likely to be shared, requirements may vary from person to person. Children, for example, require fewer calories than adults. Deaton and Zaidi (2002) and Lanjouw, Milanovic, and Paternostro (1998) provide relatively simple technical explanations and examples of the sensitivity of poverty profiles and policy conclusions based on how economies of scale and equivalence are defined.

5. When Coady, Grosh, and Hoddinott (2004) undertook their study, outcome data were only available for a few of the new proxy means tests. Since then data have become available for several more programs, all of which are quite well targeted. If these measurements had been part of the original study, proxy means tests would likely have joined the ranks of the methods that reliably produce progressive results.

6. Subsequently, some verification has been added. If reported consumption is 20 percent higher than reported income, a local program manager must investigate before forwarding information to the central level for decision. Information is cross-checked against the Ministry of Labor's income databases in some states against Department of Transport registries of automobile ownership (Lindert and others 2007).

7. The consensus around time limits was strong enough to pass the legislation mandating the time limit, but not strong enough to pass the relatively trivial budget appropriation that would have been required to implement a national database that would make the time limit more strictly enforceable.

8. Daniel Plaatjies, Executive Manager, Strategy and Business Development, South African Social Security Agency, conversation with Margaret Grosh, March 3, 2008.

9. For examples of some laws and operational manuals, see the "Implementation Matters" page at www.worldbank.org. Examples of operational manuals are in the country-specific subpages under CCT programs.

## CHAPTER 5

Benefit Levels and Delivery Mechanisms

KEY MESSAGES

To achieve its intended outcomes, a program's benefit level should be consistent with its objectives. However, budget constraints often make for hard trade-offs between coverage and benefit level. Programs with benefits that are too small will have little impact on beneficiaries and administrative costs will be high relative to the level of benefits. Programs with high benefits will have a larger impact on recipient households, but will have a higher fiscal burden, require more care in relation to design and targeting, and may induce greater work disincentives. In general in developing countries, programs with benefits that are too low are more frequent than programs with benefits that are too high.

Benefits may be differentiated by household characteristics such as poverty level, size and composition, or specific needs or behaviors. Such customization will improve the poverty impact per unit of transfer, but will complicate administration and communication with the public and are thus more common in high-capacity settings.

Participation in safety net programs has only small or moderate effects on employment or hours worked in developed countries and even smaller effects in developing countries. Moreover, policy makers have a variety of tools at their disposal to minimize work disincentives, such as limiting the program to those who are not expected to work; adopting a targeting mechanism that is not tied directly to earnings; setting benefit levels to maintain work incentives; ensuring that incentives to work remain in place by customizing benefit levels in line with earnings; and/or linking transfers to such program elements as job training or placement, education, microcredit, and social support services.

Experience is emerging with linking transfer programs to other services—voluntary or mandatory—that are designed to help households become independent. This is a promising field for experimentation. Tentative lessons suggest that mandatory links should be limited to cases where the supply of required services is ample, the services will be useful to all, or most transfer recipients already use the services. In a wide range of other cases, voluntary links through information, referrals, one-stop shops, and the like may be applicable.

Payment mechanisms should be affordable, safe, reliable, and accessible to all beneficiaries. A number of different payment instruments are available, including cash, checks, vouchers, and in-kind benefits, that can be delivered using banks, automated teller machines (ATMs), mobile pay points, private or public shops, and so on. The choice of appropriate delivery mechanisms depends on objectives, operational needs, administrative capabilities, and local infrastructure conditions. Investments in administrative systems and equipment related to payments can help increase service standards, reduce corruption and leakage, and reduce costs in the long run.

5.1 Determining Benefit Levels in Theory and Practice

This chapter takes up the one of the basics of transfer programs: paying people. This section looks at the theory concerning the size of transfers, discusses the criteria for adjusting benefit levels to household circumstances, and reviews the evidence on the generosity of safety net programs in practice.

SIZE OF TRANSFERS

A basic question in any safety net program is how generous the program should be, that is, how much to pay. No clear-cut answer to this question is available. Ultimately, the level of the benefit is one of the products of the iterative process of designing a program, that is, the program designers select a benefit level such that the overall program will fit within its budgetary, administrative, and political constraints, while maximizing its outcomes for beneficiaries. However, this summary is too general to be a useful guide for practitioners. This section tries to break down the decisions and highlight the key elements and trade-offs that occur when selecting a program's benefit level.

First and foremost, the benefit level depends on the objective of the program, and hence on the program type. The benefit level should be consistent with program theory, that is, the stylized model of how policy makers think the program's output will affect the outcomes they are trying to influence. A benefit level compatible with program theory will be the smallest transfer necessary to achieve the desired impact on intended outcomes (consumption, income, earnings, school enrollment, or use of nutritional or health services).

Last resort programs aim to reduce poverty, hence the benefit level is set as a fraction of the income gap of expected beneficiaries. This is the case for programs that select beneficiaries using a proxy means test, such as in Armenia and Georgia. A number of variations on this principle are possible. In low-income countries, benefits are often set relative to the costs of an "adequate" food basket or the food poverty line. In guaranteed minimum income (GMI) programs, which are common in Europe and Central Asia and in countries of the Organisation for Economic Co-operation and Development (OECD), the level of benefit is the difference between the eligibility threshold and the income of each family. Programs that compensate poor consumers for one element of expenditure, so-called gap formulas, are used, for example, for family allowances that cover a portion of the cost of raising a child, heating allowances that cover the seasonal increase in heating costs during the winter, and food stamps that cover only the food poverty gap.

Conditional cash transfer (CCT) programs encourage poor beneficiaries to invest in children's human capital by conditioning the benefit on the use of school, nutrition, and/or health services. The level of benefit will thus reflect two objectives: reducing current poverty among beneficiaries and providing incentives for human capital accumulation. The principles for the first objective are similar to those for last resort programs. For the second objective, the level of benefits is set to compensate households for the opportunity cost of using the services. The total benefit to a household may include a few components. An education grant will compensate households for the opportunity cost of the time children spend in school and not working, plus for the direct costs of schooling. A health and/or nutrition grant will compensate families for the cost of the time they spend taking their children for health checks and/or attending nutritional education events. Some programs, like the Programa de Asignación Familiar II (Family Allowance Program) in Honduras and the Red de Protección Social (Social Protection Network) in Nicaragua, offered a supply grant to the service providers—schools and health posts—to cover the cost of improved service. The rationale of education, health, and nutrition grants is to increase the demand for education, health, and nutrition services as illustrated in box 5.1. Sometimes programs may offer unconditional grants to any poor household, with eligibility determined by the same principles as for last resort programs.

In workfare programs, the benefit level is the wage rate. To ensure self-selection by the poor, the wage rate should be set somewhat below the wage level for unskilled workers. When other considerations, such as minimum wage laws, preclude setting such a low wage rate, programs have to ration demand by capping the total number of days of work to be

---

BOX 5.1 The Value of a CCT Program's Education Grant: From Theory to Practice

The Programa de Asignación Familiar II is a CCT program in Honduras that offers an education grant to poor children conditional on school attendance. To determine the value of the grant, the technical advice provided to the government by its consultant, the International Food Policy Research Institute, was based on both economic theory and microeconomic evidence.

Economic theory suggests that each family demands a certain level of services, such as education, up to the point where the actual value of future educational benefits from sending a child to school is equal to the marginal cost of sending the child to school. The expected value of future benefits depends on, among other factors, the family's expectations about the child's future income and the relationship between education and income. The marginal costs of sending the child to school include the direct costs incurred when the child is sent to school as well as the opportunity cost of dedicating the child's time to learning instead of using it to generate income. Based on these expected costs and benefits, each family demands that level of service that will allow it to maximize its welfare over time. This maximization process leads to a demand curve that reflects the relationship between levels of service demand and price, assuming that consumers' preferences and incomes and the prices of other products remain constant. The sum of all services sought by each family produces an aggregate demand curve that can be interpreted as the relationship between service price and the number of families willing to pay this price for its use.

The designers of the Honduran CCT program used household survey data to estimate that children provided about 3 percent of labor hours and 2 percent of household income, or about L 326 (about US$22) per year per child (about nine days of work during coffee harvest time). The direct costs of schooling were estimated to be L 6 (about US$0.40) per year for matriculation and fees; L 241 (about US$16) per year for books, uniforms, and supplies; and L 25.5 (about US$1.70) per month for 10 months for lunch and transportation money. Thus the total cost (adding up the lost income per child plus the direct costs of schooling) is about L 828 (about US$56) per child per year.

SOURCE: IFPRI 2000.

provided to individual workers. In Argentina's Trabajar workfare program, for example, the wage payment was set slightly below the legal minimum wage. As the economic crisis that began in Argentina in 1996 became more severe, unemployment and wages worsened and program wages were adjusted downward. Participation was capped at 90 days per worker. In Ethiopia's Productive Safety Net Program, the labor market is so thin in some areas that fixing a wage rate that is both below the prevailing wage and delivers sufficient value is difficult. Thus the total benefit package is designed to fill the food gap during the three months of the hungry season. In this case, the wage may be too high to induce adequate self-targeting, so the number of days of work allowed is capped at five days per person per month.

In-kind transfers have diverse objectives. If the program's objective is to provide a feeding supplement to schoolchildren, then the benefit level will be the cost of the food bundle. If the in-kind transfer is a vehicle for transferring income to poor households, then the same principles in determining the appropriate size of the transfer apply as for a cash transfer, though with some complications. If the in-kind transfer provides less of an item than the household would normally consume (is inframarginal), economic theory suggests that the subsidy is equivalent to a cash transfer of equivalent size, albeit with administrative costs that may be substantially higher. If the in-kind transfer is larger than what the household would normally consume, then the household may raise its consumption of the target good and/or may sell some portion of it, often at a discount, which will lower the real value of the transfer.

A second element that is taken into account in setting the level of benefits is the program's overall budget constraints. As an example, consider a transfer program whose objective is to reduce poverty. The process will likely start with an assessment of the poverty level in the country and then the selection of a subgroup of poor households that the program will serve (those who are "deserving" according to the values of the particular society).

The first question to address is the affordability of bringing the consumption of the poor to the poverty line. Combining information on the number of poor and their income gap,[1] policy makers can estimate the overall resource deficit among the poor. Knowing the magnitude of the overall resource deficit of the poor will inform policy makers whether measures to cover this deficit are affordable or not. Suppose that 16 percent of the population lives in poverty, the average consumption of the poor falls 25 percent short of the poverty line, and the poverty line represents 70 percent of gross domestic product (GDP) per capita. In this case, the overall resource deficit of the poor is 2.8 percent of GDP (the product of 16 percent × 25 percent × 70 percent), a crude, lower-bound estimate. The analysts should factor in that certain leakages of funds to the nonpoor are unavoidable. If the program's institutional capacity is low and income-based eligibility is not feasible, the use of more "leaky" mechanisms should be considered. For example, assuming that only 66 percent of the benefits will reach the poor, the overall financing required to bring the poor to the poverty line will rise to 4 percent of GDP (2.8 percent divided by 0.66).

Estimating the financial effort required to eliminate poverty, measured either in absolute or relative terms, is rarely the end of the story. This initial estimate is often larger than the budget available for the program. Consider that the maximum budget that can be provided for a new program is 1 percent of GDP, not 4 percent. Dealing with this imbalance will typically involve an iterative process as illustrated in figure 5.1.

FIGURE 5.1 **Reconciling Needs with Budget Constraints**

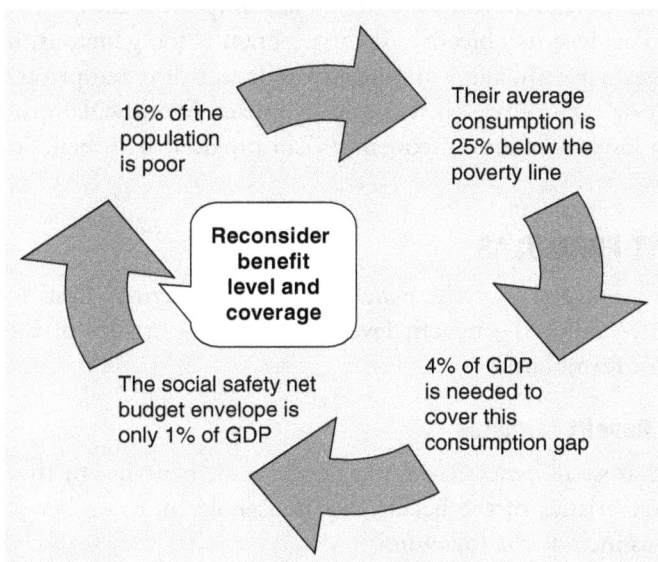

16% of the population is poor

Their average consumption is 25% below the poverty line

Reconsider benefit level and coverage

4% of GDP is needed to cover this consumption gap

The social safety net budget envelope is only 1% of GDP

SOURCE: Authors.

One option is to reconsider a program's generosity. Few safety net programs attempt to top up the consumption of their beneficiaries to the poverty line. Many programs provide benefits to bring beneficiaries up to a fraction of the poverty line or to some arbitrary level lower than the poverty line, but the utility of this approach is limited. Extremely low benefits do not protect beneficiaries from poverty—that is, they are not cost-effective—and may not justify their administrative costs—that is, they are inefficient. Peru used such a model in 2004, covering a large fraction of the population with a food-based transfer with low transfers per beneficiary unit. Lindert, Skoufias, and Shapiro (2006, p. 26), in their review of the redistributive power of social protection programs in Latin America, characterized the Peruvian safety net model as "giving peanuts to the masses." Not surprisingly, country-specific studies summarized in World Bank (2007m) find that such programs have had almost no impact on extreme poverty or nutritional status.

Another option is to restrict coverage of the program or eligibility for the program. If program designers choose to restrict coverage, they may attempt to cover as many of the poorest beneficiaries that can be reached with an adequate level of the benefit given the budget constraint. If only 1 percent of GDP can be allocated for such a program, then the program may target only a quarter of the poor, that is, the poorest 4 percent of the population. Economic theory suggests that under the circumstances, directing the available resources toward the poorest is the best welfare-enhancing solution, as the marginal value of a monetary unit is higher for the poorest. A variant of this rationing process is to focus on specific vulnerable groups (see chapter 8), or on households deprived in a number of areas, for example, poor and living in substandard housing. If program designers choose to restrict eligibility, they may choose to restrict it to a subset of the poor considered to be deserving. As mentioned in chapter 2, section 4, the notion of deserving poor varies from society to society, but the most common definition is households or individuals who cannot support themselves through work. Thus, some programs may restrict eligibility to families with more than three children and/or elderly people, who together represent about 50 percent of the poor in many countries. Many programs would combine these two options, restricting both the generosity and the coverage of the program typically to the poorest and most destitute.

In the end, defining the appropriate benefit level is a balancing act: finding a level that is neither too high to generate dependency nor too low to lack impact. If the benefit is too small, the program fails to achieve its objective. If the program is too generous, it may have adverse consequences, such as reducing work incentives or crowding out private transfers, which would diminish or even outweigh its positive impact. Worldwide, programs with benefits that are too low occur more frequently than program with benefits that are too high.

OTHER ELEMENTS OF BENEFIT FORMULAS

In addition to determining the average size of the benefit, program designers need to decide whether they would like to tailor the benefit level to the characteristics of the household, that is, to use a benefit formula.

Deciding on Flat versus Variable Benefit Formulas

Benefit formulas may be flat—that is, all beneficiaries receive the same benefit—or they may vary according to the characteristics of the beneficiary household in a number of ways. Some of the main variations include the following:

- Benefits vary by family poverty level, with larger benefits for poorer families.
- Benefits vary by family size or composition, with benefits determined by the total number of family members or of the number of family members not expected to work.
- Benefits vary by the age of family members, for example, benefits tied to education may be larger for older children in recognition of the higher opportunity costs of their time or to cover the greater number of inputs they need such as textbooks.
- Benefits vary by gender, for example, benefits tied to education may be higher for girls in countries with a marked gender gap in schooling.
- Benefits vary over time, being higher during the hungry season or the heating season or at the beginning of the school year to cover enrollment fees, uniforms, and shoes.
- Benefits vary by region to reflect differences in the cost of living in different areas.
- Benefits vary with longevity in the program, tapering down after a certain period as a way to encourage families to leave the program.
- Benefits differ in ways that promote certain behaviors even beyond a program's basic conditions. For instance, a CCT program might require school attendance all year to receive the base benefit, but provide a small bonus for good test scores at the end of the year.

In general, variable benefit formulas will make a program more efficient, that is better able to deliver the level of transfer needed to raise most families toward the poverty line and/or induce the desired behavioral changes at minimum transfer cost. However, differentiating implies both obvious administrative costs and some less obvious costs because of the complexity involved. Much more effort will be needed to explain the formulas to client families, to the public, and to program monitors and additional effort will be devoted to quality control procedures around the level of benefit determination. Private costs for applicants may also rise. Box 5.2 illustrates how Brazil's Bolsa Familia (Family Grant) program reconciled these conflicting objectives by choosing a relatively complex formula.

Determining the Recipient of the Benefits

Most programs around the world and over time have paid either the head of household or whichever member of the household carried out the transactions associated with registering for a program. Recently, however, program designers are putting much more thought into who within a household should receive payments. This reflects the growing recognition in the economics literature that households contain members with different needs, preferences, and power and that various members may allocate the funds received differently. The literature generally concurs that women will spend at least as much as men on children's welfare, in many cases more, and are less likely to favor boys over girls in doing so. The strength of this effect varies from place to place and study to study (Haddad, Hoddinott, and Alderman 1997; Quisumbing and Maluccio 2000), but the policy implication is that transfers placed in the hands of women will help children's welfare at least as much, and sometimes much more, than transfers placed in the hands of men.

Based on these findings, many new programs, especially CCT programs, explicitly deliver the benefit into the hands of the mother or a proxy for her.[2] This is done in the belief that women are more likely to invest additional monies in the well-being of their children than men and the recognition that, on average, in most countries and households, women will be the ones bearing the implicit time costs of obtaining the required health and health education services and likely shouldering a large share of the household chores children would have done had they not been attending school. A smaller number of programs, most often scholarship programs, transfer money directly to students. This is done to help motivate the students to study and ensure that they have as much influence over the money as if they had earned it themselves.

Handling Inflation

Benefits need to be increased from time to time to protect households from inflation. Many programs only do this in an ad hoc manner every few years and require special legislation or a decree each time. In such cases, the real value of the benefits and the program's impact usually plummet for a time before recovering. A more desirable procedure is to have a regular, perhaps annual, review of benefit levels as part of the budget cycle, or even an automatic indexing of benefits. In either case, program managers should consider not just how price levels have changed, but also how wages in low-skill occupations have changed.

BENEFIT LEVELS IN PRACTICE

The question of how generous safety net programs are in practice can be answered in many ways, and probably because of this, little comparative evidence is available. Some of the most common ways to express the generosity of a program are as follows:

- **By reporting the level of the benefit in local currency.** This is not always simple, however, as programs often offer different benefits to individuals or households in different circumstances. In such cases, information about the levels of benefits can be presented as a table as shown in box 5.2.

- **By reporting the level of the benefit in comparable purchasing power (in purchasing parity power dollars, for instance).** The intent is to facilitate comparisons across countries, but such information is difficult to compare, because the same type of benefit may be assigned to different assistance units (individuals, families, households) in different countries. Moreover, the adjustments for differences in purchasing power may be insufficient to characterize a benefit as generous or not across countries, as generosity is a relative concept. For instance, in the United States, a benefit of US$10 per person per month would be considered ungenerous, but in a poor country where a large fraction of the population lives on less than US$1 per day, it may be considered quite generous.

- **By reporting the level of the benefit as a share of the poverty line or other type of indicator, such as the minimum wage, the average wage, the minimum**

BOX 5.2 The Benefit Formula for Brazil's Bolsa Familia Program

Policy makers debated many options for setting the level of benefits prior to launching the Bolsa Familia program in October 2003 (see, for instance, Camargo and Ferreira 2001; Ferreira and Lindert 2003; Lindert and others 2007). Some advocated higher benefit values for families with older children to reflect the higher opportunity costs of their staying in school and the greater risk of older children dropping out of school. Others supported benefits differentiated by gender. Still others suggested that benefit amounts vary by region to reflect regional differences in the cost of living. In the end, the program designers opted for a pragmatic set of benefits that (1) was simple to administer; (2) favored the extreme poor; (3) favored families with children, but with limits to avoid promoting fertility; and (4) prevented beneficiaries eligible to receive benefits from previous programs that were being replaced from losing as a result of the reform. This latter consideration was viewed as particularly important politically. Most families actually gained from the introduction of the new Bolsa Familia program range of benefits, as their average value was significantly higher than under the prior programs. For those beneficiaries who received more under Bolsa Familia's predecessor programs because of multiple benefits, the excess amount was maintained under the new program as a so-called extraordinary variable benefit. This extraordinary benefit is to be maintained until those families who receive it no longer qualify for the program benefit. No new beneficiaries will receive the extraordinary benefit. Only 411,579 out of a total of 11.1 million families received the extraordinary benefit.

Bolsa Familia provides two types of benefits: a base benefit provided to all families in extreme poverty, regardless of their demographic composition, and a variable benefit that depends on family composition and income. For both extremely poor and moderately poor families, this variable benefit is set according to the number of children in the family (capped at three) and/or whether the mother is pregnant or breastfeeding.

As the table shows, income transfers range from R$15 to R$95 (US$7 to US$45) per family per month. The average value of benefits paid during January–May 2006 was about R$62 (US$30).

pension, the social pension, or the level of unemployment benefits. For example, in the OECD, the generosity of safety net programs is expressed as a share of the wage of the average production worker in the manufacturing sector (see annex). Such comparisons are useful for comparing a program's generosity with the generosity of other programs or types of earnings within a country, for instance, to ascertain whether the benefit level is likely to create disincentives for work. It is less useful for cross-country comparisons.

Our preference for comparing generosity is the ratio of benefits to the total consumption of beneficiary households. This measure can be estimated using household surveys that collect information on household consumption and the value of safety net benefits received during a certain period. This measure is preferable, as it takes into account many of the complexities of the provision of safety net benefits and transforms them into a single index comparable across households and countries: benefits are implicitly aggregated at the household level, the unit where they are shared and used to finance consumption.[3]

Poverty level	No. of children aged 0–15 and/or pregnant or breastfeeding women	Quantity/type of benefit	Monthly Benefit
Poor (monthly per capita family income = R$60–120)	1	1 variable	R$15
	2	2 variable	R$30
	3 or more	3 variable	R$45
Extremely poor (monthly per capita family income > R$60)	0	Base benefit	R$50
	1	Base + 1 variable	R$65
	2	Base + 2 variable	R$80
	3 or more	Base + 3 variable	R$95

SOURCES: Law 10.836 of January 2004 and Decree 5.749 of April 11, 2006.

The average value of benefit transfers has fallen from its initial level of R$75 (US$25) at the end of 2003 because the program progressed from initially covering just the extremely poor and then gradually the more moderately poor.

Unlike some other safety nets in Brazil, Bolsa Familia's benefits are not automatically indexed to inflation or minimum wage increases. The nominal benefit was held constant from 2003 until July 2007, despite a 16.7 percent increase in the cost of living. In July 2007, Decree 6.157 increased benefit amounts by 17 to 20 percent (depending on the category), thereby restoring their initial value.

SOURCES: Lindert and others 2007; www.mds.gov.br/bolsafamilia/.

This measure, however, does not adjust for one element of program generosity: the duration for which benefits are provided to eligible applicants.

We used household-level information for 55 cash transfer programs from 27 middle-income countries to illustrate how the generosity of these programs varies by program type (figure 5.2). Figure 5.3 looks at 7 CCT programs in 7 countries in Latin America and the Caribbean, and table 5.1 presents program-specific information on 49 programs in 20 countries in Europe and Central Asia.

Figure 5.2 shows key values of the distribution of generosity statistics as well as maximum and minimum values. The median value of benefits as a share of the consumption of recipient households for the programs in Europe and Central Asia is 13.0 percent for family allowances, 13.5 percent for last resort programs, 9.0 percent for CCT programs, and 19.5 percent for social pensions. While the generosity of family allowance and CCT programs is concentrated in a narrow interval, the values are more dispersed for other types of programs. The higher generosity of social pensions is not surprising: these are the programs meant to sustain households not expected to work.

FIGURE 5.2 **Generosity of Selected Safety Net Programs, Europe and Central Asia and Latin America and the Caribbean, Selected Years, 2001–4**

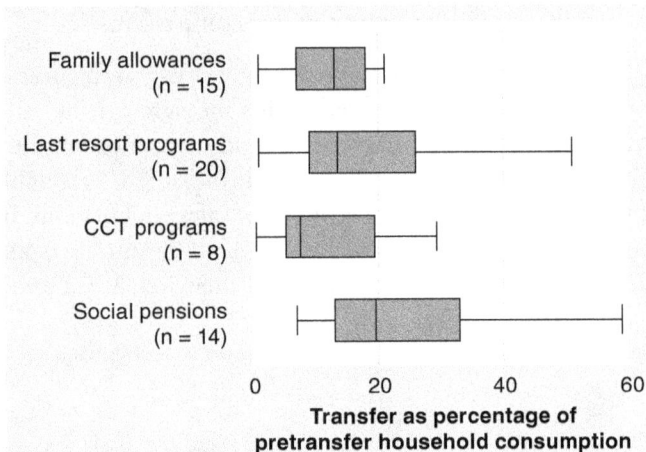

SOURCES: Tesliuc and others forthcoming; World Bank forthcoming.

NOTE: n = number of programs. The median value is the line inside the shaded rectangle, the 25th percentile is the lower value of the shaded rectangle, and the 75th percentile is the upper value of the shaded rectangle. Programs whose generosity is 1.5 times more than, or less than, the median were excluded.

FIGURE 5.3 **Generosity of Selected CCT Programs in Selected Latin American and Caribbean Countries, Various Years**

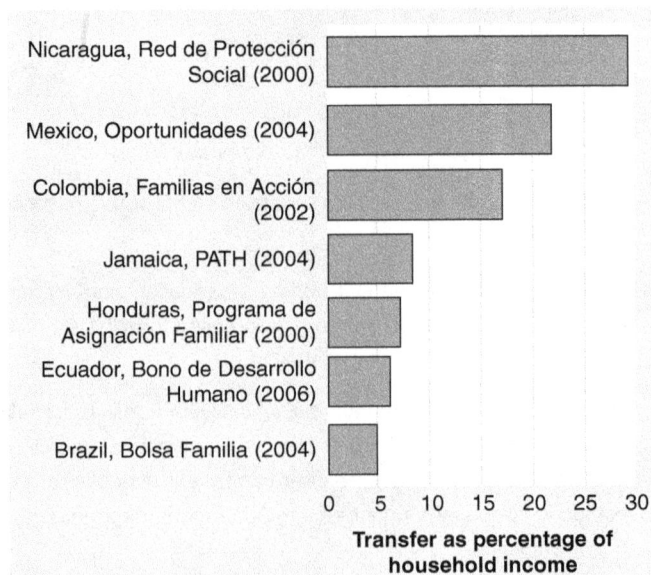

SOURCE: Based on World Bank forthcoming.

NOTE: The unit used for Brazil is the transfer as a percentage of pretransfer household income.

TABLE 5.1 **Generosity of Selected Cash Transfer Programs in Selected East European and Central Asian Countries, Selected Years 2001–4**

Country and year	Social pension programs		Family allowance programs		Last resort programs		Other programs	
	Poorest quintile	Total	Poorest quintile	Total	Poorest quintile	Total	Poorest quintile	Total
	Transfer as a percentage of pretransfer household consumption							
Albania, 2002	9	16	n.a.	n.a.	15	11	14	16
Armenia, 2003	n.a.	n.a.	26	18	26	18	24	18
Azerbaijan, 2003	15	14	3	2	3	2	8	6
Belarus, 2002	45	26	20	13	21	14	15	9
Bosnia & Herzegovina, 2001	89	40	n.a.	n.a.	27	16	58	30
Bulgaria, 2003	13	8	17	10	24	13	13	9
Estonia, 2004	n.a.	n.a.	25	12	45	34	28	13
Georgia, 2002	40	23	n.a.	n.a.	122	44	43	24
Hungary, 2002	12	12	40	21	24	19	41	22
Kazakhstan, 2003	n.a.	n.a.	n.a.	n.a.	15	11	27	19
Kyrgyz Republic, 2003	n.a.	n.a.	n.a.	n.a.	12	7	2	3
Lithuania, 2003	43	33	22	13	25	21	28	17
Macedonia, FYR, 2003	n.a.	n.a.	53	51	53	51	111	77
Moldova, 2003	18	13	13	9	13	9	18	15
Poland, 2004	65	59	18	13	36	31	31	28
Romania, 2003	21	16	13	7	35	31	18	11
Russian Fed., 2002	32	23	6	3	5	3	16	14
Serbia & Montenegro, 2003	53	41	13	18	12	9	29	32
Tajikistan, 2003	3	7	1	1	2	1	5	7
Uzbekistan, 2003	n.a.	n.a.	28	16	22	13	19	11
Median	27	20	18	13	23	14	22	16

SOURCE: Based on Tesliuc and others forthcoming.

NOTE: n.a. = not applicable. Generosity is defined as the ratio of a transfer to household consumption. Consumption is current consumption (less expenditures on durables, housing, and health.

5.2 Managing Work Disincentives

One of the most common stumbling blocks to receiving political support for transfer programs is concern about work disincentives or welfare dependency. Specifically, the concerns are that beneficiaries will work less because transfers will reduce the pressure on them to work and will also reduce the rewards from working if benefits are reduced when household income increases.

The theoretical arguments behind labor disincentives are intuitive (Ellwood 1988). First, any transfer provides unearned income, and thus inherently will reduce the pressure to work. The typical model assumes that beneficiaries will "trade" some of the extra income for more leisure.[4] Beneficiaries will feel less urgency about taking a job or having all able-bodied household members working. As a result, people will not be as likely to work as they would be in the absence of the transfer program. This is sometimes referred to as the income effect.

Second, when the amount of the benefit depends on the recipient's income (the poorer a household, the more money it gets), transfers may change the rewards from working. This situation arises for verified means-tested programs where the benefit level is reduced by a fraction of a currency unit for each additional currency unit in earnings. The implicit tax on earnings is known as the program's marginal tax rate and is sometimes referred to as the price effect. In the hypothetical naïve GMI program where the size of the benefit tops household earnings up to a minimum living standard and is reduced as income rises, the recipient whose initial income is below the guaranteed income has no incentive to work.

Thus the theoretical model predicts that the reduction in work effort will be proportional to the size of the benefit (the income effect) and the implicit marginal tax rate on earnings (the price effect). The price effect will be manifest only for means-tested programs with accurate and frequent verification of household income.

The theoretical model outlined applies in particular to a class of programs and beneficiaries in developed countries: verified means-tested GMI programs serving able-bodied households. For these programs and country settings, beneficiaries face 100 percent marginal tax rates, and households that earn less than the guaranteed income in the absence of the program have no rewards for working. To operate according to their theoretical design, GMI programs should be able to perform an accurate means test when someone applies to the program and then monitor the household's income continuously or at regular intervals to adjust the benefit level to changes in earnings. This is feasible only in countries where the informal economy is small and household incomes are monetized, documented, and verifiable. Few programs in developing countries operate under such conditions.

The concerns about work disincentives should not be applied indiscriminately to all types of safety net programs and beneficiaries. First, the concern is less pertinent for programs targeted to beneficiaries who are not expected to work, such as social pensions, disability allowances, and, sometimes, allowances for single parents. Second, the model does not fit the typical beneficiary from a low-income country well, that is, a poor, credit-constrained entrepreneur.[5] For this type of beneficiary, an injection of cash at zero interest rate may provide the additional liquidity required for a small investment, which may result in an increase in work effort. Furthermore, the model does not apply to a whole class of transfer programs such as workfare, where benefits accrue only if beneficiaries work.

EVIDENCE FROM DEVELOPED COUNTRIES

Concerns about work disincentives have traditionally been strongest in wealthy countries with generous safety nets and high unemployment rates. However, while the concerns are common in most developed countries, most of the research and evidence is limited to the United States. Some evidence of labor disincentives is apparent for generous social assistance transfers with finely tuned eligibility based on verified means testing in the case of two programs: the Aid for Families with Dependent Children (AFDC) and the negative income tax experiments. The AFDC program (box 5.3) was a relatively generous program that provided income replacement for single mothers. It contained specific features that made it especially susceptible to labor disincentives, such as reducing benefits dollar for dollar.

BOX 5.3 Lack of Applicability of High Labor Disincentives in the AFDC to Safety Nets in Middle- and Low-Income Countries

The AFDC program operated in the United States from 1935 to 1996. A number of nonexperimental studies reviewed in Moffitt (2002a) suggest that single mothers benefiting from the AFDC reduced their work effort by 10 to 50 percent. The AFDC had a number of design features that encouraged reduced work effort, namely (1) it was an income-replacement program that provided relatively generous benefits; (2) it imposed a 100 percent marginal tax rate on beneficiaries' earnings; and (3) its target group was single mothers, a group that was expected, at least during the program's early days, not to work but to care for their children. In 1996, Temporary Assistance for Needy Families, a program that incorporated many design elements that encouraged beneficiaries to work, replaced the AFDC.

Care should be exercised in extrapolating these results to other safety net programs in developed or developing countries where strictly enforced means-tested programs with positive tax rates on extra earnings are rare and programs are less generous.

SOURCES: Moffitt 1992, 2002a.

The negative income tax experiments implemented between 1968 and 1979 supplemented the incomes of poor working families by bringing them up to a fraction of the poverty line while allowing beneficiaries to keep a fraction of their extra earnings that took them above the poverty line.[6] Evaluations found that the negative income tax approach moderately reduced participant work efforts. Male beneficiaries reduced their employment and earnings by 7 percent on average. Among female beneficiaries, only 17 percent of whom were employed, employment and earnings dropped by 17 percent (Burtless 1986).

Except for these two programs, the U.S. evidence shows that participation in safety net programs has only small or moderate effects on employment or hours worked. In the United States, most studies have found no evidence of reduced work effort for a host of programs with relatively smaller benefits, such as the Food Stamp Program, nutrition programs, or child care subsidies (Blau 2003; Currie 2003). Studies obtained similar results for in-kind programs, such as housing programs or Medicaid, a program that provides health insurance coverage for the poor (Gruber 2003; Olsen 2003).

Outside the United States, the evidence on disincentives to work resulting from safety net programs is extremely scarce. In continental Europe, for example, research has focused on the impact of generous unemployment programs on the work effort of the unemployed (LaLonde 2003), not on safety net programs. This relative lack of interest is probably because GMI programs—the main culprit in terms of work disincentives—are small (in the European Union, most of them account for 0.2 to 0.4 percent of GDP and cover only 1 to 3 percent of the total population), while other programs use categorical criteria to cover population groups not expected to work (the elderly, the disabled, children) (OECD 2004a).

Another robust evaluation of the work disincentives of income-tested cash transfers comes from Ontario, Canada. There the beneficiaries of a rather generous safety net program during the 1990s reduced their work effort by 3 to 5 percent when benefits tripled from Can\$185 to Can\$507 (Lemieux and Milligan 2008).

EVIDENCE FROM DEVELOPING COUNTRIES

As concerns developing countries, the theory supports the view that the impact of safety net programs on work disincentives should be smaller in developing countries than in developed countries for the following four reasons:

- Many developing countries target their programs only to households without able-bodied adults, and in such cases the arguments are not relevant, for example, the direct support component of the Productive Safety Net Program in Ethiopia and the Kalomo District Pilot Social Cash Transfer Scheme in Zambia, or require able-bodied beneficiaries to work in return for benefits as is the case for all workfare programs and some cash transfer programs.

- Programs are less generous in developing countries. Most safety net programs complement rather than substitute for the earnings of able-bodied beneficiaries (box 5.4).

- Verified means-tested programs are rare in developing countries. Few programs use and are able to effectively enforce benefit formulas with marginal tax rates and frequent recertification of household income.

- The static model does not take into account that transfers help households make productive investments in their futures.

Relatively less empirical research on potential labor-market disincentives associated with transfer programs is available for developing countries. However, as shown in the following list, the few studies that have investigated the effect of safety net programs on adult work effort suggest limited labor disincentive impacts:

- In Armenia, Posarac, Tesliuc, and Angel-Urdinola (forthcoming) do not find that the beneficiaries of the Family Poverty Benefits Program work less because of the program. The authors compare the employment rate and the hours worked by adults in two equivalent groups, applicants accepted versus applicants denied, with a proxy means test score close to the eligibility threshold using a regression discontinuity design.

- In Brazil, Leite (2006b) simulates the potential impact of the Bolsa Escola (School Grant) program on adult work effort and finds that the transfer amounts have little impact. Even a 10-fold increase in the size of unit transfers under Bolsa Escola would result in negligible impacts on adult work effort.

BOX 5.4 Labor Disincentives in Very Low-Income Countries: The Kalomo District Pilot Social Cash Transfer Scheme, Zambia

In the Kalomo district of Zambia, a cash transfer scheme supported by the U.K. Department for International Development and the German Agency for Technical Cooperation provides about US$10 per month to destitute households. The US$10 amount is based on the price of a 50-kilogram bag of maize, which enables beneficiary households to have a second daily meal. The assistance has to be meaningful, but not so large as to engender jealousy among those not receiving the support or compromise the scheme's financial sustainability once it is extended nationwide. Households with children get a bonus of US$2.50, reflecting the higher expenses of households with children. For simplicity, the amount is irrespective of the number of children.

Evaluations of the scheme have not found that it created any disincentives for households. According to one evaluation (GTZ 2008):

> The amount that households receive per month is only enough to permit them to have a second meal per day. It thus supplements the little that households can obtain on their own with their limited capacities and is certainly not an incentive to refrain from productive work. Most of the beneficiary households have invested part of their transfers in livestock or agricultural supplies at some point of time, showing that households have a strong interest in generating extra income and engaging in small productive activities. Social transfers of this type should therefore always complement other sources of income but help to avoid negative coping strategies. The level of transfers is a question needing careful consideration and testing.

SOURCE: GTZ 2008.

- In rural Ethiopia, Abdulai, Barrett, and Hoddinott (2005) find that the receipt of food aid is not associated with lower work effort in agriculture, wage work, or self-employment. The negative correlation between food aid and various measures of labor supply that may appear to suggest the existence of work disincentives because of food aid actually reflects the placement effect, that is, that food aid is targeted to the poorest communities and to the less able-bodied members of the community. Once these characteristics are controlled for, the data suggest that food aid leads to increases in the labor supply.

- In Mexico, evidence from three studies suggests insignificant labor disincentives for the adults participating in PROGRESA. First, empirical evaluations show that the conditional transfers from PROGRESA did have a significant impact on reducing child labor, but had no measurable impact on the work efforts of adults. Specifically, Parker and Skoufias (2000) estimate that PROGRESA increased beneficiary families' average income by 22 percent and decreased children's labor force participation by 15 to 25 percent. They find no evidence of a reduction in labor force participation rates or work efforts by adults. Skoufias and di Maro (2006) find that PROGRESA did not affect the work incentives of adults from ineligible households in villages covered by the program. Finally, Freije, Bando, and Arce (2006) simulate behavioral responses and find that the Oportunidades program, the successor to PROGRESA, does not seem to affect adult labor supply. Their simulations show that such transfers would have to be far higher (more than double) before any labor disincentive effects would emerge.

- In Romania, a qualitative review of the Guaranteed Minimum Income Program (Birks Sinclair & Associates 2004) finds little evidence of an adverse impact on labor force participation. Two design elements are suspected to have mitigated the work disincentives. One is the work requirements applied to all able-bodied beneficiaries. The other is an exit threshold that is set higher than the eligibility threshold. The evaluator considered that "because there is a small bonus for employment, there may be a small positive impact on participation compared with more traditional systems of aid" (Birks Sinclair & Associates 2004, p. 27).

- In Sri Lanka, Sahn and Alderman (1996) study a rice subsidy program that induces labor disincentives through income effects. They find labor reductions of approximately 10 percent.

OPTIONS FOR MINIMIZING LABOR DISINCENTIVES

Policy makers and administrators have a variety of tools at their disposal to minimize labor disincentives as discussed in chapter 2, section 3. We summarize five of them here, focusing on how to minimize labor disincentives generated by the transfer formula (the fourth and fifth options). However, reduced work effort is not unambiguously a good or bad outcome (box 5.5).

One option is to limit programs to those who traditionally are not expected to work anyway, that is, the very young, the very old, the disabled, and so on, often referred to as the deserving poor. This is fairly common, but results in only a partial safety net (see chapters 8 and 9). One way to ensure the coverage of all the poor is to complement such programs with a workfare program. Ethiopia's Productive Safety Net Program provides an example. It covers all the extremely poor and combines a workfare program serving those who can work with cash transfers for households without labor resources.

A second option is to choose a targeting mechanism that is not tied directly to earnings, which leaves the rewards to working intact. Indeed, few developing countries use means tests or minimum income guarantee, although many transition countries do. Infrequent recertification will also minimize the labor disincentives. Most programs outside Europe recertify beneficiaries only once every two or three years or less often (see chapter 4, section 4).

A third option is to condition benefits for able-bodied beneficiaries on a work test, which is, in essence, what a workfare program does. The application of this principle is not limited to a stand-alone workfare program. Most last resort cash transfer programs in transition economies require economically inactive applicants to register with the unemployment office and actively seek work. Some last resort programs, such as Albania's Ndihme Ekonomika (Economic Assistance) program and Romania's GMI Program, take this principle further by requiring able-bodied beneficiaries to work a certain number of days per month in exchange for benefits (one day per week in Albania and one week per month in Romania). Refusal to work results in stopped payments. In Bulgaria in 2003–5, when a large percentage of GMI Program beneficiaries were long-term participants in the program, the country implemented a temporary public works program, From Social As-

---

BOX 5.5 Is Reduced Work Effort Really So Bad?

In most studies, the sensitivity of work effort to incentives is much greater for secondary work-ers—married women and children—than for men and is relatively low for men (Deaton and Muellbauer 1980). The reduction of work effort by secondary workers can be a tolerable, some-times even a valuable, outcome.

A reduction in child labor is normally viewed as a desirable outcome, not a problem, especially if less work is associated with children being able to devote more attention to their schooling. This has been the outcome of CCTs for which the condition is related to schooling, which have reduced work effort by children and youth, but not by adults, in recipient families.

Similarly for women, especially for the poorest women and the mothers of young children, fewer work hours may reduce their caloric expenditure and consequently improve their health and nutrition and/or give them time to provide better care for their children, thereby helping to reduce the intergenerational transmission of poverty (Engle, Menon, and Haddad 1999). Research on children's nutrition in poor countries shows that children may benefit from their mothers working if the child is older than one year, the substitute caretaker is an adult, the wage is good, and the woman controls the money (Smith and others 2003). This is a complex set of conditions that will not always obtain. Where the conditions are not met, a reduction in women's work effort may not always be a bad thing. Even in the United States, evaluations of the Temporary Assistance for Needy Families program reforms show that work effort by women did increase, which is generally viewed as positive, but their adolescent children showed some negative behavioral and achievement effects, apparently because of reduced supervision (Blank 2004). Moreover, the diets of children of working mothers tend to be of somewhat lower quality than those of nonworking women (Crepinsek and Burstein 2004).

---

sistance to Employment, to move the able-bodied among the long-term GMI Program beneficiaries into workfare (de Koning, Kotzeva, and Tzvetkov 2007). By combining last resort programs with a work test, program designers can reap the benefits of both worlds: they gain the freedom to set benefit levels based on poverty reduction criteria without the threat of work disincentives.

A fourth option is to set benefits at levels lower than adults can earn by working. Most programs in developing countries have extremely low benefits, often only a small fraction of the poverty line. Thus they inherently leave plenty of incentive to work. The low benefits are usually due more to fiscal constraints than concerns about work disincentives, but the result is the same. In countries with a full suite of social protection programs, this rule will translate into lower social assistance payments than unemployment insurance or the minimum pension provided by the contributory pension system.

The most widely used mechanism to partly mitigate any work disincentives is to keep benefits substantially lower than the minimum wage as done in Bulgaria and Roma-nia (World Bank 2002b, 2003h) or the earning of low-skilled agricultural laborers as in the Kyrgyz Republic (World Bank 2003g). The conceptually desirable rule is to preserve an incentive structure that ensures that work is rewarded compared with welfare by setting social assistance benefits lower than unemployment benefits and the minimum wage. At the same time, anything less than the minimum wage may be barely above a minimum survival standard. As noted earlier, social assistance benefits are rarely enough to ensure survival by themselves, but rather are a supplement that can help achieve a minimum standard of living.

In thinking about benefit levels and possible reductions in work effort, the value of any noncash benefits must be taken into account. In a number of countries (for example, China, Jamaica, and Romania), recipients of needs-based social assistance also receive subsidized or free health insurance or waivers of user fees for health care. These may add substantially to the value of assistance, and thus to the possible incentive to reduce work effort or income in order to qualify for assistance.

A fifth option for moderating labor disincentives is to use a benefit formula that reduces benefits on a sliding scale of less than one currency unit in benefit reduction for each currency unit of increased earnings. This means that additional work effort will raise incomes. In practice, this is achieved by setting exit thresholds higher than entrance thresholds using the withdrawal of benefits as income rises, the provision of earned income tax credits to help make work pay, the provision of lump sum benefits on graduation from the program, and/or the initiation or continuation of payments for allied benefits such as child care or transportation allowances for a period after work starts. These options are admittedly administratively demanding and will result in some of those above the poverty line receiving benefits.

This approach is common in OECD countries but less so in developing countries, where benefit formulas tend to be much simpler. Romania's GMI Program adopts a simplified version of this approach (box 5.6).

Households can also be encouraged to maintain their labor effort by having benefits with defined time limits or benefits that decrease over time. Both these features are incorporated, for example, in Chile's Chile Solidario and Mexico's Oportunidades program.

Finally, another option is to link transfers to program elements such as job training or placement, education, microcredit, or social support services intended to help house-

---

BOX 5.6 Managing Work Disincentives in Romania's GMI Program

The GMI Program is based on a simple idea. The GMI (often called the social minimum) is defined according to household size and composition. Households are then entitled to social assistance equal to the difference between the social minimum and their actual income from all other sources, including the imputed income from assets such as land and animals. This means that some household members could be employed in low-wage and/or part-time work and still be entitled to receive social assistance. Indeed, the existence of a working member increases the benefit entitlement by 15 percent (the entry threshold is the social minimum; the exit threshold is the social minimum plus 15 percent). Household members who are able to work are required to engage in community work if they are not otherwise employed. If they do not undertake the assigned community work, they lose their individual entitlement to assistance, although other household members will maintain their entitlements. Thus the GMI Program is a mixture of a negative income tax, social assistance, and workfare.

SOURCE: Birks Sinclair & Associates 2004.

holds move out of assistance and toward independence. These may also be administratively demanding, but are fully consistent with broad social policy objectives.

Concern about reduced work effort can lead policy makers to consider various features of program design and of the balance between social assistance of last resort, unemployment insurance, and contributory pension programs, but rarely implies abandoning social assistance as a policy tool.

5.3 Enhancing Safety Net Programs to Promote Household Independence

Recent discussions about and some innovations in enhancing safety net programs have been aimed at not only providing a transfer, but also other assistance to help households increase their incomes in the near term. Terms such as graduation, emancipation, and pathways out of poverty are used as shorthand for this notion.

Helping households increase their autonomous incomes is attractive because it

- addresses the underlying problem of poverty rather than simply helping to mitigate it,
- explicitly addresses concerns over welfare dependency,
- bundles and customizes a variety of services for poor or vulnerable households that may generate positive synergistic effects.

This section reviews some of the options and issues for program components other than basic transfers, grouping them loosely into two categories: enhancements that are explicitly part of the design of a safety net program and enhancements that link a safety net program with other interventions.

The following three main approaches to making safety net programs more explicitly promotive and not exclusively protective are available:

- **Minimizing any incentives for dependency.** As described earlier, the benefit formula can be adjusted in a variety of ways to encourage and smooth the exit from the safety net program.
- **Imposing conditions.** Receipt of the transfer may be conditioned on behaviors that are expected to help households move toward independence.
- **Introducing nonconditional links to other services.** Beneficiaries are assisted but not required to receive services meant to help them move into independence.

TRANSFERS WITH REQUIREMENTS

Imposing a condition that households do something that helps them establish an income independent of social assistance is an idea that has been sweeping the world, first in the form of labor activation policies in the United States and Europe, and then by means of the wave of CCT programs in the developing world.

Labor Activation Programs

Many OECD countries link social assistance benefits and active labor market programs that seek to increase the skills, employment, and long-run earning potential of participants through training, apprenticeships, job search assistance, subsidized job placements, and the like. In many cases participation in these is a requirement for the receipt of social assistance. In other cases participation in the labor activation programs is optional, but encouraged. Labor activation programs seek a more immediate increase in household independence than child-focused CCT programs, as they address today's earners rather than tomorrow's. Examples include Argentina's Seguro de Capacitación (Training Insurance) program and Bulgaria's From Social Assistance to Employment Program (box 5.7). Some of the most complex versions of such programs in OECD countries offer support for finding child care and provide transport subsidies and some customized assistance in helping identify and overcome individual or household-specific barriers to employment. For example, a caseworker might help potential workers who live too far from public transport or need to get to work at a time when public transport does not operate find carpools or obtain bicycles or motor scooters. Caseworkers may be able to authorize special one-time payments to cover the costs of licensing or uniforms, or they may help arrange care for elderly or disabled household members.

The concept of links to labor activation programs is appealing, but such programs can be complex and difficult to run, and the track record on increasing employment or income is mixed (box 5.8). Some proponents of such programs value the less tangible

---

BOX 5.7 Bulgaria's From Social Assistance to Employment Program

In 2002, Bulgaria started implementing its From Social Assistance to Employment Program in response to the increasingly high share of long-term unemployed relying on social assistance among the working-age population. The program's objective is to provide the able-bodied unemployed who are relying on social assistance an opportunity to work, earn their own incomes, and be reintegrated into the labor market. The program's main components are providing temporary employment through public works; having participants work in social services in nonprofit, socially beneficial activities, such as working in public recreational facilities or assisting people with disabilities; and providing adult literacy and qualification courses in parallel with employment to increase participants' employability. The program provides employers with a subsidy to help cover beneficiaries' wages for up to nine months.

The results of an interim evaluation were mixed (de Koning, Kotzeva, Tzvetkov, 2007). The program did indeed provide employment for a considerable proportion of the unemployed who would otherwise have stayed unemployed for much longer. On average, participation in the program halved the duration of unemployment. The program also generated substantial improvements in terms of participant self-confidence, social contacts, and job search motivation. Finally, the program clearly produced outputs and services that were useful to the local communities where projects were carried out. However, the program showed a low gross impact on employment: only 8 percent of program beneficiaries found regular jobs following their participation in the program, compared with 16 percent of a comparable group of nonbeneficiaries. Furthermore, some evidence indicated that about 14 percent of the program's projects were activities that would also have occurred in the absence of the program. A survey of employers revealed that the majority did not train the workers either before or during their employment.

outcome of keeping participants in the main channels of society (social inclusion) even if their earnings are not higher as a result of program participation.

BOX 5.8 **Global Experience with Active Labor Market Programs**

Active labor market programs are often targeted to the long-term unemployed; workers in poor families; and specific vulnerable groups with labor market disadvantages, such as young people, old people, and people with disabilities. Especially in industrial countries, the notion of activation of the working-age beneficiaries of transfer programs has received a good deal of attention in a renewed effort to reduce dependency on safety net transfers and counteract their possible labor disincentives. A review of 72 evaluations of such programs leads to the following general conclusions with respect to the most widely used interventions in industrial countries:

- **Employment services.** These services include counseling, placement assistance, job matching, labor exchanges, and other related services. They generally have positive impacts on participants' postprogram employment and earnings. Costs are relatively low, so the cost-benefit ratio is often favorable. However, employment services, at least by themselves, are of limited use in situations where structural unemployment is high and demand for labor is lacking. The coverage and effectiveness of such services in developing countries where many labor market transactions are informal are questionable.

- **Training for the unemployed.** Participants often benefit from these programs in terms of higher employment rates, but not in terms of higher earnings. The few evaluations in developing countries paint a less favorable picture. Programs seem to work best with on-the-job training and active employer involvement. Results are more positive for women than for men.

- **Retraining for workers following mass layoffs.** These programs generally have no positive impacts, although exceptions exist. The few successful examples typically include a comprehensive package of employment services to accompany the retraining, but these are generally expensive.

- **Training for youth.** These programs are almost always unsuccessful in improving labor market outcomes, at least in developed countries. Investing earlier in the education system to reduce the number of dropouts and other schooling problems makes much more sense. While few studies for developing countries are available, evaluations in Latin America find positive impacts for programs that integrate training with remedial education, job search assistance, and social services.

- **Wage and/or employment subsidies.** Most of these do not have a positive impact on workers and introduce substantial inefficiencies. Effective targeting may help, but at the cost of reducing take-up rates.

- **Public works programs.** These can be an effective short-term safety net, but public works do not improve participants' future labor market prospects.

- **Microenterprise development and self-employment assistance.** Some evidence suggests positive impacts for older and better educated workers; however, take-up is low.

SOURCE: Betcherman, Olivas, and Dar 2004.

Conditional Cash Transfers

Worldwide, the use of CCT programs has surged in the last decade or so. The typical CCT program links the receipt of the transfer to such conditions as regular school attendance for households' children and/or regular health center visits for a defined subset of household members, generally children and pregnant and/or lactating women, though there has been some use of cash to give incentives to other behavioral change (box 5.9). The idea of the CCT is that while the cash transfer alleviates poverty today and compensates for the costs of children's education, the conditions help guarantee that the children in the household will have better human capital when they become earners in their own right, and thus be more likely to escape the intergenerational transmission of poverty. To date, the results of impact evaluations have been positive, although they have not yet determined whether the good results depend on the conditions to which the transfers are tied, the actual transfer amounts, or the common practice of designating mothers as beneficiaries. For more details on the design of and experience with these programs, as well as the political debate surrounding them, see chapter 7, section 5.

Making a transfer payment conditional on certain behaviors by beneficiaries requires that the condition have the desired positive effect on household welfare in the short or long term for many households and negative effects on none or only a few households. The program will need sufficient administrative capacity to handle monitoring of compliance and penalties for noncompliance. Political support for the conditions is also necessary.

NONCONDITIONAL LINKS BETWEEN TRANSFER PROGRAMS AND OTHER PROGRAMS AND SERVICES

Some transfer programs are experimenting with providing links between their clients and other programs that may help them achieve greater independence. The nature of the link (provision of information, referrals, preferential treatment, or the like), as well as the types of programs that can be linked, will be largely dependent on the circumstances and characteristics of the target group. This section presents a nonexhaustive list of such programs and briefly discusses other program options.

Documentation and Other Legal Services

Lacking the right official identification documents is both a cause and a consequence of social exclusion. Participation in most public programs depends on proper documentation, and transfer programs are no exception. As the poor and the vulnerable are most likely to be lacking documentation and at the same time are the target group for many services, this poses challenges to efficient program operation. Programs that require documentation may well exclude the people who may be most in need, while programs that do not require proof of identity may end up confronting problems of inaccurate recordkeeping and possibly fraud.

A number of CCT programs are trying to address this issue explicitly by organizing outreach campaigns to inform and help people obtain documentation, even hiring lawyers to help with the process as in the case of Nicaragua's Red de Protección Social. Even without explicit efforts by the program to encourage or require beneficiaries to get their identification documents in order, increased documentation can be a positive externality of transfer programs. The first qualitative evaluation of Turkey's Social Risk Mitigation

BOX 5.9 **Cash Incentives Aimed at Behavioral Change Rather Than Income Support**

A number of programs are using the idea of giving cash or near cash as a positive incentive for changing individuals' behavior in areas other than children's health and/or education. These programs are not principally aimed at poverty, although the problems they are meant to solve may result in households being poor or facing a high likelihood of becoming poor. The following four main areas stand out.

Gender Inequality. In South Asia, a number of secondary school scholarship programs are targeted to girls to address issues of gender inequality through increased education and are explicitly conditioned on the girls remaining unmarried. However, CCT-like programs that aim to improve women's status in society much more broadly, such as the Our Daughters, Our Wealth Program in Haryana, India, are also available. This program provides a series of cash payments to girls from low-income families from the time of their birth to adulthood. Within 15 days of giving birth, the mother receives Rs 500 (about US$12) in cash to meet the baby's immediate requirements for nutrition and medical care. Within three months of giving birth, the program invests Rs 2,500 (about US$60) in the Small Savings Scheme, an amount that will have increased to about Rs 25,000 (about US$600) that will be given to the girl when she reaches 18 years if she has not yet married. Finally, for every two additional years that girls delay cashing out the benefit and remain unmarried, they receive an additional Rs 5,000 (about US$60) (Population Council 1999).

As the program was introduced in 1994, having a good picture of its full impact will not be possible until 2012, when the first group of girls turns 18. However, a 2000 beneficiary assessment (Mode Research Private, Ltd. 2000) already showed promising results: more than 90 percent of community leaders felt that the scheme had helped to reduce female infanticide and gender discrimination and had promoted school enrollment, more than 97 percent of community leaders reported increased self-esteem and self-confidence on the part of mothers after getting benefits for their daughters, 97 percent of community leaders felt that the scheme would motivate girls to wait until they were older than 18 to get married, 34 percent of mothers believed that the money would solve the dowry problem, and 77 percent of mothers reported that they were accorded more respect in society. Seventy-two percent of the mothers also reported that the behavior of their husbands and mothers-in-law were better than expected in relation to postnatal care.

HIV/AIDS and Other Sexually Transmitted Infections. A handful of pilot programs in Burkina Faso, Malawi, and Tanzania are being designed to try to reduce HIV infections. The mechanism is to make cash payments to individuals who remain free of common and cheaply curable sexually transmitted infections. Participants are screened for these often, say once every three months. If they are diagnosed with a sexually transmitted infection other than HIV/AIDS, their payments stop and they are treated immediately and then readmitted to the program. The hypothesis underlying these programs is that they will work through two channels to decrease HIV infections. First, the incentive may lower risky sexual behavior. Second, because HIV transmission rates are higher among those with other sexually transmitted infections, treatment will lower the individuals' chances of HIV infection if they have sexual contact with a person infected with HIV.

Project (Kudat 2006) indicated that because the provision of such documents was required for registration in the program, women who had not previously registered their marriages or obtained birth certificates for their children did so. Both administrators and the media recognized the increase in the registration of marriages and the number of birth certificates and citizenship cards as an important impact of the CCT program.

Transfer programs can also encourage access to and use of other legal services, whether by design or as a side effect. In the case of the Temporary Assistance for Needy Families (TANF) program in the United States, transfer recipients have free access to the services of the Child Support Enforcement Program, whereas others have to pay a fee. The latter provides assistance with locating absent parents, establishing paternity, establishing a support obligation, and/or enforcing a support obligation. States that want to receive federal TANF funds are required by law to operate a child support enforcement program. This ensures that noncustodial parents contribute to their children's welfare and reduces the burden on the state (U.S. House of Representatives, Committee on Ways and Means 2000).

Other Social Assistance Programs

Families poor enough to be eligible for one social assistance program are also often poor enough to be eligible for others, and as many countries have many programs administered by many agencies, households may be able to build a substantial package of support by receiving all the assistance for which they qualify. Recipients of a transfer program may, for example, also be eligible for housing and/or utility allowances and/or fee waivers for health or education services. In a few cases, the eligibility determination process is unified, but in many more cases, households must enroll separately with each agency administering a benefit.

One of the most common links is between countries' main social assistance benefit and access to health care via a fee waiver or subsidized health insurance payments. In 2001 in Armenia, for example, the government extended eligibility for the health services fee waiver program to all households that were receiving benefits under the Family Poverty Benefits Program (Angel-Urdinola and Jain 2006). In Jamaica, families in the PATH CCT initiative are similarly eligible for health care fee waivers, and in Colombia, families in the Familias en Acción program are eligible for subsidized health insurance (World Bank forthcoming). The link between access to health care and cash support is potentially important, as one of the most common reasons that households fall (or fall further) into poverty is because of a health shock that requires expenditures on health care and often implies missed work time and earnings.

Social Care Services

Vulnerable groups and the chronically poor may be especially at risk for having to deal with issues such as mental health problems, domestic violence, or substance abuse. While these issues are not limited to the poor or to vulnerable groups, they often face many more barriers in trying to overcome them than better-off groups, such as information and resource constraints. To effectively help these groups address these issues and their implications for overall household welfare, the receipt of income support alone through a transfer program will not suffice. They need adequate access to social care services.

Linking social assistance and social care can be achieved in a number of ways, ranging from providing clients with information on available services to providing them with a social worker who can refer them to particular social care services and coordinate their provision. While the type of intense and ongoing involvement with social workers on which Chile Solidario is based is rare in developing countries, a number of programs do try to use social workers at specific stages of programs' interaction with beneficiaries. In El Salvador, a social worker of a local nongovernmental organization (NGO) contracted for that purpose by the Red Solidaria, a CCT program, will visit households whose members are reported as not complying with the program's conditions. The social worker is responsible for determining the reasons for the noncompliance and for helping the household address them. In Brazil, the Bolsa Familia CCT program is starting a similar practice to refer households whose children do not comply with education or health conditions to municipal social assistance centers staffed with social workers to diagnose situations and establish family action plans that may include referrals to appropriate programs.

Income Generation

Interest in linking safety nets to microfinance is increasing. A number of pilots are currently being run, such as the joint Consultative Group to Assist the Poorest and Ford Foundation programs in Haiti and India and programs planned for Ethiopia and Pakistan. A number of the larger scale CCT programs, such as Bolsa Familia, Bono de Desarrollo Humano (Human Development Grant) in Ecuador, and PROGRESA in Mexico, are either considering or already starting to implement plans to link their beneficiaries to microfinance institutions. The idea is that the transfers from the safety net program are necessary for immediate poverty relief, but that access to vehicles for saving and credit, usually accompanied by some training in financial literacy or business development, can help beneficiaries raise their autonomous incomes and graduate out of social assistance. Experience to date offers some promising results in terms of the potential for such linked programs to graduate beneficiaries out of safety net programs and into microfinance.

Two models have emerged of how transfer programs and microfinance institutions can work together to achieve such results. In the first model, the safety net program provides a substantial part of the beneficiaries' preparation for accessing microfinance. In the case of the Rural Maintenance Program in Bangladesh, eligible women who are recruited to maintain earthen village roads are required to participate in a mandatory savings plan and receive training in numeracy, income-generating skills, and microenterprise management. They receive information about and are referred to local microfinance institutions. Their participation in the public works is limited to four years, but CARE, which manages the program, continues to provide business management advice for an additional year. Three years after graduating from the program, 79 percent of beneficiaries were still self-employed in microenterprise activities (Hashemi and Rosenberg 2006). The results of a similar public works and microfinance program in Malawi (Central Region Infrastructure Maintenance Programme) have been much more mixed. In this case, the successful link to microfinance institutions was missing, thus the remaining credit constraints did not allow the benefits from the program's savings mechanism and income-generating activities to lead to sustainable microenterprises (Hashemi and Rosenberg 2006).

In the second model, the microfinance institutions directly engage in the safety net program to provide savings plans and train beneficiaries to become their clients on graduation. In Bangladesh, the Income Generation for Vulnerable Groups Development Program, which distributes food grain to destitute women, organizes the beneficiaries in groups, administers a savings plan, and provides skills training, and thereafter gives them small, subsidized loans for income-generating activities. Nearly two-thirds of the 1.6 million women who have participated in the program have been able to graduate from poverty and become microfinance clients (Hashemi and Rosenberg 2006).

Experience to date indicates that key factors for a successful link between a transfer program and a microfinance program are the existence of separate and well-functioning safety net and microfinance programs, clear messages to participants about the role of each, and usually separate administration of transfers and loans. The most promising sequencing of activities is to give transfer recipients access first to a savings scheme and both numeracy and business training, as well as skills training for income-generating activities, and then follow that with small loans, possibly smaller than usual for microfinance, with eventual graduation into the microfinance institution's regular client pool.

Links to other services might also help households achieve stable, independent incomes or manage their funds and households more effectively, for example, adult education, financial literacy, and agricultural extension programs. However, little literature is available from developing countries on experiences with links of this kind to transfer programs. Chile Solidario encourages adult education for those with an incomplete secondary education and has resulted in an increase of both the take-up rates of adult literacy and education programs by about 4 to 5 percentage points and of adult literacy rates by some 5 to 10 percentage points after two years of participation in the program. In El Salvador and Ethiopia, extension programs target the same geographic areas as the transfer programs, but not necessarily the same households.

OPTIONS FOR LINKING TRANSFER PROGRAMS TO OTHER PROGRAMS AND SERVICES

Programs can operate along a continuum of closeness or integration. The following paragraphs provide brief descriptions of a number of these options and examples of programs using them. This area clearly offers scope for innovation, and program designers are currently thinking creatively about further integration of services for the poor.

Presumably the more tightly linked programs are, the more likely that individual households will actually gain benefits from both and realize any envisaged synergies. At the same time, this notion has its limits. Tighter links require much more effort to achieve. Moreover, the value of the link will vary from individual to individual; for example, a crop-based agricultural extension program will be of little help to the landless, and adult literacy classes will be fruitless for those who can already read. Thus efforts to create tighter links between transfer and other programs will generally be most worthwhile where beneficiary groups are relatively homogenous or where the services to be linked are expected to be useful to most, if not all, beneficiaries of the base transfer program. Moreover, tight linkages should be reserved for cases where the linked programs are functioning well. Experience with both CCT programs and linked social assistance and microfinance programs indicates that the transfer programs and the services to which beneficiaries are linked must be well coordinated and operate efficiently and effectively independently of each other. Linking two programs that work well on their own will be more promising than linking ineffective programs or trying to make a single program offer different services that require widely different expertise and administrative capacity.

Operating in the Same Geographic Area

At a minimum, separate services can be delivered in the same geographic areas to serve the same or similar population groups. As this does not require any institutional links or referral systems or much in the way of exchange of information between programs, it is clearly a relatively easy and low-cost way of trying to reach a target group with various services simultaneously. Its disadvantages are the possibility of high errors of exclusion, duplication of certain program functions, and lost opportunities to realize possible synergies from an integrated services approach. However, it may nonetheless be a useful approach in resource-constrained, low-capacity environments.

Ethiopia's Productive Safety Net Program provides an example of this option. Through its design it is intended to link recipient households not only to transfers via public works or direct support for families with no adults who can work, but eventually to a wider set of initiatives designed to increase food security, including agricultural extension and microcredit. In practice, both the safety net programs and the food security programs are operating concurrently in the same areas, but each program is still finding its feet and tight linkages have not yet been pursued.

Providing Information

Information campaigns about each separate service can help households become aware of the full range of programs for which they might be eligible. The office of the transfer program where beneficiaries come to apply for a transfer or payment points where they collect their benefits can make fliers, brochures, and application forms available for a number of other social programs and services. Outreach workers from other programs could also attend gatherings of program beneficiaries. Many programs have done this in a limited or sporadic manner, and an improvement would be to make such information provision more thorough or targeted.

An example of this approach is South Africa, where mobile teams from the South African Social Security Agency travel to remote areas to provide information and intake services for all of the agency's programs. These teams often arrange for similar mobile teams from the agencies involved in providing identification documents, health care, and the like to accompany them.

Locating Different Services in the Same Office

The program offices that beneficiaries need to visit to apply for and/or collect their benefits and receive services can be located in a one-stop shop office. This arrangement can help disseminate information and lower beneficiaries' transaction costs, as they will only have to visit one location rather than spending time and money traveling to separate offices for each program. One-stop shops may also increase beneficiaries' awareness of other services they might be eligible for, thereby further contributing to better outreach and higher intake rates. Ideally, locating different programs together does not only mean the physical proximity of program offices, but also that staff working for the different programs have similar working hours and a basic knowledge of each others' services so they can better serve beneficiaries and refer them to appropriate programs. This arrangement does imply the need for certain structural and behavioral changes on the part of all the programs and services involved. In addition to the logistical requirements of possibly relocating offices to be in the same location and open at similar times, staff from the different programs must be able and willing to communicate with each other and learn about each others' services. Various U.S. states use this approach, and Jamaica is designing a pilot program.

Integrating Intake Procedures

Harmonized or unified application procedures can do still more. They could result in substantial cost savings, especially in the time staff and beneficiaries spend in dealing with applications, and could also result in better outreach and lower rates of exclusion, as eligibility for all programs is determined by one process. True service integration requires that staff from all the different programs represented agree on and follow the same intake procedures and share information on all cases.

An interesting example of a one-stop shop with unified application procedures and shared information systems is the one-window experiment in the Russian city of Arzamas, which has a population of 110,000. Previously, four different agencies had separately administered 10 different benefits, most of them means tested. In 2002, the one-window pilot introduced a unified application form for all the major social assistance programs in the city. Applicants only had to visit one office and supply one set of documents verifying their eligibility for assistance, regardless of how many programs they applied for. Benefit processing was also consolidated. This reform achieved significant time savings for both staff and beneficiaries, cost savings for the programs' administration, and better outreach (box 5.10).

Service integration can, however, have its pitfalls. When the main benefit program for poor families in the United States, TANF, was reformed in 1996, this led to a significant drop in application rates for two other antipoverty programs, the Food Stamp Program and Medicaid. This occurred because the application procedure for all three programs was integrated, but the increased restrictiveness of the TANF program meant that many households did not apply anymore, and thereby did not have the chance to apply to the other two programs even though they may still have been eligible for them. With only about half of the eligible population receiving food stamps in 1998 compared with about 70 percent in the years prior to the reform, many states launched new outreach efforts, liberalized eligibility criteria for some programs, and simplified paperwork and intake procedures.

Having Social Workers Provide Ongoing Support

Vulnerable groups or the chronically poor who face multiple barriers to moving out of poverty may best be served by repeated and continued support from a social worker. This does not preclude any of the approaches already described. It does require additional processes for information sharing and referral between social workers and the programs and services their clients are beneficiaries of and/or eligible for. While the use of social

BOX 5.10 **Introduction of a One-Window Approach in Arzamas, Russia**

This case illustrates the substantial improvements in program efficiency that can be achieved by evaluating its design and implementation. In 2002, the social protection administration of Arzamas introduced a pilot one-window approach for providing social assistance benefits. The old system consisted of 10 benefits, 7 of them means tested, administered by 4 different agencies. The table shows what kinds of information needed to be verified for the three major benefits and clearly reveals the extent of duplication and the possibilities for harmonization.

Client information requiring verification	Housing allowance	Child allowance	School lunch allowance
Income from employer	X	X	X
Pension income	X	X	X
Alimony income	X	X	X
Stipend income	X	X	X
Housing authority data	X	X	X
Payment records for rent and utilities for past 3 months	X		
Employment center data	X	X	X
Passport data	X	X	X
Verification that child is in school		X	X
Bank account number		X	X

In the reorganized system, applicants can approach one specialist with all their requests for social assistance, fill in one application form, and provide one set of documents to confirm their eligibility for various benefits. Under the old system, clients had to visit four different locations to apply for, appeal denial of, or recertify for benefits, depending on the type of benefit. Under the new approach, all applications are received by small units in each neighborhood of the city and processed by a central unit.

A process evaluation documented the savings resulting from the reorganization. First, staff time savings resulted from the unified benefit processing system: staff received 40 percent fewer requests for applications, and for every 100 eligible housing allowance applicants, they spent 31 percent less time for benefit processing. Second, staff efficiency improved. Under the old system, each staff member processed 85 benefits per month; under the one-window system, each staff member processes 127 benefits per month. Third, total administrative expenditures per benefit application dropped by 32 percent. Clients also experienced a reduction in transaction costs. Under the new scheme, the average client saves between 1.3 and 2.4 hours because of the reduced time required to collect the required documents, wait in line, fill out applications, collect benefits, and travel to the local one-window office instead of the former centrally located office.

Finally, the experiment resulted in better outreach: 29 percent of clients claimed that they had learned about additional benefits during a recent visit to the one-window office.

SOURCE: Gallagher, Struyk, and Nikonova 2003.

workers would appear to be a costly option, few evaluations are available of the relative cost-effectiveness of using social workers compared with other approaches.

Chile Solidario (box 5.11) provides extensive social worker support to families to diagnose barriers to their independence and customize action plans to overcome them. The staff costs are higher than for many other cash transfer programs, but the cash benefit is low, which somewhat offsets the staff costs. The program's impacts are largely positive. Given these results, and perhaps also a growing recognition that the extremely poor and vulnerable face multiple barriers that no one program can address, other countries such as Brazil and Colombia are looking at the Chilean model and starting to emulate it.

5.4 Managing Payments

The goal of a payment system is to successfully distribute the correct amount of benefits to the right people at the right time and with the right frequency while minimizing costs to both the program and the beneficiaries. Because circumstances differ across and within countries, no one universally applicable delivery system can be used everywhere. The challenge is to select the best delivery system that takes into account the program's needs, local circumstances, and beneficiaries' current and future needs. Box 5.12 outlines the main issues pertaining to the delivery of in-kind transfers, which call for additional expenses and logistical arrangements compared with the delivery of cash.

PRINCIPLES AND GOALS

Although the choice of delivery mechanism for cash benefits must be context specific, all delivery systems have the following common goals:

- **Ensuring reliability and regularity of payments.** Reliability lowers transaction costs because people do not have to keep returning for the same payment. Moreover, beneficiaries are better able to match their income and expenditure flows if they can depend on the benefit to be delivered at the specified time and place. Even small transfers are helpful if they are frequent and reliable.

- **Maintaining accountability.** This means ensuring that all transactions are recorded and that all the funds allocated are distributed to registered beneficiaries. Effective delivery systems must be able to prevent misappropriation of funds by program officials or by ineligible or fraudulent beneficiaries. If funds are lost along the way, the amount beneficiaries receive will be reduced and political support for the program will be undermined.

- **Reducing beneficiaries' costs.** Beneficiaries face a variety of costs when they collect their benefits, including transport costs, fees to maintain and use bank accounts, identification card costs, opportunity costs of the time spent getting to the payment site and waiting, and possibly the costs of bribes and fees to receive the payment. Programs must endeavor to make the collection of benefits affordable for beneficiaries.

- **Minimizing the cost of delivery (efficiency).** This is one of the main goals of any delivery mechanism, as delivery costs can account for a substantial part of

BOX 5.11 **A Transfer Program with Strong Psychosocial Support for Families: Chile Solidario**

Even though Chile experienced years of sustained income growth during the 1990s, which translated into a reduction in the incidence of overall poverty from 33 percent in 1990 to around 15 percent in 2000, extreme poverty remained fairly steady at around 5.2 percent (World Bank 2005g).
In 2002, the government introduced Chile Solidario, a program specifically aimed at households
living in extreme poverty by using an approach that goes beyond improving the targeting performance of existing public programs or simply providing households with cash assistance.

Program Design. The program is designed to address both the demand side and the supply
side of public services serving the extremely poor and has two components. The first component targets households in extreme poverty using a proxy means test and provides them with
psychosocial support through a local social worker for two years. The social workers work with
households to assess their needs and help them devise a strategy to exit extreme poverty by
identifying specific actions that household members then commit to undertake and which become the conditions of the benefit. These specific actions could be any of 53 different so-called
minimum conditions for a family to move out of extreme poverty and are grouped in seven
categories: identification and other legal documents, family dynamics, education, health care,
housing, employment, and income. For the first six months, the degree of interaction between
social workers and households is high, starting with weekly meetings for the first two months
and slowly decreasing to meetings every other week and then monthly. After these initial six
months, social workers meet with households every other month for another six months and
finally once every three months for the second year of the program. During this two-year period,
households receive a direct cash transfer, with the amount declining over time, and preferential
access to a number of other social programs. After the two-year intensive period, households
continue to receive a smaller direct cash transfer and preferential access to assistance programs for an additional period of three years, but the social worker services are eliminated.

The second component of the program addresses the supply side of public services by ensuring coordination among different programs. This is based on the recognition that an approach
with isolated, sectoral programs does not address the multiple and interrelated material, as well
as psychosocial, deprivation of the extremely poor. The long-term objective is to move toward
a system of social protection that provides bundles of programs that are tailored to meet the
specific needs of hard-to-reach households.

Results. After the first two years of program implementation, significant gains were apparent
along a number of different dimensions. In relation to education, preschool enrollment, enrollment for children between 6 and 15, take-up of adult literacy programs, and adult literacy all
showed significant increases, ranging from 4 to 9 percentage points. In relation to health, enrollment in the public health system, as well as preventive health visits for children under six
and women, showed the most significant increases ranging from 3 to 7 percentage points. The
results also showed a strong take-up of employment programs. No significant effects on household income per capita were found. The evidence does indicate that, on average, participants
increased their awareness of social services in the community and were more likely to be more
optimistic about their future socioeconomic situation.

SOURCE: Galasso 2006.

BOX 5.12 **Delivering In-kind Transfers**

Several safety net programs deliver in-kind benefits with the objective of providing beneficiaries with take-home food rations or food that is ready to be consumed. Examples of these programs, discussed in more detail in chapter 7, are food rations, supplementary feeding, school feeding, and emergency food distribution programs.

What Is Required? The distribution of take-home food rations presents many challenges, as food is bulky and therefore expensive to store and transport, and is also subject to theft and spoilage. In some countries, the distribution of rations relies mainly on government agencies, as in Bangladesh and India, that have developed extensive systems of transport and storage facilities. In other cases, the private sector or NGOs may manage some of the distribution of rations. According to the logistics section of the World Food Programme's Web site (www.wfp.org/operations/), when emergency distribution programs are needed, United Nations organizations like the United Nations High Commissioner for Refugees and the World Food Programme have "turned the complex business of moving food into a fine art." The site describes the complex logistics needed to deliver the right amount of food to the right people at the right place at the right time.

Preparing food for on-site consumption presents additional challenges. Food needs to be acquired, stored, and prepared. In some cases local workers, teachers, health workers, or volunteers are in charge of preparing and distributing the food. Efforts to relieve pressure on local institutions for food preparation include having the private sector deliver food to schools and clinics or using snack foods and products with quicker cooking times (Del Rosso 1999 provides more details on how to simplify implementation for school feeding programs).

Where Does It Take Place? Universal and targeted food distribution programs rely on a network of government or private stores to deliver in-kind transfers to beneficiaries. Special government ration shops were common until the early 1990s in countries such as Bangladesh and Mozambique, but are now rarely used. Instead, private retail shops, which can make use of the existing retail system and marketing chain to reduce distribution costs, are being used more frequently, as in the Arab Republic of Egypt and India. Retail shops are usually paid a fee to carry out the transactions and manage the accounts. Programs must monitor the quality of the commodities that are used and ensure that the stores provide the right amount of food to the beneficiaries and do not exchange it for lower-quality products. In recent years, the use of electronic cards, which started in the U.S. Food Stamp Program and is now being incorporated in Mexico's Tortivales (Free Tortilla) program and tested in Egypt and the Indian states of Gujarat and Maharashtra, has facilitated the recording of transactions and increased accountability.

Health clinics and schools are used to deliver food subsidies and supplements to women and children to improve their health, educational achievement, and/or school attendance. Thus participating clinics and schools have to be equipped with adequate storage and cooking facilities to handle the additional requirements of managing the food.

Refugee camps or feeding centers are used to provide food to those who are either affected by natural disasters or have been displaced by conflicts. In these cases, the main challenge is to provide those affected with the proper nutritional requirements as they may not have access to any other food (Sphere Project 2004; UNHCR and WFP 1999).

overall program costs. As the program or its beneficiaries must pay delivery costs, any costs result in fewer benefits available for beneficiaries. To reduce such costs, program designers must look at context-specific factors to achieve the most effective but least costly delivery system possible. While less technologically advanced distribution systems are often less costly in the short run, investing in more modern delivery mechanisms may have long-run advantages.

- **Ensuring transparency.** This entails making sure that both beneficiaries and nonbeneficiaries know the amount of the transfer. Transparency creates confidence in the program both for the beneficiaries and for the public at large. It can be enhanced by such simple means as providing public information and having an effective complaints procedure in place.

- **Ensuring security.** The design of a benefit delivery system must address security. Security is an issue both for the program while it is transporting and distributing the benefit and for beneficiaries after they have received their benefits. Program designers must take steps to ensure that the program does not suffer losses as a result of thefts or attacks. Armed escorts may be required, and programs may have to purchase insurance to cover possible losses. This is particularly important in countries experiencing war or that are plagued by lawless groups.

DELIVERY AGENCIES AND DELIVERY INSTRUMENT OPTIONS

The methods of payment presented in this section cover the different types of delivery agencies and the means of delivering the benefits (table 5.2).

TABLE 5.2 **Distributing Agencies and Instruments**

Distributing agency	Instruments used by beneficiaries
• Banks, traveling banks, ATMs, branchless banking	• Cash
• Post offices	• Bank accounts
• Official ration stores, private retail stores	• Checks and vouchers
• Public agencies and offices, project offices, NGOs	• Debit cards, smart cards, and cell phones
• Payment centers	

SOURCE: Authors.

Distributing Agencies and Locations

As the table shows, a variety of agencies can distribute benefits from a number of locations.

Banks, Traveling Banks, ATMs, and Branchless Banking. Banks, whether private or public, can be used to deliver safety net benefits in several ways. They can be used as a payment point where cash is issued to beneficiaries against a list of individuals or families. Banks can also cash checks and vouchers distributed to beneficiaries. Finally, they can maintain accounts in beneficiaries' names in which welfare agencies or programs can deposit cash.

Regulations regarding the establishment of bank accounts vary considerably across institutions and countries. In general, one can distinguish between individual bank accounts that can be used for deposits, withdrawals, and so on and consolidated bank accounts that group some or all of the beneficiaries of a local branch under one general account. Individual bank accounts provide beneficiaries with greater freedom to make use of any additional features the bank offers; however, they might be too expensive to set up and operate. The additional benefit of a consolidated bank account is that it provides the agency implementing the program with the opportunity to retrieve funds that the intended beneficiaries have not collected after a certain time.

Banks also offer a variety of delivery opportunities in addition to their offices to cater to people who live in areas without local branches. They can improve their geographical coverage through traveling banks, ATMs, other payment centers, branchless banking, or cell phone banking. Traveling banks feature bank employees traveling with the cash to be distributed to areas with no bank branches, thereby achieving greater coverage, which results in lower transportation costs to the beneficiaries who would otherwise have to travel to the nearest branch. Bangladesh uses mobile pay stations when beneficiaries of the Primary Education Stipend Program live more than five kilometers away from a local bank branch (Ahmed 2005). One of the disadvantages of this service is that it is more costly for the bank, which may then pass those costs on to either the beneficiaries or the program. Rent seeking and kickbacks are more likely to be an issue with mobile banks because controls might be less rigid outside regular offices.[7] The potential for security problems during transport and at the payment site also needs to be evaluated.

ATMs offer all the advantages of direct payment but minimize opportunities for discretion and rent seeking. Other advantages of ATMs include accountability, automaticity, and potential for low operating costs, as well as the added feature of increased coverage and mobility. Box 5.13 describes possible uses of ATMs and their costs, together with point of service (or point of sale) (POS) machines. A combination of the state of infrastructure (especially electricity), security considerations, and costs will determine their suitability for a particular location.

In a growing number of countries, branchless banking, often referred to as mobile banks, provides a new way to deliver money and other financial services to people without bank accounts through post offices and retail outlets such as gas stations. Branchless banks use information and communication technologies, such as debit, prepaid, and smart cards and cell phones, to transmit information between the agent and the customer or the bank. Branchless banking can be operated as an extension of the banking network as in Brazil, India, and South Africa or outside the banking network as in Kenya and the Philippines (Lyman, Ivatury, and Staschen 2006; Lyman, Pickens, and Porteous 2008; Porteous 2006). In Brazil, the state-owned Caixa Econômica Federal offers a simplified current account that can be opened at any branch or correspondent using only an identification card, tax file number, and proof of residence or an address declaration. Account holders have access to Caixa's entire branch and correspondent network (Ivatury 2006). Caixa has created an impressive network of banking correspondents that covers all 5,500 municipalities in Brazil. In 2004, Caixa had about 14,300 banking correspondents that included lottery houses, supermarkets, drugstores, and gas stations, compared with about 9,000 in 2001. Counting all branches and lottery houses, of Brazil's population of 170 million people,

> **BOX 5.13 ATMs and POS Machines: Conducting Transactions Remotely Using Electronic Cards**
>
> An ATM is a computerized telecommunications device that provides a financial institution's customers with a secure method of performing financial transactions in a public space without the need for a human clerk or bank teller. ATMs range from portable stand-alone units weighing several hundred pounds to steel and concrete wall-mounted units weighing several thousand pounds to mobile units that have been incorporated into varying types of vehicles.
>
> The initial cost of an ATM ranges from US$10,000 to US$40,000. In addition, operating and maintenance costs can be as much as US$6,000 per year. Producing and distributing the cards required for accessing ATMs also incurs costs, although these are falling. Usually the program does not bear the costs of the ATM network, only of the cards for its beneficiaries. Sometimes the existence of a large program paying through ATMs will encourage the private sector to install devices in their stores as a way of attracting business.
>
> POS machines are communication devices that do not contain any money, but have the capability of authorizing transactions carried out in retail stores, restaurants, hotels, or mobile locations. Transactions can be performed in real time with connectivity to a central computer system via a telephone or the Internet or can be recorded on a smart card or computer. Shops and welfare delivery agencies can back up the records and then submit copies to banks, post offices, or welfare offices for subsequent reimbursement. POS machines, including hand-held models, can also connect to other devices such as global positioning system receivers, barcode scanners, smart card readers, cell phones, satellite phones, biometric fingerprint readers, portable printers, and audio-video devices. Costs range from US$300 to US$700 each, depending on the model.

160 million have ready access to Caixa. Those without ready access live, on average, 24 kilometers from a branch or lottery house. If other correspondent bank outlets, such as supermarkets and drugstores, are included, then everyone has ready access to Caixa (Kumar and others 2006). Bolsa Familia uses this impressive network to deliver benefits to its beneficiaries (Lindert and others 2007).

Overall, banks have much to offer as a delivery agency. They have considerable expertise in handling and accounting for cash, well-established systems of controls, and audit trails to help minimize fraud along with a management culture that actively discourages fraud. Banks are characterized by automaticity: the use of computers and software that provide internal checks on transfers and payments. In addition, the use of banks ensures that uncollected funds are not subject to theft, for example, Bangladesh's Rural Maintenance Program sends uncollected funds back to a central account (Ahmed 2005). Banks also have experience in dealing with security issues. Colombian banks, which are accustomed to operating in an insecure environment, took on complete responsibility for this aspect of the Familias en Acción program, thereby helping the program avoid additional insurance costs (Lafaurie and Velasquez Leiva 2004). A side benefit is that beneficiaries gain financial literacy and confidence in dealing with banks if they are exposed to banking by collecting a safety net benefit that is delivered through a bank. Economies of scale are attainable with banks because of their cash management experience, and this may permit savings. Further technological developments and increased competition in the banking sector are likely to improve cost-benefit ratios even more in the future.

At the same time, using banks as the main delivery agency might entail some disadvantages. To begin with, banking facilities are sometimes not available or easy to reach, especially in poor rural areas. The cost of poor geographical coverage is illustrated in Mozambique, where demobilized soldiers were given vouchers or checks to present at a bank branch or post office. Not all districts had branches or post offices, thus one-third of the beneficiaries spent between US$$2 and US$4 of their US$14 transfer on transportation (Hanlon 2004). Moreover, remote bank branches may not hold sufficient stores of cash and may be difficult to monitor (see Save the Children 2001). The poor may also have difficulties dealing with banks, understanding the transaction, or paying account fees (Ahmed 2005). Bank fees for opening accounts and transaction fees, whether borne by the beneficiary or the program, will reduce the amount of the transfer to the beneficiary. As such fees might constitute a high percentage of the transfer, the program should negotiate as low a fee as possible. The negotiation process itself is sometimes a long and difficult process that requires special skills (box 5.14).

Branchless banking promises to offer several solutions to the banking sector's constraints, but regulations pertaining to its use and the size of accounts and transactions are still being developed. In Brazil, for example, monthly transaction volumes (debits and credits) cannot exceed R$1,000 (approximately US$140) per customer. Clients are allowed four withdrawals and four account statements per month, and additional transactions are R$0.50 each. Deposits and balance inquiries cost nothing.

Post Offices. In several countries, post offices offer financial services similar to those of small banks and are being used as places to pay for goods and services other than postage and may also allow people to make financial transfers and maintain deposits. When used to make payments to beneficiaries of safety net programs, post offices usually make payments based on a list of beneficiaries provided by the program or by cashing beneficiaries' checks or vouchers.

Thus in many ways post offices may function like banks and are a good alternative to banks, as they are accustomed to dealing with cash and already have systems for transporting, controlling, accounting for, and safeguarding cash. In some countries they offer wide geographical coverage and have established delivery routes and systems, and so they can deliver payments to beneficiaries. In addition, beneficiaries who are unfamiliar with or intimidated by more formal institutions such as banks may be more familiar with post offices, making them more accessible. This is the case in India, where the post offices are used to delivering old-age pensions (Farrington and others 2003).

In some cases, despite their coverage, post offices may not be as efficient as banks in transferring resources from central or local institutions. In Lesotho, for example, post offices are used to distribute old-age pensions. To collect their money, pensioners present their pension books, which contain a photograph of the pensioner as identification, at a local post office branch. However, funds are not transferred electronically to local branches. Instead, post office officials withdraw the funds from central branches and physically distribute them to 291 pay points. This creates additional costs, including providing these officials with security escorts. Also, the delivery of funds is sometimes delayed and pensioners find that after paying for transportation or spending hours walking, they have to return later if their payments are not yet available (Devereux and others 2005).

Retail Stores. Several programs deliver in-kind transfers to beneficiaries using food stamps or vouchers, for example, the public distribution system in India and the Food Stamp Program in the United States. Beneficiaries receive their allotted amount of food upon presenting the proper documents, namely, vouchers, passbooks, identity cards, or electronic cards. When the program uses cards, official ration shops or private retail shops can authorize or record the transactions using POS machines or terminals (described in box 5.13).

The stores are responsible for managing the stocks of food and the financial transactions. This entails providing records of transactions to government officials for commodities received from the government or passing the vouchers on to banks for reimbursement of their payments for commodities they have procured.

Public Agencies and Offices, Project Offices, and NGOs. Other types of program implementation agencies may be directly involved in distributing benefits. Appropriate public agencies would be those experienced in making cash payments and handling the accounting associated with payments, including local government and welfare offices, as long as they have enough staff to perform all the necessary tasks. In Ethiopia, for example, cashiers from municipal finance departments or local branches of the Department of Agriculture disbursed payments for the Cash-for-Relief Pilot Scheme. Municipal safe boxes were used to store the cash. While early concerns about corruption and mismanagement proved to be unfounded, the cashiers viewed having to make the payments an unwelcome addition to their workload, and local officials recommended that in future, cashiers should be hired specifically to work on such projects. Municipal officials also recommended the use of separate safe boxes for any future projects (Save the Children 2001).

NGOs can also be used as cash payment sites if they have more extensive networks in a region than banks or government offices or are directly involved in managing a program. NGOs may not, however, handle cash as efficiently as the latter (Ahmed 2005).

Other possible payment locations include worksites for public works projects, a logical choice when cash is distributed directly to the beneficiaries. In this case, the workers are paid based on a list of the participants that also indicates the amount of work performed. This system is more convenient for beneficiaries, but poses several logistic and managerial challenges for program managers; for instance, they must make security and other arrangements for transporting cash safely to worksites and record all the transactions.

Payment Centers. Service point pay stations set up by government agencies or contracted out to private agencies are an attempt to reduce beneficiaries' travel costs. In this situation, government or program officials or contractors distribute transfers using simple paper and pencil recording systems or electronic devices such as POS machines or cell phones.

In Zambia, beneficiaries of the Kalomo District Pilot Social Cash Transfer Scheme who live more than 15 kilometers from the designated bank visit the closest local service point, which is usually at a school or health center. Pay point managers are responsible for collecting the money and distributing it to beneficiaries (Devereux and others 2005). This not only makes collecting the money easier for beneficiary households, but facilitates the administration of the scheme and reduces banks' workload.

BOX 5.14 Managing the Contracting Process

The social assistance agency often contracts out the processing and delivery of payments rather than managing these directly. This makes a good deal of intuitive sense, as it allows programs to take advantage of the financial sector's expertise rather than having to create parallel structures themselves. However, a few issues need to be managed in contracting out.

Demonstration Effect. In countries where a large cash transfer program has not been operated in the past, financial service providers may fear that the services will be extremely expensive, and thus may either not bid or submit bids with high prices. In the early stage of Colombia's Familias en Acción, for example, program officials knew that US$1.30 per transaction was a standard cost for an ATM charge and were expecting to pay around US$2 per transaction. The first responses from private banks quoted US$10 per transaction. As the program negotiators were knowledgeable about the banking industry, they understood the implications of offering to deposit the funds five days in advance of the start of the payment cycle. This resulted in a revised transaction fee quote of US$1.74 from the state bank. The program continued to negotiate with private banks able to provide coverage outside that of the state bank, and their quoted transaction fees were US$1.31 to US$1.52 (Lafaurie and Velasquez Leiva 2004). Other countries such as Kenya have employed similar strategies of using a demonstration effect, for example, the pilot of the Cash Transfers for Orphan and Vulnerable Children Program, to show that offering the service at a relatively low cost is feasible and then opened the process to bidding.

Contract Features and Issues. Contracts need to specify a range of issues other than the financial terms, including ownership of the database of beneficiaries. Ideally the social assistance agency should own the database used to deliver payments and maintain transaction records. At a minimum the agency should have full access rights to the database and it should be fully subject to audit if it is managed by another institution, as is the case for Bolsa Familia in Brazil (Lindert and others 2007). Issues relating to the technical features of the database will also need to be specified.

The contract should specify desirable but realistic service standards. It might, for example,

- give program clients the right to choose which of a number of alternative payment points they wish to receive payments from or give them access to multiple payment points (if

---

Sixty-five percent of the beneficiaries of the Bolsa Familia program in Brazil collected their benefits from lottery points in 2005. Caixa managed approximately 9,000 lottery outlets. These outlets use POS devices connected to the bank network to process transactions (Lindert and others 2007).

The use of pay points is appropriate where banks are not available and when their use lowers beneficiaries' transaction costs. At the same time, their use requires excellent scheduling and control mechanisms. If the transactions are recorded using paper and pencil, the control system could be operated by local observers such as community elders or local government officials who could help safeguard against corruption by ensuring that the correct people receive the cash. The use of electronic systems such as POS machines and cell phones can improve the transparency and accuracy of transactions.

payments are made through POS machines in retail stores, for example, this will allow at least some beneficiaries to comparison shop and reduce any problems with price gouging);

- require a 24-hour hotline for clients to call with questions about payments, lost or stolen cards, forgotten security codes, and the like;

- specify maximum acceptable queuing times, which can be reduced, for example, through the use of ATMs rather than teller services, but also by spreading pay days over the month rather than paying all clients on the same day.

Performance-based incentive contracts can also be used to improve the efficiency of the delivery system of contractors and other agencies. In Brazil in 2006, Bolsa Familia renegotiated its contract with Caixa for maintaining the database and delivering benefits. The new contract established 17 performance indicators to measure the level and quality of the services Caixa was providing, such as an index of duplication of registry entries, hours of availability, and delays in delivering benefits cards (Lindert and others 2007).

The biggest risk is entering into an agreement with a contractor for services that are not clearly specified or taken into account. For example, if the fees are disaggregated for each of the services provided, some costs might be overlooked. The resulting cost of the delivery system might then become much higher than expected. A 2 to 3 percent fee for each transaction seems reasonable, but if it is combined with other fees for using cards, maintaining the software and the database, and providing assistance to customers, then the fees might add up to be more than 10 percent per transaction.

Length of Contract. On the one hand, a longer contract might permit payment agencies to amortize the costs of up-front investments in technology, processing systems, and client training that will both allow low unit costs over time and good service standards. On the other hand, the fewer the overall number of contractors, merely holding a contract for a period begins to create a competitive advantage. The program does not want to end up beholden to a monopoly payment provider.

Delivery Instruments

Benefits in cash and in kind can be delivered to beneficiaries in a variety of ways, normally using one of two main methods. The first method is to have one of the distributing agencies directly distribute cash or in-kind benefits. The second method is to give the beneficiaries access to the benefits via checks, vouchers, direct deposits into personal accounts, smart cards, cell phones, and the like that can be redeemed at one of the distributing agencies.

Cash. Direct distribution of benefits in the form of cash is common in low-income countries, particularly in the case of cash-for-work programs or emergency programs. The only thing needed to process payments is a list of beneficiaries or a muster roll. The beneficiaries present some form of identification, a passbook or a checkbook for recording transactions, sign some paperwork, and receive the cash. Payments can take place in a variety of places including banks, public offices, and worksites.

Direct distribution systems are straightforward to set up. They may be the only available option in poor countries. In the Meket Project in Ethiopia, for example, beneficiaries gather along the road or at the market on the day of payment. Names are called out in groups of 10 and the first person named in the group is given the list that all 10 people sign, usually with a fingerprint, which solves the problem of illiteracy, plus the ink stains prevent duplicate collection. The first person on the list also collects the money for everyone in that group, each beneficiary is informed of his or her transfer amount, and the cash is then distributed (Devereux and others 2005).

Direct distribution of benefits by designated agents presents two main security concerns. First, security measures are required during the transfer of the funds when banks are not used, and second, systems must be in place to verify the identity of recipients.

Bank Transfers. Some programs have made arrangements to transfer cash directly into the bank accounts of individual beneficiaries. Beneficiaries can choose whether to keep the money in their accounts or withdraw it.

Direct (electronic) transfers to beneficiaries' bank accounts are advantageous, as they eliminate intermediaries, discretion, delays in payment, and rent-seeking opportunities. For example, if the central government passes funds for a safety net to local governments, any local government facing a financial crisis of some kind may temporarily borrow these funds, thereby delaying their disbursement to beneficiaries; paying beneficiaries directly prevents this from happening. Direct transfers of cash may also be an effective way to deal with security issues. Small, more frequent, disbursements help make beneficiaries less of a target after they collect their benefits.

Another advantage of this form of payment is that it introduces beneficiaries to the banking system: it provides them with the opportunity to open and operate a bank account, which they might not otherwise be able to afford. Of course the banks might charge service fees to open and maintain the accounts. To reduce such costs, the program may impose some restrictions on the banks or a number of beneficiaries may share a single account. For example, the Rural Maintenance Program in Bangladesh delivers one payment to 10 people who collect it together.

Checks and Vouchers. Instead of delivering cash or in-kind benefits directly, sometimes beneficiaries will receive a check or a voucher that entitles them to receive the benefits in cash or in kind at a later time. A voucher is typically a piece of paper that can be used as a check and exchanged for cash, or it can be exchanged for goods and/or services at designated business establishments. This method of delivering benefits is more common in middle-income countries with more established systems for printing and distributing checks and vouchers. These instruments also require a good system of banks and/or post offices to redeem checks or vouchers for cash or local stores to redeem food vouchers. The lack of an efficient system for redeeming vouchers and checks can undermine the success of a distribution system, as illustrated by a 2001 pilot project in Cundinamarca, Colombia. This pilot used vouchers that recipients could exchange for cash or use to buy goods at a designated shop. One of the problems that emerged was that retailers sometimes did not have enough cash on hand to honor the vouchers, which resulted in the majority of the recipients being dissatisfied with the arrangement (Lafaurie and Velasquez Leiva 2004).

Checks and vouchers share many of the benefits of cash: they are easily transportable, will not spoil, and do not require a large storage space. At the same time, they have the same security problems as cash (although they are less fungible) and cannot be transferred electronically. They are also more expensive than cash because of the printing costs associated with vouchers that the program must pay for. A risk is that a parallel market may emerge if beneficiaries resell their vouchers at a discounted value, which will also reduce the benefits accruing to beneficiaries. Another risk is that merchants might charge a fee to redeem vouchers or may overprice their goods, and program managers must take care not to work with such establishments. Finally, a nonfinancial cost of vouchers is that those who receive them might be stigmatized. Harvey (2005) notes that a U.K. voucher program for asylum seekers was abandoned because beneficiaries were subjected to abuse and harassment in the community.

The success of any voucher program hinges on the logistical arrangements made with merchants for redeeming the value of the vouchers (Harvey 2005). A program's efficiency will be seriously affected if merchants are not reimbursed for the vouchers they have accepted or if they are not reimbursed in a timely fashion. The program will also have to address the issue of vouchers that are not completely spent when they are redeemed.

Debit Cards, Smart Cards, and Cell Phones. A number of programs are introducing new transaction methods that seek to reduce transaction costs and the use of checks and vouchers. These methods include several types of debit cards and prepaid cards, smart cards, and cell phones. In 1993, the U.S. Food Stamp Program, for example, introduced a system based on smart cards, which is known as electronic benefit transfers, to replace paper vouchers. By December 2002, the system delivered benefits to 90 percent of the 19 million beneficiaries through 145,000 retail stores using POS terminals (O'Connor and Silbermann 2003).

Debit cards have a magnetic strip that contains information about a beneficiary's account. They can be used to withdraw cash from ATMs or to process purchases from POS machines. Each time a card is used, the stipulated amount is deducted from the cardholder's bank account. As these are electronic transactions, they are less costly than over-the-counter transactions at local banks, but as a debit card must be linked to a bank account, the account fees may cancel all or some of these savings (Lafaurie and Velasquez Leiva 2004). As debit cards require the use of ATMs or POS machines connected to telephone lines, this system may not provide adequate geographic coverage, as the high capital costs mean that equipment will only be installed where it is used frequently enough to make it profitable; however, networks of ATMs and POS machines are expanding rapidly in many countries (Ivatury 2006). At the same time, beneficiaries may find them difficult to understand or use.

Prepaid debit cards are similar to regular debit cards. The only difference is that they come with a preloaded value, and when they are used the amount is debited directly from a central account. Thus individual accounts are not required. These cards carry less risk for banks in relation to cash custody because they have a limited amount of money attached to them and can be blocked if lost or stolen. The payment settlement process is faster because the funds have already been allocated, and any ATM or POS machine within the network can be used. Security is enhanced because a personal identification number or password is required, plus beneficiaries can choose when to withdraw their benefits, thereby avoiding lines and waiting time (Lafaurie and Velasquez Leiva 2004). The transaction costs for the bank, and therefore for the program, are significantly less for prepaid cards than for individual debit cards, as the bank does not need to maintain individual accounts.

Smart cards contain an electronic chip that can hold, and sometimes also process, a large amount of information. Simple smart cards are disposable once they are used up (prepaid phone cards are an example), but some smart cards have multiple applications. More sophisticated types of smart cards can be used in POS terminals and ATMs and for storing records such as health information (Gallagher 2005).

Transactions can take place at ATMs or at POS machines at remote locations. As the required information is embedded in the card, a bank account is not needed and the POS machine does not have to be connected to a bank. Transaction records can be updated later from the card. While the transaction costs of using smart cards are even lower than those of prepaid debit cards, their main disadvantage is the higher cost of individual cards. The current cost of a smart card is approximately US$3, compared with only US$0.20 for a standard debit card.

Cell phones have also been used effectively to conduct financial transactions. Indeed, cell phones contain a smart card and can be easily connected over the network of branchless banks or to other telephones or POS remote devices. The amount of money that cell phones are allowed to carry is restricted, even though many people may have access to their own cell phone that they could use to access a financial institution that manages transactions. In the Philippines, special banking regulations allow people to transfer and hold small amounts of cash through cell phones. In South Africa, Celtel allows people to have a cell phone account and conduct transactions within the Celtel network (Porteous 2006).

Cell phones can also be used to record the delivery of cash or in-kind benefits by any authorized agent. In the Democratic Republic of Congo, cell phones are used to deliver payments to the beneficiaries of the demobilization project using any of 100 cash points, which are small booths, each with a person sitting inside with a cell phone and a cash box. Beneficiaries provide their government identification to the clerk at the cash point. The clerk enters his or her own identification number into the cell phone and sends a text message to the central financial database operated by Celtel. Ten seconds later, the clerk receives a text message confirming that the money has been credited to his or her account and containing the information about the entitlement and pays the beneficiary.

SELECTION OF A DELIVERY MECHANISM

The system selected for delivering cash and in-kind transfers to beneficiaries should consist of the appropriate combination of delivery agencies and means of payments and should be well integrated with other operational processes. In addition, the system will need to be feasible enough to be improved over time, while taking current implementation constraints into account.

Taking Appropriate Context and Political Economy Considerations into Account

Delivery mechanisms that are based on the banking system and make use of ATMs and POS machines in combination with the latest technological innovations, like smart cards or cell phones, have significant advantages where they guarantee good coverage and sufficiently low unit costs. While each instrument used for distribution has some advantages, not all of them can perform adequately in every circumstance. Therefore the choice of system must take into account country-specific constraints in relation to the financial and technological infrastructure necessary to support the proposed delivery system. An assessment of the appropriate context should include the following elements:

- A review of the country's financial infrastructure to verify the geographical coverage and efficiency of the public and private banking sectors and of the postal system, including investigation of the costs of setting up and maintaining individual and group accounts
- A review of the communications infrastructure that includes the availability of electricity, the frequency of power failures, and the availability and reliability of telephone lines and cell phones as well as the costs of using them
- A review of the capability of retail stores in relation to redeeming in-kind vouchers and stamps

In addition, the system must be compatible and integrated with other operational processes, such as the selection of beneficiaries and the reconciliation of accounts. The information about payments processed, including the number of people who received benefits and the amount of funds disbursed, has to be verified (reconciled) against the list of the program's currently eligible beneficiaries using the program's monitoring system. Therefore the level of development of the overall program's monitoring system will influence the system selected and its development. When a good, computerized management information system and communication infrastructure are in place, programs can make frequent payments using individual accounts and quickly reconcile payments. Box 5.15 shows how a CCT might be delivered using a smart card system. When the monitoring system is not particularly sophisticated, using consolidated accounting and group payment systems to facilitate recordkeeping and the transmittal of information is an easier approach.

The principles described here governing the selection of delivery mechanisms also apply to special circumstances such as the distribution of cash transfers under emergency situations—even though, in such cases as emergency situations following a natural disaster, the amount of time available for assessing options and designing alternative models may be very limited and the infrastructure disrupted. Box 5.16 describes the most common options available to deliver cash under such circumstances.

Assessing the cost of delivering transfers is complicated, and care is needed when comparing the costs of alternative delivery methods. Information on the actual costs incurred to deliver transfers is not comparable across countries and programs. One reason for this is that total administrative costs are frequently not broken down into similar subcategories of costs or they are aggregated in different ways. In other cases, the costs national banks or post offices incur are not charged to the government agency responsible for the program or they are extremely low as in Albania and Lithuania.

When the delivery of payments is outsourced to private companies and banks instead of using government institutions, the actual delivery costs charged to the program tend to be larger in nominal and percentage terms. Sometimes, to reduce both the admin-

BOX 5.15 **Processing Payments Using a Smart Card System**

The flow diagram illustrates a possible way of organizing the activities related to the payment and reconciliation process.

1. The management information system (MIS) creates the list of beneficiaries. This contains details about the amount of benefits they are supposed to receive and the type of compliance required.

2. The list of beneficiaries is sent to the bank, mobile system, or service provider from which the beneficiaries will receive payment.

3. Payment takes place. Beneficiaries collect the benefits at a bank or from a mobile system or service provider. For this transaction, they may use a card containing identification data or identifying biometrics.

4. Transaction confirmation is received from the bank, mobile system, or service provider, which is then loaded into the MIS and verified by the program administrator.

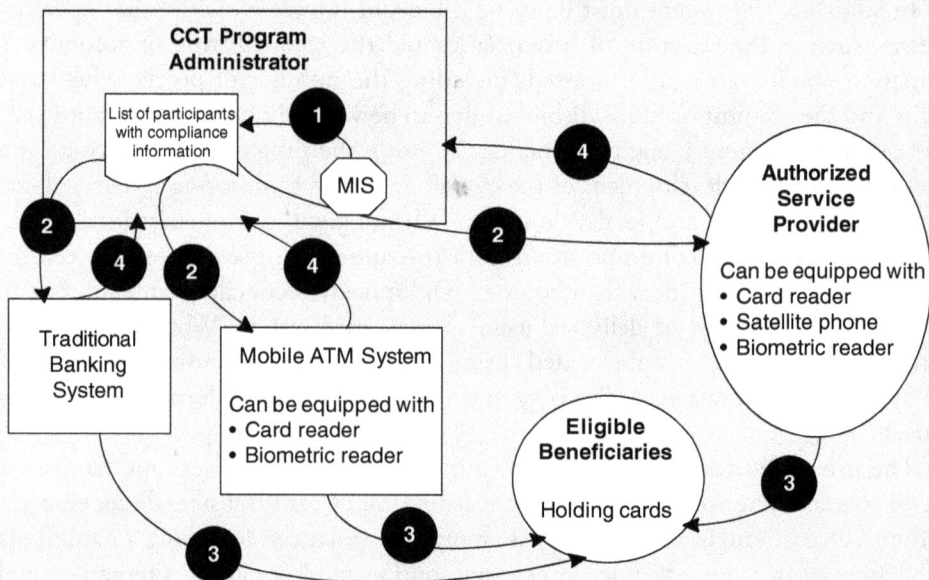

This system can be fully automated online and can process the information via the Internet or satellite while transactions are made. Alternatively, transactions can be made offline and uploaded to the main system on a daily or weekly basis by telephone, satellite, or the Internet.

SOURCES: Adapted from Gallagher 2005 and Datta 2006.

istrative and total delivery costs of transfers per beneficiary, subsidies are actually delivered every two or more months. Table 5.3 presents the costs of delivery for some countries and programs. When the actual costs of delivering benefits are low per transaction, as in Eastern Europe, payments can be made on a monthly basis. When they are higher, as in

---

BOX 5.16 **Delivering Cash in an Emergency**

The delivery of cash—and any other assistance—in an emergency may be more difficult than usual, as financial institutions, basic infrastructure, transportation systems, and communication systems may have been destroyed. Creti and Jaspars (2006) set out the following three main options for transferring cash:

- **Using the local banking system.** If a reliable, preexisting banking system is still in place and accessible to beneficiaries, payments into individual or group accounts have the advantage of being safer for recipients and project staff, because they do not have to handle cash directly. For example, in Iran after the 2004 earthquake in Bam, the banking system was still functioning and the government set up bank accounts for the beneficiaries and transferred cash directly into the accounts. Following the floods in Mozambique in early 2000, the recipients of cash transfers were given checks at designated distribution sites, where a commercial bank provided tellers protected by security personnel who could cash the checks (Harvey 2005). Similarly, the British Red Cross used a bank that provided ATM services to distribute relief transfers in Banda Aceh, Indonesia, following the 2004 tsunami (Adams and Harvey 2006).

- **Using local money transfer companies.** The use of traditional local systems for transferring cash may be an option when financial institutions, especially banks, did not exist before the emergency or were destroyed as a result of it. For example, in response to unrest in Haiti in 2004, Oxfam used local shops to transfer cash to beneficiaries. Local systems for transferring cash were also used in Afghanistan for the Emergency Support for Drought- and Conflict-Affected Populations (November 1, 2001, through March 15, 2003) and in Somalia in 2004 for the Emergency Cash Program for Drought-Affected Households (Creti and Jaspars 2006). In addition, programs can use insurance to reduce the security risks of distributing cash; for example, in Ethiopia, Save the Children takes out insurance to cover the risk of loss when transporting cash in areas that do not have banks (Harvey 2005).

- **Having an implementing agency make direct payments.** Direct disbursement may be an option when the use of banks or local systems is not feasible. It may often be the quickest delivery method to put in place, although it entails high administrative and management workloads. Various donors working in areas of Sri Lanka affected by the 2004 tsunami used this method for most of their public works programs and delivered cash through direct distribution to beneficiaries at worksites (Aheeyar 2006).

Latin America, payments are made every month or every other month. When they are even higher, as in Bangladesh, payments are made on a quarterly basis.

Political economy considerations should not be ignored when selecting and setting up new delivery systems or modernizing existing delivery mechanisms. The latter might not be easy because of resistance to new methodologies and technologies because they might be perceived as complicated and because they may require a large investment before any benefit payments can be made. A clear explanation is needed of the gains that can

TABLE 5.3 **Costs of Delivering Benefits, Selected Countries and Programs**

Country, program, and year	Average monthly transfer (US$)	Costs per transaction		Frequency of payment
		US$	As % of transfer amount	
Albania, Ndihme Ekonomika, 2004	26.0	0.13	0.5	Monthly
Bangladesh, Primary Education Stipend Program, FY2002/03	1.80	0.15	8.3	Quarterly
Brazil, Bolsa Familia, 2007	42.0	1.10	2.6	Monthly
Bulgaria, Guaranteed Minimum Income Program, 2004	25.00	0.07	0.3	Monthly
Colombia, Familias en Acción, 2004	50.0	0.60–10	1.2–2.0	Every other month
Ecuador, Bono de Desarrollo Humano, 2004	15.0	0.45	3.0	Monthly
Jamaica, PATH, 2004	45.0	0.30–0.60	0.7–1.3	Every other month

SOURCES: Authors' calculations based on Ahmed 2005; del Ninno and Ayala 2006; Handa and Davis 2006; Kolpeja forthcoming; Schady and Araujo 2006; Shopov forthcoming; personal communication with Joana Mostafa, consultant to World Bank Brazil office, April 22, 2008.

be achieved in terms of security and efficiency and the creation of strategic alliances with systems used by other government departments and the private sector. In Colombia, for example, the Department of Social Welfare is in the process of creating a sophisticated Internet-based database and payment system for the beneficiaries of all social programs. The department was able to reduce the initial setup costs of such as system by working with the private sector. The government helped to set up a payment system for all formal sector employees using a small number of banks or specialized companies that coordinate firms' payroll disbursements with individual employees' contributions to health and pension funds, thereby significantly reducing the cost of processing payroll statements.

If international or bilateral organizations finance programs, they might have additional reporting requirements that could affect the type of delivery mechanism and the frequency of payments. In the case of CCT programs in Colombia, Jamaica, and Kenya, for example, payments take place every other month to give the programs more time to undertake the reconciliation process and reporting requirements.

Adapting to Local Conditions and Avoiding Unintended Effects

The main challenge in setting up a secure and reliable delivery system for safety net programs is achieving the right balance among ensuring feasibility, reducing program costs, and reducing beneficiaries' costs. In making decisions, program managers should bear the following points in mind:

- Managers should, to the extent possible, make use of any preexisting delivery systems and local infrastructure, including bank accounts, databases, and national identity systems. In doing so, programs can take advantage of economies of scale rather than increasing up-front capital costs and focus on improving a preexisting system rather than setting up a completely new one. In Somalia, for example, money transfer companies are widespread across the country and international agencies have now set up partnerships with the remittance companies for delivering transfers for humanitarian programs (Ahmed 2006). Using or expanding a preexisting identification system can facilitate the verification of beneficiaries' identities and cross-checking of their records across databases. The use of existing systems is also preferred after a natural disaster or other emergency.

• Managers should be aware of the trade-offs among alternative options and reach an appropriate compromise. The most obvious trade-offs are between costs and efficiency on the one hand and accountability and frequency of payments on the other. For example, a less expensive system might not be able to verify beneficiaries' identities properly and give rise to fraud. Similarly, although beneficiaries might prefer more frequent payments to help them smooth their consumption, more frequent payment will result in higher administrative and transaction costs unless the marginal cost of each transaction is kept extremely low.

• Managers should select a disbursement system that makes use of locations that are accessible to most beneficiaries, thereby reducing their travel time and costs. Reducing travel and transaction costs is particularly important in poor rural areas. Another alternative is to arrange payments to coincide with other activities, for example, by providing payments at worksites. Finally, managers might wish to consider using a combination of payment providers to reduce transaction costs.

• Managers should experiment with new technologies. Introducing new systems such as smart cards and cell phones can improve the quality of delivery systems and significantly reduce costs in the long run and can also be used in low-income environments with poor infrastructure. For example, smart cards, POS machines, and cell phone pay point stations can be used in the absence of telephone lines and electricity. Moreover, even though the initial investment might be substantial, if individual transaction costs are kept low, the program's overall costs may decrease over time as occurred with the U.S. Food Stamp Program.

• Managers should consider contracting out the payment system and/or involving other supply services. In this case the challenge is to involve as many institutions as possible and then negotiate the contract with them. The negotiation process will be more difficult when only a few institutions can provide the desired coverage.

Notes

1. The income gap is the ratio between the average welfare level of the poor and the poverty line. If, as is common in the poverty and safety net literature, the welfare level is measured as per capita consumption, then an income gap of 25 percent means that the average per capita consumption of the poor is 25 percent below the poverty line.

2. An exception is the pilot program being developed in the Republic of Yemen, which will explicitly test the effect of transfers paid to the mother versus the father and of putting a share of the benefits directly into the hands of youth.

3. Cross-country comparability is enhanced if the information from different surveys uses the same recall period and the consumption aggregate is comparable, that is, it includes roughly the same components and is adjusted for differences in household size or purchasing power in the same manner. At the same time, analysts should be cautious in undertaking such comparisons without a good understanding of program eligibility criteria and of possible differences between surveys.

4. The predictions that increased transfers will reduce the labor supply of beneficiary households are based on the static labor supply model (Moffitt 2002a).

5. Poor households in low-income countries face severe credit constraints. They cannot access bank loans at market interest rates because of the small size of their businesses (and thus high overheads for banks), their lack of collateral, the informality of their businesses, and their lack of knowledge about how to deal with banks. Thus they tend to operate on parallel markets served by moneylenders who charge substantially higher interest rates than banks.

6. The United States undertook four experiments: in urban areas of New Jersey and Pennsylvania from 1968–72 (1,300 families); in rural areas of Iowa and North Carolina from 1969–73 (800 families); in Gary, Indiana, from 1971–4 (1,800 families); and in Denver and Seattle from 1970–8 (4,800 families). The negative income tax was a mirror image of the regular tax system. Instead of tax liabilities increasing with income according to a tax rate schedule, benefits varied inversely with income according to a negative tax rate (or benefit reduction) schedule. If, for example, the threshold for positive tax liability for a family of four was US$10,000, a family with only US$8,000 of annual income would, given a negative tax rate of 25 percent, receive a check from the Treasury worth US$500 (25 percent of the US$2,000 difference between its US$8,000 income and the US$10,000 threshold). A family with no income would receive US$2,500.

7. In economics, rent seeking refers to the misuse of government authority or resources.

Annex:
Generosity of Safety Net Programs of
Last Resort in OECD Countries

Table A5.1 presents the key design features for safety net programs of last resort in OECD countries (OECD 2007). These programs, commonly referred to as welfare or social assistance programs, are noncontributory income support schemes where eligibility does not depend on beneficiaries' employment record or previous earnings.

The benefit level is usually set to reflect basic needs in a country, and safety net programs are one of the main instruments of antipoverty programs. Maximum benefit amounts for a single person vary from 5 percent of the average worker's wage in the United States to 34 percent in Iceland. Claimants usually receive additional payments for dependent spouses and children depending on the number of children and their ages. In some countries such as Finland, Japan, and the Slovak Republic, benefits may be increased to cover housing, health, or education costs. Comparing the amounts paid for the first person to those granted for additional household members is particularly interesting, because they imply a determination of the relative financial needs of different household members. For a second adult in the household, typically a partner or a spouse, additions to the maximum benefit amount range from zero in Poland to 100 percent of the rate for heads of household in Denmark, Hungary, and Portugal. For children, the range is from zero in Hungary, Iceland, the Netherlands, Poland, and the United Kingdom to more than 70 percent in the Czech Republic, Finland, Sweden, and the United States.

Other design elements reviewed in table A5.1 are the presence of income disregards (a portion of the total earned income of the household or other assistance unit not taken into account when assessing income), the benefit withdrawal rate (the rate by which the amount of the benefit falls when household income increases), and some of the safety net benefits not included in the means test.

In most of the countries, social assistance benefits can complement (or top up) other incomes, whatever their source. Hence the relative generosity of countries' social assistance schemes cannot be assessed without considering the interaction of social assistance with other benefits and earnings from work. In several countries, recipients of unemployment benefits are explicitly excluded from receiving social assistance.

TABLE A5.1 **Social Assistance Benefits, Selected OECD Countries, 2005**

Country	Determination of benefit level[a]	Categorical eligibility criteria	Maximum amount (% of average wage)					Generosity of other last resort benefits	Design parameters of means test			Possible to top up unemployment benefits?
			Head of household	Spouse or partner	Children eligible for additional payments	Per child	Other last resort benefits received		Income disregards	Benefit withdrawal rate	Benefits excluded from means test	
Austria	Nat'l average		15	7		4	Rent		None	100	Family	Yes
Belgium	Nat'l rates		20	7	Depends on age & number	4–9	Rent		310 net income per year w/ children, 250 w/o children	100	Family	Rare
Canada (Ontario)[b]	Regionally determined		16	12	Depends on age & number	4–5	Rent		Depends on family size	75	Increases in nat'l child benefit	
Czech Republic[c]	Nat'l rates		23	16	Depends on age & number	13–17	Dependents	16			None	
Denmark	Nat'l rates	Age > 25	32	32	1st child	10	Rent		DKr 25,896 if part of employment scheme	100		No
		Age < 25	21									
Finland	Nat'l rates	Age > 25	14	10	Depends on age & number	7–10	Rent, health care, work-related expenses		20% of net earnings (max. 1,800)	100	None	Yes
France[d]	Nat'l rates	Age > 25	17	8	Of a single parent	8			On 100% of earnings for 6 months, then 50% for 9 months	100	Specific family & housing benefits	
					1st child of a couple	5						
					2nd child of a couple	5						
					Add'l child of a couple	7						
Hungary	Nat'l guidelines	Unemployed, & benefits exhausted, age > 18	11	11					None	100	None	No

(continued)

TABLE A5.1 (continued)

Country	Determination of benefit level[a]	Categorical eligibility criteria	Maximum amount (% of average wage)					Generosity of other last resort benefits	Income disregards	Benefit withdrawal rate	Benefits excluded from means test	Possible to top up unemployment benefits?
			Head of house-hold	Spouse or part-ner	Children eligible for additional payments	Per child	Other last resort benefits received					
Iceland (Reykjavik)	Regionally determined	Age > 17	34	21			Unemployed, age 18–24, living w/ parents; Funeral costs, dental bills, and so on	17	None	100	Child support, family & rent benefits	Rare
Ireland	Nat'l guidelines		27	18		3	Adult dependent; Rent/mortgage interest payments	18		100	Family	
Japan (Osaka, Tokyo)[c]	Regionally determined	Depends on age of family members	20	11	Depends on age & number	6	Medical, long-term care, occupational, education, maternity aid, funeral costs		Net earnings of at least ¥100,080 (up to ¥398,280 for those earning more)	100		Yes
Korea, Rep. of	Nat'l rates		14	10	Depends on number	8–9	Housing costs; Medical care, education, childbirth, funeral costs, housing costs, & self-support benefits	3	30% of income earned under specific programs	100	Single parent	No
Luxembourg	Nat'l rates	Age > 25	30	15		3	Supplementary adult (not part of family), allowance	9	30% of payment rate	100	Family	
Netherlands	Nat'l rates	Age > 22	25	11			Supplement for single parents	7	None	100	Family & housing	

(continued)

TABLE A5.1 **(continued)**

Country	Determination of benefit level[a]	Categorical eligibility criteria	Maximum amount (% of average wage)					Generosity of other last resort benefits	Design parameters of means test			Possible to top up unemployment benefits?
			Head of household	Spouse or partner	Children eligible for additional payments	Per child	Other last resort benefits received		Income disregards	Benefit withdrawal rate	Benefits excluded from means test	
Norway (Trondheim)	Regionally determined		13	8	Depends on age	2–6	Housing benefit depending on family situation	13–29	None	100	Family	
							Supplement for heating expenses & family benefit supplement in December					
Poland	Nat'l rates, social worker discretion for periodic assistance	Permanent benefit	19	0		0	Periodic assistance, temporary benefit depending on family situation		None	100		Rare
Portugal	Nat'l rates	Age > 17	15	15		7	Adult	10	Upon taking up employment 50% of earnings for 1 year	100	Family & housing	
Slovak Republic	Nat'l rates		8	6	1st child only + addition if > 4 children	5–12	Health care, housing, protective & activation allowances		25% of net income	100	Family	Yes
Spain (Madrid)	Regionally determined	Age > 24	23	4		4	4th dependent person in household	3	None	100	Family	Rare
Sweden	Nat'l guidelines, social worker discretion for supplements		13	8	Depends on age & number	6–10	Medical costs, transport, child care		None	100	None	Rare
							Housing costs					

(continued)

TABLE A5.1 (continued)

			Maximum amount (% of average wage)						Design parameters of means test			
Country	Determination of benefit level[a]	Categorical eligibility criteria	Head of household	Spouse or partner	Children eligible for additional payments	Per child	Other last resort benefits received	Generosity of other last resort benefits	Income disregards	Benefit withdrawal rate	Benefits excluded from means test	Possible to top up unemployment benefits?
Switzerland (Zurich)	Nat'l guidelines, social worker discretion for supplements		16	9		5	Supplement from 3rd person aged>16	5		100		
United Kingdom	Nat'l rates, personal amount + family premium	Age > 24 or single parent; Unmarried; age 19–24	10; 8	6	1st child of single parent,	9	Housing, basic medical costs, child care; Family premium	3	£260 for single person, £520 for a couple, £1,040 for single parent	100	Housing, council tax & family	Yes
United States[e]	Nat'l rates		5	5		4	Rent		Occasional income up to US$120	100	Earned income tax credit	

SOURCE: OECD 2007.

NOTE: All amounts are shown on an annualized basis.

a. "National rates" indicates that rates are uniform throughout the country. "National guidelines" means that national rates are recommended without being strictly enforced, in which case these guidelines are adopted for the purpose of the comparison. Where there is regional variation in payment rates, two approaches may be followed when calculating benefit amounts: the national average is known and used or the comparison relates to one particular representative region, in which case the entry is "regionally determined."

b. Basic allowance plus housing allowance.

c. The benefit is made up of two parts: an individual amount depending on the age of the child (and sometimes the parent or guardian) and a household amount that depends on the size of the household.

d. The benefit is also available for people under 25 with dependent children.

e. Amounts shown are for food stamps only.

## CHAPTER 6

Using Monitoring and Evaluation to Improve Programs

KEY MESSAGES

Monitoring and evaluation (M&E) systems are the hallmark of good public management. Yet such systems are still rarely used for safety net programs in the developing world. However, a new wave of results-oriented programs, such as conditional cash transfer (CCT) programs in Latin America and the Caribbean and workfare programs in Argentina and Ethiopia, have developed and used integrated M&E systems, which in turn have generated robust evidence that the programs are well implemented and are achieving their intended results. These programs demonstrate that strong monitoring systems support credible program evaluations and that both provide feedback for improvements in productivity, effectiveness, and impact.

A monitoring system is an essential management tool that regularly supplies information about how well a program is working so that program managers can take action to improve the program's implementation. Monitoring is a continuous process that takes place throughout a program's life and should be an integral component of any program. A good monitoring system is comprehensive, actively used, and adapted to the country and program context. Effective monitoring systems require a strategic focus and political support more than they require costly investments in information technology. They require adequate skills, management attention, and funding and take time to develop and mature.

Program evaluation refers to an external assessment of program effectiveness that uses specialized methods to ascertain whether a program meets some standards, estimate its net results or impact, and/or identify whether the benefits the program generates outweigh its costs to society. The most frequently used types of evaluation in safety net programs are process evaluation, assessment of targeting accuracy, and impact evaluation.

The value added of program evaluation is substantial, but until recently, evaluations of safety net programs have been relatively scarce in developing countries. During the last 10 years, at least minimal assessments of targeting accuracy have become increasingly available, and assessments of program impacts have become frequent for CCT and workfare programs, although they are still rare for other types of programs.

6.1 The Value of Good Monitoring and Evaluation

Program monitoring matters because it helps managers to adjust program implementation. Colombia's Familias en Acción CCT program provides an illustration. Its monitoring system uses sample-based site monitoring or spot checks. Every six months, the program undertakes interviews in 20 municipalities using questionnaires for a sample of participants, program officials, and local government officials covering 400 indicators of various aspects of the program, including enrollment processes, verification of compliance with conditions, payment systems, appeals, and quality of the health education component. The results indicate which aspects of the program are working well; how much program management varies across locations; and where changes in procedures, training, staffing, and/or other inputs are needed. For example, the monitoring revealed problems with long lines for payment, including people waiting outdoors in the rain; consequently, the program worked with banks to find various ways to address the issue. The monitoring showed that some children were not being served continuously, but experienced a gap between the preschool and school portions of the program because of the dates of their birthdays relative to the school year; as a result, the program extended the age limit for the preschool portion to ensure continuous coverage. Also, the monitoring found and the program dealt with a number of areas where staff needed more training for efficient program implementation. Without a monitoring system, financiers, policy makers, and the public will not know if a program is operating effectively and efficiently, and public funds with high opportunity costs may go to waste.

Evaluation complements the monitoring system. There are three main reasons for evaluating a safety net program: to improve the program, to inform stakeholders about the program's performance, and to draw lessons for other programs. In general, programs are evaluated in response to a request for information from management or from the supervising authority, for example, a ministry or parliament; as part of a government-wide, results-based management agenda; or to respond to a public concern, for instance, an accusation of corruption or poor management.

During the last decade, safety net programs, especially CCT programs, have been at the forefront of a new evaluation culture. Of 36 CCT programs active in 2007, 29 have either conducted or have plans to conduct impact evaluations with credible counterfactuals (World Bank forthcoming). This is a far greater percentage of programs than have normally undertaken evaluations. Moreover, in several countries the evaluations have been neither simple nor one-time undertakings: dozens have looked at various aspects of Brazil's and Mexico's CCT programs.

The new evaluations have been important in making the case for individual programs and for safety nets being part of social policy. In Colombia, Jamaica, and Mexico, for example, CCT programs have continued across changes in government and as flagship programs, something relatively rare in a region where social programs tend to rise and fall with individual chief executives or ministers. The evaluations of CCT programs in Brazil and Mexico helped spur interest in such programs elsewhere. When they were reinforced by positive evaluations from Colombia, Jamaica, and Nicaragua, the stage was set for many countries to think more about transfer policies and especially CCT programs. Indeed, the programs' success captured the attention of policy makers in the developed world as well, to the extent that Mayor Michael Bloomberg of New York has financed a pilot CCT (NYC Opportunity) since 2006, and the United Kingdom began a similar program, Opportunity Revolution, in early 2008. Evaluations of social pension programs in Bolivia, Brazil, and South Africa and of public works programs in Argentina, Bolivia, and India have provided evidence about other types of programs that strengthen the case that safety nets are beneficial.

Beyond securing budgets for the programs, the evaluations of CCT programs have been important in refining some countries' programs. Evaluations in 2000 showed, for example, that in Mexico, anemia was not declining among PROGRESA (now known as Oportunidades) program beneficiaries, as expected (Behrman and Hoddinott 2000). This led to a series of investigations and the discovery that the fortification of the food supplement provided was such that the bio-availability of iron was less than intended. Moreover, family members tended to share the supplement, and thus the targeted children received less than the intended amount. As a result, the supplement was reformulated and the program's nutrition education component was strengthened (Neufeld 2006). In Jamaica, a 2007 evaluation revealed that the increase in secondary school enrollment promoted by the PATH CCT initiative was disappointing (Levy and Ohls 2007), and the government that took office shortly thereafter decided to raise the pertinent benefits and differentiate them by grade and gender.

The demonstration effect of these evaluations has been important. Mexico paved the way for evaluations of CCT programs, and other countries have emulated its lead. Evaluations have also spread to other types of programs. The 2004 Mexican Social Development Law requires the evaluation of all new programs and established the National Council for the Evaluation of Social Development Policy. The separate Transparency Law mandates that the results be made public. External evaluations are now done, and the summaries of the results are supplied to program managers, who must inform Congress each year what they are doing in response to the evaluations (Hernandez 2006). Mexico's Ministry of Social Development, which is responsible for Oportunidades and many other programs, has adopted a system of results-based monitoring. It plans to conduct evaluations of five national programs a year and to have installed such a system in half of its subnational agencies within six years (Rubio 2007). Colombia has also been moving to a similarly systematic evaluation culture (Guerrero 1999; McKay 2007).

Despite the value of M&E, effective M&E systems have been rare in the field of safety nets until the recent explosion of evaluations of CCT programs. Often a vicious cycle arises whereby when programs are small and/or have low administrative budgets, building the systems needed for good M&E is difficult, but without good M&E, programs may perform badly, or if they perform well, they are unable to demonstrate this to their funders and thus may not garner support for improvements or expansion. By contrast, programs that have good M&E may perform better as a result and establish their case for funds more clearly. We hope that this chapter, aimed at program managers and financiers, will help expand an M&E culture to many safety net programs in the developing world.

6.2 Distinct, but Complementary, Tools

Monitoring and evaluation are distinct tools used to assess whether programs are on track and are achieving their intended results. Table 6.1 summarizes the key differences between monitoring and evaluation.

Monitoring provides information on how much money is spent, how many beneficiaries the program is reaching, and how efficiently the program is serving them. The monitoring information consists of indicators that are compared with targets to assess whether the program is on track. Managers act upon this information to correct and

TABLE 6.1 **Key Differences between Monitoring and Evaluation**

Item	Monitoring	Evaluation
Frequency	Is a continuous, routine activity that should be an integral component of any program	Is an infrequent undertaking
Coverage	Covers most programs	Covers a few programs
Depth of information	Identifies whether a program is being implemented as expected or whether the outcomes of the program show progress or not	Identifies the change in outcomes resulting from a program or whether the program's benefits are accruing to its intended target group
Cost	Involves low annual costs	Involves high costs for each study
Utility	Aims at continuous program improvement and accountability	Provides information for major decisions such as starting, ceasing, expanding, or reducing a program

SOURCE: Burt and Hatry 2005.

improve the program. Unlike monitoring, program evaluations are often one-time efforts directed at answering a few key questions about program implementation, targeting accuracy, and/or impact. An implementation or process evaluation investigates whether the program is operating as planned. An assessment of targeting accuracy asks whether the program is successful in reaching the poor. An impact evaluation looks at how the program affects key outcomes—for example, for a workfare program it would estimate how much participants' incomes have increased because of the program. As shown in table 6.1, the findings generated by program evaluations influence key decisions about the program's future. To preserve the objectivity of the assessment and because program evaluations require specialized skills, external consultants or firms typically undertake program evaluations.

Program monitoring and evaluation complement each other in two ways. First, evaluation provides answers to key questions that a monitoring system cannot address, such as what the program's impact is or whether it reaches the poor. While a good monitoring system may collect and track information on a program's key outcomes, it cannot determine whether a change in outcomes was entirely due to the program or to other factors. For example, coffee farmers covered by the Red de Protección Social (Social Protection Network) CCT program in Nicaragua lost 2 percent of their consumption (the value of everything they consumed in a month) between 2001 and 2003, despite receiving a generous benefit equivalent to roughly 30 percent of their consumption. The question was whether this loss was due to lower work effort on their part or to external income shocks. An impact evaluation (World Bank 2005m) showed that other coffee farmers, similar in all respects except for their participation in Red de Protección Social, had experienced a 31 percent drop in their consumption because of a severe coffee crisis that affected all of Central America in 2001–3. Program beneficiaries would have experienced a similar drop in consumption in the absence of the program. Only an impact evaluation, which uses specialized techniques to separate the program's influence on outcomes from that of other factors, can estimate the program's true impact. Similarly, a good monitoring system may provide a good description of program beneficiaries, but cannot determine how poor they are relative to nonbeneficiaries, as it does not collect information about the latter. Only an assessment of targeting accuracy based on a representative household survey that gathers information on household welfare and program participation can provide a reliable answer.

The integration of M&E generates substantial synergies. For example, impact evaluation requires good monitoring data for three reasons. First, the monitoring system tells the evaluator whether the necessary conditions for a program to have an impact have been met. For a CCT program, such necessary conditions include that benefits are reaching the targeted beneficiaries and that the program was implemented as designed. The monitoring system helps answer these questions by confirming who the beneficiaries are, when they joined the program, what benefits were actually delivered, and beneficiaries' compliance with conditions. Second, without a good monitoring system that covers the key parameters of the program, an impact evaluation would measure the impact of a program without knowing what the intervention really was, making any replication or scaling up of that program difficult. Third, having a monitoring system in place that collects outcome information reduces the costs and increases the quality of the impact evaluation. For example, if the monitoring system routinely collects information about the nutritional outcomes of children in a program, the only additional information needed to estimate the program's nutritional impact is information about the nutritional outcomes of an equivalent control group.

Most safety net programs have many systems that collect and process information, such as a database of beneficiaries, a payment system; an appeals and complaints system; a quality control and/ or internal audit system; a management information system (MIS); and financial, accounting, and personnel systems (figure 6.1). A substantial part of this information is used at the level it is collected, that is, by frontline staff or a specialized department, and is rarely transmitted either up or down the program hierarchy. The monitoring system aggregates a subset of this information that captures critical aspects of how the program operates and how it affects beneficiaries and passes it on to upper management, which uses it as the basis for making strategic decisions about

FIGURE 6.1 **A Typical M&E System**

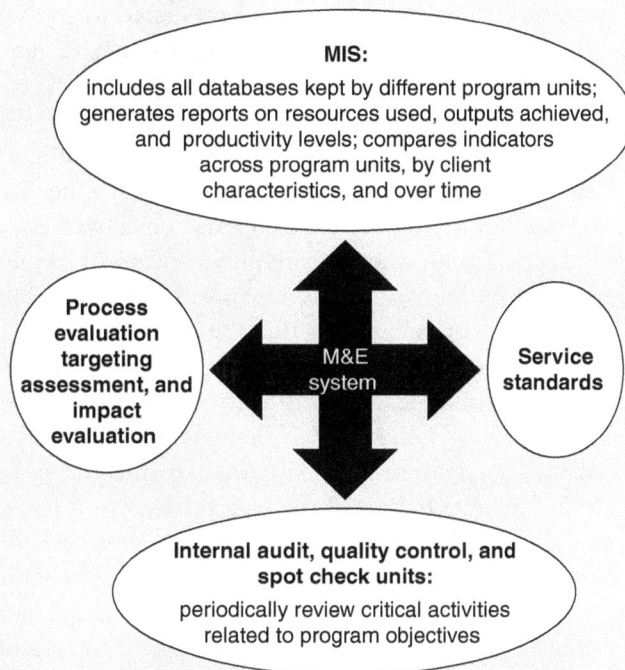

MIS:
includes all databases kept by different program units; generates reports on resources used, outputs achieved, and productivity levels; compares indicators across program units, by client characteristics, and over time

Process evaluation targeting assessment, and impact evaluation

M&E system

Service standards

Internal audit, quality control, and spot check units:
periodically review critical activities related to program objectives

SOURCE: Authors.

the program, and to external stakeholders (the finance or planning ministry, parliament, or the court of accounts—for example, the National Audit Office in the United Kingdom or the Government Accountability Office in the United States) for accountability reasons. In addition to the information the program routinely generates, both upper management and external stakeholders require information about how the program affects its beneficiaries, which is typically obtained from specialized data collection procedures—interviews, focus groups, satisfaction surveys, multitopic household surveys—used to evaluate different aspects of the program.

6.3 Development of an M&E System

The design of a good M&E system should start with a thorough understanding of what the program is trying to accomplish, that is, its goal or mission, and how it uses its inputs to generate its outputs and achieve its intended outcomes. Such an understanding shared by all key program stakeholders is essential to ensure that all the information required for decision making is collected, analyzed, and used and that extraneous information is not considered. This section discusses the development of an overall M&E system.

UNDERSTANDING THE PROGRAM'S OBJECTIVES

The first step in developing an M&E system is gaining a clear understanding of the program's objective and strategy, and the tool for this is developing the program's logical framework. The logical framework is a graphical representation of how the program is expected to help improve the condition of its beneficiaries alongside a results chain: the program uses certain inputs that are processed to generate outputs that influence certain outcomes among program participants. Inputs are resources a program uses to deliver cash or in-kind transfers, for example, employees and financial resources. Outputs are the amount of cash, goods, or social services a program delivers during the reporting period, such as the number of beneficiaries served or the number of workdays provided by a workfare program. Outcomes are events, conditions, or behaviors that indicate progress toward achievement of a program's mission and objectives. A common outcome indicator for a safety net program is the increase in beneficiaries' incomes. The main difference between outputs and outcomes is that program outputs are fully under the program's control, while outcomes are something that the program is contributing to, but that are also influenced by factors external to the program. Annex 6.1 provides some concrete examples of information and indicators to be collected for different types of safety net programs. The logical framework will identify other external factors that determine these outcomes and the risks that may impede achievement of these outcomes.

We illustrate the use of the logical framework for the development of an M&E plan using Ethiopia's Productive Safety Net Program (PSNP) as an example.[1] The program finances public works for able-bodied individuals living in food-insecure districts and cash transfers for poor households living in those districts unable to work. The public works component, in turn, creates community assets to improve the livelihoods of the poor. A review of the program documents reveals the logical hierarchy of its objectives, from program outputs to intermediate and final outcomes, as illustrated in figure 6.2.

FIGURE 6.2 **Logical Framework for Ethiopia's Productive Safety Net Program**

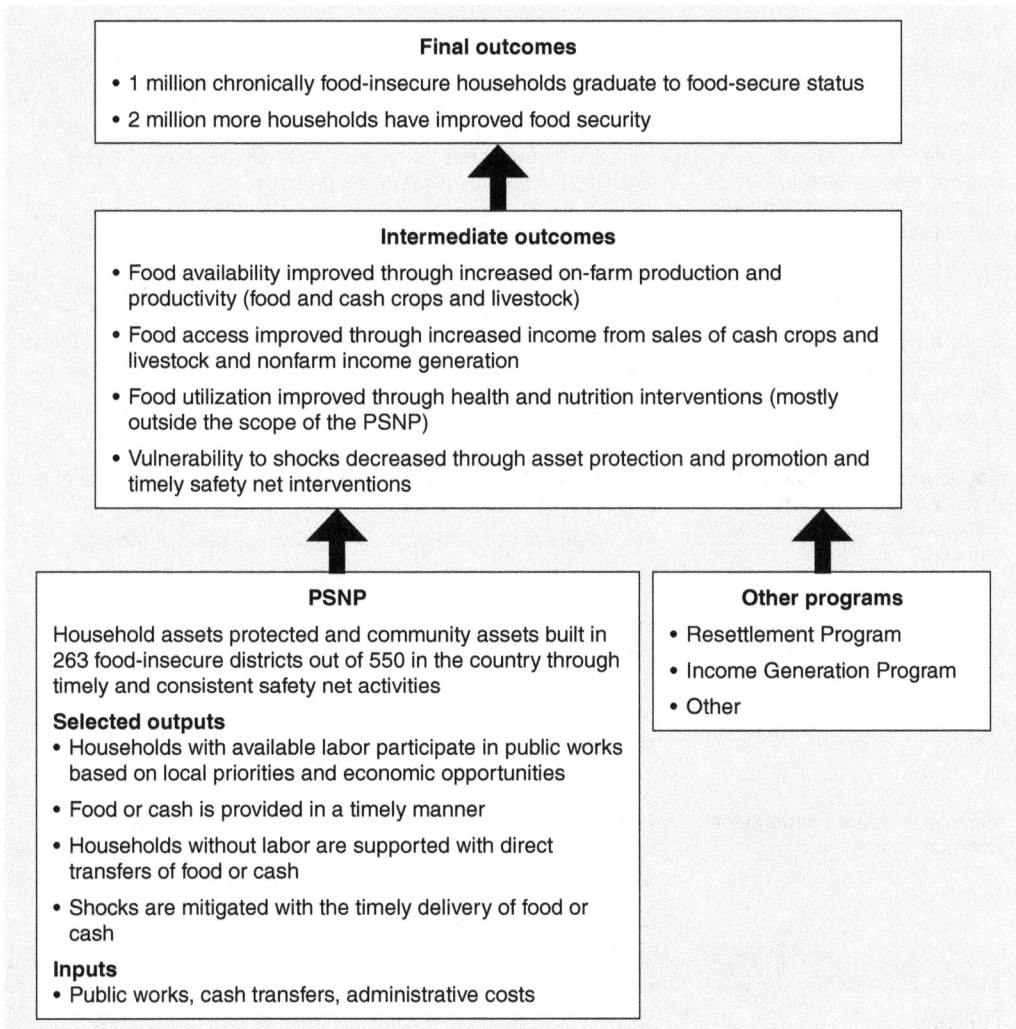

Final outcomes
- 1 million chronically food-insecure households graduate to food-secure status
- 2 million more households have improved food security

Intermediate outcomes
- Food availability improved through increased on-farm production and productivity (food and cash crops and livestock)
- Food access improved through increased income from sales of cash crops and livestock and nonfarm income generation
- Food utilization improved through health and nutrition interventions (mostly outside the scope of the PSNP)
- Vulnerability to shocks decreased through asset protection and promotion and timely safety net interventions

PSNP

Household assets protected and community assets built in 263 food-insecure districts out of 550 in the country through timely and consistent safety net activities

Selected outputs
- Households with available labor participate in public works based on local priorities and economic opportunities
- Food or cash is provided in a timely manner
- Households without labor are supported with direct transfers of food or cash
- Shocks are mitigated with the timely delivery of food or cash

Inputs
- Public works, cash transfers, administrative costs

Other programs
- Resettlement Program
- Income Generation Program
- Other

SOURCE: Food Security Coordination Bureau 2004.

However, M&E planning requires a level of detail well beyond the summary form of figure 6.2. Ethiopia's Food Security Coordination Bureau further elaborated the presentation of the PSNP's logical framework, particularly at the output, outcome, and impact levels as shown in table 6.2.

The program logical framework should also specify the main assumptions and risks that may affect the program, and the realization of these assumptions and risk needs to be monitored as well, because the program's success is based on the accuracy of certain assumptions and the absence of certain risks. For the PSNP, the key assumptions were as follows:

- Infrastructure and services, such as health, education, and roads, provided by the government but not by means of the PSNP will be supplied to rural communities at sufficient levels to adequately support the food-security status of households living within the communities.

TABLE 6.2 **Logical Framework and Selected Output and Outcome Indicators for Ethiopia's PSNP**

Objective	Indicator
Impact	
1 million chronically food-insecure households and 2 million vulnerable households attain food security within three to five years	• Percentage of households with no food gap, that is, they have sufficient food to meet their needs for all 12 months of the year, including support provided by the program
	• Percentage of households in need of food assistance over a three-year moving average
Outcomes	
Chronically food-insecure households have ensured food consumption during the program period[a]	• Percentage of program beneficiaries who report 12 months of food access from all sources including the program
	• Average number of months of household food shortages covered by the program
Household assets protected (households' short-term vulnerability to shocks reduced)	• Percentage of the average change in asset levels of chronically food-insecure households
	• Percentage of households reporting distress sales of assets
	• Percentage of households reporting consumption of seed stocks
Community assets used productively and managed in a sustainable manner	• Percentage of households reporting satisfaction or direct benefits from the community assets developed
	• Percentage of households regularly using three or more community assets developed by the program
	• Percentage of public works for which an ongoing management mechanism has been established
Markets stimulated through the shift from food to cash	• Percentage change in the number of traders/retailers in local markets
	• Percentage change in the volume of grain trade
	• Diversity of goods available in local markets
Outputs	
Public works	
Appropriate payments (food and/or cash) delivered to targeted beneficiaries in a timely and predictable manner	• Percentage of participants receiving food and/or cash resources per month versus the planned number supposed to receive food and/or cash
	• Percentage of food and/or cash delivered per month versus the amount that was planned to have been delivered
	• Percentage of districts completing 70% of distributions by end July

- PSNP staff will have appropriate capacities, materials, and financial support to carry out the program's activities in a timely and effective manner.
- Graduation from the program for most households during its three- to five-year time frame assumes an absence of extraordinary food crises. A severe crisis would slow the progress of many households toward food security.

Objective	Indicator
Targeting undertaken according to established procedures	Percentage of community members who understand targeting criteria
Community assets	
Appropriate and good quality public works constructed	• Number of public works constructed, including kilometers of roads constructed or maintained per targeted district • Number of structures constructed per targeted district (health posts, classrooms, grain stores, market structures, latrines) • Percentage of public works that conform to established standards
Soil conservation measures promoted and/or installed; degraded areas rehabilitated	• Hectares of degraded cropland and rangeland rehabilitated • Hectares covered by soil and water conservation measures • Number of tree seedlings planted • Number of communities participating in training and/or environmental rehabilitation
Small-scale irrigation and water harvesting developed, improved, or established	• Hectares of agricultural and pasture land reclaimed per targeted district • Number of irrigation and water harvesting schemes developed per district • Amount of land cultivated by small-scale irrigation
HIV/AIDS awareness campaign	Number of households receiving HIV/AIDS awareness training
Management systems for community assets established	• Percentage of communities with guidelines or bylaws developed for the management and protection of community assets • Number of visits to sites by a technical task force team per district per year • Percentage of local, district, and regional monitoring reports on actual versus planned activities delivered on time • Percentage of districts where the M&E plan is fully understood and implemented
Direct support	
Appropriate food and/or cash assistance provided accurately to targeted beneficiaries in a timely manner	• Percentage of participants receiving food and/or cash resources per month versus the planned number supposed to receive food and/or cash • Percentage of food and/or cash delivered per month versus the amount that was planned to have been delivered • Percentage of districts completing 70% of distributions by end July

SOURCE: Food Security Coordination Bureau 2004.

a. Disaggregated by male- and female-headed households and by direct support versus public works beneficiaries.

• Government decentralization will continue, and staff positions at all relevant administrative levels will be filled with capable people who will remain at their posts.

At the same time, the success of the PSNP may be threatened by certain risks, such as environmental impacts resulting from public works or negative market effects resulting from food distribution. These risks should also be monitored.

DEVELOPING THE M&E PLAN

Typically, the development of an M&E system requires drawing up an M&E plan, testing and fine-tuning the proposed system, and having internal or external experts undertake periodic reviews. The program's management can develop an M&E plan based on the logical framework. The plan will identify the information needs of the main stakeholders, the indicators that will be tracked to respond to their needs, the methods for analyzing the data, and the use made of the results and by whom. During this process, management will identify what information is available internally from the MIS, spot checks, and the like, and what information needs to be generated by means of special data collection and/ or analysis techniques such as specialized evaluations.

The outcome of this process is a written document, the M&E plan. The plan summarizes the agreements reached among program staff and key stakeholders and describes succinctly how the activities will be carried out. The M&E plan should include a section describing the institutional setup of the M&E system, the composition of the M&E unit, the unit's overall tasks, and the unit's upward and downward links and links with other stakeholders, and a diagram showing the types of information that will be collected and to whom it will be provided. A good plan will cover the following aspects:

- The information needs of each stakeholder about the program's key outcomes and outputs
- A few key indicators for each objective that should follow the logical chain of service provision, utilization, coverage, impact, and efficiency
- The information sources and data collection tools for each indicator, including frequency of collection, agency responsible, sampling system, and data storage and documentation system along with who needs the data and how they will be used
- The data analysis plan describing how the data will be analyzed; how often; by whom; how the results will be presented, discussed, and used for internal program decision making; and what information will be shared with external groups
- The resources that need to be dedicated to M&E, such as the staffing of an M&E unit and the training needs required for the personnel involved in collecting, reporting, and analyzing the data

A good M&E plan is the result of a participatory process that involves various program stakeholders, including experienced program staff; experts from the institutions that finance, regulate, and supervise the program; donors; nongovernmental organizations active in the field; and M&E experts. A process commonly used for achieving a mutual understanding among these parties is known as participatory planning.

The program team will invite these stakeholders to a planning workshop to produce the M&E plan. To this end they work, ideally under the guidance of a facilitator who understands M&E concepts, to develop the various elements of the plan as already described. The stakeholders' input and collaboration is important to the success of the M&E plan, measured by whether managers and stakeholders use the information the M&E system provides to improve the program's operations. Not involving all key users of information will result in an M&E system that will not provide feedback on some aspects of the program, that may allow potential issues in implementing the program to go undetected, and/

or that may not produce the hard evidence needed to mitigate any negative perceptions about the program.

Most experts recommend developing the M&E function from the beginning of the program. This means providing resources for an M&E unit; applying an M&E lens to program operations to ensure that the information generated by different departments and units feeds into the M&E system seamlessly and continuously; including in the job description of relevant program staff the collection, processing, and reporting of information related to their functions; and training this staff. Having an M&E system operating from the outset has a number of advantages, including the collection of baseline indicators on the characteristics of beneficiaries before the intervention, especially on those intermediate or final outcomes indicators that the program is trying to improve, and ensures a complete time series of data on critical indicators to track program performance.

Most M&E systems are, however, built incrementally. Some programs, such as Brazil's Bolsa Familia (Family Grant) program, started with an inventory of the information collected by its precursor programs and then improved or expanded the system. Programs that did not implement an M&E system from the beginning may feel the need or pressure from stakeholders to introduce one later. Whenever management or stakeholders feel they need to do this, they will use the same principals as described in this chapter; however, failure to develop the M&E plan at the beginning of the program will result in the absence of baseline information, which is critical for estimating the program's impact.

COLLECTING M&E DATA

A results-oriented M&E system requires a combination of data collection techniques. Administrative data can provide most of the input, process, and output data, as well as performance and efficiency information. Information about program outcomes and coverage requires survey data. Information on client and staff perceptions and activities undertaken by the program may require the use of rapid appraisal methods or participatory techniques. In designing the M&E system, the team should undertake an inventory of available databases (administrative data) and surveys (for instance, household surveys and public expenditure tracking surveys) and identify what indicators are readily available or could easily be estimated from these sources and where additional investments in data collection are required.

Administrative Records

Most safety net programs routinely collect and process administrative data, especially on inputs, processes, and outputs. Human resource departments manage information about program staff and accounting, and financial departments track financial flows including administrative costs and the value of program benefits. Other systems track information about the different activities performed by the program, such as eligibility determination, recertification, payments made, and verification of compliance with program rules (for both staff and clients).

Many safety net programs do not make maximum use of administrative records, which are by far the most available source of data for monitoring. Most programs do not fully exploit such data to monitor program performance and limit its use to tracking trends in inputs and outputs. Some programs do not disclose such information, and some do not collect such information to avoid accountability issues. Many programs do not invest in developing a well-conceptualized monitoring system or in the necessary infrastructure (dedicated staff, procedures, and information technology) and operate systems that may gather information lacking in relevance and validity.

Whenever possible, monitoring indicators should be derived from administrative data generated by the program, as this information has a comparatively low marginal cost. Such data are cheap whenever such records exist or can be readily modified. They are also more likely to be used by program personnel as they are familiar with the data collection system and with the procedures for transforming raw data into indicators.

Such information can be combined to generate performance indicators to monitor the efficiency or productivity of different program units and can be estimated by combining output and input information or by comparing process indicators over time or against a benchmark. Examples of such indicators are the number of beneficiaries served per program staff member, the level of administrative costs for every US$1,000 transferred, and the number of applications processed in less than a week.

The use of administrative data has several general advantages and disadvantages (table 6.3). Agency records usually do not provide sufficient outcome data, thus tracking outcome information often requires special data collection efforts. This is why identifying agency records that provide outcome information is important. For instance, CCT programs collect information about beneficiaries' compliance with conditions from service providers, such as the percentage of infants immunized and the share of school-age children with adequate attendance records or good grades.

Checking the quality of administrative data is good practice, as such data often will be incomplete, old, or unreliable. Some form of quality control is required to assess if the data cover all relevant units such as households and that information is entered accurately.

Formulating clear instructions and definitions of what data need to be collected and how the indicators should be computed is also good practice. The information generated by the administrative system is not always the information managers need, and thus data collection systems may need to be upgraded. Romania's Guaranteed Minimum Income Program, for instance, monitors the number of transactions that take place in a given

TABLE 6.3 **Advantages and Disadvantages of Using Administrative Data to Monitor and Evaluate Programs**

Advantages	Disadvantages
• Provide detailed information about clients, program outputs (transfers or services), and outcomes	• Quality of administrative data and their potential utility vary considerably
• Provide longitudinal data on beneficiaries for some programs	• Regular and systematic checking for data quality is seldom performed
• Generate data at low cost for multiple program years	• Standardized data collection procedures may not be followed across program sites
• Accommodate changes and additions to data more readily than, say, a household survey	• Privacy and permission issues may delay data access and transfer

SOURCE: Heinrich 2004.

period, but not the number of beneficiaries (more than one transaction per month for a beneficiary is a possibility) (Pop, Florescu, and Tesliuc forthcoming). Thompson (2004) reports a similar issue in relation to the Russian Federation's Child Allowance Program.

Beneficiary Surveys and Citizen Report Cards

Beneficiary surveys and citizen report cards are relatively simple tools used to obtain timely feedback from clients. Beneficiary or client satisfaction surveys assess a program's performance based on client experience with it. Such surveys are an important source of information about service quality, outcomes, client constraints in accessing public services, and responsiveness of government officials. For instance, clients can rate specific service quality characteristics, such as hours of operation, waiting times, and helpfulness of personnel. The survey can also collect information about intermediate outcomes, such as actions beneficiaries have taken because of the program and overall satisfaction. Such surveys need to be specific in relation to the constraints clients face in using the program as well as in asking for suggestions for improving services. Collecting information on a few key client characteristics (income, employment, housing, gender, age group, and the like) to disaggregate the results by group is common practice. Questionnaires are typically tailored to a program's specific organizational setup. The program M&E unit designs the terms of reference for the survey and subcontracts the work to a survey firm.

Nongovernmental organizations and think tanks in several countries have made use of citizen report cards. Similar to service delivery surveys, they have also investigated the extent of corruption encountered by ordinary citizens. A notable feature has been the widespread publication of the findings.

Representative Household Surveys

A survey of program beneficiaries cannot reveal whether a program covers its target group adequately or whether the benefits are adequately targeted toward the poor. To answer such questions, representative household surveys are needed. Two of the most common surveys found in developing countries are multitopic household surveys and core welfare indicator questionnaires.

Representative household surveys have three key advantages: (1) they generate estimates that are representative of a particular population of interest, for instance, the beneficiaries of a given program or a program's target group, with known precision; (2) they cost significantly less than a census of that population; and (3) they provide data about a wide range of client and program characteristics.

For analyzing the effectiveness of safety net interventions, these surveys should collect information about program participation, household conditions that determine eligibility for the program, and outcomes that the program seeks to influence. In some cases, such surveys will not adequately capture information about programs with low coverage. To obtain representative estimates about such programs, oversampling of the program target group is necessary.

Household surveys can be used to analyze individual programs by revealing the characteristics of program beneficiaries; the incidence of program benefits across income distribution or other groups; and the extent of take-up, for example, if it is incomplete and why. Such surveys often collect information on participation in a number of safety net programs, generating economies of scale in data collection. In such cases, the surveys can be used to investigate the incidence, coverage, and benefit adequacy of multiple safety net programs; to estimate and profile population groups that are not covered by safety nets; and to determine those groups that benefit from multiple programs.

Impact Evaluation Surveys

Estimating a program's impact on beneficiaries often requires a special household survey that will differ from the other surveys described in a few respects. First, an impact evaluation survey will cover a representative sample of program beneficiaries—the treatment group—as well as a control group that ideally is similar in all respects to the treatment group except that its members are not program beneficiaries. Unlike representative household surveys, impact evaluation surveys are not representative of the total population. Second, impact evaluation surveys collect information about a program's expected outcomes, its possible negative effects such as disincentives to work, and a fair number of household and individual characteristics to verify that the treatment and control groups are indeed similar in all respects. Third, the sample size of these surveys should be large enough to detect the minimum expected change in program outcomes that would indicate to policy makers that a program was successful. Finally, the credibility of the evaluation increases when data are collected via panel surveys, which track beneficiaries at baseline time, that is, before program implementation, and then follow up with them over time. The follow-up surveys should be spaced to provide time for the program to have had an impact on its beneficiaries.

As data collection is the mostly costly aspect of an impact evaluation, whenever possible, collecting information on a wide range of outcomes and outputs improves the survey's cost-effectiveness. The marginal cost of adding a few questions on additional outputs will likely be small; however, when different outcomes refer to different subpopulations of beneficiaries, such as the nutritional versus the education impacts of a CCT program, there may be implications for sample size as well as for the length of the questionnaire, and thus the marginal costs will be higher.

Qualitative Techniques

Qualitative data collection techniques are often a useful complement to surveys and at times are the only method that can be used to provide answers to key questions about a program's operations and performance. The most widely used techniques are key informant interviews, direct observation, and focus group (or community group) discussions. Qualitative information is collected through intensive, often repeated, interviews with individuals that are typically more in-depth than precoded questionnaires and explore why and how things are done or why people think something or respond or behave in certain ways because of the program.

When the information required for decision making is somewhat technical and requires specialized knowledge, the quality of the informant is what matters and not the representativeness of the information. The key informant interview uses a series of open-ended questions posed to individuals who are selected because of their knowledge and experience in the topic of interest. Interviews are qualitative, in-depth, and semistructured and rely on interview guides that list topics or questions. This technique is especially important when an external program evaluation is undertaken. Interviews with key staff are the fastest and cheapest way to learn about a program.

Direct observation, also known as trained observer rating, is a technique that uses a detailed observation form to record what observers see and hear at a program site. The information may concern ongoing activities, processes, discussions, social interactions, and observable results. To generate comparable and reliable information, observers should be provided with a clear rating scale that sets out what level of performance should be associated with each rating level. This technique may be suited for quality control reviews investigating whether certain procedures are being implemented as intended. Russia used this technique to investigate whether the application process for means-tested cash programs was being undertaken as intended and whether different staff or different offices were implementing the program in the same way.

Questions about program operations and performance cannot always be precoded in questionnaires or derived from administrative data. When an M&E team is at an early stage of developing an understanding about how a program influences its clients and is formulating key questions about a program's logical framework, discussions with a particular group, referred to as a focus group, can be helpful. A focus group discussion is a facilitated discussion with 8 to 12 carefully selected participants with similar backgrounds, for example, beneficiaries or program staff. The facilitator uses a discussion guide and note takers record comments and observations. A community group interview is a variant of this technique whereby the discussion is open to all community members.

While qualitative techniques lack representativeness and precision, they offer a richer understanding than surveys alone of how a program operates as well as of causality (how and why clients react to the program). Such techniques can be used before the design and deployment of quantitative data collection techniques to help formulate key hypotheses or questions to be investigated through quantitative techniques or after to investigate extreme cases or responses in depth. The general recommendation is to use these techniques in combination—a process called triangulation—to validate answers generated by different data collection processes.

REVISITING THE PLAN AND THE M&E SYSTEM OVER TIME

Once the M&E plan has been completed and the sources of data have been identified, the next step is to pilot test the M&E system and make any necessary revisions to the data collection tools. During implementation of the M&E system, the written M&E plan is expanded into an operations guide that provides practical direction on how to use the M&E tools and methods that have been developed for a specific program. A critical element of this stage is ensuring that program staff and the M&E team have sufficient training to manage the M&E system. A trial run period will help adapt the M&E system to local realities and constraints.

Once an M&E system has been implemented, it should be fine-tuned periodically in response to changes in the environment in which the program operates, changes in the program's design, or following a review of the M&E system. For example, with time the characteristics of the program's clients may change, for instance, if a local industry such as mining suffers a decline and miners' households became poor and eligible for the safety net program. In such a case, both the program's design and the M&E system need to be adapted to better serve program clients. Also, over time managers can assess which indicators are useful, which are missing, and which are useless and need to be dropped. Periodic reviews of the M&E system would detect these changes and suggest what corrections are needed. Such reviews draw on information produced by ongoing monitoring systems, but are more comprehensive and in-depth.

Periodic reviews of an M&E system should address the following questions:

- Is the program's logical framework, that is, its cause and effect reasoning, still sound?

- Are the assumptions made at the program design stage still valid or have key conditions changed?

- Has program progress been as planned or have significant discrepancies—positive or negative—become apparent? Are outputs being produced? Is the program on schedule and within budget?

- Have important procurement or technical assistance issues not been resolved?

- How well does the program team work as a unit and with its partners and stakeholders?

- Is participation in the program as extensive as anticipated?

- Are actions being taken that will help ensure the sustainability of program benefits?

- Are performance data being collected as planned, that is, will the data that are needed to demonstrate program effectiveness and impact be available as the program comes to an end?

MATCHING THE M&E SYSTEM TO PROGRAM REALITIES

This subsection illustrates how to apply the general principles of an M&E system to different settings, from high to low capacity, and from a single program to programs operating in complicated, federal, and/or multi-institution settings, using three examples of programs with good M&E systems: Brazil's Bolsa Familia, Ethiopia's PSNP, and Mexico's Oportunidades. All three programs have a number of characteristics in common: they have implemented strong, results-oriented monitoring systems complemented by one or more elements of program evaluation (of processes, targeting, and impact). While all three programs are well known primarily because of their impact evaluations, their strong monitoring systems were an important element in running the programs well enough to deliver the impacts.

A number of conditions facilitate the development of an M&E system. Developing a system for programs operated by one national agency or ministry is easier than for programs operated jointly by a number of institutions. As an extension of this case, programs operating in federal environments are more complex: monitoring is needed in particular to ensure that implementation units pursue the objectives specified by the federal center, but such systems are harder to develop than for programs that involve a single agency. Programs operating in low-capacity environments typically face additional difficulties in relation to lower levels of skills, weaker MISs, lack of availability of information technology, or even lack of basic services such as electricity and telephones in frontline offices. The development of an M&E system is further facilitated by its supervisory bodies' demand for accountability and the presence or absence of a culture of M&E in the public sector in general.

Mexico's Oportunidades program has an excellent monitoring system that operates in a high-capacity environment. From the beginning, the program was designed with a monitoring system that would serve the multiple needs of its stakeholders (figure 6.3). An operational component informs frontline and mid-level managers whether planned tasks are fulfilled in terms of quantity, quality of service, and efficiency. A strategic, results-based monitoring component informs upper-level management and external stakeholders whether beneficiaries' outcomes are improving or not.

The information different stakeholders need is supplied by different data collection and reporting tools, including the MIS, the appeals and control system, social accountability systems, and beneficiary assessments. Since the early stages of program development, Oportunidades has had three structures in place to monitor its operations and results. The first structure, the system of monitoring and management indicators, extracts information from the MIS and from the providers of health and education services to track the number of beneficiaries and their composition, the beneficiaries' compliance with conditions, the payment of program grants, the intermediate outcome indicators in relation to education and health, and the management indicators that monitor different phases of the program.

FIGURE 6.3 **M&E Strategy of Oportunidades**

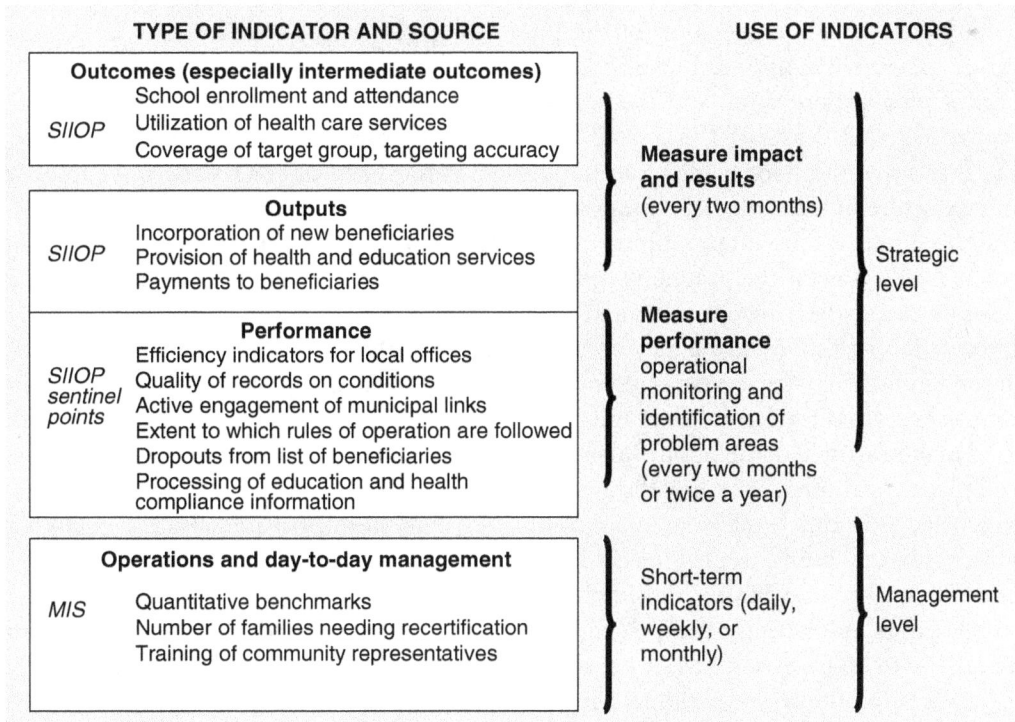

TYPE OF INDICATOR AND SOURCE	USE OF INDICATORS	
Outcomes (especially intermediate outcomes) School enrollment and attendance *SIIOP* Utilization of health care services Coverage of target group, targeting accuracy	**Measure impact and results** (every two months)	
Outputs Incorporation of new beneficiaries *SIIOP* Provision of health and education services Payments to beneficiaries		Strategic level
Performance Efficiency indicators for local offices *SIIOP sentinel points* Quality of records on conditions Active engagement of municipal links Extent to which rules of operation are followed Dropouts from list of beneficiaries Processing of education and health compliance information	**Measure performance** operational monitoring and identification of problem areas (every two months or twice a year)	
Operations and day-to-day management *MIS* Quantitative benchmarks Number of families needing recertification Training of community representatives	Short-term indicators (daily, weekly, or monthly)	Management level

SOURCE: Alvarez 2004.

NOTE: SIIOP = system of monitoring and management indicators.

The system of monitoring and management indicators has been in operation since 1998 and generates a set of 64 monitoring and management indicators every two months (see annex table A6.2.1 for selected indicators). The second structure, a survey of beneficiaries and program providers called sentinel points, has been implemented twice a year since 2000 and produces information on perceptions of service quality (see annex table A6.2.2). The third structure consists of regular assessments of program operations by external experts using the monitoring and management data. The public has access to all data and assessments on the program's Web site (www.oportunidades.gob.mx).

The example from Ethiopia exemplifies the difficulties of running an M&E system in a low-capacity, low-income country and the need for continuous adaptation and simplification. Ethiopia's PSNP, implemented in 2004 by the Food Security Coordination Bureau, offers another example of a program with a good M&E system. In 2004, a task force within the Food Security Coordination Bureau coordinated the development of an M&E plan for the newly created PSNP. The program monitoring system was designed to track progress for a range of inputs, activities, and outputs for accountability purposes as well as to allow prompt corrective action as bottlenecks were identified. The key indicators to be tracked were determined based on the program's logical framework. Government staff at the local level collect the monitoring data using standardized forms. The information is then compiled and summarized at the district, regional, and federal levels. Training was provided to federal and regional staff. At the local and district levels, the information is collected using paper and pencil and is then converted to electronic form at the regional level, processed, and transmitted to the Food Security Coordination Bureau. The system aimed for simplicity to account for the low capacity of the program's frontline units.

However, implementation of the monitoring plan encountered numerous logistical obstacles, with only 40 out of 232 districts reporting (with delays) during the first year of program operation and the remainder not reporting at all. The major stumbling blocks included the lack of local staff (25 percent of positions remained unfilled during the first year), the poor qualifications and high turnover of existing staff, and the poor infrastructure in some districts (for example, about 20 percent lacked electricity). To generate a minimum amount of monitoring data, a number of additional systems were put in place. First, to assess the program with respect to the number of beneficiaries and actual disbursements, the program instituted a sample-based emergency response system, where information was collected via telephone from around 80 districts on a twice-weekly basis. Second, four- to six-person rapid response teams were formed to perform spot checks (four times a year from the federal level and eight times per year from the regional level). Third, the Food Security Coordination Bureau instituted a system of roving audits to investigate compliance with financial rules, disbursements and payments, and appeals and complaints to provide more timely information on compliance than the normal annual auditing system. Finally, some 80 public works projects of the PSNP were reviewed twice a year to investigate both the quality of planning and implementation. In the meantime, the program further simplified its monitoring system though such steps as shortening the M&E manual from about 160 to 80 pages and invested more in training the staff involved in M&E activities.

The simplification of the M&E system and the development of a less ambitious emergency response system were appropriate responses to low capacity. Even though the formal monitoring system is now starting to show some improvement and provide more reliable data on basic program operations, the additional monitoring instruments have been kept in place, as they provide more in-depth and often more qualitative information on overall program performance.

The third example is the Bolsa Familia program, implemented by Brazil's Ministry for Social Development and the Fight against Hunger (MDS). The program developed a strong M&E system even though it had to confront two types of complications: multiple agencies coordinated the program (the MDS, the Ministry of Education, and the Ministry of Health) and the program was implemented through 5,564 municipalities (Lindert and others 2007; Vaitsman, Rodrigues, and Paes-Sousa 2006). The program's success was ensured by a combination of three factors: strong political support, gradual and ongoing drive to expand and improve the M&E system, and capacity to innovate.

From the beginning, the team that developed the system had to fight against a broader institutional culture within the government whereby the application and use of M&E tools was not widespread or mainstreamed as an integral part of public policy tools. However, the Bolsa Familia program was one of the major initiatives of President Luiz Inácio Lula da Silva's administration, and both the president and the minister for social development wanted to prove that the program was well implemented and improved its beneficiaries' welfare. To highlight the importance of M&E and ensure the presence of staff dedicated to this function, the MDS created the Secretariat for Evaluation and Information Management with the same hierarchical status as the other secretariats.

Most of the information required to monitor the program had to be obtained from other secretariats, ministries, and agencies, few of which operated nationally and most of which were local, such as schools and health centers. The solution endorsed by the M&E team was a pragmatic one: to build the system based on information available in the participating agencies, champion the use of a unique social identification number at the individual level, create a list of specifications and database of indicators, provide support for the suppliers of information (such as training and software), and simultaneously undertake a quality control function. Gradually the program has built up an impressive M&E system.

A major innovation in Bolsa Familia's M&E system was the introduction of performance-based incentives for municipalities, which played important roles in implementing various aspects of the program and in supplying information. Initially, the program faced challenges in relation to the timeliness and quality of the information received from municipalities, whose capacity varied substantially. To address this problem, the program developed an index of decentralized management that captures the quality of program implementation by each municipality. Based on their performance scores on the index, the MDS pays the municipalities a subsidy that covers some of their administrative costs for implementing the program, with higher subsidies provided for those municipalities that scored better on the index.

6.4 Monitoring

DETERMINING WHAT INFORMATION TO COLLECT

After developing the logical framework as described in the previous section, the next step is to define more precisely the indictors to use.

Define Indicators

Each category of information considered essential for decision making needs to be "translated" into an indicator. As indicated in table 6.4, indicators are numerical measurements of program inputs, processes, outputs, and outcomes typically expressed as levels (for example, the number of beneficiaries in the program as of a specific date), proportions (for instance, the percentage of beneficiaries paid on time), or ratios (such as the number of nutrition education sessions held per amount spent).

Good indicators should be valid (should measure the aspect of the program the decision maker is interested in) and reliable (conclusions based on the indicator should be the same when the indicator is measured by different people). Good indicators should also be sensitive enough to measure important changes in the situation being observed and timely (collecting and analyzing the data should be possible fairly quickly). Moreover, the process of generating the information should be cost-effective: the information gathered should be worth the time and money it costs to collect it and in line with local capabilities and resources. Effective monitoring systems start by building on information that already exists drawing on existing local data collection activities or working with indicators used for other similar programs.

For clarity, indicators should specify the reference population they refer to and the period they cover or the date when they are computed. Many programs use a template or indicator specification sheet similar to the one adapted from Brazil's Bolsa Familia program presented in table 6.4 to specify how the data will be collected, analyzed, and reported, namely, the formula for calculating the indicator, its expected (or threshold) value, the source of the information needed to compute the indicator, the frequency with which it will be calculated, the levels of disaggregation, and the main users and uses of the indicator.

A comprehensive monitoring system will track a battery of monitoring indicators capturing inputs, processes, outputs, intermediate and final outputs, and performance.

Input and Output Indicators. The bulk of inputs consists of the budget for transfers, which generally account for roughly 90 percent of program costs and are usually relatively easy to quantify at the program level using budget documents. However, the level of accuracy of the information depends on the institution that is implementing and managing the program. For example, programs run by donors and nongovernmental organizations may not be included in a government's budgetary processes; therefore information on them may be hard to access.

Staff time and other administrative resources are key to program delivery, but these inputs are much more difficult to quantify, as staff tend to work on multiple programs within an agency and programs may depend upon multiple agencies for their execution. Moreover, operational costs are often not broken down by the type of activities staff engage in, such as targeting or making payments. Thus managers often lack the basic information that would help them make decisions about improvements to administrative systems.

Output indicators track the number of beneficiaries and the transfers and other services provided to them. A good monitoring system should be able to document the number and types of beneficiaries reached and the services actually offered to them and compare the results with the program's intent.

TABLE 6.4 **Sample Indicator Specification Sheet Adapted from the Bolsa Família Program, Brazil**

Category	Indicator 1	Indicator 2	Indicator 3	Indicator 4
Name of indicator	• Coverage rate	• Average value of cash transfer	• Cash transferred by program as a whole	• Percentage of families that rose above poverty line
Description	• Percentage of families with a monthly per capita income of up to R\$100 that receive cash transfers from program in a particular location and during a particular reference period	• Average monthly value per family of cash transferred by program in a particular location and during a particular reference period	• Total cash transferred by program in a particular location and during a particular reference period	• Percentage of beneficiary families whose monthly per capita income at time of registration was > R\$50 and < R\$100 that rose above poverty line (per capita income of < R\$100 per month) as a result of cash transfer (in a particular location and during a particular reference period)
Type of indicator	• Intermediate outcome	• Output	• Output	• Outcome
Formula for calculation	• Number of families receiving Bolsa Família cash transfers divided by estimated number of families with a monthly per capita income of < R\$100 multiplied by 100	• Sum of cash transfers provided to families by program divided by number of families receiving program benefits	• Sum of cash transfers provided to families by program	• Number of beneficiary families whose monthly per capita income at time of registration was > R\$50 and < R\$100 that rose above poverty line as a result of program cash transfer divided by number of beneficiary families whose monthly per capita family income at the time of registration was > R\$50 and < R\$100 multiplied by 100[a]
Source of information	• Summary of beneficiary payrolls by municipality (National Secretariat for Citizenship Income and MDS) • Estimated number of poor families (Institute of Applied Economic Research and MDS)	• Beneficiary payroll (National Secretariat for Citizenship Income and MDS)	• Beneficiary payrolls by municipality (National Secretariat for Citizenship Income and MDS)	• Unified registry system for federal government's social programs (Caixa Econômica Federal, National Secretariat for Citizenship Income, and MDS)
Frequency	• Monthly	• Monthly	• Monthly	• Yearly

(continued)

TABLE 6.4 **(continued)**

Category	Indicator 1	Indicator 2	Indicator 3	Indicator 4
Possible level of disaggregation	• Brazil, major regions, states, districts, municipalities	• Brazil, major regions, states, districts, municipalities	• Brazil, major regions, states, districts, municipalities	• Brazil, major regions, states, districts, municipalities
Limitations	• Indicator is calculated using an estimate of the number of poor families, not a census	• Variations in data and existence of extreme values (far below or above average) may compromise indicator's ability to reflect reality • Indicator does not show exposure of each individual in the family to the benefit, as information about family size is not incorporated	• Not available	• Indicator is calculated based on self-reported income information • Methodology for calculating indicator assumes that income reported at time of registration remained static over the period and has only been modified by cash transfers, thus fluctuations in income that may occur over time are not incorporated • Interpretation of this indicator as a measurement of program impact warrants caution, as at the time of indicator calculation family income may be different from the income reported at time of registration
Interpretation	• Program coverage rate in 2001 was estimated at 58.4% of poor families with significant variation (ranging from 28.9% to 63.4%) between different areas of the country	• In March 2005, average monthly value of cash transfer received by each beneficiary family was R$65.56 for country as a whole, with amount varying between regions and states	• In March 2005, total cash transfers amounted to > R$430 million per month, with per month amount varying from < R$2 million to R$58 million depending on the state	• In March 2005, number of beneficiary families whose monthly per capita income at time of registration was > R$50 and < R$100 was 1.5 million, of whom 169,500 (11.2%) rose above the poverty line as a result of the benefit

SOURCE: MDS 2007.

a. Decree 5,749 of April 11, 2006, altered the values characterizing poverty and extreme poverty for families to R$120 per month and R$60 per month, respectively.

Monitoring input and output indicators guards against different forms of implementation failure—that is, situations where services are not provided as intended. The most common implementation failures are failure to provide any services, provision of partial services, provision of services of uneven quality, or provision of the wrong services. Factors that may lead to implementation failure include lack of accessibility to the program resulting from, for example, location of offices, office hours, and requirements or costs associated with applying to the program.

Outcome Indicators. Safety net programs are implemented to improve beneficiaries' consumption, incomes, wages, investment in human capital, or the like. To the extent possible, the monitoring system should measure these outcomes, as they provide critical information for both stakeholders and management.

Monitoring outcomes will indicate whether the social conditions the program is trying to address are being ameliorated, but will not actually reveal the net impact of the program, that is, the change in outcomes caused by the program. Measuring the impact of the program requires a comparison of outcomes of beneficiaries with and without the program, which is what impact evaluation, discussed later, does.

Nevertheless, monitoring outcome information is useful when program managers have strong reasons to believe that the provision of services by the program will have a substantial positive influence on the outcomes the program is seeking. This will happen when the influence of factors other than the program is small or insignificant. For instance, a workfare program that rehabilitates school infrastructure will directly influence the functionality and esthetics of the school. In the absence of a natural disaster that might damage the building, the outcomes can be safely attributed to the program.

While the program will generate most of the data required to monitor program performance in relation to inputs and outputs and capture it by means of its MIS, gathering information about program outcomes will often require additional data collection efforts, such as surveys of program beneficiaries. Exceptions include, for instance, a CCT program that routinely tracks information on growth monitoring or administers surveys to track the test scores of students in the program.

Table 6.5 presents guidelines for collecting outcome indicators. One difficult trade-off concerns the number of such indicators. The desire to keep data collection costs low

TABLE 6.5 **Guidelines for Collecting Outcome Indicators**

Good practice	Bad practice
• Collecting indicators for program beneficiaries	• Focusing on one or a few indicators that do not capture fully the goals of the program
• Developing indicators of preprogram to postprogram change whenever possible, but bearing in mind that change may not be due solely to the program	• Ignoring the possibility of corruptibility of indicators, which occurs when program staff has discretion in interpreting them
• Collecting information about participant satisfaction with the program	• Misinterpreting outcome indicators: changes in program outcomes are not necessarily due to the program

SOURCE: Rossi, Freeman, and Lipsey 1999.

may mean that the M&E system focuses on just a few outcome indicators, thereby failing to capture the entirety of what the program is seeking to influence.

Despite its usefulness, safety net programs rarely use one class of intermediate outcome indicators: information about the quality of services. Such indicators deal with how well a service was delivered based on characteristics important to consumers of that service (Hatry 1999). The typical service quality characteristics that could usefully be tracked include wait times, staff helpfulness and knowledge, convenience of service (accessibility of location, hours of operation), awareness of program services, condition of facilities used by program beneficiaries, and overall customer satisfaction.

Performance or Efficiency Indicators. From a managerial perspective, monitoring systems that only track information on inputs, outputs, and outcomes are operating at well below their potential. The same information can be used to develop performance monitoring indicators—indicators that capture the program's overall cost-effectiveness, or the efficiency of a subset of program operations.

Performance indicators are referred to using different labels, such as efficiency, effectiveness, or productivity indicators. Sometimes these are used interchangeably, but in this book we assign a specific meaning to each. We organize and distinguish among different performance indicators based on the logical framework, or the program's results chain, as illustrated in figure 6.4. Here we distinguish between full cost-effectiveness or cost-benefit analysis, which compare the program benefits with its costs, and indicators that capture individual dimensions that contribute to the program's overall cost-effectiveness. Every program has a value chain of delivery, from procuring the inputs, through organizing them to deliver transfers or services, and finally realizing the desired impact. Every step in this value chain is important for achieving a good cost-benefit ratio,

FIGURE 6.4 **Framework for Distinguishing among Different Types of Performance Indicators**

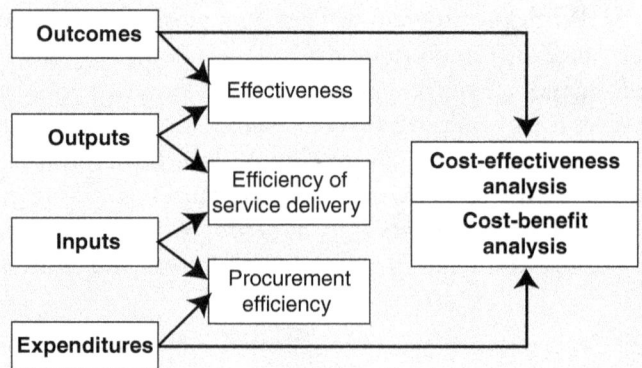

SOURCE: Authors

and failures along the line will have a negative effect on the final result. If a program is not cost-effective, it is important to know which part of the value is causing the problem. Moreover it is more often feasible to assess performance on one of the partial or proximate indicators than cost-effectiveness in total.

The value chain may be broken down into three elements:

- **Procurement efficiency,** which assesses whether the program achieved value for money in relation to purchases of inputs. Examples of procurement efficiency indicators might be the average cost of food procured for school feeding programs, of capital goods and materials for a public works program, or of the costs of staff with a given qualification.

- **Efficiency of service delivery,** which considers how efficiently inputs were employed to produce service outputs. An example of an indicator of service delivery efficiency might be the applications processed per staff member or per US$1,000 of administrative costs.
- **Effectiveness,** which examines the program's results (the change in outcomes) per unit of output. Examples of effectiveness indicators are the reduction in poverty gap per US$1,000 in transfers or the decrease in malnutrition resulting from a package or nutrition education session provided under a CCT program.

Monitoring program performance is an ongoing activity whose purpose is to understand and increase the efficiency, effectiveness, timeliness, and appropriateness of a program's activities with respect to its goals. Box 6.1 lists the key uses of performance monitoring information.

BOX 6.1 **Key Uses of Performance Indicators**

- Identify problem areas and modify practices accordingly.
- Identify the root causes of problems, develop action plans, and track progress.
- Identify technical assistance needs, supply technical assistance, and track progress.
- Tighten funding procedures and standards and reduce or eliminate funding for poorly performing programs.
- Identify the need for policy or legislative changes.
- Identify underserved groups.
- Identify and disseminate successful practices.
- Motivate staff and recognize and reward high-performing agencies, offices, and individuals.
- Allocate resources, set priorities, and develop plans and targets.

SOURCE: Hatry 1999.

Monitoring systems should also verify a program's compliance with rules and regulations and provide mechanisms to control the level of error, fraud, and corruption (EFC). A good monitoring system will support the objective of reducing EFC in a number of ways. Most fundamentally, good monitoring and proactive management will detect problem areas and address them. Important methods for preventing, detecting, and deterring EFC include hot lines that collect tips from the public; data matching systems that verify identification documents and information on well-being as reported for targeting; and internal or external controls, such as audits. Monitoring can also directly track the level of EFC detected by internal or external audit systems. Monitoring for EFC is still relatively rare (box 6.2) but useful for ensuring efficient use of public resources, guarding against political manipulation, and demonstrating program credibility, all of which are vital for maintaining public support.

Track Indicators over Time

Once the list of indicators has been finalized, they are tracked over time. The frequency with which indicators are reported will vary based on the ease with which information can

---

BOX 6.2 Tracking Error, Fraud, and Corruption

Because safety net programs channel large amounts of public resources, making sure that these reach the intended beneficiaries is important. EFC reduces the economic efficiency of safety net interventions by decreasing the amount of money that goes to the intended beneficiaries and erodes political support for the program.

Definitions. Although most safety net programs strive to transfer all their resources intended for beneficiaries to the right beneficiaries in the right amount and at the right time, a fraction is lost to EFC (see figure).

Error is an unintentional violation of program or benefit rules that results in the wrong benefit amount being paid or in payment to an ineligible applicant. Official errors are due to staff

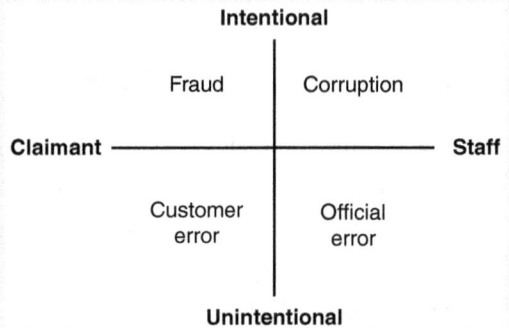

SOURCE: National Audit Office 2006.

mistakes, and customer errors occur when customers inadvertently provide incorrect information. Intentional abuses by claimants are fraud and by staff are corruption. Fraud occurs when a claimant deliberately makes a false statement or conceals or distorts relevant information regarding program eligibility or level of benefits. Corruption commonly involves manipulation of beneficiary rosters, for example, registering ineligible beneficiaries to garner political support, staff accepting illegal payments from eligible or ineligible beneficiaries, or diversion of funds to ghost beneficiaries or other illegal channels.

Losses. The evidence on the amount lost to EFC is limited, and most of it comes from developed countries. A recent study (National Audit Office 2006) finds that even well-run programs in high-capacity countries suffer from fraud and error. In five countries of the Organisation for Economic Co-operation and Development—Canada, Ireland, New Zealand, the United Kingdom, and the United States—fraud and error rates for the entire social protection system ranged between 2 and 5 percent of total social protection spending. Corruption was not an issue in these countries. Within the social protection system, means-tested safety net programs had the highest fraud and error rates (5 to 10 percent of spending), followed by unemployment benefits and disability pension programs (1 to 2 percent). Old-age pensions had the lowest rates of fraud and error (0.1 to 1.0 percent). These figures should be viewed as lower bounds for the extent be gathered; the costs of data collection, the sensitivity of the indicators, and the dynamics of the processes being tracked. For example, the number of children repeating a grade can only be measured at the end of the school year, whereas school attendance can be tracked on a daily, weekly, or monthly basis. Indicators such as the number of beneficiaries and the benefits paid can also be tracked on a weekly or monthly basis. Other indicators, especially those estimated through special surveys such as coverage of the target group, are probably generated only on an annual basis. Input and output indicators are more

of EFC, as they come from a small sample of countries and programs with high administrative capacity and adequate procedures for minimizing EFC.

The information from developing countries is scarcer, as only a few programs and countries have tried to measure the incidence of EFC, and measures to control EFC are less uniformly developed. A review of accountability in CCT programs in Latin America and the Caribbean (World Bank 2007c) did not measure EFC as such, but did document widespread use of a range of effective control tools. Elsewhere, the results are not always so encouraging.

In Bangladesh's Vulnerable Group Development Program, Ahmed and others (2004) estimate that beneficiaries as a whole receive 92 percent of their total wheat entitlement. Initially, the program distributed a certain quantity of wheat to beneficiaries from large containers. About 2.5 percent of the wheat was lost during storage and transportation, a process that is considered normal and unavoidable in the wheat merchandising business. In contravention of program rules, officials sold yet another 2.5 percent to recover the costs of transporting the wheat from warehouses to beneficiaries. Another part was lost to fraud or ad hoc distribution of rations to non-needy recipients (3.0 percent). Once these results were made public, the World Food Programme tried to reduce the extent of leakage by switching from distributing bulk wheat to distributing wheat flour in sealed 15- or 25-kilogram packages to prevent short-weight or divided rations and by increasing the amount of information provided to beneficiaries on their entitlements. In addition, the wheat flour was fortified, thereby increasing the nutritional impact of the transfer.

In India, Dev and others (2004) show that a sizable percentage of the commodities sold through the public distribution system are diverted to the open market, with the amount of fraud varying depending on the commodity and the area of the country. More than 30 percent of rice and wheat and 23 percent of sugar are diverted. Because richer people are less likely than poorer people to claim their rations of subsidized wheat and rice, shopkeepers are left with latitude for selling those commodities on the open market and doctoring records. Diversion is more extensive in the northern and eastern regions than in the southern and western regions. The government is currently thinking of introducing a smart card system (see chapter 5, section 4) to improve accountability and reduce fraud.

The two South Asian cases underscore the benefits of measuring EFC. Once it was quantified and the sources understood, both programs found that the political will and technical knowledge to address the problem were easier to marshal.

sensitive than outcome indicators; among outcome indicators, indicators of intermediate outcomes tend to be more sensitive than final outcome indicators.

Set Targets

Programs often set explicit targets to help judge whether a given level and trend of an indicator is positive or negative. Several approaches are available for setting targets in safety net programs. Targets may be determined based on, for example, assumptions about the expected relationship between inputs, outputs, and possibly outcomes or based on what should happen during each step along the program's logical framework. The performance of other similar programs may help to inform targets, for example, setting a target for the proportion of labor to nonlabor costs in a public works program or gauging whether a 5 percent change in enrollment in a CCT program is good or bad. For instance, in the case of Panama's Red de Oportunidades (Opportunity Network), the targets for the percentage of children complying with education-related conditions and showing a reduction in chronic malnutrition (table 6.6) were set based on what other CCT programs had found to be feasible.

TABLE 6.6 **Selected Targets for Panama's Red de Oportunidades**

Outcome indicator	Baseline	Year 1	Year 2	Year 3	Year 4	Year 5
Percentage of households living in indigenous jurisdictions receiving transfers	50	50	55	60	65	70
Percentage of children aged 4–17 who comply with education-related conditions	50	60	70	80	85	90
Percentage of children under 2 years old registered in the program benefiting from the strengthened health care package	0	0	20	40	65	90
Percentage point reduction in chronic nutrition among children under 2 registered in the program in indigenous jurisdictions	—	—	—	2	—	5

SOURCE: World Bank 2007l, annex 3.

NOTE: — = not available.

Targets are often set based on a program's current performance. For instance, the target may be to improve some aspect of performance by some fixed amount, say 10 percent. A more discriminating way to do this is to ascertain what is feasible by looking at the performance of an organization's better-performing units.

Some targets derive from administrative, legal, ethical, or professional standards. For example, in some cases service standards regulate such things as access to program premises (hours of operation, minimum size of the reception area, and/or presence of ramps to facilitate access by people with disabilities).

MAKING MONITORING INFORMATION USEFUL

As the implementation of a monitoring system entails costs, collecting only information that decision makers need or that is needed to ensure an adequate level of accountability in relation to stakeholders is important. In other words, the monitoring system should not become a data bureaucracy that collects information for its own sake.

To make monitoring information useful, the information should be disaggregated, compared with some appropriate benchmark, and reported in a user-friendly format. Outcome, output, and efficiency indicators should be disaggregated for different client subgroups and different service characteristics to investigate whether the service is homogenous. Table 6.7 presents some of the most common subgroups used to disaggregate monitoring indicators. If program target groups consist of a high-priority and a lowest-priority target group, then the monitoring report should capture this breakdown. In the case of Peru's Vaso de Leche program, which provides a daily glass of milk for children up to 13 years old, the priority group was preschool children, but the program's monitoring system did not break down recipients appropriately (World Bank 2007m). Eventually, an investigation by the Audit Court detected that the share of preschoolers in the program was falling, thereby prompting a revision of the eligibility rules. Had this indicator been a performance target, the situation would have been detected and resolved much sooner.

TABLE 6.7 Examples of Disaggregation Subgroups and Benchmarks

Information disaggregated by client characteristics	Information disaggregated by service characteristics	Benchmarks for comparison purposes
• Age group	• Region served (urban or rural)	• To previous performance
• Gender	• Office or facility that provided the service	• To agency targets
• Race or ethnicity		• Among categories of customers
• Household income	• Amount of assistance provided to individual clients	• Among geographical areas
• Household size	• Mode of service delivery (especially useful for testing different approaches)	• Among organizational units
• Location (urban versus rural, district, city, and so on)		• By type and amount of service
• Difficulty of improving the situation of the beneficiary (for example, very, somewhat, or not difficult)	• Individual supervisor or caseworker	• To the performance of similar programs in other countries
		• To the performance of private sector organizations

SOURCE: Hatry 1999.

Another way to increase the usefulness of monitoring information is to collect performance and outcome indicators. These measure results; hence they focus management's attention on the program's key objectives and the degree of progress toward them. Take the example of a simple cash transfer program whose mission is to protect households against income poverty and help beneficiaries achieve economic independence. A monitoring system oriented toward inputs and outputs would probably track the amount of benefits paid in a given period (the inputs) and the number of clients served (the outputs). A results-oriented system would track, in addition, the number of clients who graduated from the program. A system that focused on inputs and outputs would not signal whether the program was succeeding in helping clients achieve economic independence, nor would it highlight which welfare offices were more successful. By ignoring such issues, the program would tolerate poor performance practices or units.

Using monitoring information in decision making requires judgment. First, as outcome indicators are only partially under a program's control, decisions cannot be made based only on these indicators. Second, focusing on a narrow set of outcome indicators may jeopardize achievement of the broader program mission, as program staff would likely devote most of their effort to attainting the narrow targets, at the expense of other outcomes of interest. Finally, a monitoring system focused mainly on output indicators that does not take outcome indicators into account may generate perverse incentives. For instance, a CCT program that measures only school attendance and not academic performance incorporates incentives to bring students to school, but not for improving their knowledge and skills.

HELPING ENSURE THE SUCCESS OF A MONITORING SYSTEM

The following subsections discuss a number of factors that contribute to the success of a monitoring system.

The M&E Unit Must Be Independent

As the M&E unit fulfills an oversight function, it needs to have sufficient authority and direct access to upper management. To guarantee that monitoring information is as objective as possible, the M&E unit needs to be shielded from the influence of other program departments and placed directly under the program manager or minister. At this level, the unit will be responsible for all programs operated by the respective ministry or agency, which means that it can apply similar evaluation standards across programs and achieve economies of scale in the use of highly skilled and specialized staff. For example, in Brazil, the M&E unit of the MDS (the Secretariat for Evaluation and Information Management) was created at the same hierarchical level as other, much larger, departments that operate different transfer programs to emphasize its importance and guarantee its independence and objectivity (Vaitsman, Rodrigues, and Paes-Sousa 2006). This was an innovation in public policy in Brazil, and it is still the exception rather than the norm in most safety net programs and social protection ministries. While many program M&E units report directly to heads of agencies or ministers, as is the case for all programs operated by Armenia's Ministry of Labor and Social Protection and for Ethiopia's PSNP, typically units are headed by lower-level managers. Unfortunately, many M&E units report to program managers, who may censor any information that indicates poor performance, thereby impairing the M&E unit's objectivity and impartiality.

Coordination and Communication Are Essential, Particularly for Complex Programs

The development of a good M&E system can be a challenge for programs that involve multiple providers, such as CCTs, or that operate across different levels of government, such as programs designed and financed federally, but implemented by lower levels of government. Different actors' willingness to share the information needed to track program performance is a critical component of any M&E system. Solutions also need to be found for any logistical constraints to data sharing. For instance, the exchange of information may be hampered by differences or incompatibilities in MISs, by participating institutions tracking different indicators or defining the same indicators differently, or by the use of information technology systems that cannot communicate with each other.

Transparency Is Critical

Another well-documented example of monitoring (and evaluation) comes from the Kalomo District Pilot Social Cash Transfer Scheme in Zambia operated with technical assistance from Germany. The pilot included an external M&E system operated by the donors to measure whether the approach was cost-effective and feasible, and generated the expected impact. The monitoring focused on the quality of program management, the effectiveness of the targeting, the payment of the transfers, and the beneficiaries' use of the transfers.

Thanks to the investment in the external M&E system, the program's strengths and weaknesses are well known, and policy makers are well equipped to make decisions about its future. At the same time, the scheme has helped set standards for other programs, especially in Sub-Saharan Africa, because of its emphasis on transparency, dissemination, and accountability: all M&E manuals, reports, and survey data are accessible to any third party via the program's Web site (www.socialcashtransfers-zambia). Even though it is just a pilot, the program is better known than other large-scale initiatives in Sub-Saharan Africa because of its extensive M&E system and its transparency.

Expensive, High-Tech Systems Do Not Ensure Success

While information technology reduces the time, error rate, and costs of data collection, it is not always indispensable. Good monitoring systems existed before the advent of computers, and in many low-income countries, monitoring systems will require some combination of paper and pencil records and computerized systems.

Particularly in low-income, low-capacity countries, the use of less sophisticated systems may work better given the scarcity of qualified staff and of information technology in frontline units. Low-income countries may respond to their constraints by reducing the amount of information collected and reported, by collecting information less frequently, by collecting information from a subset of the frontline units, and/or by relying on paper and pencil systems. The earlier example from Ethiopia illustrates this point. For the PSNP, the simplification of the M&E system and the development of a less ambitious emergency response system were appropriate responses to low capacity. Donors might consider focusing their assistance on developing the M&E functions of such programs if they accompany this with sufficient training.

A Good MIS Supports and Enhances the Monitoring System

A program MIS's principal function is to help the program carry out the many transactions needed to run the program. It contains lists of people who have applied to the program, those applicants who are eligible to receive benefits, those who have complied with any conditions, those to be paid, those who have collected payments, and the like. Its fundamental purpose is to ensure that each function is carried out correctly for each client. When information from the MIS is aggregated in helpful ways or compared with information derived from other sources, the MIS produces information that is valuable for monitoring purposes. Thus while its main purpose is not monitoring, an MIS is one of the workhorse producers of information used for monitoring.

SCALING UP: A SECTORWIDE MONITORING SYSTEM

A monitoring system across the entire safety net or social protection sector is based on program-level systems. The existence of strong M&E systems at the program level—especially for large, key programs—facilitates assessment of the whole sector. The same framework and methods used at the program level apply to the sector level (Habicht, Victora, and Vaughan 1999). The systemwide system should show whether services are delivered, are used, and cover the target population adequately and whether outcomes are moving in the right direction.

Compared with program-level monitoring systems, sectorwide systems put more emphasis on tracking outcomes indicators and less on inputs and processes. Examples of sectorwide monitoring systems that emphasize intermediate and final outcomes are increasingly common in developed (Canada, New Zealand, the United Kingdom, the United States) and middle-income countries (Brazil, Chile, Mexico, the Philippines). Two examples follow, plus box 6.3 presents an example of coordination among European Union states.

The United Kingdom's Department for Work and Pensions has developed a comprehensive performance monitoring system. The department coordinates the work of four agencies that implement programs for families, the disabled, and the elderly (contributory or social pensions). The government signs performance-based agreements known as public service agreements with the department and with line agencies that specify a minimum level of outputs and outcomes to be achieved for the budgetary resources provided. For example, one objective is to ensure the best start in life for all children and end child poverty by 2020. Progress toward this objective is measured via two performance targets:

BOX 6.3 **Example of Supranational Monitoring System: The European Union's Mutual Information System on Social Protection**

The European Union established the Mutual Information System on Social Protection (MISSOC) in 1990 to promote continuous exchange of information on social protection among member states (for information on MISSOC, see http://ec.europa.eu/employment_social/spsi/missoc_en.htm). MISSOC provides basic information on the organization of social protection in each country, as well as about the financing of social protection, with highly structured and comparable information in more than 300 information categories. This information is now available in the MISSOC database, which includes information from 2004 on. The database allows users to choose what specific information categories for which countries to display for their particular uses.

MISSOC is the outcome of cooperation between the European Commission and a network of official representatives from each member state. It has become a central information source on social protection legislation, benefits, and financing in the European Union countries. Citizens use it to get basic information about social protection in other countries and to compare it with the social protection in their country—for instance, when preparing for moving to another country. Researchers and students also use it to compare social protection systems and solutions in detail and to study changes in social protection over time.

(1) reducing the number of low-income households with children (a joint target with the Treasury Department), and (2) increasing the proportion of parents participating in income-tested programs who receive income support for their children.

A second example is the monitoring system in the Philippines. The Micro Impacts of Macroeconomic and Adjustment Policies Project provides information on the welfare status of the population, particularly vulnerable groups, to policy makers, program implementers, and the general public. The system combines survey and administrative data from several levels: community volunteers collect and process selected indicators at the local level; municipal planning and development coordinators combine the data for their local governments; provincial planning and development coordinators combine the data for their municipalities; and the National Statistics Office combines data for provinces, supplemented with relevant household data derived from national surveys.

At the sector level, the emphasis is on identifying whether the safety net sector is fragmented, patchy, or neatly woven. Some issues are better addressed at this level, such as identifying poor or vulnerable populations that existing safety net programs do not cover, inefficient overlap of programs, and low take-up of certain programs. Hence the monitoring system should be able to capture any synergies and complementarities among programs and identify what program should be responsible for which functions. For example, Mexico's Oportunidades program emerged as an integrator program to ensure better access to and utilization of health, nutrition, and education services by the poor. In Chile, the Puente program fulfilled the same function.

6.5 Evaluation

Evaluation serves several important functions. First, by providing feedback during the life of a safety net program, evaluations can help improve their effectiveness. They can also help guide decisions about whether to expand, modify, or eliminate a particular program or policy. Second, evaluations permit making programs accountable to the public. Third, they can help inform government decisions about spending allocations as part of a broader, results-based management system.

Despite the usefulness of evaluation, until relatively recently, few safety net programs in developing countries were rigorously evaluated. This is beginning to change. Sound evaluations of at least a handful of programs of every type are now available, and many more are available for CCT programs. Some medium-income countries have introduced government-wide management by results reforms that mandate or provide positive incentives for regular evaluations of programs and policies. In all developing countries, donors are requesting evidence that the programs they are cofinancing produce results, thereby increasing the demand for evaluation.

Many types of program evaluation exist. For example, Rossi, Freeman, and Lipsey (1999) distinguish between the following types of program evaluations: needs assessment, process evaluation, impact evaluation, cost-benefit or cost-effectiveness analysis, and targeting accuracy evaluation. We focus on the three most common types of evaluations of safety net programs: process (or implementation) evaluation, assessment of targeting accuracy, and impact evaluation. Evaluations of cost-benefit and cost-effectiveness are also helpful, but are rare so not treated in depth here (see box 6.4).

BOX 6.4 **Cost-Benefit and Cost-Effectiveness Analysis**

An important question regarding any program is whether the costs justify the benefits, or whether it provides good value for money. Program costs and benefits are compared using two main methods. Cost-benefit analysis estimates both inputs and outputs in monetary terms to determine whether a program has net benefits to participants and to society as a whole. Cost-effectiveness analysis is used in cases where the benefits cannot be quantified monetarily, as is true for many social programs. Cost-effectiveness analysis estimates inputs in monetary terms and outcomes in nonmonetary quantitative terms. By definition, it is a comparative exercise, examining the unit cost of one program versus the unit costs of other programs.

In principle, cost-benefit or cost-effectiveness analysis involves straightforward calculations. All the costs of program operation are tallied and subtracted from the benefits of participation. Typically, the program's costs are estimated from administrative data on staff salaries, overhead, and operating costs along with estimates of participants' foregone earnings or opportunity costs of participating in the program. Benefits are taken from the impact assessment. In practice, such analyses must overcome many operational difficulties, data constraints, and measurement issues.

Comprehensive, large-scale evaluations may include a cost-benefit analysis; however, this type of analysis is frequently omitted in smaller evaluations where evaluators lack access to resources or to adequate data, and is more common in developed than in developing countries. In developing countries, full cost-benefit analyses have rarely been undertaken. For a good example of full cost-benefit analysis, see Coady (2000) on Mexico's PROGRESA and Econometría Consultores, Institute for Fiscal Studies and Sistemas Especializados de Información (2006) on Colombia's Familias en Acción.

In the case of the Colombian program, the program's benefits are the present-value of the lifetime increase in earnings of the program beneficiaries due to lowered incidence of underweight infants, lowered incidence of malnutrition and child morbidity among children aged zero to six years old, and increased years of secondary schooling. The effects of Familias en Acción on these outcomes are derived from an impact evaluation study and are then monetized using evidence from a combination of sources (for example, a net additional year of secondary school education is assumed to increase future income by 8 percent based on estimates of Mincerian rates of return; an increase of 0.4 kilograms in birthweight is assumed to increase future income by 5 percent based on international evidence). Considered were (1) program costs for the transfers and their administration, (2) private costs incurred by the household for additional food and education expenditures, (3) private household costs of collecting transfers, (4) infrastructure and input costs of additional school and health center supply, and (5) the public cost generated to finance the CCT.

Comparing the benefit and cost figures, the authors estimate a ratio of benefits to costs of 1.59, which is high by traditional benefit-cost ratio standards and suggests that the CCT is worth its cost. This ratio also means that, even if the assumptions used in this model are imperfect, costs would need to increase 59 percent relative to benefits in order to reach a point where the benefits do not justify the costs. It should be noted that this analysis does not consider other benefits, such as decrease in poverty or inequality that results from the transfer.

All three types of evaluation answer distinct, but complementary, questions. A process evaluation asks whether a program is being implemented as intended, and if not, why not. An assessment of targeting accuracy investigates whether program beneficiaries are indeed the poorest members of the population. Impact evaluation quantifies a program's net impact on the outcomes it is trying to influence, that is, it examines whether a program, as delivered, is achieving its goals. Many programs, especially CCT and workfare programs in developing countries, as well as welfare programs in the United States, have undergone all three types of evaluation, giving rise to the term comprehensive evaluations (Greenberg and Shroder 2004).

Safety net programs are increasingly being evaluated using multiple types of evaluation. The United States was the first country to pioneer this practice. Of the 146 impact evaluations undertaken in the United States between 1962 and 1996 and reviewed by Greenberg and Shroder (2004), half were complemented by a process evaluation. Recently, middle-income countries have increasingly been adopting the practice of undertaking multiple types of evaluation for a given program. In particular, CCT programs in Colombia, Jamaica, Mexico, Nicaragua, and Turkey used process evaluation to complement more focused evaluations of targeting accuracy or impact.

PROCESS EVALUATION

Process evaluation—also known as formative evaluation, implementation research, implementation analysis, or descriptive evaluation—is probably the most common type of program evaluation (Rossi, Freeman, and Lipsey 1999) and documents, assesses, and explains how a program is implemented. It can be used throughout the life of a program, from start-up to maturity, and whenever the environment in which the program is operating changes, thereby requiring adjustments of the program. This type of evaluation may cover some or all of three basic questions (Werner 2004): (1) What is happening? (2) Is it what the program's designers want or expect to happen? (3) Why is it happening as it is?

In many instances, the decision to undertake a process evaluation follows from an operational problem signaled by the monitoring system. Program managers learn about operational problems from monitoring reports, for instance, reports about complaints and appeals, quality control reviews, or audit reports. The problem may be specific to a particular client group, say low take-up among minority groups; specific to a particular service unit, for example, a high complaint rate in one office or region; or related to a program-level issue, such as a reduction in caseload below target levels. However, the monitoring system only reveals the problem. It does not indicate why the problem emerged or how to solve it. To find answers to the latter, managers can ask for an internal review or commission an external process evaluation.

In other instances, process evaluation is a substitute for a missing or a poorly performing monitoring and internal review system. Process evaluation should complement, not substitute for, internal monitoring systems. For example, Zambia's Kalomo District Pilot Social Cash Transfer Scheme included process evaluation carried out by external evaluators, but this was coupled with assistance provided by the external evaluator to the ministry to build in-house monitoring capacity.

Unlike impact evaluation, process evaluation cannot establish causality with a known margin of error. Process evaluation can uncover plausible reasons why a program is working or not, and hence can build hypotheses and theories that can be tested using an impact evaluation. In developing hypotheses about causal connections, process evaluation will use one of the following methods: (1) using stakeholders' accounts of why they take or fail to take specific actions related to program activities and goals; (2) associating variations in management, policies, operations, services, or other factors with observed differences in results; and (3) comparing actual results with predictions or expectations based on the model or theory underlying the program.

The findings from process evaluations are behind many of the improvements in effectiveness and efficiency of safety net programs. For example, in Armenia, a number of discrete process evaluations contributed to sustained capacity-building efforts that led to substantial improvements in the targeting accuracy of the Family Poverty Benefits Program (chapter 4, section 4, provides more detail). In another case in the town of Arzamas in Russia, city authorities worked with the Urban Institute to study whether the many programs the authorities were implementing had overlapping functions or stages. Finding a substantial degree of overlap across programs, the city authorities decided to replace the delivery system with a one-window approach, resulting in fewer exclusion errors, lower administrative costs, and lower transaction costs for beneficiaries (chapter 5, section 3).

During program start-up, process evaluation is used to monitor initial program implementation so that bottlenecks can be addressed speedily and good practice can be documented for future applications. After the program stabilizes and matures, a process evaluation can be used to provide ongoing feedback to management, especially when the monitoring system detects operational issues or when the factors that affect program effectiveness change, raising doubts about the continued relevance of some of its components. More generally, process evaluation is used (1) on an ad hoc basis to analyze an operational problem; (2) to complement an impact evaluation; (3) to keep stakeholders informed, that is, for accountability purposes; and (4) to substitute for an inadequate or missing monitoring system.

Emerging programs may use process evaluation to keep interest in a program alive and/or to secure support for scaling it up. In countries where the government or parliament has endorsed a management by results agenda, such evaluations can be routinely mandated to produce indicators of program performance that are tracked over time. Routine process evaluation also has other uses. Jamaica's PATH initiative, a CCT jointly financed by the government and the World Bank, uses a third party evaluator to monitor compliance with conditions and estimate the error rate in assessing eligibility. The error rate, in turn, determines the portion of the budget cofinanced by the World Bank.

If legislation requires routine process evaluations, programs are constantly exposed to public scrutiny, setting the right incentives for them to improve their effectiveness. However, evaluations mandated from above can run the risk of being irrelevant by not responding to genuine operational problems. The evaluation's sponsors may lose interest in such evaluations, or worse, fear that the results of the mandated evaluation may negatively affect the program's status quo and derail the evaluation to noncontentious areas of little importance. Process evaluations based on routine compliance with a legislative requirement to undertake them regularly have little or no value.

The questions covered by process evaluation are as diverse as the problems program managers encounter. Table 6.8 presents some examples of questions a typical process evaluation will address in the case of a safety net program.

TABLE 6.8 Examples of Questions Addressed by Process Evaluations of Safety Net Programs

Aspect evaluated	Questions
Program organization	• Is the program well organized? • Does program implementation follow a clear organizational structure? • How well do different groups involved in delivery work together (in terms of different staff within delivery teams and different programs and agencies with which the program in question must interact)?
Program resources	• Are adequate resources being used to implement the program? • Is program staffing and funding sufficient to ensure appropriate standards? • Are program resources (inputs) being used effectively and efficiently? • Are costs (per beneficiary, per benefits transferred, and so on) reasonable?
Program availability and participation	• How did people hear about the program? • What is the level of awareness among the eligible and potentially eligible population? • Do those eligible and potentially eligible understand the program's key elements? • Do all those eligible participate in the program? • Who participates and why? Who does not participate and why? Do particular groups within the target population not receive the program and why? • Do some people who are not eligible participate, and if so, does this suggest that the target population is poorly defined or that program delivery is poorly controlled?
Delivery of services and benefits	• Are participants receiving the proper amounts, types, and quality of benefits and services? • Is delivery of benefits and services consistent with the program's intent? • Are all components of the program being delivered adequately and consistently? • How much change has occurred since program implementation? • Does the program comply with professional and legal standards, for example, are appropriate complaints procedures in place?
Participant experiences	• What are participants' experiences of contact with the program, for instance, how were they invited to participate? What kinds and how many contacts with the program did they have? What was the duration and content of their contacts? • Are participants satisfied with their interactions with staff delivering the program, with program procedures, and with the services they receive? • Do participants engage in anticipated or intended follow-up behavior?
Program performance issues	• Are benefits and services delivered according to different models or by different organizations, for example, do banks distribute cash in some areas while post offices or private contractors do so in other areas? If so, how do these compare? • Are program resources and/or program delivery consistent and appropriate across all geographical locations? • Do variations exist across locations or models that provide examples of best practice or that are important interventions that should be considered elsewhere? Are variations occurring over time or for different groups? • Is the program focused on those who are easier to reach at the expense of those who are harder to reach? If so, what is the impact on the nature of the services provided and the net outcomes of these services? What would be the effect of shifting the balance between the easier and harder to reach?

SOURCES: Purdon and others 2001; Rossi, Freeman, and Lipsey 1999; Werner 2004.

Process evaluation is often undertaken as a complement to an impact evaluation. A process evaluation can significantly enrich the findings of an impact evaluation for the following reasons (Greenberg and Shroder 2004):

- A descriptive process evaluation is important for the replication or scaling up of a successful intervention that produced the expected impact. This is particularly important for complex programs such as Chile Solidario.

- The findings of a process evaluation are important for understanding the results of an impact evaluation. If an impact evaluation shows no impact, this could be due to poor program design or simply to poor implementation of a well-designed program. Programs implemented heterogeneously across sites, regions, or clients will generate a modest average impact despite their good impact in areas where the program was implemented well. The evaluator will only become aware of this problem by collecting information on the quality of implementation.

- An understanding of how and how well any intervention is actually being implemented and delivered is important before decision makers decide whether to keep or modify a program.

- The evaluator requires information from the process evaluation if the replication of a program produces different results to assess why and how the replication sites differ from the intervention that was evaluated.

The most common data collection tools used for process evaluations are interviews; observation; focus groups; and examination of the records of the program, agency, and/or ministry. Interviews are by far the dominant technique and take place at all levels with both individuals and groups. Individual interviews are advisable when the evaluator wants to inquire about aspects of the program that people will not want to discuss in front of others. Group interviews are recommended when the evaluator wants to learn about conflicting views. Observation reveals how things are actually done in practice. Focus groups are facilitated discussions with clients, former clients, applicants, and eligible clients to obtain their perceptions about how the program worked and what it did for them. Administrative records are an important source of information about the number of beneficiaries; the number of clients contacted by, accepted into, or removed from the program, and so on; timing; bottlenecks; and the like.

ASSESSMENT OF TARGETING ACCURACY

All safety net programs aim, explicitly or implicitly, to channel their benefits to the poor, or a subset of them, typically the poorest. An evaluation of targeting accuracy, also referred to as a targeting assessment, helps reveal whether this aim has been realized, asking questions such as what share of the beneficiaries of a safety net program is indeed poor? What proportion of the poor is covered or served by a safety net program? Have changes in eligibility rules succeeded in reducing the share of nonpoor beneficiaries? How much did the coverage of the poor increase after expansion of the program?

A targeting assessment is a cheaper but less precise alternative for evaluating a program's impact on poverty reduction than a full impact assessment. A reduction in poverty brought about by the program will be a function of the program's coverage, generosity, and disincentive effects, while errors of inclusion and administrative costs will raise the costs of achieving an impact. Targeting assessments quantify the program's coverage and errors of inclusion, thereby providing useful insights into why a program may or may not be having a strong impact. Moreover, a targeting assessment is feasible in many more cases than a full impact assessment, and even a partial assessment of a program can help policy makers know whether they can hope for results or need to take corrective action. Using a medical analogy (Habicht, Victora, and Vaughan 1999), one does not need to reevaluate the impact of a vaccine once it has been established that it works in many settings. If a previous impact evaluation has demonstrated that the vaccine works, for subsequent interventions, we need only demonstrate that the vaccine has reached the target groups; this is what a targeting assessment does. Note that not everyone shares our relatively positive view of targeting assessments. Ravallion (2007), for example, considers directly measuring the outcome variable of interest, which is some measure of poverty given the objectives of these programs, to be preferable. While impact evaluation is desirable, it is not always possible or sufficient.

This subsection deals with this type of evaluation at length for two reasons. First, because all safety net programs are targeted and have, at least implicitly, the objective of alleviating poverty, an assessment of targeting efficiency is critical for such programs.[2] Second, unlike other types of program evaluation, textbooks and other sources tend not to cover this type of evaluation.

Measuring Targeting Accuracy

There are many indicators of targeting accuracy, but all start with knowing who benefits from a program and who does not. This information can be reported across the whole distribution of income graphically, summarized into various single-number indexes, or reported for various subgroups. Table 6.9 summarizes some of the common measures used. In the evaluation literature on safety net programs, the assessment is typically referred to as a targeting assessment. Outside safety nets, the technique is known as benefit incidence analysis. The rest of this subsection focuses on various features of targeting assessment.

The initial question is who is the group of interest. Is it the poor or the extreme poor as defined by some explicitly delineated poverty line? Or is it the poorest x percent of the population? Both are of value, but we generally prefer the latter, because it provides information across the full spectrum of welfare. For example, knowing if the benefits that miss the poor go to the very nearly poor or to the very wealthy is helpful. Equally important, poverty lines have an element of arbitrariness about them and are rarely comparable across countries, are often not comparable within countries across time, and are often disputed. Policy makers who disagree with an analyst's definition of the poverty line will find drawing conclusions about whether a program is sufficiently targeted or not difficult if information is presented only in relation to that one disputed poverty line. In contrast, the presentation of results across the spectrum of welfare will be useful to policy makers no matter their opinions about the poverty line, will be useful to program analysts and policy makers 10 years later in the same country, and will be helpful to policy makers and analysts worldwide now and in 10 years as a comparator. Of course, to choose one does not exclude choosing the other. Both are easily computed from the same raw data and may be presented side by side.

TABLE 6.9 **Common Targeting Measures**

Measure	Definition
Concentration curve	Share of total transfers going to the poorest percentage of the population ranked by household income per person
Share going to the poor	Share of transfers going to those who are initially deemed poor (or other reference group based on income)
Normalized share	Share of transfers going to a the poorest x percent of the population divided by that share; for example, if 30 percent of the transfer goes to the poorest 20 percent of the population, the normalized share is 30/20 = 1.5
Concentration index	Area between the concentration curve and the diagonal along which everyone receives the same amount
Coverage rate	Program participation rate for the poor
Targeting differential	Difference between the coverage rate and the participation rate for the nonpoor
Proportion of type 1 errors	Proportion of program beneficiaries who are not poor
Proportion of type 2 errors	Proportion of the poor who do not benefit from the program

SOURCE: Ravallion 2007.

Looking at the Average Incidence of Benefits of a Safety Net Program

In its most basic form, a targeting assessment describes how public spending is distributed across population groups, whether defined as deciles or poor versus nonpoor.

Data Requirements. To undertake a targeting assessment, the analyst will need a household survey, representative for the entire population and for the program's target group, and with information on household welfare and program receipt. Not all countries have representative surveys that collect information on household welfare and the receipt of program benefits. Sometimes information about the receipt of program benefits is missing; in other cases, while this information may be collected, it is not representative of the subpopulation of program beneficiaries. This is particularly likely if the coverage of the safety net program is small. When this information is not available from a national survey, options include oversampling program beneficiaries and combining a survey of beneficiaries with the nationally representative household survey.

Montenegro provides an example of oversampling program participants. For its 2004 household survey, the government wanted to keep the survey small while obtaining representative information about the Family Maternal Support Program, a safety net program with low coverage. Given Montenegro's total population of about 600,000, a national survey of 600 households was considered sufficient for other issues the survey covered, but would generate an inadequate sample of program beneficiaries. Given policy makers' interest in the program's performance, the survey was augmented with a booster sample of 200 beneficiary households extracted randomly from the program lists. The same survey questionnaire was administered to 800 households. The survey weights were adjusted to take into account the oversampling of program beneficiaries (Institute for Strategic Studies and Prognoses 2004).

Jamaica decided to combine a beneficiary survey with a national household survey. To assess the targeting accuracy of the newly implemented PATH initiative, in 2003, the Statistical Institute of Jamaica fielded a beneficiary survey of 936 households one year after the regular Survey of Living Conditions had surveyed 6,976 households (Levy and Ohls 2004). The 2003 survey used the same consumption module as the previous year's survey, employed the same methodology for constructing the welfare aggregate, and was fielded just before the applicants received their benefits to generate a comparable consumption aggregate that captured beneficiaries' welfare level before the program. To assess the program's distributional incidence, the consultants hired to carry out the survey compared the 2003 data with the 2002 quintile cutoffs adjusted for inflation. To assess the inclusion and exclusion errors of the new program, the 2003 data were compared with contemporaneous poverty lines (Levy and Ohls 2004).

Sometimes programs serve only part of the population, for example, only urban or only rural areas or only areas known to be poor. Nonetheless, reference to the national welfare distribution is needed to understand program effectiveness. Using quantiles specific to that subpopulation for the analysis may be misleading. Consider a country where all the poor live in rural areas that has an antipoverty program that operates mostly in urban areas, where it successfully captures the less well-off households. Evaluated against the national income distribution, the program will show a high leakage rate, but when quantiles are constructed separately for rural and urban areas, the program will appear to be progressive. These kinds of results are not straightforward to interpret (box 6.5). For programs of national scope or that are nationally financed, we recommend always presenting the incidence of benefits based on national quantiles and qualifying the results based on quantiles estimated for subpopulations such as regions or urban and rural areas. The exception would be analyzing programs run by subnational jurisdictions, especially with their own funds; in federal countries, for example, analyses of state-level programs—such as in Brazil, India, and the United States—for state policy makers would be done for state populations.

Methodology. An analyst will estimate the incidence of benefits (or of beneficiaries) in four steps. The steps are conceptually simple, but the results can be quite sensitive to how each is performed (Demery 2000; van de Walle 2003). Thus performing a sensitivity analysis on some of the main choices made and reporting how sensitive detailed results or policy conclusions are to those choices are good practices. Reporting in detail on the choices is also important to allow proper interpretation of results and benchmarking and to allow analysts to reproduce results.

The first step is the construction of a welfare measure, which is required to correctly rank households according to their standard of living. The most typical welfare indicators are per capita consumption or income, sometimes per adult equivalent consumption or income. A good welfare measure should be comprehensive and comparable across space, time, and different types of households. To be comprehensive, a consumption indicator should capture all its components, such as food, nonfood, and services, as well as the value of goods produced and consumed by the household and the imputed value of durables or the rental value of an owner-occupied dwelling. Similarly, a comprehensive income indicator will cover the incomes earned by all household members from formal and informal sources and the value of goods produced and consumed by the household. All income

BOX 6.5 **Misleading with Targeting Statistics**

Using household surveys that are not representative of the entire population to assess the targeting performance of a national safety net program is misleading. Two contrasting examples from Ethiopia and Russia illustrate this point.

The example from Russia illustrates how a poorly targeted program can be made to appear well targeted by restricting the analysis to well-off urban areas. Since 1995, Russia has operated a cash program, the Housing Allowance Program, to compensate poor consumers for the high costs of heating. To receive the allowance, households need to submit documentary evidence of their income and their heating expenses. Because such documents are available only to urban residents living in apartment buildings connected to the urban heating grid, most rural households cannot access the program. As most of the poor live in rural areas, the program misses most of the poor. The World Bank (2006) documented the large exclusion errors and low targeting accuracy using evidence from a nationally representative survey. Struyk, Petrova, and Lykova (2006j) reached the opposite conclusion based on a household survey drawn from three upper-income towns. They find that the program identified the less well-off households from these three cities well and thus concluded that the program is well targeted.

The example from Ethiopia illustrates how a program that is probably well targeted may appear to be poorly targeted. The PSNP operates in food-insecure areas where it provides food-for-work for able-bodied individuals and cash transfers for destitute households whose members cannot work. The program's targeting efficiency was a constant concern of the authorities. A number of qualitative evaluations documented that program participants are poorer than the rest of their communities in terms of land or livestock owned. A household survey was fielded in the program areas in 2005 that Devereux and others (2006) used to present standard benefit incidence tables. Because the sample was representative only of the poorest regions in the country, the incidence results were mediocre at best: program beneficiaries came evenly from all quintiles. An uninformed reader of these results can wrongly conclude that the program is badly targeted. No assessment of the program's targeting accuracy based on the national income distribution has been carried out to date.

---

or consumption information will be totaled as a monetary value per household. Because prices differ across space and time, the purchasing power of a given level of nominal total income or consumption will differ. For comparability, the indicators will be deflated by an appropriate price index and expressed in real terms. To compare the welfare of different individuals, real per capita consumption or income is typically expressed in per capita or per adult equivalent. For guidance on constructing a consumption-based welfare measure, see Deaton and Zaidi (2002). For guidance on constructing an income-based welfare measure, see Eurostat (2003) or U.S. Census Bureau (2005). For an explanation of adult equivalencies, see box 8.2.

The second step is to construct quantiles. As Demery (2000, 2003) shows, the results of a targeting assessment can be quite sensitive to the types of quantiles the analyst uses, be they individuals or households. Constructing these so that they contain the same number of individuals, not households, is preferable except when a previous targeting assessment based on household quantiles exists, as for comparison purposes, the same methods must be used. This simplifies interpretation of the results.[3]

In the third step, the analyst has to identify the benefit given to each beneficiary (or assistance) unit—individual, family, or household. How this information is collected will depend on the type of program. For cash, quasi-cash, and workfare programs, this information is straightforward to collect via a survey. Finding this information in a multitopic household survey where each household (or individuals within the household) reports the sums of money received from the program during the reporting period is quite common. For other types of programs, notably fee waiver, subsidy, and in-kind programs, most surveys will only collect information on receipt of the program (a yes or no answer), but not the value of the benefit, especially when beneficiaries cannot estimate the cash equivalent of the goods or services received (McKay 2000b).

If the survey collects information on the value of benefits participants receive, the analyst can produce benefit incidence tables in terms of beneficiaries and benefits. If the value of the benefit is uniform across individuals, the incidence of beneficiaries will be the same as the incidence of benefits. If the benefit is customized by household characteristics, the difference in incidence by beneficiaries and benefits can differ significantly.

Sometimes even if the survey asks only about participation in the program and not the level of benefit received, it may be possible to simulate these as follows:

- Some surveys may deliberately omit to collect benefit information if the benefit formula is simple and there are no payment arrears. For example, if a child allowance program offers a flat benefit to all children aged newborn to 16 years old, collecting information on program participation is enough. The analyst can impute the amount to each household with children of eligible age.

- Some surveys gather information about individual or household circumstances that determine the level of the benefit. For example, the value of a heating subsidy whose level depends only on the type of dwelling (apartment building versus individual house) and location (municipality) can be obtained if the survey collects information on who received the program, the type of dwelling, and the municipality.

When the distinction between benefit and beneficiary incidence is important, as for price subsidy programs,[4] the analyst can try to obtain an estimate of the value of the subsidy by multiplying the number of units of the subsidized good or service consumed (as observed in the survey) by an estimate of the unit value of the subsidy made separately from the survey.

Alternative definitions of the beneficiary unit may significantly affect the results. Depending on the type of program and the target group, the direct beneficiary of a safety net program may be an individual, a family, or a household. However, in a broader sense, all household members benefit from the additional resources provided by the program, thus a strong economic rationale exists for assigning benefits to the whole household when assessing the incidence of a program. Consider a child allowance program in a country where children account for 25 percent of the population and families with children account for 60 percent of the population. If only direct beneficiaries are taken into account, the coverage of the program will be 25 percent of the population; but if all beneficiaries, direct and indirect, are counted, coverage will be 60 percent. Given the negative correlation between household size and welfare level, using households as beneficiary units for safety net programs where the assistance unit is an individual will improve both coverage and targeting accuracy statistics. Whenever possible, the analyst should report both results. If only one set of results is to be reported, we prefer those based on indirect beneficiaries, as this is the only way to compare programs that serve different types of assistance units.

Checking the quality of survey information against administrative sources is good practice, and a number of simple tests are available. The analyst can check the size of the difference between the estimated number of beneficiaries or spending level obtained from the survey with the same figure from administrative data. Is this difference statistically significant? If not, this is a necessary, but insufficient, condition indicating that the survey data are of good quality. Is the level of benefits reported by beneficiaries the same as in the program's schedule of benefits? If so, this is another indication that the survey data are of good quality. When possible, the analyst should repeat these tests for those subpopulations for which the survey is representative, such as rural and urban areas or regions. The analyst should always be careful to use the same reporting period when comparing flow quantities such as program spending or number of beneficiaries. For an example of comparing survey and administrative data to assess the representativeness of the former, see Galasso and Ravallion (2004).

Small programs—that is, those that cover a small proportion of the total population—are hard to capture by means of nationally representative surveys. The estimated coverage of such programs will be imprecise, because the sample size of a typical household survey is not large enough to capture a sufficient number of beneficiaries. In such cases, analysts cannot determine whether a discrepancy between survey data and administrative data is due to measurement error or to leakages or fraud.

Several solutions are available in this case. The first possibility is to add a booster sample to an existing household survey to have a sufficient number of beneficiaries as discussed earlier. Another possibility is to conduct a small census of the families in a village or enumeration area before selecting the beneficiaries to interview. The resulting sample of beneficiaries will be large enough to provide robust information about the characteristics of the beneficiaries, and the small census can provide better estimates of beneficiary participation. If a discrepancy between the administrative data and the small census information persists, the analyst can design a small local survey of current beneficiaries (a tracking or tracing survey) to ascertain if all the beneficiaries in specific areas actually exist. For example, the results from the initial small census carried out as part of a study of the Food Support Program in Pakistan reported a coverage rate of 0.6 percent, while administrative records reported almost 4.0 percent (World Bank 2007k). A follow-up tracing survey was able to find more than 85 percent of the beneficiaries, bringing the reported program coverage up to 3.4 percent.

The fourth and last step is the calculation, presentation, and interpretation of the results. Targeting measures are calculated using the data collected following one or more of the measures outlined in table 6.9. Once the basic calculations have been done, assessing an individual program against its stated objective and against other programs is useful. The comparators may be selected because they represent alternative uses of funds for the country or because they use a somewhat different targeting system and thus yield insights into feasible options. The selection of targeting measures used also takes into account the measures available for the proposed comparators.

As perfect targeting is not possible and programs will always fall short of their intended goal in that respect, including feasible comparators is important. For benchmarking safety net programs, Coady, Grosh, and Hoddinott (2004) provide a comprehensive compilation of the incidence of targeted transfers for 122 programs in 48 countries. Lindert, Skoufias, and Shapiro (2006) provide slightly more recent information for 56 programs in 8 countries in Latin America and the Caribbean.

Caveats. Having the right expectations of the end result of a targeting assessment is important. The targeting assessment is a descriptive analytic tool. It will not reveal why benefits are distributed as they are and what aspects of the program should be changed to close the gap between the actual and the desired allocation of program resources. It does not explain incidence outcomes, nor does it generate specific policy implications. In the end, stakeholders will learn whether the program's benefits are being distributed equitably or not and how far these results are from the intended distribution or outcome and bring understandings of the context and other dimensions of the program to bear in determining appropriate responses. At the same time, the method gives an incomplete picture of welfare effects, for example, ignoring the impact of transfers on other dimensions of welfare such as health, literacy, and nutrition. Similarly, it does not take into account the long-term effects of safety net transfers. For some interventions with positive externalities, such as the health interventions typically found in CCT programs, it wrongly assumes that the cost of provision reflects the benefit to the user: for example, the cost of immunization is low, but the benefits are large.

Undertaking More Elaborated Forms of Targeting Assessment

The advantage of the basic targeting assessment lies in its simplicity: it can be done quickly if the right data are available, it does not require exceptional analytic skills, and it produces results that are relatively easy to understand and interpret. However, this simplicity brings with it a number of limitations, some of which can be handled by more elaborated forms of targeting assessment (table 6.10).

Accounting for the Behavioral Responses of Recipients. Ideally, a targeting assessment should rank households by their level of income or consumption in the absence of the program. Only then, when the analyst knows how poor program beneficiaries would have been without the program, can he or she estimate the true incidence of the benefits. The problem is, of course, that direct observation of what recipients' welfare would have been in the absence of the program is not possible, and so some approximation of it must be made.

Two simple, or so-called naïve, estimators are possible. One method is to subtract the value of the transfer from post-transfer consumption. The assumption behind this approximation is that the extra income does not affect the wages and/or remittances received by the household, and is entirely consumed, that is, not saved or invested. If the receipt of transfers reduces the level of wages and remittances earned by the household, this method will underestimate errors of inclusion. The extent of the error will depend on the size of the behavioral changes. A second simple approximation is to use post-transfer consump-

TABLE 6.10 **Some of the Main Types of Targeting Assessments**

Policy or research question	Type of targeting assessment	Explanation
Was a counterfactual welfare distribution estimated?	Accounting	Households are grouped into quantiles based on observed consumption following safety net transfers
	Behavioral	Households are grouped into quantiles based on counterfactual consumption before (net of) safety net transfers
What distribution of benefits is of interest?	Average	Describes what shares of benefits accrue to each quantile for an existing program
	Marginal	Describes or estimates how the benefits corresponding to an increase or decrease in the program are or will be distributed
Were households ranked based on their current welfare or based on losses and gains in welfare during a given period?	Static	Ranks households by quantiles based on their level of welfare during a given period
	Dynamic	Ranks households by quantiles based on changes in their level of welfare between periods
Was the assessment done before or after the program was implemented?	Ex post	Describes how program benefits are distributed across population groups
	Ex ante	Estimates how program benefits will be distributed if certain program parameters change

SOURCE: Authors.

tion under the implicit assumption that all extra transfer income triggered a proportional reduction of other incomes from wages and/or remittances. If the transfer is large and reduces the level of wages and remittances earned by the household, this will overestimate errors of inclusion. Consider, for example, the case of a perfectly designed, perfectly implemented minimum guarantee program that gives each poor household a transfer sufficient to raise it just above the poverty line. Before the transfer, all program beneficiaries were poor; afterward, none were. A targeting assessment using post-transfer consumption would conclude that the program was failing to reach the poor, even though it was actually a success. Though neither of the naïve estimates is accurate, they provide upper- and lower-bound estimates for targeting outcomes.

To estimate a household's welfare in the absence of a program most accurately, the analyst must model changes in the household's labor supply, remittances, savings, and credit, or alternatively, obtain this information from a comparable counterfactual group, an undertaking more usually carried out under the label of impact evaluation. These changes provide an estimate of a household's welfare in the absence of a transfer and allow the calculation of correct welfare rankings.

The possible sensitivity of the results to the estimator of pretransfer welfare is dramatically illustrated by van de Walle's calculations for the Republic of Yemen (figure 6.5). The distribution of transfers is nearly equal across deciles if the observed post-transfer per capita expenditure is used, but sharply progressive if the full transfer is subtracted from per capita expenditure. Van de Walle estimates that the marginal propensity to consume out of the transfer (MPCT) is about 0.5, which means that consumption rose by 50 percent of the value of the transfer received. In this analysis, she combines all transfers: social assistance, pensions, and private transfers including remittances. Since the latter are large, they effectively raise those who receive them out of poverty and the change in ranking of households is larger than found for most social assistance programs.

The limited evidence available suggests that for safety net programs with moderate generosity, the increase in income or consumption is close to the value of transfer. In the case of five of

FIGURE 6.5 **Incidence of Social Protection Transfers Depends on the Assumed Pretransfer per Capita Consumption, Republic of Yemen, 1999**

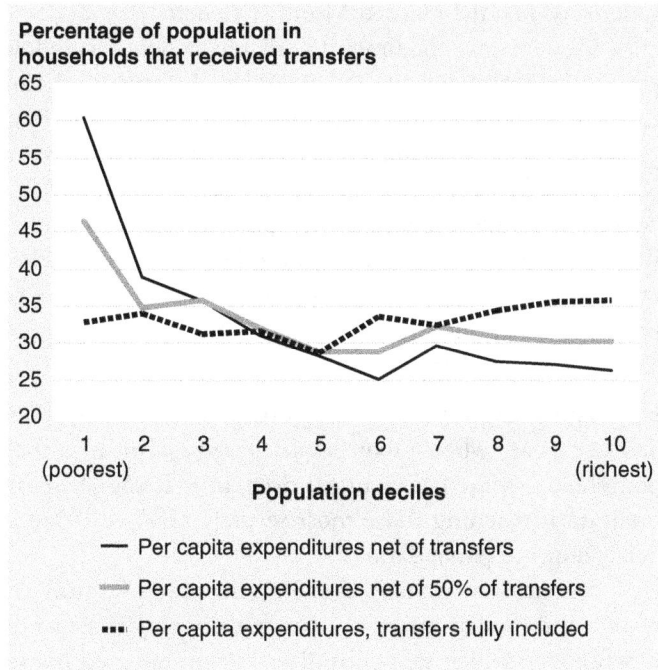

SOURCE: Van de Walle 2002a.

the six CCT programs reviewed in World Bank (forthcoming), household consumption increased by almost the whole value of the transfer, equivalent to an MPCT of 1. More generous programs with an income-replacement role, like workfare and social pension programs, but also social insurance programs, such as unemployment benefits or contributory pensions, will likely increase household consumption substantially less than 100 percent. This is because, in the absence of the program, households had to earn some income in other ways in order to survive. For example, in the case of Argentina's Trabajar workfare program, the average direct gain for participants was about half the gross wage (Jalan and Ravallion 2003), implying an MPCT of 0.5.

All methods used to account for households' behavioral responses to transfers are data intensive. Most of the CCT evaluations from World Bank (forthcoming) are randomized evaluations, with information collected from treatment and control groups. Jalan and Ravallion (2003) use propensity score matching to evaluate the distributional outcomes of Argentina's Trabajar program. Ravallion, van de Walle, and Gautam (1995) and van de Walle (2003) use panel data and instrumental variable models to estimate a reduced form equation of household consumption on transfer incomes.

In most cases, the data for a targeting assessment come from a single cross-sectional survey, and hence are insufficient to estimate the MPCT reliably. In such cases, analysts can carry out a sensitivity analysis, estimating the before transfer counterfactual consumption based on a range of possible MPCT values. E. Tesliuc (2004) provides an example of this approach for the Kyrgyz Republic's social protection programs. As expected, he finds that the results are quite sensitive to the assumed MPCT for generous programs like pensions or unemployment benefits and less sensitive for safety net programs with moderate generosity, like the Unified Monthly Benefit.

We interpret the limited available evidence as follows. For programs with high generosity and strong behavioral responses, the static targeting assessment may misspecify the counterfactual consumption, which in turn may lead to erroneous conclusions about targeting and benefit incidence (see van de Walle 2002a for an illustration from the Republic of Yemen). Thus for these programs, estimating the MPCT is important. When available data do not allow a robust estimation, analysts should at least undertake a sensitivity analysis. For safety net programs with moderate generosity, the results of a targeting assessment will not change substantially if behavioral responses are ignored. In this case, the best approximation for the counterfactual income or consumption is the observed level of income or consumption minus the value of the transfer.

Understanding Dynamic Targeting Assessment. Dynamic incidence is a term used to describe a case where quantiles are based not on households' current welfare, but on how household welfare has changed over time. It can therefore be used to describe whether a program is reaching those most severely affected by an economic shock. Dynamic incidence requires panel data.

Sumarto, Suryahadi, and Pritchett (2003) study the static and dynamic incidence of two Indonesian safety net programs: the JPS Operasi Pasar Khusus (Special Market Operations), which sells subsidized rice to targeted households, and an employment creation program in place in 1997–8 during the South Asian financial crisis. The former used administrative targeting while the latter were self-targeted via the wage. The authors classified households into static quintiles based on the consumption level in May 1997 (before the crisis) and dynamic quintiles based on the change in consumption from May 1997 to August 1998. The authors find that the employment creation scheme was much more responsive to household shocks than the sales of subsidized rice. For example, a household from the middle of the expenditure distribution before the crisis that suffered the worst shock was four times more likely to have participated in the employment creation program than a household with a positive shock, but only one-and-a-half times more likely to receive subsidized rice. The authors therefore conclude that self-targeted schemes perform better during crises.

An analysis of Hungarian programs (Ravallion, van de Walle, and Gautam 1995) looks at changes in poverty and cash benefits during the transition. It shows that social assistance was helpful in reducing poverty during a period of change accompanied by a great deal of transient poverty, though much of the effect was due to an increase in spending rather than an improvement in targeting. An analysis for Vietnam for 1992 and 1997 (van de Walle 2002b) shows that during this period of rapid growth and significant poverty reduction, the safety net was ineffective because of a combination of low spending, low coverage, and poor targeting. A good deal of movement in and out of poverty was occurring, and the safety net did not do well at targeting those who suffered shocks, although in this case the targeting was no worse than the targeting of the chronically poor. These analyses underscore the need to use dynamic analysis to look at how well transfer programs actually protect their beneficiaries from shocks.

Simulating How Changes in a Program Would Affect Incidence. Most targeting assessments describe the incidence actually observed in a program, that is, the average incidence, but policy makers often want to know how the benefits or losses occasioned by a change in a program will be distributed.

The simplest case is when policy makers are considering a proportional increase or decrease in the benefit level of a program. In this case, the standard targeting assessment is a marginal method: it gives a first-order approximation of the distributional consequences of a change in the level of benefits (Younger 2003).[5]

Changes in the benefit formula may also leave the distribution of existing beneficiaries largely unchanged, hence the standard targeting assessment can still be used to estimate the incidence of beneficiaries. However, these changes will affect the volume of benefits accruing to different quantile groups. To estimate the benefit incidence properly, analysts should use more complex methods that model the decision to participate in the program and apply this to the new schedule of benefits (Sahn and Younger 2000; Younger 2003).

A more complex case is a change in eligibility criteria. Analysts can estimate the resultant distribution with various degrees of sophistication. The most common method is a simple calculation of who would benefit without taking behavioral changes into account. Countries considering introducing a proxy means test typically simulate the distribution of benefits assuming complete take-up and without modeling changes in labor supply, savings, or the like, and countries may do the same for other program changes. Figure 6.6 shows a calculation undertaken when policy makers were thinking through proposals to replace Indonesia's energy subsidies with a cash transfer (see chapter 10, section 5, for more discussion).

Another case of topical interest is an expansion or a contraction of a program. The marginal incidence will differ from the average incidence if those brought into or removed from a program are, on average, more or less poor than those already in the program. Consider a social insurance program that covers about 70 per-

FIGURE 6.6 **Ex Ante Estimation of the Average Net Impact of Reforming Fuel Subsidies in Indonesia**

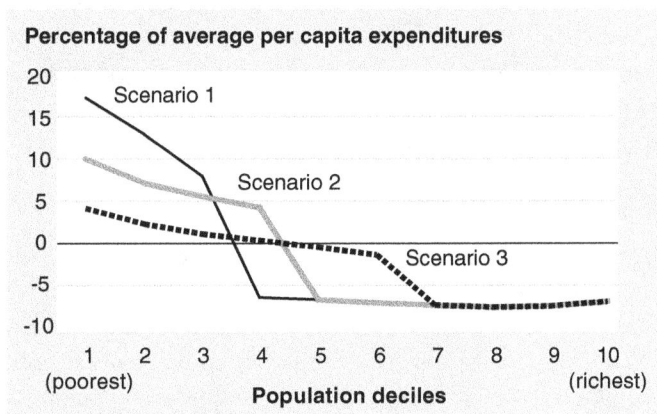

Percentage of average per capita expenditures

SOURCE: Arulpragasam 2006b.

NOTE: Scenario 1: perfect targeting of cash transfer to bottom 28 percent of the population; scenario 2: slight mistargeting, bottom 40 percent of the population receives random cash benefits; scenario 3: greater mistargeting, bottom 60 percent of the population receives random cash benefits.

cent of the population, all at the upper end of the distribution. An expansion of coverage to 80 percent could be expected to benefit only those in the bottom third of the income distribution, a much more pro-poor marginal incidence for the benefits of expansion than for the average incidence of the existing program. For a safety net program that is tightly targeted to the poorest 10 percent of the population, an expansion to cover the poorest 20 percent would also show different marginal than average incidence, but in this case the marginal incidence would be less pro-poor than the average incidence.

Lanjouw and Ravallion (1999b) develop a political economy model where the poor and the nonpoor have different amounts of political power for influencing the allocation of a program and where a given public expenditure has different costs and benefits. Lanjouw and Ravallion apply this model to three poverty alleviation programs using data from India's National Sample Survey for 1993–4—a public works program; the Integrated Rural Development Programme, a means-tested credit scheme; and the public distribution system, a food rationing scheme—and find that additional spending would be significantly more pro-poor than suggested by the average incidence of participation.

Van de Walle (2003) provides a basic reference and primer on how to compute marginal incidence with a single cross-sectional, repeated cross-sectional, or panel dataset. Younger (2003) provides a comparative assessment of different marginal targeting assessment techniques using as an example participation in secondary school in rural Peru in 1994 and 1997 and discusses when using each of the techniques is appropriate and the precision of different targeting assessment estimates.

Understanding the Value Added of a Targeting Assessment

A targeting assessment looks at an important intermediate outcome of safety net programs: do benefits reach the poor and vulnerable? If benefits do not reach them, then the program cannot have an impact on them. If benefits do reach the poor and vulnerable but many others as well, the program may operate at relatively high cost. A targeting assessment does not yield as rich information as an impact assessment, but helps policy makers understand if some of the necessary conditions for impact have been met. As targeting assessments can often be carried out with no extra data collection or with only booster samples to regularly scheduled surveys and as the analytic techniques are not excessively specialized, they can be carried out more frequently than full impact assessments.

IMPACT EVALUATION

Impact evaluation estimates a program's causal effect on the outcomes it seeks to influence—that is, it measures the changes in participants' well-being that can be attributed to a particular program.[6] The specific technique for estimating impacts varies according to the setting, but the fundamental conceptual exercise remains the same. Impacts are determined by comparing the outcomes of program participants with the outcomes those same individuals would have experienced in the absence of the program. Such an experiment is impossible in practice, of course, and all methodologies center on ways of constructing a plausible comparison group or counterfactual. For example, a CCT program that provides cash to households conditional on their children attending school and obtaining regular medical care may have three main objectives: to increase school attendance, reduce morbidity, and reduce poverty among participants. An impact evaluation would determine whether the program was actually achieving higher graduation rates, fewer sicknesses among children, and less poverty than would have been the case without the program. In this case, impact evaluation will measure the graduation rates among program participants and compare them with the estimated rates that would have prevailed for the same participants in the absence of the program. The program's impact on enrollment is the difference between the two outcomes.

Stakeholders may find impact evaluations useful in a number of respects. For example, an impact evaluation of a cash transfer program for low-income households may estimate the program's impact on beneficiaries' earnings, total income, savings, food security, and poverty status (the main objectives); on child welfare and the utilization of other safety net programs (the intermediate objectives); and on employment, remittances, fertility, and marriage (expected collateral or negative impacts). Evaluations of CCT programs in Latin America have estimated their contribution to higher school enrollment and improved academic results, lower levels of child labor and malnutrition, better access to and use of health services, and improved health status. An impact evaluation of a workfare program will typically calculate participants' net wage gains and the indirect benefits to the community of the assets created by the program.

Because a program may affect many outcomes over varying time horizons and for different subgroups of the population, impact evaluations are rarely one-time events. Often a series of evaluation reports looks at different dimensions of a program. Each wave of data collection may generate several evaluation reports and different queries may prompt the gathering of new data. Thus while we refer to "an evaluation," various products are more likely to be the case, in some situations initially planned as a complementary bundle, sometimes not planned that way, but evolving in that direction over time. The initial evaluation of PROGRESA, for example, started with a set of complementary reports looking at the program's impacts on consumption (Hoddinott, Skoufias, and Washburn 2000), health (Gertler 2000), nutrition (Behrman and Hoddinott 2005), and education (Schultz 2000, 2004). Subsequent rounds of data collection and subsequent reports have gone into more depth; they have explored other outcomes, such as adult labor supply (Skoufias and di Maro 2006), migration and fertility (Stecklov and others 2005, 2006), and household investment behavior (Gertler, Martinez, and Rubio-Codino 2006). Many other studies have sought to answer a series of questions posed by management, such as how to achieve greater reductions in anemia or the reasons for lower impacts among indigenous populations.

The results of an impact evaluation enable policy makers and program managers to answer the following questions: (1) Does the program achieve its intended goal or goals? (2) Can the changes in outcomes be explained by the program or are they the result of some other factors occurring simultaneously? (3) Do program impacts vary across different groups of intended beneficiaries, across regions, and over time? (4) Does the program have any unintended effects, either positive or negative? Armed with such evidence, policy makers can decide whether to expand, modify, or eliminate a particular program. Many examples of rigorous and well-planned impact evaluations that have proved extremely useful are available, two of which are highlighted in box 6.6. Many others form the basis of our understanding of the potential of different sorts of programs.

However, evaluations cannot answer every question policy makers might ask in relation to a particular program. In particular, they cannot address many "what if" questions. What if the program were made national? What if the proxy means-test formulas were changed? Such questions can be examined, even if not definitively, using a variety of ex

BOX 6.6 **Ignorance Has High Costs**

PROGRESA, Mexico. In Mexico, a change in government is a serious threat for the survival of social programs. Programs closely associated with the public image of a president are especially vulnerable, as are those perceived to have been abused by a specific political party for electoral purposes (Levy and Rodríguez 2005).

To prevent such risks, the CCT program PROGRESA invested in a credible impact evaluation and a transparent dissemination strategy. To ensure the credibility of the results, PROGRESA opted for a randomized evaluation undertaken by an external evaluator. The result was a series of evaluation reports. The impact evaluation showed that the program was cost-effective; that it selected its target population appropriately; and that it had a positive impact on education, health, nutrition, and diet. The results of the evaluation, including the survey data collected, have been placed in the public domain via the Internet. The results have been broadly disseminated, and special efforts have been made to ensure that Congress has complete information on the program's objectives, methodology, and results. Special efforts have been made not to associate PROGRESA with a particular political party.

In 2000, when the Zedillo administration left office, the incoming Fox administration could decide on the continuation of the program based on hard evidence. Given its demonstrated success, the program was continued and expanded from rural to urban areas. Only the name did not survive the change in government: the program is now known as Oportunidades. The program gained such credibility that in the 2006 elections, all major candidates supported it and it survived another electoral cycle.

National Job Training Partnership Programs, United States. In the mid-1980s, the U.S. Department of Labor commissioned a study of the National Job Training Partnership Act to study the effectiveness of programs funded by the act. The evaluation is one of the largest and most comprehensive of its kind ever undertaken. Some 20,000 program applicants from across the country were included in the experimental design to estimate the impacts on earnings, employment, and welfare receipt of individuals served by the programs. The ambiguous results provided by earlier, nonexperimental evaluations and the large budget for the programs triggered the decision to undertake the evaluation. The results were released to the public in 1994.

Among the findings of the study were that the act had very different effects for adults than for youth. For adults, the programs raised participants' earnings by 7 to 11 percent and provided benefits of about US$1.50 for every US$1.00 invested; however, the programs had no significant impact on earnings for youth, and the costs to society exceeded the benefits. Following the release of the evaluation findings, Congress reduced the budget for the youth component by more than 80 percent (US$500 million annually) and increased the budget for the adult component by 11 percent. Even though the evaluation took eight years to complete and cost US$23 million, it succeeded in having money shifted from a component of the program with no impact to more effective programs.

The study has also yielded longer-term benefits in terms of improved knowledge and basic research. Academic researchers and others have used its rich dataset to study a range of topics from different aspects of job training interventions to evaluation methodology itself.

SOURCES: Greenberg and Shroder 2004; Levy and Rodríguez 2005; Orr 1998.

ante simulation and modeling methods that are generally not part of standard evaluations. Impact evaluations focus on assessing the existing program as implemented.

Establishing a Counterfactual

The essential conundrum of evaluation is that evaluators want to know what would have happened to program beneficiaries in the absence of the program, but can only observe them in the context of the program. Finding a good counterfactual—a control group similar in all respects to the treatment group except for receipt of the program—is key to the reliability of an impact evaluation.

Credible evaluation uses robust statistical techniques to construct the counterfactual. These techniques include randomization or experimental design; quasi-experiments such as matching, regression discontinuity design, or double differences; and nonexperimental or instrumental variable methods (annex 6.3). All these techniques try to guarantee the comparability of the treatment and control groups by avoiding what statisticians refer to as bias (box 6.7).

As increasing numbers of safety net programs are evaluated using robust techniques to generate a counterfactual, a number of quick and easy methods used in the past are quickly falling out of favor, such as before and after program comparisons or comparisons of beneficiaries with nonbeneficiaries. The latter employed two variants: comparisons with those who chose not to enroll in the program or comparisons with those who were not offered the program. The selection of a counterfactual group is easier for before and after or with and without program counterfactuals, but the groups are rarely similar to the beneficiaries of a safety net program, as we cannot know why some people enrolled in the program while others did not. Before and after comparisons may be biased by events that occur during the life of the program and affect program outcomes. For example, a cash transfer program may increase the income of beneficiaries compared with the absence of the program, but cannot entirely mitigate a recession that reduces the incomes of the entire population. This was the case of the Programa de Asignación Familiar II (Family Allowance Program II) in Honduras. Between 2000 and 2002, an economic recession hit the country, reducing the consumption of the poor by about 14 percent. Program beneficiaries received a transfer equivalent to 6.0 to 6.5 percent of their consumption, not enough to fully mitigate the impact of the economic crisis. The impact evaluation showed that consumption by participating households was 7 percent higher than that by a comparable control group selected via randomization. A before and after comparison showed that beneficiaries' consumption fell by 6.5 percent from 2000 to 2002, and may misleadingly have led to the conclusion that the program had a negative impact on consumption.

One of the major drawbacks of the quick and easy types of evaluation is that they tend to generate different results over time. For example, two separate evaluations of Peru's social fund completed a year apart and using different methodologies and data arrived at opposite conclusions on key impacts. This and similar examples reinforce the point that evaluation design is critical.

Estimating Program Impact

Four main methods are available for estimating the impact of a program:

BOX 6.7 **The Problem of Bias**

Determining program impacts is a matter of accounting for as many of the personal, social, economic, and other factors that influence the outcome of interest to isolate the effects of participation in the program. This is usually addressed by comparing the outcomes of the treatment group with those of a comparison group where the groups are similar to each other in all respects except program participation. The similarity of the two groups in the absence of the program is therefore crucial.

Differences between the comparison and treatment groups can result in a biased estimate of program impacts in two ways:

- **Differences in observable characteristics.** If the treatment and comparison groups are very different from one another on measurable factors such as age, education, or economic status, then disentangling the effects of these variables from participation in the program becomes difficult.

- **Differences in unobservable characteristics.** The two groups may differ in ways that are not measurable but that are related to participation in the program. For example, individuals who choose to participate in a program may be more highly motivated or more able than those who decide not to participate, making them more likely to show positive outcomes even without the program. Analysts will attribute the resulting differences in the outcome of interest to the program, while in reality they may be due to the unobservable differences between the groups. This is often called selection bias.

The only way to eliminate both sources of bias is to randomly assign individuals or households that volunteer to participate in the program into treatment and control groups. This experimental design ensures that, with a large enough sample, the two groups are statistically similar in terms of observable and unobservable characteristics.

Experimental evaluation designs are expensive, however, and require advance planning and cooperation from the authorities. Careful nonrandom selection of the comparison group can significantly reduce the bias from observable characteristics and adequate data can help reduce the selection bias under certain circumstances, but there is no way to ensure that selection bias has been eliminated and no way to determine in advance how big a problem this will pose. A trade-off therefore exists between the preferred methodology of experimental design and the less expensive and timelier application of comparison group strategies.

SOURCES: Baker 2000; Orr 1998; Ravallion 1999, 2008.

- **Comparison of means** is a method of estimating impact using an experimental design that involves comparing means of treatment and control groups. A random allocation of the intervention among eligible beneficiaries creates comparable treatment and control groups. The program's impact on the outcome being evaluated can be measured by the difference between the means of the samples of the treatment group and the control group. This method can be used only if the counterfactual has been built using experimental and quasi-experimental design.

Note that this method only uses observations made at one point in time and therefore assumes that the outcomes of the treated and the counterfactual populations evolve in a similar way over time.

- **Double difference or difference-in-differences method** is another estimation method that can be used with experimental, quasi-experimental, and nonexperimental designs. Impact is estimated by comparing the outcomes for the treatment and the comparison groups (first difference) before and after the intervention (second difference). This method requires baseline and follow-up data from the same treatment and control groups, ideally as panel data. If the samples for the follow-up survey differ from the baseline survey, they should be from the same geographic clusters or strata in terms of some other variable.

- **Multivariate regression** is used with nonexperimental designs to control for possible observable characteristics that distinguish participants and nonparticipants. If controlling for all possible reasons why outcomes might differ is possible, then this method is valid for estimating the program's effects. The differences in the mean outcomes of the two groups, participants and nonparticipants, conditional on the set of variables that cause outcome and participation, constitute the program or treatment effect.

- **Instrumental variables** are used with nonexperimental design to control for selection bias. These variables determine program participation, but do not affect outcomes. Evaluators can often use geographic variations in program availability and program characteristics as instruments, especially when endogenous program placement seems to be a source of bias.

Implementing an Impact Evaluation

An impact evaluation involves several steps: (1) establishing evaluation objectives, (2) determining appropriate evaluation methods, (3) collecting data, and (4) producing and disseminating findings. A main factor that influences each of these steps is their cost.

To provide the highest value, an impact evaluation should include the following key design features:

- **Clear objectives.** Evaluation questions should be determined early during the process and should be simple and measurable.

- **Credible evaluator.** The evaluator should have the required specialized skills. An evaluator external to the agency or government is generally preferable to ensure objectivity and independence.

- **Rigorous methodology.** Experimental estimates are the ideal, but a well-chosen, matched comparison group may suffice.

- **Adequate sample size.** The sample should be large enough to detect program effects of plausible size. In addition, the size should permit assessment of program impacts on key subgroups of the target population as appropriate. Minimum detectable effects should be determined prior to implementation of the evaluation.

- **Baseline data.** These are needed to establish the appropriate comparison group and to control for observable program selection criteria.

- **Sufficient follow-up.** Follow-up data should be collected after enough time has passed to plausibly detect an impact and should measure the relevant outcome variables.

The costs of impact evaluations of safety net and other social programs vary considerably, ranging anywhere from US$200,000 to more than US$1 million, with an average for a rigorous evaluation probably amounting to around US$300,000 to US$400,000. Features affecting total costs include the number and type of policy questions to be addressed, the methodology, the extent of collection of new data, the size and scope of the program being evaluated, and the level of local capacity. The largest single cost item is usually data collection, which can vary widely depending on sample size, complexity of the survey effort, and the number of rounds of data collection. In reviewing 125 evaluations of World Bank health, education, and social protection projects, Fiszbein (2008) reports that data collection accounted for half or more of evaluation costs.

Deciding When Impact Evaluations Should Be Conducted

Impact evaluations demand a substantial amount of information, time, and resources; therefore the public actions that will be evaluated should be carefully selected. This can be done by asking three basic questions. If just one is answered affirmatively, this should support the need for a rigorous impact evaluation:

- Is the program of strategic relevance for national public policy?
- Can the evaluation results influence the design of the program?
- Will the evaluation contribute to improving the state of knowledge about a particular type of program or policy and does the information generated have potential future research value?

One important caveat is that fruitful evaluations require sufficiently mature programs. Even though programs may be testing innovative approaches, before they can be evaluated they need clearly defined objectives, well-delineated activities, and a stable institutional framework for implementation. Many programs are not ready for an impact evaluation, and some programs will never be worth a full evaluation. Before deciding to evaluate a program, assessing whether the program is "evaluable" is important. Such an undertaking can save substantial human and financial resources.

A program must fulfill a number of criteria before being evaluated (table 6.11). An evaluable intervention is stable as opposed to still developing or likely to change in major ways, is clear about its goals, is reasonably homogenous across different program sites, is substantial enough to have impacts, has enough participants to demonstrate results, and can be documented.

Politics and the political economy play an important role in the decision to conduct a program evaluation. The issues stem from principal-agent problems, where stakeholders—including the government or funding agency, the implementing agency, and the beneficiaries—do not have consistent incentives to support an evaluation.

Several factors, as follows, work against the decision to undertake an impact evaluation:

- Managers of highly constrained or poorly performing programs may fear documenting their poor results (Pritchett 2002). Negative findings have the potential

TABLE 6.11 **When to Conduct an Impact Evaluation: A Checklist**

Issue	Criterion	Question
	Well-defined objectives or not	Are the program's objectives clearly defined?
Nature of outcomes	Short or long term	Can final outcomes be assessed before the evaluation ends?
	Unique or multiple	Is expressing the effects of the program using few outcomes reasonable?
	Quantitative or qualitative	Are outcomes qualitative in nature or difficult to measure?
	Heterogeneity	Is the program a mixed bag of different interventions?
Nature of the program	Implementation	Is implementation likely to vary significantly within the program?
	Unit of analysis	Is the program directed at areas or communities and/or is its sample too small?
	Scale effect	Is the potential impact on outcomes likely to be small relative to the scale of the problem?
Context	External influences	Is the potential impact on outcomes likely to be small relative to other external influences on outcomes?
	Active or passive clients	Is the effectiveness of the program sensitive to how clients choose to respond to it?

SOURCE: Authors.

NOTE: To proceed with an impact evaluation, the first three questions should be answered "yes," and the remainder "no."

to hinder social agendas and damage political careers, thus for policy makers not to present their detractors with a club to beat them may seem easier and safer. Even managers of better-performing programs can fear results that are ambiguous or difficult to translate into policy actions.

- The time horizons of policy makers, program managers, and evaluation processes differ. National governments usually serve for only four or five years and local governments for only one or two years, but evaluations can take several years from planning to results. Managers with many competing priorities may tend to focus on actions with more immediate payoffs.

- Evaluation is a public good, yielding not only lessons that may be important to the specific program being evaluated, but to similar programs (Duflo, Glennerster, and Kremer 2008). As individual policy makers and the government do not reap the all the benefits of the evaluation, they will not have an incentive to invest fully in it.

At the same time, program officials may support evaluation of their programs either to be able to improve them or to document their successes and use that documentation for seeking funds; ministries of finance or donors may support evaluations to help them make allocation decisions; and civil society groups may support evaluations as a way to increase government accountability.

Governments and their international partners can do a number of things to encourage impact evaluation, or the broader M&E agenda, at the program level. Governments may offer to help program managers by covering the costs of M&E by subsidizing such budgets in cash or providing in-kind assistance. They may also reward managers of programs with good M&E systems through increased budgets or managerial autonomy. Governments can mandate regular cycles of M&E for all programs by law or as part of budget reviews or legislative oversight. In addition, they can put in place public information practices that implicitly raise the pressure on programs to provide information. Finally, leadership of and support for M&E can be articulated in policy statements from the chief executive on down (McKay 2007).

Notes

1. The PSNP is part of a larger safety net, the Food Security Program, deployed by the government of Ethiopia to protect chronically food-insecure households. The Food Security Program includes three initiatives: the PSNP, the Resettlement Program, and the Income Generation Program. The government agency coordinating the Food Security Program, the Food Security Coordination Bureau, developed an M&E framework for the entire Food Security Program; however, to simplify the presentation of M&E concepts, this section only presents the logical framework of the PSNP.

2. Assessing targeting efficiency is less critical for other public programs that may aim for universal coverage, such as the provision of health care and education, although the issue of whether the poor are included in such programs still remains and a targeting assessment will provide the answer.

3. If the incidence results are presented using household quantiles, judging whether the distribution of benefits is progressive or regressive will be difficult without additional information. For example, if we find that 40 percent of program benefits accrue to the poorest population quintile, then we immediately know that, on average, each individual recipient in that quintile got twice as much as they would have received if the money had been allocated randomly. If the findings refer to household quintiles, we do not know how successful the program targeting was. If the households in the poorest quintile are twice as large as the average household, then they would represent 40 percent of the population. In this case, the program targeting is no better than a blind, random allocation. We favor the use of population quantiles.

4. For normal goods, whose consumption increases with the income level of the beneficiary, rich consumers will capture a larger amount (and share) of the total subsidy. Hence beneficiary incidence will underestimate benefit incidence.

5. We term this first-order approximation, because eligible beneficiaries may respond differently to an increase or decrease in the benefit level. For example, more generous benefits may induce marginally eligible households to apply for the program.

6. This subsection draws heavily on Baker (2000); Blomquist (2003); and Prennushi, Rubio, and Subbarao (2002).

Annex 6.1 Sample M&E Indicators for Typical Safety Net Interventions

I. Cash transfers

Input indicators
- Budget allocation and expenditures
- Number of program staff by level

Output indicators
Beneficiaries
- Number of program beneficiaries (total and as a percentage of the estimated target population)
- Key characteristics of beneficiaries: gender, age, level of education, number of dependents, employment status (or employment history depending on eligibility requirements), household income, location

Benefits and services
- Amount of benefits paid (total per payment period by area)

Intermediate outcome indicators
Access and satisfaction
- Targeting efficiency as measured by inclusion and exclusion errors
- Average time of program participation
- Beneficiary satisfaction with program access and delivery

Outcome indicators
Depending on program objective
- Increase in beneficiary household consumption
- Increase in beneficiary consumption of specific products (for example, food)
- Decrease in poverty incidence or depth

Process and efficiency indicators (to be compared to targets, past performance, or other measurement units)
Entry (outreach, targeting, registration, and so on)
- Average (and range) of time for processing applications to the program (calendar days following the application)
- Number of benefits processed per month per staff member of the implementing agency

Payment
- Cost of processing payments per beneficiary
- Beneficiaries experiencing payment delays as a percentage of total beneficiaries
- Beneficiaries not collecting their payments as a percentage of total beneficiaries
- Amount of assistance provided to individual clients; office or facility that provided the assistance; method of service delivery (useful for testing different approaches); individual supervisor or caseworker

Exit
- Average (and range of) time for cancellation of the benefit (calendar days following a finding of ineligibility, fraud, or the like)
- Beneficiaries whose benefit is canceled as a percentage of total beneficiaries by reason for cancellation

Administration
- Average administrative cost of program (and range) per beneficiary
- Average benefit (and range) per beneficiary (depending on the terms of the program)
- Total amount of benefits paid as a percentage of total cost to the government of the program
- Amount used as a percentage of the amount allocated

II. Food-based transfers

Input indicators
- Budget expenditures
- Number of program staff by level
- Quantity of food available

Output indicators
Beneficiaries
Of food for education, school feeding or take-home rations programs
- Number of schools covered
- Number of children who received a ration or meal (by gender)
- Number of rations or meals distributed

Of nutrition (child and maternal health) programs
- Total number of participating health centers, community centers, village volunteers
- Number of pregnant and lactating women who received a monthly take-home ration of fortified food
- Number of children aged 6 to 59 months who received a monthly take-home ration of fortified food
- Number of pregnant and lactating women who participated in health care and child nutrition training sessions
- Number of take-home rations of fortified food distributed

Intermediate outcome indicators
Food for education, school feeding, or take-home rations
- Enrollment of poor children
- Quality of food served in schools

Nutrition (child and maternal health)
- Prevalence of poor and mothers participating in the program
- Quality of services provided (amount of waiting time)

Outcome indicators
Food for education, school feeding, or take-home rations
- School enrollment rate (by gender and grade)

- School dropout rate (by gender and grade)
- Nutritional status of children

Nutrition (child and maternal health)

- Decrease in prevalence of low body mass index among women 2 to 6 months postpartum
- Decrease in prevalence of iron deficiency anemia among pregnant and lactating women and children aged 6 to 59 months
- Decrease in prevalence of malnutrition (severe and moderate) in children

Process and efficiency indicators

Food for education

- Total number of people involved in schools per beneficiary served
- Average frequency of distribution (and range) of rations and meals
- Average cost (and range) of rations and meals (disaggregated as appropriate by region and other characteristics)
- Average program cost per beneficiary

Nutrition (child and maternal health)

- Average cost (and range) of take-home rations
- Average share in costs of fortified, blended food
- Average cost (and range) of health care and child nutrition training sessions
- Average cost per beneficiary (per child and per pregnant or lactating woman)

III. Public works programs

Input indicators

- Budget expenditures for salaries, intermediate inputs, and administration
- Amount of food available in the budget (food-for-work projects)
- Number of program staff by level

Output indicators

Projects

- Number of workfare projects by type (for example, with and without financing of materials) and by province or region
- Project specific: actual kilometers of water or sewer lines or roads maintained or built
- Wages paid to workers (per day, per month, by province, and overall)
- Amount of food distributed as wages (for food-for-work projects)

Beneficiaries

- Number of workers participating in the program
- Total number of beneficiaries employed in each activity
- Key characteristics of beneficiaries: gender, age, previous economic activity, education level, number of children, previous participation in an employment or training program, household income, confirmation of education and health certificates
- Actual number of unemployed people who received the minimum wage

Intermediate outcome indicators

Projects

- Location of projects in poor areas (correlation of number of projects and total expenditures with the incidence of poverty, number of unemployed poor, and so on within the country and within provinces)
- Quality of projects completed
- Utilization by poor communities of infrastructure built, expanded, or rehabilitated under the program

Beneficiaries

- Number of low-income workers employed in the project (total target, gender-specific target)
- Beneficiaries experiencing payment delays as a percentage of total beneficiaries

Outcome indicators

- Increase in net annual earnings of the average individual beneficiary
- Number of program beneficiaries who transitioned from workfare to formal sector employment
- If the objective is to fight seasonal hunger: percentage of beneficiaries whose diet improved
- Increase in second-round effects resulting from projects, for example, the number of people accessing roads or other infrastructure built or maintained

Process and efficiency indicators

Projects

- Average time taken to select viable projects (in calendar days)
- Number of projects appraised and evaluated per month (overall and by province)
- Number of projects evaluated as a percentage of total projects per month (overall and by province)
- Number of projects supervised per supervisor per month
- Number of supervision visits per project per month (overall and by province)
- Average number of supervision visits per project during project execution (overall and by province)
- Number of workfare activities executed by province (with and without financing of materials)
- Number of supervision visits to training courses and basic education courses
- Percentage of projects located in poor areas (quintiles 1 and 2) (target = 100 percent)
- Wages paid as a percentage of the contract amount
- Average cost (and range) per project category
- Average share of labor cost (and range) per project category
- Average share of the cost for wages in food (for food-for-work projects)

Additional related objectives (such as community involvement)

- Percentage of projects with participation by nongovernmental organizations, civil society organizations, and so on (overall and by province)
- Percentage of projects sponsored by nongovernmental organizations, municipalities, and the like (overall and by province)

Jobs

- Jobs provided per estimated target population (overall and by province)

- Poor (bottom quintile) workers as a percentage of public works laborers

Administration

- Amount spent as a percentage of the amount allocated by province
- Efficiency of employment program (value of salaries received by workers as a percentage of total government cost of program)
- Labor intensity of projects
- Unit cost, for example, by kilometer of road built
- Average cost per beneficiary by project type

IV. Conditional cash transfers

The indicators used to monitor cash transfers are also used for conditional cash transfers. In addition, the following aspects are monitored.

Output indicators

Benefits and services

- School attendance rate by children
- Health care utilization by children from birth through six years old and not enrolled in school

Intermediate outcome indicators

Access and satisfaction

- Beneficiary satisfaction with availability and access to schools
- Beneficiary satisfaction with availability and access to health care facilities

Outcome indicators

Education-based requirements

- Change in school attendance, primary and secondary school
- Change in secondary school enrollment

Health care–based requirements for children and adults

- Change in the percentage of children brought to health centers for preventive care
- Change in the number of children aged newborn through age six and not enrolled in school who have received all required immunizations on time
- Change in the number of poor pregnant and lactating women visiting health centers for timely checkups
- Change in the number of poor elderly, disabled, and other beneficiaries visiting health centers

Process and efficiency indicators

- Administrative costs for beneficiary selection, delivery of cash, and verification of compliance

Annex 6.2 Monitoring of Oportunidades, Mexico

TABLE A6.2.1 **Selected Monitoring, Evaluation, and Performance Indicators Used by Oportunidades, Mexico, 1999–2003**

	1999	2000	2001		2002		2003
Indicator	**Jan.–Feb.**	**July–Aug.**	**Jan.–Feb.**	**July–Aug.**	**Jan.–Feb.**	**July–Aug.**	**Jan.–Feb.**
% of beneficiary families monitored	95.95 (84.80–120.23)	97.44 (88.71–100.00)	97.98 (94.49–100.00)	97.95 (93.78–100.00)	97.75 (91.34–100.00)	97.97 (91.63–100.00)	97.62 (93.26–100.00)
% of children under 2 under nutritional surveillance	—	73.94 (47.19–100.00)	90.85 (74.50–100.36)	92.53 (69.09–100.00)	93.08 (65.61–125.09)	94.27 (83.04–100.00)	95.08 (81.25–99.99)
% of children aged 2–4 under nutritional surveillance	—	72.76 (43.28–100.00)	90.37 (78.15–100.00)	91.54 (68.57–100.00)	92.93 (74.86–122.70)	94.00 (82.77–100.00)	95.12 (79.90–100.00)
% of children under 2 with malnutrition	7.38 (0.00–16.52)	20.20 (3.61–33.55)	16.12 (2.22–31.89)	16.29 (4.40–32.87)	15.75 (4.73–32.66)	16.46 (5.95–32.61)	15.48 (5.14–31.63)
% of children aged 2–4 with malnutrition	10.87 (0.00–24.09)	35.82 (5.93–52.94)	28.03 (5.52–50.33)	27.16 (5.98–50.48)	25.33 (5.69–50.03)	25.96 (7.77–49.53)	24.52 (7.85–47.76)
% of pregnant mothers registered with prenatal care facilities	215.04 (129.18–498.11)	87.42 (65.28–100.90)	92.82 (67.98–100.00)	93.76 (70.47–101.03)	95.76 (76.58–125.37)	96.78 (84.36–100.00)	97.38 (83.44–100.00)
Avg. # of prenatal visits per pregnant women	5.18 (4.02–6.32)	1.78 (1.30–2.24)	1.62 (0.85–3.09)	1.81 (1.12–2.49)	1.73 (0.89–2.22)	1.81 (0.98–2.45)	1.79 (1.28–2.57)
% of nursing mothers under monitoring	78.85 (49.37–239.23)	89.26 (73.33–100.00)	93.43 (70.02–100.00)	92.70 (63.19–100.44)	94.66 (72.61–122.12)	96.16 (68.62–99.98)	97.13 (80.89–100.00)
% of children under 2 who received nutritional supplements	289.40 (34.04–857.12)	87.61 (41.76–127.09)	51.87 (20.54–94.05)	76.34 (42.40–95.92)	76.19 (35.32–104.39)	76.56 (44.48–101.12)	77.55 (53.41–101.19)
% of children aged 2–4 who received nutritional supplements	132.83 (30.50–386.00)	130.97 (70.80–363.96)	80.06 (40.00–373.35)	121.53 (78.07–462.50)	125.67 (51.17–862.35)	117.79 (46.83–322.33)	114.81 (62.50–363.60)
% of pregnant women who received food supplements	308.45 (133.16–2,083.90)	94.88 (69.66–130.47)	64.65 (25.12–98.91)	83.60 (44.23–99.66)	83.96 (59.15–104.54)	83.85 (55.21–107.41)	84.57 (62.48–109.95)

(continued)

TABLE A6.2.1 **(continued)**

Indicator	1999 Jan.–Feb.	2000 July–Aug.	2001 Jan.–Feb.	2001 July–Aug.	2002 Jan.–Feb.	2002 July–Aug.	2003 Jan.–Feb.
% of nursing mothers who received nutritional supplements	238.60 (106.07–1,407.35)	72.29 (50.25–98.46)	58.07 (33.46–98.52)	79.90 (30.17–99.56)	81.24 (49.71–104.46)	79.63 (47.26–109.14)	88.32 (63.93–140.48)
% of children under 2 who recovered from malnutrition	16.53 (2.17–542.86)	6.36 (2.35–50.00)	6.72 (2.10–274.42)	6.06 (2.14–80.00)	5.40 (0.00–64.39)	4.28 (0.00–12.27)	5.02 (1.05–15.08)
% of children aged 2–4 who recovered from malnutrition	19.74 (1.81–879.41)	6.52 (3.10–77.9)3	5.97 (2.57–111.34)	6.05 (1.72–85.87)	4.96 (2.10–31.77)	4.42 (1.68–11.71)	4.76 (1.94–14.09)
% of children under 2 with mild malnutrition	—	15.41 (3.61–23.92)	12.54 (1.78–23.51)	12.47 (4.40–23.79)	12.17 (3.96–23.82)	12.53 (5.24–23.26)	11.85 (4.55–22.59)
% of children aged 2–4 with mild malnutrition	—	28.46 (4.78–42.67)	22.66 (4.14–41.22)	22.02 (5.56–39.61)	20.69 (5.40–38.05)	21.01 (7.25–37.34)	19.87 (7.10–35.98)
% of children under 2 with moderate malnutrition	—	4.28 (0.00–8.49)	3.24 (0.43–7.30)	3.43 (0.00–9.16)	3.25 (0.35–7.88)	3.55 (0.63–8.27)	3.25 (0.55–7.94)
% of children aged 2–4 with moderate malnutrition	—	6.79 (0.83–13.99)	4.95 (0.50–11.8)8	4.77 (0.31–11.86)	4.31 (0.29–10.89)	4.60 (0.50–11.81)	4.29 (0.58–10.75)
% of children under 2 with severe malnutrition	—	0.51 (0.00–1.13)	0.35 (0.00–1.08)	0.39 (0.00–1.47)	0.33 (0.00–1.09)	0.38 (0.00–1.33)	0.39 (0.00–1.37)
% of children aged 2–4 with severe malnutrition	—	0.58 (0.00–1.38)	0.42 (0.00–1.30)	0.37 (0.00–1.13)	0.33 (0.00–1.09)	0.35 (0.01–1.13)	0.36 (0.00–1.19)
% of children with low birthweight born to beneficiaries at attended births	—	4.02 (0.90–9.74)	3.27 (0.40–33.33)	3.93 (0.00–6.94)	3.31 (0.00–15.79)	3.04 (0.00–14.29)	2.61 (0.00–5.63)
Avg. # of families served by each delivery point	—	581	504	615	534	641	680
% of total # of participating families that did not pick up their benefits	—	—	2.04 (0.75–5.48)	2.02 (0.00–8.52)	2.82 (1.71–14.70)	0.83 (0.00–3.69)	2.01 (0.003–4.48)

(continued)

TABLE A6.2.1 (continued)

	1999	2000	2001		2002		2003
Indicator	Jan.–Feb.	July–Aug.	Jan.–Feb.	July–Aug.	Jan.–Feb.	July–Aug.	Jan.–Feb.
Education grant recipients[a]							
# of recipients aged 8–17 enrolled in basic ed. as % of all children 8–17 on roster as of beginning of school year	—	—	38.46 (36.63– 40.17)		61.42 (58.35– 66.62)		—
# of recipients aged 14–20 in upper-level secondary ed. as % of all children aged 14–20 on roster as of beginning of school year	—	—	5.17 (1.85– 9.25)		13.27 (7.13– 23.46)		—
# of recipients who finished primary, lower secondary, and upper secondary ed. as % of all recipients enrolled in last grade of each level at beginning of school year	—	—	95.72 (92.04– 97.41)		94.80 (85.83– 96.38)		—
# of recipients who remained enrolled in school as % of all recipients enrolled in previous year as of beginning of school year[b]	—	—	71.68 (67.63– 75.66)		85.05 (80.77– 88.54)		—
# of recipients who finished school year as % of all recipients who began that year[b]	—	—	96.58 (91.70– 98.22)		95.12 (87.99– 96.74)		—
# of recipients enrolled in next grade as % of all recipients who finished previous year as of beginning of school year	—	—	83.94 (76.21– 92.22)		84.19 (80.26– 90.53)		—

SOURCE: Levy and Rodríguez 2005.

NOTE: — = not available. Data are national averages; ranges are indicated in parentheses and represent minimum and maximum values at the state level. Where the range extends beyond 100 percent, this reflects program expansion, when new or future beneficiaries are reported as being served by health or education facilities and this number is higher than the current number of beneficiaries.

a. The data refer to September–October of each year.

b. For 2001, the figure refers to primary education and for 2002 to lower and upper secondary education.

TABLE A6.2.2 **Indicators Collected from the Sample of Sentinel Points, by Area of Residence, in Percentages, Oportunidades, Mexico, 2000-02**

Item		2000			2001			2002		
		1st panel	2nd panel	Average	1st panel	2nd panel	Average	1st panel	2nd panel	Average
Rural (Social Security Institute and Ministry of Health)										
Human resources	Has a physician	96.01	94.70	95.35	96.05	98.50	97.28	98.15	99.20	98.68
	Has a nurse	91.90	92.65	92.28	92.65	96.00	94.33	95.75	—	95.75
	Receives S2	84.09	86.77	85.43	88.70	86.60	87.65	92.15	95.80	93.98
	Sufficiency of nutritional supplement for children	95.49	86.74	91.11	96.90	97.30	97.10	98.10	86.00	92.05
	Sufficiency of nutritional supplement for women	95.03	87.82	91.42	96.70	96.30	96.50	98.20	—	98.20
Supplies	Availability of tools	87.80	84.97	86.39	87.00	91.10	89.05	90.25	—	90.25
	Has teaching materials	81.94	84.67	83.31	88.80	90.20	89.50	87.80	—	87.80
	Sufficiency of curative materials	85.52	75.69	80.61	79.90	83.30	81.60	81.95	—	81.95
	Sufficient drugs	72.11	73.41	72.76	71.15	75.35	73.25	72.55	76.80	74.68
	Medical care	92.24	94.15	93.20	94.40	94.15	94.28	94.65	—	94.65
	Monitoring of delivery of nutritional supplement	91.61	93.06	92.33	95.05	96.70	95.88	96.80	—	96.80
	Attendance at educational sessions	92.94	95.50	94.22	94.70	98.05	96.38	97.75	94.40	96.08
	Verification of health component activities by health information system for general population	95.01	95.35	95.18	92.30	96.45	94.38	96.40	—	96.40
Records	Bimonthly preparation of nutritional supplement requirements	89.99	90.37	90.18	90.60	92.95	91.78	92.35	—	92.35
	S1s updated	75.24	71.00	73.12	81.45	85.85	83.65	85.45	—	85.45
	Absences per 2-month period in S2	95.79	97.95	96.87	97.95	97.95	97.95	97.60	—	97.60
	Timely delivery of S2	97.22	97.50	97.36	98.75	99.45	99.10	99.45	—	99.45

(continued)

TABLE A6.2.2 (continued)

Item		2000			2001			2002		
		1st panel	2nd panel	Average	1st panel	2nd panel	Average	1st panel	2nd panel	Average
Food	Monitoring of nutritional status for less than 5 years	90.33	91.87	91.10	92.90	94.45	93.68	95.30	—	95.30
	Training of mothers in preparation of supplement	95.11	94.85	94.98	94.95	98.40	96.68	97.95	—	97.95
	Waited 1 hour or more during a health clinic visit	—	—	—	—	65.00	65.00	58.60	62.10	60.35
	Pregnant or nursing women who did not receive a supplement	—	—	—	—	8.00	8.00	4.70	4.94	4.82
	Indicated not receiving a supplement for children who needed it	—	—	—	—	4.00	4.00	3.80	4.90	4.35
General	Were charged for supplement (conditions imposed)	—	—	—	—	12.00	12.00	17.30	1.30	9.30
	Indicated acute respiratory infections as common health problem among children in their community	—	—	—	—	57.00	57.00	64.40	—	64.40
	Indicated acute diarrheal diseases as common health problem among children	—	—	—	—	37.00	37.00	28.50	—	28.50
Urban (Social Security Institute and Ministry of Health)										
Human resources	Has a physician	—	—	—	96.00	94.70	95.35	98.90	99.47	99.19
	Has a nurse	—	—	—	91.90	92.65	92.28	98.43	98.10	98.27
	Receives S2	—	—	—	83.75	86.75	85.25	95.57	96.04	95.81
	Sufficiency of nutritional supplement for children	—	—	—	95.50	86.75	91.13	89.42	95.20	92.31
	Sufficiency of nutritional supplement for women	—	—	—	95.00	87.80	91.40	88.22	95.71	91.97
Supplies	Availability of tools	—	—	—	87.80	84.95	86.38	63.80	70.97	67.38
	Has teaching materials	—	—	—	82.80	84.65	83.73	64.41	73.46	68.94
	Sufficiency of curative materials	—	—	—	85.45	75.70	80.58	75.29	62.97	69.13
	Sufficient drugs	—	—	—	73.35	73.40	73.38	49.68	56.33	53.00

(continued)

TABLE A6.2.2 **(continued)**

Item	2000			2001			2002		
	1st panel	2nd panel	Average	1st panel	2nd panel	Average	1st panel	2nd panel	Average
Medical care	—	—	—	92.55	94.15	93.35	93.27	95.97	94.62
Monitoring of delivery of nutritional supplement	—	—	—	91.55	93.05	92.30	93.51	98.94	96.22
Attendance at educational sessions	—	—	—	92.90	95.50	94.20	96.15	99.10	97.63
Verification of health component activities by health information system for general population	—	—	—	94.30	91.90	93.10	84.54	97.68	91.11
Records									
Bimonthly preparation of nutritional supplement requirements	—	—	—	90.00	90.25	90.13	93.24	95.30	94.27
S1s updated	—	—	—	76.10	71.00	73.55	82.66	89.19	85.92
Absences per 2-month period in S2	—	—	—	95.80	97.95	96.88	94.80	96.33	95.57
Timely delivery of S2	—	—	—	97.20	97.50	97.35	99.33	99.77	99.55
Monitoring of nutritional status for less than 5 years	—	—	—	90.20	91.85	91.03	95.03	93.94	94.49
Food									
Training of mothers in preparation of supplement	—	—	—	95.50	49.85	72.68	98.31	98.11	98.21
Waited 1 hour or more during a health clinic visit	—	—	—	—	—	—	42.40	30.30	36.35
Pregnant or nursing mothers who did not receive supplement	—	—	—	—	—	—	9.90	5.70	7.80
Indicated not receiving a supplement for children who needed it	—	—	—	—	—	—	13.00	14.00	13.50
General									
Were charged for the supplement (conditions imposed)	—	—	—	—	—	—	13.20	16.70	14.95
Indicated acute respiratory infections as common health problem among children in their community	—	—	—	—	—	—	62.50	64.30	63.40
Indicated acute diarrheal diseases as common health problem among children	—	—	—	—	—	—	30.70	30.30	30.50

SOURCE: Levy and Rodríguez 2005.

NOTE: — = not available. The panels are for various two-month periods during the year. Upon registration at a health clinic, beneficiaries are given a booklet containing a schedule of appointments for each household member. This information is entered on an S1 form brought to the clinic by the beneficiary, ensuring that a record of attendance is kept at the clinic. The S2 is a form for registering household compliance/noncompliance with health conditions. It must be filled out by a nurse or doctor at the health unit every two months to certify that family members visited as required.

Annex 6.3 A Summary of Experimental Methods

The methods used to select the counterfactual or control group, known as evaluation designs, can be broadly classified into three categories: experimental, quasi-experimental, and nonexperimental. These three evaluation designs vary in terms of feasibility, cost, degree of clarity, validity of results, and extent of selection bias. This annex, adapted from Ravallion (2008), summarizes these designs.

The experimental (randomized) design involves gathering a set of individuals (or other unit of analysis) equally eligible and willing to participate in the program and randomly dividing them into two groups: those who receive the intervention (the treatment group) and those from whom the intervention is withheld (the control group). Experimental designs are generally considered the most robust of the evaluation methodologies. By randomly allocating the intervention among eligible beneficiaries, the assignment process itself creates comparable treatment and control groups that are statistically equivalent to one another given appropriate sample sizes. This is a powerful outcome because, in theory, the control groups generated through random assignment serve as a perfect counterfactual, free from the selection bias that plagues other evaluations.

The quasi-experimental design consists of constructing a comparison group using matching or reflexive comparisons. Matching involves identifying people who are not participating in the program who are comparable in terms of essential characteristics to participants. Matched comparison groups can be selected before project implementation (prospective studies) or afterwards (retrospective studies).

Many methods are available for selecting a counterfactual group using matching techniques, some more robust, some less robust. The following three methods are likely to produce a robust counterfactual:

- **Propensity score matching.** The most widely used type of matching is propensity score matching, in which the comparison group is matched to the treatment group by using the propensity score (predicted probability of participation given observed characteristics). This method allows the analyst to find a comparison group from a sample of nonparticipants closest in terms of observable characteristics to a sample of program participants. Score matching is a useful method when the analyst has to match many potential characteristics between a sample of program participants and a sample of nonparticipants. Instead of aiming to ensure that the matched control for each participant has exactly the same value of the control variable X, the same result can be achieved by matching on the predicted probability of program participation, P, given X, which is known as the propensity score of X. The range of propensity scores estimated for the treatment group should correspond closely to that for the retained sample of nonparticipants. The closer the propensity score, the better the match. A good comparison group comes from the same economic environment and is administered the same questionnaire as the treatment group by similarly trained interviewers.

- **Pipeline matching.** This is another widespread type of matching in which groups of beneficiaries who have already received an intervention are matched against groups of beneficiaries selected to receive the program in the near future.

- **Regression discontinuity design.** This is a combination of traditional randomized experiments and quasi-experiments. In regression discontinuity designs, participants are assigned to either the program or comparison groups on the basis of a cutoff score that was assigned before the implementation of the program; for example, the score on a proxy means test for a needs-based program of last resort or age for a child allowance or social pension. Typically those scoring above or equal to a certain cutoff value will be allowed to participate in the program and those who score below the value will not. The main assumption is that those just below and above the cutoff point will have similar characteristics other than their participation in the program.

Reflexive comparison is another type of quasi-experimental design. In a reflexive comparison, the counterfactual is constructed on the basis of the situation of program participants before the program. Thus program participants are compared before and after the intervention and function as both the treatment and the comparison group. This type of design is particularly useful in evaluations of full-coverage interventions, such as national policies and programs in which the entire population participates. There is, however, a major drawback with reflexive comparisons: the situation of program participants before and after the intervention may change for many reasons independent of the program; for example, participants in a training program may have improved employment prospects after the program. While this improvement may be due to the program, it may also be due to the fact that the economy is recovering from a past crisis and employment is growing again. Unless they are carefully done, reflexive comparisons may be unable to distinguish between the program and other external effects, thereby compromising the reliability of results.

The nonexperimental evaluation design uses statistical econometric multivariate methods to account for differences between the two groups. In this case, instrumental variables is one of the econometric techniques that can be used to compare program participants and nonparticipants correcting for selection bias. It consists of using one or more variables (instruments) that matter to participation, but not to outcomes given participation. This identifies the exogenous variation in outcomes attributable to the program, recognizing that its placement may not be random, but purposive. The instrumental variables are first used to predict program participation, then the program's impact is estimated using the predicted values from the first equation. As with quasi-experimental methods, this evaluation design is relatively cheap and easy to implement, as it can draw on existing data sources; however, it poses a number of difficulties. First, the reliability of results is often reduced, as the methodology is less robust statistically. Second, the methodology has some statistical complexities that may require expertise in the design of the evaluation and in the analysis and interpretation of results. Third, although partially correcting for selection bias is possible, full correction remains a challenge.

## CHAPTER 7

Understanding Common Interventions

KEY MESSAGES

Many different types of safety net programs exist: cash and in-kind transfers, general subsidies, public works programs, conditional cash transfers (CCTs), and fee waivers for health and education. This chapter describes the key design features, appropriate context, implementation challenges, and track record of such programs. These must be well understood if policy makers are to make appropriate choices about which programs to use to achieve their desired objectives and reach specific target groups.

The common grouping or labeling of similar programs—for example, as cash transfers or public works programs—disguises differences whereby programs with the same label may be designed and implemented in a variety of ways to make them more suitable for particular contexts. The choices about customization will affect which population groups the program will serve and the types of impacts that it can achieve. Those implementing programs should therefore not just copy programs used elsewhere: they should understand the principles underlying each type of program and how to customize it appropriately to the particular need and context.

The quality and care with which programs are designed and implemented, from the selection of beneficiaries to the provision and monitoring of benefits, have a large impact on the efficiency and effectiveness of a given program. No program is a guaranteed success, and few are guaranteed failures. The role of good systems and adroit managers in getting the most from a program cannot be overemphasized.

Improving programs is always possible: new ideas can come from within a thoughtfully managed program, from observing how other programs are operating differently, from innovating, or from new technologies. New ideas for how to design programs and how to meet the perennial challenges of targeting, payment systems, monitoring, and so on surface constantly. Program managers should stay informed and maintain a critical eye in assessing how innovations used elsewhere may be applicable to a specific program.

Developing countries employ a large number of safety net instruments to reduce and mitigate the effects of poverty and other risks on vulnerable households. The type of programs used, their objectives, their design specifics, and their implementation vary depending on a country's level of development; the amount of resources the country allocates to social programs; and the regional characteristics, including both the economic and political environments.

The types of safety net programs implemented in developing countries have been evolving. The last 20 years have seen a marked move away from generalized, universal food subsidies toward more targeted programs and from the use of food toward the use of cash. For example, universal food distribution programs were popular in North Africa, South Asia, and Sub-Saharan Africa until the early 1990s, when they were proven to be far too expensive and ineffective in reaching the poor, especially in rural areas (see Alderman and Lindert 1998 and Tuck and Lindert 1996 on the reform process in Africa and Dev and others 2004 and Mooij 1999b on India). Following the financial crises of the late 1990s, Argentina and the Republic of Korea adopted public works programs, which were previously used on a large scale mainly in South Asia. Several other countries, such as Ethiopia, Malawi, and Uganda, are now also using them. Fee waiver systems for health and education started in the 1980s and 1990s to accompany cost recovery programs, but the current trend is away from cost recovery upon service use and toward free access to education and insurance for health. A recent innovation is conditional cash transfer programs, which provide income support to families while requiring them to make the necessary investments in their children's health and education.

Three factors emerge as crucial for the success of a given safety net program in achieving the goals outlined in chapter 2. The first is selecting the right program to address the needs of the intended beneficiaries given the underlying political and administrative environment or, in other words, selecting the appropriate tool for the job. The second factor is customizing the design of the selected program. The third factor is paying adequate attention to the details in all aspects of program implementation, from the selection of beneficiaries to the distribution and monitoring of benefits.

Chapter 2 shows how safety net programs in general can make a difference in protecting the chronically poor and the transient poor and how they can promote household investment and facilitate other government policies that help reduce poverty. This chapter illustrates how different programs can achieve those goals and how well they are suited to addressing the specific issues of different population groups by severity and type of poverty and by vulnerability or other relevant categories.

Similarly, chapters 4 to 6 describe key program design functions—targeting, payment mechanisms, monitoring, and evaluation—that are common to all programs. This chapter reorients our perspective and takes a program-specific view to examine the unique design and implementation features of each type of program and how programs can be used to achieve their intended objectives for specific population groups. Furthermore, the chapter highlights the key advantages and disadvantages of each program and the challenges inherent in running effective and efficient programs.

Several criteria can be used to organize individual types of programs into meaningful groups. In this review, we have organized programs into three basic categories (box 7.1).

- **Transfer programs in cash and in kind** include programs that help protect poor households by providing them with the resources they need to maintain a minimum level of consumption. Properly crafted, they can help ensure livelihoods for the very poor and assist them in case of shocks. They include programs that deliver unconditional transfers to households in the form of cash or near cash, which includes vouchers, coupons, and stamps that provide almost the same purchasing power as cash. These are the most flexible programs and can be shaped

BOX 7.1 **Classification of Types of Programs Covered**

Programs that provide unconditional transfers in cash and in kind

- **Cash transfers, including near cash (vouchers, coupons, and the like).** Needs-based social assistance, noncontributory pensions and disability transfers, family allowances, food stamps.

- **In-kind food transfers.** Targeted food transfers and rations, other food-based programs, supplements for mothers and children, school-based feeding programs and transfers.

- **General subsidies.** Subsidies for food, energy, housing, and utilities.

Income-generation programs

- **Workfare or public works programs.** Public works programs in which the poor work for food or cash.

Programs that protect and enhance human capital and access to basic services

- **Conditional transfers.** Transfers in cash or in kind to poor households subject to compliance with specific conditions in relation to education and/or health.

- **Fee waivers for health and education.** Mechanisms to ensure access to essential public services, such as fee waivers for health care services, school vouchers, or scholarships.

to achieve any of the four goals of safety nets. Other programs provide access to food by allocating rationed and subsidized food commodities to targeted populations via ration shops; take-home rations; or supplementary feeding programs, which provide direct feeding opportunities for mothers, children, students, and/ or displaced populations in crisis situations. Food transfer programs can provide the same protection as other transfer programs and may also help improve the nutritional status of mothers and children. Finally, some programs use universal price or tax subsidies for basic commodities to ensure or increase the consumption of food and other essential commodities by poor households.

- The main focus of **income-generation programs** is to provide low-skill jobs for the poor during the course of building, repairing, or improving local infrastructure. These programs provide low wage payments in cash or in kind to members of poor households willing to work at that pay. Thus they provide some form of protection to chronically poor and vulnerable households from loss of income resulting from shocks. While the focus is on public works, other labor market interventions, such as job training, job placement, and microcredit programs, can also facilitate access to income-earning activities. Income-generation programs can complement transfers and provide opportunities for graduation out of such programs.

- **Programs to protect human capital and provide access to basic services for poor households** provide conditional transfers to encourage the use of education or health facilities or other incentive provisions to lower the cost of access to basic health and education services for the poor. Thus they also play an important role in promoting investment in human capital and provide a viable alternative in case of government reforms.

Some programs have characteristics that make them unique and therefore hard to classify, while others may fall into more than one category. Food stamps, for example, are transfer programs that provide coupons that can be treated like cash, but that may restrict purchases to certain food commodities, and can therefore also be classified as in-kind programs. Another example is food ration programs that do not restrict access to a particular segment of the population and might therefore be regarded as food transfer programs or as general price subsidies. Similarly, the Female Secondary School Assistance Program in Bangladesh can be classified as a conditional transfer program or as a scholarship. In the end, it is not the artificial classification that matters, but the design and implementation characteristics of specific programs that will ensure their success and effectiveness with respect to their broad objectives.

The rest of this chapter provides systematic coverage of individual programs based on the six main groups of interventions described in box 7.1. Appendix B briefly describes many programs organized along the same six groupings of intervention and by country and also indicates the programs' level of expenditure and coverage.

7.1 Cash and Near Cash Transfers

Cash transfer programs include the provision of assistance in the form of cash and other instruments almost like cash that can be used to transfer resources to the poor or to those who, in the absence of the transfer, face a probable risk of falling into poverty.[1] For a list of cash and near cash programs, see table B.1 in appendix B.

PROGRAM DESCRIPTION

The main objective of cash and near cash transfer programs is to increase poor and vulnerable households' real incomes. The main difference between cash, near cash—such as food stamps, coupons, or vouchers that may be used to purchase food—and in-kind transfers is the amount of choice given to beneficiaries in acquiring the types of commodities they want to consume. Cash transfers obviously allow recipients to purchase anything they wish; near cash transfers, such as food stamps, can restrict recipients' choices to certain types of commodities; while in-kind transfers limit the selection to the commodities received. Some programs deliver transfers that are partially in cash and partially in kind; and others provide vouchers, coupons, or stamps, which are something in between in cash and in kind.

The origins of cash and in-kind transfers go back to at least Roman times (Brown 2002; Hands 1968). The Alimenta (Food) Program, originally started by Trajan's predecessor Nerva and expanded by Trajan, provided food to poor children. The first example of a food stamp program is the U.S. program (USDA 2008), which operated between 1939 and 1943 and was restarted in 1964. Developing countries such as Sri Lanka in 1979 (Edirisinghe 1987) and Jamaica in 1984 (Grosh 1992) introduced food stamps to alleviate the short-term economic hardships associated with the elimination of general subsidies on food commodities or food rations.

TYPES OF PROGRAM

This subsection discusses four main types of programs: the first three are pure cash transfers for poor populations based on need or for special vulnerable groups such as the elderly or families with children (see chapter 8 for a description of the difference between regular and special poor and vulnerable groups). The fourth program, food stamps, provides a means for increasing food consumption.[2]

Needs-Based Social Assistance

Needs-based social assistance programs are mostly means-tested programs and are common in countries of the Organisation for Economic Co-operation and Development (OECD), Eastern Europe, and the former Soviet Union. Some income transfer programs based on needs are also found elsewhere in poor countries, for instance, in Mozambique and Zambia in Sub-Saharan Africa (Devereux and others 2005; Schubert 2005) and in Pakistan in South Asia (ADB 2006). The level of benefits and program coverage depend greatly on the fiscal resources available. Benefits are usually quite low, often around 5 to 25 percent of the cost of obtaining the poverty line basket of commodities. Some programs provide a regular monthly transfer, like the Food Subsidy Program in Mozambique, while others provide only occasional transfers in response to a shock (see Harvey 2005 for a description of the use of cash transfers in emergency situations). In addition, transfers can either be flat—that is, the same for all recipients—as was initially the case in the Kalomo District Pilot Social Cash Transfer Scheme in Zambia;[3] can vary depending on household resources as in the case of Romania's Guaranteed Minimum Income Program (Pop, Florescu, and Tesliuc forthcoming); or can vary with respect to household size as in Mozambique, where transfers range from US$3 to US$6 per month depending on the number of children (Devereux and others 2005).

Noncontributory Pensions

Many countries provide noncontributory pensions for some or all of those who do not fall under the country's contributory pension scheme and, in some cases, all those above a fixed age. Under these noncontributory schemes, benefits are paid without regard to past participation in the labor market. These schemes, which are discussed in more detail in chapter 8, are almost always financed from general tax revenues and are usually targeted toward the poor. The level of benefits varies from Tk 165 (US$3) a month in Bangladesh, roughly 10 percent of the average per capita income in 2003, to R 370 (US$106) a month in South Africa, equal to half the country's average household income and more than twice the median per capita income in 1993 (Bertrand, Sendhil, and Miller 2003; Duflo 2003).[4]

Family Allowance Programs

Family allowance programs are common in OECD European countries, Eastern Europe, and the former Soviet Union. Benefits are often small—a few U.S. dollars a month, representing a fraction of the cost of the food basket—although in some middle-income transition states, including the Czech Republic and Hungary, they provide a more substantial contribution to the cost of raising a child. Family allowances can take various forms, such as means-tested child benefits similar to needs-based transfers as used in the Czech Republic, Poland, and South Africa (box 7.2);[5] birth grants or universal transfers for all

BOX 7.2 **The South African Child Support Grant**

The South African child support grant is a means-tested monthly cash grant given to the primary caregivers of children living in poverty. The main objective of the program is to provide support for poor mothers and poor families to care for their children (Monson and others 2006; Samson, MacQuene, and van Niekerk 2006). The program was introduced in 1998 to replace the state maintenance grant. As of 2006, the program provides a monthly grant of R 190 (about US$28) to 7.4 million poor children younger than 14; initially, the program had covered poor children under 7. The age eligibility has been expanded gradually over the past few years, and the amount of the grant has increased with inflation, while the means test cutoffs have remained the same.

Implementation. The South African Social Security Agency, a separate national government agency, implements and administers the grant. To be eligible to participate, caregivers must present documentation showing that they have primary responsibility for caring for children, proof of the age of the children, and official proof of the employment and income status of the applicant and the spouse. To be eligible for the grant, the income of the primary caregiver and the spouse has to be R 1,100 (about US$170) or less for rural households (or households living in informal housing settlements in urban areas or shanty towns, which include communities of self-constructed shelters of unclear land tenure) or R 800 (about US$120) or less for urban households living in formal housing. The two threshold levels of income are designed to take into account the higher mean household size in rural than urban areas and the larger number of dependent children in rural areas (Rosa, Leatt, and Hall 2005).

In many areas, applicants can obtain the required certifications for affirming marriage certificates or divorce decrees, as well as making affidavits declaring the earnings of applicants and their spouses, from police officers. In some Eastern Cape sites, however, program officials or

children under a fixed age (often children under 2 or 3 years of age or those under 16 or 18), which are most common in Europe and the former Soviet Union; and programs for the employed population, often with a special system for public sector employees, which are popular in OECD countries and in some middle-income countries such as Argentina (Lindert, Skoufias, and Shapiro 2006). Moreover, the transfers can be either in cash or in kind, for example, in the form of subsidies on school uniforms or children's goods.

Food Stamp, Voucher, and Coupon Programs

Food stamps, vouchers, and coupons are near cash instruments targeted to poor households (Castañeda 1998; Grosh 1992; Hoddinott 1999; Rogers and Coates 2002) that they can use to purchase food at authorized retail locations. Retailers who accept these instruments can redeem them for cash through the banking system. The value of the food stamp is backed by the government's commitment to pay. Such programs have been implemented in Colombia, Honduras, Jamaica, Mexico, Romania (where the program was intended to help farmers after the 1997 planting season), Sri Lanka, the United States, and a few other countries.

The denomination of the stamps varies from program to program: in some cases it is in cash, in others it is in kind. The amount of the transfer is often based on the gap community leaders provide official confirmation of an applicant's situation. The program's administrative costs are low: registering a new applicant into the program costs only R 19 (about US$3), less than 1 percent of the annual payment to beneficiaries (Budlender, Rosa, and Hall 2005). Payments are managed and monitored at the national level, but disbursed by third party contractors at the provincial level.

Impact. According to some estimates (Leatt 2006), 65 percent of all children in South Africa live in families that would qualify for the program and 80 percent of these actually participate in the program. Take-up rates were lower when the program first started because of the lack of capacity of local governments and the difficulty of getting documentation for children and caregivers. Even though many improvements have been made to reduce the percentage of excluded children, a lack of documentation might still represent a constraint for poor children.

The impact of the program has generally been positive. It has been linked to reduced poverty, higher labor market participation, and increased school attainment levels. Children who receive the grant are significantly more likely to be enrolled in school in the years following grant receipt than equally poor children of the same age who did not receive the grant (Samson and others 2004).

Lessons. The government made substantial efforts and was able to increase the participation of poor children in the program, but some work remains to be done to reach those poor families without proper documentation. More work also has to be done to reduce the rate of dropouts from the program, which are likely to occur when the primary caregiver changes, often because of death from AIDS.

between the amount of resources spent on food and the amount needed to acquire a minimum basket of commodities. In practice, the benefits are often worth only a few U.S. dollars and represent a small share of the cost of the food basket. For example, in Jamaica, the value of food stamps is only 12 percent of the food budget of the lowest quintile of the population, compared with the United States, where food stamps are worth 56 to 70 percent of households' mean food expenditures (Castañeda 1998). Some programs restrict households to buying only a few specific foods, while others allow them to purchase any foods they wish. The foods authorized for purchase in the Jamaican Food Stamp Program include rice, cornmeal, skim milk, and wheat flour, which constitutes a basic local food basket (Ezemenari and Subbarao 1999; Grosh 1992). These were the same foods previously covered by general price subsidies.

KEY DESIGN FEATURES

Key challenges in delivering cash and near cash programs include making sure that programs reach their intended beneficiaries and that the funds do not disappear along the way. For efficiency, setup and delivery must be handled in a reliable and efficient manner using available technology.

Beneficiary Selection

Beneficiaries of cash transfer programs are selected using a variety of targeting mechanisms. Needs-based transfers are usually targeted using either income or means tests as in Bulgaria, Hungary, and Romania; proxy means tests as in Armenia; or a combination of proxy and means tests as in Mozambique and Zambia. In this regard, note that Mozambique also uses health status indicators, such as being chronically sick or malnourished (Devereux and others 2005). Some countries, such as some OECD nations and Mauritius, have special provisions for identifying individuals with disabilities (Tabor 2002). Either the central government can set the selection criteria, which are then applied locally, or they can be decided at the local level so as to take local conditions, preferences, and priorities into account. In Albania and Uzbekistan, communes use local information to achieve better poverty targeting than could be expected on the basis of proxy indicators alone (Alderman 2001, 2002a).

Beneficiaries of noncontributory pensions and family allowance programs are often targeted by age group and can be based simply on age and place of residence, as for Bolivia's and Lesotho's pension programs or Hungary's and Romania's family allowance programs. Selection can also be based on a means test, as in South Africa for both the pension and family allowance programs and Bulgaria and Poland for family allowances, or can be based on a proxy means test as for the pension program in Chile.

Finally, food stamp programs can include self-targeting elements. In Honduras, the Bono Escolar (Food Stamps for Schoolchildren) benefit was distributed through primary schools in selected areas and the Bono Materno Infantil (Food Stamps for Mothers and Young Children) benefit was distributed at health centers in poor areas; thus, targeting was achieved through school attendance by children or the use of health clinics by mothers. Alternatively, such programs can impose limitations on the types of commodities that can be purchased with the stamps, as in Jamaica.

Disbursement Methods

The mechanisms used to distribute cash and vouchers to beneficiaries include banking systems, post offices, local institutions such as schools, and mobile distribution units. Family allowance programs in Eastern Europe and in the Zakat ("almsgiving") Program in Pakistan, a cash transfer scheme managed by the Ministry of Religious Affairs, have made the greatest use of checks and banks. Post offices have often provided a reliable distribution mechanism for the old-age pension program in India (Farrington and others 2003), the Food Support Program in Pakistan, old-age pensions in Lesotho, and other programs elsewhere. Other delivery mechanisms include teachers in Zambia or places where other cash transactions take place, like lottery kiosks in Brazil and Western Union offices in Somalia. Namibia and South Africa use armored cars to deliver cash directly to beneficiaries. Compared with cash, more planning and preparation are needed for the distribution and reclamation of food stamps, including a reliable system for printing and distributing the stamps and a good banking system so that retailers can redeem them promptly. Recently, the use of electronic benefit transfer systems has become popular in the United States and Latin America and shows promise for reducing costs and corruption. Such mechanisms, which are discussed in more detail in chapter 5, require an effective administrative distribution process and an up-front initial capital investment.

Several programs have demonstrated that distributing cash efficiently is feasible even in difficult situations and remote locations. For example, in the 1990s, Mozambique distributed payments to demobilized soldiers and made single payments to flood victims in the form of checks, and rural residents had no difficulty in cashing the checks (Hanlon 2004).

Scope and Coverage

The amount of funds allocated and the number of people covered by cash programs vary with respect to the size of transfers and the type of program. With the exception of Hungary and South Africa, most developing countries typically allocate the equivalent of less than 2 percent of gross domestic product (GDP) to public cash transfers, while Western European countries average the equivalent of more than 2 percent of GDP on social assistance programs and a good deal more on all social programs. For the most part, the population covered varies between 1 percent of the total population (as in the Food Subsidy Program in Mozambique), to 8 percent of the total population (as in the Guaranteed Minimum Income Program in Romania), to 16 percent (as in the Ndihme Ekonomika [Economic Assistance] program in Albania), to 34 percent (in the Unconditional Cash Transfer Program in Indonesia). Participation in noncontributory old-age pension schemes in several high- and middle-income countries varies according to targeting criteria and beneficiary location. Brazil and South Africa have two of the largest programs. Brazil's rural old-age pension has a rural focus and covers 4.6 million beneficiaries, while its urban programs cover only 0.7 million elderly beneficiaries. In 1998, South Africa's program covered 1.8 people of all races nationwide. Bangladesh provides an example of a newly established program in a low-income country for poor rural people and covers 1.2 million beneficiaries annually (World Bank 2005a).

The coverage of family allowance benefits is much larger in terms of the percentage of the total population if participation is universal and is based on children's ages as in Hungary and Romania. However, the trend in Europe in the 1990s was to reduce the level of benefits and the number of children covered (Rostgaard 2004). The number of beneficiaries and total expenses are reduced when enrollment is restricted using means testing, as for Bulgaria's family benefit or South Africa's child support grant; the latter, for example, covers about 7.1 million of 13.5 million children, even though 8.8 million would be eligible based on income poverty criteria (Leatt 2006). Costs and coverage are further reduced if eligibility is restricted to families working in the public sector or in formal employment, as in Argentina and most OECD countries.

The coverage of food stamps varies greatly according to the targeting criteria used and the program's budget. Coverage amounted to 3 percent of the population in Honduras in 1992, 11 percent of the population in Jamaica in 1998, and 48 percent of the population in Sri Lanka in 1989. The U.S. Food Stamp Program acts as an insurance mechanism, as it is set up as an entitlement and all those who apply and qualify for the program are accepted. Therefore coverage varies from year to year, from 27.5 million people in 1994, to 17.2 million in 2000, and 26.5 million (about 9 percent of the total population) in 2007. The level of benefits per household varies depending on the country and the year. In Sri Lanka, for example, the level of transfers fell from 32 percent of food purchases in 1978 to 20 percent in 1982. In the United States, it is equivalent to 25 to 50 percent of the budget of a family with two children (Castañeda 1998).

Administrative Costs

The administrative costs of pure cash transfers are lower than for any other transfer program and typically range from just over 2 percent of program costs in Armenia's Family Poverty Benefits Program to about 10 percent in Bulgaria's and Romania's Guaranteed Minimum Income Programs. The costs are lower than for distributing food stamps, because of the cost of producing coupons and setting up the mechanism for retailers to reclaim cash from the government in exchange for the food stamps they accept, which may add 2 to 5 percent on top of the costs of cash transfers. The cost of delivering food stamps is 2.0 percent of the total budget in Sri Lanka (Castañeda 1998), 3.0 percent in Romania (Castañeda 1998), 10.0 percent in Jamaica (Grosh 1994), and 13.5 percent in the United States (Castañeda 1998). These costs can be kept down if the setup and delivery of food stamps relies more on markets to make food available so that governments do not have to get involved in costly marketing operations. The costs of food stamp programs are lower than for in-kind food distribution programs because transporting, storing, and distributing food in bulk is more expensive than moving food stamps around. Cash programs are less expensive than public works programs as they do not require material and tools. Finally, cash transfer programs do not require the certification of compliance that is needed for conditional transfer programs.

Implementing Institutions

Social welfare and social security ministries often administer needs-based and means-tested transfer programs, including old-age, disability, and family allowances. For example, Poland's Ministry of Social Policy administers family benefits, and national and provincial departments of social development administer pensions in South Africa. Sometimes family allowances are distributed directly through the workplace or, for those who do not work, through local agencies. In some instances, the agency that administers a country's mandatory contributory old-age pension scheme will also administer complementary noncontributory programs, as in the case of Lesotho, where the Department of Pensions of the Ministry of Finance administers the program (Devereux and others 2005).

Food stamp programs are often managed by the ministry of welfare as in Jamaica before 2002 or the ministry of agriculture as in the United States. Some countries use a combination of ministries, including the ministry of health as in the distribution of some of the benefits distributed by the Programa de Asignación Familiar (Family Allowance Program) in Honduras.

Many programs are funded centrally, but contain some elements of decentralization that may include implementation (staffing resources), financing, or design (criteria and objectives). Several Eastern European countries finance programs centrally but implement them locally. The administration of old-age pensions is often decentralized to local offices that may be part of subnational (provincial) governments, as in South Africa and Sri Lanka (Barrientos and others 2003, appendix C). Similarly, in Bulgaria, the targeted social assistance system has staff at the local level (local social assistance directorates) in the municipalities (Shopov forthcoming).

OUTCOMES, ADVANTAGES, AND DISADVANTAGES

Several studies and evaluations of cash transfer programs have shown that, in general, such programs have been effective in reaching their intended beneficiaries and had a positive impact on beneficiary consumption. Most of the results of such studies can be generalized to other transfer programs and to targeting efficiency.

Incidence

Evaluation studies show that cash transfer programs can be effective in reaching the intended poor households. Evidence from Eastern Europe shows that 50 to 80 percent of the benefits of needs-based transfers go to the poorest 40 percent of households (Tesliuc and others forthcoming). Preliminary studies of South Africa's child support grant indicate that it appears to be well targeted at children in poorer households (Barrientos and DeJong 2004; Case, Hosegood, and Lund 2005; Samson and others 2004). Family allowance programs are usually slightly better than distribution neutral, because households with children, especially those with large numbers of children, tend to have a higher than average incidence of poverty. In the case of food stamp programs, between 50 and 80 percent of benefits go to the poorest 40 percent of households. In Jamaica, the poorest 20 percent got 31 percent of the benefits; in Sri Lanka, the poorest 20 percent got 40 percent of the benefits (Castañeda 1998; Coady, Grosh, and Hoddinott 2003).

Impact

The results of impact evaluations of cash transfer programs have been broadly positive for the families of beneficiaries and have not confirmed many of the negative externalities often feared. Evidence from research on unconditional cash transfer programs in developing countries shows a positive impact on consumption and on human capital of children. In Ethiopia, Lesotho, Mozambique, and Zambia, children benefit from transfers even though they are not the programs' primary targets (Devereux and others 2005). In South Africa, the pensions, when received by women, had a large impact on the anthropometric status (weight for height and height for age) of girls, but little effect on that of boys; this was not the case when men received the allowances (Duflo 2003), suggesting that the efficiency of public transfer programs may depend on the gender of the recipient. In Bolivia, Martinez (2005) finds positive effects of the Bono Solidario program on household consumption and children's human capital. A significant fraction of this increase in consumption is derived from the consumption of home-produced agricultural products such as meats and vegetables resulting from the transfers being invested in productive activities. Child and family allowances in transition countries have proved to be effective in ameliorating the impact of structural change on households with children and have been reformed to act as safety nets (Barrientos and DeJong 2004).

Food stamp programs have been shown to be effective ways of transferring income, increasing household income by as much as 20 to 25 percent (Castañeda 1998). Without the Food Stamp Program in Jamaica, the poverty gap would have been much worse during the early 1990s, when the Jamaican dollar was being devalued: households with elderly members and young children benefited the most from the program (Ezemenari and Subbarao 1999). Evidence also indicates that food stamp programs tend to increase food consumption more than cash transfers (Breunig and others 2001; Fraker 1990; Fraker, Martini, and Ohls 1995). One possible reason for this is that households do not treat food stamps in the same way as cash. Another is that the stamps may fall under the control of women, who disproportionately favor expenditures on food and other basic needs. The impact of food stamps on nutritional status is hard to demonstrate. In a few cases, food stamp use has been associated with increased consumption of protein and micronutrients (Butler and Raymond 1996).

The possible negative effects of cash transfers include the disincentive to work; the misuse of cash resources; the change in the number of desired children; and the consumption of nonnutritious food commodities, for example, alcohol and tobacco. However, while old-age pensions may have some negative effects on the decision to work (discussed in more detail in chapter 5), people rarely seem to use cash transfers for antisocial purposes such as cigarette and alcohol consumption, and women are not necessarily disadvantaged by the use of cash rather than in-kind approaches. Concerns of corruption and insecurity may be more frequent in conflict situations (Harvey 2005). The empirical evidence shows (and sometimes program rules require) that child allowance programs do not increase the probability of having children, but rather encourage prolonged school enrollment, which leads to higher educational attainment and lower family size. The fear of crowding out might also be overstated. In Zambia, most people agree that transfers are insufficient and therefore are still willing to provide assistance, but at a reduced level (Wietler 2007). Cash transfer programs have not generally resulted in sustained price rises, even when they have successfully stimulated the local economy. In the Kalomo District Pilot Social Cash Transfer Scheme in Zambia, Schubert and Goldberg (2004) find that additional purchases of food, soap, blankets, and agricultural inputs have not resulted in local price increases.

Advantages

Cash transfers are the most direct type of intervention designed to support the poor and have a number of advantages as follows:

- Once the administrative infrastructure is in place, the cost of operating cash transfer programs is often small and far less than the cost of providing assistance in kind.
- From the recipients' point of view, cash transfers provide them with greater freedom of choice in how to use the benefit to enhance their welfare and results in a higher level of satisfaction at any given level of income than in-kind transfers. Program beneficiaries also feel that less stigma is attached to the receipt and use of cash than of in-kind benefits.
- Targeted cash transfers do not directly distort prices. In isolated and thin food markets in rural areas, cash transfers can cause an increase in the price of food, but if food markets are functioning well, cash and food stamps can strengthen local retail establishments.
- Food stamps can protect consumers from price increases and be self-targeting. If they can be redeemed easily, often, and in small quantities in local stores, they can help stimulate retail markets, in contrast to local delivery of food that might instead depress local market prices. If denominated in kind, food stamps are not subject to inflation to the same extent as food stamps denominated in value. Self-targeting can be greater than with cash transfers if the use of coupons is limited to inferior, less preferred foods.

Disadvantages

Although most of the disadvantages of cash transfer programs are common to transfer programs in general, some concerns arise in relation to possible uses of cash transfers and care is needed to limit the following disadvantages:

- Some argue that it might be difficult for women to maintain control of the resources and use them for the benefit of their children instead of promoting antisocial behavior, like the consumption of cigarettes or alcohol by men.

- Unconditional cash transfer programs may distort preferences. Where cash programs are strictly targeted based on income, they may result in a greater disincentive to work than in-kind transfers or public works programs.

- Changes in product prices affect the value of cash transfer programs. If the amount of the cash transfer is not adjusted because of unexpected surges in inflation or product prices, it can lose its value and effectiveness.

- Distribution costs tend to be higher for food stamp programs than for cash programs. In addition, food stamps are more likely to be subject to theft and fraud than food or cash, and because the use of food stamps is restricted, they are less desirable than cash.

- Cash transfers are attractive to local elites and unintended beneficiaries. As a result, they may be more difficult to target effectively, and good control mechanisms are needed (as outlined in chapter 5) to ensure that they reach the intended beneficiaries.

LESSONS AND SUGGESTIONS

Cash transfer programs are the most basic type of safety net program and can easily be adapted to different types of situations for a wide range of beneficiaries.

Most Likely Beneficiaries

Cash transfers have been used effectively to address many of the needs of poor people. The intended beneficiaries include those who are poor and have a low level of consumption for a variety of reasons. Some households might simply have too few people working at wages that are too low, and therefore require additional support that can be provided by family allowances, common in Eastern Europe, and food stamps as in the United States. Other intended beneficiaries include households that do not have anyone who, due to age or disability, can be expected to work. These households can usually be reached with pensions as in Bangladesh and South Africa, family allowances, and food stamps. Cash programs can also provide temporary cash transfers to those who have suffered losses of assets, income, and/or consumption as a result of an uninsured shock; for example, as has occurred in Indonesia, Mozambique, and Pakistan after natural disasters. See also box 7.3 on the effectiveness and flexibility of cash transfers in emergencies.

Appropriate Context and Political Economy Considerations

Cash transfers are the most obvious and simple instruments for addressing poverty in most circumstances as long as food is available in the marketplace, otherwise food prices

BOX 7.3 **Use and Effectiveness of Cash Transfers in Emergencies**

The cost-effectiveness and flexibility of cash, as opposed to in-kind support, is extremely important in an emergency, where quick delivery of assistance and adaptability to specific recipients' needs is crucial. Cash can also have positive effects on local markets and trade; however, the same disadvantages that pertain to all cash transfer programs apply in emergency situations. In particular, the security risk of moving cash around might be more pronounced than under normal circumstances (Peppiatt, Mitchell, and Holzmann 2001).

The design of a cash transfer program must take into account all these factors and be adapted to the specific emergency. In terms of program objectives, the use of cash provides the opportunity to link the relief response with longer-term development concerns, but the immediate goal in emergencies is to assist the most vulnerable and most badly affected individuals—commonly the displaced, widows, orphans, and the elderly. As the Tsunami Emergency Recovery Program in Sri Lanka in 2005 did, the targeting method can be a combination of geographical criteria (the most flood-affected areas) and categorical criteria (displaced households), with additional community identification of beneficiaries. An option Willibald (2006, p. 332) suggests in the case of cash transfers to former combatants following a conflict situation "would be to give priority access to those willing to disarm first, without excluding those who do not have a weapon."

The size and timing of the transfer depend primarily on the objective and can include the value of lost assets and a more regular transfer supporting livelihoods. In the aftermath of natural disasters in Maldives, Pakistan, and Sri Lanka, cash transfers first addressed the asset restoration objective, but also attached transfers to the status of housing reconstruction or rehabilitation.

Oxfam has developed a number of measures to create a more secure environment for the use of cash, including limiting local knowledge of cash movements; limiting access to bank transactions; having small cash transfers between banks; decentralizing responsibility for disbursement and involving a number of staff; disbursing cash on an ad hoc basis; having small, frequent cash disbursements; disseminating information to all stakeholders (community elders, committees, politicians, and nonrecipients); using long-standing staff who are local to the area and trusted by the head office and the team; and ensuring that community members choose safe locations for their cash disbursements (Creti and Jaspars 2006; Khogali and Takhar 2001).

Impact. Based on experience of cash transfers in emergencies, Harvey (2005, p. 36) concludes that "People spend the money that they are given sensibly, cash projects have not generally resulted in sustained price rises and women have been able to participate and have a say in the benefits from cash and voucher responses."

Lessons. Even in difficult situations, cash transfers can be delivered safely and provide a quick and effective means of support for vulnerable populations after a disaster. The Emergency Cash Relief Program (implemented by Horn Relief and Norwegian People's Aid and funded by Oxfam Novib Netherlands), for example, was able to distribute a total of US$691,500 to 13,830 drought-affected households in the Sool Plateau in Somalia in 2003–4, making it the largest cash response ever mounted in Somalia (Ali, Toure, and Kiewied 2005).

will increase. Thus the fact that cash transfers are the main type of safety net in the OECD countries—potentially available, in one form or another, to more than 80 percent of the population of the industrial nations according to the International Labour Office (2000)—is not surprising. Yet far fewer cash transfer programs are in effect in developing countries, and those that do exist tend to grant only small benefits mostly to those who cannot work and are equivalent to less than 2 percent of GDP.

Fewer social protection programs are based on cash transfers in developing countries for a number of reasons. First, governments' cash resources in poor developing nations are limited, as they are more likely to receive resources in the form of food aid. Second, mobilizing support for pure cash transfers can be difficult because of the lack of experience with targeting. Finally, governments and donors may give priority to programs that can relieve structural constraints to growth rather than programs to augment consumer demand or transfer income.

Despite these constraints, demand for safety nets that incorporate some form of cash transfer is growing in developing countries. This has been met by renewed interest on the part of several donor agencies in promoting the use of cash transfer programs as a response to chronic poverty, food insecurity, and AIDS in countries of eastern and southern Africa with a high prevalence of HIV infection such as Ethiopia, Malawi, and Zambia (DFID 2005; Devereux and others 2005). The intent is partly to respond to the growing unmet need for social protection with predictable cash transfers and partly to respond to the idea that regular, predictable grants in the form of cash transfers to identified vulnerable groups offer a cost-effective way to reduce poverty and realize basic human rights (Schubert and Beales 2006). They can also help reduce inequality and ensure that the benefits of growth reach those living in chronic poverty both during normal times and during emergencies.[6]

Cash and near cash programs can also be used effectively in times of crisis or for the transient poor if they have to face changing economic conditions. Coverage can be expanded either by setting the amount of the transfer without limiting the number of beneficiaries at any given point in time using current programs or by having provisions for quickly expanding the number of temporary or short-term beneficiaries. The first strategy is achieved in the U.S. Food Stamp Program, which does not limit the number of beneficiaries, although they have to be recertified often.

Among available instruments, family allowances and food stamps appear to be more politically acceptable. Policy makers often see family allowances as an important tool for preventing the intergenerational transmission of poverty. Food stamps are often claimed to be a good compromise between cash transfers and in-kind transfers, because they are tied to the merit good of foods, sometimes of particular foods. Of course, public support is likely to be larger if fewer restrictions are placed on the commodities included in the program. Food stamps also provide a way to help eliminate general food subsidies as in Jamaica and Sri Lanka. In addition, the agriculture sector and the private sector food industry often support food stamp programs because they expand the demand for food and can be supported by food aid.

The use of cash and near cash programs requires functioning markets and adequate provision of basic services to ensure that supply is sufficient to respond to increased demand (Barrientos and DeJong 2004). Indeed, these programs are only effective where food is readily available on the private market, where the problem for the poor is adequate purchasing power rather than lack of access to stocked markets, where consumers purchase most of their food at the market and the retail market operates adequately, and where the type of food offered reflects poor people's preferences.

Adapting to Local Conditions and Avoiding Unintended Effects

The following presents ways to make cash and near cash programs more effective in helping poor people given local conditions and to ensure that transfers reach the intended beneficiaries, that they are not captured by nondeserving people, and that they are not subject to corruption:

- **Specify clear program objectives and benefit levels that are widely understood and that most people agree are sound, fair, and effective to build a broadly based constituency in favor of a cash transfer program.**[7] Cash transfer programs in developing countries need not be overly generous. Given that low-income households often already derive some earnings from informal sector activities or private transfers, cash transfers can be used to partly close the gap between their current level of consumption and a minimum level of desired consumption, rather than to provide full replacement income. Furthermore, limiting transfers to those who cannot work more than they already do, whether temporarily or permanently, contains the cost of transfers and reduces the adverse labor supply effects that high benefits may foster. The amount of the food stamp transfer can be smaller or greater than the household's current expenditure on food depending on the program's nutritional objectives. However, if not denominated in quantity terms, the value of cash transfers and food stamps needs to be updated periodically to prevent the erosion of benefits because of inflation.

- **Use the best possible targeting method, given administrative capacity, to reach intended beneficiaries.** Categorical, geographic, and community-based screening approaches can be effective alternatives in circumstances in which formal income and means tests are impractical (see chapter 4 for more details on methods to improve targeting).

- **Use effective payment mechanisms.** Appropriate payment mechanisms can vary depending on administrative capacity and the availability of financial channels, from the use of banking systems as in Brazil and Colombia, for example, to post offices in India and a combination of fixed and mobile banks in Bangladesh. Emerging technologies and disbursement mechanisms (treated in more detail in chapter 5) can facilitate disbursement and reduce costs for both beneficiaries and program administration. Corruption can threaten the very existence of a program (see Datt and others 1997 for the case of Mozambique); it can be reduced by ensuring good administration and monitoring and by keeping transfers small (Farrington and others 2003).

7.2 In-Kind Food Transfers and Other Food-Based Programs

In-kind food transfers and other food-based programs provide additional resources to households by making food available when they need it the most in the form of food rations, supplementary and school feeding programs, or emergency food distribution.[8] The main difference between food programs and cash-based programs is that the former use food as a resource and give beneficiaries a limited choice in relation to the types of commodities they want to consume. For a list of in-kind food transfer and other food-based programs, see table B.2 in appendix B.

PROGRAM DESCRIPTION

The main objective of food-based programs is to provide for adequate food consumption and thus help poor consumers achieve and maintain better nutritional status when, in the absence of the intervention, people would be likely to curtail their food consumption, resulting in malnutrition, morbidity, and possibly death. At the same time, food-based programs also tend to improve vulnerable households' participation in social programs, such as primary health care (including prenatal, postnatal, and well-baby care) and education.

The use of in-kind transfers goes back to ancient Egypt and to the Roman Empire. Examples of recent food-based transfers can be found in South Asia since the 1944 Bengal famine (see Sen 1981 for an analysis of the causes of famines in which he stresses the role of unequal distribution of income).

TYPES OF PROGRAMS

The food-based programs covered in this section include food rations and other in-kind food transfers and supplementary feeding, school feeding, and emergency food distribution programs.

Food Rations and Transfers

Food rations and transfers are intended to provide access to food to vulnerable and food-insecure households.[9] In most cases, targeted households collect rations at designated public or private distribution centers either for free or at a reduced price. In India, for example, certified poor consumers, that is, those with an income below the poverty line, can purchase wheat and other commodities at reduced prices through the public distribution system (PDS). Take-home rations are a special case of rationing in which rationed quantities of food are delivered directly to beneficiary households. Many such programs are found in Africa, Latin America, and South Asia, and include the Vulnerable Group Development Program in Bangladesh (box 7.4), the Gratuitous Relief Program in Ethiopia, and the Comodores Populares (Community Kitchens) program in Peru. The main difference between these programs and general price subsidies, which are discussed later, is that they restrict access to targeted beneficiaries.[10]

Several food ration programs have their genesis in reforms of prior general food price subsidy programs. This is what happened to the PDS in India when it started to provide commodities at lower prices to households below the poverty line and to the market price stabilization interventions operated by Indonesia's National Food Logistics Agency (BULOG) when it introduced a new targeting program (box 7.5).

Many people have strong ideas about the use of food-based versus cash transfers. Food distribution programs have played an important role in social policy and development, partly because of the availability of food aid from Australia, the United States, and other OECD countries (del Ninno, Dorosh, and Subbarao 2007). The debate on the use

BOX 7.4 **The Vulnerable Group Development Program, Bangladesh**

The Vulnerable Group Development Program, which originated as a relief program in1975, is a collaborative food security intervention jointly managed and implemented by the Ministry of Women's and Children's Affairs and the World Food Programme that targets about 500,000 extremely poor rural women. The main objective is to integrate food security and nutrition with development and income generation.

Implementation. Local selection committees composed of government officials, elected local government representatives, and representatives of nongovernmental organizations select the female beneficiaries using prescribed criteria. While the program operates nationwide, it focuses on food-insecure areas. The allocation of the beneficiaries is based on a food-insecurity map, whereby more food-insecure subdistricts have more beneficiaries. Beneficiaries receive a monthly ration of 30 kilograms of wheat over a period of 24 months. Since 2002, beneficiaries in three subdistricts have been receiving 25 kilograms of fortified whole wheat flour (*atta*) instead of grain. Beneficiaries are also required to attend training in income-generating activities, such as poultry rearing, livestock raising, fisheries, and sericulture; participate in awareness sessions on social, legal, health, and nutrition issues; receive training in basic literacy and numeracy; and obtain access to credit. In addition, beneficiaries are required to make a monthly savings deposit of Tk 25 (less than US$0.50), corresponding to roughly 10 percent of the transfer, into an interest-bearing account maintained by the nongovernmental organizations providing services to the Vulnerable Group Development Program in those areas.

Impact. Evaluations have shown that the program has been extremely successful in targeting hardcore-poor women aged 15 to 49. However, only about two-thirds of these women seem to have "graduated" from absolute poverty to becoming confident microfinance clients who have not slipped back to requiring government handouts.

Lessons. The program has proven that a combination of in-kind transfers and training is an effective way to alleviate poverty in the short run and reduce it in the future.

SOURCES: Ahmed, del Ninno, and Chowdhury 2004; Ahmed 2005; Matin and Hulme 2003.

of cash rather than food has been receiving renewed attention in recent years (see Gentilini 2007 for a comprehensive discussion of the debate), partly because of the issues surrounding the use of food subsidies in Europe and the United States, which have been generating large food surpluses that are often distributed in the form of food aid. Thus the decrease in the availability of food aid resources for development has resulted in a shift away from the use of food transfers (Barrett and Maxwell 2005).

The key issue, however, is being able to determine the circumstances in which food transfers are appropriate and how to maximize their impact. Box 7.6 describes four key considerations to keep in mind to help make this assessment—the functioning of food markets, the level of transaction costs, the type and size of the transfer, and the preferences of beneficiaries.

BOX 7.5 **From Universal to Targeted Distribution, India and Indonesia**

In June 1997 in India, the existing PDS was transformed into the targeted PDS in response to the findings of several studies (for instance, Radhakrishna and others 1997) that the program suffered from poor targeting and high unit costs for handling grain. The new program differentiates the quantities households are allowed to buy and prices depend on their poverty status. The PDS used to provide all consumers with access to rice, wheat, sugar, edible oils, kerosene, coal, and standard cloth at subsidized prices through a network of registered shops. Since 1997, only households below the state-defined poverty line are entitled to a ration card, which allows them to buy a larger quantity of rice and/or wheat than before (10 kilograms in 1997, 20 in 2000, 25 in 2001) at a subsidized price equal to about 50 percent of the economic cost. Since 2001, those above the poverty line may purchase food grains at a discount rate (equal to 70 percent of the economic cost). India also increased the allocation of state quotas of poverty cards to poorer states, shifting from an allocation formula that favored states with the largest food deficits regardless of whether they were relatively poor.

In Indonesia, BULOG, a publicly owned corporation, maintained a floor price and a ceiling price in order to stabilize prices through its monopoly control over international trade in rice through 1997. In 1998, Indonesia abandoned this policy and replaced it with Operasi Pasar Khusus (Special Market Operations), renamed Beras untuk Keluarga Miskin (Rice for Poor Families) in 2001, a targeted rice subsidy program for poor consumers (Kitano, Ariga, and Shimato 1999; McCulloch 2004; Pritchett, Sumarto, and Suryahadi 2002; World Bank 2006f). The reason for the change was a shift in the exchange rate following the 1997 Asian financial crisis, which turned a policy geared toward producer subsidies into one that required massive and unsustainable consumer subsidies Under the new program, BULOG sold rice to 3.4 million households at a subsidized price of Rp 1,000 (US$0.10) per kilogram, compared with a market price of Rp 3,000 (US$0.30) per kilogram, as of August 1998. The program reached 10.4 million families in 1999 and 12 million in 2003. Each family, identified by the National Family Plan Coordination Agency using geographical and categorical indicators, was entitled to receive 10 kilograms (later 20 kilograms) of rice per month. On the whole, the operation was well implemented. In a short time, rice was being distributed in a relatively well-controlled and accountable way. The main issues were that some needy households were excluded because they did not have identity documents or were not on the preexisting rosters used to target program beneficiaries; families had to make a small copayment for the entire monthly rice ration, which meant they had to find ways to finance a payment that was larger than their usual daily purchase; and some communities chose to share rations rather than let the intended targeting stand (SMERU Research Institute 1998).

The experience in India and Indonesia shows that shifting the primary mode of intervention is possible; however, program improvements are still needed. For additional information on the reforms in India, see Ahluwalia (1993), Dev and others (2004), Government of India (2001, 2007b), Mooij (1999b), Radhakrishna and others (1997), and Tritah (2003); for Indonesia, see ADB (2006), Ahmad and Leruth (2000), Daly and Fane (2002), Perdana and Maxwell (2004), Tabor and Sawit (2001), Timmer (2004), World Bank (2006f), and Yonekura 2005.

BOX 7.6 **Cash and In-Kind Transfers: Alternatives or Complements?**

When are food transfer programs appropriate? What are the criteria to keep in mind when deciding how much to distribute in the form of rations and how much as cash? Program designers should keep the following four key considerations in mind when deciding if food transfer programs are appropriate or necessary:

- **The functioning of food markets, including access, transport, and storage, and how this is reflected in the prices of staples.** If markets are well integrated across regions, cash transfers have an advantage because of the private sector's superior ability to move food and other goods more efficiently than the public sector. Furthermore, some argue that providing cash can have a positive impact on petty trade and other economic activities (Devereux 2000). However, if markets are thin, poorly integrated across regions, or monopolistic, the provision of cash may increase prices, which reduces the value of the transfer and may cause additional hardship to those poor households that do not receive any transfers (Devereux, Mvula, and Solomon 2006). A close monitoring of prices, not of production, is needed to assess the situation.

- **The level of transaction costs for the program and for beneficiaries.** Most of the argument about transaction costs refers to the high cost of distributing food provided by donors compared with the relatively lower cost of distributing cash. Food distribution takes time to organize, requires storage and transport, and is subject to losses and pilferage, and the public sector tends not to be efficient at keeping costs down. However, in some places where marketing and transport channels are not developed, only the public sector can provide adequate supplies in local markets. Beneficiary transaction costs also need to be taken into account. These costs include the time and expense of going to local markets, which might increase if places are far or unsafe.

- **The impact of the form and size of the transfer in determining the level of food consumption.** Poor households are more likely to consume food and to eat good food if they receive a small transfer. Some claim that men might use cash transfers to purchase such commodities as cigarettes or alcohol, and the literature indicates that small food transfers result in higher food consumption than cash transfers (del Ninno and Dorosh 2003; Fraker 1990). Moreover, Hoddinott and Islam (2007) and Jacoby (2002) show that households are more likely to stick (the so-called flypaper effect) to consumption patterns and intrahousehold distributions that have a positive impact on the nutrition of children if they have access to small transfers of good food.

- **The preferences of the beneficiaries.** Beneficiary preferences may vary depending on circumstances. Even though beneficiaries may prefer cash simply because it is more flexible, they still want to maximize the level of the transfer and their control over it. This is why women in certain circumstance might prefer food to cash (see Ahmed, Quisumbing, and Hoddinott 2007 on Bangladesh and Sharma 2006 on Sri Lanka).

Supplementary Feeding Programs

Supplementary feeding programs are intended to provide food specifically to mothers and young children. The food may be prepared and eaten on-site—for example, at child feeding centers as in Bangladesh, Indonesia, and Thailand—or provided as a so-called dry ration to take home as in Chile, where food supplements are distributed on a monthly basis through the primary health care system. Bolivia, Colombia, the Republic of Congo, Guatemala, Indonesia, Jamaica, Peru, Senegal, and Thailand also have supplementary feeding programs (Gillespie 1999). Table 7.1 compares the benefits and costs of the two systems. Foods provided for on-site meals are usually a low-cost blend of grains and pulses with added fat or oil: a typical diet might consist of 500 to 700 calories per day per child (UNHCR and WFP 1999). The consumption of on-site meals presents several advantages over take-home rations. In particular, the food is consumed by the intended beneficiaries and its preparation is supervised; however, the cost is much higher.

TABLE 7.1 **Comparison of Delivery Options for Supplementary Foods**

Item	Take-home rations	On-site meals
Consumption of food by recipient	There is no guarantee that only the intended recipient, whether a child or a pregnant or lactating mother, eats the ration. Usually the household shares it, sells it, gives it to their animals, or wastes it.	All rations are eaten under supervision, and help can be given to ill and undernourished children. However, recipients may be given less food at home (referred to as substitution).
Responsibility and education of families	Families take responsibility for feeding recipients and there are fewer opportunities for education. Caregivers spend less time and effort by not having to go to feeding sites.	Responsibility for feeding may be taken away from the family, but in small feeding programs, caregivers may help prepare food and feed recipients. Feeding problems can be identified and dealt with.
Logistics, organization, and costs	Large numbers of people can be covered using fewer resources and facilities. Costs are lower.	Many resources, including well-trained staff, and extensive supervision are needed. Costs are higher, including caregivers' opportunity costs in regularly attending the feeding site.

SOURCE: Gillespie 1999.

School Feeding Programs

School feeding programs provide meals for children at school to encourage their enrollment and improve their nutritional status and ability to pay attention in class. They can vary from the provision of breakfast, lunch as in the Thailand School Lunch Project, or a midmorning snack as in Bangladesh (Ahmed 2004b), to a combination of these as in Colombia, Costa Rica, Guatemala and Peru. School feeding programs are often integrated with other interventions, such as health and nutrition education, parasite treatment, health screening, and provision of water and sanitation.[11]

A few school feeding programs also provide an income transfer in the form of food to take home. The Ethiopian World Food Programme (WFP) school feeding program provides a daily nutritious meal and a take-home ration of vegetable oil to girls in pastoralist areas who are at school for at least 80 percent of school days (WFP 2005). The Food for Education Program in Bangladesh provided wheat or rice to families that sent their children to primary school until 2001, when it was changed into a cash stipend program (Ahmed and del Ninno 2002; Ahmed, del Ninno, and Chowdhury 2004). In such cases, the food does not necessarily benefit only the enrolled child, but may be shared among the family.

Emergency Food Distribution

Emergency distribution of food includes direct provision of food; supplementary feeding for vulnerable groups; and therapeutic feeding during crises, emergencies, and situations in which people are displaced (see UNHCR and WFP 1999 for guidelines on the size and type of on-site and take-home food rations). In some cases, schools might be used for the distribution of food rations. Emergency food programs provide a safety net of last resort whose objective is to save lives by preventing starvation, malnutrition, morbidity, and possible death when public and private institutions fail to protect individual entitlements to food. In many emergency situations, such as refugee camps or camps for internally displaced populations, food transfers are the only source of food and may be the only resources households receive.

Currently, emergency operations account for a larger proportion of official development assistance than ever before. The percentage of total official development assistance devoted to humanitarian emergencies has risen from 4 percent at the end of the 1980s to 10 percent in recent years (Development Initiatives 2006; OECD Development Assistance Committee 2001). Moreover, emergency interventions represent an important component of food-based programs in general, and of food aid in particular, as food usually represents more than half of humanitarian aid. In 2005, emergency relief operations in the form of food aid accounted for 64 percent of total food aid, up from 26 percent in 1991 (Wahlberg 2008), and included interventions following conflicts in Afghanistan, Iraq, and Liberia; droughts in southern Africa in early 2000 and 2001; floods in Bangladesh in 1998; and Hurricane Mitch in Central America in 1998.

KEY DESIGN FEATURES

The implementation of food-based programs poses several logistical and implementation challenges besides the usual challenges of any other transfer program. It involves procuring and storing food, including food aid and local and international purchases; transporting food to local areas and distributing it (Jaspars and Young 1995); and finding ways to reduce waste, spoilage, and pilferage. The selection of commodities and of the geographic areas to be covered is also crucial to avoid unintended effects and achieve intended objectives.

Beneficiary Selection

The same factors that determine the success of targeting in the case of income transfers in general determine the effectiveness of the targeting of in-kind programs (see Edirisinghe 1987 on Sri Lanka). Additional targeting mechanisms can be used to improve the nutritional status of mothers and children.

The best targeting mechanisms for food transfer programs include the use of individual targeting mechanisms, such as means tests and proxy means tests; self-targeting methods through the use of inferior commodities (box 7.7); or methods based on nutritional risk criteria, for instance, age or pregnancy.[12] Targeted households usually receive a ration card that entitles them to a certain amount of food at a subsidized price as in the Arab Republic of Egypt and in India's targeted PDS. The progressiveness of transfers depends

---

BOX 7.7 **Inferior Commodities and Inframarginal Consumption**

The economics literature refers to goods that the poor consume in greater amounts than other segments of the population as inferior goods. This designation pertains to the purchasing pattern (or negative income elasticity) and not to the physical attributes of the commodity. Coarse grains, for example, may be inferior goods in the sense that households with higher incomes are less likely to consume them, but from the standpoint of nutritional quality, such grains are actually superior to the more popular highly polished or refined grains.

The economics literature defines the amount of a commodity transferred or made available at a subsidized price as inframarginal if it is smaller than the amount that consumers would have chosen to purchase at the regular market price. The impact of a subsidy of a commodity on the poor will depend largely on whether the commodity selected is inferior and whether the level of consumption is inframarginal.

Because subsidies on inferior commodities are self-targeting, the benefits of the transfer will be larger for poor people than for nonpoor. As benefits are proportional to the amount of the good the household purchases, subsidies on commodities with low, and ideally negative, elasticities will be progressive (assuming such commodities are available). If the focus of the program is narrower and the purchases of the selected commodity represent a comparatively smaller share of a consumer's budget, the amount of income that can be transferred via a self-targeted commodity subsidy decreases. Moreover, even the most favorable self-targeted commodities will only distribute between a half to two-thirds of benefits to the poorest 40 percent of the population while the most successful means-tested transfer programs have the potential to deliver more than 80 percent of benefits to the poorest two quintiles (Coady, Grosh, and Hoddinott 2004; Grosh 1994).

The magnitude of the impact of a transfer on the amount of consumption of a rationed commodity is larger if the level of the transfer of the commodity is not inframarginal, that is, it is larger than the amount usually consumed. Indeed, for an inframarginal transfer, the amount of consumption will increase in line with the increase in household income, as consumers will base their decision on how much to buy on the price available in the market. For a transfer that is larger than the amount usually consumed, the increase in consumption will be much larger and will be based on the price response. A smaller price paid (taking the transfer into account) will induce a higher level of consumption of the commodity subsidized.

The overall impact on total nutrient consumption, as measured by calorie intake, tends to increase with the level of income. While one cannot assume that all income increments are spent on increased food consumption, food consumption might increase more than proportionally (see the evidence from South Africa in Alderman and del Ninno 1999; from Bangladesh in del Ninno and Dorosh 2003; and from food stamp studies in Fraker, Martini, and Ohls 1995).

SOURCES: Alderman 2002b; Alderman and Lindert 1998.

on how well they are targeted, as well as the impact of waiting time and possible stigma on participation by poor and nonpoor households.

The typical target groups for supplemental feeding programs are pregnant and lactating women and children under the age of three or five. Many programs give more benefits to those who are malnourished (underweight or stunted) or those failing to grow according to norms. The use of public service facilities and the selection of poor and nutritionally insecure areas may introduce a significant degree of self-targeting in countries where the middle- and upper-income groups use private health care.

The selection of beneficiaries for school feeding programs presents additional difficulties, as targeting children within schools is difficult and may stigmatize them, and may therefore limit program feasibility, efficiency, and desirability.[13] Occasionally schools use differential cost recovery to target meals as in Jamaica and the United States or feed only some children outside of school hours as was previously done in Chile. The selection of schools (the institutional targets) participating in school feeding programs is therefore the main criterion that can be used to target school feeding programs as in Costa Rica, although examples of effective targeting of school feeding programs are available—for example, the U.S. School Lunch Program, which has been able to avoid stigmatizing recipients. Gender targeting can also be used if female enrollment and attendance are particularly low.

Emergency feeding is usually carried out in refugee camps or in areas affected by natural disasters. The issues related to targeting mechanisms in those situations depend on the type of intervention. Supplementary feeding programs may benefit either all members of a particular age (for example, all children under the age of two) or gender, depending on the level of malnutrition, may be targeted using anthropometric criteria (for additional details see Sphere Project 2004; Taylor and Seaman 2004).

Disbursement Methods

In most cases, governments use their own distribution channels to procure, store, and transport the food needed for food-based programs. Not surprisingly, government involvement in food marketing may lead to inefficiencies. In India, for example, program grain is procured in the northwest of the country rather than closer to the places where it is distributed to beneficiaries. The use of private retailers who are authorized to sell both nonrationed and rationed commodities is common and occurs in, for instance, Egypt, India, and Iraq. Such retailers have replaced dedicated ration shops, thereby increasing availability and reducing costs.

Because of the long distribution process and the number of transactions that take place, some of the food may not reach intended beneficiaries, resulting in leakages from fraud or spoilage. Some of the leakage may occur at warehouses or at retail shops. In the Indian targeted PDS, observers report gaps between official estimates of the amount of food provided and household consumption of between 20 and 35 percent depending on the location and the commodity (Ahluwalia 1993; Dev and others 2004; Mooij 1999a). Rao (2000) finds evidence that some retailers simply sell the subsidized grain at the open market price, thereby increasing their margins. This is not surprising, as such back-door sales are inherent in any two-tier price system.

Community organization and information can help prevent leakage and fraud. An in-depth analysis of the problems related to leakages in food distribution programs in

Bangladesh by Ahmed and others (2004) finds that leakages for the Vulnerable Group Development Program were only 8 percent, compared with the higher rates more common for other programs in South Asia, partly because of monitoring and evaluation throughout the system and partly because of women's empowerment at the local level to hold program managers accountable.

As noted earlier, supplementary feeding can be distributed in the form of take-home rations or can take place on-site. On-site feeding can be more effective in ensuring that the target population actually consumes the rations, although it may not translate into an additional supplement to the usual diet if the food intake at home is reduced. Although it is relatively expensive to set up, it is useful for therapeutic feeding of severely malnourished children and for feeding vulnerable mothers (Gillespie 1999).

The main delivery mechanisms for school feeding programs include meals prepared on-site, meals prepared in advance, bulk food, and coupons. Each model is associated with a different set of implementation issues. Preparing meals on-site in developing countries presents several challenges: the long distances to fetch water and fuel for cooking, the slow cooking facilities, and the lack of adequate personnel which is often overcome by using volunteers. In many cases, the current emphasis on the timing of meals to maximize the program's impact on educational objectives involves additional challenges. New program approaches to improve efficiency include using snack foods and products that cook more quickly and contracting out to the private sector (Del Rosso 1999).

In the case of emergency feeding, beneficiaries are totally reliant on the food supplied and must receive a complete diet. In general, the process of determining ration size and composition, frequency of distribution, and criteria for program entry and exit are subject to similar considerations as other maternal and child health supplementary feeding projects, with the additional challenge that when the diet is insufficient or inadequate, it can result in deficiency diseases, for example, pellagra if the diet is based mainly on maize (Taylor and Seaman 2004).

Scope and Coverage

Food ration programs are important in India, where the PDS distributes rationed amounts of basic food items to about 160 million families (approximately 70 percent of the population); in Egypt, which has more than 48 million beneficiaries (more than 80 percent of the population); and Indonesia, where about 12 million households receive rations (about 23 percent of the population). However, some ration programs have been discontinued, such as Mexico's Tortivales (Free Tortilla) program; others have been reorganized, such as the JPS Operasi Pasar Khusus (Special Market Operations) program in Indonesia (Yonekura 2005); and some have been replaced by other programs, such as the rice ration program in Sri Lanka, which has been replaced by a food stamp program (Edirisinghe 1987; Tabor 2002). The value of the transfer varies from extremely small percentages to 6 percent of total household expenditure for the bottom 20th percentile of the population in Indonesia (Pritchett, Sumarto, and Suryahadi 2002; Sumarto, Suryahadi, and Pritchett 2000).

The overall coverage of feeding programs varies greatly, ranging from 1 to 2 percent of the population in Honduras to 6 percent of the total population in Chile and 15 percent of the population in Peru. The coverage of specific population groups can, however, be much higher. In Chile, 80 percent of children under two and 70 percent of preschoolers and pregnant and lactating women are covered by feeding programs (Kain and Uauy 2001).

Compared with the other types of feeding programs discussed in this section, the coverage of school feeding programs is usually more limited. Basically, there are a few large programs, as in Bangladesh, where the School Feeding Program covers 1.2 million primary schoolchildren out of a total of more than 15 million in 6,126 schools, and in Kenya, where the WFP provides food to about 1.5 million poor children in 3,800 schools, and many programs that have a smaller coverage. Worldwide, a total of 16.6 million children in 72 countries benefited from WFP school feeding programs in 2004 (WFP 2005) (see the annex to this chapter for a list of programs implemented by the WFP).

Administrative Costs

The administrative costs of food transfer programs are relatively high, because transporting and storing food in bulk is costly and these costs are incurred in addition to the personnel and information system costs incurred by cash transfer programs.

In India, the cost of getting grain to recipients via the PDS was nearly 50 percent higher than the value of the grain to the consumers (Radhakrishna and others 1997; World Bank 2001e). This could have occurred because of the inefficiencies inherent in government bureaucracies and the high costs of the public distribution network.

The administrative costs of supplementary feeding programs are high and range from 5 to 25 percent of the total costs of supplementary feeding programs. In the case of school feeding programs, administrative costs account for 10 to 55 percent of total program costs. The costs of delivering 1,000 calories per student per day for a year range from US$20 in Guatemala and Honduras to more than US$100 in places like Bolivia and Tunisia and up to US$200 in Paraguay (Del Rosso 1999).

Implementing Institutions

Several institutions are involved in the delivery of food-based programs depending on the type of program and the country. Some take-home rations involve participation by a welfare department and/or a government food storage agency. This is the case for the Vulnerable Group Development Program in Bangladesh, managed by the Ministry of Women and Welfare, which collects food from local storage deposits managed by the Ministry of Food. In other cases, governments delegate distribution to private shops or special ration shops, as for the PDS in India, which uses a network of public distribution and private shops to provide rations to beneficiaries.

Ministries of health tend to run supplemental feeding programs, while the education systems run school feeding programs that provide on-site food. Some programs rely on the private sector to provide meals.

OUTCOMES, ADVANTAGES, AND DISADVANTAGES

The overall success rate of food-based programs has been mixed, depending on the type of program and its implementation, including the types of commodities used, level of benefits delivered, and delivery mechanisms used.

Incidence

The incidence of participation by the poor depends on the commodity used, the targeting mechanism employed, and the marketing channel used. In Ethiopia, even though food transfers reach some female-headed households and some of the elderly, they do not reach the poorest people who live outside traditionally food-deficit areas (Clay, Molla, and Habtewold 1999; Quisumbing 2003). India's PDS does not have a good record of reaching the poor, yet those who have access to the targeted PDS consume the subsidy in its entirety (Tritah 2003). In rural programs in the Indian states of Andhra Pradesh and Maharashtra, the poor received 49 and 41 percent of total transfers, respectively. The equivalent percentages for the states' urban programs were 33 and 31 percent, respectively (Dutta and Ramaswami 2001). Various reasons could account for this. According to Coady (2004), liquidity-constrained poor households have often not been able to take up their full ration entitlements, because they are required to purchase a larger quantity than they would normally buy at one time (Alderman and von Braun 1984; Rao 2000). In Indonesia's JPS Operasi Pasar Khusus, which was targeted to the "permanently" poor (Pritchett, Sumarto, and Suryahadi 2002; Sumarto, Suryahadi, and Pritchett 2000), the bottom 20.0 percent of the population received 26.4 percent of the transfers.

The incidence of school feeding programs is usually progressive. Some evidence indicates that school feeding programs have reached intended beneficiaries using geographic targeting. In Chile's school feeding programs, 53 percent of the benefits went to the bottom quintile; in Costa Rica and Jamaica, 33 percent of benefits went to the bottom quintile and the poorest 20 percent received between 30 and 50 percent of transfers (Grosh 1994). In some cases, as in Guatemala, the middle class captures the benefits (Lindert, Skoufias, and Shapiro 2006).

Impact

The main challenge for food-based programs is to ensure that the additional cost of delivering food transfers results in an increase in consumption of food in general and of specific foods that improve beneficiaries' nutritional status in particular.[14] In theory, the effect of food-based programs on household food consumption is equivalent to that of a cash transfer, as households have the option of fully substituting the food received for their own expenditure on food. In practice, programs' impact on nutritional status depends on whether the food distributed is a net addition to household consumption, for example, if the size of the transfer is inframarginal or not, and if the commodity used is inferior or not (Ahmed, Haggblade, and Chowdhury 2000; Barrett 2002).

Several studies show that the targeting efficiency, size of transfers, and choice of commodities determine the impact of food-based programs. The Vaso de Leche (Glass of Milk) feeding program in Peru is well targeted to poor households and to those with low nutritional status, but the impact of the food subsidies beyond their value as income transfers is limited by the degree to which the commodity transfers are inframarginal (Stifel and Alderman 2006). Del Ninno and Dorosh (2003) show that small wheat transfers in Bangladesh after the 1998 flood had a positive impact on the consumption of wheat and the total number of calories consumed and a greater impact than a cash transfer of equivalent value would have had. By taking into account the impact on food markets, they also show that the increase in the demand for wheat reduced the potentially negative price effect of food distribution programs by one-third. This might not be the case for extremely large and less well-targeted programs such as the PDS in India. Indeed, Radhakrishna and others (1997) suggest that the welfare gains of the PDS in terms of income transfer were meager and that the impact on poverty and nutritional status was minimal.

Some evidence suggests that school feeding programs help reduce short-term hunger and improve enrollment and attendance, but little evidence indicates any impact on the nutrition of schoolchildren or on learning outcomes. A variety of studies, summarized in Ahmed (2004b) and Del Rosso (1999), find that school feeding programs have a positive impact on school attendance. For example, in Bangladesh, enrollment increased by 14 percent; in Burkina Faso, Jamaica, and Malawi, small pilots led to increases in enrollment and up to a 36 percent improvement in attendance. However, in a study conducted in Kenya (Meme and others 1998), the investigators did not find a difference in attendance rates between schools with and without school feeding programs. For school feeding programs to have an impact on nutrition is more difficult to achieve, as they take place too late for them to influence the long-term nutritional status of the children fed. However, Ahmed (2004b) finds that during one year, the School Feeding Program in Bangladesh increased the body mass index of participating children by 4 percent and increased their test scores by 15.7 percent.

Advantages

The following advantages of food-based programs are due mostly to direct improvements in the level of consumption and of the well-being of beneficiaries:

- Food-based transfers are not subject to inflation to the same extent as cash.
- Food-based transfers have the potential of being self-targeted as long as the commodities are limited to inferior, less preferred foods (see Alderman and Lindert 1998 for the case of yellow maize in Mozambique).
- Evidence indicates that food-related transfers encourage increased consumption, possibly because of changes in the share of resources controlled by women.
- Food distribution programs might help satisfy the need to rotate the food stocks of governments that maintain such stocks for security purposes, as in Bangladesh and India.
- Food provided through school feeding programs may contribute to improved learning by alleviating short-term hunger in addition to its effects as a food supplement and an incentive to attend school.
- Additional benefits exist when supplementary feeding programs are linked to adequate care for children and prospective or new mothers at health centers.

Disadvantages

Food-based programs have the following disadvantages, mostly related to the difficulty of reaching intended beneficiaries and the high costs needed to implement and operate them:

- The direct provision of food limits consumers' immediate choices to the commodities that are made available.

- The costs of food-based safety net programs vary widely depending on the size of the transfer, size of the target group, and logistical difficulty of distributing the benefit. Distribution costs tend to be higher for programs distributing actual food as opposed to cash or food stamps.

- The procurement, transport, and distribution of food can potentially create distortions in food markets.

- Feeding programs might provide households with disincentives to provide children with food at home, and meals eaten on-site may be substituted for home-prepared meals.

- When feeding programs use take-home rations, it cannot be ascertained whether the intended beneficiaries benefit from the food supplied.

- Supplementary feeding programs may have an urban bias because of the higher distribution costs associated with rural areas.

- School feeding programs might be perceived as solving the problems of school-age children and therefore might deter initiatives to address other important determinants of nutrition, learning, and health.

- School feeding programs can stigmatize poor beneficiaries unless the targeting is not observable.

LESSONS AND SUGGESTIONS

The food-based programs discussed in this section address different needs and serve different population groups and should be viewed as complements to each other rather than as alternatives when adapted to local circumstances.

Most Likely Beneficiaries

The most likely beneficiaries include poor families that do not have sufficient income to purchase enough of the right foods and are more likely to achieve a better diet if they can receive specific foods or purchase them at a subsidized cost; pregnant or lactating women; or young, malnourished children enrolled in school. Feeding programs are a necessity for people who are displaced and find themselves in refugee camps or in other situations without access to food markets or livelihoods that could allow them to pay for food if it were available for purchase.

Appropriate Context and Political Economy Considerations

Often governments chose to use food-based transfers because they are concerned with high food prices or because commodities markets are inadequate and therefore they have to guarantee access to food by the poorest people. The situation can be an outcome of chronic poverty, which the PDS in India was designed to address, for example, or of a shock like drought. The latter was the situation in Ethiopia in the 1980s, when because of poor infrastructure, challenging topography, and a history of state interventions that had severely restricted trade, commodity markets were insufficiently developed for the famine relief strategy to be based primarily on income support without concurrently providing grain (von Braun, Teklu, and Webb 1999). In later years, evidence from Ethiopia suggests a positive impact of food-based programs financed by food aid in reducing household vulnerability (Dercon and Krishnan 2004; Quisumbing 2003) and in smoothing consumption and protecting assets among households facing food stress (Hoddinott, Cohen, and Bos 2003). Therefore, food-based transfers might be necessary in isolated and thin food markets in rural areas, where cash transfers can cause additional increases in the price of food, or in emergency situations to replace nonfunctioning markets.

One crucial aspect to keep in mind when governments and international organizations operate in the market is the risk of a negative impact on local markets. For example, they can cause the collapse of local agricultural commodity prices, thereby having a disincentive effect on production, or they can have a negative impact on the development of private markets. The latter is the situation in Zambia, where government imports have crowded out private sector imports (del Ninno, Dorosh, and Subbarao 2005, 2007).

Food-based programs are effective instruments when the health status of mothers and children is low and can be increased by providing direct access to nutrition support. Behrman, Alderman, and Hoddinott (2004) show that reducing hunger and malnutrition is important not only on moral grounds, but also that the gains in productivity and reduction in health care costs are worth the expenditures. At the same time, the use of school feeding programs might be biased toward richer households when enrollment among poor children is low, although the existence of such programs can help increase enrollment by poor children.

Public provision of food and feeding programs is generally more politically acceptable than cash transfers, because food is a merit good, and therefore may receive national and international support. The agriculture sector and private sector food industry often support food-based programs, because they expand demand for food, as in the case of the U.S. Food Stamp Program, as long as the commodities provided are procured locally. Additional local support might also stem from the need to rotate the government's food stocks maintained for security reasons. International or donor support may be provided if programs are designed to distribute commodities received as food aid.

Adapting to Local Conditions and Avoiding Unintended Effects

The following main challenges facing the implementation of food-based programs are related to the costs of procuring, storing, and delivering food and the ability to prevent leakage to nonintended beneficiaries:

- **The types of foods distributed should be acceptable to the local population**. Such foods could possibly be inferior commodities with a high nutritional content, taking local economic conditions, tastes, and seasonal characteristics into account.

- **The timing of food distribution programs is crucial for saving lives and supporting livelihoods after a crisis situation.** Such programs should provide more resources during times of crises than at other times. Emergency feeding programs, for example, are most effective during the acute phase of a crisis, when providing food at feeding centers or camps for displaced people or refugees, where people are much more vulnerable to morbidity and mortality from infections. Timing is also important after the initial acute phase to ensure that additional food distributed in the form of rations or transfers does not increase the local supply of food after the following harvest, assuming that it is adequate, thereby having a negative impact on local prices and future production. That is what happened in Ethiopia in 2001, when food aid resources arrived late.

- **The provision of food transfers directly to women and in conjunction with primary health care and education as an incentive for participation is suggested.** Targeting women explicitly makes food-based programs more effective from a nutritional prospective. According to Rogers (1996), giving transfers to female household heads has a higher nutritional impact on individual household members than giving them to men. When supplementary food distribution programs are provided in the context of a more comprehensive program of health care and health and nutrition education, they may have a bigger impact on health outcomes. This can be achieved, for example, by providing health care services to all family members when they pick up the food or by allowing food aid to be collected once the use of adequate health care has been demonstrated. The integration of school feeding, food distribution, and deworming has increased child health, nutrition, and school participation. In India, primary school students receiving school meals and treatment for intestinal parasites experienced a reduction in parasite infection from 71 to 40 percent at minimal additional cost. In Indonesia, the combination of deworming with school feeding had a greater impact on growth than when food alone was provided (Del Rosso 1999; Del Rosso and Marek 1996).

- **The need to avoid the stigmatizing effect of participation in food-based programs requires special care.** For example, giving school lunches to one child and not to the others is impossible.

7.3 General Subsidies

Universal price subsides and untargeted sales of subsidized commodities are general measures aimed at controlling the prices of food and other essential commodities.[15] For a list of general price subsidy programs, see table B.3 in appendix B.

PROGRAM DESCRIPTION

Contrary to targeted, in-kind distribution programs, subsidized prices or sales of commodities are not administratively targeted. This means that all consumers have access to the same commodities at the same price, albeit sometimes in a fixed amount, although even in this case, market interventions can be self-targeting to some extent in the case of inferior goods, that is, goods for which the quantity demanded falls as incomes rise (box 7.7).

The main objective of subsidies is to guarantee access to food and other essential commodities at prices that consumers can afford. Controlling the prices of staple commodities is crucial not only for poor, food-insecure households, but it also responds to the political need to prevent prices from becoming too high. Indeed, reforms to remove existing subsidies are usually difficult to implement and are often marred by general discontent, political opposition, and sometimes riots. Examples include the food riots that followed a selective raising of commodity prices in Egypt in 1977, and, more recently, the food riots that occurred in the wake of currency devaluation and subsequent increases in the costs of traded commodities in Indonesia and Zimbabwe in 1997.

Government efforts to control the prices of food and other essential commodities date back at least 4,000 years to Egypt, Babylon, Greece, and Rome.[16] Universal rationing has been used mostly in wartime to guarantee urban consumers access to minimum quantities of selected goods in the absence of functioning markets. General subsidies for food were common in North Africa, South Asia, and Sub-Saharan Africa from the 19th century to the 1990s, and several countries in Latin America and the Caribbean—for example, Argentina, Brazil, Jamaica, and Mexico—have also attempted to implement general food subsidies (Grosh 1994). Many countries still provide explicit and implicit subsidies on petroleum products and electricity, sometimes at a high fiscal cost when world prices increase as in 2005.

TYPES OF PROGRAMS

The three types of policies and programs treated in this section are those that provide universal, indirect price support for food; those that promote subsidized sales of unlimited or rationed quantities of food commodities; and those that provide universal price support for energy products.[17] Thus the commodities covered by these programs range from staple food commodities such as rice, wheat, and maize (corn meal) to lighting and cooking fuel and gasoline for transport. Some programs also include products such as beverages and soap, but these are not treated in detail in this section.

Universal, Indirect Price Support for Food

Universal, indirect price supports for food are open-ended, untargeted subsidies that attempt to lower the price the general population pays for staple foods. Often these policies are part of a general price stabilization effort by the government, as in the case of Indonesia, which intervened heavily in the market for rice from the 1960s until 1997. The interventions are implemented via indirect taxes or producer subsidies, including procurement and trade quotas or other market interventions to stabilize prices, as well as through exchange rate distortions (Krueger, Schiff, and Valdes 1991) or tax exemptions, for example, exemptions from the 14 percent value added tax (VAT) on maize and kerosene in South Africa. Most price stabilization efforts ultimately fail because of high fiscal costs. Indonesia, however, successfully stabilized prices from the early 1970s to the mid-1990s through a combination of domestic procurement, government imports, and subsidized sales of commodities through BULOG (Timmer 1991, 1996).[18]

Subsidized Untargeted Sales

Governments may also provide universal access to food or other commodities through subsidized, untargeted sales at public distribution centers or designated private outlets on a first-come, first-served basis. This is the case for bread and flour subsidies in Egypt (box 7.8). When a government does not choose to subsidize all the sales of a commodity, quantities may be rationed by the imposition of limits on the amount that any one household may purchase. In such cases, governments impose quantity limits both to reduce

BOX 7.8 **Universal Food Subsidy System for Bread and Flour, Egypt**

Egypt's food subsidy system is a major component of the safety net for the poor and a mainstay of the government's long-term policy of promoting social equity and political stability. The main objective is to guarantee the availability of affordable staples, thereby helping to reduce infant mortality and malnutrition and mitigating the adverse effects of economic reform and structural adjustment.

The food subsidy system started in 1941 and has undergone several changes over the years. The current program includes several commodities. *Baladi* (round, flat loafs baked with whole wheat) and *fino* (baguette-style bread baked with more refined flour) breads and wheat flour, which account for 62 percent and 15 percent, respectively of the subsidy, are available to all consumers regardless of their income level. Sugar, cooking oil, and other commodities, which account for less than 25 percent of the subsidies, are targeted to those with ration cards (in theory, higher-income households receive low-subsidy red ration cards and lower-income households receive high-subsidy green ration cards). The overall cost of the system reached its peak in 1977. Reforms of the bread subsides started in the early 1980s, when the price of *baladi* was first raised from 1 piaster to 2 piasters by introducing a higher-quality 2-piaster loaf alongside the 1-piaster loaf, which was later eliminated. The price was increased again, to 5 piasters, in 1989 using the same method. As a result, expenditures on bread subsidies decreased considerably. After the depreciation of the Egyptian pound in January 2003, the cost of wheat increased; in April 2004, the government introduced *fino* bread, to be sold in much smaller quantities than before, and the total cost of subsidies increased again.

Implementation. Consumers can purchase any amount of bread and flour at local, private, licensed retail outlets at a fixed price. The subsidy rates are 67 percent for *baladi* bread, 47 percent for *fino* bread, and 66 percent for wheat flour.

Impact. The current system does not target the poor well. Studies find that even though the poor consume more subsidized *baladi* bread than the well-off and that flour consumption increases slightly with income (Adams 2000; Ali and Adams 1996), the benefits are about equally distributed across income groups. Nevertheless, this is much better than the situation in the early 1980s before the reforms, when the distribution was slightly biased toward the well-off (although it contributed more to the poor as a share of income) (Alderman and von Braun 1984). However, poor targeting combined with system leakage (28 percent of the subsidized wheat flour and 12 percent of the *baladi* bread never reach the intended beneficiaries) mean that only about one-third of the subsidies go to the needy.

Lessons. The current *baladi* bread subsidy is able to provide benefits to most of the poor (75 percent of those in the bottom quintile), particularly the urban poor (90 percent coverage), helping them maintain a minimum level of consumption, albeit the subsidy is an expensive way to improve the food security and nutrition of the poor. The cost of transferring LE 1.00 to general consumers of *baladi* bread is LE 1.16, but because 61 percent of the benefit from the *baladi* bread subsidy goes to the non-needy, the cost of reaching a needy household increases to LE 2.98.

SOURCES: Ahmed and others 2001; World Bank 2005c.

consumer demand and limit the cost of the subsidies, while sales of the remaining quantities on the open market are often permitted (Pinstrup-Andersen 1988).

Subsidies for Energy and Utilities

Subsidies for energy and utilities include market interventions and subsidized sales of petroleum products and electricity.[19] The petroleum products most often subsidized include gasoline and diesel used for transport and for generating electricity for agricultural use; kerosene used for lighting and heating, and sometimes also for cooking; and liquefied petroleum gas used for cooking. The main justification for such subsidies is to ensure that households have access to these items at a reasonable cost; however, their costs can be extremely high, sometimes higher than for food subsidies, while their targeting efficiency tends to be much lower than for food.

Energy subsidies differ from food subsidies in some important ways. First, subsidies to networked utilities such as electricity require that beneficiaries be connected to the service grid. Where grid coverage is low, many will be excluded. For those who are on the network, administering multiple prices by charging a low amount for the initial kilowatts used and higher amounts for usage above a defined threshold, referred to as lifeline pricing, is easier than administering an energy subsidy. Prices can also be set to differ geographically. As for food, ensuring the ability to use a minimum amount of energy can be important, as is the case for basic electricity and heating in cold climates. Concerns about market distortions and poor targeting are similar, but often more marked.

KEY DESIGN FEATURES

The implementation of general price subsidies poses financial, administrative, and logistic, challenges. Indirect market interventions might have low administrative costs, but might have adverse impacts on markets and can result in governments incurring large fiscal losses as is the case of tax and tariff exemptions such as the VAT exemptions in South Africa (Alderman and del Ninno 1999) and the tariff exemptions in Madagascar.

Energy subsidies can also be implemented by controlling prices along the production and distribution chain without compensating the regulated companies for the ensuing losses (Baig and others 2007; Coady and others 2006). Such untargeted, direct market interventions might be a little easier to implement than targeted programs, but they face the same transportation and distribution costs and logistical challenges as other in-kind transfer programs.

Beneficiary Selection

Given the nature of general subsidy programs, beneficiaries are not selected directly, and only indirect methods can be used to ensure that the poor benefit more than the rich. The selection of inferior commodities is crucial for achieving some form of self-targeting as explained earlier. Tunisia in the early 1990s provides an example of one of the most successful attempts to shift general subsidies to self-targeted goods (box 7.9).

Geographic targeting can be used to increase the share of benefits accruing to the poor by restricting access to a fixed ration of food sold at subsidized prices to public ration shops located in areas identified as food-deficit zones or in areas that have higher prices or larger numbers of vulnerable households. However, geographic targeting of consumers of

BOX 7.9 **Reforming Food Price Subsidies, Tunisia**

The Tunisian government has been providing universal access to food subsidies on selected consumer products (cereals, cooking oil, sugar, milk, and meat) to all consumers since 1970. In the late 1980s, the government subsidized 20 to 50 percent of the value of various cereals, more than 70 percent of the value of granulated white sugar, and 30 to 40 percent of the value of milk products. Analyses undertaken throughout the 1980s concluded that the wealthiest income group benefited up to twice as much as the poorest income group as measured in mean subsidies per capita. Nevertheless, the Food Subsidy Program remained an important part of the government's safety net, with subsidies accounting for 10 percent of all government spending and 4 percent of GDP by the mid-1980s. As part of its overall structural reform efforts, in the early 1990s, the government launched a series of reforms designed to improve the targeting of subsidies. The primary components of the reform program included gradually adjusting the prices of some commodities, eliminating subsidies on certain products, and cutting the production and distribution costs of subsidized products.

The major strategic shift was toward self-targeting, achieved in part through the innovative use of packaging and marketing. For example, the government differentiated the subsidy level on different forms of milk, all of which were nutritionally equivalent. The highest subsidy was on reconstituted powdered milk sold in small plastic bags that would not stand up in the refrigerator. A lower subsidy was put on reconstituted powdered milk in small cardboard packages that would stand up in the refrigerator. The lowest subsidy was on fresh milk in bottles. When demand was not channeled into the fresh milk, the government raised the subsidy on it slightly, and enough consumers switched from the medium-subsidy to the low-subsidy product that the total cost of the subsidy declined. As concerns oils, Tunisia was receiving European television with advertising for fancy oils that stressed the health benefits of olive oils and showed plentiful images of attractive bottles. The government maintained its subsidy on cooking oil, which it dispensed into consumers' private containers from bulk drums labeled only "cooking oil" with no reference to the content of olive oil in the blend. At the same time, it sold bottled oil labeled as olive oil at market prices. As a result, many consumers switched to the more attractive and convenient unsubsidized products. In this spirit, the government also eliminated the subsidies on refined baguette-type bread.

The reforms resulted in a decrease in expenditures on food subsidies from around 4.0 percent of GDP in 1984 to 1.5 percent in 1998. The share of total transfers received by the poorest quintile increased from 8 to 21 percent, although early analysis of consumption showed an overall drop in calorie and protein intake.

SOURCES: Alderman and Lindert 1998; Tuck and Lindert 1996.

energy products might exclude the poor from participating, as they may not be connected to the national grid. This is not the case in much of the former Soviet Union and Eastern Europe (World Bank 2000b), where energy subsidies can therefore be better distributed. It is the case in Argentina, where Foster (2004) finds that focusing on subsidizing connections rather than on use of services using geographic targeting is important. In contrast, in

India, there is a large difference in consumption patterns between urban and rural areas; 60 percent of rural households have no access to electricity and use kerosene for lighting (Gangopadhyay, Ramaswami, and Wadhwa 2005). In some countries, governments have set different prices for different neighborhoods depending on their level of prosperity. Thus, Colombia has separate prices by neighborhood for electricity; Chile does the same for water.

Other targeting methods include opening stores at inconvenient times and lengthy queuing times, based on the argument that even though access is, in principle, universal, nonpoor households have higher opportunity costs of time. However, as retailers only collect cash and not the value of the time costs, this results in an excessive burden and an economic loss (often referred to as deadweight loss in economic terms) to society in general. The poor may not benefit from rationing by waiting, because market access and cash constraints may limit the amount purchased, while better-off consumers might find the time to line up. This was observed in Egypt (Alderman and von Braun 1984) and with a rice subsidy in urban Burkina Faso (Delgado and Reardon 1988), when poor households did not have the cash to buy the amount needed for the whole month. The need to make small purchases might also influence the market selected and force the poor to pay relatively high prices in unsubsidized markets (Rao 2000).

Price discrimination for energy products is possible when all consumers have access to the same commodity. For example, where connections to the grid are available, subsidies on electricity use can be rationed by guaranteeing a minimum lifeline consumption level, with prices increasing as the amount of electricity used increases, as is done in Jordan. Note, however, that in this case meters need to be available to facilitate the implementation of step pricing.

Disbursement Methods

The implementation of indirect price subsidies for food may not pose an administrative challenge when it does not involve any physical distribution. This is the case when such subsidies are implemented early in the marketing chain using exchange rates and tariff rates or taxes. This was the case for rice in Madagascar in 2004 (box 7.10) and for food and kerosene in South Africa (Alderman and del Ninno 1999). In other cases, governments become more involved in marketing operations to achieve price stabilization or subsidies, as in Pakistan, where the government subsidizes the transport and storage of grain before it is sold to flour mills (Dorosh and Salam 2008).

The implementation of subsidized sales and rations of food commodities faces the same challenges as food distribution programs. Rations can be distributed via ration shops (utility stores in Pakistan) or private retail outlets as in Egypt. In this case, the distribution requires additional logistical and administrative costs and may affect the marketing and supply chain.

Governments use two main ways to control domestic prices of petroleum products and to provide energy subsidies. In some cases, governments provide explicit (in the budget) subsidies by reducing profits or imposing losses on state-owned enterprises such as refineries or on the private sector. In other cases, the private sector can freely import and distribute petroleum products, but the government controls prices along the production and distribution chain, without compensating the companies involved. The government can set prices for domestic use with a formula that anchors domestic prices to import prices, including profit margins and taxes, or can set them on an ad hoc basis, especially after a large increase in the world market price that would have raised prices to an unpopular level, as happened in 2005 in several countries (Baig and others 2007; Coady and others 2006).

Some countries distribute commodities through ration shops. In India, kerosene is distributed through the PDS using an elaborate institutional arrangement that includes state and district officials, wholesalers, and retailers (Gangopadhyay, Ramaswami, and Wadhwa 2005; Rehman and others 2005).

Implementing Institutions

Several institutions are involved in setting prices, in price stabilization, and in procuring and delivering commodities. Often these are parastatals that have been assigned the task of operating in the market, for example, BULOG in Indonesia and the Pakistan Agricultural Storage and Services Corporation. In other cases, ministries might be involved in managing operations related to the purchase, storage, and distribution of commodities as is the case of the Ministry of Food in Bangladesh and the Ministry of Trade and Supply in Egypt. The institutions involved in implementing fuel subsidies are often the same that are used to distribute food subsidies with the addition of oil refineries.

Scope and Coverage

The use of general support programs has been evolving in recent years and has been subject to several changes and reforms, though by their nature, the coverage of such programs is quite extensive. At the same time, this does not necessarily mean that everyone can take advantage of such programs to the same extent. This will depend on the types of commodities selected.

While most price stabilization efforts and indirect price interventions in food markets have been reformed following recent trends toward market liberalization, exceptions remain. In Pakistan, provincial untargeted food subsidies in fiscal 2002/03 reached Rs 6.8 billion, a figure 12 percent greater than the total budget for the Public Sector Development Program for the Health Division. From fiscal 2001/02 to 2004/05, the government's procurement of wheat averaged 3.8 million tons per fiscal year, or 19.5 percent of national production. The government sold this wheat to millers at prices below the full costs of procurement and handling. Flour mills typically sold the wheat flour produced from government wheat in the open market; subsidized sales through utility stores accounted for only a small percentage of total sales (Dorosh and Salam 2008; World Bank 2007j). Lately governments have become more interested in other ways to intervene in food markets—for example, using VAT in South Africa (PricewaterhouseCoopers 2005) and tax and tariff reductions in Madagascar (box 7.10).

The past 20 years have seen numerous reforms in relation to the use and scope of universal rations. Ration programs are still extensive in a few countries such as Egypt, where subsidized bread and flour are available to all Egyptians in unlimited quantities, but rationed goods are available in limited quantities and only to households that hold ration cards (World Bank 2005c).

Some country programs have eliminated or phased out rations, such as Bangladesh's Palli rationing scheme (Ahmed, Haggblade, and Chowdhury 2000), Pakistan's rural rationing program, and Zambia's food distribution system. Other countries have drastically

BOX 7.10 Lowering the Cost of Rice by Adjusting Import Tariffs versus Targeted Cash Transfers, Madagascar

In 2004, the cost of rice imports rose sharply in Madagascar because of a rise in world rice prices and a large depreciation of the Malagasy franc. Faced also with a domestic production shortfall, the government attempted to stabilize domestic rice markets through subsidized sales of rice at an official price below import parity (including tariffs), a policy that actually discouraged private sector imports and ultimately led to domestic rice prices rising substantially above import parity levels. Alternative policy options, such as changing the import duties on rice and promoting private sector trade or distributing targeted direct cash transfers either alone or in combination with a smaller change in import duties, would likely have produced better outcomes for the poor.

Impact. Using a simple partial equilibrium model of rice supply and demand, Minten and Dorosh (2006) show that lowering the rice import tariff by 10 percentage points would have had only a small effect on total revenues collected, because even with inelastic overall consumer demand, import demand is price elastic. The reduction in the tariff increases the demand for rice by 14 to 24 percent, depending on the assumed magnitude of the own-price elasticity of demand. If producers are also price responsive, the effect on total tariff revenue is even smaller: only a 6 percent decline. The net benefits of this policy for net consumers would be between US$8.5 million and US$8.8 million, although the net benefits to all the poor, including rural surplus households, are only US$0.6 million to US$1.3 million.

A targeted, direct cash transfer worth the same as the net benefit of the price reduction (US$8.5 million to US$8.8 million) could avoid the welfare losses for net producers while providing the same benefits to net consumers. The administrative costs of targeting and distribution, as well as the likelihood of leakages to the nonpoor, would, however, raise the costs of such a program beyond the US$8.5 million to US$8.8 million in benefits or reduce the value of the transfer.

Lessons. The study concludes that as long as incentives for competitive private sector trade are maintained, transparent, and announced ahead of time, tariff reductions can be used to stabilize market prices with only small losses of tariff revenues. With this policy in effect, the benefits to poor net rice consumers are estimated to be 2.0 to 8.7 times the value of lost tariff revenues.

The Madagascar example shows that, in some cases, using general price subsidies to protect poor consumers from increases in the prices of staple commodities is possible. Where domestic prices are determined by the border prices of an imported commodity, adjustments to tariff rates—a policy that can be implemented quickly—can effectively stabilize policies at a low fiscal cost. Moreover, these benefits can be achieved without the high administrative costs incurred in setting up and running a new direct food transfer program. Reducing tariff rates below zero would be problematic, however, because of the potential for overinvoicing or other forms of fraud that could significantly raise costs.

SOURCES: Coady, Dorosh, and Minten 2008; Minten and Dorosh 2006.

reformed ration programs to change the types of commodities distributed and the populations covered (see box 7.9 for the example of Tunisia). In India, access to wheat rations has been restricted to those below the poverty line. A few countries have both targeted and untargeted programs depending on the commodities, including both Egypt and India.

Energy subsidy programs for petroleum products are still prevalent in two-thirds of developing countries, including both importers and exporters of petroleum products. In a number of countries, fuel subsidies have exceeded 2 percent of GDP since 2004, for example, 12.7 percent in Azerbaijan in 2005, 4.3 percent in Bolivia in 2004, 3.6 percent in Ecuador in 2005, 4.4 percent in Egypt in 2004, 3.0 percent in Indonesia in 2004, 6.6 percent in Jordan in 2005, and 9.2 percent in the Republic of Yemen in 2005. In Indonesia and the Republic of Yemen, total subsidies were higher than the health and education budgets combined (Coady and others 2006; World Bank 2005f).

Administrative Costs

The administrative costs of general price subsidies depend on the type of intervention. The administrative costs of setting exchanges rates and tariffs are quite small. Similarly, while the loss of revenues from VAT and other tax-exemption programs can be substantial, the marginal cost of administering such programs is quite small. In the case of South Africa's VAT program, the exemptions on maize and milk cost the treasury more than R 600 million in 1994, while the meat exemption would have cost the treasury R 1.8 billion if implemented (Alderman and del Ninno 1999).

The costs of intervening in food markets can be substantial, as intervention involves food procurement, storage, and distribution. The government of Pakistan procures most of the grain for its public distribution system in Punjab at the time of harvest and distributes it to other remote northwestern provinces six months later. Thus the government subsidizes both transport and storage (Minten and Dorosh 2006). Indonesia's abandonment of its use of open market sales to stabilize prices in the wake of the 1997 devaluation is not surprising, as subsidizing rice at well below import prices proved to be fiscally unsustainable and encouraged smuggling and reexport.

The costs of distributing food rations can also be high and are determined mainly by the difference between what the government pays for a unit of a commodity included in a distribution program and the price consumers pay. The full cost is often much higher if the costs of production subsidies, storage, and transportation are also taken into account.

The cost of subsidizing fuels is also large. The level of administrative costs depends on how the program is implemented. In most cases, when countries are not involved in processing petroleum products and marketing operations, administrative costs are relatively small.

An additional cost that accrues to society is the loss of the transfers that do not reach intended beneficiaries. Whenever subsidies are introduced using a long distribution chain, many opportunities arise for leakage and pilferage. In the Islamic Republic of Iran, dual markets and multiple official exchange rates led to rent seeking and leakage in consumer food subsidies estimated at 15 to 40 percent in the late 1990s. Rent-seeking behavior can lead to a diversion of supplies to private outlets at market prices, as with flour in Morocco, where the observed consumer price is 25 to 50 percent higher than the official price (World Bank 1999c). This is also the case for kerosene in India, where estimates indicate that 50 percent of the kerosene supplied through the PDS does not reach intended consumers. Regardless of attempts to control distribution by adding a blue dye to differentiate subsidized kerosene, it is often mixed with diesel fuel and sold on the open market as automotive fuel (Gangopadhyay, Ramaswami, and Wadhwa 2005; Rehman and others 2005).

OUTCOMES, ADVANTAGES, AND DISADVANTAGES

Several studies show that general subsidies have rarely been used effectively to help poor consumers.

Incidence

As general price subsidy programs do not target any group in particular, the incidence of program participation depends on the share of the budgets of the poor spent on the subsidized commodities, which is determined by consumption patterns, prices, and access. Upper-income households may opt to obtain their food in the higher-priced open market if they perceive the quality of the food sold there to be higher or if some social stigma is attached to using the ration system. Very poor consumers may not use their ration allocation if they do not have the cash to procure the full quota. Overall, the incidence of food rations and distribution programs popular in the 1980s was not pro-poor. Both quotas and take-up have, until recent reforms, varied little by income group for Egypt's ration system (Alderman and von Braun 1984). The same was true for several commodities in many other countries, including Algeria in 1991, Sri Lanka before the reforms in the 1990s, and Pakistan (Alderman 1988b; World Bank 1999c).

The proportion of low-income people who benefit from fuel subsidies is relatively low, as richer households consume more energy. The share of the total benefits to be derived from fuel subsidies for the poorest 40 percent of households ranges from 15.3 percent in Bolivia to 25.1 percent in Sri Lanka. In the countries covered by Coady and others (2006), between 75 and 85 percent of subsidy benefits accrue to the richest 60 percent of households. A study in Indonesia (World Bank 2006f) finds that before the 2005 price increase, only 20 percent of fuel subsidy benefits went to the poorest 30 percent of households: in total, the benefits accruing to the richest 10 percent were more than five times those accruing to the poorest 10 percent.

The difference in the impact of subsidy programs depends on the commodity selected for subsidization. This is illustrated by the VAT exemptions in South Africa (Alderman and del Ninno 1999). In the case of maize, 65 percent of the exemption is captured by the poorest 40 percent of the population. In the case of milk, however, only 15 percent of the exemption is captured by the poorest 40 percent of the population, reflecting the consumption pattern of the poor, who spend a much greater share of their budget on maize than milk.

Access to fair price shops, ration cards, or electricity connections can also have a large impact on the use of subsidized commodities by the poor. Obviously a subsidy on electricity will have no impact on those rural households that are not connected to the grid (Komives and others 2005).

Impact

The impact of price subsidy programs on consumers' real income is equivalent to the sum of direct and indirect reductions in the prices of the commodities consumed, which depends greatly on the incidence of participation as measured by actual consumption levels.

The direct impact of a subsidy is measured by consumers' savings resulting from the lower prices of the targeted commodity and depends on the share of their budget they devote to that commodity and the change in price.[20] The indirect impact of a subsidy is measured by the savings resulting from the impact on the prices of other commodities and on those commodities households consume when they switch to alternative commodities in response to price increases. This is particularly important in the case of petroleum products, which may constitute a large percentage of the cost of inputs into the production of many other commodities.

Tax exemptions affect consumers similarly to subsidies. The effect may be either progressive or regressive depending on whether the relative savings accrue mainly to the poor or the nonpoor. Estimating the benefits and costs of price subsidies financed by indirect taxes on producers, including procurement and trade quotas, or by exchange rate distortions, can be complicated, as they should take second-round (indirect) effects into account (Krueger, Schiff, and Valdes 1991) and will depend on whether the poor are net producers or net consumers. For example, Deaton (1989) and Trairatvorakul (1984) indicate that both the smallest and largest farms in Thailand benefit from the export tax, whereas the tax results in a net loss of income for farmers with medium-sized holdings.

A few studies report the impact of fuel subsidies on income. Coady and others (2006) find that for the five countries in their study (Bolivia, Ghana, Jordan, Mali, and Sri Lanka), a 50 percent average increase in fuel prices results, on average, in a 4.6 percent decrease in real income. Analysis of the removal of subsidies can give an indication of the magnitude of the impact of the subsidy program. The pricing reform for electricity in Eastern Europe in the 1990s increased the share of the income the poor spent on electricity, while consumption stayed the same (Lampietti 2004). Similarly, Gangopadhyay, Ramaswami, and Wadhwa's (2005) study of the effect of reducing liquefied petroleum gas subsidies in India shows that even though the kerosene subsidies are an inefficient means of subsidizing fuel use by the poor, any reductions would need to be supported by other policies that would limit the adverse impacts on the poor.

Advantages

Despite the difficulties of implementing efficient price subsidy programs, some advantages are associated with their use, namely:

- If poor people have access to the commodities subsidized, they can all take advantage of the program, thus errors or exclusions are low. In addition, general price subsidies may be easier to administer and faster to implement than income transfers. Interventions that require modifying tariffs or exchange rates may be quicker to implement and more effective than individual transfers (see the example of Madagascar in box 7.10).
- Quotas can limit the total cost of the subsidy program. A sudden rise in the local or international price of the subsidized good can result in an unplanned increase in the subsidy budget. This financial risk is reduced if the quantity of the good that is subsidized is fixed.
- Subsidies can be used to encourage a minimum level of consumption of certain goods. Such goods are sometimes referred to as merit goods and are given extra weight in economic calculations.

- Obtaining political support is sometimes easier for commodity subsidies than for direct income transfers. One reason for this support is, however, because upper-income households can then take advantage of them.

Disadvantages

Most of the following disadvantages of general subsidy programs are related to poor targeting and high budgetary costs:

- Errors of inclusion are high. If richer households consume more of the commodities subsidized than poor households, not only do too many nonpoor participate in the program, but they might even receive a larger share of its benefits. This is the case of fuel subsidies in several countries, including Egypt and Indonesia (Coady and others 2006).

- Subsidized sales distort marketing and production incentives. When the government attempts to create a parallel market infrastructure, it crowds out private trade or preempts its development, which often results in an inefficient distribution network. It can also have a negative impact on producers by distorting their incentives.

- Programs might be biased toward urban populations. If the program emphasizes the consumption patterns of urban residents, this might result in an implicit tax on small rural producers by keeping local prices much lower than they would be in the absence of subsidies.

- Price stabilization programs are expensive. This is because they involve large operations and their budgets are hard to control. If the government is committed to defending a given price level, an increase in the international price will require larger expenditures, as occurred following the increase in the price of oil in 2005.

- Popular general subsidies are difficult to reform and remove. Poor urban populations have often shown their discontent with reforms and with reduced price subsidies by rioting. A recent example is the riots that took place in the Republic of Yemen in July 2005 after fuel prices went up; these left 22 people dead and hundreds injured (Baig and others 2007).

- General subsidy programs are vulnerable to fraud and leakage to nonbeneficiaries. In situations in which the open market price of a commodity is higher than the rationed amount, dealers and retailers have an incentive to sell a portion of the commodity on the open market. This happened in a number of older programs, including in Pakistan in the 1980s and in Mozambique in the early 1990s (Alderman 1988b; Dorosh, del Ninno, and Sahn 1996), and more recently in connection with India's kerosene program (Gangopadhyay, Ramaswami, and Wadhwa 2005; Rehman and others 2005).

LESSONS AND SUGGESTIONS

General subsidy programs can have a role for poor consumer households when access to essential commodities is threatened by high prices; however, adapting them efficiently to local situations is difficult.

Most Likely Beneficiaries

Intended beneficiaries include working and nonworking poor consumer households that do not have enough resources to purchase basic staple commodities and food items and other essential commodities such as cooking and lighting fuel or electricity. The fact that consumers in urban areas are more likely to receive a larger share of transfers than those in rural areas is not surprising, as people in rural areas tend to either produce their own food or obtain what they need from neighbors and small local markets. Regarding electricity, they might not be connected to the grid. However, subsidies may be used in rural areas, as is the case for food in Pakistan and Sri Lanka and for kerosene in Egypt and India for those who do not have access to alternative sources of energy for cooking and lighting. However, whether general subsidies are the best instrument for addressing people's needs for food and other essential commodities is questionable.

Appropriate Context and Political Economy Considerations

The use of general subsidies is most relevant when the prices of essential commodities are too high and may have a negative impact on consumption by the poor. In some cases prices may have risen quickly because of a bad harvest, a natural disaster, or changing terms of trade in international markets. In Madagascar in 2004, the combination of a production shortfall and an increase in the cost of rice imports caused a rapid increase in local prices.

Many governments cite stabilization as their objective for using subsidies and ration programs, even though in many cases they are also concerned about reducing the overall cost of food consumption, as high prices can result in discontent, riots, and negative perceptions about those in power. Another reason why policy makers may favor price subsidies rather than cash transfers is that subsidies can encourage the consumption of goods that improve nutrition (Lavy and others 1996) or lead to greater household investments in health and education.

The combination of high levels of government expenditures on subsidies, lower prices of staple food commodities, and international pressure have reduced political support for price subsidy programs. This has led to a reduction in government interventions in food markets and the reform or elimination of some subsidy programs. Experience in Bangladesh and Pakistan, which have phased out ration programs and replaced them with targeted food programs (Ahmed, Haggblade, and Chowdhury 2000), and experience in Tunisia (box 7.9), where the scope and size of the ration program have been drastically reduced, show that modifying programs and reducing overall expenditures while maintaining some coverage for some of the most important commodities for the poor is possible.

In recent years, a new wave of reforms has been taking place in the energy sector. Following a series of large increases in the world market price of oil that started in late 2003 and January 2004, most countries that controlled the prices of fuel and related products were faced with either high domestic prices or unsustainable expenditures. Their first reaction was to suspend the use of automatic price increases linked to world market prices to maintain local prices at lower levels. After a while, this policy proved to be unsustainable, prompting governments to raise prices and find other ways to compensate consumers. This is what governments did in, for example, Chile, China, Ghana, and Indonesia (Bacon and Kojima 2006; Baig and others 2007).

In 2004 in Indonesia, fuel subsidies accounted for 14 percent of government expenditure, which was more than its expenditures for health and education combined. In 2005, the government decided to increase fuel prices, first by 29 percent in March, and then, as fuel prices continued to increase, by another 114 percent in October. At the same time the government introduced a new cash transfer program for 16 million poor families under which each family received Rp 300,000 (about US$30) every three months. The full annual cost of the program is estimated at nearly 0.7 percent of GDP (Baig and others 2007; World Bank 2006f, 2007h).

Other reforms are needed in poor countries such as India to provide poor households with alternatives to kerosene and biomass fuels for cooking and lighting that might be more affordable, safer, and less polluting. Such reforms include promoting the use of liquefied petroleum gas for fuel, implementing rural electrification, and marketing solar lanterns (Misra and others 2005 show that a 5-watt-peak solar lantern can provide the same amount of light as a 40-watt bulb).

Adapting to Local Conditions and Avoiding Unintended Effects

The two biggest challenges to successful implementation of general subsidy programs are reaching the intended beneficiaries and keeping the budget under control. These objectives can be achieved in a variety of ways as follows:

- **Improving targeting.** To improve the targeting efficiency of general subsidy programs, only inferior commodities should be subsidized. This can be achieved by taking into account the preferences and expenditure patterns of both poorer and wealthier income groups. Alternative approaches include rationing the amount of a commodity available for the subsidy. For example, the targeting for an electricity subsidy can be improved by providing a discount only on a small, given amount of consumption (the lifeline level) that would guarantee the household receives a minimum amount of electricity (Lampietti and others 2004).

- **Ensuring access.** The poor must have access to the subsidized commodity, for example, a connection to the electricity grid or the ability to purchase subsidized food commodities at the intended price and not from a parallel market at a higher price.

- **Reforming programs.** If the budget for general subsidies becomes too large, the government should reform the program and use the resources to provide direct transfers instead, as was recently done in Ghana, Indonesia, and Jordan (Baig and others 2007). Given the delicate political situation in regard to these programs, the nature and timing of reforms depend on many factors, including the interplay of diverse interests expressed by local groups and international agencies. Country experience has shown that the public is more likely to accept reforms if the rationale behind the reforms is explained in advance, other safety net programs that have no direct link with inefficient subsidy programs are introduced to replace them, and the replacement programs are introduced when prices increase.

7.4 Workfare

Labor-intensive public works programs have two main objectives: first, to provide a source of income to poor workers,[21] and second, to construct or rehabilitate public infrastructure.[22] In the safety net literature, the shorthand term "public works" is often used for such programs.[23] Sometimes the term workfare is used, although some reserve that term for programs that are more closely linked to labor activation programs that provide job search, training, or apprenticeships than the sort of heavy construction labor that is the traditional mainstay of labor-intensive public works. For a list of workfare programs, see table B.4 in appendix B.

PROGRAM DESCRIPTION

Public works programs are often a good choice in postcrisis countries, as in Korea following the 1997 economic crises (box 7.11) and in Argentina following the peso crises that began in 1999. They are also valuable when infrastructure reconstruction and employment generation are priorities after a natural disaster, as in Sri Lanka following the 2005 tsunami. In countries where formal unemployment insurance is infeasible or unaffordable, public works programs that guarantee employment often serve an insurance function. In addition, by providing on-the-job training, public works programs can help integrate people who are outside the mainstream labor market because they lack the necessary skills. Programs can be designed to be gender sensitive to enhance participation by women; for example, women might prefer task-based wages rather than daily wages because of the flexibility these offer.

Public works have been an important safety net intervention in both developed and developing countries since a widespread famine in England in 1817.[24] Several Western countries adopted different types of public works programs during the depression years (1931–6) and the postwar years and again during milder recessions. In much of Africa and South Asia, public works programs began at the turn of the 20th century and expanded during the 1950s in the form of food-for-work programs, in which workers were paid for their labor with food, which was in large part received in the form of food aid (Dejardin 1996).

TYPES OF PROGRAMS

Public works programs differ in relation to the type of activity involved, the type of job provided, and the level of labor intensity. The selection of activities to be carried out determines the types of jobs to be performed and the labor intensity.

Traditionally, public works programs have involved activities such as road construction and maintenance, which have generally been associated with a high level of labor intensity. Other activities often include the maintenance of public spaces and buildings and soil conservation, aimed at responding to the needs of local communities and increasing the level of labor intensity. Malawi, South Africa, and Zimbabwe, for example, have used innovative methods to include weaker populations by providing lighter tasks that involve service provision, such as child care (Oxfam 2002; Southern African Labour and Development and Research Unit 2005).

BOX 7.11 **Public Works Program, Korea**

Korea was particularly severely affected by the 1997 Asian financial crisis, which started in November of that year. The crisis caused major labor market disruptions in 1998; notably, the number of unemployed rose by more than 1.5 million, the unemployment rate rose by 4.3 percentage points, real wages fell by 9 percent, job insecurity rose, and poverty and inequality increased. The government's response was articulated along five strategies: provide income support by increasing unemployment insurance, provide public works programs, provide training, provide job retention programs, and expand public employment services. The public works program, launched in May 1998, provided employment for up to three months in a variety of labor-intensive tasks, such as building or maintaining roads, developing parks and natural areas, and creating other types of public infrastructure.

Implementation. The program wage was set at a level slightly lower than the prevailing market wage for unskilled labor to ensure that only those most in need would participate in the program. During the crisis, the prevailing market wage rate fell, and the public works wage was adjusted downward several times to keep it below the market wage to ensure that the program was self-targeting to the poorest members of society (Hur 2001). In the beginning, the wage level ranged from W 22,000 to W 35,000 (about US$16 to US$25) a day, which was far higher than the minimum wage. In response to advisory groups' opinion, the government cut the wage rate a few times; it finally ranged from W 19,000 to W 29,000 (about US$14 to US$21) a day.

Impact. By the first quarter of 1999, the program was providing 832,000 temporary jobs, though the number of applicants for such jobs was more than 1 million. Around 2.5 times more people benefited from the public works program than from unemployment insurance. The total cost of the program in 1999 was about W 2,300 billion (about US$1.9 billion).

Lessons. The public works program provided an effective and timely social insurance mechanism in response to the needs of vulnerable, able-bodied, unemployed people.

SOURCES: Hur 2001; Kwon 2002.

The level of labor intensity is crucial, because it determines the share of the program's costs that are used for wages. High labor intensity increases the amount of money that goes to the poor in the short run, but nonlabor inputs are essential to ensure the quality of the projects and their eventual economic returns. In practice, the cost of labor ranges from 40 to 50 percent of total costs for road construction projects and 70 to 80 percent for road or drainage maintenance projects, soil conservation activities, and reforestation projects (Subbarao 2003). In the Food-for-Work Program in Bangladesh, the Maharashtra Employment Guarantee Scheme (MEGS) in India, the Public Works Program in Korea, the Promotion Nationale program in Morocco, and the A Trabajar Urbano program in Peru, for example, the wage bill represented 60 to 75 percent of total program costs. In the case of Argentina's Trabajar workfare program, the share of labor costs ranged from 30 to 70 percent.

What all programs covered in this review have in common is an emphasis on creating employment and providing income transfers for a selected group of poor beneficiaries.

Many infrastructure-related projects in rural areas are referred to as public works programs and generate low-skill employment, but they are not concerned with the characteristics of those who participate in the programs; thus, they should not be viewed as safety net programs and are not covered in this section. (See Devereux 2002b for a good description of the distinction between safety net public works programs and employment-intensive public works programs and Keddeman 1998 for a broad definition of public works.)

KEY DESIGN FEATURES

The most important design features for successful public works programs are the selection of beneficiaries and the undertaking of appropriate operations at the right time of year. Many factors affect the selection of beneficiaries, and therefore participation by poor beneficiaries, including the geographic allocation of resources; the wage rate; the types of activities to be performed and their labor intensity; and the duration of the jobs created, which could range from temporary employment lasting three to six months to long-term employment lasting a year or two. In addition, program designers must pay special attention to the features needed to achieve social goals, such as providing employment opportunities to women and increasing the probability that poor people will be absorbed in the labor market at the end of a public works project.

Beneficiary Selection

The selection of participants for public works programs requires a combination of direct and indirect methods that are sometimes carried out in a series of steps. These include geographic targeting, selection of projects and schemes based on their labor intensity, self-targeting mechanisms related to the wage level, and—if these still yield more interested workers than jobs—some means of rationing them. Bulgaria, for example, uses means testing, and Malawi uses community-based targeting.[25]

The first step is to select areas where public works programs will be located. Locating programs in poor areas and communities that have a high unemployment level will increase the amount of direct benefits (in terms of transfers) and indirect benefits (in terms of the physical assets that the program creates or maintains) that go to the poor. This can be achieved by allocating budgets for public works programs to local governments in proportion to the level of poverty in their jurisdictions, as occurred in Argentina and Indonesia (Sumarto, Suryahadi, and Pritchett 2000). In the case of Trabajar, a distribution formula allocates resources by provinces according to the distribution of poor unemployed. The level of poverty of project areas is also taken into consideration in the selection of projects and in the determination of the resulting budget allocation among project areas (Ravallion 2002).

The second step is to select projects, opting for those with the highest possible labor intensity while achieving cost-effectiveness. Public works departments typically favor equipment intensity rather than labor intensity, because they perceive it to be superior and to facilitate more rapid project completion. However, equipment-intensive projects may offer greater opportunities for rent seeking (Stock and de Veen 1996), and if the work has been entrusted to private contractors, the outcome with respect to labor intensity is unpredictable. At the same time, public work projects also suffer if inadequate provisions have been made for materials and equipment, as occurred in Ethiopia's Employment Generation Program, where the lack of inputs prevented the completion of any meaningful work (Subbarao and Smith 2003). Thus flexibility in the level of labor intensity is desirable to achieve projects' objectives. For instance, in the Jawahar Rozgar Yojana (JRY, Jawahar Employment Program) in India, labor costs as a percentage of total costs fell from 70 to 50 percent from the 1980s until 2001 to ensure that local infrastructure was built well. By contrast, in Argentina, the lack of financial resources for materials, which were to be provided by municipalities, provided the incentive to implement more labor-intensive projects.

The third, and crucial, step is to determine the wage rates. For workers to self-select themselves into the program, wages should be somewhat lower than the locally prevailing market wage for unskilled labor, which will enable the poor to benefit disproportionately. A low wage rate will attract only people who have no other income-earning alternatives and who need the income the most, thereby reducing the number of overall participants and excluding the better-off. On the other hand, a lower wage rate will reduce the level of total transfers to the poor.

In practice, the ability to set a wage rate that is consistent with self-selection depends on a country's circumstances and context, including its labor regulations pertaining to the legal minimum wage. Several countries have managed to set their program wage at a level conducive to promoting self-selection and at the same time to hire skilled workers as needed at a slightly higher wage. In Burkina Faso, Senegal, and Sri Lanka, program wages were lower than market wage rates for unskilled labor. In Chile's former Cash for Work Program in 1987, the program wage rate was maintained at about 70 percent of the minimum wage. In Argentina's Trabajar program, the program could pay below the minimum wage rate, as its payments to workers were referred to as economic assistance, not wages (box 7.12). Korea's program in 1998 set the wage slightly lower than the prevailing market wage (several times higher than the minimum wage) for unskilled labor, and adjusted the wage downward as the market wage fell due to the economic crisis (box 7.11).

In some cases, the wage rate is higher than the market wage. In Botswana and Tanzania, program wages were maintained at a level higher than the market wage for comparable unskilled activities, and jobs had to be rationed, particularly during droughts, when the need of the poor to participate in public works was the greatest (Teklu 1994). In Kenya in 1992–3, the program wage was equal to the minimum wage, which was typically much higher than the prevailing market wage.[26] In Indonesia, the wage rate for public works was equal to or higher than the minimum wage. In the Philippines, the program wage, which was a combination of cash at the minimum wage plus in-kind payment, was 25 percent higher than the agricultural market wage. Not surprisingly, substantial numbers of the nonpoor were attracted to the program (Subbarao, Ahmed, and Teklu 1995). In much of the former Soviet Union and Eastern Europe, the government paid the entire wage bill for public works programs to encourage private entrepreneurs and state enterprises to hire more workers at the market rate and help address the unemployment problem.

In other countries, the wage rate for public works programs has been moving in relation to the market wage. In India's MEGS, the program wage was initially equal to the minimum wage, which was low enough to promote self-selection into the program by the poor. In 1988, when the minimum wage and the program's wage doubled, this resulted in job rationing and eroded the employment guarantee expected of the program. Targeting

BOX 7.12 **Factors Underlying the Success of Argentina's Trabajar Program**

In Argentina in 1996, the government responded to high levels of unemployment by starting Trabajar, a public works program designed to provide temporary employment benefits to poor participants. The main targeting mechanism adopted was the use of a low wage rate, supplemented by a project selection process that geographically targeted poor areas to receive projects. Under the program, more than 400,000 people participated in 16,000 projects, many of which were located in poor communities.

The initial setting and later modifications of the wage rate provided the right self-targeting mechanism. Indeed, to promote self-selection, in 2000 the wage rate was lowered from Arg$200 per month to Arg$160 per month (the figures are approximately the same in U.S. dollars), which was below the minimum wage. This was possible because the payments were considered not to be wages, but social transfers, and thus were exempt from minimum wage legislation.

An evaluation study (Jalan and Ravallion 1999) confirms the self-targeting nature of the program design, estimating that more than half the beneficiaries were in the poorest decile nationally and 80 percent of them were in the poorest quintile.

A second factor that determines whether a public works project is an effective means of assisting the poor is its labor content. For Trabajar, depending on the type of project, the share of labor costs ranged from 30 to 70 percent of total costs. The average share of labor costs for the program as a whole was 40 to 50 percent of total project costs. As the federal government covered only wage costs and municipalities covered the costs of materials, poorer municipalities in particular had an incentive to propose more labor-intensive projects.

Other factors enabled effective implementation of the program. First, the government provided clear and transparent guidelines, leaving local and municipal authorities to manage the details of implementation. Second, funds were distributed across municipalities according to the distribution of poor and unemployed people based on transparent and objective criteria. Finally, monitoring, evaluation, and supervision ensured that the targeting was working and could identify any problems.

Trabajar is an example of a well-implemented public works program that, using a low wage rate and high labor-intensity techniques, ensured that poor households received a significant share of the program's benefits.

Trabajar operated until 2001. In 2002, the government started a new program, Jefes de Hogar (Heads of Household) program, which was designed to reach a broader segment of the population that had been impoverished during the 2001 economic crisis by providing heads of households with direct income support (see chapter 10, section 3; Galasso and Ravallion 2004). The economy bounced back strongly between 2003 and 2005, reaching an average annual growth rate of 9 percent, and the program is being phased out. Almeida and Galasso (2007) evaluate the short-run effects of a program established to help Jefes de Hogar beneficiaries exit the program by providing inputs to promote self-employment.

efficiency decreased, some poor people were excluded from the program, and the total number of person-days of employment decreased (Datt and Ravallion 1994; Gaiha 2000; Subbarao 1993, 1997). In South Africa, some districts were more successful than others in setting a low wage for public works projects; for example, greening and vegetation projects offered a wage less than the market wage, but construction projects did not (Adato and others 1999; Subbarao 2003).

Additional considerations and design strategies are needed in large countries with large geographic variations in wage rates. This again can be illustrated by Argentina, where several provinces took advantage of the ability to pay a lower wage to expand participation in the program by the poor, as the wages paid reflected their own local labor conditions. By contrast, in some regions of Indonesia, the JPS Padat Karya (Labor-Intensive Public Works) program set the wage rate higher than the prevailing local wage rate to attract workers, thereby inducing those already working to switch or add jobs (Sumarto, Surya-hadi, and Pritchett 2000).

Additional criteria may be required to select beneficiaries when the wage cannot be set low enough or self-selection based only on the wage rate differential might be insufficient to exclude the nonpoor from participating in workfare projects, or because more people are willing to work at that wage than the program can accommodate. The solution has been to use a proxy means test, as in Colombia's Empleo en Acción (Employment in Action) program, or to rely on community selection of household beneficiaries, as in Ethiopia, Kenya, South Africa, and elsewhere (Adato and Haddad 2002; Government of Ethiopia 2004; Oxfam 2002).

The last aspect to consider in setting the wage rate is the choice of remuneration method between a daily rate and a piece rate. A task-based payment system might provide some flexibility to beneficiaries and therefore attract more women (Dev 1995; Subbarao and others 1997) or allow several family members to share the work. However, experience suggests that task-based payments can be difficult to administer and confusing for participants to understand, and might be exploited by gang leaders as occurred in the National Employment Guarantee Scheme in India (Pellissery 2006), thereby discouraging the poor from participating.

Finally, programs that hire people for long-term projects that are clearly targeted to specific groups require direct selection of beneficiaries. This is the case for such programs as the Rural Maintenance Program in Bangladesh; the Central Region Infrastructure Maintenance Programme in Malawi;[27] and the WFP's Integrated Food Security Program in Bangladesh, which supports the building of community-based assets such as flood and cyclone shelters, tree plantations, fishponds, and irrigation and drainage canals.

Disbursement Methods

The payment method, in cash or in kind, influences the targeting efficiency to the poor in general and to women in particular. Public works in Africa and South Asia originated as food-for-work programs that relied on food aid as a major source of financing. Currently many programs, especially outside Africa, provide wages in cash. In addition to the same issues that in-kind transfers pose, payment in kind represents an additional challenge because of the large amount of food that beneficiaries are supposed to receive, transport, and store. Beneficiaries' sales of food, sometimes even before they receive it—as happened in several public work projects in Bangladesh (del Ninno and Dorosh 2003)—are thus not surprising. By contrast, in Lesotho and Zambia, payment of 50 percent of the wage in kind as food attracted more women than men to project sites (Subbarao and others 1997). Cash payments are not immune to implementation and security challenges either. When funds are disbursed at the worksite, management issues include the transport and distribution of large sums of cash (Oxfam 2002). This issue did not arise in Argentina and Chile, where payments were made directly to beneficiaries initially via the post office, then banks, and then debit cards (see chapter 5, section 4, for a discussion of payment methods).

The frequency and reliability of payments may preclude poor people from participating in public works programs. For example, people prefer to participate in donor-funded workfare programs rather than government-funded programs largely because funds are ensured in the former but tend to be late in the latter (Subbarao and others 1997). People who do not have any savings and rely on daily wages cannot afford to wait for payment for work done (Islam 2006).

Whatever payment mechanism is selected, public works programs face the risk that not all the funds will be delivered to the participants. This may be due to underpayment to workers, the presence of ghost workers, and the padding of work and procurement of materials. Olken's (2005) study shows that in Indonesia, an average of 28 percent of the funds intended for village infrastructure projects did not reach the beneficiaries. Instances of malpractice are numerous, including manipulation of muster rolls, roads shown as built when actually nothing was done, and the like. In some countries, poor governance has often discredited public works programs.

Scope and Coverage

The scope and coverage of public works programs vary from country to country depending on government objectives. Several programs were set up following a crisis to provide relief to the unemployed on a national scale, as in Argentina and Korea. Several programs in Africa were set up to respond to natural disasters, as in Ethiopia, Mozambique, and Zambia, and have been targeted to specific affected areas. In other countries, public works programs provide an employment guarantee and risk-coping benefits similar to those provided by unemployment insurance. This is the case of the new National Employment Guarantee Scheme in India (see box 7.13 for a brief history of public works programs in India) and in Bangladesh, where most projects are offered during the slow periods of the agricultural season. In some countries, public works are scaled up or down depending on need, as in Morocco's Promotion Nationale program.

Data on actual number of days worked and employees covered are difficult to find, as outcomes are in some cases measured in terms of the number of people participating and in other cases in terms of person-days or person-months; comparisons across programs thus are sometimes difficult. Some programs that are more temporary in nature are extremely large. India's nationwide JRY employed more than 40 million people annually in the 1990s; and Korea's public works projects employed more than 1.5 million people in 1999, or about 7 percent of the economically active population. Ethiopia's Productive Safety Net Program covered about 20 percent of the economically active population in 2006, Argentina's Jefes de Hogar program covered about 11.3 percent of the economi-

BOX 7.13 **The Changing Nature of Public Works Programs, India**

India has used public works programs extensively since the 1960s to provide relief to poor households, particularly during lean agricultural seasons, following droughts and other natural calamities, or to support the unemployed rural poor. Program designs and characteristics have changed to respond to the changing needs of rural populations and to improve program effectiveness.

In 1965, MEGS was experimentally introduced in Maharashtra, and received statutory basis with the Employment Guarantee Scheme Act in 1978 (Gaiha 2005). The program guaranteed unskilled employment opportunities on a piece-rate basis to every adult in a rural area who wanted a job at a wage rate usually below the agricultural wage rate. By 1988, MEGS had proven to be extremely successful, although it had experienced a huge decline in participation after an increase in the wage rate led to rationing of jobs and poor targeting (Gaiha 1997; Ravallion, Datt, and Chaudhuri 1993).

The positive experience with MEGS prompted the 1989 launch of the JRY. It was implemented at the national level in all villages across the country through the *panchayats* (elected local bodies). The program's main objective was to generate additional gainful employment for unemployed and underemployed men and women in rural areas. Its secondary objective was to create community and social assets (Government of India various years).

Alongside implementation of the JRY, the government launched the Employment Assurance Scheme in 1993, initially in districts in drought-prone, desert, tribal, and hill areas, and then progressively expanded nationwide. The main difference from the JRY was the provision of an employment guarantee to the poor unemployed in the form of 100 days of ensured manual labor per year during lean agricultural seasons at statutory minimum wages. The scheme was demand driven, with the objective of being able to initiate projects whenever a demand for work occurred. The secondary objective was to create economic infrastructure and community assets in rural areas. Critics pointed out that the two programs spread resources too thinly at the village level and generated inadequate employment per person—only 15 to 30 days per year (Nayyer 2002)—plus they could not offer jobs to all those willing to work for a given wage, especially during lean seasons. There was also evidence of corruption with the *panchayat* system (Gaiha 2000; Gaiha and Kulkarni 2001; Lieten and Srivastava 1999).

In 1999, the government restructured the JRY into the Jawahar Grameen Smaridhi Yojana (Village Prosperity Program), which was dedicated to developing rural infrastructure at the village level, with rural employment generation becoming a secondary objective. In 2001, the government merged this program and the Employment Assurance Scheme into the Sampoorna Grameen Rozgar Yojana (Village Full Employment Program), the objective of which was to provide additional wage employment and food security in rural areas alongside the creation of durable community, social, and economic infrastructure.

In August 2005, Parliament approved the National Employment Guarantee Scheme to provide 100 days of work per year on rural public works projects during lean seasons at a minimum wage rate, with the objective of progressively replacing the existing public works programs. In the initial discussion, prior to implementation, supporters for this scheme emphasized the self targeting nature of the work requirement, critics questioned the scheme's fiscal sustainability and the magnitude of its impact on poverty (Dreze 2004; Murgai and Ravallion 2005).

cally active population in 2003, and Mexico's *Programa de Empleo Temporal* (Temporary Employment Program) covered about 1 million people or 2.5 percent of the economically active population in 2004.

The employment provided per person per year ranges from 15 to 30 days in India's JRY to 100 days in the National Employment Guarantee Scheme in Maharashtra, to 6 months in Argentina's Trabajar. Programs that run for long periods tend to cover a much smaller number of participants—for example, 42,000 women in each cycle of the Rural Maintenance Program in Bangladesh and 1,600 women in Malawi's Central Region Infrastructure Maintenance Programme.

Administrative Costs

Implementing public works program is expensive, because in addition to the cost of wages and program delivery, projects have to be designed, managed, supervised, and provided with physical inputs. Ravallion (1999a) illustrates the costs of transferring US$1 of income to the poor via a public works program in a typical middle-income country with a poverty rate of 20 percent and in a typical low-income country with a poverty rate of 50 percent. If only current benefits are considered, he estimates that the cost of transferring US$1.00 of income to the poor is $5.00 in the middle-income country and US$3.60 in the low-income country; if future gains from the assets created are included in the benefits, the cost of transferring US$1.00 to the poor drops to US$2.50 for both the middle-income and the low-income country. At the same time, public works have a comparatively lower targeting cost as long as programs are self-targeting and have a high level of targeting efficiency.

Implementing Institutions

Successful implementation requires administrative capacity to design and supervise public works projects. Countries such as Bangladesh and India have gradually built their capacity to implement public works programs, but this capacity is somewhat limited in African countries. This constraint can be eased if donors coordinate their activities and provide the technical assistance needed to build local implementation capacity. Even though international agencies, such as the WFP, the International Labour Office, and bilateral agencies, have been active in public works programs in many African countries, the record on efficiency and effectiveness is mixed (von Braun, Teklu, and Webb 1992). In Kenya's drought recovery project in 2001, for example, negligence on the part of the technical team meant that construction projects had to be pulled down and restarted (Oxfam 2002).

The administration and implementation of projects is highly centralized in, for instance, Bangladesh's Food for Work program, India's National Employment Guarantee Scheme, Indonesia's JPS Padat Karya program, and Mexico's Programa de Empleo Temporal. In some cases, local governments submit project proposals that are reviewed and supervised by national-level technical departments (departments of roads, agriculture, and so on); in other cases, the selection and supervision of projects is left up to local governments, as for the JRY in India and the Trabajar Urbano in Peru. International experience indicates that local governments are capable of selecting and implementing projects—with an interest in ensuring their quality if they have to contribute to some of the expenses—but do not have the capacity to implement larger and more complicated schemes. In the JRY, for example, *panchayats* lacked the technical expertise to formulate and implement complex projects, thereby preventing the very poor and lower-caste people from participating in them (Deshingkar, Johnson, and Farrington 2005; Islam 2006). In some countries, several institutions are involved in implementing projects. This is the case in the Philippines, where beneficiaries' irrigation associations and local municipalities are responsible for implementing water supply projects.

Other implementing institutions include the private sector (small contractors), nongovernmental organizations, and social funds. Nongovernmental organizations have played a significant role in relation to the design and implementation of public works programs in Bangladesh (CARE) and in several African countries. Social funds started to become involved in public works in Latin America and the Caribbean in the 1980s, including in Ecuador, Guatemala, Nicaragua, and Peru. This is also the case in Africa in Madagascar, Malawi, Tanzania, and Zambia. Communities submit a list of potential projects to the administration of the social funds, which screens them for feasibility using cost-benefit analysis.

When various ministries or government departments have implemented public works projects on a large scale, and when many donors are involved, a lack of coordination can stretch scarce administrative capacity; this often means that program coverage is neither extensive nor deep (see Pritchett, Sumarto, and Suryahadi 2002; Sumarto, Suryahadi, and Pritchett 2000 for the example of the JPS Padat Karya program in Indonesia, which is actually a loose, uncoordinated set of several labor-intensive programs run by a number of government departments). One problem with many public work projects in several African countries is that because donors often funded them, they were short-lived, thereby not creating any within-country capacity. This contrasts sharply with experience in South Asia, where governments fund most public works programs and run them on an ongoing basis with or without donor funds. As Subbarao and others (1997) point out, donors are part of the problem, to the extent that funds are not released in a predictable fashion and their projects are mostly short-lived. This situation was particularly challenging in Ethiopia, where before the launch of the Productive Safety Net Program a large number of donors and projects operated (McCord 2004a; Subbarao and Smith 2003). Moreover, when the source of financing is not the program's implementing agency, the best interests of the beneficiaries or the success of the program may not be the primary criteria for project design.

Programs that are entirely domestically funded seem to have more leeway in relation to program design and are more likely to create domestic capacity. Consider the example of MEGS. The scheme was financed by a special tax imposed on the urban employed who recognized that MEGS would benefit them, as it would help prevent distress migration of the poor from rural areas to urban areas. Adequate capacity to implement has been created during its 30 years of operations with assured funds. Moreover, when Maharashtra was hit by a massive drought in 1987, not a single drought-related mortality occurred, and the public works program was the mainstay for poor workers when nothing else was available (Rao, Ray, and Subbarao 1988). By contrast, in Ethiopia, droughts of a much smaller magnitude have often resulted in mortality among both humans and livestock largely because of the inability to launch a program quickly and efficiently.

OUTCOMES, ADVANTAGES, AND DISADVANTAGES

Few rigorous evaluations of public works programs in developing countries are available that cover the impact of the transfer of resources and of the physical and social assets created. However, the available evidence suggests that well-designed public works can be successful both in targeting benefits and in conferring social gains to the most needy and to society as a whole (Subbarao 2003).

Incidence

Available evaluations suggest that governments can use public works programs to transfer benefits to households. Indeed, 60 to 70 percent of the households that participated in India's JRY and MEGS (Lanjouw and Ravallion 1999) and in Argentina's Trabajar came from poor households; 80 percent of the beneficiaries of the latter program came from the poorest 20 percent of households in Argentina (Jalan and Ravallion 1999a).

In some cases, results have been mixed, as in Indonesia, the Philippines, and South Africa. In Indonesia, the JPS Padat Karya program was targeted toward those affected by the financial crisis, and, as the wages were too high, many friends of administrators participated and ghost workers were a problem (Pritchett, Sumarto, and Suryahadi 2002; Sumarto, Suryahadi, and Pritchett 2000). In the Philippines, the location of projects ensured participation by the poor, even though the relatively high wage rate meant that the nonpoor also participated, thereby excluding ultra-poor families (Islam 2006; Subbarao and others 1997). In South Africa, Adato and Haddad (2001) find that some districts with high levels of poverty and unemployment had no public works projects, while others with low levels of poverty had benefited from several. (They did find that, overall, public works projects in Western Cape Province generally outperformed hypothetical, untargeted cash transfers.)

Impact

The impact of public works programs can be measured in terms of poverty reduction and other positive impacts on poor families. For example, estimates indicate that for those participating in MEGS, the severity of poverty fell from 5.0 percent in fiscal 1979/80 to 3.2 percent in fiscal 1984/85 (Datt and Ravallion 1992). In Argentina's Trabajar, the income participants gained from working in the program accounted for about 60 percent of household income.

Public works programs have had positive effects in creating short-term jobs. Some evidence points to an increase in the numbers of days worked, as in Mexico's Programa de Empleo Temporal, and an increase in the number of hours worked, for example, by 36 percent in the case of participants in Colombia's Empleo en Acción Program. Moreover, the beneficiaries of Chile's direct employment program saw their chances of obtaining a job improve anywhere from 11 to 38 percent depending on when they joined the program (Economic Commission for Latin America and the Caribbean 2006).

While public works are an expensive way to transfer income to the poor and to build local infrastructure, any analysis of their cost-effectiveness should take the value of their indirect benefits into account and assess how they compare with those of other programs. The indirect benefits include the first-round effect of the direct value of the infrastructure built on the economy of local communities and the potential of these assets to generate second-round employment benefits. They also include the program's short- and medium-term impacts on the rural market wage rate due to the increase in wages earned by poorer workers who fill the vacancies created by workfare beneficiaries. Murgai and Ravallion (2005) confirm that if India's new National Employment Guarantee Scheme operates only for 100 days in the lean season, the scheme's real gains can be limited to the social value of the assets created, as poverty rates would fall slightly from 34 to 31 percent at a fiscal cost equivalent to less than 1.5 percent of GDP. Gaiha (2000) estimates the indirect impact of MEGS and finds that if MEGS wages were to rise by Rs 1, rural farm wages would increase by Rs 0.17 in the short run and by Rs.0.28 in the long run.

In addition to economic (transfer) gains, public works can encourage participation by women. MEGS, for example, was designed to encourage participation by women by providing employment within five kilometers of participants' homes, providing child care facilities, and eliminating male-female wage discrimination. As a result, women accounted for almost half of all participants, thereby promoting opportunities for women and gender equality. Dev (1995) notes that the Employment Guarantee Scheme also discouraged sexual barriers and inequality. Women are dressed better and their economic power has given them a better status in their families. In Korea, even though the public works program was initially designed primarily for male household heads, the projects still attracted many female workers, and at later stages gave explicit priority to female household heads (Hur 2001). In South Africa, while women were among the main target groups, they accounted for only 23 percent of the employment generated by the program.

Finally, temporary employment programs do not seem to help beneficiaries find stable jobs if they do not provide job training and placement services (Acosta and Ramírez 2004; Sojo 2003).

Advantages

When correctly implemented, public works programs have the following advantages:

- They provide income support while maintaining workers' dignity.
- They can improve the status of vulnerable populations, women, and the marginalized.
- They can be self-targeting and thus do not add financial costs in relation to beneficiary selection.
- They can be countercyclical, as the self-targeting nature of the programs is likely to attract more people at a time when regular, better-paid jobs are scarce and fewer people when the economy picks up again.
- They can provide social benefits to the community as a whole.
- They can reinforce communities' capacity to manage their own affairs by strengthening local governments and other local institutions.
- They may help the emergence and growth of small-scale private contractors.
- They are popular with both the public and with politicians.

Disadvantages

The disadvantages of public works programs are as follows:

- Unless they provide useful public goods, they can be an expensive way to transfer resources to the poor, as the amount of resources transferred to beneficiaries is typically equivalent to half the resources used for projects.
- They are administratively demanding. Projects must be well designed and implemented, materials must be selected and procured properly, and the work must be supervised to ensure that it is done correctly.
- Unless there is a proper monitoring system, public works tend to suffer from leakages of resources because of ghost workers and because of misreporting of the amount of work done (padding).
- Public works programs can have a negative impact on the labor market and can discourage people from participating if implemented in the wrong area or at the wrong time of year.

LESSONS AND SUGGESTIONS

Workfare programs can play an important role in providing temporary income earning opportunities, provided that the right projects are selected and that the wage rates are set correctly.

Most Likely Beneficiaries

The most appropriate beneficiaries of public works programs are people who are unemployed and who are willing to participate. The largest target group includes unemployed unskilled and semiskilled people who have a difficult time finding work either following a covariate shock, as occurred in Argentina and Korea, or during the agricultural slack season. Public works programs can also aim to promote participation by women and other vulnerable groups in the labor market, which can be accomplished either by creating the right environment for this to occur or by using specific targeting mechanisms, as the Bangladesh Rural Maintenance Program and the Malawi Central Region Infrastructure Maintenance Programme have done, for example.

Public works are not well suited to improving the incomes of the underemployed, as the transaction costs for underemployed people to leave their jobs to participate in a short-term public works program might be too high (Scandizzo, Gaiha, and Imai 2005). It is not surprising that McCord (2004a, 2005) for Africa and Lo Vuolo (2005) for Latin America argue that in poor countries with widespread levels of unemployment and underemployment, standard, short-term public works programs are unable to lift the chronic poor out of poverty. Instead, people outside the economically active population who have no transaction costs are encouraged to participate, but are still unlikely to enter the formal labor market. Handler (2003) for the OECD and Reinecke (2005) for Latin America find the impact of public works programs on the probability of finding a job is limited.

Appropriate Context and Political Economy Considerations

Public works programs work well in widespread crisis situations that result in high levels of open and noticeable unemployment when hiring idle people to build useful projects seems like the right thing to do. This also means that programs do not need to be permanent, but only have to last for as long as the particular situation persists. Korea, for example, used public works extensively in the 1970s to build roads, stopped such programs after the economic boom, when only old and unproductive people participated who were better served with cash transfers, but restarted them in 1997 after the East Asian financial crisis. Another obvious role for public works programs is to address seasonal labor demand shortages. Agricultural economies dominated by one cropping system, as in Bangladesh and some parts of India, have large numbers of seasonal unemployed. The timing of public works programs is crucial under such circumstances to provide income-earning opportunities to daily laborers to help them smooth their consumption. Finally, in the absence of unemployment insurance, public works can provide risk protection to the poor and offer them an employment guarantee. This is the case with India's new National Employment Guarantee Scheme. For such risk protection programs to be effective, they must have a pipeline of projects ready to be implemented as soon as the need to provide employment arises.

Public works programs enjoy political support because they satisfy the ethical principle that participants have to work to receive benefits and because they can provide public goods that everyone can use. The biggest political economy challenge is being able to set the wage rate at a low enough level to promote self-selection. This difficulty arises because of the desire to transfer enough income to guarantee a livelihood, but sometimes because of a country's history. For example, in the past the emphasis in Eastern European and Central Asian countries was on workers' rights, trade unions were strong, and the attitude toward a downward adjustment of wages generally hostile. By contrast, in more decentralized countries such as Argentina and South Africa, when communities are fully informed about program goals, the resistance to lower wages is much less (Adato and others 1999; Subbarao 2003). In all circumstances, the wage-setting process needs to be transparent if it is to be acceptable to workers, scheme providers, and implementing agencies.

If public works are generally well liked, the question arises as to why they play such a small or nonexistent role in some countries. Possible reasons are a lack of obvious open unemployment, repercussions from bad experience or corruption, or insufficient capacity. In rural areas in Pakistan, for example, the presence of large landlords might mask the presence of open periods of unemployment, and therefore demand for such programs is low.

Adapting to Local Conditions and Avoiding Unintended Effects

Public works programs can be made to be more effective in a given situation to reach the poorest and most vulnerable participants and have a positive impact on communities, while being cost-efficient, as follows:

- **Select beneficiaries primarily by setting the wage rate at a level that is no higher than the prevailing market wage for unskilled manual labor in the setting in which the scheme is introduced.** At the same time, the program wage should not be set at such a low level that it stigmatizes the work, thus leading some poor people to go hungry rather than take part in public works as was one of the problems with the English Poor Law workhouses in the 19th century (Lipton 1996). Additional selection criteria include geographic targeting to poor areas and community involvement if rationing is required. The highest possible level of labor intensity for a given project (the share of the wage bill in total costs) will maximize the income gains to the poor versus the gains from the assets created.
- **Ensure that the work performed under a project leads to the creation and maintenance of assets and the provision of services that benefit mostly the poor and**

that are well integrated with overall rural development programs and projects.
While the types of projects will depend on the country's technological level, involving communities in the decision-making process will ensure that projects address
the needs of the community as long as they are not captured by local elites (Gaiha
2000; Gaiha and Kulkarni 2001; Islam 2006; Lieten and Srivastava 1999).

- **Keep participant transaction costs low and enhance the consumption-smooth-
ing benefits to the poor by carefully deciding on the timing and duration of the
employment.** This can be achieved by locating work projects close to where people
live, paying workers on time, providing child care services, and synchronizing the
work with agricultural slack seasons or timing it for after natural disasters. Having a
pipeline of projects ready for implementation will speed up response times.

- **Ensure funding, community participation, sound technical assistance, and
proper understanding of the social structures and communities where projects are located.** This can help overcome capacity constraints and vastly increase
the effectiveness of workfare programs, reduce transaction costs, and protect
transfers to the poor from leakages. Figure 7.1 lays out the steps needed for designing and implementing public works programs. Countries introducing new
public works programs can start with a pilot program to test the capacity of the

FIGURE 7.1 **Designing and Implementing Public Works Programs**

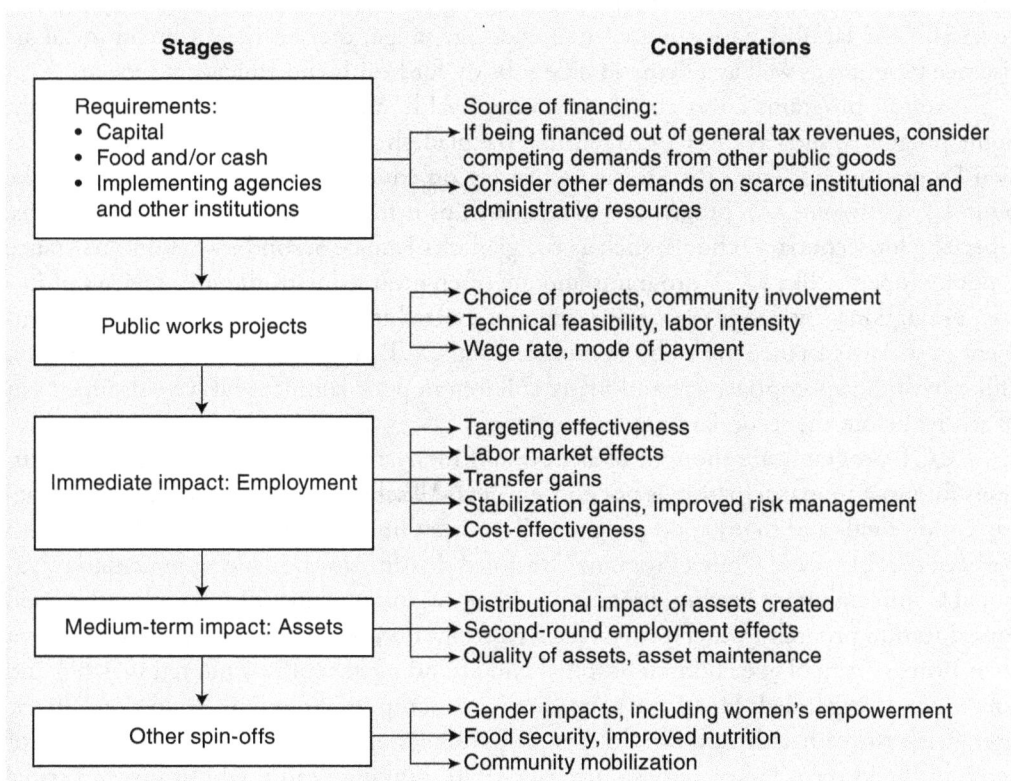

Stages	Considerations
Requirements: • Capital • Food and/or cash • Implementing agencies and other institutions	Source of financing: → If being financed out of general tax revenues, consider competing demands from other public goods → Consider other demands on scarce institutional and administrative resources
Public works projects	→ Choice of projects, community involvement → Technical feasibility, labor intensity → Wage rate, mode of payment
Immediate impact: Employment	→ Targeting effectiveness → Labor market effects → Transfer gains → Stabilization gains, improved risk management → Cost-effectiveness
Medium-term impact: Assets	→ Distributional impact of assets created → Second-round employment effects → Quality of assets, asset maintenance
Other spin-offs	→ Gender impacts, including women's empowerment → Food security, improved nutrition → Community mobilization

SOURCE: Subbarao 2003.

implementing agency and reveal lessons that can be used to scale up the program. Proper monitoring mechanisms can help reduce corruption and loss of funds and enhance program integrity.

7.5 Conditional Cash Transfers

Conditional cash transfers provide money to poor families contingent on them making investments in human capital, such as keeping their children in school or taking them to health centers on a regular basis.[28] They are an increasingly popular instrument of social assistance. For a selected list of CCT programs, see table B.5 in appendix B.

PROGRAM DESCRIPTION

CCTs have two explicit goals: to reduce the current level of poverty and to promote investments in the human capital of the poor to reduce their level of future poverty. The balance between these goals varies somewhat among programs and affects some of their design features.

The classic CCT programs, with Mexico's PROGRESA (now known as Oportunidades) as the iconic example (box 7.14), emphasize the short-run poverty relief and social assistance goal by covering children from birth to some point in the teen years. Conditions cover enrollment and minimum attendance at primary and at least junior secondary grades. These programs also have conditions for the use of a basic package of preventive health care services, at least for children from birth to age five or six. Because the programs cover all poor families with children in a wide age range, they serve as a broad social assistance program as well as a demand-side subsidy for health and education services.

Not all programs cover social assistance, health, and education objectives equally. Some programs, such as those in Argentina, Bangladesh, Brazil (the Child Labor Eradication Program), and Costa Rica focus exclusively on education requirements, though the boundary between CCT programs and scholarships is fuzzy. Some scholarship programs, especially for secondary schools, such as Bangladesh's Female Secondary School Assistance Program, operate like CCT programs and are often grouped with them in reviews of impact evaluations. By design, secondary school scholarships are much less a general instrument of social assistance than a more multisectoral CCT program: fewer families will have children of the appropriate age and many children in poor families will have dropped out of school before the secondary grades covered.

CCT programs are thought of as new and innovative, but the idea of using conditions for program participation is not entirely new. All school feeding programs are implicitly conditional, and many food programs have been linked to primary health care, with perhaps the first being Chile's Programa Nacional de Alimentación Complementaria (National Complementary Feeding Program), which was initiated in 1923. Bangladesh's Food for Education program, which provided a significant transfer to poor households that kept their primary school age children enrolled and attending school was piloted in 1993 and subsequently expanded. Honduras's separate food stamp program with conditions on the use of preventive health care for children of preschool age and on school attendance for those in the lower primary grades started in 1990. Linking health, education, and social assistance into a long-term vision of support has, however, been less common.

The well-known CCT programs deserve to be recognized as much as for their new standards for targeting, payment systems, management, and evaluation as for the innovation of their basic design concept. In general, CCT programs have handled these systems well, and, in some cases, they have been leaders in modernizing social assistance practices. Of course, technical soundness is neither inherent to nor the exclusive domain of CCT programs. Policy makers across the gamut of social policy need to understand this so that those working on CCT and other types of programs adopt some of the practices that have led to the success of the best CCT programs.

Most programs provide cash transfers, but the same sorts of impacts were observed in Bangladesh's Food for Education program, which distributed grain to the families of 2.1 million students until 2002 (Ahmed and del Ninno 2002; Ahmed, del Ninno, and Chowdhury 2004; Galasso and Ravallion 2005). Subsequently the benefit was changed to cash; the program became the Primary Education Stipend Program and was expanded to more than 5 million children.

KEY DESIGN FEATURES

CCT programs have spread so rapidly in the last 10 years that generalizing is difficult. The best known remain the most mature Latin American programs that have been thoroughly evaluated—that is, those in Brazil, Colombia, Jamaica, Honduras, Mexico, and Nicaragua—as well as in Turkey. The designers of the first wave of CCT programs paid a great deal of attention to targeting, compliance verification methods, and payment mechanisms. Careful attention to implementation details and local participation also helped CCT programs to succeed.[29]

Beneficiary Selection

CCT programs have mostly developed a combination of careful targeting mechanisms, usually involving poverty maps and proxy means tests, and sometimes community targeting, to select individual households. As is usual with targeting systems, implementation details are crucial to achieve the desired targeting outcomes (see chapter 4).

The use of conditions and the impact of the enforcement of conditions in contrast to the impact of simple cash transfers alone is subject to debate (de Janvry and Sadoulet 2006; Samson 2006; Schubert and Slater 2006) (box 7.15).

Many programs condition the transfer on the enrollment in school of households' children and their regular attendance and on regular health center visits by younger children and often by pregnant women. The conditions in relation to education may be defined by age as in the Dominican Republic and Jamaica or by grade as in Cambodia and El Salvador. Almost all CCTs require enrollment and attendance on 80 or 85 percent of school days, although Bangladesh's Female Secondary School Assistance Program is the exception, requiring only 75 percent attendance. Only a few countries have conditions pertaining to some aspect of performance. These include Nicaragua, which required promotion to the next grade at the end of the school year, and Turkey, which only allows a grade to be repeated once. In relation to health, conditions tend to apply to children from birth to five or six years old, designed to allow continuous eligibility to school age. About half the CCT programs that have conditions related to children's health also have conditions for pregnant and lactating women. Conditions pertaining to the health of other adults are

---

BOX 7.14 **The PROGRESA/Oportunidades Program, Mexico**

Mexico's PROGRESA, an integrated approach to poverty reduction initiated in 1997, is one of the flagship targeted human development programs in Latin America and the Caribbean. The program aims to eradicate extreme rural poverty by promoting investment by the poor in human capital by strengthening their demand for education and health services, while providing some support to schools and health services. Women in beneficiary households receive cash transfers, school supplies, and nutrition supplements conditional on their children's school attendance and regular preventive health care visits.

In 1999, the program reached 2.5 million households in 53,000 localities in 2,156 municipalities. Despite its substantial coverage, expenditure on the program represented around 0.2 percent of GDP. Since then, the program has been expanded nationally and was renamed Oportunidades in 2002, when several changes to the program's objectives and operational features were instituted, including an expansion to urban areas. In 2007, it reached 5 million households, or 25 million people (approximately a quarter of the population), at a total cost of US$3.3 billion or about 0.4 percent of GDP. The program was developed as a replacement for a number of poorly targeted food subsidies.

Implementation. Oportunidades targets beneficiary households in three steps. The first step identifies the localities to be included in the program using a marginality index that is constructed using socioeconomic variables associated with unsatisfied basic needs. The second step selects beneficiary households within those localities using a proxy means-testing methodology. Finally, the community reviews the beneficiary list to ensure that it has accurately identified the most needy and excluded others. Payments are made every two months in cash at temporary payment points. Conditions are thoroughly monitored and strictly enforced.

The program is centrally run by a federal agency that gathers all relevant data, applies the scoring system to determine eligibility, issues payments to households, contracts for external evaluations, and coordinates service delivery with other federal ministries and agencies. State governments are responsible for the direct provision of health and education services. Voluntary "mother leaders" are selected and trained to help provide participants with information about program rules, when and where payments will be made, which clinic to attend, what to do in case of problems, and so on.

---

less common, although these are present and well enforced in Mexico and present, albeit less well enforced, in Jamaica.

Health conditions pertaining to children vary. For example, Brazil requires children to have the complete set of immunizations, while other countries require adherence to a schedule of regular health center visits for checkups. In some countries such as Jamaica, the kinds of health services that mothers and children should receive are defined in great detail; in Honduras and elsewhere, the only stipulation is that mothers and children regularly attend health centers. Most programs with conditions related to children's health require growth monitoring two to six times a year. Health and nutrition education sessions are a feature of many Latin American programs but are less required elsewhere. Indeed, Latin

One of the program's hallmarks has been its standard-setting use of information for management and credible impact evaluation. In marked contrast to general practice at the time, from the outset the program's designers built in an impact evaluation component based on experimental designs and supported by external and independent evaluators, elaborate multistakeholder inputs, and significant funding from national resources. In addition, the data used for the evaluations were made available to the public. This effort is credited with helping improve the program over time, helping sustain it during political transitions, and engendering similar efforts in other countries.

Impact. A major achievement of the program has been to reach the hardcore poor, more than half of whom had never received any type of government transfer until PROGRESA. It achieved the following results:

- A 24 percent average increase in secondary school enrollment in rural areas (28.7 percent for girls and 15.7 percent for boys, comparing preprogram enrollment rates in school year 1996/97 with those in 2002/3)
- A 35 percent lower probability of working for rural area boys aged 10 and a 29 percent lower probability of working for rural area boys aged 14 (over the period 1997–2003)
- A 30 to 60 percent increase in visits to monitor nutritional status for infants up to two years of age and by 25 to 45 percent for children aged three to five (between 1997 and 1999, the first two years of the program)
- An 8 percent increase in the number of first-time prenatal care visits among pregnant women in their first trimester (between 1997 and 1999)
- A 10.6 percent increase in per capita food consumption in program households and a 13.5 percent increase among poorer households in comparison with consumption in nonprogram families (between March 1998 and November 1999)

Lessons. The experience of PROGRESA/Oportunidades shows that combining several objectives under one program and achieving greater effectiveness in public social spending is possible as other poorly targeted programs are phased out.

SOURCES: Behrman and Skoufias 2006; Handa and Davis 2006; Levy 2006; World Bank forthcoming; www.oportunidades.gob.mx.

American CCT programs all have health conditions of some kind, whereas these are much rarer in South Asia and Sub-Saharan Africa. Even though malnutrition and immunization are more problematic in the latter regions, services are more limited, and thus programs have not focused on these conditions.

Some programs allow exceptions or exemptions from conditions. Most common is a justification for absence from school during a specified reporting period on grounds of illness. Jamaica waives attendance requirements for children with disabilities and who are deemed unlikely to benefit from school attendance (Mont 2006). Kenya waives attendance requirements for children who do not have access to schools or clinics (Office of the Vice President and Ministry of Home Affairs 2006).

BOX 7.15 **The Debate: Conditional versus Unconditional Cash Transfers**

If one of the main objectives of a program is to increase the use of available education and health facilities, then a CCT should have a greater impact than an unconditional program. Even though a transfer alone will raise income and service use to some degree, economic theory predicts that a condition may raise service use further, because it changes the "price" of using the service. Indeed, most of the scanty available evidence shows that conditions do increase service use significantly more than an equivalent unconditional transfer (de Brauw, and Hoddinott 2008 for Mexico; Schady and Araujo 2006 for Ecuador), as do the results of simulations (Bourguignon, Ferreira, and Leite 2003). Controlled experiments that directly compare conditional and unconditional transfers of identical size for similar populations are currently being conducted and should yield further evidence on the magnitude of expected effects.

Most of the economic theory underlying social assistance concerns removing constraints from poor households rather than imposing constraints on them, which is what a condition is. Why then would conditions be justified? Theory points to some justifications: for example, when families underestimate the value of schooling or health care for their children; when they discount heavily the future gains to their children of better nutrition, health, and education; and when externalities are present such that society derives a greater benefit than that accruing to individual children. Some nascent empirical work supports the existence of these factors, though their magnitude is uncertain (World Bank forthcoming).

Many observers of CCT programs believe that the conditions have been important in garnering political support for the programs and that this has resulted in much larger social assistance budgets than would otherwise have been the case. Thus even if conditions are not needed to change incentives for households, they may be needed to reassure the public and politicians.

If a program is to be conditional, the following administrative functions are implied:

- Providing households with the information about the program's requirements
- Monitoring compliance at schools and/or health facilities
- Contacting noncompliant households to warn them about the consequences of noncompliance and to help resolve any reasons for the lack of use of services that are not related to income (optional)
- Designing a system of penalties for noncompliance ranging from a temporary reduction in benefits to permanent exclusion from the program

The marginal costs and benefits of each step in the process of enforcing conditionality are not yet known, although the median administrative costs are 7 percent for CCT programs, 9 percent for other types of cash transfers, and 10 percent over the whole range of 55 social assistance programs listed in the annex to chapter 9. Apparently the scale and generosity of mature CCT programs have been sufficient to explain their smaller share of administrative costs despite the extra administrative requirements imposed by monitoring compliance with conditions.

The zeal with which compliance with conditions is verified varies. In Mexico, the link is tight and automatic. In El Salvador, the system to verify compliance takes longer; thus it takes two months of investigation and possible adjustment of noncompliance information before the benefit is reduced or suspended. In Brazil, households are first given warnings and social workers try to visit to determine whether some sort of barrier is preventing households from accessing the services. In Ecuador, the program is called a conditional program, and households are told that it is, but adequate systems to verify compliance are not yet in place. In most countries, the reduction in benefits is delayed following the actual date of noncompliance because of the time needed to gather the information and because of the timing of payment cycles. In Mexico, for example, if a child misses too many days of school during March and April, the payment to the family will be reduced for the July and August payment cycle. The family receives a breakdown of the total payment among the different family members and conditions.

One of the distinguishing features of modern CCT programs is the need for significant information flows to link compliance with conditions to the amount of benefits paid. Precursor programs did this less intensively; for example, they required enrollment, not daily attendance. For modern CCT programs, with their more explicit conditions, the verification of compliance is more challenging and requires a system for interacting with education and health facilities, collecting records, and exchanging them with program officials and an appropriate management information system. Recordkeeping and compliance tracking can be done using paper and pencil as in Bangladesh's Primary Education Stipend Program or using more sophisticated computer databases as in most of the Latin American programs.

Disbursement Methods

The actual distribution of cash faces the same types of constraints and challenges as discussed in chapter 5, section 4. To date, most of the Latin American programs have issued payments through banking or postal systems, and thus reaped the benefits of the high degree of automaticity and accountability implied. Lower-income countries are using other means of payment. For instance, Bangladesh's Primary Education Stipend Program uses mobile banks when schools are more than five kilometers away from banks.

Scope and Coverage

In 1997, Bangladesh, Brazil, and Mexico had CCT programs. Since then, they have been implemented in most Latin American countries. Turkey had an early program, and a number of pilots are currently under way in South Asia and Sub-Saharan Africa. More than 30 countries now have active programs or pilots and many more are considering whether to add such a strand to their safety nets.

Program coverage varies in both absolute and relative terms (figure 7.2) The largest relative coverage is in Ecuador, where the 5 million beneficiaries of the Bono de Desarrollo Humano (Human Development Grant) program account for about 40 percent of the total population. The largest programs in terms of the absolute number of beneficiaries are Brazil's Bolsa Familia (Family Grant), with 46 million beneficiaries (about 24 percent of the population), and Mexico's Oportunidades, with 25 million beneficiaries (about 23 percent of the population). Bangladesh's Primary Education Stipend Program covers more than

FIGURE 7.2 **Coverage by Decile, Selected CCT Programs and Years**

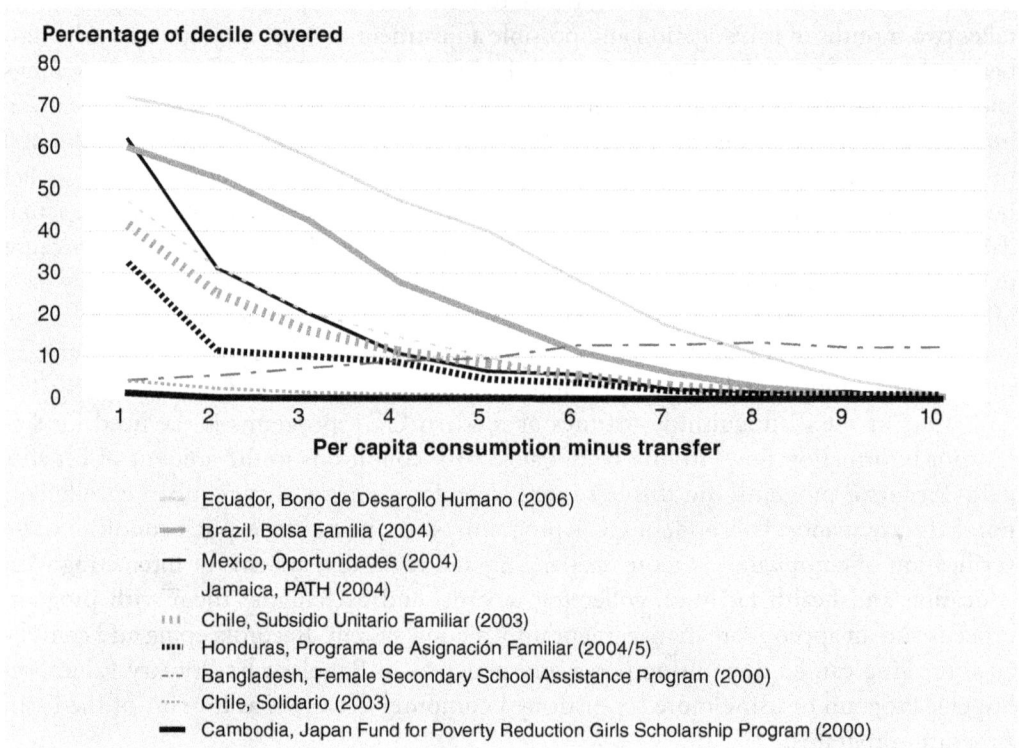

SOURCE: World Bank forthcoming.

NOTE: Welfare ranking is done using per capita household consumption less the value of transfer received. The years are the years of the surveys analyzed.

5 million beneficiaries (4 percent of the population); Turkey's Social Risk Mitigation Project covers 5 million beneficiaries (about 4.5 percent of the population). Other programs in Argentina, Costa Rica, and Nicaragua cover approximately 2 percent of the population.

Administrative Costs

The administrative costs of delivering CCTs to poor households include the costs of delivering the cash, targeting, and verifying compliance. In large, mature programs, these costs have been fairly low: about 6 percent of total costs for Mexico's Oportunidades and about 12 percent for Brazil's Bolsa Familia. Administrative costs can be higher during the pilot or if they involve supply interventions or food distribution.

Implementing Institutions

CCT programs have often been high-profile programs that are directly linked to the office of the chief executive or enjoy his or her personal support and are located in a ministry of welfare or social assistance. Programs have been designed in a top-down, centralized way, yet implementation relies on a great deal of local coordination among schools, clinics, local welfare offices, and/or municipalities. Coordination across central entities, including ministries, and local bodies is inherently challenging. In the first wave of programs, administration has been of a high caliber. Though neither unique nor inherent to CCT programs, they have generally had better than average targeting, monitoring, evaluation, administration, and troubleshooting systems.

In a number of countries, financing is entirely or largely from the national budget. In some cases, the resources have come from phasing out less efficient general subsidies or from other social assistance programs. The amount being spent on social assistance is increasing in some cases. In several countries, lending from multilateral agencies or grants from donors are important sources of finance.

OUTCOMES, ADVANTAGES, AND DISADVANTAGES

The early CCTs have a much stronger track record of credible impact evaluations than many other types of programs (reviewed in World Bank forthcoming). Broadly speaking, these show good targeting and an impact on poverty commensurate with the coverage of the program and the size of the transfer, increases in the use of services, and a more muted increase in final health and education outcomes.

Incidence

The targeting of CCT programs has in general been extremely good, with the largest share of benefits generally going to the poorest groups (figure 7.3). Except for Bangladesh,

FIGURE 7.3 **Share of Benefits Accruing by Decile, Selected CCT Programs and Years**

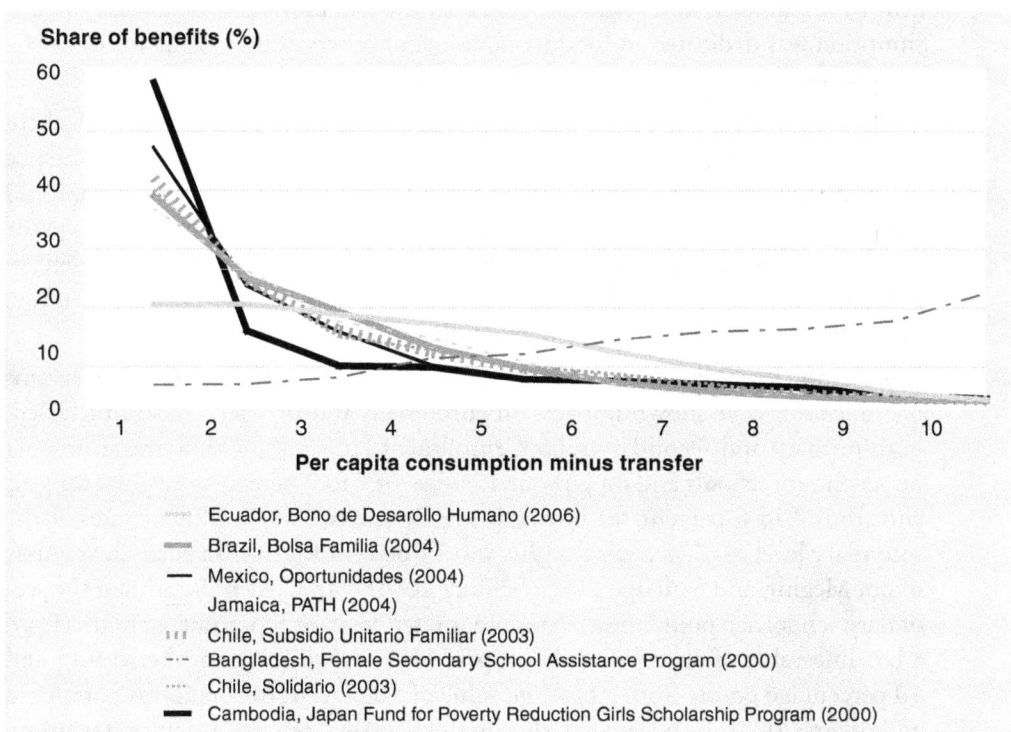

Legend:
- Ecuador, Bono de Desarollo Humano (2006)
- Brazil, Bolsa Familia (2004)
- Mexico, Oportunidades (2004)
- Jamaica, PATH (2004)
- Chile, Subsidio Unitario Familiar (2003)
- Bangladesh, Female Secondary School Assistance Program (2000)
- Chile, Solidario (2003)
- Cambodia, Japan Fund for Poverty Reduction Girls Scholarship Program (2000)

SOURCE: World Bank forthcoming.

NOTE: Welfare ranking is done using per capita household consumption less the value of transfer received. The years are the years of the surveys analyzed.

the CCT programs for which targeting outcomes are available have sharply progressive incidence, with much higher shares of benefits going to the poorest decile than to the upper end of the welfare distribution. Among the top performers, Cambodia delivers almost 60 percent of the benefits to the bottom decile, Mexico more than 45 percent, and Chile's Subsidio Unitario Familiar (Unified Family Subsidy) just over 40 percent. While properly measuring the incidence of transfers entails serious difficulties, naïve comparisons of Latin American CCT programs with other transfer programs suggest that CCT programs do a better job of concentrating benefits among the poorest.

Impact

Studies of the programs in Brazil, Colombia, Mexico, Nicaragua, and a few other countries, based on rigorous, survey-based impact evaluations, have provided clear evidence of the impact of CCT programs, particularly in the following areas:

- **Consumption and poverty.** The impact on consumption and poverty alleviation has been substantial (see Morley and Coady 2003, chapter 5, for a discussion of how to measure the impact on poverty). In Mexico, poverty was reduced by 17 percent in the PROGRESA communities, and those households obtained 7 percent more calories, largely from vegetables and animal products, and were eating better (48 percent of respondents) and eating more (19 percent of respondents) (Hoddinott and Skoufias 2004). Colombia's Familias en Acción program increased total household consumption by 19 percent in rural areas and by 9 percent in urban areas and resulted in a better diet, as most of the increase in consumption was dedicated to food (Attanasio and others 2005). Evidence from Nicaragua suggests a 17 percent increase in consumption.

- **Child labor.** The increase in school participation observed is likely to result in a reduced probability of children working. In Nicaragua, the relative prevalence of child labor in areas covered by the program fell by 2.5 percent in 2001 and 4.9 percent in 2002 among children aged 7 to 13 who had yet to complete grade 4 of primary school (Maluccio and Flores 2004). Similar results were evident in Bangladesh, Brazil, Colombia, and Mexico (Ravallion and Wodon 2000; Yap, Sedlacek, Orazem 2001, World Bank forthcoming).

- **Education.** Virtually all the many evaluations of the impact of CCT programs on education have shown impacts on enrollment and/or attendance. In Mexico, both primary and secondary school enrollment rates rose, with a greater impact on secondary schools and on girls: an increase of 7 to 9 percentage points for girls and from 3 to 6 percent for boys starting from baseline enrollment rates at the secondary level of 67 percent for girls and 73 percent for boys in rural areas (Attanasio, Meghir, and Santiago 2005; Schultz 2004).[30] In Colombia, among the secondary school age population, enrollment rates went up 5 percentage points from a baseline value of approximately 65 percent in urban areas and between 5 and 10 percentage points from a baseline value of 50 percent in rural areas (Attanasio and others 2005). In Nicaragua, during the first two years of program operation, the program's net impact on enrollment rates in grades 1 through 4 was nearly 18 percentage points from a low starting point of 68 percent and of 6 percent past grade 4, even though advancement past grade 4 was not a formal requirement of the program. In relation to the distribution of impact in the Nicaraguan program, evidence points to a much larger effect (24 percent) for the extremely poor than for the poor (13 percent) and the nonpoor (Maluccio 2001; Maluccio and Flores 2004). In Bangladesh, the estimates of increased enrollment in elementary school as a result of the Food for Education program range from 9 to 17 percent (Ahmed and del Ninno 2002; Ahmed, del Ninno, and Chowdhury 2004; Ravallion and Wodon 2000). The Chile Solidario program increased preschool enrollment by 4 to 5 percent and increased the probability that all children aged 6 to 14 were enrolled in school by 7 percentage points (Galasso 2006).

- **Nutrition and health.** Mexico saw a significant increase in nutrition monitoring and immunization rates and a lower overall incidence of severe illness. Evidence also pointed to a significant impact on increasing child growth and lowering the probability of stunting for children aged 12 to 36 months plus an 11 percent decline in infant mortality in rural areas (Barham 2005a, 2005b; Behrman and Hoddinott 2005; Gertler 2000; Gertler and Boyce 2001). In Colombia, the proportion of children under 6 enrolled in growth monitoring increased by 37 percentage points and the incidence of acute diarrhea in children under 6 was reduced by 10 percentage points in urban areas and by 11 percentage points for children under 48 months (Attanasio and others 2005). In Nicaragua, participation by children under three in a program of growth and development surveillance and promotion, a requirement of the Red de Protección Social (Social Protection Network), increased by 11 percentage points; timely immunization among children aged 12 to 23 months increased by at least 18 percentage points (IFPRI 2002; Maluccio and Flores 2004). In Honduras, the program reportedly increased coverage of prenatal care and well-child checkups by 15 to 20 percentage points. Childhood immunization series could therefore be started more opportunely, and the coverage of growth monitoring was increased by 15 to 21 percentage points (Morris and others 2004). In Jamaica, Levy and Ohls (2007) estimated that the PATH CCT initiative had a large impact on the number of preventive health visits by children, between 17 and 31 percent.

- **Labor disincentives.** So far studies have shown no decrease in adult labor effort, even in the case of Mexico, whose program has higher benefits, coverage, and longevity than most other programs. The link between benefits and service use seems to be sufficient to avoid major labor disincentives (World Bank forthcoming).

- **Fertility rates.** Some people are be concerned that CCT programs could have an adverse incentive on fertility rates. The evidence indicates that this might have happened in Honduras, where the program could have caused an increase in the birth rate of 2 to 4 percent. This was not the case in Mexico and Nicaragua (Stecklov and others 2006); in Turkey, the program was found to decrease the probability of a woman becoming pregnant by about 2 to 3 percent (Ahmed and others 2007).

Advantages

Comprehensive CCT programs have several clear advantages, namely:

- They serve as a basic needs-based social assistance program for the chronically poor with children.
- They encourage the formation of human capital among the young as a means of breaking the intergenerational cycle of poverty.
- Their conditionality changes the relationship between the program and its beneficiaries, in that those receiving transfers are now responsible and accountable for their actions. This joint responsibility has apparently been critical in changing the political acceptability of transfer programs.
- They have created a bridge between social services by trying to realize synergies in human development through their focus on the complementarities between investments in health, nutrition, and education.

Disadvantages

Despite these promising initial results, observers have voiced the following concerns about CCT programs:

- They are complex programs to mount, because they require a complex interplay of central and local actors and involve multiple ministries. In addition, the monitoring of conditions is information intensive and time sensitive.
- They may raise service use, but children's learning and health will only improve if the quality of services they receive is adequate, and CCT programs do not inherently address this. Critics contend that CCTs may distract from the more difficult task of reforming inefficient public health and education services, although proponents argue that at least at the local level, increased service use heightens pressures on local staff and facilities to perform better.
- They cannot be a complete safety net. By definition they will exclude families without children in the appropriate age group and those poor households and communities that do not have access to health or school facilities (this group also includes individuals with disabilities if the relevant facilities are not equipped to receive them). Moreover, the targeting mechanisms so far used for CCT programs are indicators of long-term welfare and are not responsive to sudden or temporary consumption shortfalls, so the programs may not serve the transient poor, although they may help families already registered in a program to withstand shocks (Sadoulet and others 2004).

LESSONS AND SUGGESTIONS

The use of conditional transfer programs is expanding rapidly. The key to their success lies in the determination of the conditions and their enforcement.

Most Likely Beneficiaries

Poor families with children with low levels of health and education benefit the most from CCT programs. These are families that may not make the right investments in their children's human capital by not taking them to health posts for checkups and vaccinations and/or not sending them to school. The beneficiaries should include families not only that have children who are not immunized or in school, but all those that need financial support and information so as to encourage and reward those families already making the right investments. If this were not the case, the program would create perverse incentives.

Appropriate Context and Political Economy Considerations

Before deciding whether to implement a CCT program, a diagnosis of what element or elements of social policy need addressing is important. Is the primary goal to provide or reform a social assistance program? Is it to solve a demand-side problem related to health and education? Or is it the lack of access to or the poor quality of health and/or education services?

In cases where the goal is a social assistance program and services are accessible, but where the poor are less likely to attend or remain in school or to use health facilities because of insufficient incomes, CCT programs may be appropriate. Because services are largely accessible, the conditions will not exclude many from the program's social assistance role, but will do much to raise the use of health and education services in presumably valuable ways. This scenario applies in most of the middle-income, high-inequality countries where CCT programs are so far most prevalent.

In cases where access to health or education services is extremely limited, conditioning social assistance on their use will exclude those, usually the neediest, without access. This is an acknowledged issue in the poorest and most remote rural areas of Brazil, Colombia, and Mexico; in poorer countries with less extensive services, this is potentially a much bigger problem. It will be especially large for programs that target not the wide age range of children aged from birth to 16, but only secondary school grades, as by this level, especially in poorer countries, many poor children will be out of school. In such cases, CCT programs could be a useful demand-side tool in increasing human capital, but will be less complete as social assistance. For CCTs to be effective as social assistance programs in low-income countries, they should serve a broad range of ages and may need to be linked to efforts to build service capacity, an increasingly common trend in CCT programs.

At the opposite end of the spectrum, where service use is all but universal, adding conditions to a social assistance program will run little risk of inducing errors of exclusion, but the potential for gains from the conditions is small, thus the extra administrative costs of verifying that conditions have been met may not be worthwhile. In such cases, programs may adopt conditions related to performance and not just service use.

Both the donor community and local politicians have expressed enthusiasm about and interest in CCT programs in the last 10 years. Donors and the public prefer to provide transfers to the deserving poor with children while being reassured that beneficiaries will do the right things for their children. Observers view the narrow targeting of programs and the absence of leakages as indicative of efficiency, and this has helped to promote national and international support. Moreover, almost all the first-generation CCT programs have been subject to thorough evaluations. The provision of sound, empirically based evidence has helped to establish and publicize the effectiveness of these programs and has facilitated the continuation of some programs and the scaling up of others in the face of fiscal constraints and political change.

Adapting to Local Conditions and Avoiding Unintended Effects

To achieve results as good as those of the well-known first-generation programs, new programs will have to achieve the same level of targeting efficiency, adopt good payment systems, require the right type of conditions, and establish effective program monitoring and management systems. The detailed implementation design will, however, have to be specific to each country, and a number of pilots are under way in low-income countries that may soon yield some helpful lessons on how best to adapt programs. The design of new programs needs to take the following considerations into account:

- New programs will need to have a **clear role within a broader social policy agenda** to ensure quality service provision and effective coordination between demand- and supply-side approaches. CCT programs alone will not be able to break the intergenerational transmission of poverty if the quality of health clinics and schools is inadequate or no jobs or adequate livelihoods are available when assisted children become earners in their own right.

- The **selection of conditions** and the objectives to be achieved need to take into account the specific human capital development shortcoming to be addressed, whether primary or secondary school enrollment, primary health care utilization, or some other aspect. In Mexico, the education impacts might be greater if the grants for secondary schoolchildren were increased and those for primary schoolchildren eliminated, but this would greatly reduce the program's ability to serve as the base social assistance program. Other countries might consider whether schooling grants should be differentiated by grade within secondary school or by gender of the student.

- Extreme care needs to be given to the **program's administrative capacity and its design and implementation** given the additional complications presented by the verification of compliance with conditions inherent in CCT programs.

7.6 Fee Waivers, Exemptions, and Scholarships

Several types of subsidy programs help poor households maintain a minimum socially acceptable standard of living, which entails having access to health and education facilities.[31] Some of these subsidies are in the form of fee waivers and exemptions to use health facilities, while others include vouchers and scholarships to help poor households send their children to school and keep them enrolled. In some ways, these program are similar to the CCT programs covered in the previous section. The fine line between the two types of programs is that fee waivers and vouchers generally reimburse households and/or service providers for actual expenditures, while CCTs provide additional resources to encourage households to use health or education facilities.

For a list of programs involving fee waivers for education and health, see table B.6 in appendix B.

PROGRAM DESCRIPTION

From the perspective of safety nets, the main objective of fee waiver, exemption, and scholarship programs is to provide poor people with the financial resources to use health facilities and send their children to school. From the perspective of service providers, a combination of user fees so they can recover their costs and waivers might be acceptable to help preserve system efficiency in places where budget constraints would prevent adequate provision of services or sufficient coverage.

Fee waivers and vouchers are relatively recent programs that were implemented in Africa as of the second part of the 1990s to counterbalance the negative effects on the poor of the introduction of fees in the health and education sectors that took place in the 1980s. In response to shrinking budgets and growing demand, many developing countries had introduced user fees for using government health facilities for all kinds of medical services, including vaccinations, to increase their efficiency and financing. Several of the countries that implemented some form of user fee system at this time were in Africa, including Kenya, Tanzania, and Uganda (Nolan and Turbat 1995; Russell and Gilson 1995). In 1994, South Africa was one of the first African countries to provide exemptions from payment for health services for pregnant women and children under five (Witter 2005). In 1998, the provision of free services was extended to all users of public primary care.

Fees of some sort are also widespread in the education sector, even for primary-level education. Fees may be official or unofficial and may cover tuition, textbooks, compulsory uniforms, community contributions for teachers' salaries (in Sub-Saharan Africa) and membership in parent-teacher associations (often used to enhance teachers' meager salaries), and/or other school-based activities. An informal survey of 79 World Bank client countries shows that fees of some sort were levied for public primary schools in all but 2 of the countries (Algeria and Uruguay) surveyed (Kattan and Burnett 2004).[32]

TYPES OF PROGRAMS

The two main types of programs discussed here are fee waivers and exemptions for health care and fee waivers and scholarships for schooling.

Fee Waivers and Exemptions for Health Care

Fee waivers and exemptions for health care are programs that enable the poor to obtain free health care even when fees are charged. The waivers may include the cost of health care services and/or drugs for which significant charges apply. Exemptions are granted to everyone for defined service and enable people to receive those services for free, such as prenatal care, immunizations, treatment for tuberculosis, and care in primary health care clinics or a subset of primary health care clinics, for example, those in rural areas. By contrast, fee waivers are granted to some individuals, usually for specific health care activities, which even though they may account for a minority of interactions with the health care system also account for the bulk of charges.

Fee Waivers and Scholarships for Schooling

Fee waivers and scholarships for schooling include a number of forms of assistance to households to meet the costs of schooling, such as stipends, education vouchers, targeted bursaries, and interventions related to tuition and textbooks. The level of benefits ranges from covering some or all of the direct costs of schooling such as fees (as in Zimbabwe and several other African countries), uniforms (India), books (Indonesia), or transport (Colombia) to compensate for a significant share of the opportunity costs of students' time.

Some programs are specifically targeted at girls in an attempt to improve their educational achievement; for example, Bangladesh, Guatemala, and Pakistan have stipend programs for girls (Braun-Munzinger 2005). In some cases, programs are complemented by grants to schools to ensure that the quality of education offered is sufficient, for instance, the Pakistan Urban and Rural Fellowship.[33] Some countries, such as Kenya and Malawi, have eliminated direct fees for primary education for all students (Wilson 2006; World Bank 2007f).

KEY DESIGN FEATURES

The manner of implementation of waiver and voucher programs is important. Those that have been carefully designed and implemented, such as the health waiver systems in Indonesia and Thailand, have had much greater success in terms of the incidence of benefits than those that have improvised, such as those in Ghana, Kenya, and Zimbabwe. Selecting beneficiaries and achieving a balance between the payment of fees and compensation for institutions and service providers are important design challenges.

Beneficiary Selection

The selection of beneficiaries for health programs can range from waivers for a few individuals to exclusions for larger groups. Programs can be designed to cover certain population groups, such as girls, pregnant and/or lactating women, or the elderly. With the exception of Cambodia, all the other countries Bitrán and Giedion (2003) review (Chile, Ghana, Indonesia, Kenya, Thailand, and Zimbabwe) have an explicit national waiver policy and all have an explicit policy for exempting certain categories of preventive services for all citizens. At the same time, most of the countries have experienced problems related to their eligibility criteria, and the lack of clear identification criteria seems to be a major problem.

In relation to health programs, three main methods are used to select individual beneficiaries, given here in approximate order of frequency. The first is a rough means test based on interviews at health facilities by social workers, clerks, or medical staff, as in Cambodia. The second is precertification by a ministry of welfare that is often associated with establishing eligibility for other programs, as in Armenia, Chile, and Jamaica. In Armenia's waiver program (box 7.16), the basic benefits package is extended to beneficiaries of the Family Poverty Benefits Program. In Jamaica, the recipients of the proxy means-tested CCT program are also included in the health system fee waiver program, as are those with Ministry of Social Affairs cards in Surinam (World Bank 2002g, annex N). In Chile, beneficiaries of the noncontributory assistance pension are automatically eligible for free access to the national public health system. The third method of selection involves selection by a community group or a committee of users of health services. In Thailand, for example, village headmen can allocate medical care cards to the poor (Giedion 2002).

Dissemination mechanisms are needed to let the poor know that they are eligible for free or subsidized care and the existence of certain exempted services. Such mechanisms must be tailored to the poor, as they often live away from major urban centers, have little access to formal media, have little education, and work long hours. The systems in Indonesia and Thailand provide a good model compared with, for example, the lack of information available in Zambia (Tien and Chee 2002).

BOX 7.16 **Heath Fee Waiver Program, Armenia**

In 1998, the government of Armenia introduced the basic benefits package to provide free access to some health care services to eligible vulnerable groups. The program's main objective was to help poor families cope with the reduced level of public financing and increased privatization of health services following the introduction of user fees in hospitals in 1993. These fees had been introduced to provide the necessary funding to service providers after the collapse of the old system, which, as was characteristic of the Soviet era, provided free services to everyone. In January 2001, the government extended eligibility for the basic benefits package program to the beneficiaries of the Family Poverty Benefits Program, which is subject to proxy means testing (World Bank 2002a). (Note that basic health services at polyclinics were and still are free for everyone, poor and nonpoor, while those not included in the basic benefits package must pay a fee for laboratory tests.)

Implementation. The State Health Agency makes payments to hospitals and polyclinics on behalf of the poor. These payments cover only about 45 percent of the cost of the health services, and hospitals tend to collect the remaining payments from patients (Lewis 2000; World Bank 2003c).

Impact. Initial analysis showed that despite the introduction of the basic benefits package, the additional costs incurred by users of the health system resulted in a 21 percent drop in utilization between 1996 and 1999 among the largest vulnerable group—families with four or more children—and a small but statistically significant positive impact on access to health care by other vulnerable groups (Chaudhury, Hammer, and Murrugarra 2003). Moreover, informal payments by patients directly to doctors had a negative impact on the availability of funds for physical investment and resulted in a deterioration of physical structures.

A later analysis conducted after the expansion of eligibility for the basic benefits package to all poor families shows that basic benefits package recipients pay approximately 45 percent less in fees than nonrecipients and display a 36 percent increase in utilization, even though the level of health care utilization remains low (Angel-Urdinola and Jain 2006). In recent years, a change in the eligibility criteria increased the utilization of health care and reduced its costs for the poor.

Lessons. Armenia's experience shows the importance of providing local institutions with alternative sources of revenue once fees have been eliminated or waived; otherwise health facilities have a strong incentive to collect informal fees directly from patients.

The possibility of stigmatization that could deter the poor from claiming waivers must also be avoided. Waiver applicants in a large public clinic in Cambodia, for example, were subjected to a public means test in the waiting room. Shame often led prospective applicants to forego their right to request a waiver.

The selection of beneficiaries of school waivers is usually done in two or more steps, beginning with geographic targeting to focus budget resources on areas with more poor students. In programs with low benefit levels, the second step is often a school- or community-based committee that determines which children will benefit, as done by Indonesia's scholarship program. In several countries, including Indonesia, an explicit quota of scholarships may be set for girls, whereby girls must be given at least 50 percent of the scholarships, and often more. In programs involving significant cash transfers, a social welfare office will be involved in a proxy means test.

Disbursement Methods

Compensation for the use of facilities can be paid either to the service providers or to the students themselves. In Indonesia, the scholarships were paid directly to the students (or their families) twice a year via a cash transfer handled by the local post office. The level of compensation is crucial to ensure the provision of quality services. Programs that compensate providers for lost revenues, as in Cambodia, Indonesia, and Thailand, are more successful that those that only provide partial compensation, as in Kenya.

When the level of compensation is not adequate or timely, health care institutions may continue to collect informal payments from patients, including the poor and vulnerable, as occurred in Armenia (box 7.16).

Scope and Coverage

The coverage for health programs is universal for exemptions, as in South Africa, and is relatively high for health fee waivers in some middle-income countries such as Chile, Indonesia, and Thailand. In Chile, about 24 percent of the total population had free access to the Fondo Nacional de Salud (National Health Fund) in 1995; in Indonesia, 18 percent of the total population had cards for the JPS Kartu Sehat health program in 2000; and in Thailand, the Low-Income Card Scheme covered about 25 percent of the total population in 1997. By contrast, in some countries coverage is extremely low, as in Colombia for education (about 0.3 percent of the population in 1997) and in Zambia for health (about 0.6 percent of the population covered in 1999). (See Keith and Shackleton 2006 for more examples on the costs of basic health care in Sub-Saharan Africa.)

Many countries provide various forms of support to facilitate access to education and to reduce schooling expenses by providing scholarships and stipends to help offset tuition costs. Others provide indirect support in the form of textbooks and other learning material. Table 7.2 shows the types of interventions and the countries that use them.

Administrative Costs

Information about the administrative costs of the programs covered in this section is not readily available. The indication is that administrative costs are generally low. For example, in the Dominican Republic, hospital fee waivers account for only 3.6 percent of total costs; in Belize, hospital fee waivers account for only 0.4 percent of total costs (Grosh 1994). Actual costs, however, may represent a significant percentage of the resources collected. For school fee waivers, administrative costs are roughly 3 to 5 percent of total program costs, or 5 to 10 percent of total program costs for programs with large transfers and more complex mechanisms (World Bank 2002g, annex N).

Implementing Institutions

Health-related programs usually fall under the auspices of the ministry of health or the social insurance system and are administered locally in the case of community financing schemes. The individual point of service (clinic or hospital) may or may not be reimbursed

TABLE 7.2 **Types of Interventions in Education by Country**

Intervention	Country examples
Tuition-related interventions—Reduce or eliminate tuition fees for the poor and the disadvantaged	China, Djibouti, Ethiopia, Jordan, Lesotho
Scholarships, stipends—Provide grants often accompanied by performance-related measures	Bangladesh, Brazil, Ethiopia, The Gambia, Ghana, Guatemala, India, Indonesia, Malawi, Mauritania, Morocco, Mozambique, Nepal, Nicaragua, Panama, Pakistan, Senegal
Targeted bursaries—Provide monetary grants to needy students	China, Colombia, India, Indonesia, Mexico, Nicaragua, Tanzania, Zambia
Textbook-related interventions	
• Replace textbook rental fee with book loan scheme	The Gambia, Vietnam
• Provide free textbooks to grades 1–7	Mali, Nigeria, Rwanda, Senegal, Pakistan
• Provide free textbooks to target groups, for example, the poor or girls	Armenia, China, Chile, Ethiopia, Guinea, India, Malaysia, Morocco, Nepal, Tajikistan, Turkey
• Provide book allowances to poor families	Bulgaria
Learning materials—Provide other learning materials such as stationery	Bangladesh, India, Mozambique
Uniforms—Provide free uniforms	India
Transport-related interventions—Provide bicycles for poor rural students to get to school	Thailand

SOURCE: Kattan and Burnett 2004.

from a central budget for the costs of services given to clients with fee waivers. Informal exemptions granted by providers based on a subjective "Robin Hood" principle are widespread. Education programs that directly provide for schooling costs and supplies tend to be run by education ministries.

OUTCOMES, ADVANTAGES, AND DISADVANTAGES

Information about program participation and program impact is still scant. The lack of monitoring and evaluation has not allowed measurement of the performance of waivers and exemptions or the imposition of corrective measures (see Bitrán and Muñoz 2000 in relation to targeting).

Incidence

Several countries have had problems with eligibility criteria, particularly in relation to distinguishing the poor from the nonpoor. For example, in Kenya, a national policy exhorted public providers to exempt so-called pauper patients from user fees, but the lack of guidelines meant that each facility adopted its own interpretation of pauper patients. In addition, large errors of exclusion appear to be commonplace, where the poor are unfamiliar with the waiver system and thus do not even seek care. Targeting in the medical program for the poor in Thailand was found to be weak, with numerous inclusion and exclusion errors because of issues with the income eligibility criteria. The third national evaluation of the Low-Income Card Scheme in 1996 showed that one-third of households surveyed were poor and that only 32 percent of them had cards (Donaldson, Pannar-unothai, and Tangcharoensathien 1999).

Low coverage in some low-income countries might be caused by the lack of incentives for service providers given inadequate levels of compensation for the provision of subsidized services. Kenyan government providers, for instance, received no compensation whatsoever; Ghanaian public providers received compensation, but funding was uneven and often delayed (Nyonator and Kutzin 1999).

Impact

The impact of user fees in health are difficult to calculate because they should take into account the net effect of exemption programs and the mobilization of resources resulting from the utilization of the fees that are charged. In Cameroon and Mauritania, for example, the improved quality of services and availability of drugs have offset the potential negative impact resulting from the introduction of user fees (Audibert and Mathonnat 2000; Litvack and Bodart 1993). In Armenia, by contrast, the introduction of the fee waiver program did not prevent a significant drop in service utilization for the most vulnerable large families (Chaudhury, Hammer, and Murrugarra 2003).

Some evidence indicates that exemptions from user fees have been accompanied by increased health service utilization and improved treatment-seeking behavior, and have thereby promoted early diagnosis. In Sudan, the greatest changes were apparent in health centers with the largest number of exemptions (Zeidan and others 2004). Evidence from Uganda shows that the removal of user fees for primary health care, accompanied by an increased budget to replace fee revenues, led to a large increase in service utilization: following the elimination of user fees in 2000, access improved, service use increased, fewer workdays were lost because of sickness, and wealthy households tended to opt out of using public services (Deininger and Mpuga 2004; Yates, Cooper, and Holland 2006). Nationwide, the number of new cases treated by health centers increased, on average, by 18 percent for children under five and 31 percent for children aged five and over; referrals increased by 26 percent. At the same time, the increase in the demand for services has put some strain on the system.

The impact of waivers on service providers' capacity to adjust to increased utilization needs to be assessed. Some evidence suggests that the introduction of waivers has created additional pressure in areas where capacity was already limited. The elimination of primary school fees has also had a large impact on the number of children going to school, and thus on the number of teachers and textbooks needed. While some countries such as Kenya have been successful in replacing lost funds, others such as Malawi have not been able to replace the lost revenues (Wilson 2006; World Bank 2007f). In Colombia, the introduction of vouchers for secondary schools placed additional stress on schools that had already reached full capacity. At that time, 1992, the secondary enrollment rate was only 75 percent overall, and as low as 55 percent for the poorest quintile of the population. The capacity constraint was overcome with a unique partnership between the private and public sectors (Braun-Munzinger 2005).[34]

Advantages

A well-designed and well-funded system of fees and waivers has the following advantages:

- Fee waivers provide both demand-side and supply-side support, as they provide resources for institutions and access to poor people.
- The incentive effects of school programs are designed to be positive, for example, to encourage enrollment and attendance or to reduce dropout rates.

Disadvantages

Program design needs to avoid several of the following common pitfalls:

- Frequently, schools and clinics are not compensated for the loss of revenue resulting from the introduction of fee waivers and exemptions leading to a lack of funds to provide adequate services.
- The reduction in beneficiaries' out-of-pocket payments may not be enough to promote access to care. The poor must often overcome access costs to health care beyond user fees, including transportation, lodging, and food costs, as well as the opportunity costs of being away from work or from home. Cambodia's Health Equity Fund not only waives user fees for the poor, but also reimburses their transportation and food costs associated with the use of health care (Bitrán and others 2003; Hardeman and others 2004).
- The impact of fee waivers on school attendance and dropout rates is questionable, as in most cases the beneficiaries are not required to attend classes. At the same time, the impact on educational outcomes might also be overstated, as most recipients might be enrolled in school in any case.

LESSONS AND SUGGESTIONS

Fee waivers and exemptions are used primarily to facilitate access to education and heath when user fees are charged for these services.

Most Likely Beneficiaries

Fee waivers, exemptions, and scholarships provide support to poor people who cannot afford to use health services or send their children to school when the use of the services is not free and their cost continues to rise. The beneficiaries of health-related programs include children and other members of indigent households who would otherwise be more likely not to use the services. Scholarships and tuitions programs are mostly targeted to poor families that otherwise would not send their children to school. They are also often targeted toward girls to encourage their participation in school, as in the case of the girls' stipend program in Bangladesh (Khandker, Pitt, and Fuwa 2003).

Appropriate Context and Political Economy Considerations

The use of fee waivers in health and education is recommended in areas that have good access to health care and education facilities, but where these are too expensive for poor people, who consequently have low levels of attendance. Such programs can only work if providers have alternative sources of revenue once fees have been eliminated or waived, as in Cambodia, Indonesia, and Thailand, where providers have been compensated for foregone revenues (Kattan and Burnett 2004).

Political support for fee waivers cannot be assessed in isolation from the existence of user fees. On the one hand, fees for health care are highly controversial (see Hutton 2004 for a description of the establishment of fees and the need for exemptions), and waiver systems are often not thought to be the solution in relation to health care. On the other hand, fee waivers and scholarships for students are popular, especially among international development agencies, because health and schooling provide the link between short-run transfer benefits and long-run human capital formation. Therefore countries want to use the fees to improve the quality of the services while finding ways not to exclude the poor.

Criticism of user fees has prompted several nongovernmental organizations to call for the abolition of fees for health services (Witter 2005), and several governments have done so in recent years. Experience with the removal of fees for health services (box 7.17)

BOX 7.17 Elimination of User Fees and Waivers, South Africa and Uganda

User fees, often combined with waivers and exemptions, have been the subject of extensive debate in recent years, and several countries have decided to eliminate user fees all together. The introduction of user fees in the 1980s and 1990s was meant to increase funding and improve the quality of public health and education services. Unfortunately, the resulting additional funds have not always been reinvested in quality improvements, and the use of services by the poor decreased because they have not always been able to receive the necessary waivers.

South Africa. In 1994, the new African National Congress government, fulfilling its mandate to remove the inequities of the apartheid era, introduced free health services for pregnant women and children under five. In 1998, the government extended fee provision to all those using public primary health care services. The removal of fees led to an increase in service utilization, but health workers felt that they were not prepared for the changes, which resulted in unnecessary tensions between workers and patients.

Uganda. User fees for health services in public facilities were introduced in 1993 and eliminated in 2001. The elimination of fees prompted an explosion in the use of services, especially among the poor (Xu and others 2005). The outcome was that drugs were frequently unavailable at government facilities, partly because of the slowness of the supply system, forcing patients to purchase them from private pharmacies, plus some deterioration was apparent in staff attitudes. Services did not suffer greatly, because the lost revenues were generally replaced with increased government budget allocations for pharmaceuticals, particularly for primary health care units in poor rural areas; recent improvements in drug supply systems appear to have been important factors in sustaining demand (Yates, Cooper, and Holland 2006).

Lessons. When the combination of fees and waivers does not promote an increase in quality without excluding the poor, eliminating user fees is possible. The experiences of South Africa and Uganda show that the removal of user fees must be carefully planned to preserve the continuity and quality of services.

shows the need for careful planning to preserve the quality of the services by ensuring that service providers and facilities continue to have access to the same levels of funding (see Gilson and McIntyre 2005; Pearson 2004). The same applies to the elimination of fees for primary education. Countries and their donor partners should focus on planning; replacing lost revenues at the local level; and ensuring sufficient capacity to handle the surge in schooling demand by providing additional books, training more teachers, providing more classroom space, and so on (Wilson 2006).

Adapting to Local Conditions and Avoiding Unintended Effects

The key challenges to successful implementation of fee waiver and scholarship programs are being able to reach the intended beneficiaries and maintaining the quality of services and efficiency without compromising equity in the absence of the revenues generated by user fees. These challenges can be addressed as follows:

- **Ensure that the criteria for granting of waivers are clear.** This will reduce confusion among those responsible for managing the system and among potential recipients. Providers need clear, written guidelines about how waivers and exemptions will work, with enough flexibility to allow for regional or local variations if necessary.

- **Disseminate information about the availability of waivers and exemptions for health widely to potential beneficiaries.** Potential beneficiaries should be aware of the criteria for granting waivers and for the receipt of financial support for other costs, such as food and transportation as in the case of health care in Cambodia. Providing information about waivers and financial support for other costs and the motivation behind the provision of such support is also necessary to counter the stigmatization associated with the provision of free health care services.

- **Train the staff responsible for administering waivers and provide them with the supplies to carry out their jobs.** Those determining eligibility should be aware of the selection criteria and be fully informed about any constraints governing the waiver process, for instance, how many waivers can be awarded in any given month.

- **Ensure that once fees are eliminated or waived, sufficient funds are available to support personnel and facilities.** Otherwise staff will have a strong incentive to collect informal fees directly from patients as occurred in Armenia and not to make expenditures for upkeep and investment.

7.7 Conclusion

This chapter, supplemented by the tables in appendix B, provides an idea of what to look for in safety net programs and what responses to expect under specific circumstances. Table 7.3 provides a summary of a number of aspects of different types of safety net programs.

All programs face the basic challenges covered in detail in chapters 4 to 6: enrolling the intended beneficiaries, defining the structure of their benefits and paying them, providing any noncash benefits, avoiding misuse of funds, and running the program effectively. Beyond that, each program faces specific challenges and its potential varies depending on the context.

The review of commonly used safety net interventions in this chapter indicates the following five general lessons:

- **The objectives of the program used should address the needs of the current or intended target population given the specific political environment.** Some interventions are extremely flexible: cash and in-kind transfers can be used for any population group. Some interventions are more easily focused on specific groups; for example, public works are best suited for those transient poor who are able to work or who have been left behind by a reform process, and CCT programs are best for chronically poor children and their families. The art of choosing an appropriate mix of interventions is taken up in chapter 9.

- **The design of the program matters.** For example, the amount of a transfer has to be adequate to meet needs at the household level, and the scale of the program has to be adequate to meet its expected function. In addition, any noncash elements have to be in place: the means for using labor effectively for public works, the supply of education and health services in CCT programs, the means to reimburse health facilities for revenues foregone when fee waivers are used, and so on. Protecting the vulnerable from shocks can be achieved by responsive administration that is able to expand a program rapidly and to include and exclude beneficiaries efficiently depending on their changing economic status.

- **The implementation and delivery mechanisms and the adequacy of administration determine the general effectiveness and efficiency of a program.** For programs to be implemented properly, a strong and well-informed administrative system is necessary. If the capacity is not available, it should be built, making use of existing structures and coordination across agencies. Starting with small pilots and eventually scaling up may be helpful, although some programs have started on a large scale and refined their systems subsequently. Both can work, but both require political will, time, and sufficient funding for administrative systems.

- **The particular country situation and political environment matter.** Many programs have been proven to work well in specific countries and under particular circumstances, but to succeed elsewhere, they need to be adapted to local conditions.

- **A country should always be open to learning about new programs and finding ways to improve current programs.** The overview of the programs presented here is by no means exhaustive. The information reported is based on the literature about programs that have been monitored and evaluated and does not include programs that have not been evaluated or that have received little publicity. New ideas and programs continue to be piloted and implemented in several countries, and advances in methods for identifying beneficiaries and for delivering benefits continue to be developed and implemented. The key is to stay informed and maintain a critical eye when assessing innovations.

TABLE 7.3 **Characteristics of Safety Net Interventions**

Type of intervention (programs)	Social protection goals	Intended beneficiaries	Advantages	Disadvantages	Appropriate context	Implementation challenges
Cash and near cash transfers • Needs based • Food stamps • Noncontributory pensions • Family allowances	• Mitigating poverty and promoting equity • Managing shocks • Facilitating reforms	• Chronically poor working families • Those not expected to work: children, the elderly, the disabled • Those needing temporary assistance	• Have lower administrative costs than many other programs • Do not distort prices • Transfers can directly meet critical household needs • Benefits can be differentiated by level of need, household size or composition, and so on	• Targeting methods can be information intensive • Transfers are fungible, therefore subject to unintended household uses	• When essential commodities are available • When consumers can purchase food in the market	• Defining clear objectives and benefit levels • Reaching the intended beneficiaries • Distributing benefits reliably and efficiently
In-kind food transfers and other food-based programs • Quantity rations and in-kind transfers • Supplemental feeding and nutrition • School feeding • Emergency food distribution	• Mitigating poverty and promoting equity • Managing shocks • Investing in human capital and nutrition • Facilitating reforms	• Chronically poor people who cannot afford to buy the food they need to improve their nutritional status • Those not expected to work: the elderly; the disabled; children in school; and malnourished, pregnant and lactating mothers • Those needing temporary relief, refugees, the displaced	• Can be effective in alleviating hunger • Can increase school attendance by poor children	• Storage and transport of food adds a large element to administrative costs • Beneficiary group is limited • Substantial errors of inclusion may occur depending on the targeting method • Often biased to urban populations • On-site feeding adds to administrative costs for programs and transaction costs for participants	• When food aid is available but cash assistance is not or when the government needs to rotate strategic food grain stocks • When prices are too high because of a lack of or inefficient markets • When programs do not have a negative impact on markets • When nutrition interventions are needed to protect food-insecure people	• Organizing efficient transport, storage, and distribution of food • Selecting commodities • Reaching needy mothers and children

(continued)

TABLE 7.3 (continued)

Type of intervention (programs)	Social protection goals	Intended beneficiaries	Advantages	Disadvantages	Appropriate context	Implementation challenges
General price subsidies • Price support for food • Subsidized sales of food • Subsidies for energy	• Mitigating poverty and promoting equity	• Chronically poor and transient poor families both working and not working	• Potentially low administrative costs depending on the delivery mechanism • Can be implemented or expanded quickly after the onset of a crisis if appropriate marketing structures exist	• High errors of inclusion to the nonpoor depending on commodity consumption patterns • Often biased to urban populations • Distort commodity prices and use • Expensive and difficult to remove once established because of pressures by interest groups	• When prices of essential commodities are too high • When used in conjunction with a defined time period	• Targeting poor populations using inferior commodities • Maintaining a reasonable budget
Public works • Usually labor-intensive infrastructure development projects	• Mitigating poverty and promoting equity • Managing shocks	• Chronically poor unemployed at the margins of the labor market • Transient poor, short-term unemployed, and seasonal workers	• Needed infrastructure is created or maintained • Self-targeting can be effective if the wage rate is low enough • Additional risk management benefits can accrue if the program is set up with an employment guarantee • Politically popular because labor disincentives can be avoided and beneficiaries can maintain the "dignity of work"	• Administratively demanding. • Trade-off between infrastructure development and poverty alleviation objectives • The ratio of net transfers to total costs is low because of the share of nonwage inputs and because of foregone earnings	• When unemployment is high after the collapse of the labor market in case of a crisis or disaster • When seasonal unemployment is high • When addressing individual unemployment in the absence of unemployment insurance	• Reaching the poorest households by self-targeting, for example, by setting the correct wage rate • Building useful infrastructure at efficient cost using as many people as possible • Keeping beneficiaries' transaction costs low • Avoiding leakages of funds

(continued)

TABLE 7.3 (continued)

Type of intervention (programs)	Social protection goals	Intended beneficiaries	Advantages	Disadvantages	Appropriate context	Implementation challenges
Conditional cash transfers • Targeted transfers conditional on school attendance or preventative health care	• Mitigating poverty and promoting equity • Investing in human capital and nutrition • Facilitating reforms	• Chronically poor and vulnerable poor families with low level of human capital, especially children and mothers	• Supports incomes of the poor • Can improve school attendance and/or health care use	• Effectiveness influenced by existing education and health infrastructure • Administratively demanding because of the need for sophisticated targeting and for monitoring compliance	• When clear human capital targets are to be achieved • When health and education services are available • When the administrative constraints are not too big	• Distributing benefits reliably and efficiently • Having a clear role within social policy • Selecting conditions • Verifying compliance with conditions
Fee waivers, exemptions, and scholarships • Health fees • School fees • Scholarships	• Mitigating poverty and promoting equity • Investing in human capital and nutrition • Facilitating reform	• Chronically poor and vulnerable poor families with low level of human capital who cannot afford the cost of health and education • Poor students that would otherwise drop out of school	• May promote human capital development	• Administratively complex and to be managed directly by health or education facilities • Effectiveness influenced by the existing education and health infrastructure	• When social services are provided for a fee and may exclude the poor • When health and education services are available • When providers have access to alternative sources of revenue	• Defining the criteria for granting waivers • Having good information systems in place • Ensuring good implementation by providers and administrators • Having funds available

SOURCE: Authors.

Notes

1. This section draws heavily on Rogers and Coates (2002) and Tabor (2002).

2. Note that in addition, some cash transfer programs require beneficiaries to provide a certain amount of public service. These are not really workfare programs, but something in between cash transfers and workfare.

3. Following complaints, the initial level of transfers of US$6 per household was raised to US$8 for families with children irrespective of their number (Devereux and others 2005).

4. Since the program's expansion to the entire population in 1993, the South African cabinet has raised the level several times (Legido-Quigley 2003). In 2005, the pension benefit was equivalent to about R 780 (US$123) a month (Samson, MacQuene, and van Niekerk 2006).

5. Universal benefits for children used to be common in Bulgaria until 2002, when they were replaced by a means-tested program conditional on school attendance.

6. Harvey (2005) shows that cash and voucher approaches remain largely underutilized in the humanitarian sector despite their effectiveness and the growing experience with such approaches.

7. Note that sometimes benefits may also need to be provided to some nonpoor households to build a broadly based constituency in favor of a cash transfer program (Tabor 2002).

8. This section draws heavily on Alderman (2002b) and Rogers and Coates (2002).

9. Public works programs frequently provide in-kind distribution of food in food-for-work programs and are discussed later in this chapter.

10. Distinguishing between the two types of programs is sometimes difficult. For instance, Egypt's food subsidy system provides restricted access to oil and sugar for the poor only, but access to subsidized bread and flour is available to everyone.

11. Note that in many ways school feeding programs are similar to CCT programs, as they provide nutritional support to children and also promote access to education. However, the two types of programs differ in other aspects such as the selection of beneficiaries.

12. Queuing and long waiting times are also sometimes used as self-targeting mechanisms to discourage participation by better-off consumers, but instead might keep needy people away.

13. Some evidence also indicates that compliance is low, as in many cases the teacher or staff person managing the program will simply divide the food into smaller portions so that all the children can participate (Sahn, Rogers, and Nelson 1981).

14. Additional benefits can be achieved if the commodities distributed are fortified. For example, a small pilot of the WFP initiative in Bangladesh delivers fortified whole wheat to beneficiaries.

15. This section is largely based on Alderman (2002b).

16. Government regulation and price controls in Egypt, Babylon, Greece, and Rome were, in most cases, designed to guarantee consumer access to essential commodities. These policies were often difficult to enforce, even when the penalty for breaking the law was death. For example, in 284 A.D., the Roman emperor Diocletian tried to control the prices of beef, grain, eggs, and other items. As a result, producers stopped bringing these products to the markets until the law was set aside (DiLorenzo 2005; Schuettinger and Butler 1979).

17. The issues involved in and the policies for addressing high prices for staple commodities are complex, because they involve domestic production, international price trends, and natural disasters. Thus for staple foods, safety net programs may need to be complemented by a broader set of food policy interventions (del Ninno, Dorosh, and Subbarao 2007; World Bank 2005h, especially chapter 7).

18. Timmer (2004) describes the political economy changes that brought an end to the stabilization policy in the wake of the 1997 Asian financial crisis despite higher grain prices and the possible negative impact on poor consumers. However, BULOG is still selling rice on the open market when approved by the minister of trade and requested by regional governments. Approval can be obtained only if the price has increased by 25 percent over the average price of the previous three months.

19. Energy subsidies are frequently examined independently from other subsidies such as for food, partly because of the scale of energy subsidies and partly because of differences in the range of instruments used for the subsidies (Alderman 2002b).

20. If the price of a commodity goes down 30 percent and consumers spend only 5 percent of their budget on that commodity, then the savings are less than 2 percent on the total amount they spend.

21. Note that the transfer is diminished by the cost of participation incurred by the participants, including any revenues they would have received if they had not participated in the program.

22. This discussion of workfare programs is based largely on Subbarao (2003).

23. In French, such programs are referred as haute intensité de main d'oeuvre, or simply as HIMO (highly labor-intensive public work).

24. At that time, Parliament passed the Poor Employment Act, which allowed the government to provide large sums of money to corporations or private individuals to invest in projects that employed many daily laborers. These projects focused on building canals and roads and draining marshes and laid the foundations of the industrial revolution. From that time, public works programs became a regular feature not only of British welfare policy, but also of economic policy (Flinn 1961; Webb 2002). A later act, the 1834 Poor Law Amendment Act, explicitly self-targeted the poor by aiming at providing pay and conditions lower than the worse possible alternatives (Himmelfarb 1984).

25. In Bulgaria, only current beneficiaries of the Guaranteed Minimum Income Program, which is means tested, can participate in the public works program. If they are asked to participate and refuse to do so, they are dropped from the Guaranteed Minimum Income Program.

26. In many poor countries, it is not unusual for the prevailing market wage for unskilled labor in the informal market to be lower than the official minimum wage.

27. See www.caremalawi.org/crimp.htm.

28. This section deals mostly with conditional cash transfers because, with the exception of the Food for Education program in Bangladesh, most programs provide cash, and this is how they are known around the world. For additional information on CCTs, see Coady (2002); Coady and Ferreira (2003); Coady, Grosh, and Hoddinott (2004); Handa and Davis (2006); Morley and Coady (2003); Patrinos (2002); Rawlings (2005); Rawlings and Rubio (2005); World Bank (forthcoming).

29. Morley and Coady (2003, p. 4) report that "For example, even centralized programs, which essentially bypass state-level governments, are designed so that community-level organizations play a crucial role. For example, in Mexico's PROGRESA the community promoter is a beneficiary, who is elected by other beneficiaries. She (the transfers are always given directly to mothers) plays the role of liaison officer between the program officials and beneficiary communities, arranging regular community meetings with beneficiaries, informing beneficiaries of their rights and responsibilities under the program, and communicating beneficiary concerns to program officials."

30. The impact on education in Mexico may be a lower-bound estimate, as Bobonis and Finan (2005) find that education policies aimed at encouraging enrollment can produce large social multiplier effects through the peer effect on nonparticipants in the program.

31. This section is based largely on Bitrán and Giedion (2003).

32. The types of fees charged vary considerably from region to region. In Sub-Saharan Africa, community contributions and parent-teacher association dues are the most common type of fee (81 percent of the countries surveyed). Other fees are less common but nonetheless significant: tuition (41 percent of the countries surveyed), textbooks (37 percent), uniforms (48 percent), and other activity fees (41 percent).

33. Orazem (2000) describes this pilot program in Baluchistan Province that is attempting to induce the creation of private schools for the poor. This study describes the program's success in urban areas and relative failure in rural areas.

34. The program sought to take advantage of excess capacity in the private sector. The Colombian government issued private school vouchers for students entering grade 6, the start of secondary school. The vouchers targeted the poorest third of the population and were renewable so long as recipients made adequate progress toward graduating from secondary school (Bettinger 2005).

Annex:
Coverage of School Feeding Programs Sponsored by the World Food Programme as of 2005

Country	Children receiving school meals		Children receiving take-home rations		Percentage receiving both school meals and take-home rations	Total children assisted by WFP	
	Number	Ratio of boys to girls	Number	Ratio of boys to girls		Number	Ratio of boys to girls
Africa, East and Central							
Burundi	72,870	1.14	33,991	0.00	46.65	72,870	1.14
Congo, Dem. Rep. of	165,647	0.83	0	n.a.	0.00	165,647	0.83
Congo, Republic of	21,084	1.12	0	n.a.	0.00	21,084	1.12
Djibouti	10,884	1.49	1,052	0.00	9.67	10,884	1.49
Eritrea	94,295	1.52	37,384	0.00	39.65	94,295	1.66
Ethiopia	638,032	1.30	67,702	0.00	10.61	638,032	1.30
Kenya	1,822,529	1.14	286	0.65	0.01	1,822,611	1.14
Rwanda	255,667	0.96	41,000	0.00	16.04	255,667	0.96
Somalia	10,000	2.33	0	n.a.	0.00	10,000	2.33
Sudan	481,331	1.12	0	n.a.	0.00	481,331	1.12
Tanzania	191,770	1.10	0	n.a.	0.00	191,770	1.10
Uganda	450,193	1.07	27,042	0.00	6.01	450,193	1.07
Africa, Southern							
Angola	163,437	1.06	0	n.a.	0.00	163,437	1.06
Lesotho	155,404	0.89	34,471	0.92	1.75	186,613	0.89
Madagascar	61,376	0.91	0	n.a.	0.00	61,376	0.91
Malawi	213,894	0.92	122,043	0.12	57.06	213,894	0.92
Mozambique	217,238	1.83	148,117	0.90	10.00	332,155	1.50
Swaziland	65,707	0.92	0	n.a.	0.00	65,707	0.92
Zambia	164,196	0.97	28,679	0.92	17.47	164,196	0.97
Zimbabwe	1,110,674	0.92	0	n.a.	0.00	1,110,674	0.92
West Africa							
Benin	32,825	1.31	0	n.a.	0.00	32,825	1.31
Burkina Faso	85,118	1.30	4,000	0.00	4.70	85,118	1.30
Cameroon	73,670	1.50	7,200	0.00	9.77	73,670	1.50

(continued)

ANNEX (continued)

Country	Children receiving school meals		Children receiving take-home rations		Percentage receiving both school meals and take-home rations	Total children assisted by WFP	
	Number	Ratio of boys to girls	Number	Ratio of boys to girls		Number	Ratio of boys to girls
Cape Verde	102,975	1.16	0	n.a.	0.00	102,975	1.16
Central African Rep.	178,040	1.47	0	n.a.	0.00	178,040	1.47
Chad	91,177	1.31	17,040	0.00	18.69	91,177	1.31
Côte d'Ivoire	1,008,160	1.39	0	n.a.	0.00	1,008,160	1.39
Gambia, The	112,979	0.98	0	n.a.	0.00	112,979	0.98
Ghana	0	n.a.	44,710	0.00	0.00	44,710	0.00
Guinea	218,848	1.44	40,300	0.00	18.41	218,848	1.44
Guinea Bissau	130,756	1.09	62,488	0.00	47.79	130,756	1.09
Liberia	475,306	1.15	3,453	0.00	0.73	475,306	1.15
Mali	95,323	1.20	31,759	0.00	33.32	95,323	1.20
Mauritania	114,996	0.82	0	n.a.	0.00	114,996	0.82
Niger	52,556	1.38	7,472	0.00	14.22	52,556	1.38
São Tomé & Principe	28,671	1.08	0	n.a.	0.00	28,671	1.08
Senegal	258,857	1.14	0	n.a.	0.00	258,857	1.14
Sierra Leone	385,461	1.22	0	n.a.	0.00	385,461	1.22
Asia							
Bangladesh	805,356	0.98	0	n.a.	0.00	805,356	0.98
Bhutan	41,396	1.23	0	n.a.	0.00	41,396	1.23
Cambodia	544,296	1.11	11,820	0.47	1.27	549,158	1.09
China	0	n.a.	10,820	0.00	0.00	10,820	0.00
Timor Leste	1,731	1.00	0	n.a.	0.00	1,731	1.00
India	818,383	1.11	0	n.a.	0.00	818,383	1.11
Indonesia	585,551	1.06	0	n.a.	0.00	585,551	1.06
Korea, Republic of	1,647,253	1.00	830,684	1.00	50.43	1,647,253	1.00
Lao PDR	55,404	1.18	29,784	0.17	53.76	55,404	1.18
Maldives	25,000	1.01	0	n.a.	0.00	25,000	1.01
Myanmar	0	n.a.	226,451	0.93	0.00	226,451	0.93
Nepal	477,731	0.95	129,759	0.00	27.16	477,731	0.96
Sri Lanka	144,955	1.10	0	n.a.	0.00	144,955	1.10
Thailand	11,255	0.86	0	n.a.	0.00	11,255	0.86

(continued)

ANNEX (continued)

Country	Children receiving school meals		Children receiving take-home rations		Percentage receiving both school meals and take-home rations	Total children assisted by WFP	
	Number	Ratio of boys to girls	Number	Ratio of boys to girls		Number	Ratio of boys to girls
Latin American and the Caribbean							
Bolivia	107,600	1.05	0	n.a.	0.00	107,600	1.05
Colombia	150,044	1.03	0	n.a.	0.00	150,044	1.03
Cuba	412,787	1.04	0	n.a.	0.00	412,787	1.04
Dominican Republic	49,186	1.20	0	n.a.	0.00	49,186	1.20
El Salvador	126,440	1.08	0	n.a.	0.00	126,440	1.08
Guatemala	75,701	1.04	0	n.a.	0.00	75,701	1.04
Haiti	293,390	0.92	0	n.a.	0.00	293,390	0.92
Honduras	364,690	1.04	0	n.a.	0.00	364,690	1.04
Nicaragua	380,089	1.06	221,142	1.07	58.14	380,089	1.06
Peru	4,243	1.04	0	n.a.	0.00	4,243	1.04
Middle East, Central Asia, and Eastern Europe							
Afghanistan	1,213,947	1.50	957,807	0.42	28.80	1,686,175	1.50
Algeria	31,323	1.10	0	n.a.	0.00	31,323	1.10
Armenia	29,640	1.01	0	n.a.	0.00	29,640	1.01
Azerbaijan	0	n.a.	5,892	1.15	0.00	5,892	1.13
Egypt, Arab Rep. of	257,894	0.99	3,530	0.00	0.88	259,133	0.98
Georgia	4,644	1.04	0	n.a.	0.00	4,644	1.04
Iran, Islamic Rep. of	0	n.a.	7,000	0.47	0.00	7,000	0.47
Iraq	1,223,655	1.38	142,043	0.00	11.61	1,223,655	1.38
Pakistan	110,000	1.00	326,874	0.00	0.00	436,874	0.14
Russian Federation	154,381	1.01	0	n.a.	0.00	154,381	1.01
Tajikistan	307,821	1.18	18,557	0.00	0.00	326,378	1.05
Yemen, Rep. of	1,400	1.22	136,300	0.00	0.00	137,700	0.01
Total	**20,265,432**	**1.13**	**3,818,652**	**0.38**	**11.16**	**21,666,573**	**1.07**

SOURCE: WFP 2006b.

NOTE: n.a. = not applicable.

## CHAPTER 8

Assisting Traditionally Vulnerable Groups

KEY MESSAGES

A number of vulnerable groups are likely to face difficulties in generating good incomes. These groups are especially likely to have a low level of education, be poorly integrated into the labor market, and own few assets. They may also face discrimination, which complicates their ability to generate independent incomes. In addition, each group faces problems specific to that group: the elderly may have declining health; people with disabilities face physical and social barriers to participation in society; the internally displaced may be restricted to certain areas or housing; former combatants may have mental health issues related to their war experiences and/or be shunned by communities; and immigrants may not have access to the full range of services, and if illegal or undocumented, may be hesitant to use those services that are provided.

The list of groups that may be especially vulnerable is long, although their size and degree of vulnerability may vary from place to place. There are particular issues involved in providing safety nets to vulnerable groups, specifically, the elderly, orphans and vulnerable children, and people with disabilities. Households with vulnerable individuals tend to be poorer than households without them, but this is not universally true. Thus categorical targeting to vulnerable individuals may be highly inaccurate.

A perennial question regarding vulnerable groups and safety nets is whether they are better served through special programs or within the social assistance programs designed for the wider population. In general, the preference is to serve vulnerable groups through a single, well-run social assistance program on grounds of equitable inclusion and efficiency of operations, but this may not always be feasible. The decision will depend in part on technical criteria, such as the caliber of alternative general social assistance programs, the accuracy of categorical targeting by vulnerability versus poverty in a specific setting, and the scope for reducing administrative costs by combining programs. More qualitative factors such as whether political support for the vulnerable groups differs, whether earmarked transfers will empower members of vulnerable groups within their households, and whether special programs would be more or less stigmatizing than general social assistance are also significant factors in the decision.

Income support is not the only public action needed to support these groups, and indeed, is often not the most important; therefore the role of income support should not be overemphasized. The integration of transfers and other services to target households is even more important for vulnerable groups than for other recipients of social assistance.

A number of vulnerable groups are likely to face difficulties in generating good incomes because of some special aspect of their situation. The list of groups that may be especially vulnerable is long, although their size and degree of vulnerability may vary from place to place and group to group. Commonly considered vulnerable groups include the elderly; orphans and vulnerable children; people with disabilities; internally displaced people; institutionalized people; those suffering from certain medical conditions, such as Hansen's disease (leprosy) or HIV/AIDS; immigrants; war veterans and former combatants; widows; and members of ethnic and migrant groups. These groups overlap, as the displaced will include orphans and old people, some of the elderly will have disabilities, and so on.

Often, members of these groups suffer from situations that make them especially likely to have a low level of education, to be poorly integrated into the labor market, and to own few assets. They may face discrimination, which complicates their ability to generate independent incomes. In addition, each group faces problems specific to that group: the elderly may have declining health; people with disabilities face physical and social barriers to participation in society; the internally displaced may be restricted to certain areas or housing; former combatants may have mental health issues related to their war experiences and/or be shunned by communities; and immigrants may not have access to the full range of services, and if illegal or undocumented, may be hesitant to use those services that are provided.

The first step in thinking about how safety nets should serve each group is to understand its size and poverty status. Is the group large or small? Are its members poorer than average for the country or not? The next consideration is whether special social assistance programs for that group are needed or desirable or whether they should be served by more general social assistance programs. If they should be included in general programs, consideration should be given to whether this will happen naturally or whether some features of the general programs need to be adjusted, and if so, how that might be accomplished.

In looking at the situation of the vulnerable groups discussed in this chapter, some common themes emerge that are likely to apply to other especially vulnerable populations as well:

- The groups and, to some extent, their problems are usually intuitively identifiable, but defining and measuring their situations are complex issues and/or pertinent data are lacking.
- The public action needed to support these groups does not just involve income support, and this is often not the most important action. Thus policy coordination, or in some cases the integration of transfers and services, is even more important than for other recipients of social assistance.
- The groups' members may not be expected to work; thus in serving them, labor disincentives are not an issue.
- The political support for assisting the groups is varied, for example, it can be quite high for the elderly but low for ethnic minorities.

This chapter focuses on two vulnerable groups—the elderly and people with disabilities—that are important in all countries and for which many countries make specific provisions in their safety nets. We give parallel treatment to orphans and vulnerable children because this is an important group in countries suffering from conflict or severe HIV/

AIDS epidemics, one that has catalyzed safety net policy in, for example, Sub-Saharan Africa. These three are not the only groups that matter in each country, but by discussing them we illustrate country- and group-specific diagnostics. Ethnicity is a cross-cutting issue (box 8.1).

8.1 Income Support for the Elderly

Concern about income support for the elderly has been a theme in social policy for decades. In recent years, frustration with stalled coverage of social security schemes in many countries has resulted in interest in the provision of noncontributory assistance to the elderly.

BOX 8.1 Including Ethnic Minorities in Safety Net Programs

Equitable social assistance programs include ethnic groups in proportion to their share of the poor. If an ethnic group is found to be underrepresented, then the cause of underrepresentation should be found and corrected. Following are some questions that can be helpful in such a diagnosis.

- Physical access
  - Does the program reach areas where the ethnic group lives, for example, specific rural or remote regions or urban neighborhoods?
  - Does the program implicitly or explicitly make participation difficult for those who have moved recently or who do so frequently, for example, immigrants, internally displaced people, migrant workers, and pastoralists?
- Cultural access
  - Are the images and language used in program information materials culturally sensitive and inclusive?
  - Do language barriers exist in the available information or between staff and potential clients?
  - Does the program employ members of the group for outreach and intake activities?
  - Do the results of monitoring of program satisfaction, especially in relation to the respect shown to clients, show differences by ethnic group?
- Program rules and benefits
  - Is the definition of the assistance unit (individual, family, household, community) consistent with the group's culture?
  - Does the form of income or assets counted in targeting criteria capture welfare equally well for different ethnic groups?
  - If community-based targeting is used, are communities homogenous or heterogeneous with respect to ethnicity?
  - Is the type of benefit appropriate, especially for in-kind benefits? For instance, supplying roofing materials to pastoralists or school lunches that include pork to Muslim children would not be useful.
  - Are any conditions attached to the receipt of benefits appropriate and are the services inclusive? For example, do schools teach in the group's language? Are health services available in the language of the group and accepted alongside traditional medicine?

THE INCREASING NUMBERS OF ELDERLY

The numbers of elderly are increasingly markedly. The United Nations estimates that worldwide, 606 million people are over the age of 60, or roughly 10 percent of the world's population, and that this number is likely to more than double to 1.6 billion by 2050, when the elderly will account for 19 percent of the world's population. Of this elderly population, 62 percent currently live in developing countries, but by 2050, 80 percent of the world's elderly will live in developing countries. Among the elderly, the fraction over the age of 80 is currently about 12 percent and is expected to increase to about 19 percent by 2050 (UN 2002).

At the same time that the number of elderly is increasing, the prospects for their independent support in old age do not seem to be improving greatly or are not doing so uniformly and reliably. Several means of support are possible, with each having different factors that affect their sufficiency as shown below:

- As individuals age, their capacity for work diminishes, although they may continue to engage in informal work or smallholder agriculture. As they become very old, their ability to rely on their own earnings will further decrease, and at the same time, their health care costs will likely increase. Formalization of the labor market makes a gradual reduction of work effort more difficult, and retirement then tends to become the norm.

- The elderly have traditionally been supported by pooled income in multigenerational families. Never a perfect safety net, this traditional source of support will become less reliable in the future as demographic changes reduce the number of children on whom the elderly can rely. Urbanization and the rise of the nuclear family increase the numbers of elderly who are not part of multigenerational households and raise the costs of supporting them because two dwellings are more expensive to maintain than one and economies of scale are lost. Moreover, if the separate households are distant from each other, the nonincome aspects of support become far harder to supply and may require payment to outsiders, raising the costs of support even higher.

- Savings are a desirable means of support for the elderly. The ability of today's workers to save may increase in those situations where poverty is declining and financial markets and instruments are improving, but many of the currently elderly or soon to be elderly will not have sufficient savings because of low lifetime earnings and the shortage of safe and reliable savings vehicles.

- Publicly mandated pension schemes are the first social protection response to aging, meant to overcome all the previous insufficiencies, but their coverage is still quite low in most regions and prospects for major improvements are disheartening.

POVERTY STATUS OF THE ELDERLY

In finding a policy response to the issue of income support for the elderly, policy makers must consider both the needs of the elderly relative to those of other groups and the choice of instruments. While thinking creatively now about how to handle the increasing numbers of elderly in the future is appropriate, policy makers should bear in mind that the elderly are not always poorer than other groups, although such diagnoses are fraught with technical problems (box 8.2).

BOX 8.2 **The Complexities of Measuring Poverty among Different Age Groups**

Measuring the poverty status of the elderly in comparison with that of other age or population groups is complex, Most elderly live in multigenerational households, which raises such conceptual issues as whether it is of interest to measure the income or assets attributed to the elderly or those of the entire household, and practical issues about how little data from household surveys are actually available at the individual level. In practice, much poverty analysis (see appendix A) divides total consumption by household size to arrive at per capita household consumption.

Accounting for the complexities in the cost structures households of different compositions and sizes face can be important. If children need less food than adults because they eat less and food accounts for a large share of household expenditure, per capita measures will, all else being equal, overstate poverty in households with many children. Adjustments for this are referred to as equivalence scales. Certain expenses, such as heating, lighting, and to a certain extent housing, are household rather than individual expenses. For such items, a number of people living together can do so more cheaply, in per capita terms, than living separately. Adjustments for this come under the heading of scale economies. Most economists recognize the conceptual desirability of the adjustments, but the debate on sensible coefficients and their proper estimation is ongoing.

Lanjouw, Milanovic, and Paternostro (1998) demonstrate the importance of carefully considering both equivalence scales and scale economies in their study of seven countries in Eastern Europe and the former Soviet Union. With no equivalence scales, in all seven countries the elderly are less than averagely poor and households with three or more children are poorer than average, sometimes markedly so. Even a modest adjustment to equivalence scales (assuming that children have consumption needs that are 70 to 90 percent those of adults) causes this ranking to be reversed. This matters powerfully for policy: should money go to pensions or to child allowances and services for children?

Deaton and Zaidi (2002) and Lanjouw, Milanovic, and Paternostro (1998) provide excellent source materials on the construction of equivalence scales and scale economies. Their general approach uses the equation adult equivalence = $(A+\alpha K)\beta$, where A is the number of adults, K is the number of children, α adjusts for age equivalences and β for economies of scale. A per capita measure of household welfare assumes that there are no economies of scale ($\beta = 1$) and that children and adults have the same requirements ($\alpha = 1$). If household consumption is largely food, as in the case of the ultra poor in very poor countries, economies of scale are few, and thus β is close to 1. As children eat less than adults, equivalence scales are important and significantly different from 1 for young children, thus $\alpha < 1$. As households and nations grow wealthier, the share of resources spent on food declines and the share of household "public" goods, such as housing and durable goods, rises, so scale economies increase, implying that $\beta < 1$. At the same time, children consume more nonfood goods such as clothing and toys, all of which add to the costs of supporting them and reduce the importance of food-based equivalence scales, causing α to rise closer to 1.

We are not aware of any worldwide comparisons of poverty among the elderly and other age groups that meet the minimum technical criteria in relation to economies of scale and equivalence, much less that use comparably defined income aggregates. Tables 8.1 and 8.2 present two regional compilations that are internally consistent within each region.

These tables show that the elderly are not always poor compared with other age groups, which in some settings runs counter to people's intuition. The technical numbers can be reconciled with that intuition in two ways. One has to do with the definition of the household, whereby the elderly may indeed have little independent income and be dependents in a larger household, but so long as the larger household is not poor, the technical numbers will not count the elderly as poor. If pride in one's own income is important or if sharing among household members is not equal, the numbers will underestimate the real welfare of the elderly. The other explanation concerns households that contain only the elderly. The perception that these will be very poor is often strong. Indeed, a lack of family support is sometimes why elderly people live alone, and this can be associated with extreme destitution. However, the elderly may live alone for other reasons. One is that they may prefer it and will do so when they can afford to. This is supported by findings in the Organisation for Economic Co-operation and Development (OECD) and is a common pattern among upper-income quintiles in developing countries (Schwarz 2003). Alternatively, the elderly may be part of strong multigenerational households in which the elderly and children remain in rural areas while working-age parents migrate to a location with better earnings possibilities and provide remittances to those left behind.

The relative poverty rates among different groups, by age as well as by other categories such as unemployed, working poor, and the like, will help determine how big a place support for the elderly should have in the overall safety net. After determining that, the issue of how to formulate that support arises.

TABLE 8.1 **Percentage of the Population Living in Poverty by Age, Selected Sub-Saharan African Countries and Years**

Country	Children aged 0–14	The elderly	All people
Burkina Faso, 1998	54.5	56.3	52.0
Burundi, 1998	62.5	59.2	61.2
Cameroon, 1996	63.6	64.2	60.9
Côte d'Ivoire, 1998	39.1	46.7	36.7
Ethiopia, 2000	41.6	43.7	40.9
Gambia, The, 1998	65.5	68.2	62.2
Ghana, 1998	47.0	45.5	43.6
Guinea, 1994	40.5	44.0	38.1
Kenya, 1997	53.5	53.8	49.7
Madagascar, 2001	66.4	55.3	62.0
Malawi, 1997	65.4	71.6	63.9
Mozambique, 1996	71.4	65.8	68.9
Nigeria, 1996	66.6	59.5	63.4
Uganda, 1999	50.1	52.2	48.2
Zambia, 1998	67.8	79.4	66.7

SOURCE: Kakwani and Subbarao 2005.

NOTE: Calorie-based equivalence scales are used and the coefficient for economies of scale is set at 0.7.

TABLE 8.2 **Percentage of the Population Living in Poverty by Age, Selected Eastern European Countries, Selected Years 1993–5**

Age (years)	Bulgaria	Estonia	Hungary	Kyrgyz Republic	Poland	Russian Federation
0–4	29.0	33.3	30.0	46.4	35.3	47.9
5–9	28.2	32.0	26.0	46.0	31.6	42.9
10–14	24.2	34.1	20.9	41.1	27.6	40.5
15–24	24.1	26.4	19.7	41.8	23.6	36.6
25–34	23.5	27.6	21.7	43.3	26.2	41.6
35–44	18.8	28.6	17.1	38.2	21.3	34.7
45–54	20.2	24.1	13.7	35.2	16.0	29.7
55–64	27.6	31.6	15.6	42.6	14.5	41.7
65–74	35.0	37.0	23.6	47.6	(18.3)	45.0
75 +	47.5	47.9	37.7	41.4	22.1	45.9
All	26.1	30.5	20.6	42.5	(23.0)	39.4

SOURCE: Braithwaite, Grootaert, and Milanovic 1999.

NOTE: OECD scales of equivalence are used where the first adult is weighted as 1, a second adult is weighted as 0.7, and a child is weighted as 0.5.

POLICY OPTIONS TO SUPPORT THE POOR ELDERLY

Four policy options are available for providing the poor elderly with income support: (1) expanding contributory pensions, (2) providing universal noncontributory or so-called social pensions, (3) providing targeted social pensions, or (4) assisting the poor elderly within a general social assistance or safety net program. Many of the poor may also need assistance with access to medical and social care services

Contributory Pensions

While often seen as the long-run solution to providing income support for the elderly, contributory pension programs are far from universal. In the typical low- to middle-income country, coverage ranges from single digits to about 50 percent, with an average of about 20 percent (Holzmann and Hinz 2005). The large share of informal employment in developing countries' economies still presents a binding constraint to formal contributory pension programs in much of the developing world, and this situation is unlikely to change soon. Even in the more formalized economies of Europe and Central Asia that had nearly 100 percent coverage during the era of central planning, the share of workers contributing to pension schemes has dropped to 75 percent and is continuing to decline as the public sector's share of the economy decreases and self-employment and the informal sector grow.

Even if coverage of contributory schemes were universal, this would not be a complete solution, as those who have been poor for their entire lives and those who have worked in the labor market intermittently may accrue rights to pensions that are too small to support them. Many of the pension reforms around the world that have taken place in the last 15 years have created tighter links between contributions and benefits and extended contribution periods and/or lowered the share of wages that the pension replaces, thereby exacerbating the problem. Another aim of many of these pension reforms is to increase coverage and contribution rates, but so far the improvements have been minor.

For more information about the role and design of contributory pensions, see, for example, Holzmann and Hinz (2005) or the papers delivered at the Closing the Gap Conference, held in Tokyo in 2008.[1] We here focus on the other options, which fall into the definition of safety nets as used in this book (noncontributory transfers targeted toward the poor).

Universal Social Pensions

The problems inherent in expanding contributory pensions, especially in countries with low coverage, is leading to a great deal of policy interest in providing social or noncontributory pensions to the elderly as evidenced by, for example, the International Labour Organisation's Global Campaign on Social Security and Coverage for All (Cichon and Hagemejer 2006; ILO 2001) and the World Bank's pension position paper (Holzmann and Hinz 2005). A growing number of countries have implemented universal, noncontributory social pensions. Their principal selling point is their apparent simplicity: by being limited to the elderly, the issue of labor disincentives does not arise as might occur with a more general social assistance program, and by being universal, the administrative and political issues of targeting are eliminated; however, by being universal, such programs will be expensive and much of the money will go to the nonpoor.

Various authors have calculated the fiscal costs of universal pensions, most often in Sub-Saharan Africa, because this is where both contributory pension schemes and more general safety nets that might provide alternatives are least developed. Schwarz (2003) calculates the cost of providing US$1 per day to all those older than 65 in 40 Sub-Saharan African countries and comes up with estimates that range from 0.1 percent of gross domestic product (GDP) in the Seychelles to 10.6 percent of GDP in Ethiopia. Confining the pension to those older than 75 reduces costs somewhat—for example, to 3.0 percent in Ethiopia. Kakwani and Subbarao (2005) simulate the impact of a transfer calibrated to be 70 percent of the country-specific poverty line to all those older than 65 in 15 Sub-Saharan African countries and find that costs for this range from 0.7 percent of GDP in Madagascar to 2.4 percent of GDP in Ethiopia.

In those developing countries that use universal social pensions, they are commonly limited to the very old and provide small benefits. This keeps costs within bounds and encourages some self-targeting, as the less poor may not find that collecting the pension is worth their while. Nepal, for example, pays Nrs 150 per month (US$2, or about 10 percent of the average per capita income) to all citizens age 75 and over, or about 1.3 percent of the population, at a cost of about 0.1 percent of GDP (Palacios and Rajan 2004). By contrast, Namibia's universal social pension is sufficient to support a family of three at the food poverty line. Targeting outcomes for social pensions are, on the scale of international transfer programs, not very good. According to Coady, Grosh, and Hoddinott (2004), programs that are targeted to the elderly deliver only 15 percent more resources to the poor than would completely universal programs. In regression analysis of outcomes and methods across targeting outcomes, demographic targeting by old age alone does not produce statistically significant results.

Universal social pensions are not without administrative challenges. They escape the problem of means testing, but they still face the challenge of establishing age, which is not easy in countries where civil registries were incomplete at the time the current elderly were born. This is quite common, especially in poor countries and for the poor within those countries, and can lower coverage or require creative ways of improving documentation. In Nepal, for example, the program requires a citizenship certificate. Twenty percent of the applicants did not have such a certificate, and so had to compile supporting documents about place of birth and age. The government allowed those with voter cards issued by the Election Commission or with horoscopes to use those as alternative forms for establishing age, which has facilitated high coverage rates.

A universal program is bigger than a needs-based option. By virtue of being large, such a scheme will require administrative capacity congruent with reaching large numbers of elderly people who will, on average, be poorer, less literate, less mobile, and more rural than the general population. In addition, as the benefit per client will be low, administration may either account for a higher than usual share of total expenditures or may be constrained to expenditures that are so low they impair service delivery.

Implementation approaches and experience are varied. The Nepalese scheme reaches about three-quarters of its eligible population through village development committees. Some of those eligible may not apply because of the low benefit, which makes the effective coverage of the target population even higher. Palacios and Rajan (2004) report few problems with corruption and relatively low transaction costs for beneficiaries and attribute the program's smooth functioning in a country with such a dispersed population to decentralization. In Namibia, by contrast, outreach to rural areas was problematic for a number of years, and total system coverage was around 50 to 60 percent, lower in poorer and more remote regions. A system of mobile cash dispensers to visit remote areas was devised and coverage has improved to 88 percent, although this required raising administrative costs from 7 to 14 percent of total program costs (Subbarao 1998).

Targeted Social Pensions

Given the high fiscal costs of a universal pension, the idea of limiting the transfer to the poor is logical. Kakwani and Subbarao (2005) note that limiting a social pension reduces costs to a little more than half of those for a universal pension for most of the 15 Sub-Saharan African countries included in their simulations. The exact savings will depend on poverty rates and trade-offs made between the breadth of coverage and the amount of the benefit.

Targeting a social pension introduces all the challenges of targeting in general (see chapter 4). While the challenges are not trivial, something effective can usually be accomplished in most settings. Moreover, the increasing number of well-implemented means-testing and proxy means-testing systems around the world suggests that at least in middle-income countries with sufficient administrative capacity, an appropriate option is available and apparently politically viable. Community-based targeting methods whereby local groups or civil society representatives decide who in the community should benefit may work satisfactorily as well, although relatively little evidence is available on their performance or on how to best organize such systems.

Any sort of targeting for a social pension program will face the issue of whose means to assess, those of the elderly alone or those of the entire households in which they live. Different philosophies prevail depending largely on attitudes about the role of family support. For example, eligibility assessments in Germany, Italy, Portugal, and Spain take children's income into account; this is not the case in Belgium, France, the Netherlands, Sweden, and the United Kingdom (de Neubourg 2008).

If the answer is to consider only the means of the elderly, an additional layer of complexity is added in trying to sort out intrahousehold ownership and allocation decisions. Targeting to the elderly may also induce households to reallocate their assets in response to the targeting rules. Whether this is good or bad for the economy or for the elderly will depend on the specific situation, but the issue bears consideration. If only the means of the elderly are considered, recertification may be performed less frequently than for the working-age population. In the U.S. Food Stamp Program, for example, recertification for households comprised only of the elderly is required every two years, while for working-age households it is required every 3 to 12 months depending on their composition.

Another possibility is to target only households comprised of the elderly or of the elderly and children with no working-age adults. This is attractive in that such households are usually a small portion of all the elderly, which lowers the total costs of a pension program, and it also seemingly solves the problems of work disincentives and of attribution of means in a multigenerational family. However, it contains an adverse incentive of its own: the possibility that families will keep their elderly in separate households rather than absorbing them as they might have done in the absence of the external support. In some cases, this can be viewed as positive in that more of the elderly who wish to live alone will be able to do so for longer, but it could also include less benign cases of households pushing out elderly family members into precarious situations in order to qualify for the support. If the benefit is small, its impact on decisions about household composition and appropriate care for the elderly may also be small given additional economic, cultural, and emotional factors.

With either universal or targeted social pensions, an important policy design issue is the level of the benefit compared to that provided by the contributory program. The higher the benefit in the noncontributory program, the more it will reduce incentives for participation in and compliance with the contributory system. This suggests that a low level of benefit should be paid, but a threshold exists below which it is not worth having a program. Problems will arise if the social pension system grants a benefit that is not much lower than the minimum the contributory system provides. In illustrating the pitfalls of either too high or too low a pension, Schwarz (2003) cites the following cases. In Uruguay, the minimum contributory pension paid at age 65 after 35 years of service is less than what the noncontributory pension makes available at age 70; consequently, contribution compliance is relatively low. By contrast, the benefits the social pension programs in Argentina and Turkey provide are so low that they do not contribute to poverty alleviation.

Inclusion in General Social Assistance

If a social pension program is to be targeted, the question arises as to whether to include the support in a more broadly based social assistance program, or if no such program exists, whether to develop a general social assistance program rather than a targeted social pension. Technically, general help provided to all those in need equally is the preferred policy, and a departure from this initial presumption makes sense only if a rationale exists for providing different groups with different services. Moreover, having a single program eliminates duplication of functions and minimizes administrative costs.

Some factors, mostly intangible, would mitigate against this default option:

- Critics of social policy and politicians often believe that the moral consensus that the elderly need support is stronger than any consensus that the poor in general need support, though as discussed in box 8.3, this may not always be the case.

- Stigmatization of beneficiaries may be less for a social pension than for a general needs-based program, especially if a social security agency rather than a welfare agency administers the social pension.

BOX 8.3 **The Political Economy of Old-Age Support**

Some people question the priority given to concerns about poverty in old-age and pension programs over concerns about other vulnerable groups and other welfare programs on efficiency grounds. James (2000), for example, notes that human capital theory supports investing in young children over the elderly. Van der Berg (2002) suggests that a focus on unemployment would be more appropriate for reducing poverty in South Africa; for Brazil, Paes de Barros and Carvalho (2004) argue for shifting public spending away from pensions and toward families with children.

Direct evidence from attitudinal surveys across societies and age groups shows that concerns about poverty in old age are strong and widely shared. Atkinson (1995) suggests that the population at large is more willing to support poor older people because old age is more easily verifiable and less subject to moral hazard, compared with unemployment insurance, for example. In addition, most people expect to be old one day, but perhaps not unemployed, or single parents, or disabled (Lund 1999).

Four main factors appear to lie behind the development of noncontributory old-age pensions in Brazil (the rural old-age pension) and South Africa. First, in both countries, government officials were committed to universalizing welfare institutions (Delgado and Cardoso 2000; van der Berg 1997). Second, in both countries, the noncontributory pension program involved an explicit redistribution from urban to rural areas to reduce internal migration. Cash transfers to poor older people appeared to be a politically acceptable, if not the most effective, instrument for injecting purchasing power into rural areas, because unlike other types of transfers, pensions are less likely to create work disincentives. Third, in both countries unpopular regimes saw noncontributory pensions as instrumental in reducing social unrest arising from agricultural liberalization and landlessness (in Brazil) and the homelands system (in South Africa). Fourth, renewal of the social contracts in Brazil with the 1988 constitution after two decades of dictatorship and in South Africa with the gradual dismantling and final fall of apartheid were key factors in the extensions of noncontributory pension programs. These events encouraged debate and consensus around the need to establish and uphold everyone's rights to social protection.

SOURCES: Barrientos 2004; World Bank 2005n.

- Advocates for the elderly suggest that receipt of pensions in their own name may empower the elderly within a household, a particularly appealing possibility where elder abuse is thought to be an issue, although little actual evidence is available to determine either how widespread elder abuse might be or to what extent an independent pension might prevent it.

The administrators of a general social assistance program may adjust certain program features to include more of the elderly or to give them larger benefits. Formulas for proxy means tests often take the demographic composition of households into account, with the elderly contributing more to the scoring of need than those of working age. Thus households with elderly members are more likely to be declared in need. Other possible adjustments include setting a higher eligibility threshold for some families than others or disregarding some income when calculating household income. In Bulgaria, the eligibility threshold for the Guaranteed Minimum Income Program is adjusted depending on family characteristics whereby it is higher for families with elderly members (Shopov forthcoming). In Jamaica's PATH initiative, the formula for the proxy means test had to be adjusted to lower the weight given to housing assets to allow significant numbers of elderly living alone to participate. The elderly receive their full payment even if children in the household default on the conditions pertinent to them and fail to qualify for their own benefits.

Social Services and Care

Income is not the only need that the elderly have. Medical care is an obvious and expensive need. Its financing and organization are beyond the topic of this book, but note that countries as diverse as Armenia, China, and Jamaica grant fee waivers for health care in the public system to beneficiaries of general social assistance programs. This approach takes advantage of a single targeting mechanism to supply two key needs of the elderly, and is thus administratively frugal.

Some elderly also need social care services to assist them with basic housekeeping and/or personal care functions. In most cases, family or community members supply such assistance, but in OECD countries an increasing range of public and private providers are also involved. The consensus is that, generally, community-based services that help keep the elderly in their own or a multigenerational household are far preferable to institutionalization, yielding better quality care and costing less, but such services are often undersupplied, particularly in developing countries.

DIVERSITY IN PRACTICE

Social pension practices vary enormously around the world (table 8.3). Such countries as Bolivia, Botswana, Mauritius, Namibia, and Nepal have universal schemes, whereas other countries such as Australia, Bangladesh, India, Italy, New Zealand Senegal, South Africa, and a number of Latin American countries employ targeted social pensions. The elderly are, by definition, included in general social assistance schemes and such programs exist almost everywhere, although they are often so underfunded as to be ineffectual. Sufficient funding and system development has been common in Europe and Central Asia and found occasionally elsewhere, for example, in China and Sri Lanka.

TABLE 8.3 **Characteristics of Social Pension Programs, Selected Countries and Years**

Country and program	% of pop. 65 or older (2002)	No. of beneficiaries (year)	Monthly pension (US$)	Expenditure (% of GDP)
Argentina, noncontributory old-age and disability pension	13	113,006 (2000)	153	0.2
Bangladesh, old-age allowance	5	403,110 (2002)	2	n.a.
Bolivia, Bono Solidario	6	n.a.	20	0.9
Botswana, universal old-age pensions	5	71,000 (1999)	24	0.4
Brazil, Beneficio de Prestação Continuada	8	1,215,988 (2000)	87	0.3
Brazil, rural old-age pension	n.a.	6,024,328 (2000)	87	1.0
Chile, Pensiones Asistenciales de Ancianidad y de Invalidez	11	163,338 (2001)	60	0.4
India, National Old-Age Pension Scheme	8	2,200,000 (2000)	2	...
Mauritius, old-age pension	9	112,000 (2001)	Age 60–89, 50; 90–99, 220; 100+, 252	2.0
Namibia, old-age pension	6	82,000 (1994)	26	0.7
Nepal, Old-Age Allowance Program	6	191,953 (2001–2)	2	n.a.
South Africa, old-age pension	6	2,002,320 (2003)	93	1.4
Sri Lanka, public assistance	10	425,477 (2000)	1.25, 4 beneficiaries max. per household	n.a.
Uruguay, old-age and disability pensions	17	64,600 (2001)	90	0.6

SOURCE: Holzmann and Hinz 2005.

NOTE: ... = negligible, n.a. = not available.

8.2 Income Support for Orphans and Vulnerable Children

Children are considered orphans when one or both parents have died. Other children are vulnerable too. Definitions of orphans and vulnerable children usually include ill children and those with sick caregivers, and sometimes other groups such as street children, children in institutions, child soldiers, child prostitutes, and other groups most of whom are not cared for in a family setting or who are involved in the worst forms of child labor. We focus on children who are currently in a family setting, because the other groups of children need much more specialized and wide-ranging assistance than given by the income support programs covered in this book.[2]

SCOPE OF THE PROBLEM

Rates of orphaning have reached huge levels in many countries because of conflict and HIV/AIDS. In Sub-Saharan Africa, 11 countries have rates of orphaning above 15 percent (figure 8.1), a further 24 countries have rates of orphaning above 10 percent, and the regionwide average is 12 percent. The issue of adequate support for orphans and vulnerable children is thus on the agenda in these countries; indeed, it has focused attention on the issue of social assistance generally. The problem is not wholly African, however. Afghanistan, Haiti, the Democratic People's Republic of Korea, and the Lao People's Democratic Republic also have rates of orphaning of about 10 percent.

Orphans and vulnerable children are more likely to be older children; more than half are 12 to 17 years old (figure 8.2). This stems from three factors. First, if the parents' deaths are caused by HIV/AIDS, those parents in-

FIGURE 8.1 **Sub-Saharan African Countries with Orphaning Rates of 15 Percent or Greater, 2003**

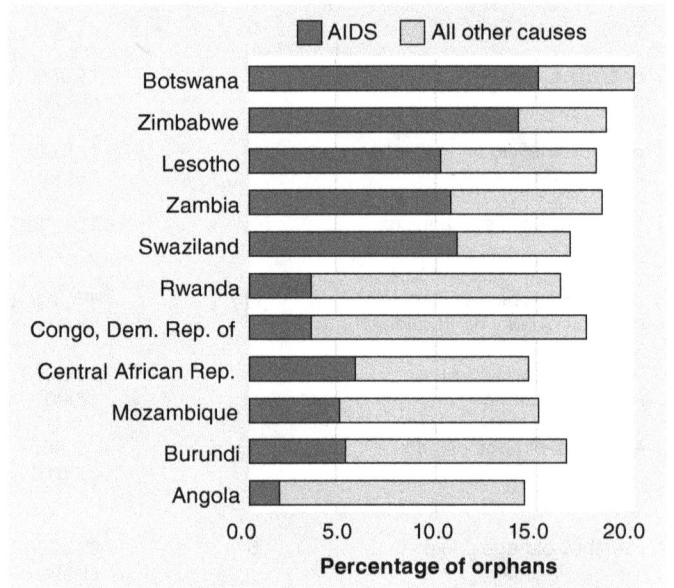

SOURCE: Author calculations from UNAIDS, UNICEF, and USAID 2004, appendix 1, table 1.

FIGURE 8.2 **Percentage of Orphans by Age, Asia, Latin America and the Caribbean, and Sub-Saharan Africa, 2003**

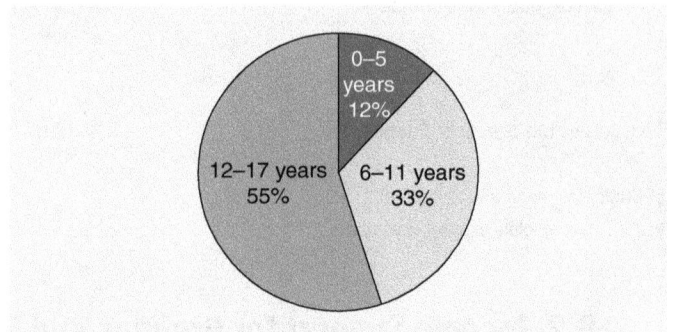

SOURCE: UNAIDS, UNICEF, and USAID 2004, reproduced with permission.

fected around the time of the child's birth or later may survive for a number of years following the child's birth. Second, children born with HIV have a short life expectancy. Third, children orphaned at young ages, especially if their mothers die, have low survival rates.

Traditionally, orphaned children are absorbed into households within the extended family or community structure. More than 90 percent of orphaned children in Africa are in the care of their extended families. This option is far preferable to institutionalization on grounds of both quality of care and cost of care; however, with orphaning rates so much higher than the 5 to 6 percent found in countries with little conflict or HIV/AIDS, traditional family support networks are being taxed to the breaking point (UNAIDS, UNICEF, and USAID 2004).

THE ORPHAN DISADVANTAGE

The literature on poverty agrees that households with higher dependency rates are more likely to be poor, and this is also likely to be true for families fostering orphans. To the extent that orphans are absorbed by those branches of the family best able to support them, this effect may be attenuated, but the inherent issue of high dependency rates remains. Deininger, Crommelynck, and Kempaka (2002), for example, find that when Ugandan households absorb foster children, their risk of poverty rises and their investment decreases by about a quarter.

Orphans and vulnerable children tend to be more at risk for poor human capital outcomes than other children. Case, Paxson and Ableidinger (2004) show that orphans are less likely to be enrolled in school than nonorphans in the same household. The magnitude of the effect of orphaning varies by country and by definition of orphanhood. Evans and Miguel (2007) find that a maternal death lowers the probability of enrollment by 9 percent in western Kenya, compared with 4 percent for a paternal death. Ainsworth and Filmer (2002) find similar variability across countries with high orphaning rates (table 8.4). The policy environment matters as well. Yamano (2007) finds that before 1974, while Kenya still had primary school fees, rural Kenyan children who lost a mother before age 15 had one year less of education than nonorphans, but after 1974, when Kenya introduced free primary education, orphans did not suffer from this disadvantage. Nevertheless, the concern that orphans and vulnerable children may face disadvantages compared with other children is intuitive and is more often than not backed empirically.

POLICY OPTIONS

To the degree that high dependency rates cause poverty and reduced human capital formation for children in the household, providing income support to families fostering or adopting orphans and vulnerable children is an appropriate policy, although income support is only part of the needed public actions. Orphans and vulnerable children also need health care; education; family law, child protective services, and other legal protection; job training; and psychosocial care. Indeed, Subbarao and Coury (2004) provide a list of interventions eight pages long that may address some aspects of the problem. Gertler and others (2004) find that orphans' enrollment in school suffers even when the economic impact of orphaning is not a factor, which underscores the need for both complementary services and services beyond income support.

Among income support programs, those most pertinent to orphans and vulnerable children are cash and in-kind transfers, whether conditional or not, and waivers for health care and education fees. Workfare programs will not affect orphans and vulnerable children directly, and the households that care for them may be relatively short on adult labor,

TABLE 8.4 **Variations in Orphans' School Enrollment, Selected Countries and Years**

	Overall country enrollment rate		
Enrollment differential	**Low (< 50%)**	**Medium (50–80%)**	**High (> 80%)**
All orphans have lower enrollment	• Benin 1996	• Cambodia 1999 • Central African Republic 1994/95 • Côte d'Ivoire 1994 • Guatemala 1999 • Madagascar 1997 • Malawi 1992 • Nicaragua 1997/98	• Brazil 1996 • Kenya 1998
Only maternal orphans have lower enrollment	• Guinea 1999	...	• Dominican Republic 1996
Only paternal orphans have lower enrollment	...	...	• Uganda 1999/2000
Only two-parent orphans have lower enrollment	...	• Mozambique 1997 • Zambia 1998	...
Maternal orphans and two-parent orphans have lower enrollment	• Burkina Faso 1992/93	• Cameroon 1998 • Haiti 1994/95	• Zimbabwe 1999
Paternal orphans and two-parent orphans have lower enrollment	• Senegal 1992/93	• Togo 1998	• Ghana 1998
Orphans equally likely to be enrolled as nonorphans	• Chad 1996/97 • Mali 1995/96 • Niger 1998	...	• South Africa 1998
Orphans more likely to be enrolled than nonorphans	...	• Nigeria 1999 • Tanzania 1996	...

SOURCE: Ainsworth and Filmer 2002.

NOTE: ... = none in sample. When an entry refers to more than one year, this indicates sample years.

especially if they are also caring for family members with HIV/AIDS. Thus workfare programs may not be effective in reaching these children even indirectly. Other actions to help improve household earning capacity, such as the provision of microfinance and agricultural assistance, may be helpful, although the same drawbacks will apply to households short of labor, which may find taking advantage of such assistance to be difficult.

As noted earlier, more than half of orphans and vulnerable children are aged 12 to 17, an age group for which both dropout rates and school costs can be high. Thus programs for orphans and vulnerable children often focus on ensuring access to education and/ or training. In its review of social protection innovations for educationally marginalized children, the Mobile Task Team (2005) identify 48 different types of intervention at the level of the child, household, school, sector, or country, some with education outcomes as the primary goal, others with these as a secondary goal. Examples range from providing various forms of transfers or fee waivers to changing curricula, providing nonformal schooling, and improving school infrastructure or management to undertaking initiatives that improve fostering or child rights, as these too will have a bearing on educational outcomes.

There is a great deal of advocacy by organizations and individuals in favor of social pensions in Sub-Saharan Africa to help handle the orphans and vulnerable children problem (see, for example, HelpAge International 2007). Grandparents are an important source of care for orphans and vulnerable children. In Namibia, the proportion of orphans who have lost both parents or one parent and are not living with the surviving parent and being taken care of by grandparents rose from 44 percent in 1992 to 61 percent in 2000. Increases have also been recorded in Tanzania and Zimbabwe (HelpAge International 2004). Impact evaluations of the social pension programs in Brazil and South Africa show that pensions are shared within households and that grandchildren benefit substantially, including by achieving improved human capital outcomes (Case 2001; Case and Deaton 1998; Carvalho 2000a; Duflo 2003). Providing support to grandparents is intuitively appealing, because households composed only of grandparents and children and with no working-age adults are likely to be limited in their capacity to earn.

The logic of providing social pensions to care for orphans and vulnerable children is, however, somewhat flawed. If the problem is the welfare of children, then a child allowance, which could be universal or targeted by poverty or status as an orphan and/or vulnerable child (OVC), is logical. It will reach all the children targeted, including those not being cared for by grandparents, who account for a large share of orphans and vulnerable children (sometimes the majority). Moreover, child allowances would be allocated per child, not per elderly person. This would be a better solution for income problems in the iconic situation of an elderly woman caring for half a dozen or more grandchildren.

The question of whether to target categorically or by need arises for orphans and vulnerable children as it does for the elderly. In terms of accuracy, categorical targeting to orphans or foster children will suffer from high errors of inclusion and exclusion. Deaths, especially from AIDS, are not concentrated among the poor, but rather are spread across the welfare distribution; thus orphans and vulnerable children will be found in families at all income levels. Of course, many of the countries greatly affected by AIDS were poor already, so they have many very poor children who are not orphans or vulnerable children.

Targeting by OVC status is attractive at first glance, because the moral case for supporting these children is so compelling; giving the support on behalf of the children to the school they attend or to teenagers themselves would seem to be helpful in relation to intrahousehold allocation issues. However, incentives related to fostering, stigmatization, and intrahousehold allocation issues are particularly relevant in the case of orphans and vulnerable children. Programs must avoid directly or indirectly influencing extended families to leave these children uncared for so that they qualify for assistance, a risk that might occur if benefits were reserved for child-headed households. International activists in this area are so concerned that assistance provided only for orphans can be stigmatizing and can create jealousy on the part of unorphaned children in the households that care for them that the programming guidance for orphans and vulnerable children (UNAIDS, UNICEF, and USAID 2004) recommends against singling out children orphaned by HIV/AIDS and thus many cases of targeting by OVC status.

Where targeting criteria are not related to OVC status but to poverty more generally, general know-how on targeting is pertinent (chapter 4), although in the poor countries where the orphaning crisis is most severe, the structures for means or proxy means tests have not been developed. Thus community-based targeting is often the method used despite limited understanding of how to do it best, where it is suited, and what outcomes can be expected.

Notwithstanding the multiagency programming guidance to the contrary, many programs do target exclusively to orphans and vulnerable children or prioritize them among other poor children. In countries with high OVC rates, poverty is high and social protection budgets are low. Therefore the use of criteria related to OVC status to help in a difficult triage is not surprising. In a review of social protection programs for educationally marginalized children, the Mobile Task Team (2005) reports those programs that had education as a primary objective did target orphans and vulnerable children in some way. Subbarao and Coury (2004) cite several examples of the use of OVC-related targeting criteria (table 8.5).

TABLE 8.5 **Targeting Criteria for OVC by Setting: Burundi, Malawi, and Selected Countries Served by World Vision**

Setting	Targeting criteria for OVC
Burundi, 2002 (postconflict country, HIV/AIDS)	OVC are ranked in order of priority as follows: • category 1—double orphans who do not receive any external support, households consisting of orphans and headed by a child • category 2—children separated from their parents who live in refugee camps or are displaced • category 3—single orphans who receive no support from their surviving parent • category 4—double orphans who are living with very poor families
Malawi (Erthemberi area), 1998 (HIV/AIDS)	Needy OVC are selected and a list of the most needy is drawn up according to the following criteria: • Orphans • Children with no food, no clothes, and no bedding material and blankets • Children who are not attending school • Children with unemployed parents who are doing small jobs for neighbors • Children of parents with mental and/or physical disabilities who are not receiving disability grants • Children living with grandmothers who are not eligible for state pensions
Various countries served by World Vision, 2002 (HIV/AIDS)	The following children are assisted: • Orphans • Children whose parents are chronically ill • Children living in households that have taken in orphans • Other children the community identifies as vulnerable

SOURCE: Subbarao and Coury 2004.

NOTE: Double orphans refers to children who have lost both parents. Single orphans refers to children who have lost one parent.

Kenya is piloting a cash transfer program meant for orphans and vulnerable children. Households within the pilot districts are eligible if they meet 14 of 18 poverty criteria and have orphans and vulnerable children, defined as orphans, chronically ill children, or children with chronically ill caregivers. These criteria yield more children in the districts covered than the budget will be able to support when the program is scaled up, so priority is given to child-headed households (and to larger households among these), then to households headed by the elderly (and among these to those with the most orphans and vulnerable children), and then to households with working-age adult caregivers (and among these to those with the most orphans and vulnerable children). A preliminary evaluation of the targeting shows that the selection of households has not been very pro-poor (Hurrell and Ward 2008). The report suggests that the selection of districts for the pilot was not well targeted geographically. This is a common phenomenon when the criteria used to select areas for pilots include ease of access or ease of implementation during start-up, but geographic targeting could be improved during program expansion. The 18 poverty criteria did not all do a good job of distinguishing poorer households and could be revised without an increase in complexity or required administrative capacity and such changes are being reviewed. The prioritization of households headed by children and the elderly was somewhat effective in prioritizing resources among those who met the poverty and OVC criteria. Errors of exclusion were large as expected given the pilot's limited resources. Overall, the pilot illustrates the difficulties of assisting orphans and vulnerable children in the context of widespread poverty and low administrative capacity. It also demonstrates the usefulness of undertaking early assessments of practice and making appropriate adjustments.

In 2001, Zimbabwe launched the Basic Education Assistance Module to help ensure that children could attend school. This is a nationwide school fee assistance program funded by the central government for vulnerable children aged 6 to 19. It assists about 1 million children a year with tuition, levies for other school costs, and examination fees. Community selection committees choose the students to receive the fee waivers. The committees are chosen annually and consist of the local school principal, two other members of the local school development committee, and six community representatives. Each school receives a budget allocation that determines how many children can receive fee waivers and compensates the school for their lost revenues. Selection criteria include orphanhood, being out of school because of hardship, and living on the street. The lists of selected students are made public for transparency. For more information on this program, see Mararike (2006).

South Africa has a means-tested child allowance, a child support grant to supplement the incomes of poor parents, and a foster child grant for orphans or others outside of parental care to replace the income that a parent might have provided. The foster child grant is paid monthly to foster parents and the benefit is about three times the child support grant. In 91 percent of cases the foster parent was a relative, in 41 percent of cases a grandparent, in 30 percent an aunt (Department of Social Development 2006). In 2006, the grant reached about 300,000 of about 1 million orphans, although many of the remainder may have benefited from the child support grant. The foster child grant is not means tested because fostering is not considered a poverty issue (Pauw and Mncube 2007).

The foster care grant seems to be an appropriate response to orphaning caused by the HIV/AIDS epidemic, but has faced some operational challenges. The application process requires that court sanction be given to fostering arrangements, but court dockets have been unable to keep up and backlogs have arisen. In addition, the administrative costs of the foster grant are high. Meintjes and others (2003) calculate the costs of a foster care placement and grant application as R 666, compared with R 30 for processing a child support grant. The terms of foster care prescribe permanent placement with the appointed guardian, whereas the normal African household structure is fluid, with both adults and children shifting between households within the extended family in response to evolving constraints and opportunities. In addition, according to program rules when children shift caregivers, the entire fostering process must start again. Critics of the system say that what the state needs to supply to most orphans is cash not care—that is, the income supplements are needed to help with the strain of higher dependency rates, but that most orphans are not in need of child protective services. They suggest that even though the foster care grant seems to be directly tailored to the problem of caring for children affected by HIV/AIDS, modifications to the child care grant might be a more practical solution to the problem (Meintjes and others 2003). This argument raises the question of whether the benefits provided by a program for orphans and vulnerable children should be viewed as a supplement to household income or an attempt to replace parental income.

Experience to date has not yet yielded a clear answer on how best to organize income support for orphans and vulnerable children and the families caring for them. Public action is still dwarfed by the scale of the problem and frustrated by the lack of general safety net systems in most of the countries affected, and much experimentation and learning remain to be done. Until more process and targeting evaluations of both OVC-specific and poverty targeting systems in low-income countries are available, program managers will have to take guidance and inspiration from practice to date, innovate from there, and ensure early assessment and fine-tuning of their innovations.

8.3 Income Support for People with Disabilities

Developing countries have paid inadequate attention to the issue of disability and safety nets. Though awareness of the need for such attention is gradually growing, a good body of experience from which to draw definitive lessons is not yet available.[3]

DEFINITIONS OF DISABILITY

Disability has often been defined as a physical, mental, or psychological condition that limits a person's activities. In the medical model of disability, the emphasis is on an impairment caused by a medical condition; thus policy responses tended to emphasize health care, and when that failed to reestablish functioning, palliative social assistance or social care. The social model, which has recently come to dominate disability research and policy discourse, emphasizes people's ability to function in their particular physical and social environment. Disability therefore arises when barriers prevent people with functional limitations caused by age, disease, injury, or other causes from participating fully in society. This approach leads to a wider range of policy options, especially with respect to accessibility to transportation, buildings, education, and employment. The World Health

Organization's *International Classification of Functioning, Disability and Health* (WHO 2001) embraces this concept and includes gradations of disability rather than focusing on a dichotomy of with disability versus without disability.

The difficulties of defining disability lead to serious problems in measuring it, both in relation to analytical work that could lead to a good understanding of the interactions between disability and poverty and in relation to operational problems encountered in directing assistance to those with disabilities.

Roughly 10 to 15 percent of the populations of developing countries have disabilities, with 2 to 3 percent typically having severe disabilities that preclude them from working and thus put them in need of long-term income support. This figure is in line with older estimates by the United Nations and surveys in several countries that have used new methods agreed on by the United Nations Washington Group on Disability Statistics (Mont 2007; WHO 2008).

FIGURE 8.3 **Prevalence of Disability by Age Group, Selected East European Countries and Years**

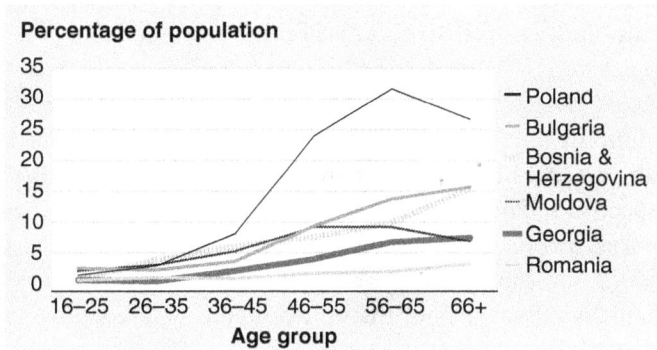

SOURCE: Mete 2008.

Disability is extremely heterogeneous. It can range from mild to moderate to severe. It can be mental, physical, sensory, or psychosocial. It can be acquired at any age, but disability rates are usually highest among the elderly (figure 8.3).

POVERTY AND DISABILITY: A TWO-WAY STREET

Poverty can cause disability through, for instance, lack of preventive and curative health care, poor nutrition, poor occupational safety, and unsafe transport systems; thus we would expect the poor to have a higher incidence of new disabilities than the nonpoor (Elwan 1999).

Disability can also lead to poverty among those who were not poor before acquiring a disability for the following three main reasons:

- People with disabilities may no longer be able to earn as much as they did before acquiring the disability either because of the actual physical impairment or because of such factors as a lack of appropriate transportation to get to work, a lack of access to retraining, a lack of accommodation in the job, or discrimination (Braithwaite and Mont 2008c; Mont 2004).

- The family of a person with a disability may dedicate a good deal of time to caring for the person rather than working. Thus a caretaker may earn less than otherwise or even withdraw from the labor force entirely.

- The disability imposes extra costs on the household. In addition to the obvious costs for medical care and assistive devices, the household may incur additional costs for other services. For example, a person with a disability may not be able to use public transport but may need a taxi or may need to be accompanied by a companion, thereby doubling the fares for each trip. Measurements of such extra costs are complicated and depend greatly on context. In the United Kingdom, Tibble (2005) cites estimates ranging from none to 69 percent of household income. In India, Mohapatra (2004) reports that recurring costs such as medical care and repair of aids and devices are equivalent to the income of a household at the poverty line and that paying an attendant plus one-time costs such as getting a certificate of disability, purchasing aids and appliances, and modifying housing add to the total costs. In Bangladesh, the average costs of extra care for children with a disability are reported to be equivalent to about four months of wages (Chowdhury 2005).

Few studies undertake detailed quantification of the links between poverty and disability. Braithwaite and Mont (2008c), for example, review all 154 poverty assessments done by the World Bank over the last 20 years and find that only 11 quantified the poverty rate of households with disabled members, that these studies were heavily concentrated in Eastern Europe and Central Asia, and that the definitions of disability used were often linked to the receipt of a disability pension rather than to a direct measurement of disability. Elwan (1999) made a much quoted "guesstimate" that 20 percent of the poor may have a disability with little hard data to support the figure. While people with disabilities may be less likely than others to have high personal incomes, most are likely to be part of families with earners across the income spectrum. Thus even though disability will be somewhat concentrated among the poor, not all people with disabilities or families with members with disabilities will be poor. Mete (2008) shows that disability rates in five Eastern European countries are only slightly higher among the poor than the nonpoor whether poverty is measured by consumption (figure 8.4) or assets; however, these findings are based on poverty lines unadjusted for the greater needs of households with members with disabilities. Braithwaite and Mont (2008c) argue that when allowances are made for these extra costs, poverty rates among households with members with disabilities will be higher, as illustrated by Kuklys (2005) for the United Kingdom.

FIGURE 8.4 **Disability Rates by Poverty Status, Selected East European Countries and Years**

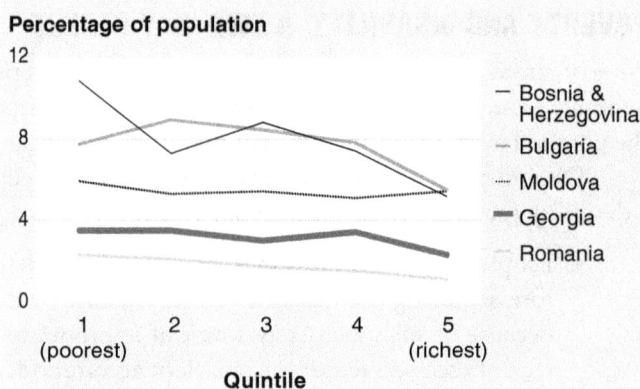

SOURCE: Mete 2008.

POLICY OPTIONS

The two basic options for income support for people with disabilities are providing them with specific disability-targeted programs (contributory or not) and/or including them in general social assistance programs in addition to complementing these options with other services.

Targeting Programs to People with Disabilities

Contributory social insurance programs usually make provisions for disability; however, fewer than 30 percent of the world's labor force is covered by such programs. Most of those covered work in the formal sector. Those working in rural areas, the self-employed, and low-income workers are poorly covered. Coverage has been relatively constant for many years or has even decreased in some countries (Mete 2008). Thus contributory disability insurance programs are not by themselves sufficient to solve the problem of providing income support to people with disabilities. In addition to contributory disability insurance programs, some countries have disability-targeted programs that do not require prior affiliation with social security such as those shown in table 8.6.

TABLE 8.6 **Social or Family Assistance Programs for People with Disabilities, Selected Countries**

Country	Type of program	Disability test	Means test	Coverage Adult	Coverage Children	Benefit
Asia						
Hong Kong (China)	Social assistance	100% loss of earning ability or profoundly deaf	Yes	Yes	No	Two flat rate benefits
Kyrgyz Republic	Social assistance	Inability to work, attendant needed, loss of mobility	No	Yes	No	Flat rate (% of minimum wage)
Turkmen-istan	Social assistance	Inability to work, attendant needed	Yes	Yes	Yes	Flat rate for full and partial disability
Latin America and the Caribbean						
Barbados	Social assistance	Incapable of work because of defective eyesight or serious hearing/speech problems	Yes	Yes	No	Flat rate
Bermuda	Social assistance	Incapable of employment	Yes	Yes	No	Flat rate
Brazil	Social assistance	Unable to work or unable to live independently	Yes	Yes	Yes	Flat rate (minimum wage)
Trinidad and Tobago	Social assistance	Age 40 or older if certified as blind and needy	Yes	Yes	No	Flat rate
Sub-Saharan Africa						
Liberia	Social assistance	Inability to work	Yes	Yes	No	—
South Africa	Social assistance	Inability to work	Yes	Yes	Yes	Flat rate

SOURCE: Mitra 2005.

NOTE: — = not available.

The crucial operational issue with regard to disability-targeted programs, whether contributory or noncontributory, is assessing disability. Most programs handle this by means of a medical assessment, a complex and difficult process. The definitional issues are significant (table 8.7). Such assessments also demand significant resources. We do not have firm estimates of costs, but a medical assessment of disability would likely be more expensive than a means test, if only because the doctors who usually do the assessments and other medical staff who may be involved in managing records or assisting are more highly paid than social assistance clerks.

TABLE 8.7 Advantages and Disadvantages of Alternative Approaches to Operational Definitions of Disability in Medical Assessments

Definition	Advantages	Disadvantages
Based on general and outcome-oriented terms such as "inability to work"	• Conceptually appropriate • Allows discretion to consider full set of medical and other circumstances • Definition is sensitive to the context (accessibility of transportation and buildings, types of jobs and livelihoods available)	• Discretion implies variability among assessors and/or expensive systems to minimize discretion through the use of multiple assessors or review panels
Based on a list of impairments or diagnoses	• Simpler to guarantee equal treatment of people with the same conditions	• Does not recognize differences in severity of the same diagnosis • Does not recognize interactions among multiple conditions • Lists can be politically difficult to agree on

SOURCE: Authors.

Many disability-targeted programs are also means tested. Indeed, of the 18 programs in developing countries that Mitra (2005) describes as providing social assistance to people with disabilities, 16 are means tested but only half are disability tested.

Because the goal of disability insurance programs is to provide a substitute income to those with disabilities, the benefit is sometimes a relatively high share of average income. In Latin American disability insurance programs, for example, the range is from 35 to 70 percent of mean income, with most providing about 50 percent (Grushka and Demarco 2003). This is much more generous than most safety net programs, which are intended to supplement rather than replace income (figure 5.2 and table 5.1). Moreover, the benefit is likely to be sustained for the life of the beneficiary rather than for a specified period as for poverty-targeted programs.

The combination of relatively high benefit levels, longevity of benefits, and difficulties in assessing disability mean that disability benefits are especially subject to fraud. In practice, disability programs often serve as substitutes for unemployment benefits. Workers may prefer disability pensions, as they are permanent and often higher than unemployment benefits, while firms may prefer putting workers on disability rather than making severance payments. Such issues are not uncommon in Europe, with the Netherlands (de

Jong 2003) and Poland (Hoopengardner 2001) commonly cited as countries with problems that have led to subsequent incentive and gatekeeping reforms (Mont 2004). The differences in disability prevalence rates across countries with reasonably similar incomes and health circumstances suggest that the issue of gatekeeping has indeed been a problem. In Croatia, more than 8 percent of the labor force receive disability benefits, whereas in the former Yugoslav Republic of Macedonia, the figure is closer to 2 percent (Mete 2008). At their highest levels in the early 1990s, about 11 percent of labor force participants in the Netherlands qualified as disabled (de Jong 2003), compared with only 0.4 percent in Switzerland (Hoopengardner 2001).

OECD countries have increased their efforts to boost employment among people receiving disability benefits including through a range of activation measures such as job training, subsidies to employers, or provision of supportive measures ranging from job coaches to transportation services. Where a return to work is sought, the eligibility rules for disability-tested benefits need to allow those receiving such benefits to experiment with working without immediate withdrawal of the benefits or eligibility; for example, the rules could permit part-time work or a trial period of employment. Belgium allows a three-month trial period while the Netherlands, Norway, and Sweden allow three years. Even if cash payments are not made during the trial period, the right to revert to receiving benefits without undergoing a new eligibility screening should reduce the risk to workers in attempting a return to work. In the United States, benefits can continue for up to nine months during a trial period and eligibility can remain in effect for three years. Canada does not maintain eligibility, but has an expedited procedure for reestablishing it (Mont 2004).

The low coverage of disability insurance in developing countries implies that other safety net programs will have to handle disability issues. However, the gatekeeping difficulties of disability insurance programs and the fact that people with disabilities may not live in poor households suggest that adequate and effective disability-targeted programs will be difficult to establish.

Mainstreaming People with Disabilities into General Social Assistance Programs

An alternative approach is to mainstream people with disabilities into general safety net programs. Where these people are poor, this should occur to some extent even without explicit action, but special attention may be needed to ensure that programs are inclusive.

As discussed in chapter 4, access to information and the transaction costs associated with participating in safety net programs are significant determinants of coverage, and these issues are likely to be even more significant for people with disabilities. To promote inclusion of this group, program administrators should redouble their efforts to lower transaction costs. For example, they should be particularly sensitive to reducing the number of trips, the extent of travel, and the waiting time for submitting paperwork and collecting benefits. They should also consider the physical accessibility of pertinent buildings and transport systems. Allowing designated proxies to conduct many of the transactions is likely to be helpful. Outreach will be especially important, as people with disabilities are less likely to be literate if they acquired their disability early in life and more likely to be homebound; some will have visual or hearing impairments that limit their use of the kinds of media generally used for outreach. Social assistance programs may find that cooperation with organizations for people with disabilities is useful for ensuring that programs are known to these people and for facilitating enrollment.

Programs may need to make some accommodations for the disability. For example, cash transfer programs might provide higher payments to beneficiaries with disabilities to help compensate for their higher costs of living. Romania's Guaranteed Minimum Income Program does this by setting a higher eligibility threshold and guarantee for households with members with disabilities.

In conditional cash transfer programs, if education is not inclusive, children with disabilities may in practice be excluded by the requirement to enroll in and attend school. While inclusive education is the right long-run answer to this problem, in the interim, the conditions can be waived for such children. In Jamaica, for example, the PATH conditional cast transfer initiative waives the school attendance requirement if the child has a disability certificate and the program officer judges that the school is not sufficiently inclusive to allow the child to benefit from attending it.

Workfare programs can make various sorts of accommodations. To begin with, some consideration of what sorts of jobs those with a disability can do is required. Traditional workfare has mostly required heavy manual labor unsuitable for those with mobility and physical impairments, but perhaps manageable by those who are deaf or have a cognitive impairment. Even traditional public works jobs may require other types of labor, for example, recordkeeping for payroll and/or supplies. Such jobs require lighter labor, but literacy, and might serve those with a different set of disabilities. This is the approach implied when governments require that a certain percentage of jobs be reserved for people with disabilities, the so-called quota-levy systems. South Africa's Expanded Public Works Program has a target of 2 percent of places reserved for workers with disabilities; the result is that only about 0.5 to 0.6 percent of the workers have a disability (Marriott and Gooding 2007). In India, 3 percent of jobs in the Sampoorna Grameen Rozgar Yojana (Village Full Employment Program) are reserved for those with a disability certification. Although data indicate that this target has not been met, state reports show that between 0.3 and 1.7 percent of jobs were effectively reserved for workers with disabilities (World Bank 2006h). In many transition countries, employers opt to pay fines rather than hire workers with disabilities.

In some middle-income countries, workfare or public service requirements have taken on a quite different range of activities, including such jobs as working in libraries, assisting teachers, and serving as clerks in health facilities. These provide less physically demanding jobs than traditional public works types of jobs, but still require some mobility and often higher literacy and education than manual labor. They may therefore be able to accommodate people with a range of disabilities.

Even after matching potential beneficiaries with disabilities against such slots, it may be difficult to find jobs on the workfare program in proportion to the share of those with disabilities in the target population. Therefore some programs waive the requirement for work. Bulgaria's Guaranteed Minimum Income Program does this for those who have formal disability certification (Shopov forthcoming). In Ethiopia, the Productive Safety Net Program allows up to 20 percent of beneficiaries to come from households with a labor shortage; such beneficiaries are not required to work. Disability is included as a reason for a household labor shortage.

As noted earlier, some programs provide labor activation measures in addition to income support. In these cases, the activation measures need to be sensitive to disability. Case officers may need to coordinate not only with potential workers, but with potential employers to discern whether some accommodations in relation to equipment, job structure, work flow, or work hours are required for a job placement. The Netherlands and the United Kingdom now make aggressive use of this approach.

The contradiction in adjusting general social assistance programs to include clients with disabilities as fully as possible is that this requires knowing who has a disability, the very thing that makes disability targeting difficult. In some cases, the adjustment is done only for those with formal disability certificates such as those used in disability-targeted programs. In other cases, the assessment of a disability in order to waive the requirements of a general social assistance program is much less formal than for a disability-tested program and may be done by a social assistance clerk, other staff in the local program office, or the community. This may be less reliable, but it costs less; in addition, potential beneficiaries would already have had to meet the program's poverty-targeting criteria. Thus erroneously waiving a condition such as school attendance or work for a poor person who does not have a disability would simply result in an unconditional transfer to a poor person, which is not an unacceptable outcome in its own right, though it is possibly inequitable with regard to other poor people who face a condition attached to the support. A worse outcome would be failing to detect and accommodate a poor person's disability and excluding him or her from a program altogether.

Few studies have examined disability assessments by communities. In Ethiopia's Productive Safety Net Program, communities were given the responsibility of choosing all beneficiaries suffering from inadequate food consumption for more than three months a year and were allowed to excuse up to 20 percent of households from the work requirement on the grounds of being short of labor. This included not only adults with disabilities, but women who were due to give birth within 3 months or had done so in the previous 10 and households with no prime-age adults (Sharp, Brown, and Teshome 2006). The targeting assessment showed that the households excused from work were indeed poorer than those who did work, indicating that the community assessments were reasonably accurate. Twenty percent of households excused from the work requirement had a member with a disability (Sharp, Brown, and Teshome 2006).

South Africa presents a contrasting case. Because of the challenges of medical assessment, especially providing such assessment in rural areas, the government experimented with allowing communities to assess disability since 2001. The assessment panels included six members expected to have some familiarity with disability or care dependency and with local social and economic conditions, such as social security officials, rehabilitation specialists, community members, staff of agencies that support services to or advocacy on behalf of people with disabilities, or medical professionals. The results were mixed. Potential beneficiaries had better access to panels, but issues of comparable assessment were intensified, as some provinces used medical assessments and some used assessment panels, but neither had effective means of ensuring that similar cases were similarly assessed (Marriott and Gooding 2007). The assessment panels appear to have been more lenient than the medical assessors. This resulted in significant increases in certification rates high enough that the government reverted back to medical assessments.[4]

Other Public Action

Public policy toward disability needs to do many things in addition to just providing social assistance. Medical care is needed for prevention; for rehabilitation, including providing assistive devices; and for meeting the ongoing medical needs of people with disabilities. Inclusive education, job training, and employment are needed to sever the link between disability and poverty. Transportation and public buildings must be universally accessible for people with disabilities to be able to participate fully in society and attitudes of acceptance rather than discrimination are fundamental for social inclusion. Action on these fronts is needed irrespective of the form that income support to people with disabilities takes. To the extent that these measures of social inclusion succeed, they will reduce the risk that people with disabilities are poor and diminish their needs for social assistance.

Within the community of people with disabilities and their advocates and service providers, attitudes toward social assistance are somewhat divided. Some see it as unwanted charity or fear that it will reinforce patterns of exclusion. Others see the pragmatic benefits of income support as part of a larger package of needed public policies. Some even see increasing provision of social assistance as a tool helpful for achieving progress on other policy fronts pertinent to people with disabilities (Marriott and Gooding 2007).

Notes

1. http://cis.ier.hit-u.ac.jp/English/society/conferences01.html.

2. Guidance on OVC issues, including those pertinent to children not living in a family setting, is provided in World Bank (2005i). UNICEF Innocenti Research Centre (2003a, 2003b, 2003c) addresses a difference set of OVC issues: it provides guidance on how to reduce the institutionalization of children in Eastern Europe and Central Asia.

3. The chain of logic and conclusions in this section are heavily influenced by Mitra (2005) and reinforced by Marriott and Gooding (2007).

4. Daniel Plaatjies, Executive Manager, Strategy and Business Development, South African Social Security Agency, conversation with Margaret Grosh, March 3, 2008.

## CHAPTER 9

Weaving the Safety Net

KEY MESSAGES

Policy makers and sector specialists need to choose the right mix of safety net policies and programs to meet national goals related to reducing poverty and vulnerability as set out in national or sector strategies.

Our vision of a good safety net system is one that addresses the needs of the poor and vulnerable in a given country; that is adequate, equitable, cost-effective, incentive compatible, sustainable, and dynamic; and that is well adapted to the country's circumstances and constraints.

The general framework for assessing the safety net sector involves three steps: (1) Diagnosing the sources of poverty and vulnerability using the key tools of poverty assessments, risk and vulnerability assessments, and/or poverty and social impact analysis. (2) Evaluating the individual safety net interventions against the criteria listed. (3) Evaluating the mix of programs against the criteria listed. We refer to a key diagnostic tool: the public expenditure review of the safety net sector.

Such assessments are useful whenever significant reforms are contemplated or new needs arise. Moreover, they are warranted periodically because old strategies may become obsolete as new problems and priorities emerge, or simply because the world has learned how to solve old problems in more efficient ways.

Moving from the status quo toward the vision of a good safety net implies overcoming challenges with respect to financial constraints, political feasibility, and administrative capacity. Different types of reforms will face different combinations of these challenges and how binding each is will vary over time in a given setting. In most settings some sort of improvement will be feasible, though sometimes improvements will come incrementally over a number of years and stages.

9.1 What Is a Good Safety Net?

Safety net systems are usually woven of several programs, ideally complementing each other as well as complementing other public or social policies. A good safety net system is more than a collection of well-designed and well-implemented programs, however; it also exhibits the following attributes.

- **Appropriate.** The range of programs used and the balance between them and with the other elements of public policy should respond to the particular needs of the country. Each program should be customized for best fit with the circumstances.

- **Adequate.** The safety net system overall covers the various groups in need of assistance—the chronic poor, the transient poor, those affected by reforms, and all the various subsets of these groups. Individual programs should provide full coverage and meaningful benefits to whichever subset of the population they are meant to assist.

- **Equitable.** The safety net should treat beneficiaries in a fair and equitable way. In particular, it should aim to provide the same benefits to individuals or households that are equal in all important respects (horizontal equity) and may provide more generous benefits to the poorest beneficiaries (vertical equity).

- **Cost-effective.** Cost-effective programs channel most program resources to their intended target group. They also economize the administrative resources required to implement the program in two ways. First, at the level of the whole safety net system, they avoid fragmentation and the subsequent need to develop administrative systems without realizing economies of scale. Second, they run efficiently with the minimum resources required to achieve the desired impact, but with sufficient resources to carry out all program functions well.

- **Incentive compatible.** Safety nets can change households' behavior, for better or worse. To ensure that the balance of changes is positive, the role of safety nets should be kept to the minimum consistent with adequacy. The safety net system often may include programs that explicitly help build assets or incomes of their individual clients or communities by linking transfers to required or voluntary program elements. Public works programs can provide physical assets to communities. Conditional cash transfer (CCT) programs build the human capital of households. Links to financial, job search, training, or social care services may help households raise their incomes.

- **Sustainable.** Prudent safety net systems are financially sustainable, in that they are pursued in a balanced manner with other aspects of government expenditure. Individual programs should be both financially and politically sustainable so that stop/start cycles of programs are avoided, as these result in enormous lost opportunities for efficient administration and the achievement of programs' promotive aspects. In low-income countries, programs started with donor support are gradually incorporated into the public sector.

- **Dynamic.** A good safety net system will evolve over time. The appropriate balance of programs will change as the economy grows and changes, as other elements of policy develop, or when shocks occur. The management of specific programs should also evolve as problems are solved and new standards set.

9.2 Know Your Target Group

Policy makers and sector specialists cannot choose an appropriate mix of safety net policies without first obtaining a good understanding of the population groups that need safety net programs on a permanent basis: the chronically poor or a subset of these, the transient poor or a subset of these, and other vulnerable groups.

The analytical tools that provide a better understanding of the groups that need safety net programs are poverty analysis and risk and vulnerability analysis. Poverty analysis provides information on the level, severity, and depth of poverty; describes the characteristics of the poor; and identifies the factors associated with poverty. When repeated over time, it depicts the trends, duration, and dynamics of poverty among particular groups and identifies the factors associated with poverty. Risk and vulnerability analysis complements poverty analysis by providing insights into the risks the poor face, as well as the size and characteristics of the population at risk of becoming poor in the event of a shock. Many countries are prone to a variety of interlocking risks that feed off each other; for example, natural disasters destroy potable water and sewage systems and may therefore be followed by epidemics. The poor and those hovering just above the poverty line are particularly vulnerable to such risks. This vulnerability, combined with low levels of assets, high variability of income, and lack of effective risk management instruments can have a disastrous impact on people's livelihoods. Risk and vulnerability analysis can identify prevention and mitigation activities that would help prevent the transmission of poverty over time (see Hoogeveen and others 2004 for a guide to risk and vulnerability analysis). The two types of analyses are complementary and together can provide powerful insights that can result in the most appropriate policy responses, including responses other than safety net interventions. The analysis of poverty and vulnerability to poverty will indicate whether existing safety net programs are appropriate given the magnitude, depth, characteristics, and causes of poverty and vulnerability.

DETERMINING THE SIZE OF THE TARGET GROUP

The first step in designing a safety net is to understand the dimensions of the problem to be addressed.

How Many People Are Poor or Vulnerable?

Knowing the size of the poor and vulnerable population helps to determine the scope of the safety net, both in terms of coverage and budget. Another important and simple poverty statistic that informs the design of safety net programs is the income gap—that is, the average deficit of the poor's resources relative to the poverty line. When policy makers are considering introducing new programs, the income gap informs them how generous a program should be to cover this deficit or a given fraction of it. For existing programs, the income gap provides an estimate of the remaining consumption deficit of the poor despite the existence of the current programs. However, as discussed in chapter 3, section 1, the income gap is only one factor taken into consideration when setting the benefit level of a program. Other important factors are the type of program and its objective, the budget constraint, and the institutional capacity to administer programs with differentiated benefits, along with political economy factors. In general, policy makers will try to find the right balance between providing enough protection from poverty while maintaining adequate incentives for self-sufficiency and work effort.

How Does Poverty Evolve over Time?

When the information available to assess poverty includes repeated cross-sectional surveys, policy analysts can track changes in the level and depth of poverty in the aggregate or for selected subgroups.[1] This information can, in turn, be used to assess whether existing programs offer effective protection against poverty. For example, such comparisons have shown that in Chile in the 1990s, the indigent did not share in the general prosperity of the country (table 9.1). From 1987 to 1992, Chile made substantial progress in reducing poverty. After 1992, however, further progress was observed for total poverty, but not for the indigent. Thus the indigent were left out during a period of sustained growth. Responding to these findings, the government of Chile developed the Chile Solidario program, which helps the indigent escape from poverty via a combination of cash assistance, priority access to public services, and personalized support (World Bank 2005g).

TABLE 9.1 **Failure to Reduce Indigence Despite Growth, Chile, Selected Years**

Item	1987	1990	1992	1994	1996	1998	2000
Mean income (peso)	90,598	101,075	122,353	126,644	142,892	159,821	160,441
Gini index	0.5468	0.5322	0.5362	0.5298	0.5409	0.5465	0.5457
Poverty headcount (%)	40.0	33.1	24.2	23.1	19.9	17.0	15.7
Extreme poverty headcount (%)	12.7	9.0	4.7	5.1	4.2	3.9	4.2

SOURCE: World Bank 2005g.

How Many People Are Vulnerable to Poverty?

As the recent crises in East Asia (1997), the Russian Federation (1998), and Argentina (2002) demonstrated, countries need flexible safety net systems that can be scaled up in times of need to help the poorest and most affected cope with the hardship brought about by a crisis. Poverty and risk and vulnerability analyses can help identify prospectively those who may become poor in the event of a severe shock and those at risk of poverty. Even crude estimates based on a cross-sectional survey can be used to identify potential threats to the living standards of the population. Estimating the share of the population just above the poverty line may indicate the share of the population at risk of poverty during economic downturns. Table 9.2 illustrates this for Indonesia just before the 1997 East Asian crisis. In 1996, 15.7 percent of the population was poor, but a large share of the population was living just above the poverty line, indicated by the fact that the income shares for the second and third population quintiles

TABLE 9.2 **Percentage Share of Income by Quintile, Indonesia, 1996**

Share of	Quintile				
	1	2	3	4	5
Income	8.0	11.3	15.1	20.8	44.9
Population	15.7 poor		84.3 not poor		

SOURCES: World Bank 2000e, 2001i.

NOTE: Quintile 1 is the poorest; quintile 5 the richest.

were similar. When the crisis hit, many of those living at the border of poverty became poor; by 1999, 27.1 percent of the population was poor.

PICTURING THE TARGET GROUP

Poverty profiles based on household surveys reveal who the target group is and can be useful both for suggesting how to reach them and indicating what sort of assistance they may need. We provide four typical examples of how the information generated by poverty profiles informs safety net policy making.

Identify Easily Identifiable Characteristics of the Poor That Can Be Used for Categorical Targeting

The poverty profile will show policy analysts whether poverty is concentrated in groups identified by easily observable characteristics such as ethnicity or location. When poverty is concentrated in easy-to-identify groups, reaching these groups may be simple. For example, an assessment of poverty in Cambodia in 1997 found that 90 percent of rural inhabitants were poor and that most of the poor lived in rural areas (World Bank 1999b). Under these circumstances, restricting program eligibility to rural areas would result in high coverage of the poor and low leakage. Situations where poverty is dispersed may necessitate implementation of a household targeting system, which in turn requires greater administrative capacity and resources.

Distinguish between Chronic and Transient Poverty

When panel data—data based on a survey that revisits the same households over time—are available, they can shed light on the dynamics of poverty, which in turn informs the selection and design of appropriate safety net interventions. Typically, households are classified according to the time they spend in poverty and the frequency of their spells as transient poor or chronically poor. Classifying households by the duration of their poverty spell can inform the content of safety net programs and policies. When a large share of poverty is chronic, governments may consider more permanent safety net programs and less frequent recertification. Some targeting instruments, notably proxy means testing, are more appropriate for such contexts.

Dercon (1999) uses a two-period panel survey to analyze movements into and out of poverty in Ethiopia during the 1990s (table 9.3). Between 1989 and 1995, the overall poverty rate declined from 61 to 46 percent of the population; however, the aggregate decrease in poverty masked significant flows in and out of poverty, which became apparent only when examining the panel structure of the data. The overall decrease in poverty by 15 percentage points was the result

TABLE 9.3 **Percentage of Population Moving Into and Out of Poverty, Rural Ethiopia, 1989 and 1995**

Status in 1989	Status in 1995		
	Poor	Nonpoor	Total
Poor	31	30	61
Nonpoor	15	24	39
Total	46	54	100

SOURCE: Dercon 1999.

of two offsetting tendencies. On the one hand, a large population group amounting to 30 percent of the total population was poor in 1989 but escaped poverty in 1995. On the other hand, another group equal to 15 percent of the population was not poor in 1989 but fell into poverty in 1995. The large flows in and out of poverty are a clear sign of vulnerability to poverty.

Account for Seasonal Variations in Poverty or Vulnerability

Poverty and/or vulnerability have a markedly seasonal nature when livelihoods are tied to seasonal events; when climate induces extra expenditure needs, for instance, for heating; or when illness has seasonal patterns that both reduce work effort and require expenditures for health care. Box 9.1 provides an example from Mozambique.

Quantify the Contribution of Various Population Subgroups to Total Poverty

Poverty profiles have generated similar qualitative findings across many countries: poverty is more frequent or intense for larger households with higher dependency rates and is negatively correlated with the education level of the adults, their level of physical and financial capital, the quality of their dwelling, and/or their endowment with durable goods. In many cases, rural populations, including farmers, are at higher risk of poverty than the general population.

While the observable characteristics of the poor tend to be similar across countries, the relative importance of these characteristics is country specific. For example, households headed by illiterate people represent a deep pocket of poverty in both Chile and Zambia. While the poverty rate among this subgroup will be high in both countries, their share in the total poor population will be low in Chile, where few adults are illiterate, and high in Zambia, where the opposite is true. Putting actual figures on the contribution of each characteristic to total poverty or on the fraction of poor people who share given characteristics is therefore important for the design or review of a safety net program.

A poverty and vulnerability profile will provide clues as to who the poor are and how they may be identified, often based on such indicators as living in a home without electricity. It will not, however, tell us the root cause of their poverty.

UNDERSTANDING CAUSES OF POVERTY AND VULNERABILITY

Understanding the causes of poverty and vulnerability is of paramount importance to select policies and programs that can reduce or eliminate poverty, including safety nets. In general, poverty is generated by a lack of assets, uninsured exposure to shocks, or a combination of these factors. Poverty analysis and risk and vulnerability analysis will inform the choice of intervention: whether to use a safety net program and which type of safety net program would be more appropriate.

With Respect to Which Assets Are the Poor Most Disadvantaged?

Most often, the policies that build the assets of the poor lie outside the social protection sector in sectors such as health, education, microfinance, land reform, or infrastructure to provide basic services. As chapters 2 and 7 indicate, increasing evidence suggests that safety net policies are effective in helping the poor build their assets: public works programs can help build the infrastructure needed to improve income for today's earners

BOX 9.1 **Seasonality of Vulnerability in Two Localities in Mozambique**

Angoche. The small town of Angoche used to be an important fishing town with several processing plants for cashews, rice, and the like. All but one were shut down in the 1990s. The closure of these plants led to a rapid rise in unemployment and underemployment and to the near collapse of the local economy. Most households resorted to artisanal fishing, informal and petty trade, and subsistence agriculture. A few fortunate people remain employed in the formal sector in public institutions; stores; and a small, recently opened shrimp processing plant.

December through March coincides with the shrimp protection period, when shrimp trawling and fishing are not allowed. Well-being normally begins to deteriorate in January and February, and March and April are the most critical months. During this period the supply of fish is at its lowest and the prices of staple goods, particularly dried cassava, are at their highest. In addition, the beginning of the school year strains household budgets with payments due for matriculation (for children in secondary school), school materials, and uniforms. This time is also when households normally suffer the most from ill health caused by malaria, diarrhea, and even cholera in bad years.

Conditions improve in May and June. Fish, shrimp, and scallops are abundant, both for eating and selling, and agricultural produce (fresh and dried cassava, maize, sorghum, and rice) can be bought at fairly low prices. Well-being remains high into July and August, with a boost from good fishing conditions. Conditions start to decline again in November and December as a result of bad fishing conditions, the onset of shrimp protection, and higher prices for agricultural products.

Xilembene. Xilembene is a peri-urban town. Central to the agricultural engine of Mozambique during colonial times, it has a rich history and is known across Mozambique as the birthplace of Samora Machel, the country's first president. Until recently, it benefited from an extensive and sophisticated system of irrigation canals that stretched across much of southern Mozambique, but the region's infrastructure for agricultural support—which previously included several processing plants, an agricultural seed production factory, and several credit institutions—gradually fell apart because of a lack of maintenance and investment. Irrigation has been in a state of permanent disrepair since the 2000 floods, leaving the fields of hundreds of households without easy and regular access to water. The gradual collapse of agricultural production and marketing devastated local subsistence farmers. Nevertheless, households in Xilembene appear to face smoother and less severe changes in well-being during the year than those in Angoche.

September means the end of the good times. The food situation becomes severe from late October until February or March, with most households eating fewer than two meals a day. The most vulnerable—orphans and female-headed households—rarely get more than one meal a day. This period also coincides with the warm and rainy season, which brings with it malaria and diarrhea. January burdens many households with schooling expenses. The winter months from April through July are times of abundance, with harvests bringing in enough food for most people. In good years, production is sufficient to sell the excess.

SOURCE: World Bank 2008b.

while CCT programs work to build human capital for tomorrow's earners. If infrastructure and human capital are the assets that the poor most lack, then safety nets may not only help them cope with the underlying problem of a lack of assets, but may also be part of the solution.

What Are the Major Sources of Risk?

Exposure to uninsured risk is another channel that determines poverty. Various means can be used to identify the major sources of risk the poor face. Analyses for several Latin American countries categorize the population into age groups, list the risks each age group theoretically faces, marshal data on the basic indicators of each risk, and use those data to assess whether the potential problem represented by each risk should be a priority for attention. For example, one would look at indicators of nutritional status to see if children's health and development are threatened. If the malnutrition rate is low, higher priority should be given to other risks. Such analysis can be enriched by systematically distinguishing between different population groups by gender, ethnicity where pertinent, and level of poverty. This approach has the advantages that most audiences find it easy to understand and that programs to address unacceptable outcomes match well with this approach. Its disadvantage is that in grouping together individuals of different ages and needs, it ignores the role of the family.

What Are the Characteristics of the Risks?

Once the sources of risk have been identified, each type of risk should be assessed as to its severity, scope (in terms of the numbers and groups of people affected), and types of effects and their expected frequency within the particular country context. An important aspect of this assessment is determining whether the identified risks affect specific individuals or households and are therefore idiosyncratic (such risks include noncommunicable illnesses, individual short-term unemployment, and family breakup), or whether they affect entire regions or groups of households and are therefore covariate (such as drought, seasonal price volatility, war, or a financial crisis that affects an entire community at the same time). Risks can be either single or repeated events, with examples of the latter being droughts or floods. Covariate, repeated, or compounded (covariate and repeated) shocks are typically difficult to handle through informal means such as savings, loans, or gifts, and an appropriate response to catastrophic events may be long-term net transfers. In contrast, noncatastrophic events that occur frequently but whose effects are not severe, such as transitory illness or temporary unemployment, do not always require long-term net transfers, because affected households may be able to cope using savings, loans, reciprocal gifts, or, in some cases, private insurance. For extremely poor households, however, even these types of events can be devastating. Figure 9.1 gives an example of one phase of a risk and vulnerability analysis for Guatemala.

Are Safety Nets the Appropriate Response to Poverty and Vulnerability?

Once the groups affected by various causes of poverty and their characteristics have been identified, the role that safety nets can play, in conjunction with interventions in other sectors and at the macroeconomic level, can be investigated. Other social protection programs, notably, labor market programs and pensions, and policies to ensure macroeco-

FIGURE 9.1 **Losses by Households That Experienced Shocks, Guatemala, 2000**

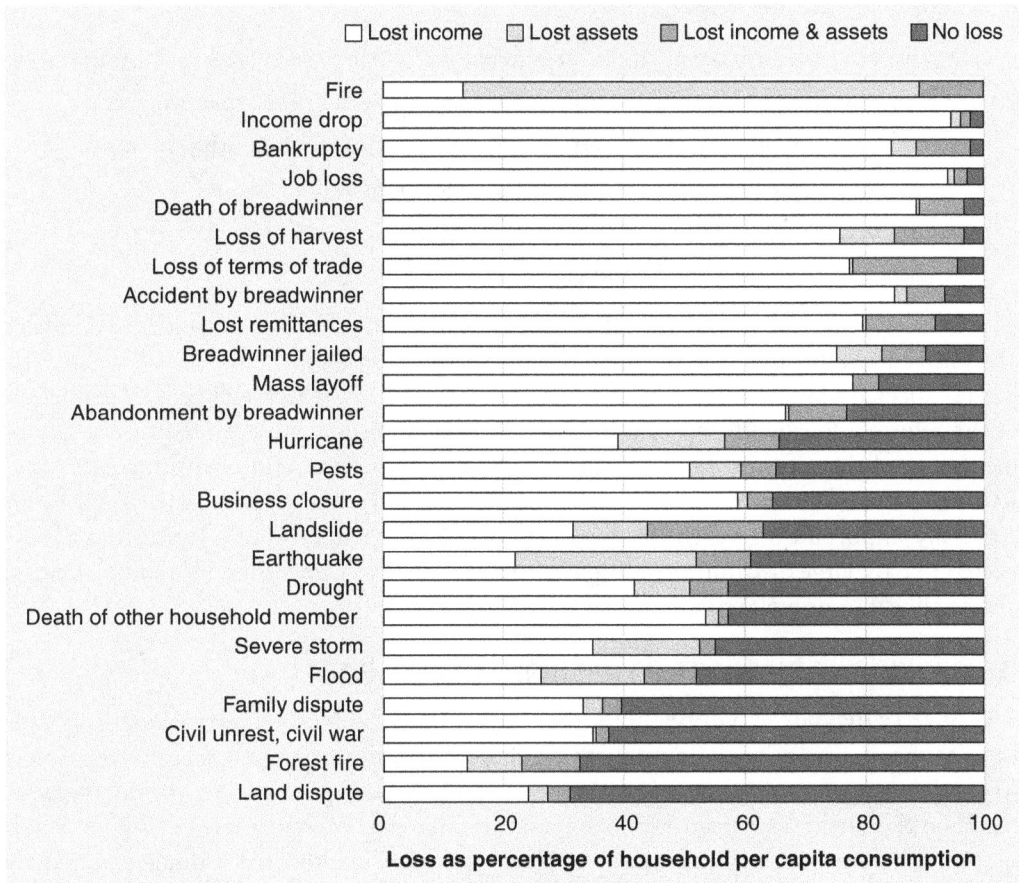

SOURCE: Tesliuc and Lindert 2004, figure 4.

nomic stability, rural development, and human capital formation are especially important. Safety nets are typically used to fill in where other policies cannot deliver sufficient
results in the short run.

MODIFYING THE DIAGNOSTIC WHEN SAFETY NETS ARE USED TO MITIGATE THE NEGATIVE CONSEQUENCES OF NEEDED REFORMS

In one special instance, safety net programs are called for that require a slight modification of the diagnostic outlined in the rest of this section—that is, when safety net programs are used to compensate those who lose from needed economic reforms. In this case
they act as safety nets for politicians as well as for the poor.

The analytical approach used to identify the appropriate compensation mechanism
is a form of distributional analysis that in recent years has become known as poverty and
social impact analysis (good references on the topic are Coudouel and Paternostro 2006a,
2006b, 2006c; World Bank 2004b). Poverty and social impact analysis is an examination
of the distributional impact of policy reforms on the well-being and welfare of various
stakeholder groups, particularly the poor and vulnerable. Increasingly, this kind of analysis

is being applied to promote evidence-based policy choices and foster debate on policy reform options, thereby helping to

- examine the link between policy reforms and their poverty and social impacts,
- consider trade-offs among reforms based on their distributional impacts,
- enhance the positive impacts of reforms and minimize their adverse impacts,
- design mitigating measures and risk management systems,
- assess the risks of policy reforms,
- build country ownership and capacity for analysis.

Unlike poverty analysis and risk and vulnerability analysis, poverty and social impact analysis is not a distinct analytical technique. The process begins with an ex ante analysis of the expected poverty and social impacts of policy reforms, which will help in the design of the reforms. Ideally, the approach then involves monitoring the results during implementation of the reforms. Finally, where possible, ex post evaluations of the poverty and social impacts of the reforms are carried out. Poverty and social impact analysis can be an especially important ingredient in the design and implementation of reforms that are expected to have large distributional impacts, are prominent in governments' policy agendas, and are likely to provoke significant debate.

IMPROVING THE DIAGNOSTICS REQUIRES BETTER DATA

The poverty diagnostic will be more informative for the safety net practitioner if it captures as many dimensions of poverty as possible, which in turn depends on having access to good data. Simple diagnostics tend to focus on monetary poverty, identifying the poor based on their income, consumption, or asset endowment. More complex diagnostics will incorporate nonmonetary indicators of poverty, which identify individuals affected by poor health; poor nutritional status; low level of education or illiteracy; lack of access to basic services; social exclusion; insecurity due to violence, gang activity, or political repression; and/or lack of freedom, voice, or empowerment. Richer diagnostics will incorporate the temporal dimension of poverty. By examining the dynamics of household welfare, such diagnostics quantify the duration of poverty for different population subgroups, separate the chronically poor from the transient poor, and may incorporate an analysis of risk-induced poverty or vulnerability. Table 9.4 summarizes the value added of collecting in-depth information pertaining to different dimensions of household welfare to quantify the need for poverty alleviation programs, including safety nets.

In addition, program diagnostics require data of three sorts: the details of specific programs; an overview of the full panoply of safety net programs; and comprehensive information about all complementary programs in the areas of social insurance, health, education, and poverty reduction.

Conducting in-depth analysis will only be possible for a selected subset of programs. These should include programs that receive substantial budget allocations or that affect large groups of people; smaller interventions that appear to address important, largely unmet needs; and programs for which good evaluations are already available.

A broad overview of the full range of safety net interventions is needed. This might provide only limited information on budget and design features, such as intended target

TABLE 9.4 **Types of Data Required for Different Types of Diagnostics**

Item	Data requirements	Type of analysis
Dimension of poverty: monetary	Cross-sectional survey with information on monetary welfare (consumption, income, assets)	• Level and severity of poverty • Poverty profile • Factors associated with poverty
	Panel survey with information on monetary welfare	• Chronic versus transient poverty • Transition in and out of poverty • Duration of poverty • Factors causing poverty
Dimension of poverty: monetary, nonmonetary	Cross-sectional survey with information on monetary and nonmonetary welfare	• Level of monetary and nonmonetary poverty • Households deprived in different dimensions of well-being (for example, nutrition, health, education, housing, social capital) • Poverty profile for vulnerable groups
	Repeated cross-sectional survey with information on monetary and nonmonetary welfare	• Trends in poverty, total and by subgroups
Vulnerability to poverty	Cross-sectional survey with information on welfare, shocks, and risk management strategies and instruments	• Main sources of risk to household welfare • Households with high exposure to risk • Households with low coping capacity
	Panel survey with information on welfare, shocks, and risk management strategies and instruments	• Proximate factors of vulnerability: low consumption versus variable consumption • Factors causing vulnerability

SOURCE: Authors.

group and benefit levels, and little on actual performance. It should, however, be comprehensive in conducting an inventory of the main public safety net programs run by all ministries and across various levels of government. This sounds relatively straightforward, but may be quite difficult in practice, because the safety net "sector" consists of many programs spread across different agencies and levels of government. Especially where a country has many small or medium programs, they may be insignificant individually, but important in aggregate. For example, in Madagascar, 18 different international aid agencies have financed and/or delivered safety net interventions and together accounted for about 74 percent of the total safety net budget in 2004. The remainder was funded from the government's general revenues (including the Heavily Indebted Poor Countries Initiative) through five ministries. Chapter 3, section 5, shows that this is not unusual, and indeed, that countries that are not as poor often have even more programs running simultaneously. A second complication arises when countries have safety net policies whose cost is hard to estimate, such as quasi-fiscal subsidies, and such policies are likely to be omitted from the analysis. Typical examples of underreporting include subsidy programs for privileged citizens in the countries of the former Soviet Union and quasi-fiscal subsidies such as energy and water subsidies. Omitting these policies from the diagnostic is likely to be misleading, because they may account for a large volume of inefficient spending. For example, the quasi-fiscal cost of the subsidies provided to privileged citizens in Russia in 2002 represented 2 percent of Russia's gross domestic product (GDP), or about a third of the entire social assistance budget.

As the safety net needs to fit into broader social policy, understanding the coverage and adequacy of other social services is important, that is, contributory pension systems, health insurance, education coverage, housing policy, and the like (see the discussion in chapter 2, section 2). In a complete review of a country's social protection strategy, these elements may receive parallel treatment to safety nets. In a safety nets assessment, the safety net programs will be the focus, but some information on the context may also be included.

9.3 Assessing the Performance of Individual Programs

The basic issue in assessing an individual program is determining whether it is a "good" version of whatever sort of program it is. The desirability of a public works program versus a needs-based cash transfer is context specific, but obviously a good public works program or cash transfer is always better than a bad one. Ideally, a full cost-effectiveness exercise can be carried out to ascertain how good a program is. In the numerous cases where this is not possible, reviewing individual facets of the program can be helpful, often by benchmarking against other feasible options or against best practice (chapter 7 summarizes some elements of best practice for each type of program). This assessment should be complemented by a review of the program's actual performance. The diagnostic tools and standards for understanding actual performance are much clearer than for looking at systems as a whole.

The performance of a program is multifaceted, thus acknowledging that and considering explicitly different elements of the program is useful. This section discusses four facets of a program: its adequacy, equity, cost-effectiveness, and sustainability. Analysts may work with different numbers of dimensions, title them differently, group them differently, and/or break out factors that contribute to these four dimensions (for example, quality of delivery systems) or add complementary process indicators (for instance, transparency). Indeed, adequacy, equity, and cost-effectiveness together determine whether the program has the desired impact or not, so some writers would lump these features together. We separate them to continue with the multifaceted discussion of impact in chapter 6, to help us understand which feature or features may be working well and which less so, and to enable us to make some judgments in the all-too-frequent cases when policy decisions must be made in the absence of a strong information base.

This book provides only a brief explanation of what we mean by each of the four dimensions. More information is provided in the social protection chapter of the toolkit for preparing public expenditure reviews found at www.worldbank.org/hdpers. The toolkit provides a checklist of topics for analysis (summarized in box 9.2), notes with explanations or references to methodological materials and comparators, and illustrations of some of the types of analyses suggested.

ADEQUACY

A program is adequate if it provides "sufficient" benefits to "enough" people for "long enough." These are, of course, relative terms. The profile of poverty and vulnerability will provide an indication of the level of need. Considering possible disincentive effects may limit the generosity of a program somewhat; considering fiscal constraints may do so even more. Simplifying a bit, assessing the overall generosity of a program implies taking into account coverage, benefit level, and duration.

Coverage

At its simplest, coverage refers to the total number of people benefiting from a particular safety net intervention. A meaningful analysis should further refine the coverage to make it relevant to the context, for example, calculating total coverage in relation to the number of people in the poorest quintile or two and/or including their geographic location (urban versus rural, specific region) and social characteristics (ethnic group, age, gender).

The analysis should assess whether all the poor are covered by the existing safety net or by other social protection interventions. The most accurate estimation of the gap in coverage among the poor would require survey data with information about household welfare and program receipt. Given this information, the analyst can estimate both the gap in coverage of the overall safety net or social protection intervention (given the complementarities among income replacement benefits such as contributory pensions and unemployment insurance) and the extent to which multiple safety net programs overlap.

Even when no survey data on program receipt are available, the analyst can assess whether the program is large enough to reach all the poor by comparing the fraction of the population that is poor with the caseload of existing programs. For example, if 20 percent of the population lives in poverty and existing programs cover only 10 percent of the population, we know that the safety net is not reaching a large share of the poor. However, comparing the fraction of the poor with program caseloads may be a crude way to gauge how many poor are not being reached by the safety net for two reasons. First, not all the beneficiaries of a safety net program will be poor. In some programs, the eligibility criteria may not be closely linked with poverty, and even where they are, some applicants may cheat to gain eligibility while others bordering eligibility may be accidentally included or excluded from the program. Second, some beneficiaries of safety net programs may be eligible for more than one program, and therefore adding up administrative data on the caseloads of all programs may overestimate the total coverage of the safety net. For instance, in the early 1990s, the Bulgarian authorities were happy with the take-up of the Guaranteed Minimum Income Program, because both the program's caseload and the number of extreme poor (the explicit target group of the program) were similar, around 10 percent of the population. However, as subsequent survey analyses have shown (World Bank 2002b), more than one-third of the existing beneficiaries were not extremely poor, and thus one-third of those who were extremely poor were not served.

A good analysis will take the coverage of other programs into account. Adequacy has to be judged in relation to needs: if social policy has only a small hole, then a small program may be sufficient. In Chile, the proxy means-tested social pensions program covers only 13 percent of the population, but 64 percent of the population is already covered by the contributory system, and presumably not all those who are not covered by contributory pensions are poor, so even though it is small in absolute size, the program makes a meaningful start at meeting needs (Rofman 2005).

BOX 9.2 The Public Expenditure Review Lens: Analysis of Individual Programs

A public expenditure review should assess how well a selection of the most important programs is working and provide guidance on any necessary or contemplated reforms. Such analysis should usually cover elements within each of the following areas:

- Adequacy
  - Coverage, which may be disaggregated as pertinent by location (rural versus urban), state, age, gender, formal versus informal sector of employment, and so on. May include demographic projections for pensions.
  - Adequacy of benefit level. Benchmarks will vary by program; for example, social pensions could be compared with the poverty line, unemployment assistance with average wages and the poverty line, social assistance with the poverty line, wages for public works jobs with the market wage for similar work, and the like.
  - Duration of benefit.
- Equity
  - Incidence of benefits received and participation rates and exclusion should always be presented by welfare group, for instance, consumption quintile, when available.
  - Where poverty profiles or program goals indicate or where full distributional information is not available, presenting breakdowns by other pertinent groups—age or gender, location (urban versus rural), covered or uncovered sector—may be useful.
  - Where pertinent, the review should contrast the incidence of participation and of payments made where benefits are not uniform.
- Cost-effectiveness (the specific indicators will vary greatly by program and here we provide only a few examples)
  - Does program design conform to good international practice? Are relevant parameters in line with benchmarks or international comparators?

Comparing the dynamics of poverty with that of program caseloads—for programs aimed explicitly at the poor—may highlight ineffective targeting, as was the case with Russia's Child Allowance Program. The eligibility for child allowances is determined by a simple income test, whereby a child may benefit from the program if the household's per capita income is below the poverty line. During 2000–5, child poverty fell by half, but the caseload fell only by about a fifth. These findings prompted the authorities to launch an in-depth study to investigate why the targeting performance of income-tested programs is mediocre.

Benefit Level

The main issue concerning the benefit level is to determine the adequacy of the transfer in helping program beneficiaries fulfill their basic needs. Several benchmarks can be used to measure the adequacy of benefits depending on the type of transfer and its objectives. The amount of cash or the value of an in-kind transfer could be compared with the income gap between the beneficiary's income level and the poverty line. Similarly, a feeding intervention may assess the nutritional supplement it provides against the nutritional deficit

- Is the level of administrative costs appropriate, that is, high enough to allow adequate administration, but low enough to be efficient?
- Does the intended budget reach the beneficiaries or are there indications of resources being siphoned off for unintended or illegal uses?
- What are unit costs? For example, for public works, what is the share of unskilled labor in total costs? For food programs, what is the cost per calorie provided? For training programs, what is the cost per trainee? How do unit costs compare with appropriate local benchmarks or good international practice?
- Does the program have significant effects on labor markets, for instance, to what degree do social assistance benefits discourage work effort?

- Sustainability
  - Is the burden on the budget sustainable? How do any foreseeable trends brought about by changes in poverty levels or fiscal status affect the answer?
  - What is the budget or expenditure allocation for each social protection program as a percentage of total government expenditure and of social protection expenditure?
  - What is the source of financing for each program (external or internal)? Are funds earmarked? Are there issues of intergovernmental financial flows?
  - Is this source of finance likely to shrink or to grow over time in concert with need?
  - Is the program in conflict with existing policy, legal, or regulatory frameworks that could undermine its sustainability?
  - What is the unit cost of the intervention, for example, to transfer US$1 to the target group of a social assistance program?

SOURCE: Adapted from www.worldbank.org/hdpers.

of a child, and the adequacy of transfers made through a public works program could be measured by the level of wages it offers compared with the prevalent minimum or market wage or the number of days of employment provided compared with the average number of days of idleness during the slack season. Note that a household may benefit from several programs at the same time or over the course of a year, and therefore the analysis may need to take the combination of several programs into account to assess the adequacy of safety net programs. Finally, a good analysis of benefit level should also address possible work disincentive risks.

Duration

A further dimension of adequacy is the duration of the benefit. Some programs are meant to provide seasonal or episodic support, in which case they can be judged against the length of the season of need. For example, does the heating allowance provide assistance for the entire winter or only for six weeks? Does the school feeding program run out of food before the school year ends? Other programs are designed to provide continuous support, although sometimes for limited periods. In such cases, considering whether the family's underlying need is likely to have changed before the program ends is useful—that is, will they have had enough time to increase their assets or likelihood of employment so that they will no longer need assistance?

EQUITY

Equity analysis examines the distribution of benefits across pertinent groups, showing both who is included in the program and who is excluded. One of the most common goals of safety net programs is redistribution, so looking at patterns of inclusion and exclusion across the distribution of welfare, as measured by consumption (or income or assets) is always pertinent. Looking at rates of participation and exclusion among various other groups is usually also wise, with analysis carried out by age, gender, ethnic group, geographic location, economic sector, and so on to see whether patterns of exclusion other than income or consumption are addressed. Moreover, the goals of some safety nets are to reach those affected by specific shocks for which some of these household characteristics may be proxies.

The benchmarks to be used in judging whether the patterns of benefit are acceptable are not absolute. First, they depend on the definitions of the target groups. Safety nets are usually meant to help certain groups in society, such as the poor, those who have suffered specific shocks, those believed to be vulnerable, and so on. The definition of target groups may differ from place to place and time to time, and is sometimes kept rather vague so as to build coalitions of support across advocates for different groups. (See chapter 4, section 2, for benchmarks with respect to errors of inclusion in relation to the welfare dimension and chapter 6, section 5, for a methodological treatment of the analysis.)

Second, the benchmarks should relate to feasible alternatives. For example, serving the same population group is more costly if it is dispersed than if it is concentrated in few locations. A country with a significant share of its population dispersed in remote areas will have inherently bigger challenges in covering all the poor than one that is more densely settled or has extensive transport systems. A country with a long history of exclusion of ethnic groups or women may wish to benchmark itself against countries with similar legacies but recent progress and not only against countries where such discrimination does not exist.

COST–EFFECTIVENESS

Good programs are cost-effective: they improve the livelihood of participants using the least amount of resources. As discussed in chapter 6, section 4, a cost-effectiveness ratio (or cost-benefit ratio when outcomes can be expressed in monetary terms) can be estimated for a program as a whole or for different parts of a program's production function. This subsection illustrates the usefulness of these indicators and examines the related issue of whether a program has sufficient resources to fulfill all its functions.

Efficiency and Effectiveness

Full cost-effectiveness or cost-efficiency analysis is rarely undertaken for safety nets. Rather, individual dimensions that contribute to the program's overall cost-effectiveness are examined, in particular: (1) efficiency in procurement, which assesses whether the program achieved value for money in relation to purchases; (2) efficiency in service delivery, which compares the program's output with the inputs used to generate the output; and (3) effectiveness, which examines the program's results (change in outcomes) per unit of output. These indicators cover different parts of the program functions logically along the program's results chain.

Efficiency in procurement is important for in-kind transfer programs such as food distribution, school feeding, and public works programs. For example, nonlabor inputs and capital goods should represent 30 to 50 percent of the costs of a productive public works program, and obtaining the best value for money for these items can reduce the program's overall costs and increase the amount of resources that goes to beneficiaries. In getting good value for money, the program should examine how costs and quality vary depending on the source of the purchases—for example, whether they are bought locally, domestically, or on the international market—and should follow transparent procurement practices. In general, using locally produced inputs rather than importing them from abroad is preferable, especially for food, as this tends to cost less because of savings on transport costs and has less of an impact on local production. However, this is not always feasible or true. The effectiveness of school feeding programs is enhanced when the food is fortified, and this may be less easily done for community-level local purchases. For all types of programs, having transparent procurement procedures and monitoring the cost and quantity of inputs is important.

Another aspect that may be examined is how efficiently the program transforms its inputs into outputs. Table 9.5 provides an example of cost-efficiency analysis where the measure is the cost of delivering 1,000 calories via various school feeding programs. This is a fairly straightforward case with closely comparable outputs and inputs across different programs.

TABLE 9.5 **Cost-Efficiency of Various School Feeding Programs, Panama, 2005**

Item	Milk	Porridge	Cookie	Lunch
Subsidy per ration (B)	0.21	0.09	0.13	0.13
Calories per ration	159	161	150	645
Subsidy per 1,000 calories per day (B)	1.33	0.55	0.84	0.20
Grams of protein per ration	8.1	4.0	2.2	16.3
Subsidy per 100 grams of protein per day (B)	2.62	2.22	5.70	0.80

SOURCE: World Bank 2000c, table A16.1.
NOTE: Subsidy amounts are given in Panamanian balboas.

Table 9.6 illustrates a more complex and less common cost-effectiveness analysis that compares the costs of reducing the poverty gap using different kinds of programs (a ratio of program cost per unit of output). Here it was necessary to assume that gross and net benefits were equal. To calculate how gross and net benefits may differ requires full modeling of behavioral changes, an enterprise that more closely resembles impact evaluation (chapter 6, section 5). If full modeling is not possible, the results of such modeling for similar programs in similar contexts may give an idea of what to expect.

When performing a complete efficiency analysis is not possible, judgments may be based on consideration of whether a program seems to have incorporated good practice in its design and have sufficient implementation capacity (chapter 7). These elements may not

TABLE 9.6 **Cost-Effectiveness of Transfers to Reduce Poverty, Guatemala, 2000**

Program	Quetzal of cost for each quetzal of reduction in poverty gap
All social assistance programs	1.4–2.0
School feeding	1.5
School transport subsidies	6.0
Scholarships	3.0
Energy subsidy	8.0
Social insurance	5.0–9.0

SOURCE: World Bank 2003f.

NOTE: The cost-effectiveness of poverty reduction estimated in the table are purely static and thus inappropriate for comparing programs with different expected future returns, for example, education-related programs versus cash transfers.

be sufficient to produce an efficient program, but are probably necessary. A 2003 analysis of the Gratuitous Relief Program, a food-for-work program in Ethiopia, concluded that the program was inefficient and had a low impact because the works part of the program had too few nonlabor inputs, the works selection was not integrated into appropriate planning systems, and works were poorly supervised (World Bank 2004a). Because the food was often received late and during the rainy season when works were difficult or impossible to undertake, the labor requirement was often not enforced, but the food was nevertheless distributed to avoid a humanitarian crisis. Thus none of the usual elements of a good public works program (as described in chapter 7, section 4) were fully in place.

Adequate Funds for Administrative Costs

Understanding administrative costs is important for understanding program efficiency. To maximize the level of transfers reaching beneficiaries, the obvious desire is to minimize administrative costs. At the same time, delivering cash or in-kind transfers is like any production process: to reach the intended beneficiaries with the desired transfer or service, programs have to finance a set of critical functions, such as receiving and processing applications, dealing with appeals, processing payments, undertaking monitoring and evaluation, and exercising oversight over how program resources are used. Programs that allocate insufficient resources to perform these functions tend to perform poorly. As a result, sector specialists often ask what a reasonable level of administrative costs is.

After sifting through all available studies (see the annex to this chapter) and making whatever allowances for differences in methods of assembling data on administrative costs and program design and implementation factors that we could,[2] we arrive at the conclusion that the administrative costs of well-executed cash or near cash programs cluster in the range of 8 to 15 percent of total costs (figure 9.2). Anything much less may imply underdeveloped administration, though it may also imply significant economies of scale and/or an extremely generous program. For example, both factors explain the low share of admin-

FIGURE 9.2 **Share of Administrative Costs in Program Budget, Median Value by Type of Program, Selected Programs and Years**

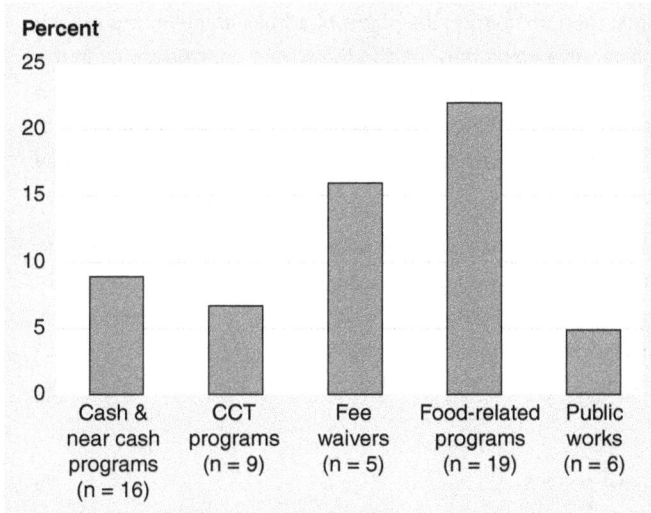

SOURCE: See the annex to this chapter.

istrative costs for Mexico's Oportunidades program (about 6 percent of total program costs) and for Armenia's Family Poverty Benefits Program (about 2 percent). Anything beyond about 12 to 15 percent of total costs bears close examination to see why administrative costs are relatively high. They may be entirely appropriate because the program is providing good service to a narrow target group or noncash services that the analyst has considered to be administration, but conveys a direct benefit, or it may be a sign that the program could be improved.

On average, the share of administrative costs is larger for food-related programs because of the logistical costs of transportation, storage, preparation, and related losses during these phases of such programs. For the 19 food-related programs presented in the annex to this chapter, the average share of administrative costs was 22 percent.

This benchmark must be used thoughtfully. As described in chapter 4, section 2, arriving at a reasonable estimate of administrative costs for a single program can be difficult, and arriving at numbers that are comparable across countries is likely to be still more difficult. We present a proposal for an indicator that will allow cross-program and cross-country comparability in box 9.3. Even when approximately comparable numbers are available, interpretation may be open to several subtleties. In examining a number, the following key questions should be asked:

- **Is the number high because the scale of the program is small or the program is just starting up?** This is the case for the administrative cost numbers often cited for Nicaragua's CCT program or the initial year or two of Oportunidades (Caldés, Coady, and Maluccio 2006). Now that several CCT programs are operating to scale and have undergone credible impact evaluations, and the findings of those evaluations have been positive, we know that a good CCT program can be run with administrative costs on the order of 6 to 12 percent (Lindert, Skoufias, and Shapiro 2006).

- **How does the program's level of generosity affect conclusions about the share of administrative costs?** In 2000–7, Russia's child allowance program had administrative costs of about 10 percent of the total, which sounds fine, but the program's benefits were low, equivalent to only 25 percent of median family allowance benefits in 22 European and Central Asian countries. Compared with

BOX 9.3 A Proposal for Benchmarking Administrative Costs

If generosity differs across programs, then comparing the share of administrative costs in total costs with the usual share of administrative costs may lead to the wrong conclusion, as in the Russian example cited in the text. To assess whether a program's administrative costs are within the normal range, we prefer to compare the administrative costs per beneficiary, expressed in purchasing power parity terms. We encourage analysts to report this information whenever they examine a program's administrative costs.

Alternatively, analysts can multiply program generosity, calculated as the ratio of benefits to the consumption of the beneficiary household based on household survey data, with the share of administrative costs and compare this index across safety net programs of the same type, for example, cash programs, public works programs, or school feeding programs. The following figure reports this index for a sample of programs from Europe and Central Asia and Latin America and the Caribbean.

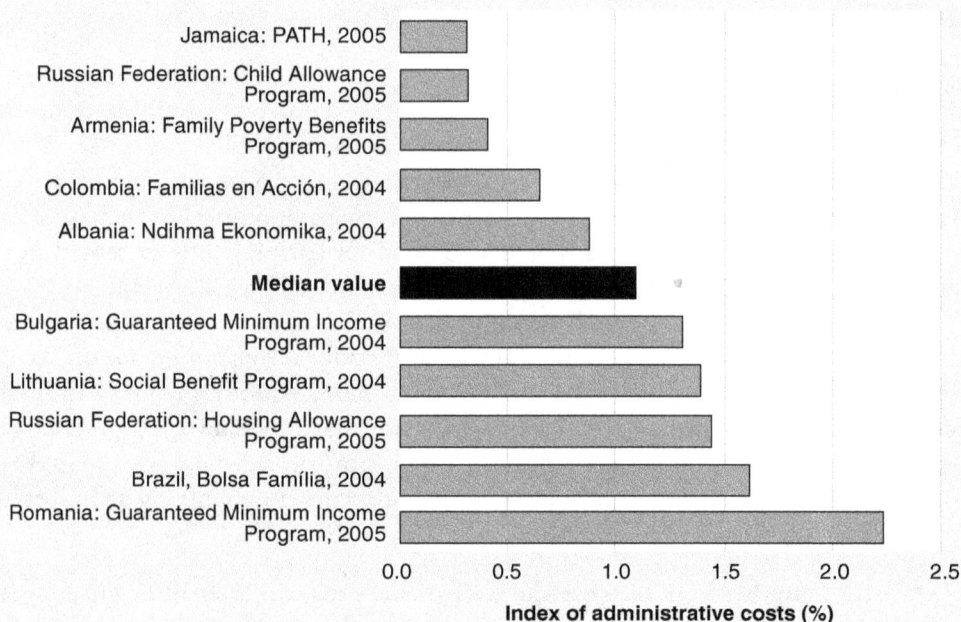

Index of administrative costs (%)

SOURCE: Tesliuc and others forthcoming.

NOTE: Index of administrative costs = Generosity × Share of administrative costs in total program budget.

similar programs in that region, the staff of the Russian program needed to make ends meet with only a quarter of the budget provided elsewhere. The program achieved its low administrative costs by underinvesting in some program functions that are critical for accurate targeting, such as third-party verification of claimants' incomes and assets, recertification, and adequate monitoring and evaluation. Employee workloads became huge, with one staff member serving 1,655 beneficiaries. In contrast, the workload in well-targeted programs in Armenia and Romania was only 180 and 93 beneficiaries per staff member, respectively. In qualitative interviews with employees of the Russian program they cited lack of time as the key reason for their superficial treatment of important program functions. Not surprisingly, the program's targeting accuracy remained low, with more than 60 percent of the children being served falling outside the target group.

- **Is the number high because of an inherent design problem?** This was the case with Mexico's old Leche Industrializada Compania Nacional de Subsistencias Populares (National Subsistence Commodities' Industrialized Milk Program), which provided subsidized fresh milk to the urban poor through dedicated stores. This design was expensive compared with many other possible variants. By using dedicated stores for a single product rather than selling the milk through commercial outlets, it had to maintain a large physical and staff infrastructure for a relatively small throughput. By selling a highly perishable product, the program had to deal with the complications of refrigeration, rotation of inventories, and spoilage that ration stores that sell cereals do not face to the same extent. By focusing on milk, transferring calories was inherently expensive (Grosh 1994).

- **Is the number too high because of leakages or losses?** Food transfer programs in South Asia have high administrative costs because they procure, store, and transport food commodities; in addition, they suffer from leakages and losses resulting from pilferage and spoilage. In India, the estimated cost of transferring Rs 1 of food grains under the targeted public distribution system in fiscal 1999/2000 was Rs 1.11 without leakages, but Rs 1.59 once estimates of leakage were taken into account (World Bank 2001e).

- **Would additional administrative expenses or systems pay off in relation to efficiency or improved impact?** The U.K. government estimates that it spent about £1 million on a hotline to reduce fraud in all social protection programs, and as a result identified about £21 million in overpayments (Barr 2007).

SUSTAINABILITY

Sustainability has fiscal, political, and administrative dimensions as follows:

- **Fiscal sustainability** depends on both the level and sources of financing. Less costly programs or programs in countries with fewer fiscal pressures will be sustained more easily. Programs wholly financed by current tax revenues are more likely to be sustained than those reliant on deficit spending, borrowing from international aid agencies, or grants from donor agencies. Low-income countries with low tax bases tend to rely on donor funding to support their safety net interventions, and this reduces the sustainability of their programs.

- **Political sustainability** is difficult to write about with certainty, because both public attitudes about poverty and safety net programs differ from place to place, and because the specifics of governmental structures and party dynamics differ as well. Whether a program targeted to the very poorest or a more general program aimed at a larger group of still mostly poor people is more politically sustainable is a disputed issue, and is probably context specific. Nevertheless, a program that is well run; that demonstrates good results; and that communicates these results effectively to its supervisory agencies, interested advocacy groups, the press, and the public is on much firmer ground than one that can only appeal to the idea that it is doing "good works."

- **Administrative sustainability** requires building and maintaining a minimal administrative apparatus (or capacity) and a sufficient administrative budget. A minimum administrative capacity is required if there is a need to scale up a program or to maintain program know-how across political cycles. As is clear from chapters 4 through 8, a program cannot be well run without a basic level of inputs. Contracting out or allocating functions to entities other than the main safety net agency can lower the number of staff directly on the program's payroll, but requires that arrangements with the contributing agencies are sustainable and that appropriate incentives and monitoring arrangements are in place. It may even raise the level of sophistication of required systems.

9.4 Assessing the Performance of the Entire Safety Net System

An assessment of individual programs will result in an understanding of which are performing well or badly and of areas where improvements might be possible. Targeting systems might be fine-tuned, benefit levels revised, or systems for monitoring and management action developed. When considering reforms of existing programs, the safety net system as a whole also needs to be examined. Perhaps the most important action may be not to fix each existing program individually, but rather to discontinue or consolidate some programs or add others.

A good safety net system depends not only on individual programs being "good," but on the mix of programs being appropriate and fitting well into broader poverty reduction, risk management, and social policies. The entries presented in box 9.4 will help the analyst examine this issue. The analysis matches the needs revealed by the poverty and vulnerability assessment discussed at the beginning of this chapter with what we know about the advantages and disadvantages of various types of programs from chapters 7 and 8 and the evaluations of specific programs.[3]

APPROPRIATENESS

A first set of questions examines whether the safety net programs are appropriate: whether a safety net is the best policy response to the country's problem, whether it complements other social protection and antipoverty policies well, whether it incorporates an efficient way to target the main groups, and whether the overall budgetary effort is reasonable. These questions are as follows:

- **How much of the poverty or vulnerability problem is best addressed by safety nets?** Often, reducing poverty and vulnerability requires public interventions other than safety nets or can be accomplished using multiple policy instruments. For example, a review of agriculture policy in Sub-Saharan African countries (Krueger, Schiff, and Valdes 1991) shows that several countries were taxing their farmers, most of whom were poorer than their urban counterparts, through a combination of export tariffs and marketing policies. The implicit tax on the value added of the

BOX 9.4 **The Public Expenditure Review Lens: Sectorwide View**

This part of the analysis investigates the overall composition of social protection expenditures and addresses whether the mix of programs and their size is adequate or sensible given constraints. It normally addresses the following issues:

- Get the big picture
    - List the country's main public programs: child allowances, noncontributory pensions, needs-based social assistance, food programs, public works, targeted fee waivers, any other social assistance programs, unemployment insurance and assistance or active labor market policies, contributory pensions, and so on.
    - List pertinent nongovernment programs: private pensions, large programs by nongovernmental organizations, unusually large international remittances, and local interhousehold transfers.
- Obtain an overview of budget allocations, trends, and processes
    - List public expenditures by program and calculate the safety net and social protection sector total as a share of GDP and of total public expenditures and in absolute values.
    - Assess intergovernmental financing arrangements, including defining and describing the operations of any subvention mechanisms.
    - Obtain trend information to show whether program expenditures are countercyclical and whether the balance between programs is changing over time.
    - Review issues pertaining to budget formulation, execution, and auditing and the incentives conveyed therein that affect the sector or its subsectors.
- Identify gaps, overlaps, and inefficiencies
    - Does the program mix have an appropriate blend of social insurance and social assistance? Of coverage in the formal and informal sectors?
    - Is the mix of public and private programs suitable?
    - Does the program mix provide an adequate balance of efforts to assist the chronically poor, transient poor, and special groups that may need aid even if overall poverty is low?
    - Given the risk profile, do large gaps exist in areas of intervention? Significant overlaps? Duplication? Fragmentation?
    - Is the overall level of effort sensible? Too high? Too low?

SOURCE: Adapted from www.worldbank.org/hdpers.

agriculture sector was used to finance government consumption and urban investments and was, in effect, a transfer from the poor to the rich. In such settings, rural poverty can be tackled more effectively by removing the agricultural price distortions than by using rural safety nets. Safety net policies may complement this approach, for instance, by providing transfers to poor, landless households in rural areas. Similar trade-offs often arise in other sectors as well. To reduce high unemployment, a government may finance a workfare program in a depressed area or develop the infrastructure for a free trade zone. If primary school enrollment is low, a government may build schools in areas with high poverty, provide free primary education for all children, or give scholarships to poor children. If high out-of-pocket expenditures block access by the poor to public health services, the government may build health posts in poor areas, provide a free package of health interventions, or give health waivers to the poor. Often, the optimal response is not to choose one option, but to combine a number of options.

- **Does the safety net system fit well within the range of complementary social insurance and poverty reduction policies?** Is the system unbalanced, providing too little for safety nets and too much for social insurance? Is the balance of demand-side (social protection) and supply-side (health and education) programs suitable for human capital formation? Do programs dovetail well enough; for example, are social pensions and contributory pensions functioning in a coordinated way to providing adequate income support for the elderly? Or does the social pension unduly undermine incentives to contribute to the employment-based scheme? Does the social assistance of last resort program unduly undermine job search or work in the informal economy?

- Do programs cover the main groups that should be covered? Does the program mix provide an adequate balance of efforts to assist the chronically poor, the transient poor, and special groups that may need aid even if overall poverty is low? Brazilian social policy in the 1990s, for example, was often criticized for devoting radically more resources to the elderly than to children despite much higher poverty rates among children and the evidence on the importance to human capital and lifelong outcomes of ensuring adequate child welfare. This was partly redressed with the expansion of the Bolsa Familia (Family Grant) program. Other countries use a single program of last resort to address the needs of different groups, such as the guaranteed minimum income programs in transition economies that give benefits to children, the elderly, people with disabilities, and others living in poor households.

- Are resources dedicated to an efficient mix of programs within the safety net? In addition to seeing that each program operates as well as it can, looking at the balance of programs is important. For example, in 2004, the Arab Republic of Egypt spent the equivalent of 10.5 percent of GDP on general food and energy subsidies that benefited the nonpoor more than the poor (World Bank 2005e) and distorted incentives for the production and consumption of these goods. Meanwhile targeted safety net programs received only 0.3 percent of GDP, and poverty remained at 20 percent. Clearly the safety net could play a greater role if resources were shifted from general subsidies that mostly benefit the nonpoor to targeted safety net interventions.

- Are resources reasonable? Resources are rarely adequate to do all that a government might want to in the area of social policy. One can judge whether resources are reasonable by comparing spending with the cumulative income gap of the poor, or perhaps spending with the poverty gap of the poorest 10 or 15 percent of the population. Looking at the resources put into targeted safety nets versus into contributory social insurance and subsidies in other sectors—electricity, fuel, water, health, education, and so on—is useful. In doing this, it makes sense to think about whether transfers would be as good or better as a way to meet equity or risk management goals than some of the other options and about whether progress toward other goals and services is more or less constrained than for safety nets. One can also benchmark against what other countries spend on safety nets.

Box 9.5 lists a number of common mistakes made in reforming safety net systems.

BOX 9.5 **Common Pitfalls in Reforming Safety Net Systems**

When developing reform plans, avoiding common pitfalls such as the following is important.

- **Having unrealistic expectations.** Safety net programs can never fully compensate for macroeconomic instability or eliminate the causes of poverty, although they can be helpful when used in conjunction with policies that address the root problems of these.

- **Avoiding conflicts between policies and programs.** Safety net programs cannot be expected to, for example, solve an unemployment problem caused by excessively restrictive labor market regulation or rural poverty caused by distortions in agriculture markets.

- **Avoiding having too many programs.** International experience is rife with countries that have too many programs, each with low coverage, low benefits, inadequate administrative systems, and high overheads. Having fewer, larger programs would allow them to achieve economies of scale. In countries with too many programs, they often overlap and are not sufficiently coordinated to achieve the best possible synergies.

- **Preventing an imbalance in target groups.** Programs may be excessively based in the formal sector or favor "virtuous groups" such as children or the elderly while failing to cover other groups, such as minorities or those with disabilities.

- **Rationing entry into a program by budget rather than by eligibility threshold.** When the funding for a program is insufficient to allow all those who meet the defined eligibility criteria to be included, horizontal inequity is created, transparency declines, and opportunities for rent seeking are created whereby eligibility intake officers may demand bribes or give favorable treatment to those with whom they share an interest or affiliation.

- **Having insufficient administrative effort, monitoring, and evaluation.** Programs are often set up in a hurry with only rudimentary systems. They may die altogether or fade away after a few years, especially if a change in government occurs. Developing and fine-tuning the most effective safety net systems takes time.

INCENTIVE COMPATIBILITY

A second set of questions examines whether the interactions between different safety net programs stimulate work and economic independence for beneficiaries as opposed to creating poverty traps. These questions are as follows:

- **Does the safety net contain elements that help households avoid irreversible losses?** One of the most compelling reasons for safety nets is to prevent irreversible losses to households' or individuals' long-term welfare resulting from a short-term coping strategy. Childhood malnutrition is perhaps the most irreversible and most costly example. A notable feature of current interest in relation to CCTs in Sub-Saharan Africa is that proposals and discussions tend to focus only on links to the education system despite a substantial improvement in primary school enrollment rates, while malnutrition is still high and worsening.[4] Allowing households to retain their land, animals, tools, or other inputs to their livelihoods is important everywhere, thus a minimum goal would be to avoid such losses.

- **Does the safety net contribute as much as is appropriate to the long-term reduction of poverty?** As described in chapter 7, a number of safety net programs contribute to long-term poverty reduction: CCT programs can improve the human capital of children and public works programs can improve the physical capital of communities. Recently, a handful of programs has been experimenting with other ways to move households into independence through links to other efforts, such as obtaining documentation, or through training and access to microfinance.

9.5 From Diagnosis to Action

The review of the mix of programs and how well each functions is likely to lead to ideas for reform, as few systems are optimal. Changes may be dramatic and entail eliminating or merging some programs and creating others, or may be more moderate and involve a change in the relative size of programs or modifications to one or more programs.

ASSESSING REFORM OPTIONS

Using the information generated during the preceding steps, the team responsible for designing the action plan for reforms can put together a list of interventions to address existing gaps and needs. The next step is to prioritize the interventions and determine their implications for existing programs or policies. This exercise will result in one or more proposals for a more appropriate mix of safety net and social protection interventions. These proposals may differ from the status quo in one or more of the following ways:

- **Changing the budget envelope for safety net interventions.** Often a country will find that it is spending too little to have an effective safety net. It may need to scale up existing programs (sometimes reforming them first for greater efficiency) or add new programs to its safety net. Some countries will find that they are spending too much on programs that are aimed at redistribution or at protecting equity, but are actually based on inefficient general subsidies or on social insurance programs that are ineffective in reaching the poor.

- **Reforming one or more existing interventions to make them more effective or to change their purpose.** Often, modifying existing safety net interventions is helpful. In some cases, changes in a program's rules or administration can markedly improve its effectiveness. In these cases, the program should already be reasonably well suited to the poverty situation in the country in question.

- **Creating a new intervention.** Introducing a new safety net intervention is often tempting, especially when a major risk or cause of poverty is largely unaddressed.

Despite a valid justification for the program in such cases, the value of the new program with regard to other uses of funds must be assessed. Establishing a new program that addresses an issue that should have been addressed by other, poorly performing programs is tempting, and particular care must be taken in such situations. Sometimes starting a new program is appropriate, as when small local programs cannot be scaled up without losing their effectiveness, but in many cases, starting a new program rather than resolving an old one's flaws can prove costly in the long run. The forces that led to the need to reform the old program or that made it difficult to reform may, over time, affect the new program, leaving the country with two poorly performing programs. Moreover, neither program will have as much opportunity to achieve full economies of scale.

- **Replacing or removing existing interventions entirely.** This may be desirable if the interventions are ineffective and cannot be feasibly modified or if they address low-priority groups or risks. To make such a move palatable, a government usually has to show that the funds (and sometimes the staff and structures) will be used for some other intervention in support of a broadly similar goal.

Table 9.7 provides some examples of recent safety net reforms.

ADOPTING AN ACTION PLAN

The purpose of an action plan is to ensure that medium-term and long-run goals are accomplished by ensuring that the immediate and intermediate steps are taken. At a minimum, the plan should include details on (1) the steps required to get from the status quo to the goal, (2) the resources required, (3) the timetable, and (4) the assignment of who is responsible for each action. Including other factors, such as how stakeholders will be consulted and the indicators that will be adopted to monitor progress, may also be useful. Many of the issues that must be addressed when developing an action plan for the safety net sector are generic to action planning generally.

Often the plan will need to be developed iteratively. For example, a first, general version might include an entry such as "reform the public works program." A more detailed version should elaborate on subcomponents of the reform, such as "get an exemption from the minimum wage law," "develop a poverty map," and "develop a manual of unit costs for tools and materials with suitable regional variations." A third version should detail the steps required to pass legislation or to gather the data for the unit cost manual. As successive levels of detail are added, inconsistencies across goals, resources, and time frames may emerge. Identifying these so that they can be resolved is important. The different levels of detail are also useful for the various users of the plan. Pamphlets for dissemination to the general public may reflect only broad goals and minimal detail, for example, but those who are actually implementing the plan will need much more detail if the work is to stay on track, especially where work by multiple offices has to be coordinated. Detailed development of the plan is also an important way of verifying that the goals in the general version are actually achievable.

The resources required can be specified in several ways, with the one-time investment requirements and annual recurrent costs specified separately. Each will need to fit within the respective budget envelopes. Specifying the administrative resources required

TABLE 9.7 **Examples of Recent Reforms by Type**

Type of reform	Country	Year	Action
Improving individual programs	Argentina	2005	Transition from emergency Jefes de Hogar (Heads of Household) cash transfer program to the Seguro de Capacitación (Training Insurance) program, a medium-run employment services approach
	Ethiopia	2005	Transformation from relief-oriented food aid to a meaningful public works program complemented by transfers to those who cannot work
Adding significant new programs	Colombia	2000	Creation of the Familias en Acción CCT program
	India	2007	Nationwide extension of the Employment Guarantee Scheme
	Lesotho	2004	Creation of a universal social pension
Merging several programs	Brazil	2004	Merger of the Bolsa Escola, Bolsa Alimentação, Cartão Alimentação, and Auxilio Gás programs into Bolsa Familia
	Jamaica	2001	Merger of the Food Stamp Program, the Outdoor Poor Relief Program, and public assistance into the PATH
Replacing some programs with others	Armenia	1999	Replacement of 26 categorically targeted payments with a single proxy means-tested family benefit
	Ecuador	2003	Replacement of the Bono Solidario and Beca Escolar programs with Bono de Desarrollo Humano, a program with greater coverage and generosity and a stronger beneficiary identification system
	Georgia	2007	Replacement of most existing, fragmented social assistance programs with a proxy means-tested targeted poverty benefit
	Mexico	1997	Replacement of a range of in-kind food and price subsidies with PROGRESA
Reducing subsidies and creating compensatory programs	Brazil	2002	Elimination of gas subsidies and the creation of Auxilio Gás
	Indonesia	2006	Reduction in fuel subsidies and the creation of a cash transfer program
	Jamaica	1984	Elimination of food subsidies and the creation of the Food Stamp Program
	Romania	1997	Replacement of heating and utility subsidies with targeted, seasonal heating allowances

SOURCE: Authors.

(personnel, training, equipment, processes) in detail can be useful. Even though their financial cost may be small relative to the program's benefits, making them available may require significant lead time—for example, if significant training is required, if new tasks are to be accomplished so that new staff must be hired or jobs redesigned, or if databases or administrative systems need to be built from scratch. Identifying specific needs makes it possible to see what measures are required to meet them and how the program might be phased.

Specifying who is responsible for each action can be particularly important for safety net strategies, because so many actors carry out safety net interventions. No single head of sector is available as, for example, a ministry of education would be for all matters relating to education. For instance, unless specified, who would be responsible for such cross-cutting actions as ensuring that safety net programs carry out impact evaluations at least once every five years would be unclear. A single decision-making unit, usually in the ministry of planning or finance or the prime minister's office, may be assigned to monitor progress and provide technical assistance, but many agencies will have to carry out evaluations of their own programs. Furthermore, many individual programs involve multiple actors, such as a central ministry and local offices, a municipality, a nongovernmental organization, and grassroots groups. Note that donor agencies have a large role in some safety net programs and may have to take some actions to bring about the desired reforms. The assignment of responsibility in the action plan is to ensure that every action is carried out, with none being omitted because the parties involved were unaware of their responsibilities. Such assignment may also reveal the complexity of the process or highlight potential synergies wherein, for example, several actors might carry out a common consultative process jointly rather than each undertaking it separately.

ADDRESSING THE CHALLENGES OF THE REFORM PROCESS

All reform programs face challenges. Here we discuss common elements related to financial constraints, political feasibility, and administrative capacity. The many technical challenges related to specific kinds of programs or their specific functions are discussed in greater detail in chapters 3 through 8.

Different types of reforms will face different combinations of challenges. A new program creates new winners among beneficiaries and program officials, so the political feasibility issues may be easy, but obtaining sufficient financing may be hard. Setting up new systems will require building administrative capacity, but starting from a clean slate may be technically easier than merging or transforming several legacy systems as a program merger or upgrade would require. In contrast, closing programs is politically challenging, but relatively simple in relation to financial and administrative issues. Reforming an existing program will involve both political and technical challenges, but may not pose financial challenges. The creation of new safety net programs may occur more often than the reform or discontinuation of programs in part because this is easier to accomplish.

Financial Constraints

Any action plan should fit within its budget constraint, that is, any new program or proposed reform must be financially feasible. This may seem obvious, but numerous strategy exercises, many of which never bear fruit, fail to look at financial sustainability issues.

The first step in determining what is affordable is to estimate what a program might cost. Table 9.8 shows the illustrative costing exercise done in Pakistan as part of the development of the social protection strategy (Government of Pakistan 2007). It sought to put options on the table for a consultation process intended to garner support to expand the safety net system. The safety net part of the strategy suggested an increase in spending for targeted safety nets program from PRs 11.3 billion in 2004 (0.2 percent of GDP) to PRs 35.8 billion in 2010 (0.63 percent of GDP), resulting in an increase in coverage of

TABLE 9.8 Estimated Annual Costs and Expected Coverage of a Proposed Safety Net Reform Package, Pakistan, 2006–10

Programs	Current situation (FY2003/04)		Targets: minimum requirement	
	Cost (billion PRs)	Beneficiaries (thousands of households)	Cost (billion PRs)	Beneficiaries (thousand of households)
Cash transfers	10.0	2,069	18.0	3,150
Zakat (almsgiving) Program (cash and other transfers)	5.9	800	5.9	800
Food Support Program	4.0	1,250	2.2	700
Child Support Program (CCT program)	n.a.	n.a.	8.8	1,300
Pilots, such as for child and bonded labor programs	0.1	10	1.1	350
Public works programs	n.a.	n.a.	15.0	2,110
School feeding programs	0.7	500	1.6	800
Social care services (people with disabilities, vulnerable children)	0.6	50	1.2	100
Total social assistance	11.3	2,610	35.8	6,160

SOURCE: Government of Pakistan 2007.

NOTE: n.a. = not applicable.

the programs from 10 percent of the population in 2004 to 24 percent by 2010, or from 2.6 to 6.2 million households. The proposed increase would bring Pakistan more closely in line with average spending in the region.

Taking into account the population's poverty and vulnerability profile, the strategy proposed the introduction of a new CCT program, for which part of the unconditional cash transfer spending would be reoriented, and new workfare programs that would help the poorest households earn higher and more stable incomes. Some of the likely benefits of the proposed reform would include higher and more stable incomes for poor and vulnerable households; enhanced food security (diversity, quality, and quantity of food consumed); significant increases in school enrollment, attendance, and completion; reduced levels of child labor; lower levels of rural to urban migration; a more vibrant rural economy; and moderately lower income inequality.

In assessing the financial sustainability of the proposed strategy, the authors carefully considered different alternatives for creating the fiscal space for needed safety net programs. Although the proposed increase in targeted program spending is substantial, it starts from a low base: combined spending for social insurance and assistance is less than 0.5 percent GDP in fiscal 2003/04 and only 3 percent of pro-poor expenditure as set out in the Poverty Reduction Strategy Paper. The overall increase in spending will account for only a small fraction of the agreed increase in pro-poor spending, from 4.25 in 2005 to

6.49 percent in 2010. Part of the cost of the strategy will be financed by eliminating unnecessary programs and waste and by reorienting some programs.

The budget must be consistent with the eligibility threshold and benefit levels. When the funding for a program is insufficient to allow all those who meet the defined eligibility criteria to be included in the program, horizontal inequity is created and transparency declines as eligibility intake officers gain discretionary power over who among those eligible may enter the program, thereby creating opportunities for corruption.

Thinking about various time horizons is also important, for example, whether the program is intended to solve a crisis and likely to be radically reduced or terminated after a couple of years. However, as discussed in chapter 3, many such programs stay in place after crises because they really targeted the chronically poor rather than the transient poor, and so were still needed after the crisis had passed. Even programs designed for those who were made transiently poor by a covariate shock may be continued after a large covariate shock abates and program designers realize that idiosyncratic shocks are present that cause transient poverty, and thus that a permanent program to serve those affected may be useful. Alternatively, a program may stay in place for less technically sound but still powerful reasons, for instance, that removing a program or dismissing the civil servants who are administering it may be politically unpopular.

Looking at the time horizon thoughtfully is also important for programs intended to be permanent from the outset such as social pensions. Sometimes governments set up programs to assist the very old that provide a modest income supplement and are therefore affordable, but two factors may increase their budget over time. First, demographic changes are leading to more people surviving to older ages, leading to a predictable increase in the number of beneficiaries if the program's parameters remain constant. Second, and perhaps more important, the government may face political pressure to increase the size of the transfer or to lower the age of eligibility. This has been the case in Mauritius, and policy makers in Lesotho foresee the same trajectory for their new social pension scheme.

Political Feasibility

Reforms that are accomplished relatively easily in some contexts can seem impossible to policy makers in other contexts. The following circumstances are the most propitious for reform, or at least for some types of reforms:

- When a major crisis occurs, such as those that followed the breakup of the Soviet Union, the East Asian financial crisis, and the tequila crisis, dramatic changes occur in needs, means, and/or public attitudes toward redistribution and render inaction unacceptable. Action on the safety net agenda is almost guaranteed. Such periods often result in wholesale system redesign and/or the addition of simple programs geared to protecting the poor during massive shocks.
- When times are good and policy makers are optimistic that the numbers that need to be served should be decreasing or that they may be able to serve those covered better, the environment may be propitious for reforms that lead to more sophisticated targeting methods or respond to concerns about labor disincentives. At such times simple programs may be transformed into sophisticated programs.
- When the proposed changes create few losers, for example, the expansion of a program during a time of growth, making changes to the system may be easy.

- When a program is so egregiously bad or so costly that it cannot be sustained, changes may be possible, though difficult. This is what has occurred with the reform or replacement of some of the general energy and food subsidy programs.

- Where political parties agree on the need for and direction of the reform, this can allow action, especially in building the capacity for sophisticated programs over time. This seems to be happening in several of the maturing Latin American CCT programs.

- Where changes in government are common, programs often depend on a specific government, or even minister. In such a setting, the electorate and beneficiaries can become accustomed to programs starting and stopping or shrinking into insignificance rather often, and do not protest the demise of each. This lends itself to the accumulation of many fragmented, neglected programs that do not add up to a coherent policy, but does allow for experimentation that yields some interesting new possibilities.

Although the underlying circumstances can make reforms easier or harder, and sometimes impossible, political feasibility is not a given. Policy makers can influence it. Making a reform politically acceptable is an art, with the specifics highly dependent on the context. We can thus only suggest the following general stratagems that may be of use. How to craft each, and the relative emphasis on each, will have to be left to the reform team itself.

- **Make the case for reform**. If people understand why and how badly changes are needed, they are more likely to accept them. If the current program or system is performing badly, measure that (as described in chapter 6), publicize the results, and explain how much better the new program would be. Craft a communication campaign using appropriate terms and venues to reach the entire range of stakeholders: the politicians and civil servants in all affected parts of the government, the opinion makers, the nongovernmental organization or advocacy community, the program's beneficiaries, and the general public (box 9.6).

- **Craft rule changes in ways that do not create more losers than necessary.** For example, when Sri Lanka converted from an in-kind food ration to a food stamp program, the value of the transfer was maintained, and only its form changed initially. In the U.S. welfare reform, the federal government imposed new rules for work requirements, but the budgets for the states were set for five years at the high levels then prevalent. State offices did not initially lose funding, and would have increased discretion over the use of those funds if they managed to reduce their caseloads by implementing the reforms. The strong economy meant that many welfare recipients found a fairly easy path back to employment, which validated the basic design change and gave states a big increase in their welfare budgets that they could use for innovative programs.

- **Decide whether and how much to compensate losers.** If an existing program is to be eliminated, reduced, or reformed, some people are likely to lose out. The question then arises as to whether and how to compensate them as discussed earlier. A number of cash transfer programs were created as partial compensation for the reduction or elimination of energy or utility subsidies. These usually sought to compensate consumers toward the bottom to middle of the welfare distribution. Elsewhere, governments changed the eligibility rules for programs or successor programs. When new eligibility requirements are put in place, sometimes those eligible under the old rules are grandfathered in, at least for a period. When Ecuador converted from its Bono Solidario program to the new Bono de Desarrollo Humano program, for example, it allowed elderly beneficiaries of the former program who fell just above the eligibility threshold to remain in the new program for a year. Similarly, when Georgia moved from categorical targeting to proxy means testing for its social assistance benefit, it allowed former beneficiaries who did not qualify under the new eligibility criteria to maintain their previous benefit for a certain period.

- **Have a credible option.** If a program is being offered as compensation, the promise has to be credible. This is true at the moment of announcing the reform plan, and credibility must be maintained in the ensuing first months of delivery. In Zambia, when the government introduced a food stamp program in the 1980s as part of a package of maize price reforms, it failed to budget and manage cash well enough to ensure that it could immediately reimburse retailers for the stamps. Once the retailers experienced payment delays from the government, they refused to accept food stamps from the public, and the program's credibility collapsed.

Administrative Capacity

The key questions in determining administrative feasibility is what capacity is needed and where it should be located. This issue, like others, must be handled at both the program level and at the level of the entire safety net system.

No single standard is available for what capacity is needed at the level of the individual program. New programs, especially those set up during emergencies, are often run with only rudimentary capacity for processing eligibility and payments and minimal monitoring and auditing systems. Mature, permanent programs will have more sophisticated versions of these, as well as developed outreach mechanisms; systems to recertify eligibility periodically; established grievance or appeals systems; and much more developed monitoring and accountability mechanisms, perhaps including some performance-based incentives. Programs differ in their inherent complexity: a universal child allowance or social pension program is quite simple compared with a means-tested CCT program or public works program. The degree of completeness or sophistication will also vary by context, with simpler or more rudimentary systems generally being used in countries with lower administrative capacities and incomes.

At the whole system level, having a body that can review the entire system, make corrections in relation to balance, bring about cooperation among agencies or synergies across programs, and so on is desirable, but rarely achieved.

When a new program is to be created, policy makers have options about where to put it, each with its advantages and disadvantages (table 9.9). Some goals with respect to program placement are to put them where they can be well run, take advantage of institutional capacity where it exists rather than duplicating it, and put them where they can more readily be coordinated with other programs. Sometimes these goals come into conflict. Ministries of welfare are the natural location for most social assistance programs,

---

BOX 9.6 **Communication Strategy: A Key Component of Reform**

What Is a Communication Strategy? Communication strategies define objectives, target groups, and messages that will help achieve objectives.

Preparations for a communication strategy might include the following components:

- An assessment of the country's media climate, the specific needs of the planned reform program, and the level of awareness and acceptance of the reform
- A list of the main stakeholders, including government officials, parliamentarians, journalists, union members, members of professional associations, employees and employers in sectors affected by the reform, and members of social groups at which the reform is directed
- A program to develop the skills of spokespeople, opinion leaders, and champions of the reform by holding workshops, setting up communication units, training media advisors, training officials in strategic communication, and organizing placements and study tours to countries that have implemented similar reforms
- A set of guidelines for the institution implementing reform on how to become user-friendly, for example, by developing newsletters and interactive Web sites

The communication strategy may include these elements:

- A mass media campaign using radio and television spots, advertisements in print media, and articles in targeted periodicals and/or press conferences
- A program to develop media capacity on reporting on a given issue, including workshops for journalists, databases for the media, and awards for reporting
- A program of face-to-face presentations for key groups of stakeholders ranging from seminars for legislators, speeches at conferences, and so-called town hall meetings for union members and the general public
- An awareness program directed at potential beneficiaries through organizations they trust, such as schools, and nongovernmental organizations
- A set of feedback mechanisms—formal and informal consultations with stakeholders, media monitoring, and focus group and opinion research—to allow adjustment of the communication strategy or reform as needed

A communication strategy as described here is a relatively short, intense effort that precedes and accompanies a specific reform. It goes well beyond the normal outreach efforts that stable programs need to ensure that potential clients are aware of the programs. It is episodic, whereas outreach should be continuous.

Why Have a Communication Strategy? An effective communication campaign builds awareness of and trust in a reform and neutralizes criticism based on misconceptions. It improves the chances the reform will be completed and increases the chances that future reforms can be carried out.

---

but are often technically and politically weaker than other options, so that sometimes governments tend to locate them elsewhere, especially in the case of an emergency program or one that is the flagship of a new government.

Launching a major reform without an adequate communication campaign is risky, as illustrated by the Russian government's attempt to replace in-kind subsidies for privileged citizens with cash equivalents on January 1, 2005. Politically, the reform was difficult because the subsidies were large and reached about half of Russia's population. The fiscal and quasi-fiscal cost of the subsidies amounted to almost 6 percent of GDP. Even though the government was aware that the subsidies were regressive, it did not attempt to make them more pro-poor, fearing that middle-class beneficiaries would derail a reform that would make them worse off. For the same reason, the government decided to implement the reform in phases, starting with federal employees and pensioners, who represented one-third of the beneficiaries. Regional governments were supposed to monetize the rest of the subsidies at a later unspecified date.

Given the political economy constraints, the design of the reform was appropriate. The government opted for full cash compensation, taking beneficiaries' average consumption patterns and the cost of the subsidized services into account. The reform was income neutral for the middle class, increased the incomes of poor privileged citizens who consumed fewer subsidies than the average beneficiary, and reduced the level of subsidies for the well-off. (In Russia, some of the poor are granted privileged status and qualify for certain subsidies. The subsidies are not universal for all Russians.)

Details about the reform measures and their expected impact were not widely discussed or disseminated before the changes suddenly took place. A few days after they were implemented, pensioners took to the streets in Moscow, St. Petersburg, and a few other large cities to protest the reform. Even though federal privileges were monetized on January 1, 2005, the appetite for similar reforms by the regions disappeared. By the end of 2005, of Russia's 98 regions, only 8 had chosen to monetize the subsidies.

What Determines the Objectives and Scale of Communication Efforts? The timing and scale of communication efforts may range from a one-time poster information campaign or press conference to a comprehensive, multiyear communication program with a large budget. The following is a generic list of activities that might be included, with some indicative budget figures in parentheses: organizing training for journalists (project budget of around US$100,000); laying the basis for a government-led communication strategy (US$150,000); and developing communication capacities that involve setting up and hiring the staff for a spokesperson's office, training journalists, running a press and broadcasting information campaign, conducting public opinion research, maintaining the project's Web site, running a radio feature show, producing television news items and a soap opera on a reform, purchasing equipment for the news office, launching and maintaining a specialized magazine, and running a field theater in villages on the project issue (US$2.5 million). Large-scale efforts will be needed for reforms that are complex, affect large benefits or groups of people, are controversial, or are to be carried out when dissent would be particularly costly to reformers or society.

Quite often, the capacity to run even a single program is not located in a single agency. Some functions will correspond to different levels of government, and often programs will try to take advantage of existing capacity by dividing responsibility among

TABLE 9.9 **Options for Institutional Locations for Safety Nets**

Option	Advantage	Disadvantage
Program level		
In ministry of social welfare	• Is often the natural location • Can easily allow programs to share structures for targeting, monitoring, payment, and so on • Will make the long-run development and balancing of a safety net easier if most programs respond to a single ministry	• Ministries of welfare often have low administrative capacity and little political clout
In president's or prime minister's office	• Is often associated with more modern administrative systems and sometimes with higher salaries, leading to better capacity • Can give the program clout when dealing with partners	• May clutter the institutional landscape • May be harder to keep the program free from political interference in reality or perception or to achieve continuity across electoral cycles
In sectoral ministry	• Allows the integration of supply- and demand-side actions to increase service use	• Implies duplication of systems for targeting and the like across ministries and programs • Makes coordinating benefits and ensuring that the combined package across all programs is fair and sufficient difficult, but does not induce too many disincentives
In municipalities	• Has good possibilities for outreach, appeals mechanisms, and so on • Can be especially useful for ensuring that public works programs are well integrated with systems for planning infrastructure	• May give rise to horizontal inequity if not financed centrally • Gives rise to the need to manage performance incentive issues if financed centrally • Is likely to give rise to substantial variability in relation to program implementation
System level		
In cabinet	• Is the natural home	• May be so high a level that it remains perfunctory without getting to the required technical level
In special technical secretariat	• May provide significant clout and enhance results	• Can cause confusion of roles • Can clutter the institutional landscape, especially if the secretariat becomes less important with a change of government or priorities but is not abolished
In planning ministry	• Can be a sensible place to locate functions that can be shared across programs in different sectors	• Divides responsibilities for a single program and makes accountability mechanisms less clear

SOURCE: Authors.

agencies, sometimes on a cooperation basis, sometimes on a contract basis. Ensuring that the parts fit together is important. Chapter 3, section 6, discusses the issues pertaining to assigning different functions to different levels of government overall; chapter 4, section 4, discusses the role of central and local offices in targeting; chapter 5, section 4, discusses issues relevant to contracting out payment functions; and chapter 6 discusses monitoring, especially performance-based monitoring, which is particularly important when different agencies are involved in running a program.

9.6 How Often Should Safety Net Strategies Be Revised?

The last two decades have witnessed growing efforts to measure, monitor, and understand the nature of poverty, as well as to design effective policies to combat it, including safety nets. This effort has been made possible because of the greater availability of household survey data, an increase in computing capacity, and a growing trend toward open access to microdata. Such advances have been facilitated by the advocacy and capacity-building role played by international organizations and developing countries' increased capacity to rigorously analyze poverty, vulnerability, and the role played by existing safety net policies. While safety net programs have figured permanently in policies to reduce poverty since the early 1990s, their level of sophistication has increased over time. Data-intensive methods to identify the poor, such as proxy means testing or poverty maps, have emerged thanks to these advances, and have given governments the tools to replace more expensive categorical programs with more effectively targeted programs.

The way in which safety net programs are designed and implemented in developing countries will continue to become more sophisticated. The demands for improved performance by safety net programs are increasing with the emphasis governments, financiers, nongovernmental organizations, and the general public place on being accountable, delivering results, and demonstrating clear impact through rigorous impact evaluations. All these pressures call for regular reviews of the safety net sector as old strategies become obsolete because of the emergence of new problems and priorities, as progress in solving the first level of a problem reveals the next generation of issues, or simply as governments have learned how to solve old problems in more efficient ways.

With regard to when countries need a broad review of their safety net policy, the answer is "right away" for countries without a sector strategy. The same is true for countries that are considering introducing new programs or are substantially changing their mix of programs. For most other countries that have a strategic blueprint on file, assessments or reviews of the safety net strategy are probably warranted at least every 5 to 10 years.

In the interim period between such assessments, program-level assessments will likely be needed. While more limited in scope, program-specific assessments account for the majority of reforms in the safety net sector. They trigger the adaptation of safety net programs to changing circumstances through incremental improvements in design and operations.

Notes

1. Comparing poverty rates for population subgroups over time using cross-sectional surveys may be misleading. For time-invariant characteristics, say, gender or an age cohort born in

1965–70, this type of comparison is valid. For other characteristics, say rural inhabitants, the observed changes will reflect both changes in the welfare of the initial group as well as changes in the composition of the group. When membership of a group changes significantly between successive surveys, for example, rural households during a period of high migration to urban areas, the resulting change in poverty may be driven by the selection process, not by real changes in the welfare of the original group. For instance, the survey may indicate that poverty in rural areas is rising. This may be due to a fall in rural incomes, but it may also be the result of better-off households migrating to urban areas.

2. A handful of studies have tried to put together comparable numbers across a number of programs. Grosh (1994) provides information for 26 programs in Latin America. Lindert, Skoufias, and Shapiro (2006) provide information for 14 programs, also in Latin America. Coady, Grosh, and Hoddinott (2004) report administrative cost information for several programs in their appendixes, but found the sources too disparate in relation to methods to make strong comparisons. Caldés, Coady, and Maluccio (2006) provide numbers for three Latin American CCT programs and provide a useful method for disaggregating them by program function. Tesliuc and others (forthcoming) apply that method to six Europe and Central Asia programs. In addition, a variety of estimates of individual programs are available.

3. This section is based on Coudouel and others (2002) and Grosh (1995).

4. In Sub-Saharan Africa, the net enrollment ratio in primary school increased from 49 percent in 1991 to 68 percent in 2006 (World Bank 2008e). The average malnutrition rate as measured by weight for age in children under five was 27 percent in 2006 (World Bank 2008e) and is projected to increase (De Onis and others 2004).

Annex:
Administrative Costs by Type of Intervention

Region	Country	Year	Program	% of total costs	Source
			Cash and near cash programs		
Europe and Central Asia	Albania	2004	Ndihme Ekonomika	7.2	
	Armenia	2006	Family Poverty Benefits Program	2.2	Tesliuc and others (forthcoming)
	Bulgaria	2004	Guaranteed Minimum Income Program	9.9	
	Bulgaria	1992/93	Child allowances	5.6	Coady, Grosh, and Hoddinott (2004)
	Kyrgyz Republic	2005	Unified Monthly Benefit Program	9.3	
	Lithuania	2004	Social Benefit Program	6.5	Tesliuc and others (forthcoming)
	Romania	2003	Guaranteed Minimum Income Program	9.8	
Latin America and the Caribbean	Honduras	1992	Food stamps for female-headed households	12.0	
	Honduras	1992	Bono Materno Infantil)	6.0	
	Jamaica	1992	Food Stamp Program	10.0	Grosh (1994)
	Mexico	1992	Tortivales	12.0	
	Venezuela, R. B. de	1992	Food scholarship	4.0	
Middle East and North Africa	Yemen, Republic of	2001	Social Welfare Fund	8.5	Coady, Grosh, and Hoddinott (2004)
South Asia	Sri Lanka	1982	Food Stamp Program	2.0	Castañeda (1998)
Sub-Saharan Africa	Namibia	1993/94	Old-age pension	9.5	Coady, Grosh, and Hoddinott (2004)
	Zambia	2005	Pilot Social Cash Transfer Scheme	16.6	Devereux and others (2005)
			Median	**8.9**	
			Mean	**8.2**	
			Conditional cash transfer programs		
Latin America and the Caribbean	Brazil	2003	Bolsa Familia	12.3	Lindert, Skoufias, and Shapiro (2006)

(continued)

ANNEX (continued)

Region	Country	Year	Program	% of total costs	Source
	Colombia	2000/4	Familias en Acción	10.5	Lindert, Skoufias, and Shapiro (2006)
	Dominican Republic	2006	Solidaridad	5.9	
Latin America and the Caribbean	Ecuador	2005	Bono de Desarrollo Humano	4.1	World Bank (2006a)
	Jamaica	2004/5	PATH	13.0	
	Mexico	2003	PROGRESA/ Oportunidades	6.0	Lindert, Skoufias, and Shapiro (2006)
	Peru	2006	Juntos	11.6	World Bank (2006a)
South Asia	Bangladesh	2002	Primary Education Stipend Program	4.0	Ahmed (2005)
	Pakistan	2005/6	Child Support Program (pilot)	6.7	World Bank (2006k)
			Median	6.7	
			Mean	8.2	
Fee waivers					
	Colombia	1992	Student loans	21.0	
Latin America and the Caribbean	Costa Rica	1992	University tuition waivers	16.0	
	Jamaica	1992	Student loans	30.0	Grosh (1994)
	Belize	1992	Hospital fee waivers	0.4	
	Dominican Republic	1992	Hospital fee waivers	3.6	
			Median	16.0	
			Mean	14.2	
Food-related programs					
	Bolivia	2003	School feeding, WFP	55.5	
	Brazil	1997	Programa Nacional de Alimentación Escolar	28.9	
Latin America and the Caribbean	Colombia	2003	School feeding, WFP	20.5	
	Dominican Republic	2003	School feeding, WFP	9.4	Lindert, Skoufias, and Shapiro (2006)
	El Salvador	2003	School feeding, WFP	46.2	
	Guatemala	2003	School feeding, WFP	14.0	
	Honduras	2003	School feeding, WFP	30.1	

(continued)

ANNEX **(continued)**

Region	Country	Year	Program	% of total costs	Source
	Nicaragua	2003	School feeding, WFP	38.3	Lindert, Skoufias, and Shapiro (2006)
	Chile	1992	Food supplements	6.0	
	Costa Rica	1992	Day care food packets	9.0	
Latin America and the Caribbean	Dominican Republic	1992	Proyecto Materno-Infantil	12.3	Grosh (1994)
	Jamaica	1992	Nutribuns	6.8	
	Peru	2005	School feeding, WFP	19.2	WFP (2006a)
	Peru	1992	Programa de Alimentacion y Nutricion para Familias de Alto Riesgo	22.0	
					Grosh (1994)
	Mexico	1992	Leche Industrializada Compania Nacional de Subsistencias Populares	28.5	
South Asia	Bangladesh	2001	Income Generation for Vulnerable Group Development Program	10.0	Ahmed (2005)
	Benin	2005	School feeding, WFP	37.2	
Sub-Saharan Africa	Malawi	2005	School feeding, WFP	35.8	WFP (2006a)
	Mali	2005	School feeding, WFP	52.0	
			Median	**22.0**	
			Mean	**25.4**	
			Public works		
Latin America and the Caribbean	Argentina	2004	Jefes de Hogar	1.6	Lindert, Skoufias, and Shapiro (2006)
	Bolivia	1992	Emergency Social Fund	3.5	Grosh (1994)
	Peru	2002–3	A Trabajar Urbano	23.0	Chacaltana (2003)
Middle East and North Africa	Morocco	1990s	Promotione Nationale	6.0	World Bank (2001g)
	Yemen, Republic of	2003	Second Public Works Programs	3.7	Al-Baseir (2003)
South Asia	Bangladesh	2001	Rural Maintenance Program	24.0	Ahmed (2005)
			Median	**4.9**	
			Mean	**10.3**	

SOURCE: Authors.

NOTE: WFP = World Food Programme.

## CHAPTER 10

Customizing Safety Nets for Different Contexts

KEY MESSAGES

There is no single recipe for a safety net system, as needs and capacities differ by context. Both the program mix and the handling of individual programs should vary from place to place.

Safety nets in low-income countries will be subject to the harshest triage. They will usually focus on ameliorating the worst of destitution, trying to prevent households from suffering irreversible losses, and helping households to invest in their children. Safety net systems should be built up from a few programs maintained over time to allow institutional capacity to be developed. Individual programs may be relatively simple.

Safety net systems in middle-income countries may aspire to cover all target groups and motivations for safety nets, although they tend to focus on helping the chronically poor. Individual programs may be quite sophisticated, but innovations may not have spread to all programs in the country that might benefit from them.

Safety net systems following an economic crisis or in the face of rising food prices have two primary objectives: to protect incomes and avoid irreversible losses of physical assets and human capital and to help maintain political consensus around the policies needed to resolve the crisis. Scaling programs up quickly is difficult, so some compromises with respect to targeting, incentive compatibility, and accountability may be needed. Such compromises will be less likely if the country has a base program that it can modify and expand than if it must start from scratch.

The key role of safety nets following a natural disaster is to help households avoid irreversible losses that could ensue after the actual disaster. Effective safety net systems should be seen as a complement to larger efforts to protect livelihoods and undertake reconstruction and recovery. Again, given the difficulties of scaling up programs quickly, countries with existing safety net systems that they can modify will be better placed to deliver safety nets following natural disasters. They may need to adjust procedures during the response, and afterwards they will need mechanisms to return to normal procedures.

In relation to policy reform, safety nets can play two linked but somewhat separate roles. They can help compensate the poor for any losses suffered, and beyond that they can help engender political tolerance of the reform. Some programs with a primarily temporary political economy goal may be at a scale that is too large to sustain, and thus must have a clear sunset clause built in. Other programs with a clearer poverty focus may be meant to be permanent, and so must be designed to be sustainable. If launched quickly, they will need an enduring period of institutional development and process reform.

The main objective of this chapter is to show how to apply the principles of safety net design in different settings. As no single recipe for a safety net exists, chapter 9 advises on how to craft a safety net by outlining the process used to arrive at country-specific programs and policies. Needs differ by context, and multiple ways of addressing them are usually available. This chapter moves a step toward concreteness and specificity by discussing different types of contexts and what they may imply for sensible safety net design and implementation, with illustrations for each.

Appropriate safety net policy varies not only from place to place, but over time in the same country as the context changes. The experience of countries acceding to the European Union illustrates this well (box 10.1).

BOX 10.1 Eastern European Safety Nets: From Central Planning through Transition to Accession

Under central planning, income distribution was relatively equal, access to health care and education was free, housing markets were highly controlled, and the prices of many basic goods were subsidized. Generous pensions provided income for the elderly, and individuals with special needs were placed in special institutions. Little need therefore existed for a social assistance system to take account of income differences or special needs. The number of children made the biggest difference in determining household welfare. Family benefits in the form of child allowances were, therefore, central to social assistance, generous, and universal.

With the transition from planned to market economies, many of the constituent parts of the system changed. Open unemployment emerged, income inequality rose sharply, price subsidies were eliminated, access to health and education declined in some cases or became more reliant on fees, and the real value of child allowances often declined. Early in the transition poverty was widespread, but was often relatively shallow or transient. As reforms progressed and growth was reestablished, overall poverty rates declined, but not all prospered equally, and pockets of chronic and deep poverty emerged. These changes resulted in the need for two new kinds of assistance: unemployment benefits and needs-based social assistance. These required new capacities, and countries struggled to build the political understanding and administrative systems to handle these new programs, which continued alongside the still important child allowances.

With their accession to the European Union, these countries are now facing new challenges to their social assistance policies. Accession-related legislation does not govern social assistance, and the European Union is using the open method of coordination to harmonize policies. The European Union's social policy has ambitious goals for reducing poverty and increasing social inclusion. Policy measures are not binding or uniform, but promote the provision of a guaranteed minimum income (to all residents, not just nationals) with accompanying labor activation measures. The emphasis on social inclusion brings to the fore the need for accession countries to better integrate minorities and reintegrate those previously cared for in institutions.

SOURCE: Sipos and Ringold 2005.

In each country setting we sketch the general context using the same diagnostics: needs assessment, review of individual program capability, and safety net systems as a whole. We then discuss how the safety net might be constructed. This relates not only to the mix of programs (cash versus in kind), but also to specific details of program design features. For example, should a cash program be an entitlement or rationed? Should it be means or proxy means tested? What features should be used to limit work disincentives? Such differences are how a good deal of the accommodation to different contexts is made.

10.1 Safety Nets in Very Low-Income Countries

The idea that safety nets are an important component of economic policy in low-income countries has only started to be accepted in recent years, so practice is still relatively nascent. Even when accepted, safety nets are subject to harsh triage decisions about how to use scarce resources that characterize all policy choices in such countries. Nonetheless, a number of very poor countries are making promising progress.

GENERAL CONTEXT

In very low-income countries, incomes are low and vulnerability is high. Such countries are characterized by an extremely low per capita gross domestic product (GDP) of the order of US$300–600 per year and a poverty rate greater than 40 percent. Growth is often slow, with little prospect of improvement in poverty rates. This situation applies to countries such as Chad, Ethiopia, Malawi, Mali, Nepal, and Niger. Many of the very low-income countries are landlocked, possess limited physical infrastructure, are facing pressures from their large populations, and are poorly endowed with natural resources. Their main challenges include the low productivity of labor working in subsistence agriculture and a lack of off-farm employment opportunities. The role of contributory social insurance schemes is extremely limited because of the small size of the formal sector. Growth is more robust in some larger low-income economies, but they still account for large numbers of the world's poorest people who are often concentrated in particular social groups or live in particular geographic areas as is the case in, for instance, Bangladesh, India, Kenya, Uganda, and Vietnam.

In addition to the widespread and generalized poverty and low asset base prevalent in very low-income countries, people living in such countries are extremely vulnerable to both idiosyncratic and covariate shocks. Risk management strategies of the traditional, informal, community-based type are largely ineffective in dealing with widespread poverty and tend to collapse during large and/or repeated covariate shocks.

Capacity

Overall government capacity is weak in most aspects in these countries, including management, accounting, and logistical and financial controls. Safety net programs will not be able to take advantage of other systems to the degree that they can in other countries: household surveys for diagnosing need and on which to piggyback the monitoring of targeting and evaluation studies will be outdated, civil registries and identification documentation will be incomplete, databases of taxes and/or incomes will be too limited for use by targeting systems, and banking or postal banking systems will only reach urban areas and therefore be unsuitable for use as payment mechanisms.

Safety Net Systems

Most very low-income countries have minimal government-financed safety net systems that usually operate with too few resources to have an impact and have only rudimentary administrative systems. Public resources are extremely limited, especially given competing demand for other basic services. With a total tax collection of 10 to 15 percent of GDP (World Bank 2007r), a country with a per capita GDP of US$500 per year will have US$50 to US$75 per year per person for all public functions, from combating malnutrition to providing schools, improving physical infrastructure, addressing low agricultural productivity, and providing all other services. In general, little help is available for families facing idiosyncratic shocks or with special vulnerabilities. Funding for programs for the destitute, and even more so for those suffering from covariate shocks, is likely to come from donors; donor management is thus a critical issue. Countries should seek long-term commitments from donors, develop only a few permanent programs, and channel support to these to build and preserve institutional capacity to realize economies of scale.

A few low-income countries, such as Bangladesh, India, and Sri Lanka, have supported domestically financed safety nets and/or have largely resolved problems of donor management and have had long-standing programs. The best of these programs have many, though sometimes not all, the features of good practice—for example, the Maharashtra Employment Guarantee Scheme and the Bangladesh Food for Education Program—but many other programs could be made more effective through reforms to their basic design and improved implementation.

Potential Role for Safety Net Systems

The huge needs and limited resources of very low-income countries mean that a severe triage of objectives and detailed attention to implementation are called for. Safety nets in these countries should, and usually do, focus on supplementing the incomes of the poorest to prevent irreversible losses of human capital or livelihoods. Even these will focus on a subset of the poorest, not everyone below the poverty line. Programs for covariate shocks may be funded intermittently, almost always by donors. Programs to address idiosyncratic shocks and social care services are usually not well developed or funded, and the informal sector tends to provide whatever support is available.

Interventions and Implementation

Workfare will be a commonly selected program because it can help build or maintain much-needed infrastructure and because it can be self-targeted. A seasonal program in rural areas can help bridge families through the hungry season, larger versions may be appropriate after droughts or floods, and operations in urban areas can assist if commodity price instabilities bring shocks to the urban economy. Public works should use labor to improve infrastructure such as roads, irrigation systems, or drainage systems that will help raise productivity. In very low-income countries, public works programs can have fairly high labor intensity and workers can be organized in traditional construction or work gangs.

A public works program could be complemented by a small transfer, possibly seasonal, to the most destitute. Because of difficulties in accurately distinguishing shades of poverty, the program might be categorically targeted—for example, aimed at widows in South Asia, orphans in southern Africa, people with disabilities anywhere. Community-based targeting may also be used, and communities often choose to focus support on such groups even when this is not a program requirement. Several low-income countries have recently implemented new proxy means tests to identify the poorest, but lessons from these are not yet clear.

Where malnutrition is an issue, the country should have a strong nutrition program, within which a transfer element may be helpful. The target group for such programs is pregnant and lactating women and children from birth to two years old, the age group for which nutrition programs can have the largest impact. If resources permit, fee waivers for health care and education for a slightly wider segment of the population will help safeguard or form human capital. The larger a program is, the more important it will be to arrange maximum links to health and education services to ensure that in addition to relieving misery, the program builds human capital.

A score or more Sub-Saharan African countries are working on proposals or pilots for new cash transfer schemes. We hope that in the coming years we will begin to see modest, but well-implemented, programs in many of these countries. Meanwhile, the Productive Safety Net Program (PSNP) in Ethiopia illustrates many of the issues pertinent to safety nets in very low-income settings.

ETHIOPIA'S PRODUCTIVE SAFETY NET PROGRAM

Since the mid-1980s, images of severe drought and large-scale starvation have become inexorably linked to Ethiopia.[1] In 1999/2000, 42.2 percent of the population lived below the national poverty line, and 22.5 percent of households were extremely poor and lived below a food poverty line of 1,650 kilocalories per person per day. Most poor households are engaged in subsistence farming on small plots of degraded land. On a daily basis they must manage hunger, extreme hardship, and multiple sources of uncertainty. Climatic variability is high. The variability in rainfall is among the highest in the world, and fluctuations in rainfall are inversely related to mean incomes: the larger the coefficient of variation in rainfall, the lower is consumption (World Bank 2005d). One risk is the failure of the rains. In addition, health risks, including both malaria and HIV/AIDS, exacerbate the vulnerability of the poor, driving many thousands of people into poverty traps.

As a result, every year for more than two decades the government of Ethiopia had to launch an international emergency appeal for food aid. This annual emergency assistance was designed to meet the consumption needs of both chronically and transitorily food-insecure households.[2] Even though the total amount of humanitarian assistance provided was substantial (estimated to average about US$265 million a year between 1997 and 2002) and saved many lives, evaluations have shown that it was unpredictable for both planners and households, often arriving late relative to need. The delays and uncertainties meant that the emergency aid could not be used effectively in the public works it was meant to support and thus did little to protect livelihoods, prevent environmental degradation, generate community assets, or preserve household assets (physical or human capital). Thus, despite the large food aid inflows, household-level food insecurity remained both widespread and chronic. Indeed, chronic food insecurity had been increasing in the aftermath of repeated droughts as vulnerable households failed to manage their effects and slide deeper into poverty. As part of the same phenomenon, rural growth had also stagnated.

Given these shortcomings of the emergency aid regime, the Ethiopian government decided that an alternative instrument was needed to support chronically food-insecure households and to address some of the major underlying causes of food insecurity. In 2005, it started implementation of a new program, the Productive Safety Net Program. The PSNP replaced the emergency humanitarian appeal system as the chief instrument in the country's safety net. It is currently operational in 234 chronically food-insecure districts (of a total of 692 districts).

The PSNP provides resources to chronically food-insecure households in two ways: through payments to the able-bodied for participation in labor-intensive public works activities and through direct grants to households composed of the elderly or those who cannot work for other reasons. Community committees decide on entrance into the program and determine which households are to participate in public works versus receiving unconditional cash transfers. Eligible households are those that face more than three months a year of food insecurity year after year. The program provides beneficiaries with up to six months of consumption support per year.

The program involved a number of reforms to the public works program to improve the value of works done, namely, earmarking 20 percent of the funds for nonlabor inputs; providing a multiyear, predictable flow of resources so that adequate planning can be undertaken and works can take place in the dry season when construction is feasible; and integrating the planning and selection of works in district development plans. Public works planning has adopted an integrated approach to watershed planning that aims to reverse the severe environmental degradation and raise agricultural incomes over the long run.

Despite various teething problems associated with capacity constraints, in 2006 the PSNP made about six rounds of payments to about 7.3 million beneficiaries. The PSNP public works are operated on a large scale and generated more than 172 million person-days of labor in 2007. Most of the works are focused on soil and water conservation activities (table 10.1). The works have been found to have already brought demonstrable benefits to the communities in the form of environmental transformation. For example, improved water conservation has led to increased agricultural productivity and an increase in groundwater recharge such that dry springs have started to flow again. In addition, the communities have enhanced income generation from area closure, and improved access to markets, education and health facilities.

A 2005 beneficiary survey found that the PSNP has had a significant positive effect on beneficiaries' well-being as calculated by both subjective and objective indicators. The survey found that three in five beneficiaries avoided having to sell assets to buy food in 2005, and according to 90 percent of the households, this was a result of their participation in the PSNP. Almost half the beneficiaries surveyed stated that they had used health care facilities more in 2005/6 than in 2004/5, and 76 percent of these households credited the PSNP with this enhanced access. More than one-third of surveyed households enrolled more of their children in school; 80 percent of them attributed this to participation in the PSNP.

TABLE 10.1 **Sample of Public Works Supported under the PSNP, 2007**

Project	Result
Soil embankment construction (kilometers)	482,542
Stone embankment construction (kilometers)	443,148
Pond construction and maintenance (number)	88,936
Spring development (number)	598
Hand-dug well construction (number)	491
Land rehab. through area enclosure (hectares)	530
Small-scale irrigation canals (kilometers)	2,679
Tree nursery site establishment (number)	285
Seedlings produced (number)	301,778,607
Seedlings planted (number)	12,883,657
Rural road construction (kilometers)	8,323
Rural road maintenance (kilometers)	20,458
School classroom construction (number)	340
Animal health post construction (number)	71
Farmer training center construction (number)	119

SOURCE: Food Security Coordination Bureau 2007.

Significant work is planned to further improve implementation capacity and bring systems to a level of functioning not previously possible with fragmented and temporary programs. Work is also beginning on a contingent grant mechanism that will trigger extra resources for the safety net in affected districts where the program works in years when rainfall is particularly inadequate.

The PSNP is complemented by a larger Food Security Program that tries to help households raise their incomes by means of resettlement grants, household income-generating packages, and water harvesting. Households that benefit from the PSNP are also entitled to assistance under other parts of the Food Security Program. Food security interventions financed by donors that fall outside the PSNP are, however, as yet rarely coordinated with the PSNP at local levels, and links to basic rural services such as marketing or veterinarian services are also weak.

The transformation of the prior emergency appeal system into the PSNP illustrates many of the issues that surround safety nets in very low-income countries:

- The program is moving in a clearly beneficial direction by means of a basic design that not only seeks to use resources in ways that save lives, but also that assist in livelihoods. The progress in implementation to date suggests that this is possible even in a very low-income setting.

- The design process and implementation planning have undergone a fairly harsh triage. Even when fully realized, the program will only provide a safety net in about a third of the country. The districts selected are appropriately the poorest, but many poor people also live in the unserved districts. Even in the included districts, the eligibility threshold is low: households that have been food insecure for more than three months per year. Richer countries might have tried to serve all those who were food insecure, but in this setting, that would have been impossible. Moreover, the program has phased its implementation. It is focusing first on consolidating the basic PSNP. It hopes to enrich it eventually in a number of dimensions, but program managers and donors have realized that everything could not be accomplished right away. Thus, for example, the contingent fund for droughts was not implemented until the third year of the PSNP. The government recognized that it needs to develop a modified version of the program for pastoralist groups, but decided to consolidate the basic program first. Household specific linkages with agriculture extension, microcredit, and other elements of the wider Food Security Program are planned but were not pursued in the first phases until both the PSNP and the Food Security Program were functioning smoothly.

- Good implementation requires diligent and sustained effort. By 2007, the program had many positive outcomes, and early qualitative assessments of its targeting and impacts are positive, but more remains to be done to consolidate implementation. Good implementation also requires flexibility and innovation. For example, the government was initially having problems with the program's monitoring system. In the interim, it deployed so-called rapid response teams to visit districts to identify and solve implementation problems. This gave managers a sense of what was going well and what was not and whether adjustments were needed in individual districts or at a more systemic level. Meanwhile, the design of the monitoring system was simplified and a pilot to computerize it is under way.

- An important part of the reform is the shift to a multidonor, multiyear framework rather than an annual emergency appeal system with each donor running a separate initiative. This is complemented by the decision to deliver the program through regular government systems rather than the special implementation units common in donor-funded programs. The multiyear framework and the reduction in fragmentation should permit the development of much more effective administrative systems. The multidonor framework should also aid in resilience, in that withdrawal or a reduced commitment by a single donor will have a less deleterious effect.

10.2 Safety Nets in Middle-Income Countries

Middle-income countries contain half the world's population and a third of the world's poor. These countries have many types of safety nets and have recently undertaken a great deal of experimentation with evaluating and learning about good design and implementation. Individual programs, and sometimes the suites of programs in some of the upper-middle-income countries, approach those in countries of the Organisation for Economic Co-operation and Development in terms of targeting, care in handling incentives to work, and evaluation and are reasonably generous. Other countries have more of a mix of programs than an integrated system and their individual programs are more basic.

GENERAL CONTEXT

The label middle income hides a great deal of heterogeneity among countries, and often within individual countries. Income per capita varies from US$1,000 in Azerbaijan to

US$10,000 in Antigua and Barbuda. Gini coefficients vary from 0.28 in Ukraine to 0.58 in Uruguay. On the whole, growth has been strong in recent years, with growth rates of 3.7 percent from 1995 through 2000 and nearly 5 percent from 2001 to 2005 for middle-income countries as a whole. With respect to poverty, in 11 middle-income countries, more than 40 percent of their populations live on less than US$2 per day; in 12 countries, less than 5 percent of their populations live on less than US$2 per day. Many other middle-income countries have strong national economies, but significant pockets of poverty among specific ethnic groups or regions (World Bank 2007d, 2007r).

Macroeconomic shocks have been a significant feature for many countries, for example, the 1997 financial crisis in East Asia and its spillover effects, crises in Russia and Turkey, and repeated debt or financial crises in Latin America. These shocks have been influential in shaping safety net policy in a number of the countries, with many current safety net programs having begun as initiatives to ameliorate crises.

Capacity

Safety net programs in middle-income countries can usually take advantage of systems developed by other institutions for other purposes. National identification systems or civil registries may be well enough developed to be used as the main identifiers for individuals within and across programs; income and property tax systems, labor registries, and utility billing mechanisms may be useful in targeting; and banking systems or postal banks are usually sufficiently developed to provide useful channels for payments. Data for understanding poverty and vulnerability are usually available, and a fair body of analysis of existing social policies and at least partial impact evaluations of some programs may be available. One or two of the flagship programs in each country may well incorporate quite sophisticated features for targeting, payment, provision of noncash benefits, fraud and error control, monitoring, and evaluation.

Safety Net Systems

Most middle-income countries have partial, but significant, safety net systems, although a great deal of diversity is apparent. In countries in the Middle East and North Africa, expenditures can be significant, and the main instruments are general food subsidies and, often, fuel subsidies. Many Latin American countries have a long tradition of truncated welfare states, with social protection systems built on contributory social insurance based on attachment to the formal labor market but large informal sectors. Because as many as half of all workers, and a much higher proportion of the poor, work in the informal sector and are not covered by social insurance, they derive little benefit from such schemes. An increasing number of these countries have begun to develop the social assistance side of the welfare state by creating conditional cash transfer (CCT) programs, several have adopted noncontributory pensions, and a few have extended health insurance or fee waivers to the poor. Countries of the former Soviet Union have moved away from the Soviet legacy of categorically based in-kind "privileges" to targeted cash transfers and child allowances. East Asian countries' publicly supported safety nets are still quite small, and the countries tend to rely on high growth and family support to prevent poverty.

Potential Role for Safety Net Systems

Complete safety nets cover the chronic poor, those hit by shocks, and those with special vulnerabilities. Few middle-income countries have achieved full coverage in all three areas; in general, the programs for the chronic poor are the best developed.

These countries are relatively unconstrained in their choices of how to construct their safety net systems. Their selection will depend on the starting point. Many countries are introducing targeted cash transfer systems to meet the needs of the chronically poor, but for different reasons: in Europe and Central Asia to replace a system of privileges unrelated to economic need; in Latin America and the Caribbean to address the truncation of the welfare state; and in a few countries elsewhere to replace substantial, untargeted commodity subsidies. Programs aimed at vulnerable groups are increasingly a focus of attention, in Europe and Central Asia because the inherited system of institutionalized social care services yielded poor care and was unsustainably expensive, and in other regions to address needs that had previously not been met. Because more countries are developing strong base programs, when the next crises hit, something to build on may be in place, but as yet few countries have an explicit ex ante design for crisis management.

The safety net may include some or all of a range of other services to improve social inclusion. Often these are not fully to scale. Some countries are working to ensure coverage of ethnic minorities or indigenous groups. Social care services for people with disabilities, the elderly, children with inadequate parental care, and the like are being developed, albeit unevenly. Countries in Latin America and the Caribbean are developing programs to ensure that the poor and vulnerable have adequate documentation, especially of births, marriages, identity, social security numbers, and/or voter registration to help households take full advantage of economic opportunities or government programs.

Interventions and Implementation

Middle-income countries have been innovating extensively in relation to safety nets in recent years, contributing much to the understanding of what is desirable and feasible. Some relatively sophisticated features and programs are clearly feasible in at least some settings, and elements of the best programs should be replicated more generally, both across countries, but especially from the flagship program in each country to other programs in the same country.

Cash transfers will play a larger role in stable, middle-income countries than in other settings, in part because means testing and proxy means testing are feasible and will permit the good targeting required for significant cash transfers. The programs may use one or more features to keep labor disincentives low. For instance, they might configure benefits to be higher for households with higher dependency ratios; they might add a requirement for public service, work, or enrollment in some sort of training or job search; or they might be complemented with an earned income tax credit. In countries with extensive health and education networks but inadequate use of these, benefits might be conditional on households obtaining adequate preventive care for themselves, undertaking health education, and/or enrolling their children in school.

A needs-based cash transfer may integrate coverage of all age groups or be complemented by separate child allowances or social pensions, possibly using the same administrative apparatus. Cold countries might provide a seasonal heating allowance using essentially the same administrative structures, though possibly with a higher threshold for eligibility. The same targeting procedures, perhaps with a different income threshold, will grant access to subsidized health insurance or fee waivers for health care. In countries with a small informal labor force and good macroeconomic stability, a needs-based cash transfer could become an entitlement program and serve to protect not just against chronic poverty, but against shocks as well.

Public works programs in middle-income countries should be designed to accommodate the complexity of their infrastructure and their larger formal labor markets. To accommodate the generally more adequate infrastructure, such programs usually select works at the local government level and may have a lower labor content so that more equipment and/or more materials are used to construct higher-quality or more complex works. Alternatively, the labor hours may be used for a completely different range of public service activities. For example, beneficiaries may work in parks, in libraries, in schools, or in hospitals or may act as home aides for the elderly or those with disabilities. This usually means that workers are allocated across many different agencies rather than working in large labor gangs on a few construction sites. Where the labor market is mostly formal, public works programs sometimes subsidize employment in private firms or count training or job search as labor effort. Such programs add the goal of improved future earnings to the more modest goal of immediate income support typical of public works programs. All these variations to the basic public works scheme make supervising the labor effort, finding suitable placements for workers, monitoring the program, evaluating it on its multiple objectives, and the like much more difficult.

FOOD SUBSIDIES IN THE ARAB REPUBLIC OF EGYPT: AS ENDURING AS THE PYRAMIDS

Egypt's story is one of entrenchment and the difficulty of making lasting changes to subsidy systems.[3] Egypt is a middle-income country with a per capita GDP of US$1,250, a Gini coefficient of 0.35, and a poverty headcount of about 20 percent. Poverty is fairly shallow, so extreme hardship is uncommon. At the same time, many households are just above the poverty line and are vulnerable to falling into poverty as the result of small, negative shocks. The most important correlations of poverty are location (poverty is higher in Upper Egypt than in Lower Egypt and is higher in rural areas than in urban areas), low educational attainment of the head of household, and work in agriculture or construction activities. As an oil-producing nation, Egypt looks to redistribute commodity revenues for the public good. This objective, combined with the country's tendency toward governments with long political tenure, favors the maintenance of a safety net system based on general subsidies.

Energy subsidies have come to dominate redistributive spending, accounting for 8 percent of GDP in fiscal 2004. The largest subsidies are for natural gas, diesel, and liquefied petroleum gas. In the 1980s and early 1990s, the government raised energy prices gradually but significantly to reduce energy subsidies, then did not raise domestic prices at all between 1997 and 2004. Not surprisingly, the subsidies are not well targeted: the richest quintile of the population receives about three times the value than the poorest quintile. Moreover, the subsidy reduces incentives to conserve energy, which leads to high consumption, pollution, and lower export revenues.

Egypt is perhaps the iconic case of food subsidies, as these dominate the social assistance budget. Today they account for about 1.6 percent of GDP, compared with 0.12 percent for social assistance defined more traditionally. Expenditures on the Social Fund run another 0.16 percent. The government put the food subsidy system in place in 1941 to avert famine during World War II. It did not immediately repeal it after the war, but the subsidy remained relatively small throughout the 1960s. Anwar Sadat greatly increased subsidies and the range of subsidized commodities, especially after 1977. Major and politically difficult reforms in the 1980s limited the range of commodities covered, reduced the fiscal cost of the subsidies, and improved targeting.

Baladi and *shami* breads, which are made from two grades of wheat flour, are subsidized in unlimited quantities and to a substantial extent (47 to 67 percent of the price). Cooking oil, sugar, tea, ghee, beans, lentils, rice, and pasta are subsidized in defined quantities and mostly with lower subsidy rates per item than for bread. In principal, all households are eligible for a subsidy ration card, which can be either green (high rate of subsidy) or red (low rate). The red cards are available to those who meet any one of 18 criteria. Of these criteria, three are pro-poor: eligibility for other targeted programs, divorced homemakers, and seasonal and temporary agricultural laborers. All the other criteria are regressive; for example, recipients must be public sector employees or pensioners. More than 80 percent of the value of the subsidy accrues to nonpoor households, and 25 percent of the poor do not benefit. The benefit is equivalent to about 8 percent of consumption expenditure, and about 5 percent of the population is lifted out of poverty as a result of the program. Recent increases in the world price of wheat have reversed the reduction in costs achieved by means of prior reform efforts, which underscores the difficulties of managing subsidy systems.

Reform of Egypt's food subsidy system is a perennial topic on the agenda of the international community, with suggestions offered on ways to improve it by changing the eligibility criteria, the mix of commodities and the subsidy rates on them, the regional targeting of subsidized food stocks, and the self-targeting by means of the location of ration shops, and so on or replacing it with various alternative safety net elements. The program has, however, been politically sensitive and enduring. Reform rather than replacement seems more likely, and even that is much easier to envision technically than politically.

The social assistance program is small and rather underdeveloped. Fewer than 12 percent of the poor participate and transfers are relatively small—for example, equivalent to about 8 percent of the poverty line for a family with two adults and three children in rural Upper Egypt. Administrative structures are basic. Serious reductions in the general food or energy subsidies would require a much larger and better developed social assistance program, possibly based on the existing program or complemented by other programs yet to be determined.

The Egyptian case illustrates three general lessons about safety net policy. The first is how hard reform can be, especially of general subsidy systems. The second is that not all expenditures made in the name of safety nets are equally efficient or defensible. The third is the "chicken and egg" conundrum that is common to safety nets. The social assistance program is small and has long played a marginal role in the overall system, so the government has not invested in its administrative systems and the program has not demonstrated its effectiveness persuasively. Because it has not done so, it does not inspire the confidence of policy makers or the public as being worthy of expansion or improvement.

BULGARIA: SAFETY NET POLICY IN A NEW MEMBER STATE OF THE EUROPEAN UNION

Bulgaria offers an example of a comprehensive safety net that is well embedded in the larger social protection system.

Changing Safety Nets for Changing Times

Bulgaria is a middle-sized, middle-income country with a population of 7.7 million and a GDP of about US$31 billion in 2006 (approximately US$79.05 billion in purchasing power parity terms) (World Bank 2007r). GDP per capita was about US$4,000 at the official exchange rate and US$10,000 in purchasing power parity terms. In part a heritage of the country's socialist past and its strong redistributive policies, inequality is low to moderate; the Gini index of per capita consumption was 0.3 in 2003. The extent of redistribution is substantial. Government revenues represent about 40 percent of GDP and are used to finance a wide range of public policies, notably in the areas of health, education, social protection, and infrastructure. The key social protection issue that confronts Bulgaria is providing adequate pensions for the elderly, the unemployed, and the poor. The elderly represent about 17 percent of the population (in 2005), the national poverty headcount is estimated at around 14 percent (in 2003), and the unemployment rate is around 12 percent (in 2006).

The social protection system consists of three main categories of programs: (1) social insurance programs, including pensions and benefits to cover such risks as death of the breadwinner, illness, and disability, plus benefits for pregnant women; (2) passive and active labor market measures; and (3) safety net programs. Social protection programs redistribute a large share of GDP and cover a sizable proportion of the population. In 2005, social protection spending amounted to 10.5 percent of GDP, or about a quarter of total government spending. The coverage of the social protection system was extremely broad, with 76 percent of the population benefiting from some form of social protection transfer in 2003, either directly or indirectly through the sharing of benefits within the household. Eighty-seven percent of the poorest decile received some form of cash support. About 90 percent of social protection spending covers pensions and unemployment benefits, while safety net programs account for the remaining 10 percent, equivalent to 1.2 percent of GDP.

The core safety net system consists of five programs for low-income and vulnerable households. The main programs include the Guaranteed Minimum Income (GMI) Program, which is a cash benefit paid to low-income households below a particular income threshold; an energy benefit that consists of cash benefits paid to low-income households during the winter heating season; a family benefit paid under the Birth Promotion Act that includes child allowances, maternity leave, and birth grants for uninsured households; cash and in-kind benefits for the disabled, which include medical and transportation benefits; and social care services and institutions. The GMI Program, energy benefits, and child allowances are means tested. A temporary workfare program has been operating since 2003 with the objective of placing able-bodied, long-term GMI Program beneficiaries in the labor market.

The main role of the safety net programs is to close the coverage gap in social protection programs for the poor, as well as help beneficiaries reenter the labor market or gain access to essential basic services. For example, the GMI Program covers only 20 percent of the poorest decile, even though everybody in the poorest decile is eligible. The rest of the poorest decile is covered by other social protection programs, notably, unemployment benefits and pensions (including social pensions), which are more generous than the GMI Program. In relative terms, safety net spending represents only 2 to 3 percent of total governmental spending.

Institutional Actors and Roles

The design and implementation of the three means-tested safety net programs is centralized. The Ministry of Labor and Social Protection formulates and oversees policy that is implemented by the Social Assistance Agency through its 28 regional and 272 municipal directorates. The administrative systems for the three programs are based on the same procedures, although thresholds and benefit levels vary. Applicants must present detailed information, including certificates relating to their income and assets, to their local social assistance directorate. The information is verified by an interview; a home visit; and cross-checks with other institutions, including the tax authorities, employment bureaus, social insurance offices, and other state and municipal institutions. Recertification is done annually, with the beneficiary responsible for notifying the local social assistance directorate of changes in the interim. Payments are made monthly in cash, with most being made directly to recipients' bank accounts and the remainder paid out by the local social assistance directorates.

Distributional Outcomes

The outcomes of the safety net program are good, especially for the GMI Program (table 10.2): about 50 percent of the program's benefits go to the poorest decile. Errors of exclusion are low. The generosity of the program is adequate: it supplies about half of the income of the poorest decile. The program's administrative costs are reasonable, estimated at 10 percent of total program costs.

Lessons from Two Decades of Economic Transition

In the last two decades, Bulgaria has engineered a major shift in its economic system, breaking with the socialist model in 1989, navigating through a difficult transition period until 1997, and then entering a period of recovery and stabilization. In the early 1990s, the economy declined dramatically, first because of the loss of traditional export markets in the former Soviet Union, and then because of a hesitant reform agenda that triggered a severe economic and financial crisis in early 1997.[4] During 1990 to 1997, the country experienced negative growth for six of the eight years, resulting in GDP being 40 percent less than its level before transition. In 1997, the government adopted a comprehensive economic reform program as a response to the crisis, supported by international financial institutions and other development partners that included major trade and price liberalization; social sector reform; and restructuring of the financial, enterprise, agriculture, and energy sectors, including the divestiture of state-owned enterprises. The country then entered a period of steady economic growth that averaged 5 percent per year in per capita terms. In January 2007, Bulgaria joined the European Union.

TABLE 10.2 **Targeting Outcomes of the GMI Program, Bulgaria, 2003**

Quantile	Share participating (%)			Share of accrued benefits (%)			Generosity (program benefits as % of recipient household consumption)		
	Total	Urban	Rural	Total	Urban	Rural	Total	Urban	Rural
Poorest quintile	8	7	10	58	57	58	47	41	54
2nd poorest quintile	3	2	4	19	19	18	21	21	21
3rd poorest quintile	2	1	3	14	11	17	16	14	17
4th poorest quintile	0	0	1	3	2	5	14	6	17
Richest quintile	1	1	0	7	11	1	12	13	9
Total	3	2	4	100	100	100	35	31	39
Poorest decile	13	11	15	47	44	50	54	50	60

SOURCE: Tesliuc and others forthcoming.

NOTE: Household consumption is determined as the average for a given group. Quantiles are based on per capita household consumption.

At the outset of the transition, Bulgaria had little poverty. It rose thereafter, initially slowly, affecting 5.5 percent of the population by 1995, and then rapidly, affecting 36.0 percent of the population by the time of the 1997 crisis (World Bank 1999a). It declined continuously thereafter, falling to about 12.9 percent of the population by 2001 and about 10.0 percent by 2003 (C. Tesliuc 2004).[5] These changes in overall poverty mirrored changes in the profile of the poor. At the peak of the crisis, poverty affected a large number of able-bodied adults with a good education and labor market skills. After the crisis, higher wage incomes and pensions lifted most of the active population and the elderly out of poverty, leaving poverty concentrated among ethnic minorities, notably Roma, and in rural areas. The large discrepancy between the welfare of the Roma and the rest of the population brought this issue to the forefront of European domestic and regional policy (Ringold, Orenstein, and Wilkens 2005).

The current social protection system is a mix of old and new programs that are continuously being reformed in response to changing social needs and opportunities to provide social transfers or services more efficiently. Some of these programs were inherited from the socialist period, such as pensions and family benefits. Other programs have been added since, such as unemployment benefits, which were initiated during the 1990s to meet the needs of a market economy, and needs-based social assistance programs. Prior to 1991, guaranteed employment served as the main safety net mechanism. Social assistance had a relatively small role, with limited programs for those who were unable to work, such as the elderly and those with disabilities. With the economic restructuring and reforms of the late 1990s, the social protection system expanded to encompass welfare programs that explicitly help households cope with the new risks of poverty and unemployment (box 10.1). The GMI Program was initiated in 1992 and energy benefits were introduced in 1995.

The 1997 crisis was a turning point not only for economic policy, but also for safety net policy. The first response to the crisis was to expand those safety net programs with the most accurate targeting—the GMI Program and energy benefits—and to increase the programs' generosity. At that time, concerns about labor disincentives were minimal, and programs were dominated by the need to provide protection from poverty as rapidly and efficiently as possible. The government was able to respond quickly to the crisis because it had a number of programs in place that it could scale up.

Once the crisis was over, successive governments promoted a number of reforms that increased the effectiveness and efficiency of the safety net system and programs. In 1997, the GMI Program and energy benefits were consolidated under the same agency and operated under similar procedures except for eligibility criteria and benefit levels. In 2002, eligibility for the universal child allowance program, which had been established in 1986, became means tested and conditional on school enrollment. The child allowance program used the same administrative procedures and institutional framework as the GMI and energy benefit programs. After 2000, with the economy thriving, concerns about benefit dependency began to dominate the policy debate. The government responded with the temporary workfare program described earlier.

One of the government's experiments in its search for a more efficient safety net policy was less successful: its attempts to decentralize the financing of the GMI Program. From 1998 to 2003, the government experimented with different cost-sharing formulas between the central and local authorities. In 1999, the cost-sharing arrangement called for a 50 percent contribution by the central government and 50 percent by local authorities, but this arrangement led to arrears or to partial payment of benefits because some local governments did not contribute their share. By the end of 1999, arrears represented 10 percent of the entitlements. In 2002, the cost-sharing rule was changed to 75 percent by the central government and 25 percent by local authorities, but the arrears continued. A new social assistance law in 2003 centralized the financing and implementation of means-tested programs and the arrears ended.

The key factors that determined the success of the safety net system in Bulgaria, especially of the means-tested programs, can be divided into the following two categories:

- **Overall design features.** The centralization of the design, administration, and financing of the system has been crucial. In addition, the different aspects of social protection are well coordinated. The design of the GMI Program benefit balances protection of the poor while rewarding work effort, as the benefit is worth less than the minimum wage or unemployment compensation. Complementary programs seek to help the unemployed find work.

- **Good implementation.** Procedures are developed and staff are well trained and sufficient. Social protection agencies cooperate by exchanging information about their clients. Errors of inclusion are reduced through the assiduous use of home visits and verification of information. Errors of exclusion are reduced by lowering transaction costs for beneficiaries: the required documents are all free, much information is obtained directly from other sources rather than requiring applicants to present certificates, and payment through bank accounts or post offices is convenient.

10.3 Safety Nets for an Economic Crisis Situation

In times of crisis governments are galvanized to provide safety nets, even in countries that have been unwilling to fund them in stable times. Without a base to build on, the response to a crisis will be constrained, although crisis responses are often the start of more permanent safety nets. Even with a base to build on in a crisis, the speed and scale of action needed to address the crisis may entail temporary compromises in relation to the usual standards for targeting, incentive compatibility, and accountability.

GENERAL CONTEXT

Economic crises can disproportionately affect the poor, and substantially raise poverty rates as a result of increasing unemployment or declining wages, relative price changes such as increased food prices, and lower returns on physical and financial assets. Cuts in public spending in the social sectors often exacerbate the reduction in households' autonomous incomes. Decreased use of health services is common, malnutrition and other health outcomes may worsen, and poor children may drop out of school. These conditions tend to aggravate chronic poverty and may lead to irreversible losses in human capital among the poor and vulnerable, undermining an economy's ability to recover and sustain growth. The increases in poverty can also lead to longer-term erosion of social capital within communities marked by deteriorating political consensus and increasing crime and violence.

Capacity

Few of the countries facing recent macroeconomic and financial crises in Asia (1997–9), Europe (Russia 1998, Turkey 2001), and Latin American (the debt crises of the 1980s and the financial crises of 1994–5, 1999, 2001–2) had strong safety nets in place before the crisis. Thus countries had to choose among imperfect options. The first was to expand whatever existed regardless of how good or bad it was and what target group it served. Mexico chose this response in reaction to the so-called tequila crisis when it scaled up retraining and employment programs and targeted food distribution. The second option was to start up new programs in a hurry, which runs the inevitable risk of poor initial implementation, as occurred in Indonesia's JPS Padat Karya (Labor-Intensive Public Works) program, and/or a delay of many months between the onset of the crisis and the time the program is operational on a fairly large scale, as occurred in Colombia's Familias en Acción program. Many more countries now have some elements of a safety net system in place, usually to serve the chronically poor. However, countries have had little experience as yet with how to modify their programs during a crisis or how well they can be modified, though some indications from the Central American coffee crisis of 1998–2001 suggest that preexisting CCT programs helped beneficiary households accommodate the shock to their incomes.

Potential Role for Safety Net Systems

The primary objectives of safety nets in times of crisis are to protect incomes and avoid irreversible losses of physical assets and human capital and to help maintain political consensus around the policies needed to resolve the crisis. Permanent and appropriately financed programs can also act as automatic fiscal stabilizers, although programs with permanency, appropriate finance, and guaranteed countercyclical finance are rare (see chapter 3, section 3).

A perennial issue in relation to safety nets for postcrisis situations is whether to target the chronically poor or those most affected by the crisis. The logic of a postcrisis program is to address the income losses caused by the crisis, but while the newly poor are often politically vocal, they are not necessarily the poorest. The chronically poor are likely to become poorer as a result of the crisis and may be most at risk of suffering irreversible losses. Countries' fiscal constraints mean that not all can be served as much as needed, giving rise to competing pressures. Even though the philosophical disputes underlying the debate as to which options to chose can be intense, the practicalities of limited targeting options often render any debate somewhat moot.

Interventions and Implementation

Where countries operate fully needs-based cash transfers, as in much of Europe and Central Asia, a separate crisis response program will not be needed. The number of beneficiaries will automatically expand as more households fall into poverty and become eligible for the program. The main adjustment needed is to ensure that funding will be available to cover the increased number of beneficiaries and higher level of benefits where benefits are differentiated by beneficiaries' degree of poverty. Supplemental staffing may also be needed to handle the larger than usual number of applicants.

In countries without a well-developed unemployment insurance program, public works are a commonly used response to economic crises and have been employed in such situations by, for example, Argentina, Bolivia, Chile, Colombia, Indonesia, the Republic of Korea, and Peru. The self-targeting through a low wage is a highly desirable feature that is especially valuable in a postcrisis setting. Where unemployment is high, public works programs are a logical response to some of the social, as well as economic, issues for newly unemployed workers. However, such programs often encounter difficulties in absorbing enough labor to fully address the problems. Argentina's Trabajar workfare program devised in response to the 1996 crisis was successful in terms of targeting, impact on workers' incomes, and value of works done, but was relatively small, covering only 1.6 percent of the economically active population. During the next crisis, Argentina implemented the Jefes de Hogar (Heads of Household) program on a much larger scale, reaching about 13 percent of the economically active population at its peak, but could not effectively enforce the work requirement for so many people, so the value of the works done was less and the targeting not as excellent, though it was still good.

Public works programs are less applicable where labor adjustments that occur as a result of a shock are mostly through a widespread reduction in wages rather than through unemployment. This was the case in Mexico's tequila crisis, and thus public works programs were a limited part of the response and were included more because some existing programs could easily be expanded than because they were the single best answer. Public works programs may also be difficult to implement quickly and at high labor intensity where infrastructure is well developed or sophisticated, as the works tend to be more complex, involve longer planning horizons, and be more capital intensive. This was a problem Argentina and Colombia faced in their large cities.

In addition to public works programs, crisis responses usually include as much protection as possible for the budgets for basic health and education services and sometimes include new scholarship or fee waiver programs to help avoid irreversible losses of human capital. Colombia's Familias en Acción CCT program, Indonesia's JPS Scholarship and Grant Program, and Zimbabwe's Basic Education Assistance Module of school fee waivers all started under such circumstances.

The crisis itself is likely to make targeting difficult. Even countries with well developed survey capacity and information on poverty will find that their data quickly become out of date and of limited use after a crisis hits, as was the case in Argentina, Indonesia, and Mexico. Means tests would have to be readministered every few months to keep pace with changing household circumstances, a feat that few countries could manage. Moreover, the informal economy almost always grows during a crisis, so the reliability of the means test will decline as those who lose their formal jobs take up informal activities. Proxy means tests are geared toward indicators of chronic poverty and will not usually identify the newly poor, who may still live in a decent house and neighborhood, but now have no money to put food on the table, buy medicine, or pay school fees. Occasionally categorical targeting is possible by giving assistance to those laid off from formal enterprises, but these are often not the most poor, plus such programs are usually limited to severance pay for those in downsized state-owned industries. Self-targeting is thus a highly desirable option and is most viable via public works programs, which is why they are so commonly used in postcrisis settings. Community-based targeting may also be applicable.

Exit strategies, often for entire programs, must be considered from the outset for both political and administrative reasons. For example, when their economies improved, Argentina and Korea closed down their postcrisis public works programs. This is sometimes appropriate, but has some disadvantages. The closure of programs means that most of the institutional capacity to run them is lost, and if a new crisis hits, the whole start-up process will have to be repeated. Moreover, safety net programs initiated in response to a crisis will often serve those who are suffering from idiosyncratic shocks and/or some of the chronically poor as well, therefore scaling down a program is often more desirable than eliminating it altogether. This requires thinking about exit strategies for individual households. These may be automatic, for example, when households recover their economic activity they may no longer accept public works jobs, or they may require explicit design or implementation actions, for example, through recertification by a means or proxy means test or by having established a time limit for the benefit early on.

ARGENTINA'S RESPONSE TO THE 2002 CRISIS

In 2002, a severe financial crisis hit Argentina following three years of economic slowdown.[6] Real output fell by 11 percent after a cumulative decline in real GDP of more than 9 percent during the previous three years. Unemployment soared to 22 percent, and the share of those working in the informal sector increased while the quality of jobs deteriorated. The main impact of the crisis was on real wages, which collapsed by nearly 30 percent as a result of uncontrolled inflation. Overall poverty increased by 50 percentage points during 1998–2002, more than during any other previous crisis, peaking with 58 percent of the population classified as poor by the end of 2002. This outcome was accompanied by a deterioration in basic services that reflected an increased demand for health services by the larger number of uninsured and a decline in the rate of collection of utility fees.

The government's response to the crisis was a combination of restoring macroeconomic stability and protecting key social programs. While overall real government spending fell by 38 percent during the crisis and social spending fell by 32 percent, spending on targeted pro-poor programs increased by 21 percent. This increase was insufficient to stabilize the real value of this spending per poor person because of the dramatic increase in poverty; thus spending per poor person fell by 16 percent.

In April 2002, the government created a massive new workfare program as part of its emergency response—the Jefes de Hogar program—spending 7 percent of the federal budget on it. The program transferred about US$50 per month to its beneficiaries. Participants had to meet four eligibility criteria: be unemployed; be a head of household; (3) live in a household with a child under age 18, a pregnant woman, or a person with disabilities; and work or participate in education or training activities for four to six hours per day. The program was scaled up relatively rapidly, and by May 2003 had 2 million participants. Incidence and coverage were both good, with about 80 percent of the benefits concentrated among the two poorest quintiles of the population. A third of those in the poorest quintile participated.

The good incidence was achieved despite some problematic features of the program. First, the government could not completely enforce the eligibility criteria. The program ran cross-checks against lists of contributors to social security, but only half of employment in Argentina was formal, so this was not fully effective in ensuring that participants really were unemployed. Moreover, the scale of the program, its rapid expansion, and some lapses in accountability meant that the work requirement was not fully enforced. In 2004, only 70 percent of participants fulfilled their work requirement, and in the first half of 2005, only 55 percent did so. Applicants also self-reported whether they were household heads, and subsequent research showed that some 40 percent of the beneficiaries were women who had entered the labor market as additional family earners and were probably not the head of household as usually defined. To go to scale quickly, the registration process allowed civil society groups to nominate participants, which resulted in some highly controversial registrants and affected the program's reputation.

The program was designed with a sunset clause, meaning that it would remain in effect only for as long as the emergency continued, but the emergency decree was extended each time the program was due to expire. A new government came to power in May 2003. It closed registration for the program and made some significant improvements to its administration that resulted in the dropping of about 300,000 beneficiaries (about 15 percent of the peak number). The government also developed a three-pronged strategy to transition out of the program, whereby (1) some participants were expected to move off the rolls as they found formal employment opportunities; (2) families living in any of 400 large municipalities with two or more children would move to a new CCT program that would offer similar levels of support; and (3) others could move to a new noncontributory training and unemployment insurance program that was gradually being rolled out and that offered slightly higher benefit levels for up to two years. By early 2008, the number of beneficiaries had declined to about 700,000, about a third of the peak level, because of a combination of further administrative improvements, a strengthened economy that led to participants withdrawing from the program as they found jobs, and the implementation of the transition strategy.

The government succeeded in moving rapidly, facilitated in part by its experience with the Trabajar program. Even though the latter had been discontinued, some of the same people who had worked on the Trabajar program were still available in the central ministry and municipalities, so not all the capacity had been lost. The other factor that facilitated the speed of response was the design compromises made in relation to targeting criteria and enforcement of the work requirements.

The government might have been able to avoid some of the considerable controversy around the Jefes de Hogar program by making a few minor design changes that would have aligned the program's rules and practices more closely—for example, by having as its announced target group households with families and without formal jobs and rationing participation to one person per household. It could have called itself by some name other than the Jefes de Hogar program and run a publicity campaign to emphasize that it was intended for the poor working in the informal sector. The outcomes would probably have been much the same, as these changes would merely have announced the criteria that the program did actually enforce, but the changes might have eliminated the criticism that the program did not follow its own rules with the implication that it might be massively corrupt in a much worse sense than giving a benefit to poor secondary earners rather than poor principal earners. With such changes, the program's reputation might have been much better. For such a large program to enforce its work requirement would still have been difficult, although given the requisite political will, the rate of compliance could have increased over time as the agencies built capacity.

Argentina's experience with the Jefes de Hogar program illustrates some common features of safety nets in postcrisis settings: finding a practical targeting mechanism to reach those who the government really wants to target can be difficult, scaling up a program quickly and still maintaining all the desired quality control features can be hard, and considering exit policies from the outset is important.

10.4 Safety Nets after Natural Disasters

Until fairly recently, safety nets were not thought of as part of the response to disasters beyond the immediate humanitarian relief phase. Once that was over, attention turned largely to reconstructing public infrastructure and restoring service delivery, with less attention paid to helping households safeguard or reestablish their livelihoods. Policy makers are increasingly recognizing the role of safety nets following natural disasters, but practice is still relatively underdeveloped. As for responses to economic crises, safety nets following natural disasters are more feasible where a base to build on exists and when temporary compromises in systems and standards are made if necessary.

GENERAL CONTEXT

Natural disasters can affect both the poor and the nonpoor. Earthquakes, floods, and hurricanes can cause significant losses of life and wreak significant physical destruction. These and slower-onset shocks such as droughts can lead to regional health and food price shocks and significantly increase poverty. The poor are particularly exposed to natural disasters and have limited access to risk management instruments, but many nonpoor will be affected as well, especially by rapid-onset disasters.

The economic impact of disasters varies, depending on the extent of the damage relative to the size of the economy, the geographic scope of the damage, the initial level of economic development, and the success of crisis response actions. The social impact may also vary depending on the extent of displacement, of postdisaster trauma (especially among children), of damage to social capital and informal coping mechanisms, and of disability.

Capacity

As natural disasters occur worldwide, the initial safety net base is highly varied. Running a good transfer program is a demanding task and setting systems up takes time. It is impossible to do well, or often at all, overnight, and even more difficult when regular communications, transport systems, and markets are disrupted. The easiest approach is to respond to a disaster by modifying an existing program. For example, the government may scale up a public works program in affected areas, shortcut certain elements of the planning and selection process for works, and eliminate the local funding requirement for nonlabor inputs. For a cash transfer program the government may increase payments to existing beneficiaries, add temporary beneficiaries in affected areas using specially adapted targeting procedures, and alter payment procedures temporarily where systems are disrupted. For existing programs to have contingency plans in place for scaling up would be useful, but is uncommon.

Informal coping mechanisms tend to collapse during large shocks. Natural disasters during the last two decades and the economic and social consequences that have affected many countries in Central America, East Asia, and South Asia have demonstrated that informal and group-based coping mechanisms that form the backbone of traditional community- and family-based safety nets tend to be insufficient and may be unsustainable in the face of such large covariate shocks. Examples of such disasters include Hurricane Mitch in Honduras in 1998, repeated floods in Bangladesh, the 2004 tsunami in Indonesia, and the 2005 earthquake in Pakistan.

Potential Role for Safety Net Systems

The key role of safety nets following a natural disaster is to help households avoid irreversible losses that could ensue after the actual disaster. Effective safety net systems should be seen as part of and as a complement to the larger efforts pertaining to livelihood protection, reconstruction, and recovery.

Ideally, disaster management strategies are part of larger government or development policy and balance ex ante and ex post actions. For example, ex ante prevention (such as dikes, dams, or irrigation works) or mitigation (for example, insurance) may decrease the probability of crop loss or replace income lost because of crop loss. Ex post interventions provide mechanisms for coping after a disaster. Effective disaster management strategies are based on a good understanding of who is exposed and the role of potential instruments and the political will to take action ahead of time. In general, ex ante natural disaster management tends to be insufficient, focusing more on infrastructure, and with much less thought given to how to safeguard livelihoods.

Ex post interventions can be divided into three categories. In the immediate aftermath of the disaster, search and recovery operations and humanitarian assistance may be needed, especially for rapid-onset events such as earthquakes or typhoons. This kind of specialized assistance is beyond the scope of this book. In the medium term, households will require support to prevent the further loss of assets and to allow them to start reinvesting in their livelihoods. Safety nets of the sort discussed in this book can play a role here. The longer-term response will focus on reconstructing public infrastructure and services.

Interventions and Implementation

Immediate assistance after rapid-onset disasters is often humanitarian and in kind, for instance, food, water, blankets, and tents. How long this period lasts will depend on the severity of the disaster and the extent to which it disrupts markets. Once transport systems and markets begin to function again, transfers can be in cash, which provides households with greater flexibility and can be provided with fewer logistical complications. Public works are also particularly attractive for both ex ante (for example, protecting watersheds and installing flood controls) and ex post (including reconstruction and rehabilitation of basic community infrastructure) parts of a crisis management strategy.

Following a disaster, the speed of the response is critical, thus there is little time to set up complex systems. Targeting criteria are therefore one or a combination of the following: geographic, meaning assistance is provided to everyone in defined areas; categorical, with categories defined by the extent of loss of life or disability, of total or partial damage to dwellings, and of other physical losses; and/or self-targeting, whereby public works jobs or feeding are provided to all who come to feeding centers.

Needs can change rapidly in the aftermath of a disaster if bad weather further affects those without shelter, if epidemics develop, or if the scale of the response is greater than expected. Planning and responses thus have to be flexible. Monitoring systems need to be agile and be based on statistics from sentinel sites or on qualitative methods. Coordination will involve a large number of actors: national and local governments, many sectors, and probably many nongovernmental organizations and international agencies.

After a disaster, large amounts of funds and food aid flow through hastily improvised channels. This can bring with it challenges in relation to controlling corruption. Strong political leadership, community involvement, close coordination, and a transparent monitoring system with proper oversight and fraud control are crucial, and yet must not be so onerous as to slow the response.

BANGLADESH'S "FLOOD OF THE CENTURY"

In September 1998, Bangladesh was inundated by a huge flood.[7] At its peak, the flood covered two-thirds of the country, causing severe damage to the rice crop that was due to be harvested in November and December. Total rice production losses exceeded 2 million tons, or about 10 percent of annual consumption. Despite the damage to the rice harvest and the major disruption of the rural economy and employment opportunities, in marked contrast to the famine that followed the 1974 flood, no major food crisis occurred. The flood did exact a heavy cost in terms of increased private debt because of extensive borrowing in private markets, a major coping strategy of the poor.

The government used two major instruments to respond to the disaster: it allowed large-scale, private rice imports and it provided direct transfers to households. Both these responses were possible because of groundwork laid in the years preceding the flood.

By 1998, the private rice market was well established. The government had liberalized trade in the early 1990s, and this was followed by an expansion in the number of traders; in the size of the market; in investments in infrastructure (roads, bridges, electricity, and telecommunications); and in an easing of restrictions on private sector trade including, for example, the lifting of a ban on commercial bank credit for the food grain trade. The government had also begun to encourage increased rice imports from India early in 1998 when the first harvest of the year had been somewhat poor, and stepped up the policy as the damage caused by the flood became apparent. The private sector imported 2.4 million tons of rice during July 1998 to April 1999. Price increases were thus held to 12 percent, and price variations across regions remained small.

The second leg of the response consisted in the use of two existing, albeit dormant and not well-funded, transfer programs. The first was an immediate relief effort, the Gratuitous Relief Program, designed to provide emergency relief to disaster victims from August to September 1998. The second was a medium-term program, the Vulnerable Group Feeding Program, which ran from September 1998 through April 1999.

The Gratuitous Relief Program provided immediate transfers of 50,000 tons of rice targeted by location to flood-affected households. The Vulnerable Group Feeding Program covered the entire country and was administratively targeted to poor households that were selected by local committees. The program provided 4 million households with an allotment of 16 kilograms of grain per month, half rice and half wheat in October and all wheat thereafter. It was not well targeted to households directly affected by the flood, but it was relatively well targeted to poor households. The two programs did help, but were small relative to need. The Food for Work Program began on a large scale only in December 1998, when the soil was dry enough to permit manual construction of earthworks.

The Bangladesh example underscores two main messages about safety nets in post-disaster settings. First, effective action is feasible if its basis has been laid earlier. Second, even when the worst outcomes, such as famine, are avoided, more subtle issues may arise, such as increased debt, from which households may take a long time to recover.

HURRICANE MITCH AND THE HONDURAN SOCIAL FUND

On October 30, 1998, Mitch, a massive, slow-moving hurricane, hit Honduras.[8] Three weeks of rain had already soaked the countryside before the storm pounded the country for three days. Torrential winds, floodwaters, and mudslides destroyed villages, shattered social and economic infrastructure, paralyzed production, and left up to three feet of mud and debris throughout the country. Communities cut off from economic activity and basic services faced immediate health concerns and security risks. Some 6,000 people died, 8,000 were missing, 13,000 were wounded, and more than a million were left homeless.

Honduras called upon its Social Fund, its main social protection instrument at the time, for the response. The Social Fund had been operational for eight years and was well established. The fund took advantage of the flexibility of its legal framework and lean structure to change operating procedures for its crisis response. It established 11 temporary regional offices and delegated responsibilities and resources to senior staff appointed as regional directors. Its technical experts were in northern Honduras within hours of receiving news of the hurricane's impact to assess the damage from mudslides that had buried extensive areas. Regional offices worked closely with community members and municipal representatives to assess immediate needs for cleaning up mud and debris and repairing or replacing water and sanitation systems, access roads, bridges, health centers, and schools. Recognizing the need for quick action, the Social Fund simplified its subproject cycle, reducing the required number of steps from 50 to 8, and increased its use of standardized subprojects and simplified procurement methods. It also established safeguards in each of the regional offices to ensure accountability and transparency.

Within 100 days, the fund had approved 2,100 projects with a total value of US$40 million. By the end of 1999, about 3,400 emergency subprojects had been financed, representing an implementation rate four times higher than the average before Mitch. The fund's immediate focus on restoring economic activity and basic social services prevented the emergency from aggravating poverty. Indeed, because it financed highly labor-intensive projects (labor accounted for 25 to 30 percent of the value of most subprojects and as much as 70 percent of cleanup activities), the fund generated temporary employment in precisely those communities where productive activities had been disrupted. The Social Fund created about 100,000 person-months of employment during the first three months, on a par with workfare programs in other countries, such as Argentina's Trabajar program.

The following are among the specific lessons learned from the Social Fund's work in the wake of Hurricane Mitch:

- A strong partnership with municipalities and communities is invaluable.

- The ability to decentralize and delegate is essential.

- The establishment of contingency procedures (and agreeing on them with financing agencies) ahead of time is wise. Many social funds now have contingency manuals.

- The use of streamlined institutional procedures, less complete documentation, and longer working hours may be appropriate during emergencies, but may not be desirable over the longer term.

- The rapid deployment of Social Fund staff and the changes in subproject processing procedures created some confusion and undermined some of the advances that had been made under prior institutional strengthening. Thus social funds should attempt to isolate their emergency responses so that they can return to normal operations as quickly as possible. Nicaragua's Emergency Social Investment Fund was able to reestablish normal operating procedures after Hurricane Mitch much more quickly, because it allocated a specific amount of money (US$12 million) for a set period of time (three months) to emergency activities.

- The urgent and immediate needs that arise following a natural disaster can affect long-term goals because of trade-offs between quick response times and long-term quality of investments. In addition, users cannot always be thoroughly trained in operations and maintenance during emergencies.

- The full gamut of social needs will not be met by cleanup and reconstruction activities, although these can provide temporary employment in the hardest hit areas.

10.5 Safety Nets to Facilitate Reforms

The need for compensation for a reform commonly arises when a country has operated a program or policy with intertwined equity and efficiency goals. Such policies often result in conflicting objectives and inefficiencies, and so de-linking the two objectives and using different instruments to address them is often preferable. For example, rather than having a utility company subsidize residential consumers so that they can stay warm in the winter, allowing the utility company to price at cost and providing transfers or vouchers to poor consumers through a social assistance framework may be much more efficient. The same holds true for general food subsidies, fertilizer subsidies, and the like. Indeed, Kanbur (2005) and World Bank (2005c) suggest that the use of a generalized redistributive mechanism is preferable to having to design specific compensatory packages for each reform option. During the 1990s, all the transition economies inherited heating subsidies that they replaced in some cases with targeted heating allowances as in Bulgaria and Romania or basic social assistance programs as in Armenia. General fuel subsidies are common around the world, and periodically countries reduce or eliminate them and use targeted cash transfers as compensation. Indonesia provides a recent example. Replacing general food subsidies with targeted subsidies is also common.

GENERAL CONTEXT

The need for compensation will depend in part on the pattern of benefits of the program to be reformed—that is, who it reached and how important the program was to them. In the case of food subsidy reforms, the poor often receive a low share of the absolute benefits, but these low benefits are nonetheless an improvement in their welfare. Sometimes, however, the poor have benefited little from the subsidy to be reduced, for example, if electricity were subsidized but the poor were not connected to the grid. An indirect feature of the needs assessment (see chapter 9 for guidance on how to carry out a needs assessment) concerns the political economy of reform. Is there consensus on the need for reform or not? Who opposes it and why? Would a compensatory targeted cash transfer help make the reform more acceptable?

Capacity

Such reforms are applicable in a diverse range of contexts: in both high- and low-income countries, in times of relative stability or crisis, and so on. A possible common feature is a high degree of state intervention in the economy.

Safety Net Systems

Often countries that need to provide compensation for reforms do not have good poverty-based cash transfer programs in place. Indeed, the lack of such a program may have been what led the government to try to accomplish its redistributive goals through other less efficient instruments. In these cases, a major addition to the safety net system may be required. In some cases governments slowly and methodically build up the compensatory system as they gradually dismantle the old one. Mexico's replacement of food subsidies with the PROGRESA (now known as Oportunidades) initiative is such a case. Probably more often, however, the government mounts its compensatory program in a rush, giving itself little time to develop adequate systems before beginning large-scale operations. Where such programs become permanent, they will need to be refined over time.

Where a poverty-based cash transfer program is already in place, introducing compensatory measures may be simpler. Jamaica already had a progressively targeted food stamp program in operation in 1995, thus when the government eliminated kerosene subsidies, it was able to boost the value of the food stamp benefit as a compensatory measure for the poor and did not have to mount a separate program.

Potential Role for Safety Net Systems

In supporting policy reforms, safety nets can play two linked, but somewhat separate, roles. They can help compensate the poor for any losses suffered; beyond that, they can help engender political tolerance of the reform. In the case of reforms of general price subsidies, such as for fuel, utilities, or food, the loser is the general public—or at least the large share of it that benefited from the subsidy. The art of compensation is to provide an alternative benefit to a subset of beneficiaries that is large enough to calm opposition to the reform. Helping the poor lowers their direct opposition and also weakens the arguments that elites with a self-interest in maintaining the status quo can make on behalf of the poor. For instance, energy producers or millers may not gain much sympathy if they say they are afraid of having to become efficient, but may gain much attention if they say they are concerned about the poor and that that is what keeps them from being competitive. A direct transfer to protect the poor will disarm such arguments.

Compensation may also be due when the eligibility criteria for a program are changed. These kinds of reforms commonly convert categorically targeted benefits to poverty-based criteria. In this setting the losers are clearly defined, and the compensation process is less costly, but possibly still important. It may take the form of grandfathering such beneficiaries into the new program for a defined period.

Interventions and Implementation

The compensation policies for which this book is pertinent are mostly cash transfers or near cash transfers such as food stamps or heating vouchers. Other compensatory mechanisms, such as lifeline utility pricing for low-volume users or training programs for workers laid off from state enterprise reform, are common elements accompanying such reforms, but are outside the scope of this book.

In designing cash transfer programs as part of a reform package, governments may take either of two approaches. In one, the government moves directly to a benefit targeted to the poor that is expected to have a long duration and is designed accordingly. Several prominent safety net programs, including Brazil's Bolsa Familia (Family Grant) program and Mexico's Oportunidades had their roots in compensatory programs. In Brazil, the

Bolsa Familia program was created by combining four prior programs, one of which, Auxilio Gás (Cooking Gas Grant), was a transfer designed to compensate poor households for the removal of subsidies on cooking gas. In Mexico, the aim was to redirect monies spent on less efficient food distribution programs. In the other approach, the government uses a more generous definition of poverty than usual for its target population. When this is the case, such programs should be instituted on a temporary basis whereby they are gradually discontinued, become more narrowly targeted, or announce their sunset rules up front as in the case of Indonesia's fuel subsidy reform.

REFORM OF FUEL SUBSIDIES IN INDONESIA

Indonesia has traditionally had little in the way of targeted safety nets.[9] For many years, Indonesia had universal price subsidies on fuel, with price levels fixed well below world prices. By 2005, with the rise in world fuel prices, the cost of the subsidy was equivalent to 5 percent of GDP. Between 1998 and 2005, fuel subsidies averaged three-quarters of the social protection system's total subsidies and transfers. As common with such subsidies, they were highly regressive (figure 10.1).

The government introduced the first large programs following the 1998 financial crisis. Some of these remain, but coverage of the scholarship and health card programs is quite low and the targeting is mediocre. Coverage of the rice subsidy is higher, but it has significant cost-effectiveness issues.

In 2005, the government reduced fuel subsidies by about US$10 billion. It reduced total expenditures by half that amount. A quarter of the funds were used to fund a targeted, unconditional cash transfer program;

FIGURE 10.1 **Incidence of Diesel, Gasoline, and Kerosene Subsidies, Indonesia, 2004**

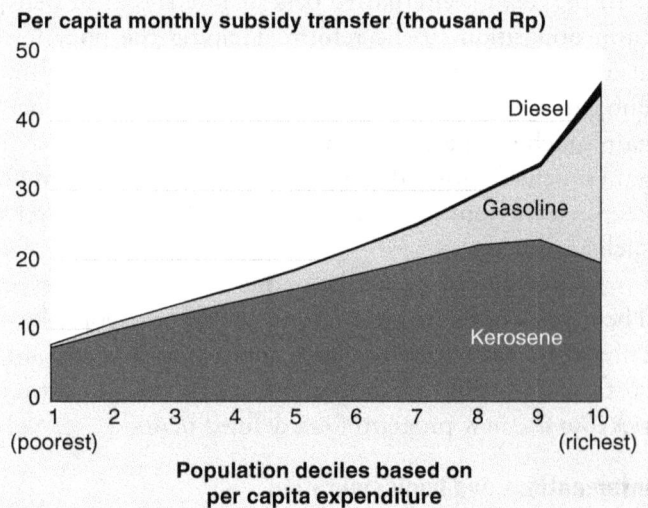

SOURCE: World Bank 2006f.

and the remainder was used for block grants to schools, basic health care and health insurance for the poor, and a village improvement program. Given the concentration of people just above the poverty line, the government decided to target the cash transfer not just to the 16 percent who fall under the poverty line, but to the near poor as well. The cash transfer program thus reached 19 million poor and near poor households, or 28 percent of the population. Under the program, each beneficiary family received about US$10 per month paid quarterly. The benefit was equivalent to about 17 percent of per capita consumption of the poorest decile.

FIGURE 10.2 **Coverage and Incidence of the Unconditional Cash Transfer Program, Indonesia, 2005**

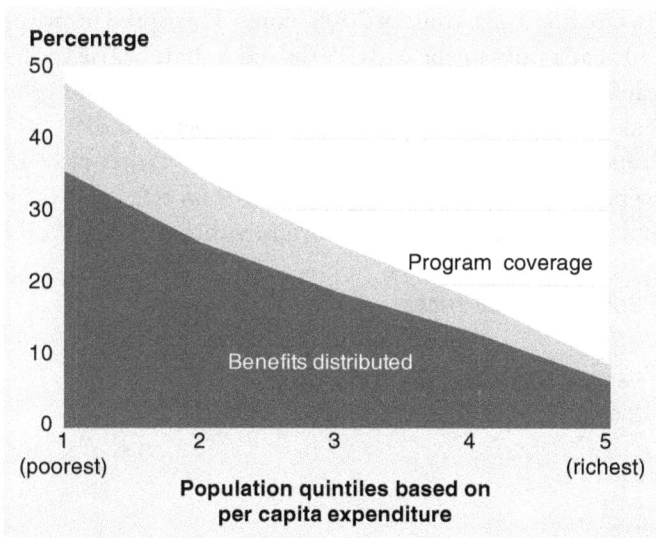

SOURCE: World Bank 2006f.

The cash transfer program was rolled out rapidly, with the basic decision to implement the program being taken in August 2005 and the first quarterly payment being made in October. As expected with such a rapid rollout, some initial difficulties arose. The targeting was progressive and a dramatic improvement over the prior regressive fuel subsidies, but the haste with which the program was set up showed up in moderately high errors of inclusion (figure 10.2). Early reports also showed that information provided to the public and participants about the program's purpose and procedures was less than optimal, and channels for handling complaints were not well defined. The government worked on these issues, starting with an initial assessment of the program after the first payment in 2005, and initiated actions to improve program administration. Significant fuel price increases, including for kerosene, were implemented without major public protests.

The compensation was intended to last just one year, and did last just that long. However, the experience led to interest in adding an element to Indonesia's antipoverty policy, which has had little in the way of safety nets and no poverty-targeted cash transfers. In 2007, the authorities began piloting a CCT program that would build and improve on the former cash transfer program.

Indonesia's experience illustrates some of the lessons of safety nets in reform settings and in general. First, cash transfer programs can be useful for compensating households so that they do not suffer sharp changes in welfare. Second, they can reduce opposition to reform. Third, while mounting a program quickly is possible, perfecting it is likely to take longer.

10.6 Safety Nets for Rising Food Prices

As this book was going to press, the world's attention began to focus on dramatic increases in food prices.[10] Newspapers around the world were full of coverage of the issue, many countries saw food riots, and governments and the international agencies that work with them went into overdrive trying to address the problem. This crisis underscores the need for safety nets and the importance of building them during stable times so that they are available in times of crisis.

GENERAL CONTEXT

Food grain prices have more than doubled since January 2006 (figure 10.3), with more than 60 percent of this increase occurring since January 2008 alone. This spike in prices has had few parallels in the last 50 years: only in the early 1970s did a sharper rise in the real prices of cereals such as wheat and corn occur. Several structural factors, such as the increased use of biofuels, the weak U.S. dollar, and the shifts taking place in diets, are key drivers of the trend. The recent sharp increase in the international market price of rice may also have been driven by policy factors, including restrictions on rice exports by some exporters and large-scale tenders by rice importers in a currently thin market (World Bank 2008a).

The observed increase in food prices is unlikely to be a temporary phenomenon, but to persist in the medium term. Food crop prices are expected to remain high in 2008 and 2009 and then begin to decline as supply and demand respond to high prices; however, for most food crops, prices are likely to remain well above 2004 levels through 2015 (World Bank 2008d).

FIGURE 10.3 **Food Prices**

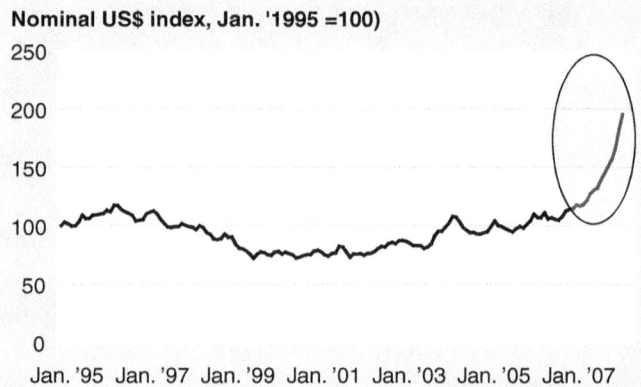

Nominal US$ index, Jan. '1995 =100)

SOURCE: World Bank 2008c.

The rising food prices may have a negative impact on human development by increasing poverty, worsening nutrition, reducing the use of education and health services, and depleting the productive assets of the poor. As argued in chapter 2, disinvestment by the poor in their human and physical capital will have large and lasting effects of a kind that are well documented and quantified in the development literature. These effects can be ameliorated if governments can provide a positive policy response, primarily through direct income transfers.

As a result of the current increases in food prices, many of the 2.3 billion people living on less than US$2 a day will became poorer, and another 100 million will fall into poverty (Ivanic and Martin 2008). The immediate impact of rising food prices on the number of poor and the depth of poverty in each country will depend on the consumption patterns of the poor, their economic activity (especially whether they are net consumers or net producers of those commodities whose prices are rising), their location, and the prices they face. In urban areas, the poor are almost all net consumers, and those on fixed incomes are especially vulnerable. In rural areas, the majority of the poor in most countries are net consumers of staple commodities, including grains. Higher food prices will reduce the real incomes of these groups of poor over the short to medium term. While wages tend to adjust over time, empirical evidence shows that they typically do not mitigate the full impact of price increases or are slow in responding. In many contexts the very poorest groups—rural landless households and people in households that lack labor—will be among the most severely affected. The consequences of increased food prices will differ across countries depending on the extent of price increases and initial conditions. Where both are unfavorable, the need for action is the most urgent.

Capacity

Rising food prices are affecting countries of all income levels, including countries spanning the full gamut of existing capacity, in terms of both general government systems and administration of safety net programs. A particularly important element is countries' capacity to confront the costs of good policy responses to rising food prices. At the start of the crisis, some countries, such as Indonesia, Mexico, and Tunisia, had a strong fiscal stance and do not face a terms of trade problem. Some had a reasonably good fiscal stance, but suffered terms of trade shocks (including Burkina Faso, Ethiopia, and Honduras) and/ or political crises (including Kenya and Pakistan). Some countries, such as Mongolia and Zambia, had a weak fiscal stance but have experienced favorable terms of trade movement. Finally, some countries such as Burundi, Eritrea, Grenada, Haiti, Jamaica, and Nepal had weak fiscal positions that have now been compounded by terms of trade shocks (World Bank 2008a).

Role of Safety Net Systems

The overall policy response to rising food prices should be multisectoral and should generally encompass improving grain price policies; production, transport, and logistics; safety nets to improve food security at the household level; nutrition programs; and management of the macroeconomic consequences of both the food price increase and the costs of responding to it.

Safety net programs play a triple role in response to rising food prices:

- Safety nets partially forestall the increases in poverty and inequality that would result from the price increases.

- In so doing, safety nets help households maintain their access to food and the essential health and education services that are critical to the well-being and human capital of their children.

- Safety nets can be important in maintaining social equilibrium and thereby help governments avoid having to quell social pressures with policies that would further aggravate the problem.

Countries differ significantly in the types of safety nets they employ. Countries with well-designed programs can mitigate the impact of the crisis on poor consumers by expanding their transfer programs in one way or another—for example, by ensuring funding so that all families that meet the established eligibility threshold can participate, by raising the eligibility threshold, or by increasing the benefit level. In some cases, the changes are "stroke of the pen" actions that imply few changes in program administration. In other cases, the program's capacity may need to increase to deal with new claimants. Countries such as Brazil, Bulgaria, Ethiopia, Mexico, South Africa, and Ukraine can increase coverage quite easily. They have programs that already have good coverage of the poor and mechanisms that could allow new applicants into the programs with relatively minor changes in rules and capacity. For the subset of countries with such programs in place and with relatively good fiscal capacity, the safety net part of the response to rising food prices should be relatively straightforward.

Unfortunately, many more countries have much less adequate initial safety nets. Their systems provide partial, fragmented, or inefficient safety nets as in Haiti and Malawi. Some countries, such as Mozambique and Sierra Leone, may have little in the way of existing safety nets. In such cases adequate responses are much more constrained and are likely to involve significant trade-offs between speed of response and coverage and other desirable features of good safety nets, especially equity, efficiency, and sustainability.

Interventions and Implementation

The short-run response is to scale up existing programs. Countries with sound and comprehensive systems already in place will be in a good position to react to the food price increases by increasing the value and/or coverage of benefits. Countries with poor systems will have to scramble to start programs quickly and in the interim will have to either leave needs unmet or use costly, distortive, regressive, and difficult-to-remove general pricing or tax measures.

The medium-term response is to work toward a sound safety net system if it does not already exist. Many countries are finding their policy responses constrained to mediocre programs or undesirable policies because they do not have good safety net programs or a household targeting system in place. Those countries that took quick but inefficient action, such as reducing tariffs or value added taxes or increasing or instituting general food price subsidies, will want to work their way out of these altogether or they may want to change their mix of programs, for example, increasing the role of targeted cash transfers relative to school feeding programs. Or having implemented "quick and dirty" programs, they may need work on various elements of implementation, for example, targeting systems, accountability, monitoring, and management, especially for programs that will remain in place in the long run.

Short-run responses should try to avoid actions that will work against the medium- to long-run development of a sounder social protection system. For example, in the absence of social protection programs that can be scaled up, many governments are resorting to general food price subsidies, which are usually distortive and regressive and well-known to be hard to remove. Avoiding or minimizing reliance on these is worthwhile, and where they are used, the government should announce up front that they are temporary. Countries should also avoid setting up household targeting systems so quickly that the targeting errors and the political backlash resulting from them are so high that they damage the prospects of developing a sound household targeting system over time. Initially using combinations of geographic, demographic, and self-targeting mechanisms until a good household targeting system can be built might be preferable.

The decision as to which programs to scale up should be made based on a quick assessment of three criteria: Which are "good" or "best" (according to the criteria used throughout this book and explained in full in chapter 9)? Which have administrative capacity for a quick scale up? Which have sources of funding amenable to a quick scale up? Often an adequate short-term response will require compromises in relation to targeting accuracy and the quality of implementation, and will in general be less concerned with incentive compatibility and sustainability than will the core elements of safety nets in more stable times.

Policy responses must be chosen based on country context, but there is a loose ranking of programs for the short-run response.

- Targeted cash transfers of adequate coverage, generosity, and quality are the best option.

- Increasing the benefits for non-earnings-linked social pensions, survivorship pensions, disability pensions, unemployment benefits, and the like can be helpful where they cover the poor.

- Food stamps have slightly higher administrative costs than cash, but can be politically popular.

- In-kind food distribution is appropriate where markets are functioning poorly, where foreign assistance is only available in kind, or where strategic grain reserves need to be rotated. Elsewhere, in-kind programs will have higher than necessary administrative costs per unit of value transferred but can be a vehicle for significant income transfer. Among them are the following:
  - Take-home rations can be targeted at the household level and serve much like cash transfers; they also have lower administrative costs than on-site feeding.
  - School feeding programs generally can be targeted only at the school level and not at the household level; thus, if they have wide coverage, they will involve high errors of inclusion, but may improve children's concentration and therefore learning.
  - Distribution of fortified, calorically dense weaning food for children 6–24 months old, especially as part of a nutrition education program, can be an important nutrition intervention.
  - On-site feeding through health centers is logistically complex and imposes high transaction costs on beneficiaries to come to the centers for meals. This type of program is usually best reserved for children who are severely or moderately malnourished.
  - Targeted market sales can be used for more general income transfers when other programs do not exist.

- Fee waivers or vouchers for health and scholarships for education help households maintain access to services even if they are poorer.

- Public works programs rarely achieve coverage sufficient to be the whole response to rising food prices. Where public works programs exist, increasing their benefit or coverage may help.

- Where conditional cash transfer programs already exist, increasing their benefit or coverage may be a key part of the response. However, establishing new CCTs may take too long and exclude the neediest in low income countries or fragile states

- General food price subsidies are regressive, distortive, costly, and hard to eliminate.

In some cases, scaling back on social protection interventions will be appropriate as food prices find their new long-term level and households adjust to it. Where the response to increased food prices results in improvements to grossly insufficient or inefficient safety net programs, leaving these improvements in place in the medium and long run—and indeed, building on them—may be desirable. Where the response results in coverage or benefit levels above prudent long-run levels, programs may need to be scaled down. Those countries that use less preferable policies or programs in their short-term response may need to replace them with better ones.

Countries can scale down short-run responses in various ways. One option is to announce up front that entire programs, top-up benefits, or relaxed eligibility criteria are temporary and then discontinue them on schedule. For poverty-targeted programs, recertification every year or every two years will gradually reduce the number of beneficiaries as the economy and households adjust to changes in food prices. For self-targeted programs, households will voluntarily withdraw as their needs become less acute. Benefits set in nominal terms will gradually erode away, which may be a sufficient exit strategy for top-up benefits. For stand-alone benefits, the decline in benefits will minimize people's concerns about canceling a whole program, but bureaucratic interests may dictate its continuation. This can result in programs with benefits that are too small to substantially improve welfare and inefficiently high administrative costs as a portion of total costs.

COUNTRIES' EXPERIENCES

A great many countries are mobilizing a wide variety of policy responses to rising food prices, but because the crisis is so recent, we can only discuss how countries have begun to confront it and not how their safety net policies will be affected in the long run. To date, countries' policy responses are tilted heavily toward general subsidies rather than targeted safety nets. A poll of World Bank country economists taken at the beginning of March 2008 shows that the most common short-run responses to household food insecurity in 80 countries have been price changes or market restrictions rather than more targeted safety nets (figure 10.4). Economists generally consider these kinds of across-the-board measures to be inefficient and distortive, and thus the least favored. Their predominance points to the need to build safety net capacity immediately so that countries using them have a way to back out of them as soon as possible.

Chile's response illustrates a "first-best" response made possible by a good preexisting social protection system. Chile is an upper-middle-income country with per capita GDP of about US$6,000 and low poverty. By February 2008, food price inflation had risen to 16 per-

FIGURE 10.4 **Types of Mitigating Policies Adopted by Selected Countries, Early March 2008**

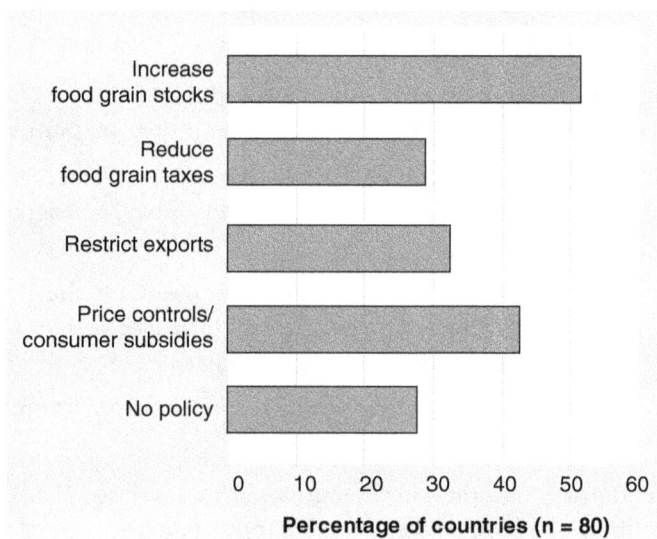

SOURCE: Zaman and others forthcoming.

cent year-on-year, with total inflation of 8 percent. The government moved swiftly, announcing a special one-time cash payment of Ch$20,000 (about US$45) to 1.4 million poor households on April 9, with immediate congressional approval and with the funds being received by households in May. The 1.4 million households include three groups: current participants in Chile Solidario, a CCT program intended to help the poorest 5 percent of the population combat various barriers to social exclusion (300,000 families); participants in the Subsidio Unitario Familiar (Unified Family Subsidy), a family allowance for the poor (516,000 families); and families that receive a family allowance for those who are employed but whose monthly income is equal to or less than Ch$250,000 (US$555) per month (600,000 families). In all, the cash payment benefited 5.6 million people, the bottom 40 percent of the income distribution, at a total cost of US$62 million.

Ethiopia was also able to respond quickly, but based only in part on its existing rural safety net.[11] Food price inflation in April 2008 reached approximately 40 percent year-on-year, raising serious concerns about the impact on the poor. The government took a three-pronged approach as follows, relying on assistance from donors and accelerated disbursements from World Bank credits to finance the responses:

- At the national level, the government suspended the value added tax and turnover taxes on all cereals.

- In rural areas, the government is relying on its Productive Safety Net Program, a cash and food-for-work program and the mainstay of Ethiopia's safety net system. The program covers 7.3 million food-insecure people and is targeted geographically and to the most food-insecure households in the participating rural districts. The cash wage rate was increased by 33 percent in January 2008, raising the annual transfer to food-insecure households in rural areas to an average of US$120 per year. Donors are supporting the government by bringing in additional maize from outside the country to ensure the availability of grain for the food transfers made under the program.

- In urban areas, the government has started providing subsidized wheat to households. The subsidy amounts to more than US$75 per household per year in urban areas. Current estimates indicate that about 4.5 million people (900,000 households) are benefiting. This scheme, while operating exclusively in urban areas, is meant to stabilize wheat prices in both urban and rural areas.

Political pressures in Haiti dictated the use of a general rice subsidy in addition to scaling up existing social protection instruments.[12] By March 2008, year-on-year inflation had doubled to 16 percent and food inflation had tripled to 20 percent. As the prices of basic food staples rose in early 2008, public protests grew large and violent. An attempt to storm the presidential palace in April 2008, thwarted by United Nations peacekeepers, led the Senate to vote the prime minister and his cabinet out of office. Prior to the riots, a multisectoral working group chaired by the prime minister and supported by the international community had been developing a strategy to deal with rising food prices, including, for the short-term, generating employment through labor-intensive public works programs; providing agricultural inputs to revitalize production; and expanding food assistance programs, including feeding programs for schoolchildren, mothers, and infants.

The riots indicated a need for more immediate and visible action. Thus in April, the government announced a temporary subsidy to reduce the price of rice. Analysis of the most recent available data (from 2001) shows that almost all Haitian households (86 percent) consume rice, that rice expenditure as a percentage of income is much higher among the poorest Haitians, and that the 76 percent of the population living on less than US$2 a day consumes roughly 70 percent of the rice. The subsidy is close to distributionally neutral—that is, less sharply targeted than most good safety net programs—but less regressive than is usual for commodity subsidies. Moreover, errors of exclusion are lower than would be expected from the employment generation, agricultural input, and food assistance programs, as these often do not reach the poorest households in Haiti.

The government set up a working group to develop a plan for gradually moving back to market prices and initiated work with donors on complementary efforts to strengthen agricultural productivity and improve the targeting and coverage of social protection instruments. The first step in relation to social protection is to design a household targeting system that will eventually underpin more streamlined programs.

Romania's experience a decade ago shows how a country can successfully navigate from a short-term response to a permanent and effective safety net (Tesliuc, Pop, and Tesliuc 2001). Until February 17, 1997, 70 percent of the bread produced was price controlled, with controls enforced from wheat production, distribution, and intermediate products (flour) to bread and other bakery products. At that time, the government liberalized wheat, flour, and bread prices despite considerable uncertainty about the level of inflation (including for bread) that would follow. The price of bread rose by 80 percentage points in March compared with February, against a backdrop of consumer inflation of 31 percent.

As bread is the major staple in the food basket of urban consumers, the government was concerned that a rise in the price of bread would hurt the poor and the middle class and that their opposition would undermine the reforms. To win support for the price liberalization and avoid a costly policy reversal that might be necessitated by social unrest, it offered temporary compensation to a population group substantially larger than the number of poor, over and above the existing, well-woven, safety net.

The government implemented the bread compensation program between April and September 1997, to facilitate the adjustment to the new relative price of bread for the poor and middle-class consumers. The introduction of temporary bread compensation was feasible because an effective safety net was already in place. The poorest quintile of the population was already covered by survivors' pensions and a variety of social protection programs for the elderly, people with disabilities, and the unemployed and by the Guaranteed Minimum Income Program before the price liberalization. To protect the purchasing power of the poor, the generosity of this safety net was maintained by indexing the cash benefits to overall inflation.

The bread compensation program provided a fixed subsidy of lei 13,500 (approximately US$2) per month to all those earning less than lei 600,000 (US$85) per month; all pensioners with pensions of less than lei 450,000 (US$65) per month; and all those who were unemployed, had disabilities, or were beneficiaries of the social assistance program of last resort (the GMI Program). The eligibility threshold for employees and pensioners was almost twice as high as the prevailing poverty line, and the target group was almost double the poverty headcount (slightly more than half the population, compared with a poverty headcount of 19.4 percent).

A simulation of the distributional impact of the bread compensation under the assumption of perfect implementation showed that it was weakly pro-poor and that a substantial share of the benefits went to middle-class households (Tesliuc, Pop, and Tesliuc 2001). However, the bread compensation was more progressive than the former bread price controls and cost the government less.

10.7 Summary

One of the core messages of this book is that no single recipe for a safety net is available. Appropriate policy is context specific, and this chapter illustrates how safety net solutions vary across contexts. The variation is apparent in the mix of programs, in how each is customized, and in the expectations for each.

Thus program mix varies from setting to setting. Egypt, for example, has massive food and energy subsidies. Indonesia is moving away from such subsidies, replacing general price supports with a targeted price subsidy for rice, reducing massive fuel subsidies alongside providing compensation via a temporary cash transfer program, and introducing a pilot for a CCT program. Bulgaria has also moved from primary subsidies to a means-tested cash transfer complemented by a seasonal heating allowance.

Context affects how programs are implemented. In several of the cases presented in this chapter, governments used public works programs, but customized the approach to the setting. In Ethiopia's PSNP, the work is seasonal and rationed by means of community-based selection of who is most food insecure. The works involve heavy manual labor, and much of the labor is used for soil and water conservation projects. The program is intended for the long run; consequently, the selection of works is being integrated into district-level planning. By contrast, Argentina's Jefes de Hogar program has open-ended and self-targeted benefits. While some projects use heavy manual labor with workers organized in traditional work gangs, a good deal of work is physically lighter unskilled labor, with small groups of workers working in schools, hospitals, and parks, caring for the elderly, and the like. The program was started quickly, so planning for the use of labor was more rudimentary than in Ethiopia, but as in Ethiopia, was left to the local level. Honduras's response to Hurricane Mitch also employed public works as a key piece of the response, where they were used both for cleanup and reconstruction and as a temporary financial support for households whose livelihoods had been impaired. Participation was self-targeted, but rationed. The institutional homes of the programs are also different: the Ministry of Labor in Argentina, the Food Security Bureau in Ethiopia, and the Social Fund in Honduras. These various accommodations fit the programs to the needs of the countries.

The most sophisticated programs and systems are in stable, middle-income countries or in transition countries that have been working on developing systems for some time. In very low-income settings, systems will be constrained and greater simplicity will be sensible. Following economic shocks or natural disasters, the speed of response is critical as the situation changes rapidly, thus compromises in design and implementation standards will be needed.

A final lesson emerges from the settings and cases presented: safety net systems and programs should be dynamic. The mix and design of programs should respond as needs change, and the implementation of individual programs should involve a constant search for improvements. Bulgaria presents a clear example of such dynamics, with the balance and implementation of programs changing significantly over time. Ethiopia's program has evolved in ways meant to remedy past deficiencies. Even Egypt's food subsidies, which seem to be enduring, have changed over the years to become somewhat more effective than they were at their height. Responses to crises, natural disasters, and policy reforms are, of course, inherently dynamic.

Notes

1. This subsection is based on World Bank (2006n).

2. Food insecurity is defined as a lack of access to enough food for an active, healthy life. Chronic food insecurity refers to the persistence of this situation over time, even in the absence of idiosyncratic or covariate shocks.

3. This portion is taken largely from Sadowski (1991) and World Bank (2005c).

4. In July 1997, after several months of chaos involving a sharp decline in GDP and per capita incomes, the collapse of the banking sector, and a major foreign exchange crisis, Bulgaria adopted a currency board arrangement.

5. According to the National Statistical Institute, nearly 14 percent of the population was living below the poverty line in 2003. The institute defined the national poverty line as an income equivalent to the cost of 60 percent of the overall monthly consumer expenses per person in a household (about €52). This figure differs from the 4.5 percent of the population below the poverty line of US$2.15 (purchasing power parity) per day and from the calculations based on the World Bank poverty lines used in a series of poverty assessments in 1999, 2002, and 2005 and reported in the text. The World Bank poverty levels are the only ones comparable across time.

6. This subsection draws heavily on Baldacci (2006) and World Bank (2006b).

7. This subsection is based on del Ninno, Dorosh, and Smith (2003).

8. This subsection is drawn from Warren (2003).

9. This subsection draws on Arulpragasam (2006a), Indrawati (2005), and World Bank (2006f).

10. This section is drawn from World Bank (2003a, 2008a, 2008c, 2008d).

11. Briefing provided May 22, 2008, by Trina Haque, Sunil Rajkumar, and William Wiseman of the World Bank Africa Region, Human Development Department, Social Protection Sector.

12. Briefing provided May 28, 2008, by David Warren of the World Bank Latin America and the Caribbean Region, Human Development Department, Social Protection Sector.

Basic Concepts of Poverty and Social Risk Management

This appendix defines various social policy concepts used throughout this book and highlights how they differ from one another or where they sometimes overlap. This information is presented for readers who may not be familiar with these terms and to ensure a common understanding among those who are.

A.1 Poverty, Vulnerability to Poverty, and Vulnerable Groups

Understanding and measuring poverty and vulnerability to poverty are crucial for designing effective poverty alleviation policies and programs. Here is an attempt to briefly illustrate the multiple dimensions of poverty and the methods often used to define and measure poverty and vulnerability to poverty.

POVERTY

Poverty generally is defined as an unacceptable level of welfare. In this context, welfare covers a broad range of dimensions such as consumption or income poverty, inadequate nutrition, lack of access to health and education, insecurity due to conflicts, and lack of political freedom, among others. Thus, poverty encompasses more than low income or consumption alone (Narayan and others 2000; Sen 1999; World Bank 2000f). Although deprivation is often related to income poverty—as when low income prevents people from achieving sufficient nutrition or from obtaining remedies for treatable illness—poverty is not always closely related to income. Rather, poverty may arise from a lack of access to public facilities and programs (such as health or education) or from the denial of political, civil, and economic liberties. Throughout this book, to make the analysis manageable, we focus on one or a few important welfare dimensions, depending on the specific country context.

The measurement and analysis of poverty requires some measure of welfare. Ideally, such a measure would capture the multidimensional aspects of poverty and be observable and measurable in a consistent way across households, space, and time. One-dimensional welfare measures, whether monetary or nonmonetary, are more common. Monetary indicators of poverty and living conditions include income, consumption, and assets. Nonmonetary indicators include malnutrition; access to health, education, and basic services; and perceptions of poverty or deprivation. Since no single measure fully captures all such features, living conditions should be monitored over time using a battery of indicators rather than a single measure.[1] Two composite indicators that attempt to capture the multidimensionality of poverty are the Human Development Index developed by the United Nations Development Programme and various basic needs indexes that aggregate different dimensions of deprivation (such as poor-quality housing and lack of adequate education).

The two monetary indicators that top researchers' preferences as indexes of household welfare are per capita (or per adult equivalent) consumption and income.[2] Of these, the use of consumption is generally preferred because it is fairly comprehensive; these data tend to be more reliable than income data because of incomplete measurement or underreporting; consumption tends to fluctuate less than income (which can even go to zero in certain months due to seasonality), making it a better indicator of living standards; and consumption is less subjective than basic needs indexes, which rely on some form of subjective weighting across their components. Unlike income, consumption reflects the ability of a household to borrow or mobilize other resources in time of economic stress.

The level of poverty can be measured by comparing the index of household welfare with a cutoff point that separates the poor from the nonpoor. This cutoff point is the poverty line, which can be monetary (for example, a certain level of consumption) or nonmonetary (for example, a certain level of literacy). Sometimes multiple lines are used to help in distinguishing among different levels of poverty. In practice, most analysts measure poverty by comparing the per capita (or per adult equivalent) consumption or income with a monetary poverty line. Households whose consumption falls below the poverty line are counted as poor.

ABSOLUTE VERSUS RELATIVE POVERTY

Because poverty lines can be either relative or absolute, there are consequently two types of poverty: absolute and relative poverty. Relative poverty lines are defined in relation to the overall distribution of income or consumption in a country; for example, the poverty line could be set at 50 percent of the country's mean income or consumption. Absolute poverty lines are anchored in some absolute standard of what households should be able to count on in order to meet their basic needs. For monetary measures, these absolute poverty lines are often based on estimates of the cost of basic food needs—that is, the cost of a nutritional basket considered minimal for the health of a typical family—to which a provision is added for nonfood needs. Because large parts of the populations of developing countries survive with the bare minimum or less, reliance on an absolute rather than relative poverty line often proves to be more relevant. On the other hand, in designing or reviewing safety net programs, relative poverty seems to be more useful. In a hypothetical example where absolute poverty is 40 percent but budget considerations constrain the coverage of a program to 10 percent of the population, an analysis of the poorest 10 percent would be most informative for program design.

CHRONIC VERSUS TRANSIENT POVERTY

The concept of poverty has been expanding over the last few years to include dynamic considerations that take into account the realization that over time poor households are not the same (Baulch and Hoddinott 2000). Poverty can thus be classified as chronic or transient, depending on the duration of poverty periods over time. The transient poor are households that are not poor in good years but occasionally experience poverty. Chronically poor households are poor in every period; they cannot escape poverty even in good years. The concept of chronic poverty also implies a deeper level of severity of poverty since there is no means available to the household to escape poverty.

Figure A.1 illustrates the consumption levels relative to the poverty line of two households, A and B, over a period of eight years. Based on the transitions into and out of poverty, household A is classified as transient poor.

FIGURE A.1 **Households in Chronic versus Transient Poverty**

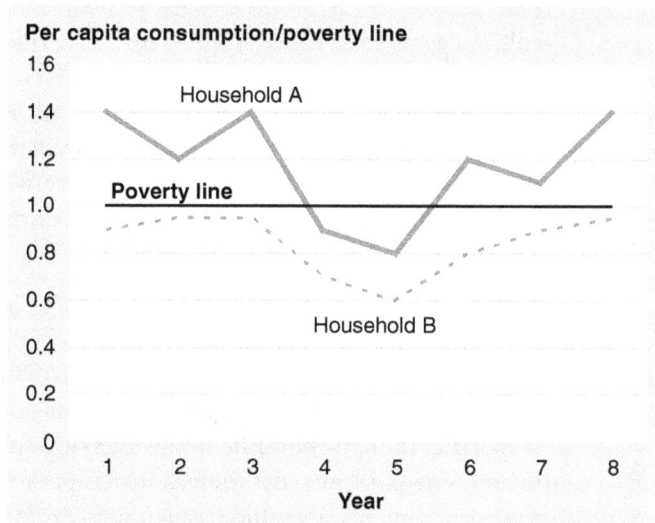

SOURCE: Authors.

Although it has, on average across the eight years, a consumption (or income) level 1.2 times the poverty line, it was poor in years 4 and 5. Household B is classified as chronically poor. It has an average consumption (or income) of 0.8 times the poverty line and has lived in poverty in all eight years.

Estimation of chronic and transient poverty requires panel data measuring the welfare of a representative sample of households over several periods.

VULNERABILITY TO POVERTY

What causes nonpoor households to become poor, at least for a period of time? The concept of vulnerability to poverty provides a useful framework to answer this question. Vulnerability to poverty is defined as exposure to uninsured risk, leading to a socially unacceptable level of well-being. This definition comprises several ideas worth parsing (see Hoogeveen and others 2004 for a more detailed treatment).

- **Exposure to risk.** Not all risks lead to unacceptable welfare outcomes, and some level of exposure to risk is desirable. For example, given the costs of labor monitoring, some job insecurity provides the flexibility and incentives needed for labor markets to offer high levels of employment. Quick financial liberalization may in some circumstances be substantially better for economic growth than a less crisis-prone, steady pace of financial liberalization. Exposure to risk may even be enjoyable and sought after, as with gambling or entrepreneurship. Exposure to risk becomes unacceptable if it leads to socially unacceptable low levels of welfare. Unemployment that leads to destitution is likely to be deemed unacceptable, and society may choose to alleviate its consequences or reduce the risk of unemployment itself. In a health context, a frequently occurring risk such as diarrhea may be unacceptable if it mainly affects poor households with limited access to medical care or clean water and therefore results in increased early childhood mortality. But if diarrhea is mostly an inconvenience affecting wealthy families that eat frequently at restaurants, the risk may be acceptable and not a focus for vulnerability analysis.

- **Insured versus uninsured risk.** Once insured, risk ceases to be a concern since the manifestation of a shock will not affect welfare outcomes. Market-based insurance and self-insurance both prevent negative welfare consequences from occurring. In practice, full insurance is not attained; thus, uninsured risk remains even in the presence of insurance mechanisms.
- **Socially.** The use of the term "socially" refers to society and the context-specific set of norms and values that it deems important. What some societies consider socially unacceptable levels of well-being may be acceptable in others.
- **Acceptable level of well-being.** Which welfare outcomes are unacceptable is context specific, though the Millennium Development Goals of the United Nations provide some guidance, defining as unacceptable welfare outcomes falling below the poverty line; being malnourished; not completing primary education; experiencing unequal gender outcomes; high early childhood and maternal mortality; and a high exposure to diseases such as HIV/AIDS, tuberculosis, and malaria.

The manifestation of risk or the exposure to risk may be seen as one of the many dimensions of poverty for households with low coping capacity such as the poor. The manifestation of risk (as a shock) leads to undesirable welfare outcomes. Apart from the physical and psychological consequences for well-being from experiencing a shock, the economic consequences can be highly undesirable. A shock can push an already poor household further into poverty or drive a nonpoor household below the poverty line. A shock can cause children to be taken out of school, permanently affect people's health, or reduce life expectancy.

Exposure to risk also has a direct negative impact on well-being. In an attempt to avoid risk exposure, households may take costly preventive measures which in turn contribute to poverty. The decision not to invest in a high-risk but high-return activity not only means foregone income but also a higher likelihood that a household is poor. If security concerns force parents to take children out of school, the children are disenfranchised from their right to basic education. And if credit and insurance markets are poorly developed, exposure to risks may induce households to hold portfolios of assets that, while possibly well suited to buffering consumption, are not necessarily the most productive.

The exposure to uninsured risk causes undesirable welfare outcomes such as consumption (or income) poverty, malnutrition, low education levels, and low life expectancy. The exposure to or manifestation of risks alone may not lead to unacceptable outcomes in well-being. If households have the option to insure against the negative consequences of shocks, risk will have a limited impact on welfare.

RELATIONSHIP BETWEEN POVERTY AND VULNERABILITY TO POVERTY

Most analysts use the term vulnerability to poverty to mean the likelihood or probability that a household will pass below the defined acceptable threshold of a given indicator and fall into poverty. Such an adverse outcome can stem from one or a combination of three factors: starting below the threshold (chronic poverty); exposure to risks or shocks, especially for those close to the poverty line; and having few risk management tools available. It is important to know how prevalent each of these problems is and how they interact, as each should be addressed with different interventions.

Other analysts use the term vulnerability to poverty to report the variability in consumption (or income) even when the average level is above the poverty line. Understanding variability in consumption (or income), even for those who start somewhat above the poverty line, is important in understanding poverty and the concerns of households and policy makers with respect to social protection mechanisms.

The relationship between poverty and vulnerability to poverty in a dynamic environment with many risks can be conceptualized using a public health analogy—specifically, to consider poverty as a disease, as illustrated in figure A.2. Most diseases have a stochastic component: it is always somewhat uncertain who will fall ill and when. At any point in time, some individuals are ill, and others are not. Among the sick, some are likely to recover (transient sick); others are chronically ill. Among the healthy, some are at risk of becoming ill, and others are not. Those who are ill may transmit the disease to others, in particular, their children.

FIGURE A.2 **Poverty as a Disease**

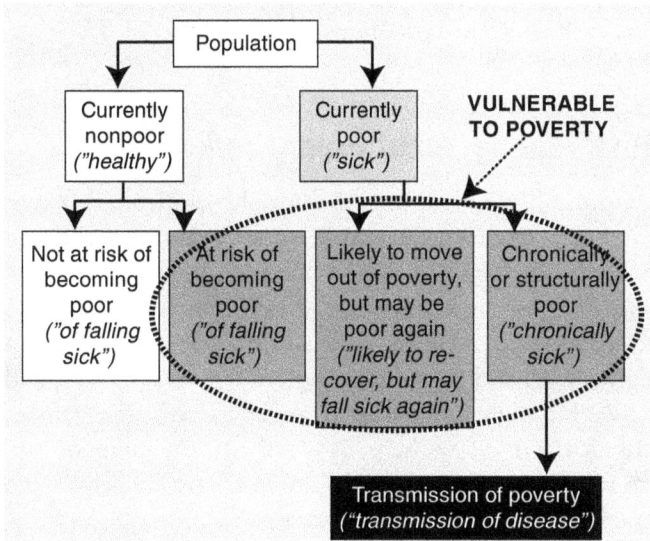

SOURCE: Authors.

These categories have a direct correspondence with the different groups who are poor or vulnerable to poverty. Those poor at a given moment can be divided into chronic (stuck in poverty) or transient (temporarily poor). The chronically poor are not only stuck in poverty; they are likely to transmit this poverty across generations. Among those not poor at a given moment, there are households at risk of becoming poor—if, for instance, they suffer a severe shock. The population vulnerable to poverty is the sum of those currently poor and those at risk of becoming poor.

What are the implications of this categorization for poverty reduction policy? A public health intervention analogy can be used in this regard. To respond to transmission mechanisms, public health interventions typically have three elements: treatment for those who are ill, preventive measures to reduce the risks of contracting or recontracting the disease, and programs to halt the transmission of the disease. Similarly, poverty reduction strategies must simultaneously incorporate three elements: programs to help the currently poor, such as transfers to alleviate poverty and/or programs to help them build assets and thus their independent incomes; programs to reduce the likelihood of the nonpoor becoming poor, such as unemployment or health insurance; and programs to prevent the intergenerational transmission of poverty, such as programs to guarantee adequate nutrition, health care, and schooling for poor children.

VULNERABLE GROUPS

Vulnerability is often used somewhat differently than it as defined here to indicate weakness or defenselessness, and is typically used to describe groups that are weak and prone to serious hardship. These vulnerable groups are people with disabilities, orphans, those infected with HIV, the elderly, ethnic minorities, certain castes, refugees or internally displaced persons, households headed by widows or deserted women, or households headed by children. These groups are described as vulnerable in the common usage of the term, but (uninsured) risk is not a core characteristic of their problems, although for some of them shocks may have contributed to their destitution or precarious circumstances. Any uninsured risk is especially difficult for them because their options to manage risk are likely to be limited. These groups often receive income support through safety nets, either via separate categorical programs or by using indexes of vulnerability in determining entry or benefit levels in more general cash assistance programs.

A.2 Social Risk Management Framework

All individuals, households, and communities are exposed to multiple risks from different sources. But the poor are more vulnerable to these, since they are typically more exposed to risks and have access to fewer risk management instruments that can allow them to deal with these risks (Holzmann 2003). This exposure to risks and lack of ability to address this exposure has two important consequences: (1) the poor are severely affected when shocks do occur, accentuating their poverty; and (2) the poor become more risk averse and unwilling (or unable) to engage in risky but higher return activities. Social risk management aims to provide instruments to the society to allow the poor—and also the nonpoor—to minimize the impact of exposure to risk and change their behavior in a way that helps them exit poverty and lower their vulnerability (Holzmann and Jorgensen 2000).[3]

RISK MANAGEMENT STRATEGIES

Social risk management can take place at different points both before and after risk occurs. The goal of ex ante measures or strategies is to avoid the risk's occurrence (risk prevention) or, if this is not possible, to reduce its impact (risk mitigation). If risk prevention and mitigation are insufficient or inadequate, households are left with the residual option of coping with the shock once it occurs (ex post).

Prevention strategies for risk reduction are implemented before a risk event occurs. Reducing the probability of an adverse risk has intrinsic welfare benefits and increases people's expected income and reduces their income variance. Preventive interventions include measures designed to reduce risks in the labor market (the risk of unemployment, for instance), preventive health care measures (such as vaccination, use of mosquito nets, or information campaigns), and the development and implementation of standards (such as building standards in areas prone to earthquakes). Prevention strategies implemented by households or individuals may be very costly and could even be a cause for (income) poverty, for instance when farmers grow low-return but drought-resistant crops or when people seek protection from violence by moving to camps for internally displaced persons.

Mitigation strategies aim to address risk before it occurs by helping individuals reduce the impact of a future risky event. For example, households may pool uncorrelated risks through informal or formal insurance mechanisms. While formal insurance mechanisms are best placed to pool a large number of risks over many participants, information and enforcement constraints limit the coverage actually offered (both geographically and by type of risk). Many people therefore participate in informal insurance mechanisms that are less successful in pooling risk but more effective in sharing information and in enforcement. Mitigation strategies can also be implemented in isolation; for instance, when a household or individual saves money as a precaution for a rainy day, or when food is stored in preparation for an adverse weather event.

Coping strategies are designed to relieve the impact of risk once it has occurred. The main forms of coping consist of individuals using their savings and selling assets, borrowing, or relying on public or private transfers. When individuals or households have not saved enough to handle repeated or catastrophic risks, the government has an important role to play by providing transfers—this is necessary, for example, when asset prices plummet and food prices soar because the population is selling assets to obtain money to buy food following a covariate shock.

INSTITUTIONAL ARRANGEMENTS FOR RISK MANAGEMENT

Different kinds of social risk management arrangements to deal with exposure to risk have evolved. These fall into three main categories: informal, market-based, and public arrangements. In an ideal world with perfectly symmetrical information and complete and well-functioning markets, all risk management arrangements can be market based. In reality, all three risk management arrangements play a role.

Informal arrangements have existed for a long time and still constitute the main source of risk management for the majority of the world's population. In the absence of (or with incomplete) market institutions and public support, individual households respond to risk by protecting themselves through informal and personal arrangements. Although they sidestep most of the information and coordination problems that cause market failure, they may not be very effective in helping a household weather adverse events. Nonetheless, the introduction of market or public arrangements may have negative consequences for the functioning of informal arrangements. For instance, the introduction of a public arrangement such as a food-for-work program may lead to the withdrawal from an informal insurance arrangement of able-bodied individuals, leaving less-able-bodied individuals (such as the elderly) uninsured.

Market-based arrangements have great potential, and, where available, households and individuals take advantage of the financial products offered by insurance companies and banks. In practice, many of these financial instruments are not available to the poor because of market failures; thus, their use is restricted until financial markets become more developed. Because formal market institutions have difficulty in lending to households (or in providing them with insurance) without secured earnings, microcredit and insurance arrangements are potentially interesting instruments for social risk management.

Public arrangements take various forms. Where informal or market-based risk management arrangements do not exist, the government can provide or mandate social insurance programs for risks such as unemployment, old age, work injury, disability, widowhood, and sickness. Mandatory participation in a risk pool can circumvent issues of adverse selection, in which individuals with low-risk profiles avoid participation in insurance pools while high-risk profiles join. Because these programs typically apply to those in formal employment, their coverage in developing countries is generally low. Governments have an array of other instruments to help households cope after a shock hits, such as direct assistance, free medical care, subsidies on basic goods and services, and public works programs. Through its legislative abilities, government is also able to introduce prevention strategies such as building codes in disaster-prone areas, protection of widows' rights to assets, and so on. Finally, many sectoral government programs (in health, education, infrastructure, and the like) also play an important role in risk prevention.

INTERACTION OF RISK MANAGEMENT STRATEGIES AND ARRANGEMENTS

Table A.1 provides examples of various risk management strategies and arrangements.

Risk management strategies will typically be multisectoral and need not be limited to social protection. For example, in Sub-Saharan Africa, risks are numerous, severe, and widespread, but little is spent on social protection. Instead, management of risks here focuses mainly on nonsocial protection instruments such as health care, education, rural development, and infrastructure development.

In the matrix of risk management strategies and arrangements illustrated in table A.1, safety net programs appear as public interventions aimed primarily at risk coping (ex post). However, as discussed in chapter 2, some safety net programs may incorporate design elements that will augment their role in risk mitigation or risk reduction, such as guaranteed minimum income transfers or workfare programs with employment guarantees.

A.3 Poverty and Vulnerability Reduction Strategies and Policies

Promoting policies and strategies for poverty and vulnerability reduction is a top priority of the World Bank. *World Development Report 2006: Equity and Development* (World Bank 2005n) reiterates the message of *World Development Report 2000/2001: Attacking Poverty* (World Bank 2000f) in proposing a strategy for attacking poverty by promoting opportunity, facilitating empowerment, and enhancing security:

- **Promoting opportunity.** Poor people consistently emphasize the centrality of material opportunities. This means jobs; credit; roads; electricity; markets for their produce; and the schools, water, sanitation, and health services that underpin the health and skills essential for work. Overall economic growth is crucial for generating opportunity. So is the pattern or quality of growth. Market reforms can be central in expanding opportunities for poor people, but reforms need to reflect local institutional and structural conditions. Mechanisms need to be in place to create new opportunities and compensate the potential losers in transi-

TABLE A.1 **Examples of Social Risk Management Strategies and Arrangements**

Arrangement/ strategy	Informal	Market based	Public
Risk reduction and prevention	• Less risky production • Migration • Proper feeding and weaning practices • Engaging in hygiene and other disease-preventing activities	• In-service training • Financial market literacy • Company-based and market-driven labor standards	• Labor standards • Preservice training • Labor market policies • Child labor reduction interventions • Disability policies • Good macroeconomic policies • AIDS and other disease prevention
Risk mitigation			
Portfolio	• Multiple jobs • Investment in human, physical, and real assets • Investment in social capital (rituals, reciprocal gift giving)	• Investment in multiple financial assets • Microfinance	• Multipillar pension systems • Asset transfers • Protection of poverty rights (especially for women) • Support for extending financial markets to the poor
Insurance	• Marriage/family • Community arrangements • Share tenancy • Tied labor	• Old-age annuities • Disability, accident, and other personal insurance • Crop, fire, and other damage insurance	• Mandated/provided insurance for unemployment, old age, disability, survivorship, sickness, and so on
Risk coping	• Sale of real assets • Borrowing from neighbors • Intracommunity transfers/ charity • Sending children to work • Dissaving in human capital	• Sale of financial assets • Borrowing from banks	• Transfers in cash and in kind • Subsidies • Public works

SOURCE: Holzmann 2003.

tions. In societies with high inequality, greater equity is particularly important for rapid progress in reducing poverty. This requires action by the state to support the buildup of human, land, and infrastructure assets that poor people own or to which they have access.

- **Facilitating empowerment.** The choice and implementation of public actions that are responsive to the needs of poor people depend on the interaction of political, social, and other institutional processes. Access to market opportunities and to public sector services is often strongly influenced by state and social institutions, which must be responsive and accountable to poor people. Achieving access, responsibility, and accountability is intrinsically political and requires active collaboration among poor people, the middle class, and other groups in society. Active collaboration can be greatly facilitated by changes in governance that make public administration, legal institutions, and public service delivery more efficient and accountable to all citizens—and by strengthening the participation of poor people in political processes and local decision making. Also important is removing the social and institutional barriers that result from distinctions of gender, ethnicity, and social status. Sound and responsive institutions are not only important to benefit the poor but are also fundamental to the overall growth process.

- **Enhancing security.** Reducing vulnerability—to economic shocks, natural disasters, ill health, disability, and personal violence—is an intrinsic part of enhancing well-being and encourages investment in human capital and in higher-risk, higher-return activities. This requires effective national action to manage the risk of economywide shocks and effective mechanisms to reduce the risks faced by poor people, including health- and weather-related risks. It also requires building the assets of poor people, diversifying household activities, and providing a range of insurance mechanisms to cope with adverse shocks—from public work to stay-in-school programs and health insurance.

- **There is no hierarchy of importance.** The elements are deeply complementary. Each part of the strategy affects underlying causes of poverty addressed by the other two. For example, promoting opportunity through assets and market access increases the independence of poor people and thus empowers them by strengthening their bargaining position relative to state and society. It also enhances security, since an adequate stock of assets is a buffer against adverse shocks. Similarly, strengthening democratic institutions and empowering women and disadvantaged ethnic and racial groups—say, by eliminating legal discrimination against them—expand the economic opportunities for the poor and socially excluded. Strengthening organizations of poor people can help to ensure service delivery and policy choices responsive to the needs of poor people and can reduce corruption and arbitrariness in state actions as well. And if poor people do more in monitoring and controlling the local delivery of social services, public spending is more likely to help them during crises. Finally, helping poor people cope with shocks and manage risks puts them in a better position to take advantage of emerging market opportunities. That is why this report advocates a comprehensive approach to attacking poverty.

A.4 The Role of Safety Nets within Social Protection and Social Policy

Social policy in general and social protection and safety nets in particular are critical in reducing poverty and deprivation. The relationship between social policy, social protection, and safety nets is illustrated in figure 2.1, and their respective roles are delineated below.

SOCIAL POLICY

Social policy is that part of public policy pertaining to human development and social issues. Social policy aims to improve human welfare and meet human needs for education, health, housing, and social protection. In an academic environment, social policy refers to the study of the welfare state and the range of responses to social need.

SOCIAL PROTECTION

An adequate social protection system is an important element of any comprehensive strategy to reduce poverty and vulnerability. Social protection systems include "the set of public interventions aimed at supporting the poorer and more vulnerable members of society, as well as helping individuals, families and communities to improve their risk administration" (Holzmann and Jorgensen 2001). This set of interventions includes social insurance, labor market policies, social funds, social services, and safety net (social assistance) programs.

Social insurance programs, for example, are designed to help households insure themselves against sudden reductions in income. They include publicly provided or mandated insurance against unemployment, old age (pensions), disability, death of the main provider, and sickness. Social insurance programs are contributory. Beneficiaries receive benefits or services in recognition of contributions to an insurance scheme.

Because the aim of social protection programs is to reduce vulnerability by improving the instruments available to manage risks and/or by helping the extremely poor, social protection interventions can be viewed as both a safety net and a springboard. Put another way, while they prevent people from falling deeper into poverty, they also provide poor people with the capacity to climb out of poverty altogether.

SAFETY NETS

Safety nets are noncontributory transfer programs targeted in some manner to the poor or those vulnerable to poverty and shocks. These programs are often referred to as social assistance or social welfare programs. Social assistance programs are generally designed to help individuals or households cope with chronic poverty or transient declines in income that would otherwise cause them to sink into poverty or worse poverty. As such, they help alleviate poverty and reduce nonpoor households' vulnerability to becoming poor. There is no universal consensus on the types of interventions covered under the safety net label; those covered in this book are as follows:

- **Cash transfers:** needs-based transfers, food stamps, noncontributory pensions, family allowances
- **Food and nutrition:** quantity rations and in-kind transfers, supplemental feeding and nutrition, school feeding, emergency food distribution
- **General commodity price subsidies:** price support for food, subsidized sales of food, subsidies for energy prices
- **Public works:** in which the poor work for food or cash
- **Conditional cash transfers:** transfers to poor households conditional on specific behavior

- **Fee waivers:** health fees, school fees, scholarships

The book does not cover microcredit initiatives, although these are often labeled as safety net programs.

Notes

1. Extensive empirical evidence exists that monetary indicators can reliably capture nonmonetary dimensions of deprivation.
2. Most countries in the Organisation for Economic Co-operation and Development or Latin America use income to assess household well-being and poverty. In contrast, transition economies, as well as countries in Asia and Africa, primarily use consumption. The Russian Federation uses both income and consumption, although only consumption data are reliably collected.
3. This section draws on World Bank (2001b).

Main Features of Selected Safety Net Programs

TABLE B.1 **Cash and Near Cash Programs**

NEEDS-BASED TRANSFERS

Albania: Ndihme Ekonomika (Economic Assistance)

Description	This is an income transfer to households that have no or insufficient income from market or nonmarket sources to meet their minimal subsistence requirements. Eligibility for the program is based on a means test, with the income eligibility threshold based on household size and composition. Additional exclusion criteria, added in 1995, are related to access to income-generating assets, refusal of paid work or professional training, or a household member being employed. The benefit is determined based on monthly income testing. Generally, every month the household head has to visit a program office to claim the benefits and provide the necessary information. An eligible household receives a cash transfer equal to the difference between the eligibility threshold and its actual income from all sources, including imputed income from assets.
Start date	1993 with changes in 1994–5
Expenditure	2004: lek 3.99 billion (US$38.8 million), or about 0.5% of GDP
Coverage	2004: about 125,000 households (500,000 people) or 16% of the population
Sources	Alderman (1998, 2002a); Kolpeja (2005, forthcoming); Tabor (2002)

Armenia: Family Poverty Benefits Program

Description	Since 1999, the program has replaced the system of state compensation and humanitarian assistance in the sphere of social assistance. The program aims to reduce the number of extremely poor families and to ease their burden. The new system introduced a proxy means-tested targeting mechanism, whereby households are ranked based on a single index formula that includes individual and household indicators. The use of the targeting mechanism based on proxies, not income, was motivated by the highly informal nature of economic activities in Armenia. Each family that qualifies receives a basic monthly benefit.
Start date	1999
Expenditure	1999: dram 21 billion (about US$39 million) or 2.1% of GDP; 2003: dram 13.2 billion (about US$25 million), or 0.89% of GDP
Coverage	1999: 211,555 families (657,071 individuals), or about 21.2% of the population; 2003: 141,218 families (505,560 individuals), or about 16.6% of the population
Sources	Ghukasyan (forthcoming); World Bank (2003b, 2003c)

(continued)

TABLE B.1 **(continued)**

NEEDS-BASED TRANSFERS

Bulgaria: Guaranteed Minimum Income Program

Description	The program provides a means-tested cash benefit to the poor. Its objectives are to increase the income of the poor to reach a minimum defined by law and stimulate their social integration and integration into the labor market. The level of applicants' own incomes must be below a defined limit known as the differentiated minimum income. This is calculated by adjusting the value of the guaranteed minimum income using a set of coefficients, taking into account household size and composition, with preferential treatment for some vulnerable population groups (people with disabilities, the elderly, single parents with small children). This differentiated approach ensures consistency between the amount of social assistance benefits and other minimum incomes (the minimum wage, the social pension, unemployment benefits), while ensuring priority to specific population groups. Social workers also check the beneficiaries' property status to determine if the size of their housing meets legal requirements and if their movable and unmovable assets could be an income source.
Start date	1992
Expenditure	2004: US$55 million or 0.22% of GDP
Coverage	2004: 527,000 beneficiaries or 6.8% of the population
Sources	Shopov (forthcoming); World Bank (2002c)

Hungary: social assistance

Description	The social assistance system covers many means-tested assistance programs for which local governments are responsible. The three main forms of social assistance are cash benefits, in-kind benefits, and personal care. Cash benefits include the regular social assistance and also cover housing, medical fees, temporary assistance, and funeral benefits. The beneficiaries of regular social assistance are working-age people who have lost 67% of their working capacity or are blind and their per capita monthly income is less than 80% of the minimum old-age pension, and working-age people who are unemployed with an income less than 70% of the minimum old-age pension.
Start date	1993
Expenditure	1997: Ft 38,391 million (about US$211 million) or 0.46% of GDP
Coverage	1997: approximately 2.3 million recipients or about 22.3% of the population
Sources	Grootaert (1997); Ringold and Kasek (2007); World Bank (2001d)

Indonesia: unconditional cash transfer

Description	The government initiated this program to compensate poor families for the short-term impacts of the fuel price increase. It was implemented after the removal of the fuel subsidy and the decision to reallocate funds saved in programs that benefited the poor. Each beneficiary family, selected through a proxy means test based on households' economic and social characteristics, receives about US$10 per month, paid quarterly. The plan is to convert the program into a conditional cash transfer program following a pilot program in 2007 that is still ongoing.
Start date	2005–6
Expenditure	2006: about US$2.4 billion or 0.66% of GDP
Coverage	2006: 19.2 million poor and near poor households or about 34% of the population
Sources	World Bank (2006f)

(continued)

TABLE B.1 **(continued)**

NEEDS-BASED TRANSFERS

Lithuania: Social Benefit Program

Description	This means-tested cash transfer program is meant to ensure a minimum level of subsistence for low-income individuals. To be eligible, family members must be permanent residents of the country and the family's per capita income over the last three months must have been less than LTL135 (US$52) per month. In addition, the value of the household's property must be less than a certain threshold set by the government and based on household size and place of residence. The program is autonomously administered by social assistance departments in municipalities.
Start date	1990
Expenditure	2004: US$27.5 million or 0.1% of GDP
Coverage	2004: 84,000 families or 2.4% of the population
Sources	Ringold and Kasek (2007); Zalimiene (forthcoming)

Mozambique: Food Subsidy Program

Description	The program is managed and implemented by the National Institute for Social Action under the auspices of the Ministry for Women and Social Action. The program provides a monthly cash transfer to recipient households. The value of the transfer is low and depends on the size of the household, starting at Mt 70,000 (US$3) per month for a one-person household and rising to a maximum of Mt 140,000 (US$6) for households with five or more members. Despite its name, the program is not a subsidy, but a cash transfer for the poor to buy food. Target groups include people who are temporarily or permanently unable to work or satisfy their subsistence needs. Eligibility is determined by a combination of proxy indicators (age, disability), means testing (per capita monthly income below Mt 70,000), and health status (chronically sick or malnourished). This program replaced an earlier cash transfer program that had been in effect during 1990–7.
Start date	1997
Expenditure	Not available
Coverage	2005: approximately 69,000 households or 160,000 people or about 1% of the population
Sources	Datt and others 1997; Devereux and others (2005)

Pakistan: Food Support Program

Description	The program, managed by the Pakistan Bait-ul-Maal (Government Charitable Fund), an autonomous body under the umbrella of the Ministry of Social Welfare and Special Education, targets the poorest of the poor to provide relief from increased wheat prices since 2000. The program is administered in collaboration with the post office and provincial governments. Eligibility criteria are needy individuals with no support or source of income, including individuals with major ailments or disabilities, widows with dependent children, invalids with dependent children, orphans, and the destitute. The scheme provides assistance on an annual basis and selected households receive PRs 3,000 a year as of FY2005/06.
Start date	2000
Expenditure	FY2003/04: Rs 2,062.9 million (about US$36 million) or about 0.04% of GDP
Coverage	2007: 1.46 million households or about 5.5% of total population
Sources	ADB (2006); *Dawn* (2003); Pasha, Jafarey, and Lohano (2000); World Bank (2007k)

(continued)

TABLE B.1 **(continued)**

NEEDS-BASED TRANSFERS

Romania: Guaranteed Minimum Income Program

Description	Local authorities provide the benefit in the form of an income-tested monthly benefit. It is calculated as the difference between the minimum guaranteed income threshold (established by law) and the monthly net income of poor households. Differentiated minimum income thresholds have been established in accordance with the number of people per household. The program uses a two-tier testing system: an administrative testing of personal income based on applicants' declarations of their incomes (including imputed income from assets such as land and animals) and a verification of means procedure based on inquiries at the claimant's domicile. Provisions include work requirements for those able to work. Beneficiaries are also entitled to health insurance and heating subsidies.
Start date	2002
Expenditure	2002: 0.28% of GDP; 2004: 0.19% of GDP
Coverage	2002: 619,000 families or about 8% of the population 2004: 422,157 families or roughly 1.3 million people or about 6% of the population
Sources	Pop, Florescu, and Tesliuc (forthcoming); World Bank (2003h)

Zambia: Kalomo District Pilot Social Cash Transfer Scheme

Description	The pilot provides cash transfers for incapacitated and destitute households affected by AIDS. The targeted households initially received a monthly cash transfer of K 30,000 (about US$7.50), or enough cash to buy one 50 kilogram bag of maize. Following complaints that this amount was insufficient to meet basic needs especially for large households with many dependents, the cash transfer was increased to K 40,000 (about US$10) a month for households with children. The amount does not depend on the number of children, as all households with children get the same amount. A combination of targeting criteria is used that includes proxy indicators and means testing.
Start date	2003
Expenditure	2005: about K 500 million (about US$112,000) or about 0.0015% of GDP
Coverage	2005: approximately 1,100 households or about 0.05% of the population
Sources	Devereux and others (2005); MCDSS and GTZ (2007); Schubert (2005)

NONCONTRIBUTORY OLD-AGE PENSION SCHEMES

Bangladesh: old-age allowance

Description	The old-age allowance is a monthly transfer of Tk 165 (about US$3) targeted to low-income citizens in rural areas aged 65 and older, half of whom have to be women, subject to a means test. The Ministry of Social Welfare manages the scheme.
Start date	1998
Expenditure	FY2003/04: about US$31 million or 0.05% of GDP
Coverage	Annually: about 1.2 million beneficiaries, or about 0.9% of the population
Sources	Barrientos (2004); World Bank (2005a)

(continued)

TABLE B.1 **(continued)**

NONCONTRIBUTORY OLD-AGE PENSION SCHEMES

Bolivia: Bono Solidario (Solidarity Grant)

Description	This benefit consists of a universal fixed cash transfer to all Bolivian citizens over 65. Initially established as an annuity of US$248, the program has three primary objectives: to return the equity in Bolivia's recently privatized state enterprises to the people, to cover the large majority of elderly Bolivians not covered by a pension program, and to help reduce poverty by targeting a particularly poor and vulnerable segment of the population.
Start date	1997, suspended from 1998–2000, reinstated in 2001–2
Expenditure	Annually: about US$90 million in payments or about 1% of GDP
Coverage	1997: 53,647 individuals or about 0.7% of the population
Sources	Barrientos and Lloyd-Sherlock (2002); Martinez (2005); Tabor (2002)

Brazil: prêvidencia rural (rural old-age pension)

Description	The age of pension eligibility is 60 for men and 55 for women (65 before 1991). Since 1991, entitlement to old-age, disability, and survivor pensions has been extended to workers in subsistence activities in agriculture, fishing, and mining and to those in informal employment. The pensions are financed through a tax on the first sale of agricultural produce, which covers 1/10th of benefit expenditures, and subsidies from the social insurance system, which cover 9/10ths of expenditures.
Start date	1963, reformed in 1991
Expenditure	1998: US$10 billion or about 1% of GDP
Coverage	1998: 4 million households include at least one beneficiary; 2000: around 4.6 million beneficiaries or about 2.6% of the population
Sources	Barrientos (2004); Barrientos and others (2003); Barrientos and Lloyd-Sherlock (2002)

Chile: Pensiones Asistenciales de Ancianidad y de Invalidez (Old-Age and Disability Pension Program)

Description	This noncontributory pension is provided to those over 65 and to people with disabilities provided that their total income is lower than 50% of the guaranteed minimum pension. Targeting is based on proxy means testing that takes housing characteristics, education levels, and labor market activity into consideration. Beneficiaries are automatically eligible for free access to the national public health service.
Start date	1975
Expenditure	2000: CH$143 614 millions (about US$270 million) or roughly 0.36% of GDP
Coverage	2000: 358,813 elderly and people with disabilities or 2.3% of the population
Sources	Bertranou, Solorio, and van Ginneken (2002); Larrañaga (2005); Lindert, Skoufias, and Shapiro (2006); Valdés-Prieto (2004)

Lesotho: old-age pension

Description	This is a universal noncontributory pension for all Basotho older than 70. It is not means tested. It appears to have been generated entirely by a domestic political economy agenda and financed out of domestic resources with no technical or financial support from international donors.
Start date	2004
Expenditure	2005: about US$20 million or 1.37% of GDP
Coverage	2005: 69,046 individuals or about 3.8% of the population
Sources	Devereux and others (2005)

(continued)

TABLE B.1 **(continued)**

NONCONTRIBUTORY OLD-AGE PENSION SCHEMES

Namibia: old-age pension

Description	Individuals aged 60 and older qualify for a monthly pension of N$160. Prior to independence in 1990, whites received a pension of R 382 per month whereas 90% of blacks received a minimum pension of R 55 per month. Following independence, pensions were equalized and the minimum was N$135 per month in 1994, which was roughly adjusted for inflation to N$160 in 1996.
Start date	1949: program extended to black Namibians in 1973
Expenditure	1998: N$158.7 million (about US$29 million) or about 0.8% of GDP
Coverage	1998: an estimated 82,670 beneficiaries or about 4.7% of the population
Sources	Devereux (2001); Subbarao (1998)

South Africa: old-age pension

Description	This is a noncontributory pension that covers all women above 60 and all men above 65 subject to a means test. As of 2005, the pension benefit was R 780 a month (about US$130). In the 1980s and 1990s, there was a gradual move toward parity in benefit levels, which was completed in 1996. When the program first started, it covered the white population only, but blacks are now the main beneficiaries. The program is reasonably well administered and reaches the poorer rural areas. It is funded through general taxes.
Start date	1928
Expenditure	2000: 1.4% of GDP
Coverage	1999: 1.8 million people or about 4.2% of the population
Sources	Barrientos and others (2003); Barrientos and Lloyd-Sherlock (2002); Devereux (2001); Legido-Quigley (2003); Tabor (2002)

FAMILY ALLOWANCES

Bulgaria: child allowances

Description	This is a means-tested child allowance intended to help low-income parents raise their children and to promote school enrollment. The intended beneficiaries are low-income pregnant women, families with children less than one year old, and families with children starting first grade through age 20 as long as they are still in school. To be eligible, a household's average monthly income has to be lower than a certain threshold. In FY2003/04, the threshold was Lev 200 (US$127) per family member per month. The requirement for children to attend school is an important additional criterion for households to have access to the monthly allowances and to receive the one-time allowance given when a child enrolls in the first grade.
Start date	2002
Expenditure	2004: US$160 million or 0.65% of GDP
Coverage	2004: approximately 1.3 million children or 16.7% of the population
Sources	Rostgaard (2004); Shopov (forthcoming); Tabor (2002)

(continued)

TABLE B.1 **(continued)**

FAMILY ALLOWANCES

Czech Republic: child benefit

Description	This program provides means-tested allowances for each child under 15 years old (until the end of compulsory education) or under 26 years old if in full-time education or vocational training or if the child has a disability.
Start date	1995
Expenditure	2000: about 0.7% of GDP
Coverage	2000: 1.91 million people or about 18.6% of the population
Sources	Ministry of Labor and Social Affairs (2000); Potucek (2004); Rostgaard (2004)

Hungary: Családi Pótlék (Family Allowance)

Description	Hungary has one of the most complex family benefit systems in Europe and consists of both universal and means-tested benefits. In terms of coverage, the main program is the Family Allowance, a universal benefit financed from the central government's budget. It is paid to parents starting with a child's birth and continuing until the child completes his or her compulsory school (usually through age 16), and continues during secondary school or vocational training up to 24 years of age. The amount depends on the number of children in the family, whether the parent is a single parent, and whether the child has a disability. Eligibility conditions were modified several times in the 1990s.
Start date	Ongoing during the 1990s
Expenditure	2004: Ft 188 billion (estimated) (about US$927 million) or about 0.9% of GDP
Coverage	2004: 2.1 million children or about 20.8% of the population
Sources	Grootaert (1997); Ringold and Kasek (2007); Rostgaard (2004); Tabor (2002); World Bank (2001d)

Kyrgyz Republic: Unified Monthly Benefit Program

Description	The benefit is the main poverty reduction program in the country. It is a means-tested cash benefit intended to bring the income of the poorest families up to a line known as the guaranteed minimum level of consumption. The process of determining eligibility involves two filters: a means test plus categorical criteria. First, only households whose per capita income is less than the guaranteed minimum level of consumption are eligible for the program. Second, only certain family members are eligible for the benefit, namely, children under 16 or until they are 21 if they are full-time students. The program underwent a number of modifications and assumed its current form in 1998, when a new unified monthly benefit became the basis for a simplified cash social assistance policy.
Start date	1995
Expenditure	2005: US$14.5 million or 0.58% of GDP
Coverage	2005: 507,400 beneficiaries or 9.8% of the population
Sources	Kyrgyzstan Center for Social and Economic Research (forthcoming); E. Tesliuc (2004)

(continued)

TABLE B.1 **(continued)**

FAMILY ALLOWANCES

Mongolia: Child Money Program

Description	To qualify for a transfer, households must satisfy all of the following conditions: (1) earn an income below the minimum subsistence level, (2) have at least one child aged 18 or younger, (3) enroll all school-age children in school, (4) ensure that all children have received their mandatory immunizations, (5) must be the parents or legal guardians of the children living with them, and (6) ensure that their children are not engaged in illegal child labor. The program employs proxy means testing for targeting.
Start date	2005
Expenditure	2006: about 1.4% of GDP (expected)
Coverage	December 2005: 303,000 households or 609,000 children or about 24% of the population
Sources	Araujo (2006); Batjargal (2006); World Bank (2006g)

Poland: family benefits

Description	Family benefits in various forms are granted for a child under age 16 (age 20 if in full-time education). Benefits are subject to means testing.
Start date	Mid-1990s, new regulations in effect since 2004
Expenditure	2003: Zl 3.3 billion (about US$848 million) or about 0.4% of GDP
Coverage	2003: 5.9 million beneficiaries or about 15.4% of the population
Sources	Ministry of Economy and Labor (2004); Rostgaard (2004)

Romania: child allowances

Description	The state child allowances are a universal benefit granted monthly for all children under the age of 16 (18 if with disabilities or in secondary education), provided that they attend school regularly. The supplementary child allowance was introduced in 1997 for families with two or more children. Starting in January 2004, the government decided to stop this type of allowance and to introduce a means-tested one, the complementary family allowance.
Start date	1993, new law came into effect in 1997
Expenditure	2004: 0.47% of GDP for the universal child allowance and 0.12% of GDP for the complementary family allowance
Coverage	2004: approximately 4.2 million beneficiaries of the universal child allowance and 667,905 beneficiaries of the complementary family allowance, or about 22.5% of the population (both allowances)
Sources	Pop, Florescu, and Tesliuc (forthcoming); Rostgaard (2004); Tabor (2002); World Bank (2003h)

(continued)

TABLE B.1 **(continued)**

FAMILY ALLOWANCES

South Africa: child support grant

Description	This is a cash grant to help poor households or caregivers provide for children aged 1–14. When the grant was first introduced, only children under the age of 6 were eligible. In 2003, the government announced an age extension for the grant; between 2003 and 2005, the age eligibility was increased in phases, first to children under 9, then to children under 11, and as of April 2005 to children under 14. The grant is means tested to target the poorest families.
Start date	1998
Expenditure	Not available
Coverage	2006: approximately 7.4 million children or about 15.6% of the population
Sources	Children's Institute (2006); Leatt (2006); Samson, MacQuene, and van Niekerk (2006)

FOOD STAMP PROGRAMS

Honduras: Bono Escolar, Bono Materno Infantil (Food Stamps for Schoolchildren, Food Stamps for Mothers and Young Children)

Description	Honduras implemented two food stamp programs in 1990 to protect the poor during a period of economic structural adjustment. One was for poor primary schoolchildren, which was distributed throughout primary schools in selected areas of the country. The other was for poor, pregnant women and/or with children under five years of age who attended periodic prenatal, immunization, and growth checks clinics for their children and training programs in health and nutrition. Food stamp recipients could use the stamps to purchase any food they wanted, school supplies, and medicines.
Start date	1990, replaced by the Family Allowance Program in 2000
Expenditure	1991: US$4.6 million for Bono Escolar and US$1.4 million for Bono Materno Infantil or about 0.2% of GDP (both programs)
Coverage	1992: 125,700 schoolchildren and 56,200 children aged birth to five, pregnant women, and nursing mothers or about 3% of the population
Sources	Castañeda (1998); Rogers and Coates (2002); Sanghvi and others (1995)

Jamaica: Food Stamp Program

Description	The program was part of an effort to reduce the fiscal deficit in a context of structural economic adjustment and currency devaluation, but still protect the poor. It was targeted to all pregnant and lactating women, children under six, the elderly poor, people with disabilities, and selected poor families. Families were eligible if the threshold family income was less than the equivalent of 40% of the minimum wage (in 1996). Beneficiaries were limited to the purchase of specific food items, including rice, cornmeal, skim milk, and wheat flour. Stamps could be redeemed at food stores across the country. In 2002, the program was replaced by the PATH.
Start date	1984; ended 2002
Expenditure	1998: US$8 million or about 0.1% of GDP
Coverage	1998: 263,000 individuals or roughly 11% of the population
Sources	Castañeda (1998); Ezemenari and Subbarao (1999); Grosh (1992); Rogers and Coates (2002); World Bank (2001f)

(continued)

TABLE B.1 **(continued)**

FOOD STAMP PROGRAMS

Sri Lanka: Food Stamp Program

Description	The program replaced the previous economically unsustainable, untargeted consumer food price subsidies with a targeted food stamp program that subsidized the consumption of basic goods for the poorest households. The program was targeted to the poorest 20% of the population, with eligibility determined by a means test based on self-reported household income with a marginal adjustment made for household size. Recipients could use the stamps to buy basic foods (rice, wheat flour, bread, sugar, milk products, and pulses) and kerosene for cooking. The program was replaced by cash transfers and subsidies following changes in 1989 and 1995.
Start date	1979; ended 1989
Expenditure	1984: 1.3% of GDP
Coverage	1989: about 8 million people or about 48% of the population
Sources	Castañeda (1998); Edirisinghe (1987); Rogers and Coates (2002)

United States: Food Stamp Program

Description	This national program is intended to help low-income families meet their nutritional requirements by increasing their food purchasing power to enable them to obtain a more nutritious diet. They can use the stamps at regular retail stores. Recipients are free to purchase any food they want. The program covers 56% to 70% of recipients' monthly mean food expenditures. Standards for eligibility and benefit levels apply across the country. Most eligible households must have a monthly gross income of less than 130% of the federal poverty level (US$2,097 for a family of four in FY2006), a monthly net income of less than 100% of the poverty level, and assets of less than US$2,000. Households with elderly and disabled members are exempt from the gross income limit and must have assets of less than US$3,000. Eligible households must also meet some nonfinancial criteria, including citizenship and work requirements. In FY2007, the program provided an average monthly benefit worth US$95 per person.
Start date	1964
Expenditure	1995: US$24 billion plus US$3.2 billion in administrative costs or about 0.37% of GDP FY2007: US$33,165.5 million or about 0.25% of GDP
Coverage	1995: 27 million people or 10.4% of the population; FY2007: 26,465,816 people or about 9% of the population
Sources	Castañeda (1998), annex 1; Gundersen and others (2000); Rogers and Coates (2002); Department of Agriculture 2005; www.fns.usda.gov/fsp/

SOURCE: Authors.

NOTE: GDP = gross domestic product.

TABLE B.2 **In-Kind Food Transfers and Other Food-Based Programs (Targeted Programs)**

RATION PROGRAMS

Arab Republic of Egypt: food subsidy system

Description	Cooking oil, sugar, tea, margarine, beans, lentils, rice, and pasta are available at subsidized prices on a monthly quota basis to those with ration cards. Eligibility for the cards is based on self-reported income. Egypt has been able to reduce the overall costs of its subsidies by raising food prices, reducing the number of ration card holders, and reducing the number and quantity of subsidized food items.
Start date	1941
Expenditure	2004: 0.4% of GDP
Coverage	1992: about 10.9 million ration card holders or 48 million beneficiaries or about 86% of the population; 1997: about 9.9 million card holders
Sources	Adams (2000); Ahmed and Bouis (2002); Alderman (1988a, 2002b); World Bank (1999b, 2005c)

India: public distribution system

Description	The system is managed by state governments and provides rationed amounts of basic food items (rice, wheat, sugar, and edible oils) and nonfood products (kerosene, coal, and standard cloth) at below-market prices. In 1992, the subsidy on food grains was increased for people in tribal, drought-prone, and desert areas. Until 1997, access to the system was universal. In 1997, it was replaced by the targeted public distribution system in which targeting was shifted from poor regions to poor households that were entitled to ration cards that allowed them to buy higher quantities at a subsidized price. Specific amounts of food grain were available at a highly subsidized price per family per month for families below the poverty line. Since 1997, those classified as nonpoor have not received any subsidy unless they live in drought-prone areas, though they are served by a network of more than 462,000 fair price shops. In 2001, the government decided to allocate food grains to families above the poverty line at a discounted rate of 70% of the economic cost of the grain.
Start date	Since World War II with major changes in 1997, 2000, and 2001
Expenditure	FY2002/03: US$4.3 billion or 0.7% of GDP
Coverage	About 160 million families per year or approximately 70% of the population); FY2004/05: 83% of all households hold a ration card, of which 33.7% are below the poverty line
Sources	Alderman (2002b); del Ninno, Dorosh, and Subbarao (2005); Dev and others (2004); Government of India (2001); Mooij (1999a, 1999b); World Bank (2007p)

Indonesia: JPS Operasi Pasar Khusus (Social Safety Net Special Market Operations)

Description	The program was introduced after the 1997 Asian economic crisis. Under the program, the National Food Logistics Agency, a publicly owned corporation, sells rice to low-income families at a subsidized price of Rp 1,000 per kilogram. Each family is entitled to receive a specified allocation of rice per month. The program's aim is to distribute low-quality rice at below-market prices to poor households and provide a stable source of income to the poor farmers from whom most of the rice is procured. Beneficiaries are selected based on geographic and categorical household targeting. Renamed Beras untuk Keluarga Miskin (Rice for Poor Families Program) in 2001.
Start date	1998
Expenditure	2003: Rp 4,831 billion (about US$563 million) or about 0.24% of GDP

(continued)

TABLE B.2 (continued)

RATION PROGRAMS

Coverage	2003: 12 million households or about 23% of the population
Sources	ADB (2006); Ahmad and Leruth (2000); Alderman (2002b); Daly and Fane (2002); Perdana and Maxwell (2004); Pritchett, Sumarto, and Suryahadi (2002); Sumarto, Suryahadi, and Pritchett (2000); Timmer (2004); Yonekura (2005)

Mexico: Tortivales

Description	The program, which replaced the Tortibonos Food Stamp Program, allowed urban low-income households to receive 1 kilogram of tortillas each day from participating tortilla shops at no cost. The program adopted the use of "smart" cards, which were issued to families based on a means test implemented through certain retail stores and the Trust Fund for Tortilla Subsidy Payments. Mexico has phased out the program as part of broader social assistance reforms.
Start date	1990; ended 199 when it became a component of PROGRESA (see table B.5)
Expenditure	Not available
Coverage	1990: 2.1 million low-income households or about 6% of the population
Sources	Alderman (2002b); Grosh (1994); Gundersen and others (2000); Mckenzie (2002)

Philippines: Food Subsidy Program

Description	The program, implemented by the National Food Authority, was designed to provide rice at a subsidy of ₱2.50 per kilogram to families below the food poverty threshold. The beneficiaries are given discount cards to use when they purchase rice from accredited rice retail stores.
Start date	1998
Expenditure	1998: ₱6.208 billion (about US$152 million) or 0.23% of GDP
Coverage	1995–8: about 11% of the country's 14 million households
Sources	Economic and Social Commission for Asia and the Pacific (2001)

TAKE-HOME RATIONS

Bangladesh: Vulnerable Group Development Program

Description	This is a nationwide targeted program aimed at improving the lives of the poorest and most disadvantaged women in rural areas. Participants receive a monthly ration of 30 kilograms of wheat over a period of 24 months. Two nongovernmental organizations provide training in such income-generating activities as poultry rearing, livestock raising, fisheries, and sericulture; raising participants' awareness of social, legal, health, and nutrition issues; providing basic literacy and numeracy training; and providing access to credit. Participants are required to make a monthly savings deposit of Tk 25 into an interest-bearing account maintained by the nongovernmental organizations.
Start date	1975
Expenditure	Annually: US$40 million or about 0.09% of GDP in 2000
Coverage	2000: about 500,000 extremely poor rural women annually or about 0.4% of the population
Sources	Ahmed and others (2004); Ahmed (2005); Alderman (2002b); del Ninno and Dorosh (2003); del Ninno, Dorosh, and Subbarao (2005); Mujeri (2002); World Bank (2005a)

(continued)

TABLE B.2 **(continued)**

TAKE-HOME RATIONS

Ethiopia: Gratuitous Relief Program

Description	This program distributes cereals such as wheat, maize, and sorghum to those who are unable to participate in public works for reasons such as ill health or old age.
Start date	1993
Expenditure	US$70–US$500 million per year
Coverage	2–5 million beneficiaries during a normal year and up to 10 million during a bad year
Sources	Adams and Kebede (2005); del Ninno, Dorosh, and Subbarao (2005); Humphrey (2002)

SUPPLEMENTARY FEEDING PROGRAMS

Bangladesh: National Nutrition Program

Description	The program consisted of a large array of community-based nutrition services, with one of its key goals being to significantly reduce malnutrition, especially among poor women and children. It provided food supplements and counseling on nutrition and health to pregnant and lactating mothers and food supplements to children under two. The services provided were area-based community nutrition services, including growth monitoring and promotion, supplementary feeding, national-level nutrition services, training, and behavioral change communication. This program replaced the Integrated Nutrition Project.
Start date	2000; ended 2006
Expenditure	2000–6: total budget of about US$90 million or about 0.2% of GDP
Coverage	2000–6: approximately 4 million women and children or about 3% of the population
Sources	World Bank (2000a, 2002f, 2004d, 2005k, 2007b)

Chile: Programa Nacional de Alimentación Complementaria (National Complementary Feeding Program)

Description	Originally a public milk distribution program for working mothers, the program was significantly strengthened in the 1950s with the creation of the National Health Service. In 1983, a new "enhanced" program helped mothers and children under six at high risk for hunger. Currently, the supplements distributed are full-fat powdered cow's milk fortified with vitamins and minerals and a milk-cereal blend fortified with iron and rice. Food supplements are distributed at public clinics on a monthly basis as an integral part of the primary health care system. Every pregnant woman and child is eligible for the free food supplements.
Start date	1924
Expenditure	1996: US$70 million or 0.1% of GDP
Coverage	2000: 900,000 children under six and 100,000 pregnant and/or lactating women or about 6% of the population
Sources	Grosh (1994); Kain and Uauy (2001); Uauy, Albala, and Kain (2001)

(continued)

TABLE B.2 **(continued)**

SUPPLEMENTARY FEEDING PROGRAMS

Peru: Vaso de Leche (Glass of Milk)

Description	The program provides milk and milk substitutes to low-income pregnant women, children up to age 13, tuberculosis patients, and the elderly. The program uses community-based targeting operated at the local level. The milk or milk substitute is delivered by a network of mothers' clubs and Glass of Milk committees. It was introduced as a pilot in Lima in 1984 and was expanded nationally during the economic crises in the late 1980s and early part of the 1990s.
Start date	1984
Expenditure	2001: US$93 million or about 0.17% of GDP
Coverage	2001: 4 million beneficiaries or about 15% of the population
Sources	Rogers and others (2002); Ruggeri Laderchi (2001); Stifel and Alderman (2006)

SCHOOL FEEDING PROGRAMS

Bangladesh: School Feeding Program

Description	The government and the World Food Programme launched this program in chronically food-insecure areas of the country to provide incentives directly to children in primary school as opposed to providing cash or food to parents for sending their children to school. The program provides a midmorning snack of eight fortified wheat cookies to more than 1 million children in approximately 6,000 primary schools in highly food-insecure rural areas plus four slum areas in Dhaka. At a cost of US$0.06 per packet of eight, the cookies provide 300 kilocalories and 75% of the recommended daily allowance of vitamins and minerals.
Start date	2002
Expenditure	2002–4: total cost of about US$30 million or about 0.06% of GDP
Coverage	2003: 1.21 million primary schoolchildren in 6,126 schools or about 0.9% of the population
Sources	Ahmed (2004b)

Costa Rica: School Cafeterias Program

Description	This program offers breakfast and lunch to all students attending urban high-priority schools (education centers in marginal and remote areas) one-teacher schools, and education centers located in cantons where, according to the 1997 weight and height census, the student population suffers from serious nutritional problems.
Start date	1974
Expenditure	2004: C 9.964 million (about US$23 million) or 0.12% of GDP
Coverage	2004: 515,684 children or about 12% of the population
Sources	Ministry of Public Education (2004); World Bank (2002e)

(continued)

TABLE B.2 **(continued)**

EMERGENCY FEEDING PROGRAMS

Kenya: food assistance to drought-affected people in Kenya (a World Food Programme program)

Description	The failure of the rains at the end of 2003 resulted in poor pasture and browse, which affected livestock and led to food insecurity among communities in semi-arid areas who rely on milk, other livestock products, and marginal crop production for their livelihoods. The program provides assistance through general food distribution, supplementary feeding, food-for-work, and an expanded school feeding program. The program uses a community-based targeting and distribution system, which empowers communities, especially women, to participate in program planning and management.
Start date	Initially August 2004–January 2005; subsequently extended through June 2008
Expenditure	Total cost: more than US$370 million or about 2.2% of GDP
Coverage	2.1 million beneficiaries or about 6% of the population
Sources	www.wfp.org/operations/current_operations/countries/countryproject.asp?section=5&sub_section=7&country=404#EMOP

Pakistan: food assistance to affected persons following the South Asia earthquake (a World Food Programme program)

Description	At the request of the government and in cooperation with other partners, the World Food Programme provided fortified food commodities for 1 million earthquake victims, with those located in more remote areas lacking cooking facilities initially provided with ready-to-eat foods. Distribution of dry food rations was expanded to cover all beneficiaries as cooking facilities become available.
Start date	October 15, 2005, to April 14, 2006
Expenditure	Total cost: about US$56 million or 0.05% of GDP
Coverage	1 million beneficiaries targeted or about 0.6%of the population
Sources	www.wfp.org/operations/current_operations/project_docs/104910.pdf

SOURCE: Authors.

NOTE: GDP = gross domestic product.

TABLE B.3 **General Subsidy Programs**

UNIVERSAL INDIRECT PRICE SUPPORT FOR FOOD

Indonesia: rice subsidy

Description	Indonesia succeeded in stabilizing rice prices through the National Logistic Agency. The agency defended a floor price and a ceiling price through a combination of monopoly control over international trade in rice; access to an unlimited line of bank credit; procurement of as much rice as necessary by the agency's local-level bureaus to lift the price in rural markets to the policy-determined floor price; and extensive facilities, including a nationwide complex of warehouses, which permitted storage of substantial quantities of rice. After the 1997 Asian financial crisis, the sector was liberalized and the National Logistic Agency now sells rice at a subsidized price through a targeted program. In 2003, the National Logistic Agency was reorganized into a public corporation.
Start date	Late 1960s; ended 1997
Expenditure	FY1991/92: total annual cost of US$1.5 billion, or about 1.2% of GDP
Coverage	Universal coverage
Sources	Alderman (2002b); Perdana and Maxwell (2004); Robinson and others (1997); Timmer (2004); Yonekura (2005)

Pakistan: wheat subsidy

Description	The government purchases wheat from farmers and resells it to flour mills. A portion of the flour is then sold at a fixed price though utility stores at the same price throughout the country.
Start date	Not available
Expenditure	FY2003/04: 0.14% of GDP
Coverage	Universal coverage
Sources	Dorosh and Salam (2008); Faruqee (2005); World Bank (2007k)

South Africa: value added tax exemptions

Description	The value added tax was introduced in 1991. Maize and brown bread were exempted shortly thereafter. By mid-1993, 19 food commodities had been exempted and roughly the same number of additional exemptions had been proposed, including several "luxury" foods, such as meat and dairy products, which were never exempted.
Start date	1991
Expenditure	1993: R 1,570 million (about US$480 million), calculated as the fiscal revenue loss associated with granting the exemption, or 0.37% of GDP
Coverage	Universal coverage
Sources	Alderman (2002b); Alderman and del Ninno (1999); Alderman and Lindert (1998)

(continued)

TABLE B.3 **(continued)**

SUBSIDIZED, UNTARGETED FOOD SALES

Algeria: food price subsidies

Description	The general subsidy scheme provided 16 categories of staple foods, including bread, flour, rice, and oil, at affordable prices to low-income groups. The aim was to maintain farm incomes and insulate the economy from short-term international price fluctuations. Increasing costs and leakages to the nonpoor led to reforms of the food subsidy program. Starting in 1992, over the course of four years, food subsidies were completely eliminated. To compensate for welfare losses, the government introduced safety nets targeted to the elderly, people with disabilities, and the poor unemployed.
Start date	1973; ended 1996
Expenditure	1991: 4.7% of GDP 1992: 3.3% of GDP 1995: 0.9% of GDP
Coverage	Universal coverage
Sources	Alderman (2002b); Belkacem (2001); World Bank (1999c)

Bangladesh: statutory rationing

Description	Statutory rationing began in the major towns of East Bengal in 1956. All urban residents, regardless of income level, received a ration card that allowed them to purchase a weekly allotment of heavily subsidized basic foods, including wheat and oil. The subsidies decreased through the 1980s.
Start date	1956; ended 1994
Expenditure	Not available
Coverage	All urban residents
Sources	Ahmed, Haggblade, and Chowdhury (2000), chapter 11

Arab Republic of Egypt: food subsidy system (bread and flour)

Description	Subsidized bread and wheat flour are available to all consumers without any quantity restrictions. Egypt has been able to reduce the overall costs of its subsidies by shifting to a self-targeting mechanism using lower-quality products.
Start date	1941
Expenditure	2004: 1.3% of GDP
Coverage	Universal coverage
Sources	Adams (2000); Ahmed and Bouis (2002); Ahmed and others (2001); Alderman (1988a, 2002b); World Bank (1999c, 2005c)

Islamic Republic of Iran: consumer food subsidies

Description	General food subsidies on wheat flour and bread employ price controls and an overvalued exchange rate. After the 1992 reforms, price controls on a range of staples (sugar, vegetable oil, cheese, rice, meat, chicken, and eggs) were lifted, and the commodities became available for purchase using coupons.
Start date	Reforms launched around 1992
Expenditure	FY1991/92: 2.0% of GDP FY1994/95: 2.9% of GDP FY1995/96: 2.7% of GDP
Coverage	Universal coverage
Sources	World Bank (1999c)

(continued)

TABLE B.3 **(continued)**

SUBSIDIZED, UNTARGETED FOOD SALES

Jordan: consumer food subsidies

Description	Jordan's food subsidy system started as a general subsidy program available to all Jordanians. The first set of reforms occurred in 1990, when general subsidies on several food items were replaced by a targeted subsidy scheme that consisted of universal subsidies on barley and wheat; and a coupon system whereby fixed quantities of rice, sugar, and powdered milk were made available at subsidized prices initially to every Jordanian citizen, and from 1994 on, were subject to means-testing criteria. In 1996, the general wheat subsidies were replaced by targeted, means-tested cash transfers that were eliminated in 1999.
Start date	1970s through 1996 with major reforms in 1990 and 1994
Expenditure	1990: 3.4% of GDP 1995: 1.4% of GDP; 1999: 0.3% of GDP
Coverage	Universal coverage
Sources	Shaban, Abu-Ghaida, and Al-Naimat (2001); World Bank (1999c)

Morocco: food subsidies

Description	Sugar, cooking oil, and low-grade flour are universally available at subsidized prices and in unlimited quantities. The subsidy can be characterized as a tax subsidy scheme in which taxes on particular commodities finance subsidies. Since July 1996, some aspects of the regulatory framework have been reformed. Currently local production and domestic markets are protected only via customs tariffs using a variable levy mechanism.
Start date	1941
Expenditure	1992: 1.3% of GDP 1998: 1.7% of GDP
Coverage	Universal coverage
Sources	World Bank (1999c, 2001g)

Sri Lanka: food subsidy scheme

Description	The scheme included a major subsidy on rice, the staple food of the entire population. Other major commodities such as wheat flour, sugar, and powdered milk, were subsidized at various times. The amount of the subsidies and consumer entitlements have undergone changes influenced by fiscal and political considerations. In 1978, the subsidy was replaced by a targeted program of rice rations (means-tested based on self-reported household income), and in 1979 was replaced by food stamps.
Start date	1942; ended 1978
Expenditure	1977: Rp 1,424 million (about US$160 million) or about 4% of GDP
Coverage	Universal coverage
Sources	Alderman (2002b); Edirisinghe (1988); Yapa (1998)

(continued)

TABLE B.3 **(continued)**

SUBSIDIZED, UNTARGETED FOOD SALES

Tunisia: food subsidy

Description	The government provided general food subsidies on major food commodities (cereals, cooking oil, sugar, and milk) until the first half of the 1990s, when it introduced self-targeting and quality differentiation. Specific measures involved improved targeting through a shift to subsidies on inferior goods, price increases for superior goods (goods consumed disproportionately by the rich), and reduced production and distribution costs of subsidized commodities.
Start date	1970
Expenditure	1984: 4.0% of GDP 1993:.2.0% of GDP 1995: 1.7% of GDP 1998: 1.5% of GDP
Coverage	Universal coverage
Sources	Alderman (2002b); Alderman and Lindert (1998); Tuck and Lindert (1996); World Bank (1999c)

Republic of Yemen: food subsidies

Description	General subsidies were provided on wheat and wheat flour. Quantities and prices were set along the import and marketing chain through overvalued official exchange rates (through which the government distributed a sizable direct subsidy to importers) and fixed prices. The authorities embarked on a medium-term program to completely eliminate subsidies in 1996.
Start date	Early 1990s; ended 1999
Expenditure	1996: 7.9% of GDP 1997: 5.2% of GDP 1998: 3.6% of GDP
Coverage	Universal coverage
Sources	World Bank (1999c, 2000d)

SUBSIDIES FOR ENERGY AND UTILITIES

Bolivia: LPG, gasoline

Description	In 2004, of the total consumer subsidy equivalent to 4.3% of GDP, only 2.6 percentage points showed up in the budget in the form of explicit subsidies and forgone revenue. An automatic pricing formula for setting the domestic prices of petroleum products was introduced in 1996 as part of sectoral reforms but was abandoned in the late 1990s. Low prices are maintained by explicit subsidies, low producer prices, and low taxation. The outcome has been an increase in subsidies, the smuggling abroad of subsidized items, and demand shortages.
Start date	Not available
Expenditure	2004: 4.3% of GDP
Coverage	Universal coverage
Sources	Coady and others (2006)

(continued)

TABLE B.3 (continued)

SUBSIDIES FOR ENERGY AND UTILITIES

Arab Republic of Egypt: electricity, LPG, gasoline, kerosene, natural gas, diesel, and fuel oil

Description	The government has controlled the domestic prices of all energy products for decades. In the 1980s and early 1990s, the government raised energy prices significantly, but gradually, to reduce energy subsidies. There was no change in the nominal domestic price of any petroleum product between 1997 and 2004.
Start date	Subsidies for kerosene during World War II, program expanded thereafter
Expenditure	FY2004: financial cost of LE 21.7 billion (about US$3.5 billion) or 4.4% of GDP[a]
Coverage	Universal coverage
Sources	World Bank (1999c, 2005c)

Ghana: LPG, gasoline, and kerosene

Description	Explicit subsidies are provided to the refinery and to distributors to compensate for below-formula prices. The government introduced the pricing formula in January 2003 while simultaneously increasing prices by an average of 90%. The formula was effectively abandoned when continued increases in world prices were not passed on to consumers.
Start date	Not available
Expenditure	2004: 2.2% of GDP
Coverage	Universal coverage
Sources	Coady and others (2006)

India: kerosene and LPG

Description	The subsidies on both kerosene and LPG are general and not targeted. The subsidized fuels are widely used for lighting and cooking. The public distribution system distributes the subsidized kerosene, quantities of which are limited, and dealers working with state-owned oil companies are responsible for distributing the subsidized LPG, which has no quantity limits.
Start date	Since World War II
Expenditure	FY2003/04: about Rs 65 billion (about US$1.4 billion) or 0.23% of GDP
Coverage	Universal coverage
Sources	Gangopadhyay, Ramaswami, and Wadhwa (2005); Komives and others (2005); Misra and others (2005)

Indonesia: diesel, gasoline, and kerosene

Description	The government reduced the universal fuel subsidies in 2005, thereby freeing up US$10 billion, and redirected the savings to development programs in education, health, rural development, and infrastructure and to establishing a cash transfer program (see table B.1).
Start date	Not available

(continued)

TABLE B.3 **(continued)**

SUBSIDIES FOR ENERGY AND UTILITIES	
Expenditure	2001: 4.1% of GDP 2003; 1.5% of GDP 2005: 3.4% of GDP 2006: 2.1% of GDP 2007: 1.8% of GDP (estimated)
Coverage	Universal coverage
Sources	World Bank (2006f, 2007h)

Mali: energy subsidies

Description	Mali introduced a formula in 1994, but abandoned it in 2003. Until mid-2005, domestic prices tracked world prices and included a significant element of taxation. Since then, price increases have been restrained by reducing excise tax rates. Petroleum products have traditionally been taxed, with the tax component of pump prices ranging from more than 20% for kerosene to nearly 50% for gasoline.
Start date	Not available
Expenditure	2004: 2% of GDP (lost tax revenues because of decreasing tax rates and exemptions for some sectors, especially mining)
Coverage	Universal coverage
Sources	Coady and others (2006)

Sri Lanka: LPG, diesel, gasoline, kerosene, and electricity

Description	Sri Lanka introduced a pricing formula in 2002, but suspended it in early 2004. Formula prices included value added taxes on diesel and gasoline as well as excise taxes on all products. The value added tax on diesel was eliminated in August 2005.
Start date	Not available
Expenditure	2004: 2.1% of GDP
Coverage	Universal coverage
Sources	Coady and others (2006)

Republic of Yemen: gasoline, kerosene, diesel, and LPG

Description	The net subsidy on petroleum products is the difference between the retail price at the distribution center gate and the economic price to which distribution costs and taxes have been added. In 2003, the total cost to the government of petroleum product subsidies amounted to 13% of all government spending and 63% of development spending.
Start date	Not available
Expenditure	2001: Yrls 63 billion (US$370 million) or about 4% of GDP; 2003: Yrls 97 billion (about US$530 million) or about 4.8% of GDP
Coverage	Universal coverage
Sources	World Bank (2005f)

SOURCE: Authors.

NOTE: GDP = gross domestic product, LPG = liquefied petroleum gas.

a. With more appropriate accounting of the opportunity costs of energy products, the economic cost of the subsidies would be much higher, estimated at LE 38.4 billion (8.1 percent of GDP) in FY2004).

TABLE B.4 **Public Works Programs**

PUBLIC WORKS PROGRAMS

Argentina: Jefes de Hogar (Heads of Household)

Description	In response to the severe economic crisis that hit Argentina in 2001, this program sought to reach a broad segment of the population that had been impoverished to provide affected heads of households with direct income support. The program transferred Arg$150 (about US$48) per month to beneficiaries who met the following criteria: (1) be unemployed; (2) be the head of a household; (3) live in a household with at least one minor below the age of 18, a pregnant woman, or a handicapped person of any age; and (4) work or participate in training or education activities for 4–6 hours a day (no less than 20 hours a week) in exchange for the payment. The transfer amount was set at a level slightly below the going wage for full-time work for unskilled workers. Program enrollment declined since mid-2003, reflecting the government's continued application of controls to identify and drop from the program those beneficiaries who no longer were eligible and efforts to strengthen the program's governance; improved employment opportunities; the transfer of beneficiaries to the Familias conditional cash transfer program as of March 2005; and beginning 2006, transfers to a new program promoting self-employment by beneficiaries through a set of activities designed to strengthen their long-term capacity to generate income (completing basic education, participating in training courses, combining the work requirement with on-the-job training, and participating in subprojects intended to provide experience and skills for future jobs).
Start date	2002; ended 2006
Wage level	Wpr < Wmin < Wmk
Expenditure	2004: US$1,255 million or 0.82% of GDP
Coverage	2002: 574,000 beneficiaries (about 3.3% of economically active population); 2003: nearly 2 million (about 11.3%) 2004: 1.7 million (about 9.5%); 2006: 1.2 million (about 6.4%)
Sources	Almeida and Galasso (2007); Galasso and Ravallion (2004); Latin American Economic System (2005); Reinecke (2005); Tcherneva and Wray (2005); World Bank (2003a, 2006b, 2007a)

Argentina: Trabajar (To Work)

Description	The government introduced this program in the wake of a sharp rise in unemployment and evidence that this was hurting the poor more than others. The first objective was to provide short-term work opportunities to unemployed poor workers subject to a strictly enforced work requirement of 30–40 hours per week. The program tried to locate socially useful projects in poor areas that involved maintaining and building local infrastructure. The main targeting mechanism adopted was the low wage rate, supplemented by a project selection process that geographically targeted poor areas to receive projects.
Start date	1996; ended 2001
Wage level	Wpr = Wmin < Wmk Lowered in 2000: Wpr < Wmin < Wmk
Expenditure	1998–2001: about US$200 million per year or about 0.07% of GDP
Coverage	About 240,000 people (August 1998–October 1999) or about 1.5% of the economically active population
Sources	Arriagada, Castañeda, and Hall (2000); Galasso and Ravallion (2004); Jalan and Ravallion (1999, 2003); Latin American Economic System (2005); Ravallion (2002); Reinecke (2005); Subbarao (2003)

(continued)

TABLE B.4 **(continued)**

PUBLIC WORKS PROGRAMS

Bangladesh: Food-for-Work Program

Description	The program's short-term aim is to provide employment for landless rural families during the slack agricultural season. To this end, it creates work mostly in construction and maintenance of rural roads, river embankments, and irrigation channels. The program's long-term objectives are to improve the performance of the agricultural sector, increase communication among communities, and reduce the physical damage and loss of human life caused by floods and other natural disasters. The program is self-targeted, as it provides a relatively low wage and requires arduous manual labor that would be performed only by those in dire need of employment. Wage payments are made in kind (in wheat) rather than in cash.
Start date	1974
Wage level	Wpr < Wmk
Expenditure	FY2001/02: about US$124 million (about 0.26% of GDP); FY2003/04: about US$41million (about 0.08%); FY2004/05: about US$89 million (about 0.16% of GDP)
Coverage	About 1 million participants annually or about 1.7% of the economically active population in 2000
Sources	Ahmed and others (1995); Kabeer (2002); World Bank (2002f, 2005a)

Bangladesh: Rural Maintenance Program

Description	Women are recruited and employed for four years during which they receive wages for maintaining earthen village roads; accumulate savings for investment; and participate in comprehensive training in road maintenance, health and health awareness, numeracy, human rights, gender equity, nutrition, business management, and preparation for income-generating activities. The program, managed by CARE Bangladesh, helps women become self-reliant and prepares them to be better able to face day-to-day challenges.
Start date	1982
Wage level	Participants are paid a wage of Tk 51 per day and required to save Tk 10 a day
Expenditure	Annually: US$16 million or about 0.03% of GDP in 2000
Coverage	About 42,000 rural women annually or less than 0.1% of the economically active population
Sources	Ahmed (2005); Hashemi and Rosenberg (2006); World Bank (2005a)

Bolivia: Plan Nacional de Empleo de Emergencia (National Plan for Emergency Employment)

Description	The program was created as a temporary intervention with the objective of generating employment for poor families in urban and rural areas as a response to increasing unemployment among the poor since 1998. Types of works include constructing, maintaining, and cleaning community infrastructure. The program has since been extended and is now a component of the Red de Protección Social (Social Protection Network).
Start date	2001–4, when it became a component of the Red de Protección Social
Wage level	Wpr < Wmk (about two-thirds of the average Wmk)
Expenditure	2002: US$28 million or about 0.35% of GDP

(continued)

TABLE B.4 **(continued)**

PUBLIC WORKS PROGRAMS	
Coverage	2002: 170,000 participants or about 4.5% of the economically active population
Sources	Landa (2003, 2004); Latin American Economic System (2005); Reinecke (2005); www.rps.gob.bo/rps/pages/RPSMain.htm

Chile: direct employment programs

Description	This group encompasses several employment programs implemented by different agencies. They share the same objectives, namely, to create short-term employment for the most vulnerable families following a large increase in the unemployment rate.
Start date	1993
Wage level	Wpr = Wmin plus social security contributions
Expenditure	2001: 0.24% of GDP
Coverage	2001: 7.79% of the economically active population
Sources	Latin American Economic System (2005); Oficina Internacional del Trabajo (2006); Reinecke (2005)

Colombia: Empleo en Acción (Employment in Action)

Description	This program, together with Familias en Acción (Families in Action) and Jovenes en Acción (Youth in Action), formed the Red de Apoyo Social (Social Support Network). Its objective was to provide temporary employment for unskilled workers in the bottom income quintile and incomes for their families and to maintain and build community infrastructure in poor urban areas to alleviate the negative impacts of the economic recession on the most vulnerable. The program was unable to set the wage below the minimum wage to encourage self-targeting because Colombia's labor laws prevent hiring workers for less than the minimum wage.
Start date	2001; ended 2004
Wage level	2001–March 2004: 205,298 beneficiaries or less than 1% of the economically active population
Expenditure	2001–March 2004: US$290 million or 0.35% of GDP
Coverage	Wpr = Wmin < Wmk
Sources	Departamento Nacional de Planeación (2004); Latin American Economic System (2005); World Bank (2002d)

Ethiopia: Productive Safety Net Program (PSNP)

Description	The main component of the program is labor-intensive public works through which the chronically food insecure are employed on rural infrastructure projects such as road construction and maintenance, small-scale irrigation, and reforestation. The second component is Direct Support, an unconditional transfer of cash or food to vulnerable households with no able-bodied members who can participate in public works projects. The objectives are to provide transfers to the food-insecure population in a way that prevents asset depletion at the household level and creates community assets.
Start date	2005
Wage level	Wpr < Wmk (cash and/or food)

(continued)

TABLE B.4 **(continued)**

PUBLIC WORKS PROGRAMS

Expenditure	FY2005/06 budget: US$225 million or about 2% of GDP
Coverage	2005: approximately 5 million chronically food-insecure people (about 14.6% of the economically active population); 2006: 7.2 million people (about 20.4%)
Sources	Adams and Kebede (2005); Devereux and others (2006); Government of Ethiopia (2004); Lind and Jalleta (2005); Sharp, Brown, and Teshome (2006); World Bank (2006i, 2007n)

India: Jawahar Rozgar Yojana (Jawahar Employment Program)

Description	The program's main objective is to generate supplementary wage employment for the unemployed and underemployed rural poor by creating rural economic infrastructure and community assets. It is largely implemented through elected bodies at the village level. The program was restructured in 1999 and renamed the Jawahar Gram Samridhi Yojana (Jawahar Village Prosperity Program). It is no longer a wage employment program but a rural infrastructure program. In 2001, it was merged with the Employment Assurance Scheme to create the Sampoorna Grameen Rozgar Yojana (Village Full Employment Program) with the objective of providing additional wage employment in rural areas and food security alongside the creation of durable community, social, and economic infrastructure in rural areas.
Start date	1989, restructured in 1999 and 2001
Wage level	$W_{pr} = W_{min} > W_{mk}$
Expenditure	FY1997/98: 0.14% of GDP
Coverage	800 million person-days annually
Sources	Kabeer (2002); Rohini (2002); Subbarao (2003)

India: Maharashtra Employment Guarantee Scheme

Description	The program was established by the 1978 Employment Guarantee Scheme Act, which states that all adults in rural Maharashtra have a right to work as unskilled manual laborers and that work must be provided to every job seeker within 15 days of a formal request for employment. Self-targeting is built into the program, and no choice of work is offered. The types of works performed help develop rural, especially agricultural, infrastructure. In September 2005, Parliament approved the National Rural Employment Guarantee Act to extend the program nationally. Building on the experience of the Maharashtra Employment Guarantee Scheme, the national program offers up to 100 days of employment per rural household per year on public works at the prevailing minimum unskilled wage rate. The aim is to boost the rural economy and enhance overall economic growth.
Start date	1979, extended nationally in 2005
Wage level	1975–88: $W_{pr} < W_{mk} < W_{min}$; after 1988: $W_{pr} = W_{min} > W_{mk}$
Expenditure	1980: Rs 1 billion (about US$130 million) or 0.07% of GDP; 1997: Rs 4.13 billion (about US$114) or 0.03%; 2003: Rs 6.67 billion (about US$143 million) or 0.02%; FY2006/07 (for the national program): Rs 88 billion (about US$2 billion) or 0.22%
Coverage	1980: about 205 million person-days; 1997: about 94 million person-days; 2003: 154 million person-days; FY2006/07 (for the national program): 905 million person-days
Sources	Gaiha (2005); Murgai and Ravallion (2005); Overseas Development Institute (2005); Rohini (2002); Scandizzo, Gaiha, and Imai (2005); Sjoblom and Farrington (2008); Subbarao (2003); Subbarao and others (1997); Government of India (2007a); World Bank (2006d); http://nrega.nic.in

(continued)

TABLE B.4 **(continued)**

PUBLIC WORKS PROGRAMS

Republic of Korea: public works projects

Description	After the 1997 Asian financial crisis, the government undertook a number of emergency measures to help those affected. Among those interventions, the public works projects provided temporary work opportunities for the low-income unemployed who were not eligible to collect unemployment benefits. The work included activities ranging from infrastructure maintenance, social service provision, and environmental cleanup to information technology projects.
Start date	1998; ended 2000
Wage level	As of 1999, when wages were cut: Wpr = Wmin < Wmk
Expenditure	1998: W 0.9 billion (about US$660 million) or about 0.19% of GDP; 1999: W 2.3 trillion (about US$1.9 billion) or about 0.43%; 2000: W 1.5 trillion (about US$1.3 billion) or about 0.25%
Coverage	1998: 438,000 beneficiaries (about 2% of the economically active population); 1999: about 1.5 million (about 6.8%); 2000: 886,000 (about 4%)
Sources	Hur (2001); Kwon (2002); Subbarao (2003)

Malawi: Central Region Infrastructure Maintenance Programme

Description	Poor women's communities select them for the program, in which they participate for 18 months to carry out maintenance work on the road network. They receive part of their salary in cash; part is held in a savings account for them. The intent is that by the end of the program, the participants will have built some assets and be able to start income-generating activities that will lead them out of destitution.
Start date	1999; ended 2002
Wage level	Average monthly income of MK 825 (about US$12)
Expenditure	Not available
Coverage	Total of 1,600 women
Sources	Hashemi and Rosenberg (2006); www.caremalawi.org/crimp.htm

Malawi: Public Works Program

Description	The program is a component of the Malawi Social Action Fund strategy, which aims to improve the livelihoods of the most vulnerable and marginalized groups. The program creates labor-intensive temporary employment for poor households in targeted poor rural and urban areas. Projects include road building, afforestation, and environmental rehabilitation.
Start date	1995
Wage level	2004: Wpr < Wmin
Expenditure	1998–2003: about US$76 million or about 4% of GDP
Coverage	1998–2003: about 535,700 people or about 10% of the economically active population
Sources	Benson (2002); Chirwa and others (2004); World Bank (2004c)

(continued)

TABLE B.4 **(continued)**

PUBLIC WORKS PROGRAMS

Mexico: Programa de Empleo Temporal (Temporary Employment Program)

Description	This program was created as a response to the severe economic crisis in the mid-1990s. It was aimed at providing income to the poorest people by generating highly labor-intensive jobs in rural areas while rehabilitating and improving social and productive infrastructure. Since 2002, the program's objectives have been broadened and it has become more permanent.
Start date	1995
Wage level	Wpr < Wmin
Expenditure	1995: 0.29% of GDP
Coverage	1995: 660,000 beneficiaries, or about 1.8% of the economically active population 2000: 1 million beneficiaries or about 2.5% of the economically active population
Sources	Latin American Economic System (2005); Samaniego (2002); www.sedesol.gob.mx/index/index.php?sec=3007&len=1

Peru: A Trabajar Urbano (Urban to Work)

Description	The program was initiated in response to the 1998–2001 economic downturn, which resulted in an increase in poverty and unemployment. The objective is to provide temporary employment at low wages for unskilled workers negatively affected by the crisis in poor urban areas. The program aims to improve social and economic urban infrastructure through highly labor-intensive projects and to promote participation by communities in local development.
Start date	2002
Wage level	Wpr < Wmin
Expenditure	2003: about US$50 million or 0.08% of GDP
Coverage	2003: 76,886 four-month jobs
Sources	Chacaltana (2003); Latin American Economic System (2005); Reinecke (2005); World Bank (2005j)

South Africa: Expanded Public Works Program

Description	The program is one element of a broader government strategy to reduce poverty by alleviating and reducing unemployment. It provides short-term employment opportunities for the unemployed coupled with training.
Start date	2004
Wage level	Wpr ≤ Wmin
Expenditure	FY2004/05: R 823 million (total wages paid out) (US$128 million) or about 0.06% of GDP; FY2005/06: R 636 million (US$100 million) or about 0.04%; FY2006/07: R 917 million (US$135 million) or about 0.05%
Coverage	FY2004/05: 174,845 work opportunities; FY2005/06: 208,898; FY2006/07: 316,810
Sources	Department of Public Works (various years); McCord (2004b); Phillips (2004)

(continued)

TABLE B.4 **(continued)**

PUBLIC WORKS PROGRAMS

Republic of Yemen: public works projects

Description	The government has sought to mitigate the short-term effects of the adjustment program designed to stabilize the economy and stimulate sustainable growth on the country's most vulnerable people by providing a safety net and creating jobs. In particular, projects provide needed infrastructure to improve services and environmental conditions (particularly those affecting women and children) and create short-term employment. The government seeks to ensure the sustainability of projects through community involvement in project selection, preparation, and implementation and the development of local contracting and consulting firms.
Start date	1996
Wage level	Wpr < Wmin
Expenditure	1996–2000: US$28 million (about 0.48% of GDP); 2000–4: US$60 million (about 0.63%); 2005–10: US$52 million (about 0.31%)
Coverage	1996–2000: 66,000 person-months of employment 2000–4: about 95,000 person-months of employment
Sources	World Bank (2003k, 2004f)

SOURCE: Authors.

NOTE: GDP = gross domestic product, Wmin = minimum wage, Wmk = market wage, Wpr = program wage.

TABLE B.5 **Conditional Cash Transfer Programs**

CONDITIONAL CASH TRANSFER PROGRAMS

Argentina: Programa Nacional de Becas Estudiantiles (National Scholarship Program)

Description	The program is designed to promote long-term human capital accumulation among young people and to reduce poverty. The program targets poor children aged 13–19 who are entering their eighth and ninth years of study in public schools and are at risk of leaving school before completing their education. Eligible students come from families with a monthly total income of less than Arg$500 (about US$170) who do not receive any similar benefit from another organization. The transfer is conditional on the students' school attendance and annual grade progression.
Start date	1997
Size of transfer	Annual scholarship of Arg$400 (US$140)
Expenditure	2003: US$46 million or 0.03% of GDP
Coverage	2004: 350,000 beneficiaries or about 0.9% of the population
Sources	de Andraca (2006); Heinrich (2007); Heinrich and Cabrol (2005)

Bangladesh: Female Secondary School Assistance Program

Description	The objectives of this program are to increase school enrollment among girls of secondary school age; improve the secondary schooling completion rate for girls; and increase the age at which girls marry. The program provides a stipend that covers tuition fees and other personal costs of educating girls after they enroll for sixth grade, conditional on school attendance of at least 75% and attainment of 45% of class-level test scores. The students must remain unmarried.
Start date	1994
Size of transfer	As of 2001: stipend varies by grade from Tk 300 (US$5) to Tk 720 (US$12) per student per year In addition, tuition costs of Tk 120 (US$2) to Tk 240 (US$4) per student per year; annual book costs of Tk 250 (US$4) for 9th graders, and examination fees of Tk 500 (US$8) for 10th graders
Expenditure	2002–9 (second phase): about US$145 million
Coverage	1994: 187,320 girls 1999: 875,858 girls 2002: 1,068,064 girls
Sources	Braun-Munzinger (2005); Herz and Sperling (2004); Hove (2007); Kattan and Burnett (2004); Khandker, Pitt, and Fuwa (2003); Mahmud (2003); World Bank (2003d, 2005a)

Bangladesh: Food for Education Program

Description	The program's aim was to increase primary school enrollment, promote attendance, and reduce dropout rates among children from landless and very poor families. It provided rice and/or wheat transfers to poor households conditional on minimum school attendance by the children (85% per month) in primary school. The program was converted into a conditional cash transfer program (Primary Education Stipend Program) in 2002.
Start date	1993; ended 2002

(continued)

TABLE B.5 **(continued)**

CONDITIONAL CASH TRANSFER PROGRAMS

Size of transfer	A ration of 15 kilograms of wheat or 12 kilograms of rice per month for a household that had only one child of primary school age (6–10) who attended school; a maximum ration of 20 kilograms of wheat or 16 kilograms of rice per month per household with more than one child if all children of primary school age attended school
Expenditure	FY1993/94: Tk 683 million (US$17 million) or about 0.05% of GDP, distribution of 79,553 metric tons of food grains FY1999/2000: Tk 3.94 billion (US$77 million) or about 0.17% of GDP, distribution of 285,973 metric tons of food grains
Coverage	2000: 2.1 million students or about 1.5% of the population
Sources	Ahmed and Arends-Kuenning (2003); Ahmed and del Ninno (2002); Barrientos and DeJong (2004); Morley and Coady (2003); Tietjen (2003)

Bangladesh: Primary Education Stipend Program

Description	The program aims to increase enrollment and attendance rates, reduce dropout rates, and promote performance by children of primary school age from poor families by providing cash payments to targeted households. Cash benefits are conditional on school attendance of a minimum of 85% of school days and obtainment of at least 40% on annual examinations.
Start date	2002
Size of transfer	Tk 100 (about US$1.7) per month per household with one student or Tk 125 (about US$2) per month per household with more than one student
Expenditure	Annually: approximately US$100 million or about 0.2% of GDP
Coverage	About 5.3 million beneficiaries every year or about 4% of the population
Sources	Ahmed (2005); Tietjen (2003); World Bank (2005a)

Brazil: Bolsa Escola (School Grant)

Description	This program, which was piloted in 1995 and expanded nationally in 2001, targeted families with children aged 6–15 and per capita monthly incomes no greater than R$90 (US$43). It provided education grants for poor children aged 6–15 reporting at least 85% school attendance in a three-month period. This program, along with other programs, was merged with Bolsa Familia in 2003.
Start date	1995; ended 2003
Size of transfer	R$15 (US$7) per month per child up to a maximum of three children
Expenditure	2001: more than US$680 million or about 0.13% of GDP
Coverage	2001: 8.2 million children or 4.8 million households 2002: 8.6 million children from 5 million families or 4.8% of the population
Sources	Barrientos and DeJong (2004); Cardoso and Souza (2004); de Janvry and others (2005); Herz and Sperling (2004); Lindert, Skoufias, and Shapiro (2006); Morley and Coady (2003); Nigenda and González-Robledo (2005); Rawlings (2005); World Bank (2001a, 2003j)

(continued)

TABLE B.5 **(continued)**

CONDITIONAL CASH TRANSFER PROGRAMS

Brazil: Bolsa Familia (Family Grant)

Description	This program integrated four cash transfer programs (school and health grants, a cash transfer for cooking gas, and a food card program) into a single program. It targets poor and extremely poor families. As of 2006, the income ceilings for program eligibility were set at a monthly per capita family income of R$120 (about US$57) for moderately poor families and R$60 (about US$28) for extremely poor families. It provides poor families with children up to 15 years old and/or pregnant or breastfeeding women with a monthly transfer that varies depending on per capita family income and family size and composition. The benefits are conditional on compliance with health and nutrition requirements for children from birth through age 6 and pregnant and lactating women, enrollment in school and attendance of at least 85% for each child of school age, and participation in nutritional education.
Start date	2003
Size of transfer	Basic benefit of R$58 (about US$30) for extremely poor families and variable benefit of R$18–R$54 (about US$9–US$28) per child (up to three children) per month for both extremely poor and moderately poor families (benefit amounts were increased to these levels in July 2007)
Expenditure	2005: R$6.7 billion (about US$3 billion) or 0.31% of GDP 2006: R$8.3 billion (about US$4 billion) (budgeted) or about 0.36% of GDP
Coverage	2006: 11.1 million beneficiary families or about 46 million people or about 24% of the population
Sources	de Janvry and others (2005); Lindert and others (2007); Lindert, Skoufias, and Shapiro (2006); World Bank (2005b); www.mds.gov.br/bolsafamilia

Brazil: Child Labor Eradication Program

Description	The program's purpose is to stop the worst forms of child labor, such as work in charcoal or sugarcane production, while increasing educational attainment and reducing poverty. Eligible households must have an income per capita less than half the minimum wage (about US$65 a month). The program includes an income transfer for poor families with children and adolescents aged 7–14 reporting at least 80% school attendance and participation in the program's afternoon school program. Families must participate in social education and income-generating activities and must ensure that their children are not involved in child labor. The income transfer part of the program (not the afternoon school program) was incorporated into Bolsa Familia in 2005.
Start date	Piloted in 1996 and extended to all areas in 1999–2005
Size of transfer	Varies across states from R$25–R$39 (US$11–US$17) per child per month
Expenditure	2002: R$472.4 million (about US$162 million) or 0.03% of GDP
Coverage	2002: 866,000 children or 0.5% of the population
Sources	Barrientos and DeJong (2004); Cardoso and Souza (2004); Lindert, Skoufias, and Shapiro (2006); Lindert and others (2007); Nigenda and González-Robledo (2005); Rawlings (2005); Yap, Sedlacek, and Orazem (2001); World Bank (2001c)

(continued)

TABLE B.5 **(continued)**

CONDITIONAL CASH TRANSFER PROGRAMS

Chile: Chile Solidario

Description	Benefits are targeted to households in extreme poverty identified through a proxy means test. Households receive both tailored conditional cash transfers and personalized assistance in one of seven possible areas (health, education, employment, housing, income, family life, or legal documentation). Participation is conditional on signing and complying with contracts that commit households to participating in the activities identified by their personal social workers who monitor their progress.
Start date	2002
Size of transfer	US$20 per month for the first 6 months, US$15 for the second 6 months, US$10 for the third 6 months, and US$6 (equivalent to the Subsidio Unitario Familiar) for the next 42 months
Expenditure	2003: about US$22 million or 0.02% of GDP
Coverage	2006: about 290,000 of households or about 6% of the total population
Sources	Barrientos and DeJong (2004); Galasso (2006); Lindert, Skoufias, and Shapiro (2006); World Bank (2005g); www.mideplan.cl/final/categoria.php?secid=1&catid=8

Chile: Subsidio Unitario Familiar (Unified Family Subsidy)

Description	This is a family cash transfer targeted to mothers in eligible families who have school-age children attending school or who are pregnant or caring for invalids. The beneficiaries of the education subsidy have to regularly take their children under age 6 to health clinics and send their children aged 6–18 to school. Eligibility is based on a proxy means test.
Start date	1981
Size of transfer	Average of US$6 per child per month
Expenditure	1998: US$70 million or about 0.09% of GDP
Coverage	1998: 954,000 students or about 6.3% of the population
Sources	Morley and Coady (2003)

Colombia: Familias en Acción (Families in Action)

Description	This program provides a nutritional grant to poor families with children from birth through age 6 conditional on regular health care visits to monitor their growth and development every two months and an educational grant for families with children aged 7–17 enrolled in school conditional on at least 80% school attendance in a two-month cycle (maximum of eight unjustified absences/month).
Start date	2001
Size of transfer	Education grant of Col$14,000 (US$6) per child per month in primary school and Col$28,000 (US$12) per month per child in secondary school; health subsidy of Col$46,500 (US$20) per month per family regardless of the number of children under seven
Expenditure	2005: US$95 million or about 0.08% of GDP

(continued)

TABLE B.5 **(continued)**

CONDITIONAL CASH TRANSFER PROGRAMS	
Coverage	2004: 340,000 families or about 3% of the population 2005: 400,000 households in 700 municipalities or about 3.6% of the population
Sources	Attanasio and others (2005, 2006); Ayala (2006a); Barrientos and DeJong (2004); Lindert (2005b); Lindert, Skoufias, and Shapiro (2006); Nigenda and González-Robledo (2005); Rawlings (2005); Rawlings and Rubio (2005); World Bank (2003j, 2005b)

Costa Rica: Programa Superémonos (Let's Overcome Program)

Description	The program provides a monthly food coupon to poor households on the condition that all children in the household aged 6–18 attend school. The program requires letters of commitment signed by fathers or mothers in which they promise that their children will not drop out of school while they are receiving the benefit and acknowledge that the benefit will be suspended automatically if they do so. Participating households receive a coupon each month for the 10 months of the school year that they can redeem for food in any supermarket.
Start date	2000
Size of transfer	Monthly coupon worth C 10,000 per month (approximately US$30)
Expenditure	2002: US$3.45 million or 0.02% of GDP
Coverage	2001: 12,234 families or about 1.2% of the population
Sources	Duryea and Morrison (2004); World Bank (2003j)

Dominican Republic: Solidaridad (Solidarity)

Description	The program provides monthly transfers to poor households conditional on school enrollment and attendance of at least 85% for children aged 6–16 and visits to health units for preventive care and early detection of health problems for children from birth through age 5. Transfers are conditional on attendance at capacity-building sessions for household heads and their spouses every four months and on obtaining identity documents (birth certificates, identify cards) for family members who lack them.
Start date	2005
Size of transfer	Monthly food component of RD$550 (US$17); education component of RD$300 (US$9) for households with one or two minor children, RD$450 (US$14) for households with three minor children, and RD$600 (US$19) for households with four or more minor children
Expenditure	2006: US$57 million or 0.19% of GDP
Coverage	2006: 230,000 families or about 9% of the population
Sources	Regalia and Robles (2005); World Bank (2006a); www.gabsocial.gov.do/solidaridad/

Ecuador: Bono de Desarrollo Humano (Human Development Grant)

Description	This program targets transfers to households with children from birth to 16 in the poorest two quintiles and poor households with elderly and/or disabled members. Payments are conditional on the fulfillment of certain health and education responsibilities. Children through age 1 are expected to visit a health center every two months for checkups. Children aged 1–5 are expected to visit a health center every six months for checkups. During these checkups the children's weight and height are monitored to detect any signs of malnutrition and vaccinations are given. Children aged 6–16 are expected to enroll in school and have attendance rates of at least 80% for each school year they are in the program.

(continued)

TABLE B.5 **(continued)**

CONDITIONAL CASH TRANSFER PROGRAMS	
Start date	2003
Size of transfer	US$15 per month per household with children and US$11.5 per household with elderly and/or disabled members
Expenditure	2006: approximately US$200 million or 0.5% of GDP
Coverage	Targeted to families in the poorest two quintiles, or approximately 5.2 million people or 1.2 million households or about 40% of the total population
Sources	Armas (2005); Schady and Araujo (2006); World Bank (2005b, 2006a, 2006l)

Honduras: Programa de Asignación Familiar II (Family Allowance Program II)

Description	This program provides demand- and supply-side incentives for education and health care. On the demand side, education vouchers are given to poor households with children aged 6–12 who have not yet completed the fourth grade of primary school conditional on school enrollment and a school attendance rate of at least 85%. A maximum of up to three children per family are eligible. Health vouchers are given to pregnant women and/or mothers of children under age 3. Vouchers are provided only to women who have visited a health clinic every month. Each family may receive up to three health vouchers per month. On the supply side, the program provides monetary transfers to health centers and to primary school parent-teacher associations.
Start date	2000
Size of transfer	Education vouchers of about US$5 per child per month (limit of three children per family), health vouchers of US$4 per family per month (limit of three health vouchers per family), average school incentive of US$4,000 a year, and average health facility incentive of US$6,000 a year
Expenditure	2005: US$25 million or 0.3% of GDP
Coverage	2005: 411,000 households or about 28% of the population
Sources	Barrientos and DeJong (2004); Glewwe, Olinto, and de Souza (2003); Handa and Davis (2006); Morley and Coady (2003); Nigenda and González-Robledo (2005); Rawlings (2005); Rawlings and Rubio (2005); World Bank (2003j, 2006a); www.ifpri.org/themes/praf.htm

Indonesia: JPS Scholarship and Grant Program

Description	The program aims to maintain enrollments in primary and lower and upper secondary schools and the quality of education in these schools at the same level as before the 1997 Asian economic crisis. It consists of two components. The first is scholarships for the poorest students attending primary, junior secondary, and senior secondary schools that are paid directly to the students or their families twice a year via a cash transfer handled by the local post office. Poorer districts and schools receive a relatively larger allocation of scholarships. The number of scholarships to particular schools and students relies heavily on local knowledge and community participation. Beneficiary selection is based on the families' socioeconomic situation using criteria such as families living in poverty, single parents, large households, or welfare status. At least 50% of the scholarships must be awarded to girls. The second component is block grants for primary, junior secondary, and senior secondary schools serving predominantly poor communities.
Start date	1998

(continued)

TABLE B.5 **(continued)**

CONDITIONAL CASH TRANSFER PROGRAMS

Size of transfer	Scholarships amounted to Rp 10,000 (US$1.2) per month for students in primary school, Rp 20,000 (US$2.4) per month for students in junior secondary school, and Rp 25,000 (US$3) per month for students in senior secondary school
Expenditure	FY1998/99: Rp 1,138 billion (about US$145 million) or 0.15% of GDP FY1999/2000: Rs 1,251 billion (about US$150 million) or 0.11% of GDP FY2000: Rp 667 billion (about US$80 million) or 0.05% of GDP[a]
Coverage	Target for the scholarship program: 1.8 million primary school students, 1.65 million junior high school students, and 500,000 senior high school students Target for block grants: 104,000 primary school schools, 18,000 junior high school schools, and 9.5 senior high school students
Sources	Economic and Social Commission for Asia and the Pacific (2001); Haryadi (2001); Perdana and Maxwell (2004); Pritchett, Sumarto, and Suryahadi (2002); Sparrow (2007); Sumarto, Suryahadi Widyanti (2002)

Jamaica: Program of Advancement through Health and Education (PATH)

Description	This program replaced several fragmented income support and targeted transfer programs. It has two components. The first is child health and education grants for eligible poor children through age 17. The receipt of health grants is conditional on children up to age 6 not enrolled in school visiting a health clinic every two months during the first year and twice a year thereafter. The receipt of education grants is conditional on school attendance for at least 85% of school days by poor children aged 6–17. The second component is a social assistance grant for poor pregnant or lactating women; poor people older than 65; and poor, disabled, and destitute adults younger than 65. Initially, the receipt of benefits was conditional on adults making regular visits to health clinics. This was changed shortly after the program was launched, and benefits for adults are no longer conditional. Targeting is based on a proxy means test.
Start date	2001
Size of transfer	Each grant is J$530 (about US$9) per month per beneficiary
Expenditure	2005: US$16 million or 0.16% of GDP
Coverage	2005: 220,000 people or about 8% of the population
Sources	Ayala (2006b); Ayala and Endara (2005); Barrientos and DeJong (2004); Handa and Davis (2006); Levy and Ohls (2007); Nigenda and González-Robledo (2005); Rawlings (2005); Rawlings and Rubio (2005); World Bank (2003j, 2005b, 2006a)

Mexico: Programa de Educación, Salud y Alimentación (PROGRESA)/ Oportunidades (Education, Health, and Employment Program/Opportunities)

Description	The program provides demand-side subsidies and supply-side support for education, health, and nutrition. Education grants are targeted to poor families with children aged 8–18 enrolled in primary and secondary school conditional on school enrollment and minimum attendance of 85%, both monthly and annually, and completion of middle school. The health and nutrition component includes cash transfers for family food consumption; a basic health package for all family members; and nutritional supplements for children 4–23 months, undernourished children aged 2–5, and women who are pregnant or nursing and is conditional on health care visits by all household members and mothers' attendance at health and nutrition lectures. The program provides cash transfers or in-kind support to improve the supply of schools and health services. In 2002, PROGRESA changed its name to Oportunidades and broadened its objectives. The program now aims to create income-generating opportunities for poor households through preferential access to microcredit, housing improvements, and adult education. The program has expanded from a rural program to a national program.

(continued)

TABLE B.5 (continued)

CONDITIONAL CASH TRANSFER PROGRAMS	
Start date	1997
Size of transfer	Grant for primary education varies by grade from US$11–US$22 per child per month plus US$21 per child/per year for school supplies; for secondary education, grant varies by grade and gender from US$32–US$40 per child per month plus US$26 per child per year for school supplies; for upper secondary and higher education, grant varies by grade and gender from US$53–US$69 per child per month plus US$26 per child per year for school supplies; US$300 in saving account upon completion of middle school; health grant is US$16 per household per month; US$23 per month per adult over 70 who is part of a beneficiary family
Expenditure	2007: Mex$36 billion (about US$3.3 billion) or about 0.4% of GDP
Coverage	2007: 5 million households or about 25 million people or about 23% of the population
Sources	Barrientos and DeJong (2004); de Janvry and others (2006); Garcia (2005); Government of Mexico (2007); Handa and Davis (2006); Levy (2006); Lindert (2005b); Lindert, Skoufias, and Shapiro (2006); Morley and Coady (2003); Rawlings (2005); Rawlings and Rubio (2005); Schultz (2004); Skoufias (2001); World Bank (2003j, 2005b); www.oportunidades.gob.mx/

Nicaragua: Red de Protección Social (Social Protection Network)

Description	The program provided demand-side incentives such as a nutritional grant (to be used to purchase the food necessary to improve family nutrition) that was conditional on health care visits, vaccinations, and attendance at health and nutrition talks; a basic health care package for children from birth to age 5; and an education grant for poor families with children aged 6–13 who were in the first through fourth grades of primary school conditional on school enrollment, less than six days of absence from school in a two-month period, and passage to the next grade. It also provided a supply grant to mothers to give to schools to motivate teachers to buy school supplies.
Start date	2000; ended 2006
Size of transfer	Nutritional grant of C$480 (US$34) per family every two months; educational grant of C$240 (US$17) per family every two months; school material support of C$275 (US$20) per year per child; supply incentive of C$10 (US$0.70) per student every two months
Expenditure	2004: US$6.37 million or 0.14% of GDP
Coverage	2004: 21,619 families or about 2.2% of the population
Sources	Barrientos and DeJong (2004); Handa and Davis (2006); Herz and Sperling (2004); Maluccio and Flores (2004); Maluccio and others (2005); Morley and Coady (2003); Rawlings (2005); Rawlings and Rubio (2005); World Bank (2003j, 2005b)

Pakistan: Child Support Program

Description	The program's benefits are targeted to extremely poor families with children aged 5–12 conditional on school enrollment and attendance of at least 80% of classes. Initially the program will cover all beneficiaries of the Food Support Program with at least one child of primary school age.
Start date	2006 (pilot)

(continued)

TABLE B.5 **(continued)**

CONDITIONAL CASH TRANSFER PROGRAMS	
Size of transfer	Rs 200 (about US$3.5) per month for a family with one child and Rs 350 (about US$6) per month for a family with two or more children of school age enrolled and going to school
Expenditure	FY2005/06: budget of US$7 million or about 0.006% of GDP
Coverage	Pilot phase: 125,000 households or about 0.5% of the population
Sources	World Bank (2006a, 2007k)

Peru: Juntos (Together)

Description	The program provides transfers to the poorest households in rural communities conditional on school attendance of at least 85% for children aged 6–14 and regular health visits for pregnant women and children under age 5.
Start date	2005
Size of transfer	Financial incentive equivalent to S/. 100 (US$33) per month
Expenditure	2006: S/. 300 million (US$100 million) or about 0.1% of GDP
Coverage	November 2007: 336,555 households or about 5.3% of the population
Sources	World Bank (2006a); www.juntos.gob.pe/intro.php

Turkey: Social Risk Mitigation Project

Description	The project is aimed at improving the education and health status of the poorest 6% of Turkey's population. It provides proxy means-tested education and health grants to extremely poor households with children from birth to age 6, school-aged children aged 6–17, and women of child-bearing age. Benefits are paid to mothers with children under age 7 or attending school conditional on school attendance of at least 80% of total monthly education days and not repeating the same grade more than once. Also included are health care visits for children younger than school age. Benefits for pregnant and lactating women are conditional on regular attendance at health clinics and on giving birth at a health clinic.
Start date	2001
Size of transfer	Monthly education grant for primary school of US$13 for boys and US$16 for girls and for secondary school of US$21 for boys and US$29 for girls; health grant of US$12.50 per month per child, US$12 per month during pregnancy, US$41 for birth at a health clinic.
Expenditure	Total of US$360 million or about 0.2% of GDP
Coverage	2006: 870,660 families or about 4.5% of the population
Sources	Adato and others (2007); Ahmed and others (2007); Kudat (2006); Rawlings and Rubio (2005); World Bank (2003j, 2005b, 2006a)

SOURCE: Authors.

NOTE: GDP = gross domestic product.

A. In 2000, the government changed its fiscal year from April–March to January– December. Thus, FY2000 was only nine months long, April– December.

TABLE B.6 **Fee Waivers for Health and Education**

HEALTH

Armenia: basic benefits package

Description	To help poor families cope with reduced public financing and increased privatization of health services, the government provides a basic package of services free of charge to eligible individuals in vulnerable groups, such as people with disabilities, orphans under 18, veterans, those affected by the Chernobyl accident, and families of war victims. In January 2001, the government extended program eligibility to the beneficiaries of the Family Poverty Benefits Program (table B.1).
Start date	1998
Expenditure	Not available
Coverage	Not available
Sources	Chaudhury, Hammer, and Murrugarra (2003); Murrugarra and others (2004)

Cambodia: Health Equity Fund

Description	The fund finances the cost of health services provided at no charge or at reduced prices to the poor. A local nongovernmental organization manages the fund. When poor patients arrive at a hospital, their socioeconomic status is identified through interviews that rely on indicators such as ownership of land and productive assets, housing characteristics, occupation, food security, and household size and structure. The fund's target group consists of the extremely poor and those poor who risk falling into extreme poverty. The level of support is determined on a case-by-case basis and ranges from partial payment of the admission fee to full coverage of the total cost of hospitalization, including transport, food, and basic items. Waiver policies vary widely among provinces and districts.
Start date	2000
Expenditure	September 2000–September 2002: US$27,100
Coverage	September 2000–September 2002: 1,437 patients (16% of hospitalized patients)
Sources	Bitrán (2002); Bitrán and Giedion (2003); Hardeman and others (2004); Jacobs and Price (2006)

Chile: Fondo Nacional de Salud (FONASA) (National Health Fund)

Description	Chile's health care system includes both public and private provision of care. The fund is the only large public insurer. In addition there are multiple, competing private health insurers and traditional commercial indemnity insurance firms. The fund covers middle-, lower-middle-, and low-income people whose eligibility is based on their income and age. The fund identifies the indigent through a means test based on individual assessments. The indigent obtain a health care card for free access to health services and are not required to contribute to the fund.
Start date	1980
Expenditure	1995: Ch$175.3 billion (about $441 million) or 0.6% of GDP
Coverage	1995: total of 8.47 million beneficiaries of which 3.4 million or about 23.6% of the population were classified as indigent
Sources	Bitrán and Giedion (2003); Bitrán and Muñoz (2000); Bitrán and others (2000)

(continued)

TABLE B.6 **(continued)**

HEALTH

Ghana: national health exemption policy

Description	Official fee levels and exemption categories were established in 1985. Whole or partial exemption from payment of user fees was initially targeted to the poor, but also to selected service user subgroups, which included psychiatric patients, lepers, malnourished children, and pregnant women. Those with specific diseases of public health concern, such as tuberculosis, yaws, and cholera, also fell under the exempt category. Later, health staff and their immediate families (spouse and up to four children) were exempted from user fees. In subsequent years, the target groups and conditions allowing exemptions have been broadened through policy changes made in response to critical emerging issues.
Start date	1985
Expenditure	Not available
Coverage	No systematic monitoring, but according to some data, exemptions granted to fewer than 2% of patients
Sources	Bitrán and Giedion (2003); Nyonator (2002); Nyonator and Kutzin (1999)

Indonesia: JPS Kartu Sehat (Social Safety Net Health Card)

Description	The program was initially implemented in an effort to mitigate the adverse effects of user fees on the poor and received additional impetus following the 1997 Asian economic crisis. Local leaders are given cards for distribution in their districts based on the estimated number of poor along with guidelines on the criteria to use when distributing the cards to households. The criterion for eligibility is the household's "prosperity status," whereby they are deemed to be in need when they have insufficient funds for any one of the following: (1) worshipping according to the tenets of their faith, (2) eating twice a day, (3) having different clothes for school or work and home, (4) having a floor not made of earth, or (5) having access to modern medical care for their children or to modern contraceptive methods. This information is collected by the National Family Planning Board via a census. Local leaders maintain a good deal of leverage to distribute health cards based on their own insights as to who might need them. Those holding cards are entitled to free access to health services provided by designated public health care centers for basic medical care, family planning purposes, prenatal care, and childbirth.
Start date	1994
Expenditure	FY1998/99: Rp 1,043 billion (about US$133 million) or about 0.14% of GDP FY1999/2000: Rp 1,030 billion (about US$122 million) or about 0.09% of GDP FY2000: Rp 867 billion (about US$103 million) or about 0.06% of GDP[a]
Coverage	FY2000: 9.3 million poor households or about 18% of the population
Sources	Bitrán and Giedion (2003); Bitrán and Muñoz (2000); Economic and Social Commission for Asia and the Pacific (2001); Perdana and Maxwell (2004); Pritchett, Sumarto, and Suryahadi (2002); Saddah, Pradhan, and Sparrow (2001); Sumarto, Suryahadi, and Widyanti (2002); World Bank (2006f)

(continued)

TABLE B.6 **(continued)**

HEALTH

Kenya: exemptions

Description	To mitigate the negative effects of user fees on access by the poor, the Ministry of Health introduced a system of exemptions for categories of patients afflicted with certain illnesses. Since 1992, the number of exemption categories has been reduced. For example, before 1995 children under age five were waived from fees in all primary care facilities; after 1998, only about half of all facilities kept this waiver in place. Facility staff determines whether they will grant waivers to the poor on the basis of income and health status following approval by the medical superintendent.
Start date	1990
Expenditure	Not available
Coverage	On average, two exemptions per month per facility, but systematic information is not available
Sources	Bitrán and Giedion (2003); Owino and Abagi (2000); Owino and Were (1998)

Thailand: Low- Income Card Scheme

Description	Qualified beneficiaries of this program, who are subject to geographic targeting and means testing, have free access to health facilities. During the 1990s, eligibility was expanded to include not only the poor, but the elderly, children under 12, veterans, people with disabilities, monks, and other groups. Those who qualify for the scheme are given a beneficiary card that is valid for three years. The card specifies one or two designated health facilities, normally local health centers or district hospitals, that beneficiaries should visit in case of illness or injury.
Start date	1975
Expenditure	1997: B 6,703 million (about US$216 million) or 0.14% of GDP
Coverage	1997: about 15 million people or about 25% of the population
Sources	Bitrán and Giedion (2003); Giedion (2002); Economic and Social Commission for Asia and the Pacific (2001)

Zambia: Public Welfare Assistance Scheme

Description	The scheme was intended to address inequalities in access. It has a structure of welfare assistance committees at the district, subdistrict, and village levels. Chronically ill patients who cannot pay are referred to a district social welfare office for assessment, and the scheme pays approved fees to the district's health management board on behalf of the patient.
Start date	1995
Expenditure	1999: K 1.52 billion (about US$640,000) or about 0.02% of GDP
Coverage	1999: 66,210 people or about 0.6% of the population or 29% of 228,558 applicants
Sources	Republic of Zambia (2002)

(continued)

TABLE B.6 **(continued)**

EDUCATION

Colombia: Programa de Ampliación de Cobertura de la Educación Secundaria (PACES) (Plan for Increasing Secondary School Coverage)

Description	The program was introduced to enable poor students to attend secondary school in areas where public schools had reached capacity limits. Students receive school vouchers to pay for tuition at private schools. The government covers 80% of voucher costs and participating municipalities cover 20%. To receive voucher funds, a school has to be situated in one of the participating towns, which include all major cities. The program targets students from low-income families, specifically, students entering the sixth grade and living in low-income areas who have previously attended public primary schools and who cannot obtain a place at a public secondary school.
Start date	1992
Expenditure	Not available
Coverage	1997: more than 125,000 students or about 0.3% of the population
Sources	Angrist and others (2002); Braun-Munzinger (2005); Herz and Sperling (2004); Kattan and Burnett (2004)

Guatemala: Eduque a la Niña (Educate the Girl) pilot under the Basic Education Strengthening Project

Description	The program provided payments to girls and their parents in the form of scholarships or stipends. While the pilot made use of parent committees and community outreach workers, its most innovative tool was a small scholarship payable each month for 11 months a year and renewed for the following year conditional on promotion to the next grade that was provided to girls enrolled in grades 1, 2, and 3 in 12 rural communities. Communities selected were those with the highest gender disparity in school enrollment and attendance. Within the chosen communities, girls were selected based on income criteria.
Start date	1993; ended 1996
Expenditure	1995: US$37,464
Coverage	1995: 442 recipients
Sources	Braun-Munzinger (2005); Kattan and Burnett (2004); Liang and Marble (1996); USAID (1999)

Pakistan: Quetta Urban Fellowship Program

Description	The purpose of this program was to determine whether establishing private girls' primary schools in poor neighborhoods was a cost-effective means of expanding primary education for girls in Quetta's lower-income urban neighborhoods. The program encouraged private schools, which were controlled by the community, to establish new facilities by paying subsidies directly to the schools. Schools were assured of government support for three years. This subsidy was sufficient to cover typical tuition fees at the lowest-priced private schools.
Start date	1995; ended 2000
Expenditure	First year: US$0.11 million
Coverage	1995–8: the program grew from 11 schools with about 2,000 students to 40 schools with 10,000 students

(continued)

TABLE B.6 **(continued)**

EDUCATION	
Sources	Alderman, Kim, and Orazem (2003); Herz and Sperling (2004); Kim, Alderman, and Orazem (1999a); Liang (1996); Orazem (2000)

Pakistan: Rural Fellowship Pilot

Description	The pilot was built around a model that used government funds to leverage private sector involvement in the provision of education to poor communities. Communities donated land and buildings, and the government provided funding for teachers' salaries. The transfers were used to target girls, set minimum and maximum class sizes, and encourage retention.
Start date	1995; ended 1998
Expenditure	First year: about US$0.14 million for the direct costs of establishing 30 rural schools in Balochistan
Coverage	First year: 1,570 students
Sources	Alderman, Kim, and Orazem (2003); Kim, Alderman, and Orazem (1999b); Liang (1996); Orazem (2000)

Zimbabwe: Basic Education Assistance Module

Description	The program aims at reducing the number of needy children aged 6–19 dropping out of school or not attending because of economic hardships. It provides targeted fee waivers at the primary and secondary school levels in both urban and rural areas. Local school selection committees comprised of people with some knowledge of the socioeconomic realities of the communities are in charge of identifying the most deserving children for assistance.
Start date	2001
Expenditure	2005: about Z$195 billion (about US$9 million) or about 0.25% of GDP
Coverage	2005: about 970,000 children or about 7% of the population
Sources	Regional Hunger and Vulnerability Programme (2007); Subbarao, Mattimore, and Plangemann (2001); World Bank (2006a); www.wahenga.net/index.php/views/country_update_view/zimbabwe_the_basic_education_assistance_module_beam/

SOURCE: Authors.

NOTE: GDP = gross domestic product.

a. In 2000, the government changed its fiscal year from April–March to the calendar year, thus FY2000 only covers nine months, April–December.

Glossary

Absolute poverty lines. Poverty lines anchored in some absolute standard of what households should be able to count on in order to meet their basic needs. For monetary measures, these absolute poverty lines are often based on estimates of the cost of basic food needs, that is, the cost of a nutritional basket considered minimal for the health of a typical family, to which a provision is added for nonfood needs.

Active labor market programs (or labor activation programs). Programs aimed at increasing the skills, employment, and long-run earning potential of participants through training, apprenticeships, job search assistance, subsidized job placements, and the like.

Adequacy. A program is adequate if it provides sufficient benefits to enough people for long enough. Information on which to judge adequacy is usually provided in positive rather than normative terms—the transfer as a share of income of the recipients, the share of recipients in the population or among the poor, and so on.

Administrative costs. All the costs required to deliver the transfers (and, in some cases, other related services). These activities include the identification of target population receiving and processing applications, dealing with appeals, processing payments, undertaking monitoring and evaluation, and exercising oversight over how program resources are used.

Administrative costs of targeting. Costs to the program of gathering information to help make the decision about who should be admitted. These costs are part of the total administrative costs of the program and include program staff time to determine eligibility and verify reported levels of income as well as systems for registration procedures and applicant databases.

Cash transfer programs. Programs that transfer cash to eligible people or households. Common variants include child allowances, social pensions, needs-based transfers, and conditional cash transfers.

Categorical targeting. A targeting method in which all individuals in a specific category (for example, a particular age group, geographic location, gender, or demographic composition) are eligible to receive benefits.

Chronic poverty. Poverty that endures year after year, usually as a result of long-term structural factors faced by the household, such as low assets or location in a poor area remote from thriving markets and services.

Community-based targeting. A targeting method in which a group of community members or leaders (whose principal functions in the community are not related to the transfer program) decide who in the community should benefit.

Comparison of means. Method of estimating program impact using an experimental design that randomly allocates eligible applicants to treatment and control groups. The program's impact on the outcome being evaluated can be measured by the difference between the mean outcomes of the samples of the treatment group and the control group. This method uses observations at one point in time and therefore assumes that the outcomes of the treatment and control groups evolve in a similar way.

Coping strategies. The subset of risk management strategies designed to relieve the impact of risk once a shock has occurred. The main forms of coping with shocks that decrease income consist of individuals using their savings and selling assets, borrowing, or relying on public or private transfers to maintain current consumption.

Conditional cash transfers. Provide money to poor families contingent on them making investments in human capital, such as keeping their children in school or taking them to health centers on a regular basis.

Cost-benefit analysis. Compares the value of a program's net impacts on final outcomes, expressed in monetary terms, with the extra costs associated with implementing the program, also expressed in monetary terms.

Cost-effectiveness. Estimates the costs in monetary terms required to obtain a change in final outcomes expressed in quantitative nonmonetary terms, for example the cost of lowering the poverty gap by one point. Such analysis is used in lieu of cost-benefit analysis when outcomes cannot be valued well in monetary terms.

Countercyclical financing. Cases where funding for a program increases when gross domestic product decreases and vice versa.

Covariate shock. An uncertain (in realization, timing, or magnitude) event that affects many or all members of a group or community, such as drought, earthquake, or macroeconomic crisis.

Decile. One-tenth of an ordered population; for example, the poorest or richest one-tenth of the population. See quantile.

Demographic targeting. A targeting method in which eligibility is based on age.

Dependency ratio. The ratio of non-income-earning (or dependent) to income-earning members in the household.

Disability. A physical, mental, or psychological condition that limits a person's activities. The social model of disability emphasizes people's ability to function in their particular physical and social environment. Disability therefore arises when barriers prevent people with functional limitations caused by age, disease, injury, or other causes from participating fully in society.

Double difference or difference-in-differences method. Method of estimating program impact by comparing the outcomes for the treatment and comparison groups before (first difference) and after (second difference) the intervention.

Dynamic targeting assessment (or dynamic incidence). Ranks households not by current welfare but by changes in welfare in a recent period. It can therefore be used to describe whether a program is reaching those most severely affected by an economic shock. It requires panel data.

Economically active population. Synonymous with the labor force; includes both the employed and the unemployed.

Equity. Concept of fairness in economics. Equity analysis examines the distribution of benefits across pertinent groups (poor/nonpoor, men/women, rural/urban, and so on). Horizontal equity requires that the same benefits or taxes apply to individuals or households that are equal in all important respects. Vertical equity implies that benefits or taxes are differentiated by ability to pay or need.

Error of exclusion. The exclusion of a person who meets eligibility criteria from a program.

Error of inclusion. The inclusion of a ineligible person in a program.

Evaluation designs. Methods used to select the counterfactual or control group for impact evaluations. They can be broadly classified into three categories: experimental (randomized) design, quasi-experimental design, and nonexperimental design.

Experimental (randomized) design. Impact evaluation design that involves gathering a set of individuals (or other unit of analysis) equally eligible and willing to participate in a program and randomly dividing them into two groups: those who receive the intervention (treatment group) and those from whom the intervention is withheld (control group). Experimental designs are generally considered the most robust of evaluation methodologies.

Family allowance. Cash transfer for families with children. Family allowances can take various forms, such as means-tested child benefits, birth grants, or universal transfers for all children under a fixed age.

Fee exemption. Exemption granted to everyone for a defined class of service, for example, vaccination or prenatal care.

Fee waivers and scholarships for schooling. Also known as stipends (usually paid in cash to households), education vouchers (coupons that households use to purchase education or inputs to education), targeted bursaries, and interventions related to tuition and textbooks. All such mechanisms are meant to assist households in meeting the costs of schooling.

Fee waivers for health. Waivers granted to individuals based on their personal characteristics (such as poverty), relieving them of the need to pay for health services for which charges usually apply.

Food insecurity. Lack of access to enough food for an active, healthy life. Chronic food insecurity refers to the persistence of this situation over time, even in the absence of idiosyncratic or covariate shocks.

Food stamps, coupons, or vouchers. See near cash transfers.

Food rations. In-kind food transfers intended to provide access to rationed quantities of food to vulnerable and food-insecure households

Food transfers. See in-kind food transfers.

General subsidies. Measures aimed at controlling the prices of food and other essential commodities or services.

Generosity. The level of a program benefit as a share of the poverty line or other type of indicator, such as the minimum wage, the average wage, or the total consumption of beneficiary households.

Geographic targeting. A targeting method in which location determines eligibility for benefits or allocates budget to concentrate resources on poorer areas.

Idiosyncratic shock. An uncertain (in realization, timing, or magnitude) event that affects one individual or household, such as illness or the loss of a job.

Impact evaluation survey. Covers a representative sample of program beneficiaries—the treatment group—as well as a control group that ideally is similar in all respects to the treatment group except that its members are not program beneficiaries. Impact evaluation surveys are not representative of the total population.

Incentive compatibility. Implies that a program reinforces certain behaviors considered virtuous by a society. For example, it does not encourage recipients to work or save less, but instead encourages them to invest in schooling, nutrition, and health care.

In-kind food transfers. Provide additional resources to households by making food available when they need it most in the form of food rations, supplementary and school feeding programs, or emergency food distribution.

Incentive (or indirect) costs of targeting. Costs that arise when eligibility criteria induce households to change their behavior in an attempt to become beneficiaries.

Income elasticity. Measures the responsiveness of the quantity demanded of a good to the change in the income of the people demanding the good. Income elasticity is calculated as the ratio of the percentage change in quantity demanded to the percentage change in income.

Income gap. Ratio between the average welfare level of the poor and the poverty line among the poor. For example, if the welfare level is measured as per capita consumption, an income gap of 25 percent means that the average per capita consumption of the poor is 25 percent below the poverty line.

Inferior goods or commodities. Goods that have negative income elasticities; thus, the quantity demanded falls as incomes rise.

Informal transfers. See private transfers.

Inframarginal. The amount of a commodity transferred or made available at a subsidized price that is smaller than the amount that consumers would have chosen to purchase at the regular price.

Input indicators. Numerical measurements of the resources (such as staff and financing) used to provide program activities, tracked by the monitoring system.

Instrumental variables. Variables used in nonexperimental design program impact estimates to control for selection bias. These variables determine program participation but do not affect outcomes.

Labor disincentives. Features of program design that discourage labor effort by potential beneficiaries (who may reduce work effort in order to qualify for a benefit) or actual beneficiaries (who may choose a different combination of labor and leisure once they have income from the program benefit).

Last resort programs. Needs-based, usually means-tested, programs designed to help those who are not assisted, or not assisted enough to prevent poverty, by social insurance (pensions, unemployment insurance) or universal programs (child allowances, education, and the like).

Leakage. In discussions of targeting, the leakage rate is the proportion of those who are reached by the program who are classified as nonpoor (errors of inclusion). In discussions of accountability, the term is often used more broadly to include funds that, through various forms of negligence or malfeasance, are diverted from legitimate (though possibly nonpoor) beneficiaries to other uses.

Living standards measurement surveys (or multitopic household surveys). Multisubject, integrated surveys that gather data on a number of aspects of living standards to inform policy. The surveys cover spending, household composition, education, health, employment, fertility, nutrition, savings, agricultural activities, and other sources of income.

Management information system (MIS). Includes all the databases kept by the various program units in the performance of their functions—registry of beneficiaries, payments, and so on.

Means test. A targeting method based on income that seeks to collect comprehensive information on household income and/or wealth and verifies the information collected against independent sources.

Merit good. A commodity that society or policy makers think individuals should have on the basis of a norm other than respecting consumer preferences; education is a broad example of such a good, milk a narrower one.

Mitigation strategies. Risk management strategies implemented by individuals or households before a risk event occurs aimed at reducing the impact of a future risky event. For example, households may contribute to informal or formal insurance mechanisms that will help cover the cost of losses in the event of drought or flood.

Monitoring indicators. Numerical measurements of program inputs, processes, outputs, and outcomes typically expressed as levels (for example, the number of beneficiaries in the program as of a specific date), proportions (for instance, the percentage of beneficiaries paid on time), or ratios (such as the number of sessions held per amount spent). These indicators are tracked by the monitoring system.

Monitoring system. An essential management tool that regularly supplies information about how well a program is working so that program managers can take action to improve its implementation. Monitoring is a continuous process that takes place throughout a program's life.

Moral hazard. The prospect that people insulated from risk may behave differently from the way they would behave if they were fully exposed to the risk. For example, a person receiving unemployment insurance might search less strenuously for a job because the negative consequences of being uninsured are (partially) borne by the insurance.

Multivariate regression. A statistical technique used for the modeling and analysis of numerical data consisting of values of a dependent (response) variable and one or more independent (explanatory) variables.

Near cash transfers. Include food stamps, coupons, or vouchers that may be used by households to purchase food at authorized retail locations. These instruments can nominally or actually restrict recipients' choices to certain types of commodities but effectively alleviate the budget constraint in fungible ways.

Needs-based social assistance. Provide transfers for poor populations based on need.

Noncontributory pensions (or social pensions). Benefits paid to the elderly from tax-financed (rather than contribution-financed) sources and without regard to past participation in the labor market.

Nonexperimental design. A design for impact evaluation that uses multivariate statistical methods to account for differences between program beneficiaries and others.

Orphans and vulnerable children. Orphans (children who have lost one or both parents) and other groups of children who are more exposed to risks than their peers such as children with HIV and those with sick caregivers, street children, children in institutions, child soldiers, child prostitutes, and others who are not cared for in a family setting or who are involved in the worst forms of child labor.

Point-of-service (or point-of-sale) (POS) machines. Communication devices that do not contain any money, but have the capability of authorizing financial transactions carried out in retail stores, restaurants, hotels, or mobile locations.

Political costs of targeting. The costs arising if the degree of targeting negatively affects the program's budget.

Poverty analysis. Provides information on the level, severity, and depth of poverty; describes the characteristics of the poor; and identifies the factors associated with poverty. When repeated over time, poverty analysis depicts the trends, duration, and dynamics of poverty among particular groups.

Poverty and social impact analysis. Examination of the distributional impact of policy reforms on the well-being and welfare of various stakeholder groups, particularly the poor and vulnerable.

Poverty gap. The mean difference between the poverty line and household income divided by the poverty line (the nonpoor have a gap of zero) calculated over the whole population. The income gap multiplied by the headcount equals the poverty gap.

Poverty lines. Cutoff points separating the poor from the nonpoor. They can be monetary (for example, a certain level of consumption) or nonmonetary (for instance, a certain level of literacy). The use of multiple lines can help in distinguishing among different levels of poverty. Also see absolute poverty lines and relative poverty lines.

Prevention strategies. Subset of risk management strategies implemented by individuals or households before a risk event occurs to lessen the likelihood of an occurrence.

Price elasticity. Measures the responsiveness of the quantity demanded of a good to the changes in its price.

Private transfers. Transfers or exchanges between households of cash, food, clothing, informal loans, and assistance with work or child care.

Private costs of targeting. The costs to an applicant of applying for a program, including the time or cash costs of collecting the necessary information, traveling to the registration site and queuing for registration, complying with any preconditions, and so on.

Process evaluation. Also known as formative evaluation, implementation research, implementation analysis, or descriptive evaluation. Process evaluation documents, assesses, and explains how a program is being implemented.

Program evaluation. An external assessment of program effectiveness that uses specialized methods to determine whether a program meets certain standards, to estimate its net results or impact, and/or to identify whether the benefits the program generates outweigh its costs to society.

Proxy means test. A targeting method by which a score for applicant households is generated based on fairly easy-to-observe household characteristics, such as the location and quality of the household's dwelling, ownership of durable goods, demographic structure, education, and so on.

Public works programs (or workfare). Where income support for the poor is given in the form of wages (in either cash or food) in exchange for work effort. These programs typically provide short-term employment at low wages for unskilled and semiskilled workers on labor-intensive projects such as road construction and maintenance, irrigation infrastructure, reforestation, and soil conservation. Generally seen as a means of providing income support to the poor in critical times rather than as a way of getting the unemployed back into the labor market.

Quasi-experimental design. An evaluation design in which a comparison group is constructed using either matching (comparison with a population similar to program participants in terms of their essential characteristics) or reflexive comparison (comparison of the circumstances of program participants before and after their participation in the program).

Quantile. Generic term for equally sized groups of population resulting from ranking from the lowest to the highest on the basis of some characteristic such as household income. The groups resulting from dividing a population into five equally sized groups (each representing 20 percent of the population) are called quintiles; deciles result from division into 10 groups; and percentiles from division into 100 groups.

Quintile. One-fifth of an ordered population; for example, the poorest or richest one-tenth of the population. See quantile.

Relative poverty lines. Poverty lines defined in relation to the overall distribution of income or consumption in a country; for example, the poverty line could be set at 50 percent of the country's mean income or consumption.

Risk and vulnerability analysis. Complements poverty analysis by providing insights into the risks the poor face, as well as the size and characteristics of the population at risk of becoming poor in the event of a shock.

Risk management strategies. Strategies introduced by individuals, households, or communities dealing with risks that may temporarily or permanently affect their well-being. Ex ante strategies look to avoid the risk's occurrence (prevention strategies) or, if this is not possible, to reduce its impact (mitigation strategies). Ex post strategies are aimed at dealing with the shock once it occurs (coping strategies).

Safety nets. Noncontributory transfer programs targeted in some manner to the poor and those vulnerable to poverty and shocks. Analogous to the U.S. term "welfare" and the European term "social assistance."

Safety net system. A collection of programs, ideally well-designed and well-implemented, complementing each other as well as complementing other public or social policies.

School feeding programs. In-kind food transfers that provide meals or snacks for children at school to encourage their enrollment and improve their nutritional status and ability to pay attention in class.

Self-targeted programs (or self selection). Self-targeted programs are technically open to everyone, but are designed in such a way that take-up is expected to be much higher among the poor than the nonpoor, or the level of benefits is expected to be higher among the poor.

Shock. See covariate shock and idiosyncratic shock.

Social assistance. See safety nets.

Social costs of targeting. The costs arising when participation in a program carries with it some sort of stigma.

Social funds. Multisectoral programs that provide financing (usually grants) for small-scale public investments targeted at meeting the needs of the poor and vulnerable communities and at contributing to social capital and development at the local level.

Social pensions. See noncontributory pensions.

Social insurance. Contributory programs designed to help households insure themselves against sudden reductions in income. Types of social insurance include publicly provided or mandated insurance against unemployment, old age (pensions), disability, the death of the main provider, and sickness.

Social policy. Public policy dealing with social issues. Social policy aims to improve human welfare and to meet human needs for education, health, housing, and social protection.

Social protection. The set of public interventions aimed at supporting the poorer and more vulnerable members of society, as well as helping individuals, families, and communities manage risk. Social protection includes safety nets (social assistance), social insurance, labor market policies, social funds, and social services.

Social risk management. A framework that can be used to analyze the sources of vulnerability, how society manages risks, and the relative costs and benefits of various public interventions on household welfare. Risk management strategies include prevention, mitigation, and coping and may use government, for profit, or private informal mechanisms.

Social safety nets. See safety nets.

Stigma. Negative social labels attached to beneficiaries participating in targeted programs.

Subsidized untargeted sales. Provide universal access to food or other commodities at public distribution centers or designated private outlets on a first-come, first-served basis.

Supplementary feeding programs. In-kind food programs intended to provide food to mothers and young children.

Sustainability. The ability of a program to be continued over a long period.

Target group (or target population). The intended beneficiaries of program benefits.

Targeting. The effort to focus resources among those most in need of them.

Targeting assessment (or benefit incidence analysis). Describes how public spending is distributed across population groups, whether defined as deciles, poor versus nonpoor, geographic areas, ethnic groups, and so on.

Targeting errors. When program eligibility is based on imperfect information, program officials or the targeting rules they use may mistakenly identify nonpoor people as poor or poor people as nonpoor. When the former are admitted to a program, it is an error of inclusion; when the latter are denied access to the program, it is an error of exclusion.

Targeting method. Approach taken to identify the target group and thus determine eligibility for program benefits.

Transient poverty. Poverty among households that are poor in some years but not all. They may be poor in some years due to idiosyncratic or covariate temporary shocks ranging from an illness in the household or the loss of a job to drought or macroeconomic crisis.

Universal, indirect price support for food. Open-ended, untargeted subsidies that aim to lower the price the general population pays for staple foods.

Vulnerability. The likelihood or probability that a household will pass below the defined acceptable threshold of a given indicator and fall into poverty.

Vulnerable groups. Typically including the elderly, orphans, widows, people with disabilities, people with HIV/AIDS, refugees or internally displaced persons, among others. Vulnerable groups face special difficulties in supporting themselves because of some particular aspect of their situation.

Welfare dependency. See labor disincentives.

Workfare. See public works programs.

References

Abdulai, A., Christopher Barrett, and John Hoddinott. 2005. "Does Food Aid Really Have Disincentives Effects? New Evidence from Sub-Saharan Africa." *World Development* 33 (10): 1689–704.

Acosta, Olga, and Juan Carlos Ramírez. 2004. *Las redes de protección social: modelo incomplete*. Financiamiento del desarrollo 141 (LC/L.2067-P). Santiago: Economic Commission for Latin America and the Caribbean.

Adams, Lesley, and Paul Harvey. 2006. *Learning from Cash Responses to the Tsunami: Disbursement Mechanisms*. London: Overseas Development Institute, Humanitarian Policy Group.

Adams, Lesley, and Emebet Kebede. 2005. "Breaking the Poverty Cycle: A Case Study of Cash Interventions in Ethiopia." Background paper. London: Overseas Development Institute, Humanitarian Policy Group.

Adams, Richard H. 1998. "The Political Economy of the Food Subsidy System in Bangladesh." *Journal of Development Studies* 35 (1): 66–88.

———. 2000. "Self-Targeted Subsidies: The Distributional Impact of the Egyptian Food Subsidy System." Policy Research Working Paper. Washington, DC: World Bank.

Adato, Michelle, and Lawrence Haddad. 2001. "How Efficiently Do Public Works Programs Transfer Benefits to the Poor? Evidence from South Africa." Discussion Paper 108. Washington, DC: International Food Policy Research Institute.

———. 2002. "Targeting Poverty Programmes: Community-Based Public Works Programmes: Experience from South Africa." *Journal of Development Studies* 38 (3): 1–36.

Adato, Michelle, Lawrence Haddad, D. Horner, N. Ravjee, and R. Haywood. 1999. *From Works to Public Works: The Performance of Public Works in Western Cape Province, South Africa*. Washington, DC: International Food Policy Research Institute.

Adato, Michelle, Terence Roopnaraine, Natalia Smith, Elif Altinok, Nurfer Çelebioğlu, and Sema Cemal. 2007. *An Evaluation of the Conditional Cash Transfer Program in Turkey: Second Qualitative and Anthropological Study*. Washington, DC: International Food Policy Research Institute.

ADB (Asian Development Bank). 2006. *Social Protection Index for Committed Poverty Reduction*. Manila: ADB.

Adema, Willem. 2006. *Social Assistance Policy Development and the Provision of a Decent Level of Income in Selected OECD Countries*. OECD Social Employment and Migration Working Papers No. 38. Paris: Organisation for Economic Co-operation and Development.

Aheeyar, M. 2006. "Cash Delivery Mechanisms in Tsunami-Affected Districts of Sri Lanka." Background Paper. London: Overseas Development Institute, Humanitarian Policy Group.

Ahluwalia, Deepak. 1993. "Public Distribution of Food in India: Coverage, Targeting and Leakages." *Food Policy* 18 (2): 33–54.

Ahmad, Ehtisham, and Katherine Baer. 1997. "Colombia." In Teresa Ter-Minassian, ed., *Fiscal Federalism in Theory and Practice*, pp. 457–503. Washington, DC: International Monetary Fund.

Ahmad, Ehtisham, and Luc Leruth. 2000. *Indonesia—Implementing National Policies in a Decentralized Context: Special Purpose Programs to Protect the Poor.* Washington, DC: International Monetary Fund, Fiscal Affairs Department.

Ahmed, Akhter U. 2004a. "Assessing the Performance of Conditional Cash Transfer Programs for Girls and Boys in Primary and Secondary Schools in Bangladesh." Project report prepared for the World Bank. Washington, DC: International Food Policy Research Institute.

———. 2004b. *Impact of Feeding Children in School: Evidence From Bangladesh.* Washington, DC: International Food Policy Research Institute.

Ahmed, Akhter U., Michelle Adato, Ayse Kudat, Daniel Gilligan, and Refik Colasan. 2007. "Impact Evaluation of the Conditional Cash Transfer Program in Turkey: Final Report." Washington, DC: International Food Policy Research Institute.

Ahmed, Akhter U., and Mary Arends-Kuenning. 2003. "Do Crowded Classrooms Crowd Out Learning? Evidence from the Food for Education Program in Bangladesh." Discussion Paper 149. Washington, DC: International Food Policy Research Institute.

Ahmed, Akhter U., and Howarth E. Bouis. 2002. "Weighing What's Practical: Proxy Means Tests for Targeting Food Subsidies in Egypt." *Food Policy* 27 (5): 519–40.

Ahmed, Akhter U., H. Bouis, T. Gutner, and H. Lofgren. 2001. "The Egyptian Food Subsidy System: Structure, Performance, and Options for Reform." Research Report 119. Washington, DC: International Food Policy Research Institute.

Ahmed, Akhter U., and Carlo del Ninno. 2002. "The Food for Education Program in Bangladesh: An Evaluation of Its Impact on Educational Attainment and Food Security." Food Consumption and Nutrition Division Discussion Paper 138. Washington, DC: International Food Policy Research Institute.

Ahmed, Akhter U., Carlo del Ninno, and Omar Haider Chowdhury. 2004. "Investing in Children Through the Food for Education Program." In P. C. Dorosh, C. del Ninno, and Quazi Shahabuddin, eds., *The 1998 Floods and Beyond: Towards Comprehensive Food Security in Bangladesh*, pp. 271–311. Dhaka and Washington, DC: University Press and International Food Policy Research Institute.

Ahmed, Akhter U., Agnes R. Quisumbing, and John F. Hoddinott. 2007. "Relative Efficacy of Food and Cash Transfers in Improving Food Security and Livelihood of the Ultra Poor in Bangladesh." Draft. Washington, DC: International Food Policy Research Institute.

Ahmed, Akhter U., Shahidur Rashid, Manohar Sharma, and Sajjad Zohir. 2004. *Food Aid Distribution in Bangladesh: Leakage and Operational Performance.* FCND Discussion Paper 173. Washington, DC: International Food Policy Research Institute.

Ahmed, Akhter U., Sajjad Zohir, Shubh K. Kumar, and Omar Haider Chowdhury. 1995. "Bangladesh's Food-for-Work Program and Alternatives to Improve Food Security." In J. von Braun, ed., *Employment for Poverty Reduction and Food Security*, pp. 46–74. Washington, DC: International Food Policy Research Institute.

Ahmed, Ismail. 2006. "New Regulations Restrict Somalia Remittances." In *Sending Money Home: Can Remittances Reduce Poverty?* id21 insights 60. Brighton, UK: University of Sussex, Institute of Development Studies.

Ahmed, Raisuddin, Steven Haggblade, and Tawfiq-e-Elahi Chowdhury. 2000. *Out of the Shadow of Famine: Evolving Food Markets and Food Policy in Bangladesh*. Washington, DC: International Food Policy Research Institute.

Ahmed, Shaikh. 2005. "Delivery Mechanisms of Cash Transfer Programs to the Poor in Bangladesh." Social Protection Discussion Paper 0520. Washington, DC: World Bank.

Ainsworth, Martha, and Deon Filmer. 2002. "Poverty, AIDS, and Children's Schooling: A Targeting Dilemma." Policy Research Working Paper 2885. Washington, DC: World Bank.

Al-Baseir, Ali Kasim Ismail. 2003. *Final Report for Socio-Economic Impact Assessment: A Study for Assessing Project Impacts on Poverty Reduction, Employment and Community Livelihoods*. Sana'a, Republic of Yemen: Ministry of Planning and International Cooperation.

Alderman, Harold. 1988a. "Food Subsidies in Egypt: Benefit Distribution and Nutritional Effects." In Per Pinstrup-Andersen, ed., *Food Subsidies in Developing Countries: Costs, Benefits, and Policy Options*, pp. 171–82. Baltimore: Johns Hopkins University Press.

———.1988b. "The Twilight of Flour Rationing in Pakistan." *Food Policy* 13 (3): 245–56.

———. 1998. "Social Assistance in Albania." Living Standards Measurement Study. Working Paper 134. Washington, DC: World Bank.

———. 2001. "Multi-Tier Targeting of Social Assistance: The Role of Intergovernmental Transfers." *World Bank Economic Review* 15 (1): 33–53.

———. 2002a. "Do Local Officials Know Something We Don't? Decentralization of Targeted Transfers in Albania." *Journal of Public Economics* 83 (3): 375–404.

———. 2002b. "Subsidies as a Social Safety Net: Effectiveness and Challenges." Social Protection Discussion Paper 0224. Washington, DC: World Bank.

Alderman, Harold C., and Carlo del Ninno. 1999. "Poverty Issues for Zero Rating VAT in South Africa." *Journal of African Economies* 8 (2): 182–208.

Alderman, Harold, and Trina Haque. 2006. "Countercyclical Safety Nets for the Poor and Vulnerable." *Food Policy* 31 (4): 372–83.

Alderman, Harold, Jooseop Kim, and Peter F. Orazem. 2003. "Design, Evaluation, and Sustainability of Private Schools for the Poor: The Pakistan Urban and Rural Fellowship School Experiments." *Economics of Education Review* 22 (3): 265–74.

Alderman, H., and Kathy Lindert. 1998. "The Potential and Limitations of Self-Targeted Food Subsidies." *World Bank Research Observer* 13 (2): 213–29.

Alderman, Harold, and Joachim von Braun. 1984. *The Effect of the Egyptian Food Ration and Subsidy System on Income Distribution and Consumption*. Report 45. Washington, DC: International Food Policy Research Institute Research.

Alesina, Alberto F., Arnaud Devleeschauwer, William Easterly, Sergio Kurlat, and Romain T. Wacziarg. 2002. "Fractionalization." Research Working Paper 1959. Cambridge, MA: Harvard Institute.

Alesina, Alberto, and Edward L. Glaeser. 2004. *Fighting Poverty in the US and Europe*. Oxford, UK: Oxford University Press.

Alesina, Alberto, and Guido Tabellini. 2005. "Why Is Fiscal Policy Pro-cyclical?" NBER Working Paper 11600. Cambridge, MA: National Bureau of Economic Research.

Ali, Degan, A. Fanta Toure, and Tilleke Kiewied. 2005. *Cash Relief in a Contested Area: Lessons from Somalia*. Network Paper 50. London: Overseas Development Institute, Humanitarian Practice Network.

Ali, Sonia, and Richard Adams, Jr. 1996. "The Egyptian Food Subsidy System: Operation and Effects on Income Distribution." *World Development* 24 (November): 1777–91.

Almeida, Rita, and Emanuela Galasso. 2007. "Jump-Starting Self-Employment? Evidence among Welfare Participants in Argentina. Policy Research Working Paper 4270. Washington, DC: World Bank.

Alvarez, Carola. 2004. "Evaluating Safety Net Programs: The Family Allowance Program from Honduras and Oportunidades from Mexico." Presentation at the World Bank Social Safety Nets Core Course, November 29–December 10, 2004.

Angel-Urdinola, Diego, and Shweta Jain. 2006. "Do Subsidized Health Programs in Armenia Increase Utilization among the Poor?" Policy Research Working Paper 4017. Washington, DC: World Bank.

Angrist, Joshua, Eric Bettinger, Erik Bloom, Elizabeth King, and Michael Kremer. 2002. "Vouchers for Private Schooling in Colombia: Evidence from a Randomized Natural Experiment." *American Economic Review* 92 (5): 1535–58.

APEC (Asia and Pacific Economic Consortium). 2001. "Safety Nets and Response to Crisis: Lessons and Guidelines from Asia and Latin America." Unpublished report. Washington, DC: World Bank.

Araujo, M. Caridad. 2006. "Mongolia: Assessment of the Child Money Program and Properties of Its Targeting Methodology." Working Paper Series on Mongolia 2006-1. Washington, DC: World Bank.

Ardington, E., and F. Lund. 1995. "Pensions and Development: Social Security as Complementary to Programmes of Reconstruction and Development." *Development Southern Africa* 12 (4): 557–77.

Armas, Amparo. 2005. *Redes e institucionalización en Ecuador: Bono de Desarrollo Humano*. Santiago: United Nations.

Arriagada, Ana Maria, Tarcisio Castañeda, and Gillette Hall. 2000. "Managing Social Risks in Argentina." Washington, DC: World Bank, Human Development Department, Social Protection Group.

Arribas-Baños, Maria, and Cesar Baldeón. 2007. "Strengthening the MIS in Social Protection Programs: A Toolkit." Presentation to Workshop on Fraud and Error Control in Social Protection Programs, May 16–17, 2007, Washington, DC.

Arulpragasam, Jehan. 2006a. "An East Asian Case: Indonesia's CCT Pilot." PowerPoint presentation, Poverty Reduction and Economic Management Network Learning Week, World Bank, Washington, DC, April 23, 2006.

———. 2006b. "Making Expenditures Work for the Poor in Indonesia: The Case of Reallocating Indonesia's Fuel Subsidy." PowerPoint presentation, Cost-Benefit Analysis Course, World Bank, Washington, DC, May 12, 2006.

Attanasio, Orazio, Erich Battistin, Emla Fitzsimons, Alice Mesnard, and Marcos Vera-Hernández. 2005. "How Effective Are Conditional Cash Transfers? Evidence From Colombia." IFS Briefing Note 54. London: Institute for Fiscal Studies.

Attanasio, Orazio, Emla Fitzsimons, Ana Gomez, Diana Lopez, Costas Meghir, and Ana Santiago. 2006. *Child Education and Work Choices in the Presence of a Conditional Cash Transfer Programme in Rural Colombia*. London: Institute for Fiscal Studies.

Attanasio, Orazio, Costas Meghir, and Ana Santiago. 2005. "Education Choices in Mexico: Using a Structural Model and a Randomized Experiment to Evaluate Progresa." Unpublished manuscript. London: Institute for Fiscal Studies.

Atkinson, Anthony B. 1995. *Incomes and the Welfare State: Essays on Britain and Europe*. Cambridge, UK: Cambridge University Press.

———. 1999 *The Economic Consequences of Rolling Back the Welfare State*. Cambridge, MA: Massachusetts Institute of Technology Press.

Audibert, M., and J. Mathonnat. 2000. "Cost Recovery in Mauritania: Initial Lessons." *Health Policy and Planning* 15 (1): 66–75.

Ayala, Francisco. 2006a. "Familias en Acción, Colombia." Policy Brief 2. London: Overseas Development Institute.

———. 2006b. "The Programme for Advancement through Health and Education (PATH), Jamaica." Policy Brief 4. London: Overseas Development Institute.

Ayala, Francisco V., and Cristina Endara. 2005. "Cash Transfers: Lessons Learnt from the Design and Implementation of a Conditional Cash Transfer Programme. Jamaican Case: Programme for Advancement through Health and Education." Policy case study draft prepared for the Inter-Regional Inequity Facility. Quito.

Bacon, Robert, and Masami Kojima. 2006. "Phasing Out Subsidies: Recent Experiences with Fuel in Developing Countries." Financial and Private Sector Policy Note 310. Washington, DC: World Bank.

Baig, Taimur, Amine Mati, David Coady, and Joseph Ntamatungiro. 2007. "Domestic Petroleum Product Prices and Subsidies: Recent Developments and Reform Strategies." Working paper. Washington, DC: International Monetary Fund.

Baker, Judy L. 2000. *Evaluating the Impact of Development Projects on Poverty: A Handbook for Practitioners*. Washington, DC: World Bank.

Baldacci, Emanuele. 2006. "Managing Economy-Wide Shocks: Lessons for Social Protection in Latin America and Caribbean Countries." Unpublished paper. Washington, DC: World Bank, Latin America and the Caribbean Region, Social Protection Unit.

Baldacci, Emanuele, Arye L. Hillman, and Naoko C. Kojo. 2004. "Growth, Governance, and Fiscal Policy Transmission Channels in Low-Income Countries." *European Journal of Political Economy* 20 (3): 517–49.

Barham, Tania. 2005a. "The Impact of the Mexican Conditional Cash Transfer on Immunization Rates." Final report. Berkeley, CA: University of California-Berkeley.

———. 2005b. "Providing a Healthier Start to Life: The Impact of Conditional Cash Transfers on Infant Mortality." http://ssrn.com/abstract=1023786.

Barr, David. 2007. "Reducing Fraud and Error in the UK: What It Takes?" Presentation at the World Bank Workshop on Fraud & Error Control in Safety Net Programs, Washington, DC, May 16–17, 2007.

Barr, Nicholas. 2004. *Economics of the Welfare State.* Oxford, UK: Oxford University Press.

Barrett, Christopher B. 2002. "Food Security and Food Assistance Programs." In B. L. Gardner and G. C. Rausser, eds., *Handbook of Agricultural Economics*, 2nd ed., vol. 2, pp. 2103–90. Amsterdam: Elsevier.

Barrett, Christopher, and Daniel Maxwell. 2005. *Food Aid after Fifty Years: Recasting Its Role.* London: Routledge Press.

Barrientos, Armando. 2004. "Cash Transfers for Older People Reduce Poverty and Inequality." Draft background paper for the *World Development Report 2006: Equity and Development.* Manchester, UK: University of Manchester, Institute for Development Policy and Management.

Barrientos, Armando, and Jocelyn DeJong. 2004. *Child Poverty and Cash Transfers.* Report 4. London: Save the Children and the Childhood Poverty Research and Policy Centre.

Barrientos, Armando, Monica Ferreira, Mark Gorman, Amanda Heslop, Helena Legido-Quigley, Peter Lloyd-Sherlock, Valerie Møller, João Saboia, and Maria Lucia Teixeira Werneck. 2003. *Non-Contributory Pensions and Poverty Prevention: A Comparative Study of South Africa and Brazil.* London: HelpAge International and Institute for Development Policy and Management.

Barrientos, Armando, and Peter Lloyd-Sherlock. 2002. *Non-Contributory Pensions and Social Protection.* Issues in Social Protection Series. Geneva: International Labour Organisation.

Batjargal, Uranbileg. 2006. *The Newest Poverty Targeting Program in Mongolia—Child Money Program: Evaluation and Assessment of Its Targeting Methodology.* Tokyo: University of Tokyo, Graduate School of Economics.

Baulch, Bob, and John Hoddinott. 2000. "Economic Mobility and Poverty Dynamics in Developing Countries." *Journal of Development Studies* 37 (6): 1–24.

Beecroft, Erik, Wang Lee, and David Long. 2003. *The Indiana Welfare Reform Evaluation: Five-Year Impacts, Implementation, Costs and Benefits.* Cambridge, MA: Abt Associates.

Behrman, Jere R., Harold Alderman, and John Hoddinott. 2004. "Hunger and Malnutrition." Paper prepared for the Copenhagen Consensus 2004.

Behrman, Jere, and John Hoddinott. 2000. "An Evaluation of the Impact of PROGRESA on Pre-School Child Height." Washington, DC: International Food Policy Research Institute.

———. 2005. "Programme Evaluation with Unobserved Heterogeneity and Selective Implementation: The Mexican PROGRESA Impact on Child Nutrition." *Oxford Bulletin of Economics and Statistics* 67 (4): 547–69.

Behrman, Jere R., and Mark Rosenzweig. 2001. "The Returns to Increasing Body Weight." Working Paper No. 01-052. Philadelphia: University of Pennsylvania, Penn Institute for Economic Research.

Behrman, Jere R., and Emmanuel Skoufias. 2006. "Mitigating Myths about Policy Effectiveness: Evaluation of Mexico's Antipoverty and Human Resource Investment Program." *Annals of the American Academy of Political and Social Science* 606 (1): 244–75.

Belkacem, Laabas 2001. *Poverty Dynamics in Algeria*. Kuwait: Arab Planning Institute.

Benson, Todd. 2002. *The Poverty Targeting Efficiency of Public Works Programs: An Application of Poverty Mapping in Malawi*. Washington, DC: International Food Policy Research Institute.

Bertrand, M., Mullainathan Sendhil, and Douglas Miller. 2003. "Public Policy and Extended Families: Evidence from Pensions in South Africa." *World Bank Economic Review* 17 (1): 27–50.

Bertranou, Fabio M., Carmen Solorio, and Wouter van Ginneken, eds. 2002. *Pensiones no contributivas y asistenciales: Argentina, Brazil, Chile, Costa Rica y Uruguay*. Santiago: Oficina Internacional del Trabajo. www.oitchile.cl/pdf/publicaciones/pro/pro012.pdf.

Besley, Timothy, Robin Burgess, and Imran Rasul. 2003. "Benchmarking Government Provision of Social Safety Nets." Social Protection Discussion Paper 0315. Washington, DC: World Bank.

Betcherman, Gordon, Karina Olivas, and Amit Dar. 2004. "Impacts of Active Labor Market Programs: New Evidence from Evaluations with Particular Attention to Developing and Transition Countries." Social Protection Discussion Paper 0402. Washington, DC: World Bank.

Bettinger, Eric. 2005. "Private School Vouchers in Colombia." Draft paper prepared for the conference, Mobilizing the Private Sector for Public Education, World Bank and Kennedy School of Government, Harvard University, Cambridge, MA, October 5-6, 2005.

Bezuneh, Mesfin, Brady Deaton, and George Norton. 1988. "Food Aid Impacts in Rural Kenya." *American Journal of Agricultural Economics* 70 (1): 181–91.

Bienen, H., and M. Gersovitz. 1986. "Economic Stabilization, Conditionality, and Political Stability." *International Organization* 39 (4): 729–54.

Birks Sinclair & Associates Ltd. 2004. "Evaluation of the Implementation of the Minimum Income Guarantee (Law 416/2001)." Draft final report for U.K. Department for International Development and World Bank. Durham, UK: Mountjoy Research Centre.

Bitrán, Ricardo. 2002. "Waivers, Exceptions, and Implementation Issues under User Fees for Health Care: Equity Funds and Other Waiver Systems in Cambodia: A Case Study." Presentation at the World Bank seminar on Protecting the Poor: User Fees for Health Services, Washington, DC, June 26, 2002.

Bitrán, Ricardo, and Ursula Giedion. 2003. "Waivers and Exemptions for Health Services in Developing Countries." Social Protection Discussion Paper 0308. Washington, DC: World Bank.

Bitrán, Ricardo, and C. Muñoz. 2000. *Targeting Methodologies: Conceptual Approach and Analysis of Experiences*. The Regional Initiative of Health Sector Reform for Latin America and the Caribbean. Washington, DC: Partnerships for Health Reform Project.

Bitrán, Ricardo, Juan Muñoz, Paulina Aguad, Mario Navarrete, and Gloria Ubilla. 2000. "Equity in the Financing of Social Security for Health in Chile." *Health Policy* 50 (3): 171–96.

Bitrán, Ricardo, Vincent Turbat, Bruno Meessen, and Wim Van Damme. 2003. *Preserving Equity in Health in Cambodia: Health Equity Funds and Prospects for Replication*. Washington, DC: World Bank Institute.

Blank, Rebecca M. 2002. "Can Equity and Efficiency Complement Each Other?" NBER Working Paper 8820. Cambridge, MA: National Bureau of Economic Research.

———. 2004. "What Did the 1990s Welfare Reform Accomplish?" Revised version. Paper prepared for the "Berkeley Symposium on Poverty, the Distribution of Income, and Public Policy: A Conference Honoring Eugene Smolensky," Berkeley, CA, December 12–13, 2003.

Blau, David. 2003. "Child Care Subsidy Programs." In Robert Moffitt, ed., *Means-Tested Transfer Programs in the United States*, pp. 443–515. Chicago: University of Chicago Press.

Blomquist, John. 2003. "Impact Evaluation of Social Programs: A Policy Perspective." Draft. Washington, DC: World Bank, Social Protection Unit.

Bobonis, Gustavo, and Frederico Finan. 2005. "Endogenous Peer Effects in School Participation." Working paper. Berkeley, CA: University of California at Berkeley.

Bose, Niloy, Jill Ann Holman, and Kyriakos C. Neanidis. 2004. "The Optimal Public Expenditure Financing Policy: Does the Level of Economic Development Matter? *Economic Inquiry* 45 (3): 433–52.

Bourguignon, François, Francisco Ferreira, and Phillippe Leite. 2003. "Conditional Cash Transfers, Schooling, and Child Labor: Micro-Simulation Brazil's Bolsa Escola Program." *World Bank Economic Review* 17 (2): 229–54.

Braithwaite, Jeanine, Christian Grootaert, and Branko Milanovic. 1999. *Poverty and Social Assistance in Transition Countries*. New York: St. Martin's Press.

Braithwaite Jeanine, and Daniel Mont. 2008. "Disability and Poverty: A Survey of World Bank Poverty Assessments and Implications." Social Protection Discussion Paper 0805. Washington, DC: World Bank.

Braun, Miguel, and Luciano Di Gresia. 2003. "Towards Effective Social Insurance in Latin America: The Importance of Countercyclical Fiscal Policy." Paper presented at Dealing with Risk: Implementing Employment Policies Under Fiscal Constraints seminar, Milan, March 23, 2003.

Braun-Munzinger, Corinna. 2005. "Education Vouchers: An International Comparison." Working paper. New Delhi: Centre for Civil Society.

Breunig R., I. Dasgupta, C. Gundersen, and P. Pattanaik. 2001. "Explaining the Food Stamp Cash-Out Puzzle." Food Assistance and Nutrition Research Report 12. Washington, DC: U.S. Department of Agriculture, Economic Research Service, Food and Rural Economics Division.

Brown, Peter. 2002. *Poverty and Leadership in the Later Roman Empire*. London: University Press of New England.

Brueckner, J. K. 2000. "Welfare Reform and the Race to the Bottom: Theory and Evidence." *Southern Economic Journal* 66 (January): 505–25.

Budlender, Debbie, Solange Rosa, and Katherine Hall. 2005. *At All Costs? Applying the Means Test for the Child Support Grant*. Cape Town: University of Cape Town, Children's Institute.

Burt, Martha, and Harry Hatry. 2005. "Monitoring Program Performance." Presentation at the World Bank, Training Course on Monitoring and Evaluating Social Programs, Washington, DC, July 26, 2005.

Burtless, Gary. 1986. "The Work Response to a Guaranteed Income: A Survey of Experimental Evidence." In Alicia H. Munnell, ed., *Lessons from the Income Maintenance Experiments*. Washington, DC: Federal Reserve Bank of Boston and Brookings Institution.

Butler, J. S., and J. E. Raymond. 1996. "The Effect of the Food Stamp Program on Nutrient Intake." *Economic Inquiry* 34 (4): 781–88.

Caldés, Natàlia, David Coady, and John A. Maluccio. 2006. "The Cost of Poverty Alleviation Transfer Programs: A Comparative Analysis of Three Programs in Latin America." *World Development* 34 (5): 818–37.

Camargo, José Márcio, and Francisco H. G. Ferreira. 2001. "Single Social Benefit: A Proposal for Social Policy Reform in Brazil." Discussion Paper 443. Rio de Janeiro: Pontifical Catholic University of Rio de Janeiro, Department of Economy.

Cameron, Lisa. 2002. "Did Social Safety Net Scholarships Reduce Drop-Out Rates during the Indonesian Economic Crisis?" Policy Research Working Paper 2800. Washington, DC: World Bank.

Cardoso, Eliana, and Andre Portela Souza. 2004. *The Impact of Cash Transfers on Chile Labor and School Attendance in Brazil.* Paper 04-W07. Nashville: Vanderbilt University, Department of Economics.

Carter, Michael R., and Christopher B. Barrett. 2006. "The Economics of Poverty Traps and Persistent Poverty: An Asset-Based Approach." *Journal of Development Studies* 42 (2): 178–99.

Carter, Michael R., Peter D. Little, Trevodaj Morgues, and Workneh Negatu. 2004."Shocks, Sensitivity and Resilience: Tracking the Economic Impacts of Environmental Disaster on Assets in Ethiopia and Honduras." BASIS Research Program on Poverty, Inequality and Development. Washington, DC: U.S. Agency for International Development.

———. 2007. "Poverty Traps and Natural Disasters in Honduras and Ethiopia." *World Development* 35 (5): 835–56.

Carvalho, Ireneu Evangelista. 2000a. "Elderly Women and Their Living Arrangements in Brazil." Unpublished manuscript. Cambridge, MA: Massachusetts Institute of Technology.

———. 2000b. "Household Income as a Determinant of Child Labor and School Enrollment in Brazil: Evidence from a Social Security Reform." Draft. Cambridge, MA: Massachusetts Institute of Technology, Department of Economics.

Case, Anne. 2001. "Does Money Protect Health Status? Evidence from South African Pensions." NBER Working Paper 8495. Cambridge, MA: National Bureau of Economic Research.

Case, Anne, and Angus Deaton. 1998. "Large Cash Transfers to the Elderly." *Economic Journal* 108 (45): 1330–61.

Case, Anne, Victoria Hosegood, and Frances Lund. 2005. "The Reach of the South African Child Support Grant: Evidence from Kwa-Zulu Natal." *Development Southern Africa* 22 (4): 467–82.

Case, Anne, Christina Paxson, and Joseph Ableidinger. 2004. "Orphans in Africa: Parental Death, Poverty, and School Enrollment." *Demography* 41 (3): 483–508.

Castañeda, Tarcisio. 1998. *The Design, Implementation and Impact of Food Stamp Programs in Developing Countries.* Washington, DC: World Bank.

Castañeda, Tarcisio, and Kathy Lindert. 2005. "Designing and Implementing Household Targeting Systems: Lessons from Latin America and the United States." Social Protection Discussion Paper 0532. Washington, DC: World Bank.

Castañeda, Tarsicio, and Kathy Lindert, with Bénédicte de la Brière, Luisa Fernandez, Celia Hubert, Osvaldo Larrañaga, Mónica Orozco, and Roxana Viquez. 2005. "Designing and Implementing Household Targeting Systems: Lessons from Latin American and the United States." Social Protection Discussion Paper 0526. Washington, DC: World Bank.

Chacaltana, Juan J. 2003. *Impacto del programa "A Trabajar Urbano": Ganancias de ingreso y utilidad de las obras.* Final report. Lima: Centro de Estudios para el Desarrollo y la Participación.

Chamberlin, Jeffrey. 2004. "Comparisons of US and Foreign Military Spending: Data from Selected Public Sources." Order Code RL32209. Report for Congress. Washington, DC: Congressional Research Service.

Chaudhury, Nazmul, Jeffrey Hammer, and Edmundo Murrugarra. 2003. "The Effects of a Fee-Waiver Program on Health Care Utilization among the Poor: Evidence from Armenia." Policy Research Working Paper 2952. Washington, DC: World Bank.

Chen, Shaohua, and Martin Ravallion. 2007. "Absolute Poverty Measures for the Developing World." Policy Research Working Paper 4211. Washington, DC: World Bank.

Children's Institute. 2006. *South African Child Gauge.* Cape Town: University of Cape Town.

Chirwa Ephraim, Anna McCord, Peter Mvula, and Caroline Pinder. 2004. "Study to Inform the Selection of an Appropriate Wage Rate for Public Works Programmes in Malawi." Unpublished report prepared for the Government of Malawi, National Safety Nets Unit.

Chowdhury, J. 2005. "Disability and Chronic Poverty: An Empirical Study on Bangladesh." M.Phil. thesis. Oxford, UK: Oxford University.

Chowdhury, Tawfiq-e-Elahi, and Steven Haggblade. 2000. "Dynamics and Politics of Policy Change." In Raisuddin Ahmed, Steven Haggblade, and Tawfiq-e-Elahi Chowdhury, eds., *Coming Out of the Shadow of Famine: Evolving Food Markets and Food Policy in Bangladesh*, pp. 165–88. Baltimore: Johns Hopkins University Press.

Chronic Poverty Research Centre. 2004. *Chronic Poverty Report 2004–05.* Manchester, UK: University of Manchester, Institute for Development Policy and Management.

Chu, Ke-young, Hamid Davoodi, and Sanjeev Gupta. 2000. "Income Distribution and Tax and Government Social Spending Policies in Developing Countries." Working Paper WP/00/62. Washington, DC: International Monetary Fund.

Chu, Ke-young, and Sanjeev Gupta. 1998a. "Economic Reforms, Social Safety Nets, and the Budget in Transition Economies." In Ke-young Chu and Sanjeev Gupta, eds., *Social Safety Nets: Issues and Recent Experiences*, pp. 63–93. Washington, DC: International Monetary Fund.

———. eds. 1998b. *Social Safety Nets: Issues and Recent Experiences.* Washington, DC: International Monetary Fund.

Cichon, Michael, and Krzysztof Hagemejer. 2006. "Social Security for All—Investing in Global Social and Economic Development: A Consultation." Issues in Social Protection Discussion Paper 16. Geneva: International Labour Office.

Clay, Daniel C., Daniel Molla, and Debebe Habtewold. 1999. "Food Aid Targeting in Ethiopia: A Study of Who Needs It and Who Gets It." *Food Policy* 24 (4): 391–409.

Coady, David. 2002. "Social Safety Nets, Human Capital and the Poor: Evidence from Recent Program Evaluations." Paper prepared for the Asian Development Bank and Inter-American Development Bank Workshop on Social Protection for the Poor in Asia and Latin America: Concepts and Experiences, Manila, October 21-25, 2002.

———. 2004. "Designing and Evaluating Social Safety Nets: Theory, Evidence, and Policy Conclusions." Food Consumption and Nutrition Division Discussion Paper 172. Washington, DC: International Food Policy Research Institute.

Coady, David, Paul Dorosh, and Bart Minten. 2008. "Evaluating Alternative Approaches to Poverty Alleviation: Rice Tariffs Versus Targeted Transfers in Madagascar." Working Paper 08/9. Washington, DC: International Monetary Fund.

Coady, David, Moataz El-Said, Robert Gillingham, Roland Kpodar, Paulo Medas, and David Newhouse. 2006. "The Fiscal and Social Costs of Fuel Subsidies: Evidence from Bolivia, Ghana, Jordan, Mali and Sri Lanka." Review paper. Washington, DC: International Monetary Fund.

Coady, David, and Francisco Ferreira. 2003. "Proactive States: Smart Instruments for Redistribution." In *Inequality and the State in Latin America and the Caribbean*, pp. 361–95. Washington, DC: World Bank.

Coady, David, Margaret Grosh, and John Hoddinott. 2003. "Targeting Outcomes, Redux." Food Consumption and Nutrition Division Discussion Paper 144. Washington, DC: International Food Policy Research Institute.

———. 2004. *Targeting of Transfers in Developing Countries: Review of Lessons and Experience*. Regional and Sectoral Studies. Washington, DC: World Bank.

Coady, David, and Rebecca Lee Harris. 2004. "Evaluating Targeted Cash Transfer Programs: A General Equilibrium Framework with an Application to Mexico." Research Report 137. Washington, DC: International Food Policy Research Institute.

Combariza, Rita. 2006. "The Impact of the Conditionalities of Familias en Acción." Paper presented at the Third International Conference on Conditional Cash Transfers, Istanbul, June 26–30, 2006.

Conning, Jonathon, and Michael Kevane. 2001. "Community Based Targeting Mechanisms for Social Safety Nets." Social Protection Discussion Paper 0102. Washington, DC: World Bank.

Coudouel, Aline, Kene Ezemenari, Margaret Grosh, and Lynn Sherburne-Benz. 2002. "Social Protection." In *A Sourcebook for Poverty Reduction Strategies*, pp. 164–200. Washington, DC: World Bank.

Coudouel, Aline, and Stefano Paternostro. 2006a. *Analyzing the Distributional Impact of Reforms: A Practitioner's Guide to Trade, Monetary and Exchange Rate Policy, Utility Provision, Agricultural Markets, Land Policy and Education*, vol. 1. Washington, DC: World Bank.

———. 2006b. *Analyzing the Distributional Impact of Reforms: A Practitioner's Guide to Pension, Health, Labor Markets, Public Sector Downsizing, Taxation, Decentralization, and Macroeconomic Modeling*, vol. 2. Washington, DC: World Bank.

———. 2006c. *Poverty and Social Impact Analysis of Reforms: Lessons and Examples from Implementation*. Washington, DC: World Bank.

Cox, Donald, and Emmanuel Jimenez.1997. "Coping with Apartheid: Inter-Household Transfers over the Life-Cycle in South Africa." Draft working paper. Boston College and World Bank.

Crepinsek, Mary Kay, and Nancy R. Burstein. 2004. *Maternal Employment and Children's Nutrition*. Bethesda, MD: Abt Associates, Inc.

Creti, Pantaleo, and Susanne Jaspars. 2006. *Cash-Transfer Programming in Emergencies*. Oxford, UK: Oxfam.

Currie, Janet. 2003. "US Food and Nutritional Programs." In Robert Moffitt, ed., *Means-Tested Transfer Programs in the United States*, pp. 199–259. Chicago: University of Chicago Press.

Dahlberg, Matz, and Karin Eadmark. 2004. "Is There a Race to the Bottom in Setting Welfare Benefit Levels? Evidence from a Policy Intervention." Working Paper 2004: 19. Uppsala, Sweden: Uppsala University, Department of Economics.

Daly, Anne, and George Fane. 2002. "Anti-Poverty Programs in Indonesia." *Bulletin of Indonesian Economic Studies* 38 (3): 309–29.

Datt, Gaurav, and Martin Ravallion. 1992. "Behavioral Responses to Workfare Programs: Evidence for Rural India." Living Standards Measurement Study Working Paper. Washington, DC: World Bank.

———. 1994. "Transfer Benefits from Public Works Employment: Evidence for Rural India." *Economic Journal* 104 (427): 1346–69.

Datt, Gaurav, Ellen Payongayong, James L. Garrett, and Marie Ruel. 1997. "The GAPVU Cash Transfer Program in Mozambique: An Assessment." Food Consumption and Nutrition Division Discussion Paper 36. Washington, DC: International Food Policy Research Institute.

Datta, Gora. 2006. "The Dream: A Smooth and Efficient CCT. Possible Uses of ICT." CAL2CAL Corporation. Paper presented at the Third International Conference on Conditional Cash Transfers, Istanbul, June 26–30, 2006.

Davis, Jeffrey M., Rolando Ossowsky, and Annalisa Fedelino. 2003. *Fiscal Policy Formulation and Implementation in Oil-Producing Countries.* Washington, DC: International Monetary Fund.

Dawn. 2003. "Bait ul Maal Rejects 50pc Recommendations of Politicians." November 5.

de Andraca, Ana María. 2006. "Programas des Becas Estudiantiles. Experiencias latinoamericanas." Instituto Internacional de Planeamiento de la Educación Research papers. Paris: United Nations Educational, Scientific and Cultural Organization.

Deaton, Angus. 1989. "Rice Prices and Income Distribution in Thailand: A Non-Parametric Analysis." *Economic Journal* 99 (Supplement): 1–39.

Deaton, Angus, and John Muellbauer. 1980. *Economics and Consumer Behaviour.* Cambridge, UK: Cambridge University Press.

Deaton, Angus, and Salman Zaidi. 2002. "Guidelines for Constructing Consumption Aggregates for Welfare Analysis." Living Standards Measurement Study Working Paper 135. Washington, DC: World Bank.

de Brauw, Alan, and John Hoddinott. 2008. "Must Conditional Cash Transfer Programs Be Conditioned to Be Effective? The Impact of Conditioning Transfers on School Enrollment in Mexico." Discussion Paper 00757. Washington, DC: International Food Policy Research Institute.

De Ferranti, David, Guillermo Perry, Francisco Ferreira, and Michael Walton. 2004. *Inequality in Latin America: Breaking with History?* Washington, DC: World Bank.

De Ferranti, David, Guillermo E. Perry, Indermit Gill, and Luiz Serven. 2000. *Securing Our Future in a Global Economy.* Latin American and Caribeean Studies. Washington, DC: World Bank.

Deininger, Klaus, Anja Crommelynck, and Gloria Kempaka. 2002. "Long-Term Welfare and Investment Impact of AIDS-Related Changes in Family Composition: Evidence from Uganda." Social Protection Discussion Paper 0207. Washington, DC: World Bank.

Deininger, Klaus, and Paul Mpuga. 2004. "Economic and Welfare Effects of the Abolition of Health User Fees: Evidence from Uganda." Policy Research Working Paper 3276. Washington, DC: World Bank.

de Janvry, Alain, Frederico Finan, Elisabeth Sadoulet, Donald Nelson, Kathy Lindert, Bénédicte de la Brière, and Peter Lanjouw. 2005. "Brazil's Bolsa Escola Program: The Role of Local Governance in Decentralized Implementation." Social Protection Discussion Paper 0542. Washington, DC: World Bank.

de Janvry Alain, Frederico Finan, and Elisabeth Sadoulet, and Renos Vakis. 2006. "Can Conditional Cash Transfer Programs Serve as Safety Nets in Keeping Children at School and from Working When Exposed to Shocks?" *Journal of Development Economics* 79 (2): 349–73.

de Janvry, Alain, and Elisabeth Sadoulet. 2006. "When to Use a CCT Versus a Conditional Cash Transfer Approach." Comment on a presentation at the Third International Conference on Conditional Cash Transfers, Istanbul, June 26–30, 2006.

de Janvry, Alain, Elisabeth Sadoulet, Pantelis Solomon, and Renos Vakis. 2006. "Uninsured Risk and Asset Protection: Can Conditional Cash Transfer Programs Serve as Safety Nets?" Social Protection Discussion Paper 0604, Washington, DC: World Bank.

Dejardin, Amelita King. 1996. "Public Works Programmes—A Strategy for Poverty Alleviation: The Gender Dimension." Issues in Development Discussion Paper 10. Geneva: International Labour Office.

de Jong, Philip R. 2003. "New Directions in Disability (Benefit) Policy: The Dutch Experience." In Raija Gould and Sini Laitinen-Kuikka, eds., *Current Trends in Disability Pensions in Europe,: Proceedings from a Seminar Held in Helsinki on 8th April 2003*, pp. 49–70. Helsinki: Finnish Centre for Pensions.

de Koning, Jaap, Mariana Kotzeva, and Stoyan Tzvetkov. 2007. "Mid-Term Evaluation of the Bulgarian Programme 'From Social Assistance to Employment.'" In Jaap de Koning, ed., *Employment and Training Policies in Central and Eastern Europe*. Amsterdam: Dutch University Press.

Delgado, G. C., and J. C. Cardoso, eds. 2000. *A Universalização de Direitos Sociais no Brasil: a Prêvidencia Rural nos anos 90*. Brasilia: Instituto de Pesquisa Econômica Aplicada.

Delgado, Christopher, and Thomas Reardon. 1988. "Why the Urban Poor Pay More for Their Grain: Transaction Derived Cereal Prices in Burkina Faso." Paper presented at the American Association of Agricultural Economics Annual Meeting, July 1988.

del Ninno, Carlo, and Francisco Ayala. 2006. "Basic Operations—Payments." Paper presented at the Third International Conference on Conditional Cash Transfers, Istanbul, June 26–30, 2006.

del Ninno, Carlo, and Paul Dorosh. 2003. "Impacts of In-Kind Transfers on Household Food Consumption: Evidence from Targeted Food Programmes in Bangladesh." *Journal of Development Studies* 40 (1): 48–78.

del Ninno, Carlo, Paul Dorosh, and Lisa Smith. 2003. "Public Policy, Market and Household Coping Strategies in Bangladesh: Avoiding a Food Security Crisis Following the 1998 Floods." *World Development* 31 (7): 1221–28.

del Ninno, Carlo, Paul Dorosh, and Kalanidhi Subbarao. 2005. "Food Aid and Food Security in the Short- and Long Run: Country Experience from Asia and Sub-Saharan Africa." Social Protection Discussion Paper 0538. Washington, DC: World Bank.

———. 2007. "Food Aid, Domestic Policy and Food Security: Contrasting Experiences from South Asia and sub-Saharan Africa." *Food Policy* 32 (2007): 413–35.

Del Rosso, Joy Miller. 1999. *School Feeding Programs—Improving Effectiveness and Increasing the Benefit to Education: A Guide for Program Managers*. Oxford, UK: UK Partnership for Child Development.

Del Rosso, Joy Miller, and Tonia Marek. 1996. *Class Action: Improving School Performance in the Developing World through Better Health and Nutrition*. Washington, DC: World Bank.

Demery, Lionel. 2000. *Benefit Incidence: A Practitioner's Guide.* Washington, DC: World Bank, Africa Region, Poverty and Social Development Group.

———. 2003 "Analyzing the Incidence of Public Spending." In François Bourguignon and Luiz. A. Pereira da Silva, eds., *The Impact of Economic Policies on Poverty and Income Distribution. Evaluation Techniques and Tools,* pp. 41–68. Washington, DC: World Bank.

de Neubourg, Chris. 2002. "Incentives and the Role of Institutions in the Provision of Social Safety Nets." Social Protection Discussion Paper 0226. Washington, DC: World Bank.

———. 2008. "Social Assistance Programs in the EU: Its Role within Social Protection, Differences and Similarities and Coverage." Presentation at the course For Protection and Promotion: The Design and Implementation of Effective Social Safety Nets, World Bank, Washington, DC, February 25–March 7, 2008.

de Neubourg, Chris, Julie Castonguay, and Keetie Roelen. 2007. "Social Safety Nets and Targeted Social Assistance: Lessons from the European Experience." Social Protection Discussion Paper 0718. Washington, DC: World Bank.

De Onis, Mercedes, Monika Blössner, Elaine Borghi, Edward A. Frongillo, and Richard Morris. 2004. "Estimates of Global Prevalence of Childhood Underweight in 1990 and 2015." *Journal of the American Medical Association* 291 (21): 2600–6.

Departamento Nacional de Planeación. 2004. *Documento Programa Empleo en Acción: Condiciones Inciales de los Beneficiarios e Impactos de Corto Plazo.* Evaluación de Políticas Públicas 2. Bogota: Departamento Nacional de Planeación.

Department of Public Works. Various years. *Quarterly Reports.* Pretoria: Government of South Africa.

Department of Social Development. 2006. *Report on Incentive Structures of Social Assistance Grants in South Africa.* Pretoria: Republic of South Africa.

Dercon, Stefan. 1997. "Wealth, Risk and Activity Choice: Cattle in Western Tanzania." Oxford, UK: Oxford University.

———. 1999. "Who Benefits from Good Weather and Reforms? A Study of Ethiopian Villages." Paper presented at the conference on Poverty in Africa: A Dialogue on Causes and Solutions, Center for the Study of African Economies, University of Oxford, UK, April 15–16, 1999.

———. 2006. "Risk, Growth and Poverty: What Do We Know, What Do We Need to Know." Queen Elizabeth House Working Papers No. 148. Oxford, UK: Oxford University.

Dercon, Stefan, and Pramila Krishnan. 2004. "Food Aid and Informal Insurance." In Stefan Dercon, ed., *Insurance against Poverty,* pp. 306–30. Oxford, UK: Oxford University Press.

Deshingkar Priya, Craig Johnson, and John Farrington. 2005. "State Transfers to the Poor and Back: The Case of the Food-for-Work Program in India." *World Development* 33 (4): 575–91.

Dev, S. Mahendra. 1995. "India's (Maharashtra) Employment Guarantee Scheme: Lessons from Long Experience." In J. von Braun, ed., *Employment for Poverty Reduction and Food Security,* pp. 108–43. Washington, DC: International Food Policy Research Institute.

Dev, S. Mahendra, C. Ravi, Brinda Viswanathan, Ashok Gulati, and Sangamitra Ramachander. 2004. "Economic Liberalisation, Targeted Programmes and Household Food Security: A Case Study of India." Markets, Trade, and Institutions Division Discussion Paper 68. Washington, DC: International Food Policy Research Institute.

Dev, S. Mahendra, Kalanidhi Subbarao, S. Galab, and C. Ravi. 2007. "Safety Net Programmes: Outreach and Effectiveness." *Economic and Political Weekly Special Articles* (September): 3555–65.

Devarajan, Shanta, Karen Theirfelder, and Sethaput Suthiwart-Narueput. 2001. "The Marginal Cost of Public Funds in Developing Countries." In Amedeo Fossati and Wolfgang Wiegard, eds., *Policy Evaluations with Computable General Equilibrium Models*, pp. 39–55. New York: Routledge Press.

Development Initiatives. 2006. *Global Humanitarian Assistance 2006.* Evercreech, UK: Development Initiatives.

Devereux, Stephen. 2000. *Social Safety Nets for Poverty Alleviation in Southern Africa.* Economic and Social Research Unit Research Report R7017. London: Department for International Development.

———. 2001. "Social Pensions in Namibia and South Africa." Discussion Paper 379. Brighton, UK: University of Sussex, Institute of Development Studies.

———. 2002a. "Can Social Safety Nets Reduce Chronic Poverty?" *Development Policy Review* 20 (5): 657–75.

———. 2002b. *From Workfare to Fair Work: The Contribution of Public Works and other Labour-Based Infrastructure Programmes to Poverty Alleviation.* Geneva: International Labour Office, Recovery and Reconstruction Department.

Devereux, Stephen, Jenni Marshall, Jane MacAskill, and Larissa Pelham. 2005. *Making Cash Count: Lessons from Cash Transfer Schemes in East and Southern Africa for Supporting the Most Vulnerable Children and Households.* Report for the United Nations Children's Fund. London and Brighton: Save the Children, HelpAge International, and Institute of Development Studies.

Devereux, Stephen, Peter Mvula, and Colette Solomon. 2006. *After the FACT: An Evaluation of Concern Worldwide's Food and Cash Transfers Project in Three Districts of Malawi, June 2006.* Brighton, UK: University of Sussex, Institute of Development Studies.

Devereux, Stephen, Rachel Sabates-Wheeler, Mulugeta Tefera, and Hailemichael Taye. 2006. *Ethiopia's Productive Safety Net Programme—Trends in PSNP Transfers within Targeted Households: Final Report.* Sussex and Addis Ababa: University of Sussex, Institute of Development Studies and Indak International.

DFID (Department for International Development). 1999. *Learning Opportunities for All: A Policy Framework for Education.* London: DFID.

———. 2005. *Social Transfers and Chronic Poverty: Emerging Evidence and the Challenge Ahead.* DFID Practice Paper. London: DFID.

———. 2006. "Eliminating World Poverty." White Paper on International Development. London: DFID.

DiLorenzo, Thomas J. 2005. *Four Thousand Years of Price Control.* Auburn, AL: Ludwig von Mises Institute.

Donaldson, Dayl, Supasit Pannarunothai, and Viroj Tangcharoensathien. 1999. *Health Financing in Thailand Technical Report.* Boston: Management Sciences for Health.

Dorosh, Paul, Carlo del Ninno, and David Sahn. 1996. "Market Liberalization and the Role of Food Aid in Mozambique." In David Sahn, ed., *Economic Reform and the Poor in Africa*, pp. 339–65. Oxford, UK: Clarendon Press.

Dorosh, Paul A., and Abdul Salam. 2008. "Wheat Markets and Price Stabilization in Pakistan: An Analysis of Policy Options." *Pakistan Development Review* 44 (1): 71–88.

Dreze, Jean. 2004. "Employment as a Social Responsibility." *The Hindu*, November 22.

Duflo, Esther. 2003. "Grandmothers and Granddaughters: Old Age Pension and Intrahousehold Allocation in South Africa." *World Bank Economic Review* 17 (1): 1–25.

Duflo, Esther, Rachel Glennerster, and Michael Kremer. 2008. "Using Randomization in Development Economics Research: A Toolkit." In T. Paul Schultz and John A. Strauss, eds., *Handbook of Development Economics*, vol. 4, pp. 3895–3962. Amsterdam: North-Holland.

Duryea, Suzanne, and Andrew Morrison. 2004. "The Effect of Conditional Transfers on School Performance and Child Labor: Evidence from an Ex-Post Impact Evaluation in Costa Rica." Working Paper 505. Washington, DC: Inter-American Development Bank.

Dutta, Bhaskar, and Bharat Ramaswami. 2001. "Targeting and Efficiency in the Public Distribution System: Case of Andhra Pradesh and Maharashtra." *Economic and Political Weekly* 36 (18): 1524–32.

Econometría Consultores, Institute for Fiscal Studies, and Sistemas Especializados de Información. 2006. "Evaluación del Impacto del Programa Familias en Acción. Subsidios Condicionados de la Red de Apoyo Social. Final Report." Bogotá.

Economic and Social Commission for Asia and the Pacific. 2001. "Strengthening Policies and Programmes on Social Safety Nets: Issues, Recommendations and Selected Studies." Social Policy Paper 8. New York: Economic and Social Commission for Asia and the Pacific.

Economic Commission for Latin America and the Caribbean. 2006. *Shaping the Future of Social Protection: Access, Financing and Solidarity*. Santiago: Economic Commission for Latin America and the Caribbean.

Edirisinghe, Neville. 1987. "The Food Stamp Scheme in Sri Lanka: Costs, Benefits, and Options for Modification." Research Report 58. Washington, DC: International Food Policy Research Institute.

———. 1988. "Food Subsidy Changes in Sri Lanka: The Short-Run Effect on the Poor." In Per Pinstrup-Andersen, ed., *Food Subsidies in Developing Countries: Costs, Benefits, and Policy Options*, pp. 253–66. Baltimore: Johns Hopkins University Press.

Ellwood, David. 1988. *Poor Support: Poverty in the American Family*. New York: Basic Books.

Elwan, Ann. 1999. "Poverty and Disability: A Survey of the Literature." Social Protection Discussion Paper 9932. Washington, DC: World Bank.

Engle, Patrice L., Purnima Menon, and Lawrence Haddad. 1999. "Care and Nutrition: Concepts and Measurement." *World Development* 27 (8): 1309–37.

Esping-Andersen, Gøsta. 1990. *The Three Worlds of Welfare Capitalism*. Oxford, UK: Polity.

Eurostat. 2003. "'Laeken' Indicators: Detailed Calculation Methodology." Paper presented to the Working Group on Statistics on Income, Poverty and Social Exclusion, Luxembourg, April 28–29, 2003.

Evans, David D., and Edward Miguel. 2007. "Orphans and Schooling in Africa: A Longitudinal Analysis." *Demography* 44 (1): 35–57.

Ezemenari, Kene, and Kalanidhi Subbarao. 1999. "Jamaica's Food Stamp Program: Impacts on Poverty and Welfare." Policy Research Working Paper 2207. Washington, DC: World Bank.

Fafchamps, Marcel, Christopher Udry, and Katherine Czukas. 1998. "Drought and Saving in West Africa: Are Livestock a Buffer Stock?" *Journal of Development Economics* 55 (2): 273–305.

FAO (Food and Agriculture Organization). 2002. *The State of Food Insecurity in the World.* Fourth edition. Rome: FAO.

———. 2003. "Safety Nets and the Right to Food." Intergovernmental Working Group for the Elaboration of a Set of Voluntary Guidelines to Support the Progressive Realization of the Right to Adequate Food in the Context of National Food Security Information Paper. Rome: FAO.

Farrington, John, N. C. Saxena, Tamsyn Barton, and Radhika Nayak. 2003. *Post Offices, Pensions and Computers: New Opportunities for Combining Growth and Social Protection in Weakly Integrated Rural Areas?* Natural Resource Perspectives 87. London: Overseas Development Institute.

Faruqee, Rashid. 2005. "Reforming Wheat Policy in Pakistan." Draft. Washington, DC: World Bank.

Ferreira, Francisco H. G., and Kathy Lindert. 2003. *Principles for Integrating and Reforming Social Assistance in Brazil.* Brasilia: World Bank.

Ferreira, Francisco, Giovanna Prennushi, and Martin Ravallion. 1999. " Protecting the Poor from Macroeconomic Shocks." Policy Research Working Paper 2160. Washington, DC: World Bank.

Fiszbein, Ariel. 2004. "Beyond Truncated Welfare Status: *Quo Vadis* Latin America?" Draft. Washington, DC: World Bank.

———. 2008. "Impact Evaluation across the Human Development Network: Status Report and Future Challenges." Presentation at the Human Development Network Management Meeting, World Bank, Washington, DC, April 30, 2008.

Flinn, M. W. 1961. "The Poor Employment Act of 1817." *Economic History Review* 14 (1): 82–92.

Food Security Coordination Bureau. 2007. "2007 PSNP Annual Report." Addis Ababa: Federal Democratic Republic of Ethiopia, Ministry of Agriculture.

———. 2004. *Food Security Programme: Monitoring and Evaluation Plan, October 2004–September 2009.* Addis Ababa: Federal Democratic Republic of Ethiopia.

Foster, Vivien. 2004. "Toward a Social Policy for Argentina's Infrastructure Sectors: Evaluating the Past and Exploring the Future." Policy Research Working Paper 3422. Prepared in collaboration with the Argentine Business University, Center for the Economic Study of Regulation. Washington, DC: World Bank.

Fox, Louise. 2003. "Safety Nets in Transition Economies: A Primer." Social Protection Discussion Paper 0306. Washington, DC: World Bank.

Fraker, T. 1990. *The Effects of Food Stamps on Food Consumption: A Review of the Literature.* Alexandria, VA: Food and Nutrition Services.

Fraker, T., A. Martini, and J. Ohls. 1995. "The Effect of Food Stamp Cashout on Food Expenditures: An Assessment of the Findings from Four Demonstrations." *Journal of Human Resources* 30 (4): 633–49.

Frankenberg, Elizabeth, Duncan Thomas, and Kathleen Beegle. 1999. "The Real Costs of Indonesia's Economic Crisis: Preliminary Findings from the Indonesia Family Life Surveys." Labor and Population Program Working Paper Series 99-04. Santa Monica, CA: Rand.

Freije, Samuel, Rosangela Bando, and Fernanda Arce. 2006. "Conditional Transfers, Labor Supply and Poverty: Microsimulating Oportunidades." *Economia: Journal of the Latin American and Caribbean Economic Association* 7 (1): 73–108.

Gaiha, Raghav. 1997. "Rural Public Works and the Poor: The Case of the Employment Guarantee Scheme in India." In S. Polachek, ed., *Research in Labor Economics*, pp. 235–69. Stamford, CT: JAI Press.

———. 2000. "Do Anti-Poverty Programmes Reach the Rural Poor in India?" *Oxford Development Studies* 28 (1): 71–95.

———. 2005. "Does the Employment Guarantee Scheme Benefit the Rural Poor in India? Some Recent Evidence." *Asian Survey* 45 (6): 949–69.

Gaiha, Raghav, and Vani Kulkarni. 2001. "Panchayats, Communities and the Rural Poor in India." *Journal of African and Asian Studies* 37 (2): 38–82.

Galasso, Emanuela. 2006. *With Their Effort and One Opportunity: Alleviating Extreme Poverty in Chile.* Washington, DC: World Bank, Development Research Group.

Galasso, Emanuela, and Martin Ravallion. 2004. "Social Protection in a Crisis: Argentina's Plan Jefes y Jefas." *World Bank Economic Review* 18 (3): 367–99.

———. 2005. "Decentralized Targeting of an Anti-Poverty Program." *Journal of Public Economics* 89 (4): 705–27.

Gallagher, L. Jerome, Raymond J. Struyk, and Ludmila Nikonova. 2003. "Savings from Integrating Administrative Systems for Social Assistance Programmes in Russia." *Public Administration and Development* 23 (2): 177–95.

Gallagher, M. 2005. "A Technology White Paper on Improving the Efficiency of Social Safety Net Program Delivery in Low Income Countries." Social Protection Discussion Paper 0522. Washington, DC: World Bank.

Gangopadhyay, Shubhashis, Bharat Ramaswami, and Wilima Wadhwa. 2005. "Reducing Subsidies on Household Fuels in India: How Will It Affect the Poor?" *Energy Policy* 33 (2005): 2326–36.

Garcia, Marito. 2005. "Going to Scale: International Experience in Designing and Implementing Conditional Cash Grants to Families." Presented at the Going to Scale Workshop, Pretoria, June 27–28, 2005.

Gauthier, Anne Helene, and Jan Hatzius. 1997. "Family Benefits and Fertility: An Econometric Analysis." *Population Studies* 51 (3): 295–306.

Gelbach, Jonah B., and Lant Pritchett. 2002. "Is More for the Poor Less for the Poor? The Politics of Means-Tested Targeting." *Berkeley Electronic Press Journal of Economic Analysis and Policy* 2 (1), Article 6.

Gentilini, Ugo. 2007. *Cash and Food Transfers: A Primer.* Rome: World Food Programme.

Gertler, Paul. 2000. *The Impact of PROGESA on Health.* Final Report. Washington, DC: International Food Policy Research Institute.

Gertler, Paul, and Simone Boyce. 2001. "An Experiment in Incentive-Based Welfare: The Impact of PROGRESA on Health in Mexico." Berkeley, CA: University of California at Berkeley.

Gertler, Paul, Sebastian Martinez, David Levine, and Stefano Bertozzi. 2004. "Lost Presence and Presents: How Parental Death Affects Children." Draft. Berkeley, CA: University of California at Berkeley.

Gertler, Paul, Sebastian Martinez, and Marta Rubio-Codino. 2006. "Investing Cash Transfers to Raise Long Term Living Standards." Policy Research Working Paper 3994. Washington, DC: World Bank.

Ghukasyan, Hasmik. Forthcoming. "Program Implementation Matters for Targeting Performance—Evidence and Lessons from Eastern and Central Europe: Report on Administrative Costs of Armenia Family Benefits Program. Country Study: Armenia." Social Protection Discussion Paper. Washington, DC: World Bank.

Gibson, John, Susan Olivia, and Scott Rozzelle. 2006. "How Widespread Are Non-Linear Crowding Out Effects? The Response of Private Transfers to Income in Four Developing Countries." Working paper. Hamilton, New Zealand: University of Waikato, Department of Economics.

Giedion, Ursula. 2002. "The Case of Thailand." Presentation at the World Bank seminar on Protecting the Poor: User Fees for Health Services, Washington, DC, June 26, 2002.

Gillespie, Stuart. 1999. *Supplementary Feeding for Women and Young Children*. Washington, DC: World Bank, Human Development Network.

Gilson, Lucy, and Di McIntyre. 2005. "Removing User Fees for Primary Care in Africa: The Need for Careful Action." *British Medical Journal* 331 (7519): 762–65.

Glewwe, Paul, and Gillette Hall. 1998. "Are Some Groups More Vulnerable to Macroeconomic Shocks Than Others? Hypothesis Tests Based on Panel Data from Peru." *Journal of Development Economics* 56 (1): 181–206.

Glewwe, Paul, Pedro Olinto, and Priscila Z. de Souza. 2003. "Evaluating the Impact of Conditional Cash Transfers on Schooling in Honduras: An Experimental Approach." Draft. Rio de Janeiro: Escola de Pós-Graduação em Economia.

Government of Ethiopia. 2004. *Productive Safety Net Programme: Programme Implementation Manual*. Addis Ababa: Ministry of Agriculture and Rural Development.

Government of India. 2001. *Public Distribution System and Food Security for the Tenth Five Year Plan (2002–2007)*. New Delhi: Planning Commission.

———. 2007a. *National Rural Employment Guarantee Act 2005 (NREGA): Report of the Second Year April 2006–March 2007*. New Delhi: Ministry of Rural Development, Department of Rural Development.

———. 2007b. *Public Distribution System of Essential Commodities as a Social Safety Net: A Study of Uttar Pradesh*. Final Report. Allahabad: Govind Ballabh Pant Social Science Institute.

———. Various years. *Annual Report*. New Delhi: Ministry of Rural Development.

Government of Mexico. 2003. *Diaro Official*, May 23, p. 129.

———. 2007. *Oportunidades: Un Programa de Resultados*. Mexico City: Secretaría de Desarrollo Social.

Government of Pakistan. 2007. *A Social Protection Strategy to Reach the Poor and the Vulnerable*. Islamabad: Planning Commission, Center for Poverty Reduction and Social Policy Development.

Greenberg, David, and Mark Shroder. 2004. *The Digest of Social Experiments*, 3rd ed. Washington, DC: Urban Institute Press.

Greenberg, Mark, Jodie Levin-Epstein, Rutledge Hutson, Theodora Ooms, Rachel Schumacher, Vicki Turetsky, and David Engstrom. 2002. "The 1996 Welfare Law: Key Elements and Reauthorization Issues Affecting Children." *The Future of Children* 12 (1): 27–57.

Grogger, Jeffrey, and Lynn Karoly. 2006. *Welfare Reform: Effects of a Decade of Change.* Cambridge, MA: Harvard University Press.

Grootaert, Christiaan. 1997. "Poverty and Social Transfers in Hungary." Policy Research Working Paper 1770. Washington, DC: World Bank, Environment Department, Social Policy Division.

Grosh, Margaret. 1992. "The Jamaican Food Stamps Programme: A Case Study in Targeting." *Food Policy* 17 (1): 23–40.

———. 1994. *Administering Targeted Social Programs in Latin America: From Platitudes to Practice.* Washington, DC: World Bank.

———. 1995. "Five Criteria for Choosing among Poverty Programs." In Nora Lustig, ed., *Coping with Austerity: Poverty and Inequality in Latin America,* pp. 146–86, Washington, DC: Brookings Institution.

Gruber, Jonathan. 2003. "Medicaid." In Robert Moffitt, ed., *Means-Tested Transfer Programs in the United States*, pp. 15–77. Chicago: University of Chicago Press.

Grushka, Carlos O., and Gustavo Demarco. 2003. "Disability Pensions and Social Security Reform: Analysis of the Latin American Experience." Social Protection Discussion Paper 0325. Washington, DC: World Bank.

GTZ (German Agency for Technical Cooperation). 2008. "Social Cash Transfer Scheme: Dependency." GTZ.

Gundersen, Craig, Mara Yañez, Constanza Valdez, and Betsey Kuhn. 2000. "A Comparison of Food Assistance Programs in Mexico and the United States." Food Assistance and Nutrition Research Report 6. Washington, DC: U.S. Department of Agriculture, Economic Research Service.

Gupta, Sanjeev, Luc Leruth, Luiz de Mello, and Shamit Chakravarti. 2001. "Transition Economies: How Appropriate Is the Scope and Size of Government?" Working Paper 01/55. Washington, DC: International Monetary Fund.

Guerrero, Pablo, R. 1999. "Evaluation Capacity Development in Developing Countries: Applying the Lessons from Experience." In Richard Boyle and Donald Lemaire, eds., *Building Effective Evaluation Capacity: Lessons from Practice*, pp. 177–94. New Brunswick, NJ: Transaction Publishers.

Gurenko, Eugene, and Rodney Lester. 2004. "Rapid Onset Natural Disasters: The Role of Financing in Effective Risk Management." Policy Research Working Paper 3278. Washington, DC: World Bank.

Haber, Stephen H. 2001. "Political Institutions and Banking Systems: Lessons from the Economic Histories of Mexico and the United States, 1790–1914." Unpublished paper. Stanford, CA: Stanford University, Department of Political Science.

Habicht, J. P., C. G. Victora, and J. P. Vaughan. 1999. "Evaluation Designs for Adequacy, Plausibility, and Probability of Public Health Programme Performance and Impact." *International Journal of Epidemiology* 28 (1): 10–18.

Haddad, Lawrence, John Hoddinott, and Harold Alderman. 1997. *Intrahousehold Resource Allocation in Developing Countries: Models, Methods, and Policy.* Baltimore: Johns Hopkins University Press.

Hamilton, Gayle. 2002. "Moving People from Welfare to Work. Lessons from the National Evaluation of Welfare-to-Work Strategies." Prepared by Manpower Demonstration Research Corporation under a contract with the U.S. Department of Health and Human Services.

Handa, Sudhanshu, and Benjamin Davis. 2006. "The Experience of Conditional Cash Transfers in Latin America and the Caribbean." *Development Policy Review* 24 (5): 513–36.

Handler, Joel F. 2003. "Social Citizenship and Workfare in the US and Western Europe: From Status to Contract." *Journal of European Social Policy* 13 (3): 229–43.

Hands, Arthur R. 1968. *Charities and Social Aid in Greece and Rome.* Ithaca, New York: Cornell University Press.

Hanlon, Joseph. 2004. "It Is Possible to Just Give Money to the Poor." *Development and Change* 35 (2): 375–83.

Hardeman, Wim, Wim Van Damme, Maurits Van Pelt, and Ir Por, Heng Kimvan, and Bruno Meessen. 2004. "Access to Health Care for All? User Fees Plus a Health Equity Fund in Sotnikum, Cambodia." *Health Policy and Planning* 19 (1): 23–32.

Harrison, Kathryn. 2006. *Racing To The Bottom? Provincial Interdependence in the Canadian Federation.* Vancouver: UBC Press.

Harvey, Paul. 2005. "Cash and Vouchers in Emergencies." Humanitarian Policy Group Discussion Paper. London: Overseas Development Institute.

Haryadi, Yadi. 2001. "Scholarship and Block Grant Program for Primary and Secondary Schools in Indonesia." Paper presented at the workshop on Targeting and Rapid Assessment for Social Programs, Jakarta, May 22–23, 2001.

Hashemi, Syed, and Richard Rosenberg. 2006. *Graduating the Poorest into Microfinance: Linking Microfinance and Safety Net Programs to Include the Poorest.* Focus Note 34. Washington, DC: Consultative Group to Assist the Poorest.

Hatry, Harry. 1999. *Performance Measurement: Getting Results.* Washington, DC: Urban Institute Press.

Heinrich, Carolyn J. 2004. "Program Evaluation and Development Effectiveness." Presentation at the Third Meeting of the Social Policy Monitoring Network, Buenos Aires, November 22–23, 2004.

———. 2007. "Demand and Supply-Side Determinants of Conditional Cash Transfer Program Effectiveness." *World Development* 35 (1): 121–43.

Heinrich, Carolyn, and Marcelo Cabrol. 2005. *Programa Nacional de Becas Estudiantiles: Impact Evaluation Findings.* Washington, DC: Inter-American Development Bank, Office of Evaluation and Oversight.

HelpAge International. 2004. *Age and Security: How Social Pensions Can Deliver Effective Aid to Poor Older People and Their Families.* London: HelpAge International.

———. 2007. *Stronger Together: Supporting the Vital Role Played by Older People in the Fight against the HIV and AIDS Pandemic.* London: HelpAge International.

Henninger, Norbert, and Mathilde Snel. 2002. *Where Are the Poor? Experiences with the Development and Use of Poverty Maps*. Washington, DC and Arendal, Norway: World Resources Institute, United Nations Environment Programme, and GRID-Arendal.

Hentschel, Jesko, Jennie Lanjouw, Peter Lanjouw, and Javier Poggi. 2000. "Combining Census and Survey Data to Trace the Spatial Dimensions of Poverty: A Case Study of Ecuador." *World Bank Economic Review* 14 (1): 147–65.

Hernandez, Gonzalo. 2006. "M&E of Social Programs in Mexico." In Ernesto May, David Shand, Keith MacKay, Fernando Rojas, and Jaime Saavedra, eds., *Towards the Institutionalization of Monitoring and Evaluation Systems in Latin America and the Caribbean: Proceedings of a World Bank/Inter-American Development Bank Conference*, pp. 47–52. Washington, DC: World Bank.

Hernanz, Virginia, Franck Malherbet, and Michele Pellizzari. 2004. "Take-Up of Welfare Benefits in OECD Countries: A Review of Evidence." Social, Employment, and Migration Working Paper 17. Paris: Organisation for Economic Co-operation and Development.

Herz, Barbara, and Gene B. Sperling. 2004. *What Works in Girls' Education: Evidence and Policies from the Developing World*. New York: Council on Foreign Relations.

Himmelfarb, G. 1984. *The Idea of Poverty*. London: Faber.

Hines, James R., and Richard H. Thaler. 1995. "Anomalies: The Flypaper Effect." *Journal of Economic Perspectives* 9 (4): 217–26.

Hoddinott, John. 1999. *Principles and Practice in the Design of Food-Based Targeted Assistance*. Washington, DC: World Bank.

Hoddinott, John, Marc J. Cohen, and María Soledad Bos. 2003. *Food Aid in the 21st Century: Current Issues and Food Aid as Insurance*. Washington, DC: International Food Policy Research Institute.

Hoddinott, John, and Mahnaz Islam. 2007. *Evidence of Intra-Household Flypaper Effects from a Nutrition Intervention in Rural Guatemala*. Washington, DC: International Food Policy Research Institute.

Hoddinott, John, and Bill Kinsey. 2001. "Child Growth in the Time of Drought" Halifax, Nova Scotia: Dalhousir University.

Hoddinott, John, and Agnes Quisumbing. 2003. "Investing in Children and Youth for Poverty Reduction." Washington, DC: International Food Policy Research Institute.

Hoddinott, John, and Emmanuel Skoufias. 2004. "The Impact of PROGRESA on Food Consumption." *Economic Development and Cultural Change* 53 (1): 37–61.

Hoddinott, John, Emmanuel Skoufias, and Ryan Washburn. 2000. "The Impact of PROGRESA on Consumption: A Final Report." Washington, DC: International Food Policy Research Institute.

Holzmann, Robert. 2003. "Risk and Vulnerability: The Forward Looking Role of Social Protection in a Globalizing World." In E. Dowler and P. Mosely, eds., *Poverty and Social Exclusion in North and South*. New York: Routledge Press.

Holzmann, Robert, and Richard Hinz. 2005. *Old Age Income Support in the 21st Century: An International Perspective on Pension Systems Reform*. Washington, DC: World Bank.

Holzmann, Robert, and Steen Jorgensen. 2000. "Social Risk Management: A New Conceptual Framework for Social Protection and Beyond." Social Protection Discussion Paper 0006. Washington, DC: World Bank.

————. 2001. "Social Protection as Social Risk Management: Conceptual Underpinnings for the Social Protection Sector Strategy Paper." *Journal of International Development* 11 (7).

Honohan, Patrick, and Daniela Klingebiel. 2000. "Controlling the Fiscal Costs of Banking Crises." Policy Research Working Paper 2441. Washington, DC: World Bank.

Hoogeveen, Johannes, Emil Tesliuc, Renos Vakis, and Stefan Dercon. 2004. *A Guide to the Analysis of Risk, Vulnerability and Vulnerable Groups*. Washington, DC: World Bank.

Hoopengardner, Tom. 2001. "Disability and Work in Poland." Social Protection Discussion Paper 0101. Washington, DC: World Bank.

Horton, Susan. 1999. "Opportunities for Investments in Nutrition in Low-Income Asia." *Asian Development Review* 17 (1,2): 246–73.

Hove, Jennifer. 2007. *Barriers to Girls' Secondary School Participation in Rural Bangladesh*. Center for Policy Research Commentary 5. Dhaka: International University of Business Agriculture and Technology.

Howell, Fiona. 2001. "Social Assistance: Theoretical Background." In Isabel Ortiz, ed., *Social Protection in Asia and the Pacific*. Manila: Asian Development Bank.

Humphrey, Liz. 2002. "Food-for-Work in Ethiopia: Challenging the Scope of Project Evaluations." Working Paper 81. Brighton, UK: University of Sussex, Institute of Development Studies.

Hunter, Wendy, and Timothy Power. 2007. "Rewarding Lula: Executive Power, Social Policy and the Brazilian Elections of 2006." *Latin American Politics & Society* 49 (1): 1–30.

Hur, Jai-Joon. 2001. "Economic Crisis, Income Support, and Employment Generating Programs: The Korea's Experience." Paper prepared for the United Nations Economic and Social Commission for Asia and the Pacific regional seminar, Evaluation of Income/Employment Generating Programs to Alleviate Socio-Economic Impacts of the Economic Crisis, Bangkok, May 23–25, 2001.

Hurrell, Alex, and Patrick Ward. 2008. "Kenya OVC-CT Programme Operational and Impact Evaluation." Draft baseline survey report. Oxford, UK: Oxford Policy Management.

Hutton, Guy. 2004. *Charting the Path to the World Bank's "No Blanket Policy on User Fees": A Look Over the Past 25 Years at the Shifting Support for User Fees in Health and Education, and Reflections on the Future*. London: Department for International Development, Health Systems Resource Centre.

IFPRI (International Food Policy Research Institute). 2000. *Second Report—Implementation Proposal for the PRAF/ IDB Project: Phase II*. Washington, DC: IFPRI.

————. 2002. *Sistema de evaluación de la fase piloto de la Red de Protección Social de Nicaragua: Evaluación de focalización (informe final)*. Washington, DC: IFPRI.

ILO (International Labour Office). 2000. *World Labour Report 2000: Income Security and Social Protection in a Changing World*. Geneva: ILO.

————. 2001. *Social Security: A New Consensus*. Geneva: ILO.

IMF (International Monetary Fund). 2001. *Government Finance Statistics Manual 2001*. Washington, DC: IMF.

Indrawati, Mulyani. 2005. **"**Moving Forward to Achieve the MDGs: A Strategy to Help the Poor While Reducing Fuel Subsidies." Speech at the Consultative Group for Indonesia Mid-Term Review Meeting, Jakarta, October 3.

Institute for Strategic Studies and Prognoses. 2004. "Montenegro Household Survey, Basic Information Document." Unpublished report. Podgorica, Montenegro: Institute for Strategic Studies and Prognoses.

Institute for Urban Economics, Independent Institute for Social Policy, and Urban Institute. 2006. "Russian Federation: Policy Note on Good Practices and Lessons Generated by Reforms to Improve Social Assistance." Unpublished report. Moscow: Institute for Urban Economics.

Islam, Nurul. 2006. *Reducing Poverty in Rural Asia: Challenges and Opportunities for Microenterprises and Public Employment Schemes*. New York: Haworth Press.

Ivanic, Maros, and Will Martin. 2008. "Implications of Higher Global Food Prices for Poverty in Low-Income Countries." Policy Research Working Paper 4594. Washington, DC: World Bank.

Ivatury, Guatam. 2006. *Using Technology to Build Inclusive Financial Systems*. Focus Note 32. Washington, DC: Consultative Group to Assist the Poorest.

Jacobs, B., and Neil Price. 2006. "Improving Access for the Poorest to Public Sector Health Services: Insights from Kirivong Operational Health District in Cambodia." *Health Policy and Planning* 21 (1): 27–39.

Jacoby, Hanan G. 2002. "Is There an Intrahousehold 'Flypaper Effect'? Evidence from a School Feeding Programme." *Economic Journal* 112 (476): 196–221.

Jalan, Jyotsna, and Martin Ravallion. 1999. "Income Gains to the Poor from Workfare: Estimates for Argentina's Trabajar Program." Policy Research Working Paper 2149. Washington, DC: World Bank, Development Research Group, Poverty and Human Resources.

———. 2002. "Household Income Dynamics in Rural China." Discussion Paper No. 2002/10. New York: United Nations University, World Institute for Development Economics Research.

———. 2003. "Estimating the Benefit Incidence of an Antipoverty Program by Propensity-Score Matching." *Journal of Business and Economic Statistics* 21 (1): 19-30.

James, Estelle. 2000. "Coverage under Old Age Security Programs and Protection for the Uninsured: What Are the Issues?" In Nora Lustig, ed., *Shielding the Poor: Social Protection in the Developing World*, pp. 149–74. Washington, DC: Inter-American Development Bank and Brookings Institution Press.

Jaspars, Susanne, and Helen Young. 1995. *General Food Distribution in Emergencies: From Nutritional Needs to Political Priorities*. Relief and Rehabilitation Network, Good Practice Review 3. London: Overseas Development Institute.

Jensen, Robert. 1998. "Public Transfers, Private Transfers, and the 'Crowding Out' Hypothesis: Evidence from South Africa." John F. Kennedy School of Government Faculty Working Paper. Cambridge, MA: Harvard University.

Jorgensen, Steen, Margaret E. Grosh, and Mark Schacter. 1992. "Bolivia's Answer to Poverty, Economic Crisis, and Adjustment: The Emergency Social Fund." Living Standard Measurement Study Working Paper No. 88. Washington, DC: World Bank.

Kabeer, Naila. 2002. "Safety Nets and Opportunity Ladders: Addressing Vulnerability and Enhancing Productivity in South Asia." Working Paper 159. Brighton, UK: University of Sussex, Institute of Development Studies.

Kain, Juliana, and Ricardo Uauy. 2001. "Targeting Strategies Used by the Chilean National Supplementary Feeding Programme." *Nutrition Research* 21 (4): 677–88.

Kakwani, Nanak, and Kalanidhi Subbarao. 2005. "Aging and Poverty in Africa and the Role of Social Pensions." Social Protection Discussion Paper 0521. Washington, DC: World Bank.

Kanbur, Ravi. 2005. "Pareto's Revenge." Ithaca, NY: Cornell University. www.people.cornell.edu/pages/sk145.

Kattan, Raja Bentaouet, and Nicholas Burnett. 2004. *User Fees in Primary Education*. Washington, DC: World Bank, Human Development Network, Education Sector.

Kaufmann, Daniel, Aart Kraay, and Massimo Mastruzzi. 2005. *Governance Matters IV: Governance Indicators for 1996–2004*. Washington, DC: World Bank.

Keddeman, Willem. 1998. "Of Nets and Assets—Effects and Impacts of Employment-Intensive Programmes: A Review of ILO Experience." Socio-Economic Technical Paper 1. Geneva: International Labour Office.

Keith, Regina, and Peter Shackleton. 2006. *Paying with Their Lives. The Cost of Illness for Children in Africa*. London: Save the Children.

Khandker, Shahidur, Zaid Bakht, and Gayatri Koolwal. 2006. "The Poverty Impact of Rural Roads: Evidence from Bangladesh." Policy Research Working Paper 3875. Washington, DC: World Bank.

Khandker, Shahidur, Mark M. Pitt, and Nobuhiko Fuwa. 2003. *Subsidy to Promote Girls' Secondary Education: The Female Stipend Program in Bangladesh*. Washington, DC: World Bank.

Khogali, H., and P. Takhar. 2001. *Evaluation of Oxfam GB Cash for Work Programme, Kitgum/Pader District, Uganda*. Oxford, UK: Oxfam GB.

Kim, Jooseop, Harold Alderman, and Peter F Orazem. 1999a. "Can Private School Subsidies Increase Enrollment for the Poor? The Quetta Urban Fellowship Program." *World Bank Economic Review* 13 (3): 443–65.

———. 1999b. *Evaluation of the Balochistan Rural Girls' Fellowship Program: Will Rural Families Pay to Send Girls to School?* Report 24339-AM. Washington, DC: World Bank, Europe and Central Asia Region, Human Development Sector Unit.

Kitano, Naohiro., Hiromichi Ariga, and Harue Shimato. 1999. *Current Situation of Rice Distribution System in Indonesia*. Tokyo: Japan Bank for International Cooperation, Research Institute for Development and Finance.

Kolpeja, Vilma. 2005. "Ndihma Ekonomika (NE) "Program Implementation Matters for Targeting the Performance: Evidence and Lessons from Albania." Paper prepared for meeting on Program Implementation Matters for Targeting Performance: Evidence and Lessons from Eastern and Central Europe, Bucharest, June 6–7, 2005.

———. Forthcoming. "Program Implementation Matters for Targeting Performance: Evidence and Lessons from Eastern and Central Europe. Country Study: Albania." Social Protection Discussion Paper Series. Washington, DC: World Bank.

Komives, Kristin, Vivien Foster, Jonathan Halpern, and Quentin Wodon. 2005. *Water, Electricity, and the Poor. Who Benefits from Utility Subsidies?* Washington, DC: World Bank.

Kopits, George, and Steven Symansky. 1998. "Fiscal Policy Rules." Occasional Paper 162. Washington, DC: International Monetary Fund.

Krueger, Anne, Maurice Schiff, and Alberto Valdes. 1991. *The Political Economy of Agricultural Pricing*. Baltimore: Johns Hopkins University Press.

Kudat, Ayse. 2006. *Evaluating the Conditional Cash Transfer Program in Turkey: A Qualitative Assessment*. Washington, DC: International Food Policy Research Institute.

Kuklys, Wiebke. 2005. *Amartya Sen's Capability Approach: Theoretical Insights and Empirical Applications, Studies in Choice and Welfare*. Berlin: Springer-Verlag.

Kumar, Anjali, Ajai Nair, Adam Parsons, and Eduardo Urdapilleta. 2006. "Expanding Bank Outreach through Retail Partnerships: Correspondent Banking in Brazil." Working Paper 85. Washington, DC: World Bank.

Kwon, Huck-Ju. 2002. "Unemployment and Public Work Projects in Korea, 1998–2000." Reference material prepared for the Asian Development Bank Institute Seminar on Social Protection for the Poor in Asia and Latin America, Manila, October 21–25 2002.

Kyrgyzstan Center for Social and Economic Research. Forthcoming. "Program Implementation Matters for Targeting Performance—Evidence and Lessons from Eastern and Central Europe: Country Study: Kyrgyz Republic." Social Protection Discussion Paper Series. Washington, DC: World Bank.

Lafaurie, Maria Teresa, and Claudia A. Velasquez Leiva. 2004. "Transferring Cash Benefits through the Banking Sector in Colombia." Social Protection Discussion Paper 0409. Washington, DC: World Bank.

LaLonde, Robert. 2003. "Employment and Training Programs." In Robert Moffitt, ed., *Means-Tested Transfer Programs in the United States*, pp. 517–85. Chicago: University of Chicago Press.

Lampietti, Julian, ed. 2004. "Power's Promise: Electricity Reforms in Eastern Europe and Central Asia." Working Paper 40. Washington, DC: World Bank.

Lampietti, Julian, Hernan Gonzalez, Margaret Wilson, Ellen Hamilton, and Sergo Vashakmadze. 2004. "Revisiting Reform in the Energy Sector. Lessons from Georgia." Working Paper No. 21. Washington, DC: World Bank.

Landa, Casazola Fernando. 2003. *Transferencia De Recursos Hacia Los Mas Pobres. Un Analisis del PLANE-I con Escenarios Contrafactuales*. La Paz: Unidad de Análisis de Políticas Sociales y Económicas.

————. 2004. *PLANE-II Una Iniciativa para Adquirie Experiencia en el Mercado Laboral*. La Paz: Unidad de Análisis de Políticas Sociales y Económicas.

Lanjouw, P., B. Milanovic, and S. Paternostro. 1998. "Poverty and the Economic Transition: How Do Changes in Economies of Scale Affect Poverty Rates for Different Households?" Policy Research Working Paper 2009. Washington, DC: World Bank.

Lanjouw, Peter, and Martin Ravallion. 1999. "Benefit Incidence, Public Spending Reforms, and the Timing of Program Capture." *World Bank Economic Review* 13 (2): 257–73.

Larrañaga, Osvaldo. 2005. "Focalización de programas Sociales en Chile: el Sistema CAS." Social Protection Discussion Paper 0528. Washington, DC: World Bank.

Latin American Economic System. 2005. *Strategies and Programmes for Poverty Reduction in Latin America and the Caribbean*. Caracas: Latin American Economic System.

Lavy, Victor, John Strauss, Duncan Thomas, and Phillippe de Vreyer. 1996. "Quality of Health Care, Survival and Health Outcomes." *Ghana Journal of Health Economics* 15 (3): 333–57.

Leatt, Annie. 2006. "Grants for Children: A Brief Look at the Eligibility and Take-Up of the Child Support Grant and Other Cash Grants." Working Paper 5. Cape Town: University of Cape Town, Children's Institute.

Lee, Woojin, and John E. Roemer. 2004. "Racism and Redistribution in the United States: A Solution to the Problem of American Exceptionalism." *Journal of Public Economics* 90 (6–7): 1027–52.

Legido-Quigley, Helena. 2003. "The South African Old Age Pension: Exploring the Role of Poverty Alleviation in Households Affected by HIV/AIDS." Paper prepared for the International Social Security Association Fourth International Research Conference on Social Security, Social Security in a Long-Life Society, Antwerp, May 5–7, 2003.

Leite, Phillippe. 2006a. "An Ex Ante Evaluation of Labor and Schooling Incentives under Brazil's Bolsa Família Program." Draft. Washington, DC: World Bank.

———. 2006b. "Effects of Bolsa Escola on Adult Labor Force Participation." Draft. Washington, DC: World Bank.

Lemieux, Thomas, and Kevin Milligan. 2008. "Incentive Effects of Social Assistance: A Regression Discontinuity Approach." *Journal of Econometrics* 142 (2): 807–28.

Lentz, Erin, and Christopher Barrett. 2005. "Food Aid Targeting, Shocks and Private Transfers among East African Pastoralists." Draft. Ithaca, NY: Cornell University, Department of Economics.

Lentz, Erin, Christopher Barrett, and John Hoddinott. 2005. "Food Aid and Dependency: Implications for Emergency Food Security Assessments." Rome: World Food Programme, Emergency Needs Assessment Branch.

Levy, Dan, and Jim Ohls. 2004. "Evaluation of Jamaica's PATH Program: Targeting Assessment." Washington, DC: Mathematica Policy Research, Inc.

———. 2007. "Evaluation of Jamaica's PATH Program: Final Report." Washington, DC: Mathematica Policy Research, Inc.

Levy, Santiago. 2006. *Progress Against Poverty: Sustaining Mexico's Progresa-Oportunidades Program.* Washington, DC: Brookings Institution Press.

Levy, Santiago, and Evelyne Rodríguez. 2005. *Sin herencia de pobreza: el programa Progresa-Oportunidades de México.* Washington, DC, and Colonia Florida, Mexico: World Bank and Editorial Planeta Mexicana.

Lewis, Maureen. 2000. *Who Is Paying for Health Care in Eastern Europe and Central Asia?* Washington, DC: World Bank, Human Development Sector Unit.

Liang, Xiaoyan. 1996. *Pakistan: Balochistan Pilot Fellowships.* Washington, DC: World Bank, Human Development Department.

Liang, Xiaoyan, and Kari Marble. 1996. *Guatemala—Eduque a la Niña: Girls' Scholarship.* Washington, DC: World Bank, Human Development Department.

Lieten, G. K., and Ravi Srivastava. 1999. *Unequal Partners: Power Relations, Devolution and Development in Uttar Pradesh.* New Delhi: Sage.

Lind, Jeremy, and Teriessa Jalleta. 2005. "Poverty, Power and Relief Assistance: Meanings and Perceptions of 'Dependency' in Ethiopia." Background paper. London: Overseas Development Institute, Humanitarian Policy Group.

Lindert, Kathy. 2005a. "Implementing Means-Tested Welfare Systems in the United States." Social Protection Discussion Paper 0532. Washington, DC: World Bank.

———. 2005b. "Reducing Poverty and Inequality in Latin America: The Promise of Conditional Cash Transfers." Presentation for the International Training Center of the International Labour Organisation, Brazil Country Office, World Bank, Brazil, November 25, 2005.

Lindert, Kathy, Anja Linder, Jason Hobbs, and Bénédicte de la Brière. 2007. "The Nuts and Bolts of Brazil's Bolsa Familia Program: Implementing Conditional Cash Transfers in a Decentralized Context." Social Protection Discussion Paper 0709. Washington, DC: World Bank.

Lindert, Kathy, Emmanuel Skoufias, and Joseph Shapiro. 2006. "Redistributing Income to the Poor and the Rich: Public Transfers in Latin America and the Caribbean." Social Protection Discussion Paper 605. Washington, DC: World Bank.

Lindert, Peter H. 2004. *Growing Public: Social Spending and Economic Growth since the Eighteenth Century.* Cambridge, UK: Cambridge University Press.

Lipton, Michael. 1996. "Successes in Anti-Poverty." Discussion Paper 8. Geneva: International Labour Office.

———. 1997. "Editorial: Poverty—Are There Holes in the Consensus?" *World Development* 25 (7): 1003–07.

Litvack, J., and C. Bodart. 1993. "User Fees Plus Quality Equals Access to Health Care: Results of a Field Experiment in Cameroon." *Social Science and Medicine* 37 (3): 369–76.

Lokshin, Michael, and Martin Ravallion. 2000. "Short-Lived Shocks with Long-Lived Impacts?: Household Income Dynamics in a Transition Economy." Policy Research Working Paper 2459. Washington, DC: World Bank.

Lovei, Laszlo, Eugene Gurenko, Michael Haney, Philip O'Keefe, and Maria Shkaratan. 2000. "Scorecard for Subsidies: How Utility Subsidies Perform in Transition Economies." Public Policy for the Private Sector Note No. 218. Washington, DC: World Bank.

Lo Vuolo, Ruben M. 2005. "Social Protection in Latin America: Different Approaches to Managing Social Exclusion and Their Outcomes." Paper presented at the Economic and Social Research Council Seminar Series on Social Policy, Stability and Exclusion in Latin America, London, June 2–3, 2005.

Lund, Frances. 1999. "Understanding South African Social Security through Recent Household Surveys: New Opportunities and Continuing Gaps." *Development Southern Africa* 16 (1): 55–67.

Lyman, Timothy R., Gautam Ivatury, and Stefan Staschen. 2006. *Use of Agents in Branchless Banking for the Poor: Rewards, Risks, and Regulation.* Focus Note 38. Washington, DC: Consultative Group to Assist the Poorest.

Lyman, Timothy R., Mark Pickens, and David Porteous. 2008. *Regulating Transformational Branchless Banking: Mobile Phones and Other Technology to Increase Access to Finance.* Focus Note 43. Washington, DC: Consultative Group to Assist the Poorest.

Mahmud, Simeen. 2003. "Female Secondary School Stipend Programme in Bangladesh: A Critical Assessment." Final draft. Dhaka: Bangladesh Institute of Development Studies.

Maluccio, John A. 2001. "Education and Child Labor: Experimental Evidence from a Nicaraguan Conditional Cash Transfer Program." Unpublished. Washington, DC: International Food Policy Research Institute.

Maluccio, John A., Michelle Adato, Rafael Flores, and Terry Roopnaraine. 2005. *Nicaragua—Red de Proteccion Social: Mi Familia. Breaking the Cycle of Poverty.* Washington, DC: International Food Policy Research Institute.

Maluccio, John A., and Rafael Flores. 2004. "Impact Evaluation of a Conditional Cash Transfer Program: The Nicaraguan *Red de Protección Social.*" Discussion Paper 184. Washington, DC: International Food Policy Research Institute.

Mararike, Ngoni. 2006. "Zimbabwe: The Basic Education Assistance Module." Wahenga, Zimbabwe: Regional Hunger and Vulnerability Programme.

Marriott, Anna, and Kate Gooding. 2007. *Social Assistance and Disability in Developing Countries.* Haywards Heath, UK: Department for International Development and Sightsavers International.

Martin, Will, and James Anderson. 2005. "Costs of Taxation and the Benefits of Public Goods: The Role of Income Effects." Policy Research Working Paper 3700. Washington, DC: World Bank.

Martinez, Sebastian. 2005. "Pensions, Poverty and Household Investments in Bolivia." Draft. Berkeley, CA: University of California at Berkeley, Department of Economics.

Matin, Imran, and David Hulme. 2003. "Programs for the Poorest: Learning from the IGVGD Program in Bangladesh." *World Development* 31 (3): 647–65.

McCord, Anna. 2004a. "Policy Expectations and Programme Reality: The Poverty Reduction and Labour Market Impact of Two Public Works Programmes in South Africa." Economics and Statistics Analysis Unit working paper. London: Overseas Development Institute.

———. 2004b. "Public Works and Overcoming Under-Development in South Africa." Paper presented at the Conference on Overcoming Under-Development in South Africa's Second Economy, Pretoria, October 29.

———. 2005. "Win-Win or Lose? An Examination of the Use of Public Works as a Social Protection Instrument in Situations of Chronic Poverty." Paper presented at the University of Manchester, Institute for Development Policy and Management, conference on Social Protection for Chronic Poverty Risk, Needs, and Rights: Protecting What? How?, Manchester, England, February 23–24, 2005.

McCulloch, Neil. 2004. "Trade and Poverty in Indonesia: What Are the Links?" Paper presented at the Thematic Workshop on Trade and Industry, Why Trade and Industry Policy Matters?, Jakarta, January 14–15, 2004.

MCDSS (Ministry of Community Development and Social Services), and GTZ (German Agency for Technical Cooperation). 2007. *Final Evaluation Report: Kalomo Social Cash Transfer Scheme.* Lusaka: Ministry of Community Development and Social Services and German Agency for Technical Cooperation.

McKay, Andrew. 2000a. "Should a Survey Measure Total Household Income?" In Margaret Grosh and Paul Glewwe, eds., *Designing Household Survey Questionnaires for Developing Countries: Lessons from Fifteen Years of the Living Standard Measurement Study,* vol. II, pp. 83–104. Oxford, UK: Oxford University Press.

———. 2000b. "Transfers and Other Non-labor Income." In Margaret Grosh and Paul Glewwe, eds., *Designing Household Survey Questionnaires for Developing Countries: Lessons from Fifteen Years of the Living Standard Measurement Study,* vol. 1, pp. 273–92. Oxford, UK: Oxford University Press.

MacKay, Keith. 2007. *How to Build M&E Systems to Support Better Government.* Washington, DC: World Bank, International Evaluations Group.

Mckenzie, David. 2002. "Are Tortillas a Giffen Good in Mexico?" *Economics Bulletin* 15 (1): 1–7.

MDS (Ministry of Social Development and the Fight against Hunger). 2007. *Catalog of Indicators for Monitoring the MDS' Programs.* Brasilia: MDS.

Meintjes, Helen, Debbie Budlender, Sonja Glese, and Leigh Johnson. 2003. "Children in Need of Care or in Need of Cash? Questioning Social Security Provisions for Orphans in the Context of the South African AIDS Pandemic." Working paper. Cape Town: Children's Institute and University of Cape Town, Centre for Actuarial Research.

Meme, M. M., W. Kogi-Makau, N. M. Muroki, and R. K. Mwadime. 1998. "Energy and Protein Intake and Nutritional Status of Primary School Children 5 to 10 Years of Age in Schools with and without Feeding Programmes in Nyambene District, Kenya." *Food and Nutrition Bulletin* 19 (4): 334–42.

Mete, Cem, ed. 2008. *Economic Implications of Chronic Illness and Disability in Eastern Europe and the Former Soviet Union.* Washington, DC: World Bank.

Micklewright, John, Aline Coudouel, and Sheila Marnie. 2004. "Targeting and Self-Targeting in a New Social Assistance Scheme." Discussion Paper 1112. Bonn: Institute for Labor Study.

Ministry of Economy and Labour. 2004. *Poland 2004 Report. Labor Market and Social Security.* Warsaw: Ministry of Economy and Labor, Economic Analyses and Forecasting Department.

Ministry of Labor and Social Affairs. 2000. *The First Report on the Implementation of the European Social Charter: The First Part.* Prague: Government of the Czech Republic.

Ministry of Public Education. 2004. *Nacional Inform the Development of Education Costa Rica.* San José: Department of Plans and Programs, Division of Planning and Educational.

Minten, Bart, and Paul Dorosh, eds. 2006. "Rice Markets in Madagascar in Disarray: Policy Options for Increased Efficiency and Price Stabilization." Africa Region Working Paper Series 101. Washington, DC: World Bank.

Misra, Neha, Ruchika Chawla, Leena Srivastava, and R. K. Pachauri. 2005. *Petroleum Pricing in India: Balancing Efficiency and Equity.* New Delhi: Energy and Resources Institute Press.

Mitra, Sophie. 2005. "Disability and Social Safety Nets in Developing Countries." Social Protection Discussion Paper 0509. Washington, DC: World Bank.

Mobile Task Team. 2005. *Education Access and Retention for Educationally Marginalised Children: Innovations in Social Protection.* Durban, South Africa: University of KwaZulu-Natal, Health Economics and HIV and AIDS Research Division.

Mode Research Private, Ltd. 2000. "Study on Evaluation of Apni Beti Apna Dhan Scheme in Haryana." New Delhi: Mode Research Private, Ltd.

Moffitt, Robert. 1992. "Incentive Effects of the US Welfare System: A Review." *Journal of Economic Literature* 30 (1): 1–61.

———. 2002a. "Economic Effects of Means-Tested Transfers in the US." *Tax Policy and Economy* 16 (1): 1–35.

———. 2002b. "Welfare Programs and Labor Supply." NBER Working Paper 9168. Cambridge, MA: National Bureau of Economic Research.

————, ed. 2003. *Means-Tested Transfer Programs in the United States*. National Bureau of Economic Research Conference Report. Cambridge, MA: National Bureau of Economic Research.

Mohapatra, C. 2004. "Poverty and Disability in India." Paper presented at Disability Management in India: Challenges and Perspectives workshop, Ministry of Social Justice and Empowerment and the Indian Institute of Public Administration, New Delhi, March 4–5, 2004.

Monson, Jo, Katherine Hall, Charmaine Smith, and Maylene Shung-King, eds. 2006. *South African Child Gauge 2006*. Cape Town: University of Cape Town, Children's Institute.

Mont, Daniel. 2004. "Disability Employment Policy." Social Protection Discussion Paper 0413. Washington, DC: World Bank.

————. 2006. "Disability in Conditional Cash Transfer Programs: Drawing on Experience in LAC." Paper presented at the Third International Conference on Conditional Cash Transfers, Istanbul, June 26–30, 2006.

————. 2007. *Measuring Disability Prevalence*. Social Protection Discussion Paper 0706. Washington, DC: World Bank.

Mooij, Jos. 1999a. *Food Policy and the Indian State: The Public Distribution System in South India*. New Delhi: Oxford University Press.

————. 1999b. "Real Targeting: The Case of Food Distribution in India." *Food Policy* 24 (1): 49–69.

Morduch, Jonathan, 1999. "Between the State and the Market: Can Informal Insurance Patch the Safety Net?" Washington, DC: World Bank.

Morley, Samuel, and David Coady. 2003. *From Social Assistance to Social Development*. Washington, DC: Center for Global Development and International Food Policy Research Institute.

Morris, Saul, Rafael Flores, Pedro Olinto, and Juan Manuel Medina. 2004. "Monetary Incentives in Primary Health Care and Effects on Use and Coverage of Preventive Health Care Interventions in Rural Honduras: Cluster Randomised Trial." *Lancet* 364 (9450): 2030–37.

Mujeri, Mustafa K. 2002. *Bangladesh: Bringing Poverty Focus in Rural Infrastructure Development*. Geneva: International Labour Office, Recovery and Reconstruction Department.

Murgai, Rinku, and Martin Ravallion. 2005. "Is a Guaranteed Living Wage a Good Anti-Poverty Policy?" Policy Research Working Paper 3640. Washington, DC: World Bank.

Murrugarra, Edmundo, Nazmul Chaudhury, Rodica Cnobloch, and Jeffrey Hammer. 2004. "Poverty-Targeted Social Assistance and Health: Impact of Eligibility Expansion on Health Care Utilization in Armenia." Working Paper 04/11. Washington, DC: World Bank.

Musgrave, Richard. 1959. *The Theory of Public Finance: A Study in Public Economy*. New York: McGraw-Hill.

Narayan, Deepa, Robert Chambers, Meera Shah, and Patti Petesch. 2000. *Voices of the Poor: Crying Out for Change*. Oxford, UK: Oxford University Press.

National Audit Office. 2006. "International Benchmark of Fraud and Error in Social Security Systems." Report by the Comptroller and Auditor General. London: National Audit Office.

Neufeld, Lynette M. 2006. "Nutrition in the Oportunidades Conditional Cash Transfer Program: Strengths and Challenges." Paper presented at the Third International Conference on Conditional Cash Transfers, Istanbul, June 26–30, 2006.

Nielsen, Mette E., and Pedro Olinto. 2007. "Do Conditional Cash Transfers Crowd Out Private Transfers? Evidence from Randomized Trials in Honduras and Nicaragua." Paper prepared for World Bank Latin American and Caribbean Regional Studies Program. Washington, DC.

Nigenda, Luz, and María González-Robledo. 2005. *Lessons Offered by Latin American Cash Transfer Programmes, Mexico's Oportunidades and Nicaragua's SPN: Implications for African Countries.* London: Department for International Development, Health Systems Resource Centre.

Nolan, B., and V. Turbat. 1995. "Cost Recovery in Public Health Services in Sub-Saharan Africa." Economic Development Institute Technical Material. Washington, DC: World Bank.

Nyonator, Frank. 2002. "Mechanisms to Protect the Poor When User Fee Systems are in Place: The Ghana Case Study." Presentation at the World Bank seminar on Protecting the Poor: User Fees for Health Services, Washington, DC, June 26, 2002.

Nyonator, Frank, and Joseph Kutzin. 1999. "Health for Some? The Effects of User Fees in the Volta Region of Ghana." *Health Policy and Planning* 14 (4): 329–41.

Oates, Wallace. 1972. *Fiscal Federalism.* New York: Harcourt Brace Jovanovich.

O'Connor, Thomas, and Lizbeth Silbermann. 2003. "Using Technology to Improve Social Safety Nets: Experience with Electronic Benefit Transfers in the US Food Stamp Program." Presentation to World Bank, March 26, 2003.

OECD (Organisation for Economic Co-operation and Development). 2004a. *Benefits and Wages: OECD Indicators.* Paris: OECD.

———. 2004b. OECD Social Expenditure Database. www.oecd.org/els/social/expenditure.

———. 2007. *Benefits and Wages.* Paris: OECD.

OECD (Organisation for Economic Co-operation and Development) Development Assistance Committee. 2001. *Aid Activities in Least Developed Countries, 1999.* Paris: OECD.

Office of the Vice President and Ministry of Home Affairs. 2006. *Cash Transfers for Orphan and Vulnerable Children (OVC).* Programme Design Cash Transfer Pilot Project. Nairobi: Office of the Vice President and Ministry of Home Affairs.

Oficina Internacional del Trabajo. 2006. *Superando la Crisis Mejorando el Empleo: Políticas de Mercado de Trabajo, 2000–2005.* Santiago: Oficina Internacional del Trabajo.

Okun, Arthur M. 1975 *Equality and Efficiency: The Big Tradeoff.* Washington, DC: Brookings Institution.

Olken, Benjamin A. 2005. "Monitoring Corruption: Evidence from a Field Experiment in Indonesia." Working Paper 11753. Cambridge, MA: National Bureau of Economic Research.

Olsen, Edgar. 2003. "Housing Programs for Low-Income Households." In Robert Moffitt, ed., *Means-Tested Transfer Programs in the United States*, pp. 365–441. Chicago: University of Chicago Press.

Orazem, Peter F. 2000. *The Urban and Rural Fellowship School Experiments in Pakistan: Design, Evaluation, and Sustainability.* Washington, DC: World Bank.

Orr, Larry. 1998. *Social Experiments: Evaluating Public Programs with Experimental Methods.* Thousand Oaks, CA: Sage.

Overseas Development Institute. 2005. "The Maharastra Employment Guarantee Scheme." Policy Brief 6. London: Overseas Development Institute.

Owino, Wasunna, and Okwach Abagi. 2000. "Cost Sharing in Education and Health in Kenya." Draft. Nairobi: Institute of Policy Analysis and Research.

Owino, Wasunna, and Maureen Were. 1998. "Enhancing Health Care among the Vulnerable Groups: The Question of Waivers and Exemptions." Discussion Paper DP/014/98. Nairobi: Institute of Policy Analysis and Research.

Oxfam. 2002. *Cash for Work Programming. A Practical Guide.* Nairobi: Oxfam GB Kenya Programme.

Paes de Barros, R. and M. Carvalho. 2004. *Targeting as an Instrument for a More Effective Social Policy.* Washington, DC: Social Equity Forum.

Palacios, Robert, and S. Irudaya Rajan. 2004. *Safety Nets for the Elderly in Poor Countries: The Case of Nepal.* Pension Reform Primer. Washington, DC: World Bank.

Parker, Susan W., and Emmanuel Skoufias. 2000. "Final Report: The Impact of PROGRESA on Work, Leisure, and Time Allocation." Washington, DC: International Food Policy Research Institute.

Pasha, Hafiz A., Sumaira Jafarey, and Hari Ram Lohano. 2000. "Evaluation of Social Safety Nets in Pakistan." Research Report 32. Karachi: Social Policy and Development Centre.

Patrinos, Harry Anthony. 2002. "A Review of Demand-Side Financing Initiatives in Education." Draft. Washington, DC: World Bank.

Pauw, Kalie, and Liberty Mncube. 2007. "Expanding the Social Security Net in South Africa: Opportunities, Challenges and Constraints." Working Paper 07/127. Cape Town: University of Cape Town, Development Policy Research Unit.

Paxson, Christina, and Norbert Schady. 2004. "Child Health and the 1988–1992 Economic Crisis in Peru." Policy Research Working Paper 3260. Washington, DC: World Bank.

Pearlstein, Steven. 2007. "The Grand Bargainer." *Washington Post.* February 7, 2007.

Pearson, Mark. 2004. *Issues Paper: The Case for Abolition of User Fees for Primary Health Services.* London: Department for International Development, Health Systems Resource Centre.

Pellissery, S. 2006. *Do Public Works Programmes Ensure Employment in the Rural Informal Sector? Examining the Employment Guarantee Scheme in Rural Maharashtra, India.* Department of Social Policy and Social Work. Oxford, UK: Oxford University, Barnett House.

Peppiatt, David, John Mitchell, and Penny Holzmann. 2001. *Cash Transfers in Emergencies: Evaluating Benefits and Assessing Risks.* London: Overseas Development Institute, Humanitarian Practice Network.

Perdana, Ari, and John Maxwell. 2004. "Poverty Targeting in Indonesia: Programs, Problems and Lessons Learned." Economics Working Paper Series 083. Jakarta: Centre for Strategic and International Studies.

Perry, Guillermo, Omar Arias, Humberto Lopez, William Maloney, and Luis Serven. 2006. *Poverty Reduction and Growth: Virtuous and Vicious Circles.* Washington, DC: World Bank.

Phillips, Sean. 2004. "The Expanded Public Works Programme (EPWP)." Presentation to the Conference on Overcoming Under-Development in South Africa's Second Economy, Pretoria, October 29, 2004.

Pinstrup-Andersen, Per, ed. 1988. *Food Subsidies in Developing Countries: Costs, Benefits, and Policy Options.* Baltimore: Johns Hopkins University Press.

Piron, Laure-Hélène. 2004. "Rights-Based Approaches to Social Protection." Paper prepared for the U.K. Department for International Development. London.

Planning and Development Collaborative International. 2001. *How to Create a Transparent Appeals System for the Social Benefits*. Report 16. Yerevan, Armenia: Planning and Development Collaborative International.

Polity IV Project. 2008. "Polity IV Project: Political Regime Characteristics and Transitions, 1800–2006." www.systemicpeace.org/polity/polity4.htm.

Pop, Lucian, Richard Florescu, and Emil Tesliuc. Forthcoming. "Program Implementation Matters for Targeting Performance—Evidence and Lessons from Eastern and Central Europe: Country Study Romania." Social Protection Discussion Paper Series. Washington, DC: World Bank.

Population Council. 1999. *Our Daughters Our Wealth: Investing in Young Girls*. New Delhi: Population Council, South and East Asia Office.

Porteous, David. 2006. *The Enabling Environment for Mobile Banking in Africa*. Report commissioned by the U.K. Department for International Development. Boston: Bankable Frontier Associates.

Posarac, Alexandra, Emil Daniel Tesliuc, and Diego Angel-Urdinola. Forthcoming. "The Impact of the Poverty Family Benefit Program on Work Effort." Washington, DC: World Bank.

Potucek, Martin. 2004. "Accession and Social Policy: The Case of the Czech Republic." *Journal of European Social Policy* 14 (3): 253–6.

Prennushi, Giovanna, Gloria Rubio, and Kalanidhi Subbarao. 2002. "Monitoring and Evaluation." In *A Sourcebook for Poverty Reduction Strategies*, pp. 107–30. Washington, DC: World Bank.

PricewaterhouseCoopers. 2005. *VAT in Southern and Eastern Africa*. Cape Town: PricewaterhouseCoopers.

Pritchett, Lant. 2002. "It Pays to Be Ignorant: A Simple Political Economy of Rigorous Program Evaluation." *Journal of Economic Policy Reform* 5 (4): 251–69.

————. 2005. "A Lecture on the Political Economy of Targeting." Social Protection Discussion Paper 0501. World Bank, Washington DC.

Pritchett, Lant, Sudarno Sumarto, and Asep Suryahadi. 2002. "Targeted Programs in an Economic Crisis: Empirical Findings from Indonesia's Experience." Working Paper 95. Cambridge, MA: Harvard University, Center for International Development.

Purdon, Susan, Carli Lessof, Kandy Woodfield, and Caroline Bryson. 2001."Research Methods for Policy Evaluations." Research Working Paper 2. London: UK Department for Work and Pensions.

Quisumbing, Agnes R. 2003. "Food Aid and Child Nutrition in Rural Ethiopia." *World Development* 31 (7): 1309–24.

Quisumbing, Agnes R., and John A. Maluccio. 2000. "Intrahousehold Allocation and Gender Relations: New Empirical Evidence from Four Developing Countries." Food Consumption and Nutrition Division Discussion Paper 84. Washington, DC: International Food Policy Research Institute.

Raczynski, Dagmar, and Pilar Romaguera. 1995. "Chile: Poverty, Adjustment, and Social Policies in the 1980s." In Dominique van de Walle and Kimberly Nead, eds., *Public Spending and the Poor: Theory and Evidence*, pp. 275–333. Baltimore: Johns Hopkins University.

Radhakrishna, R., and K. Subbarao, with S. Indrakant and C. Ravi. 1997. "India's Public Distribution System: A National and International Perspective." Discussion Paper 380. Washington, DC: World Bank.

Rainwater, Lee. 1982. "Stigma in Income-Tested Programs." In I. Garfinkel, ed., *Income-Tested Transfer Programs: The Case for and Against*, pp. 19–46. New York: Academic Press.

Rao, C., S. K. Ray, and Kalanidhi Subbarao. 1988. *Unstable Agriculture and Droughts: Implications for Policy.* New Delhi: Vikas Publications.

Rao, Vijayendra. 2000. "Price Heterogeneity and 'Real' Inequality: A Case Study of Poverty and Prices in Rural South India." *Review of Income and Wealth* 46 (2): 201–11.

Ravallion, Martin. 1991. "Reaching the Rural Poor through Public Employment: Arguments, Evidence and Lessons from South Asia." *World Bank Research Observer* 6 (2): 153–76.

———. 1999a. "Appraising Workfare." *World Bank Research Observer* 14 (1): 31–48.

———. 1999b. "The Mystery of the Vanishing Benefits: Ms. Speedy Analyst's Introduction to Evaluation." Policy Research Working Paper 2153. World Bank, Washington, DC.

———. 2002. "Are the Poor Protected from Budget Cuts? Evidence for Argentina." *Journal of Applied Economics* V (1): 95–121.

———. 2007. "How Relevant Is Targeting to the Success of an Antipoverty Program?" Policy Research Working Paper 4385. Washington, DC: World Bank.

———. 2008. "Evaluating Anti-Poverty Programs." In T. Paul Schultz and John A. Strauss, eds, *Handbook of Development Economics*, vol. 4, pp. 3787–3846. Amsterdam: North-Holland.

Ravallion, Martin, Gaurav Datt, and Shubham Chaudhuri. 1993. "Does Maharastra's Employment Guarantee Scheme Guarantee Employment? Effects of the 1988 Wage Increase." *Economic Development and Cultural Change* 41 (2): 251–75.

Ravallion, Martin, Dominique van de Walle, and Madhur Gautam.1995. "Testing a Social Safety Net." *Journal of Public Economics* 57 (2): 175–99.

Ravallion, Martin, and Quentin Wodon. 2000. "Does Child Labor Displace Schooling? Evidence on Behavioral Responses to an Enrollment Study." *Economic Journal* 110 (March): C158–C176.

Rawlings, Laura B. 2005. "A New Approach to Social Assistance: Latin America's Experience with Conditional Cash Transfer Programmes." *International Social Security Review* 58 (2–3): 133–61.

Rawlings, Laura B., and Gloria M. Rubio. 2005. "Evaluating the Impact of Conditional Cash Transfer Programs." *World Bank Research Observer* 20 (1): 29–55.

Republic of Zambia. 2002. *Zambia Poverty Reduction Strategy Paper 2002–2004.* Lusaka: Ministry of Finance and National Planning.

Regalia, Ferdinando, and Marcos Robles. 2005. *Social Assistance, Poverty and Equity in the Dominican Republic.* Economic and Sector Study Series. Washington, DC: Inter-American Development Bank.

Regional Hunger and Vulnerability Programme. 2007. *Zimbabwe: National Inventory of Social Protection Policies, Institutions and Frameworks.* Johannesburg: Regional Hunger and Vulnerability Programme.

Rehman, Ibrahim, Hafeezur Preeti Malhotra, Ram Chandra Pal, and Phool Badan Singh. 2005. "Availability of Kerosene to Rural Households: A Case Study from India." *Energy Policy* 33 (17): 2165–74.

Reinecke, Gerhard. 2005. "Income Protection through Direct Employment Programmes: Recent Concepts and Examples from Latin America." *International Social Security Review* 58 (2–3): 163–83.

Ringold, Dena, and Leszek Kasek. 2007. "Social Assistance in the New EU Member States: Strengthening Performance and Labor Market Incentives." Working Paper 117. Washington, DC: World Bank.

Ringold, Dena, Mitchell A. Orenstein, and Erika Wilkens. 2005. *Roma in an Expanding Europe: Breaking the Poverty Cycle.* Washington, DC: World Bank.

Robinson, S. Moataz El-Said, Nu Nu San, Achmad Suryana Hermanto, Dewa Swastika, and Sjaiful Bahri. 1997. "Rice Price Policies in Indonesia: A Computable General Equilibrium (CGE) Analysis." Trade and Macroeconomics Division Discussion Paper 19. Washington, DC: International Food Policy Research Institute.

Rodrik, Dani. 1998. "Globalization, Social Conflict and Economic Growth" *World Economy* 21 (2): 143–58.

———. 1999. "Where Did All the Growth Go? External Shocks, Social Conflict, and Growth Collapses." *Journal of Economic Growth* 4 (4): 385–412.

Rofman, Rafael. 2005. "Social Security Coverage in Latin America." Social Protection Discussion Paper 0522. World Bank, Washington," DC.

Rogers, Beatrice Lorge. 1996. "The Implications of Female Household Headship for Food Consumption and Nutritional Status in the Dominican Republic." *World Development* 24 (1): 113–128.

Rogers, Beatrice Lorge, and Jennifer Coates. 2002. *Food-Based Safety Nets and Related Programs.* Social Safety Net Primer Series 0225. Washington, DC: World Bank.

Rogers, Beatrice Lorge, Serena Rajabiun, James Levinson, and Katherine Tucker. 2002. "Reducing Chronic Malnutrition in Peru: A Proposed National Strategy." Discussion Paper 2. Medford, MA: Tufts University.

Rohini, Nayyer. 2002. "Contribution of Works and Other Labour-Based Infrastructure to Poverty Alleviation—The Indian Experience: Issues in Employment and Poverty." Discussion Paper 3. Geneva: International Labour Office.

Rosa, Solange, Annie Leatt, and Katharine Hall. 2005. *Does the Means Justify the End? Targeting the Child Support Grant.* Cape Town: University of Cape Town, Children's Institute.

Rossi, Peter H., Howard E. Freeman, and Mark W. Lipsey. 1999. *Evaluation: A Systematic Approach,* 6th ed. Thousand Oaks, CA: Sage.

Rostgaard, Tine. 2004. *Family Support Policy in Central and Eastern Europe: A Decade and a Half of Transition.* Early Childhood and Family Policy Series 8. Budapest: United Nations Educational, Scientific, and Cultural Organization, Education Sector.

Rubio, Gloria. 2007. "Construyendo un Sistema de Evaluación y Monitoreo basado en Resultados de los Programas Sociales." Paper presented at the Conference on Social Programs, Inter-American Development Bank, Washington, DC, November 15, 2007.

Ruggeri Laderchi, C. 2001. "Killing Two Birds with the Same Stone? The Effectiveness of Food Transfers on Nutrition and Monetary Policy." Paper presented at the Latin American Economic Association Conference, Montevideo, October 18–20, 2001.

Russell, S., and L. Gilson. 1995. *User Fees in Government Health Services: Is Equity Being Considered? An International Survey*. Public Health and Policy Publication 15. London: London School of Hygiene and Tropical Medicine.

Saaddah, Fadia, Menno Pradhan, and Robert Sparrow. 2001. "The Effectiveness of the Health Card as an Instrument to Ensure Access to Medical Care for the Poor during the Crisis." Washington, DC: World Bank.

Sadoulet, Elisabeth, Alain de Janvry, and Benjamin Davis. 2001. "Cash Transfer Programs with Income Multipliers: PROCAMPO in Mexico." *World Development* 29 (6): 1043–56.

Sadoulet, Elisabeth, Frederico Finan, Alain de Janvry, and Renos Vakis. 2004. "Can Conditional Cash Transfer Programs Improve Social Risk Management?" Social Protection Discussion Paper 0420. Washington DC: World Bank.

Sadowski, Yahya M. 1991 *Political Vegetables? Businessmen and Bureaucrats in the Development of Egyptian Agriculture*. Washington, DC: Brookings Institution.

Saghir, Jamal. 2005. "Energy and Poverty: Myths, Links and Policy Issues." Energy Working Notes No. 4. Washington, DC: World Bank, Energy and Mining Sector Board.

Sahn, David E., and Harold Alderman. 1995. "Incentive Effects on Labor Supply of Sri Lanka's Rice Subsidy." In Dominique van de Walle and Kimberly Nead, eds., *Public Spending and the Poor: Theory and Evidence*, pp. 387–410. Baltimore: Johns Hopkins University.

———. 1996. "The Effect of Food Subsidies on Labor Supply in Sri Lanka." *Economic Development and Cultural Change* 45 (1): 125–45.

Sahn, David E., Beatrice L. Rogers, and David Nelson. 1981. "Assessing the Uses of Food Aid: PL 480 Title II in India." *Ecology of Food and Nutrition* 10 (3): 153–61.

Sahn, David E., and Stephen Younger. 2000 "Expenditure Incidence in Africa: Microeconomic Evidence." *Fiscal Studies* 21 (3): 329–48.

Samaniego, Norma. 2002. *Las políticas de mercado de trabajo en México y su evaluación*. Santiago: Comisión Económica para America Latina y el Caribe, División de Desarrollo Económico.

Samson, Michael. 2006. "Are Conditionalities Necessary for Human Development?" Paper presented at the Third International Conference on Conditional Cash Transfers, Istanbul, June 26–30, 2006.

Samson, Michael, Una Lee, A. Ndlebe, Kenneth MacQuene, Ingrid van Niekerk, Viral Gandhi, Tomoko Harigaya, and Celeste Abrahams. 2004. *The Social and Economic Impact of South Africa's Social Security System: Social Grants Help Reduce Poverty, Promote Job Search and Increase School Enrolment Rates in South Africa*. Cape Town: Economic Policy Research Institute.

Samson, Michael, Kenneth MacQuene, and Ingrid van Niekerk. 2006. "Social Grants, South Africa." Policy Brief 1. London: Overseas Development Institute.

Sanghvi, T., B. L. Rogers, P. Tatian, Jere Behrman, M. Calderón, S. Crelia, and M. García. 1995. *The Effect of Food Assistance and Cash Transfers on Health and Nutrition: An Evaluation of the Programs of Bonos and Supplementary Maternal and Child Feeding (PL 480 Title II)*. Bethesda, MD: International Science and Technology Institute.

Save the Children. 2001. "Cash-for-Relief Piloting." Review report. Addis Ababa: Save the Children.

Scandizzo, Pasquale, Raghav Gaiha, and Katsushi Imai. 2005. "Option Values, Switches and Wages: An Analysis of the Employment Guarantee Scheme in India." Paper presented at the University of Manchester, Institute for Development Policy and Management, conference on Social Protection for Chronic Poverty Risk, Needs, and Rights: Protecting What? How?, Manchester, England, February 23–24, 2005.

Schady, Norbert R., and Maria Caridad Araujo. 2006. "Cash, Conditions, School Enrollment, and Child Work: Evidence from a Randomized Experiment in Ecuador." Policy Research Working Paper 3930. Washington, DC: World Bank.

Schubert, Bernd. 2005. *Social Cash Transfers. Reaching the Poorest: Health, Education and Social Protection Sector Project: Systems of Social Protection. A Contribution to the International Debate Based on Experience in Zambia.* Eschborn, Germany: German Agency for Technical Cooperation.

Schubert, Bernd, and Sylvia Beales. 2006. *Social Cash Transfers for Africa: A Transformative Agenda for the 21st Century.* London: HelpAge International.

Schubert, Bernd, and Jörg Goldberg. 2004. *The Pilot Social Cash Transfer Scheme: Kalomo District, Zambia.* Lusaka: German Agency for Technical Cooperation.

Schubert, Bernd, and Rachel Slater. 2006. "Social Cash Transfers in Low-Income African Countries: Conditional or Unconditional?" *Development Policy Review* 24 (5): 571–78.

Schuettinger, Robert, and Eamon Butler. 1979. *Forty Centuries of Wage and Price Controls.* Washington, DC: Heritage Foundation.

Schultz, T. Paul. 2000. "Final Report: The Impact of PROGRESA on School Enrollments." Washington, DC: International Food Policy Research Institute.

———. 2004. "School Subsidies for the Poor: Evaluating the Mexican Progresa Poverty Program." *Journal of Development Economics* 74 (1, special issue): 199–250.

Schwabish, Jonathan, Timothy M. Smeeding, and Lars Osberg. 2004. "Income Distribution and Social Expenditures: A Crossnational Perspective." Luxembourg Income Study Working Paper 350. Luxembourg.

Schwarz, Anita. 2003. "Old Age Security and Social Pensions." Unpublished report. Washington, DC: World Bank, Social Protection Unit.

Sen, A. 1981. *Poverty and Famines: An Essay on Entitlement and Deprivation.* Oxford, UK: Oxford University Press.

———. 1999. *Development as Freedom.* Oxford, UK: Oxford University Press.

Shaban, Radwan A., Dina Abu-Ghaida, and Abdel-Salam Al-Naimat. 2001. *Poverty Alleviation in Jordan in the 1990s: Lessons for the Future.* Washington, DC: World Bank, Middle East and North Africa Region.

Sharma, M. 2006. *An Assessment of the Effects of the Cash Transfer Pilot Project on Household Consumption Patterns in Tsunami-Affected Areas of Sri Lanka.* Washington, DC: International Food Policy Research Institute.

Sharp, Kay, Taylor Brown, and Amdissa Teshome. 2006. *Targeting Ethiopia's Productive Safety Net Programme.* London, Bristol, and Addis Ababa: Overseas Development Institute, IDL Group, and A-Z Capacity Building Consult.

Shopov, Georgi. Forthcoming. "Program Implementation Matters for Targeting Performance—Evidence and Lessons from Eastern and Central Europe. Country Study: Bulgaria." Social Protection Discussion Paper. Washington, DC: World Bank.

Singh, Anoop, Agnes Belaisch, Charles Collyns, Paula De Masi, Reva Krieger, Guy Meredith, and Robert Rennhack. 2005. "Stabilization and Reform in Latin America: A Macroeconomic Perspective of Experience Since the 1990s." Occasional Paper 238. Washington, DC: International Monetary Fund.

Sinha, Saurabh, and Michael Lipton. 1999. "Damaging Fluctuations, Risk and Poverty: A Review." Background paper for *World Development Report 2000/2001*. Brighton, UK: University of Sussex, Poverty Research Unit at Sussex.

Sipos, Sandor, and Dena Ringold. 2005. "Social Safety Nets." In Nicholas Barr, ed., *Labor Markets and Social Policy in Central Europe: The Accession and Beyond*, pp. 89–134. Washington, DC: World Bank.

Sjoblom, Disa, and John Farrington. 2008. *The Indian National Rural Employment Guarantee Act: Will It Reduce Poverty and Boost the Economy?* Project Briefing 7. London: Overseas Development Institute.

Skoufias, Emmanuel. 2001. *PROGRESA and Its Impacts on the Welfare of Rural Households in Mexico*. Research Report 139. Washington, DC: International Food Policy Research Institute.

———. 2003. "Economic Crises and Natural Disasters: Coping Strategies and Policy Implications." Washington, DC: Inter-American Development Bank.

———. 2005. "PROGRESA and Its Impacts on the Welfare of Rural Households in Mexico." Research Report 139. Washington, DC: International Food Policy Research Institute.

Skoufias, Emmanuel, and Vincenzo di Maro. 2006. "Conditional Cash Transfers, Work Incentives, and Poverty." Policy Research Working Paper 3973. Washington, DC: World Bank.

SMERU Research Institute. 1998. *Results from a SMERU Rapid Appraisal in Five Provinces*. Monitoring the Social Crisis from the Field 2. Jakarta: SMERU Research Institute.

Smith, Lisa, C. Ramakrishnan, Aida Ndiaye, Lawrence Haddad, and Reynaldo Martorell. 2003. *The Importance of Women's Status for Child Nutrition in Developing Countries*. Research Report 131. Washington, DC: International Food Policy Research Institute.

Smith, W. James, and Kalanidhi Subbarao. 2003. "What Role for Safety Net Transfers in Very Low Income Countries?" Social Protection Discussion Paper 0301. Washington, DC: World Bank.

Sojo, Ana. 2003. *Social Vulnerability, Insurance and Risk Diversification in Latin America and the Caribbean*. Review 80 (LC/G.2204-P/E). Santiago: Economic Commission for Latin America and the Caribbean.

Southern African Labour and Development and Research Unit. 2005. *Addressing Social Protection Challenges in the Context of HIV and AIDS: A Role for PWPs in East and Southern Africa?* Cape Town: University of Cape Town.

Sparrow, Robert. 2007. "Protecting Education for the Poor in Times of Crisis: An Evaluation of a Scholarship Programme in Indonesia." *Oxford Bulletin of Economics and Statistics* 69 (1): 99–122.

Sphere Project. 2004. *The Sphere Humanitarian Charter and Minimum Standards in Disaster Relief.* Geneva: Sphere Project.

Squire, Lyn, and Herman G. van der Tak. 1975. *Economic Analysis of Projects*. Baltimore: Johns Hopkins University Press.

Stecklov Guy, Paul Winters, Marco Stampini, and Benjamin Davis. 2005. "Do Conditional Cash Transfers Influence Migration? A Study Using Experimental Data from the Mexican PRO-GRESA Program." *Demography* 42 (4): 769–90.

Stecklov, Guy, Paul Winters, Jessica Todd, and Ferdinando Regalia. 2006. "Demographic Externalities from Poverty Programs in Developing Countries: Experimental Evidence from Latin America." Working Paper No. 2006-1. Washington, DC: American University.

Stifel, David, and Harold Alderman. 2006. "The 'Glass of Milk' Subsidy Program and Malnutrition in Peru." *World Bank Economic Review* 20 (3): 421–48.

Stock, Elizabeth, and Jan de Veen. 1996. "Expanding Labor-Based Methods for Road Works in Africa." Technical Paper 347. Washington, DC: World Bank, Africa Technical Department.

Struyk, Raymond, Ekaterina Petrova, and Tatiana Lykova. 2006. "Targeting Housing Allowances in Russia." *European Journal of Housing Policy* 6 (2): 191–220.

Subbarao, Kalanidhi. 1993. "Interventions to Fill Nutrition Gaps at the Household-Level: A Review of India's Experience." In B. Harriss, S. Guhan, and R. H. Cassen, eds., *Poverty in India: Research and Policy*. Mumbai: Oxford University Press.

———. 1997. "Public Works as an Anti-Poverty Program: An Overview of Cross-Country Experience." *American Journal of Agricultural Economics* 79 (May): 678–83.

———. 1998. "Namibia's Social Safety Net: Issues and Options for Reform." Policy Research Working Paper 1996. Washington, DC: World Bank.

———. 1999. "Financial Crises and Safety Nets: Old and the New Poor in Korea." Unpublished report. Washington, DC: World Bank.

———. 2003. "Systemic Shocks and Social Protection: The Role and Effectiveness of Public Works." Social Protection Discussion Paper 0302. Washington, DC: World Bank.

Subbarao, Kalanidhi, Akhter Ahmed, and Tesfaye Teklu. 1995. "Philippines: Social Safety Net Programs: Targeting, Cost-Effectiveness and Options for Reform." Discussion Paper 317. Washington, DC: World Bank.

Subbarao, Kalanidhi, Aniruddha Bonnerjee, Jeanine Braithwaite, Soniya Carvalho, Kene Ezemenari, Carol Graham, and Alan Thompson. 1997. *Safety Net Programs and Poverty Reduction: Lessons from Cross-Country Experience*. Washington, DC: World Bank.

Subbarao, Kalanidhi, and Diane Coury. 2004. *Reaching Out to Africa's Orphans: A Framework for Public Action*. Africa Region Human Development Series. Washington, DC: World Bank.

Subbarao, Kalanidhi, Angel Mattimore, and Kathrin Plangemann. 2001. *Social Protection of Africa's Orphans and Other Vulnerable Children: Issues and Good Practice Program Options*. Washington, DC: World Bank, Africa Region.

Subbarao, Kalanidhi, and William James Smith. 2003. "Safety Nets Versus Relief Nets: Towards a Medium-Term Safety Net Strategy for Ethiopia." Draft. Washington, DC: World Bank.

Sumarto, Sudarno, Asep Suryahadi, and Lant Pritchett. 2000. "Safety Nets and Safety Ropes: Who Benefited from Two Indonesian Crisis Programs: The 'Poor' or the 'Shocked?'" Policy Research Working Paper 2436. Washington, DC: World Bank.

———. 2003. "Safety Nets or Safety Ropes? Dynamic Benefit Incidence of Two Crisis Programs in Indonesia." *World Development* 31 (7): 1257–77.

Sumarto, Sudarno, Asep Suryahadi, and Wenefrida Widyanti. 2002. "Designs and Implementation of Indonesian Social Safety Net Programs." *Developing Economies* XL-1 (March): 3–31.

Tabor, Steven. 2002. "Assisting the Poor with Cash: Design and Implementation of Social Transfer Programs." Working Paper, Social Safety Net Primer Series. Washington, DC: World Bank.

Tabor, Steven, and M. Husein Sawit. 2001. "Social Protection Via Rice: the OPK Rice Subsidy Program in Indonesia." *Developing Economies* XXXIX–3 (September): 267–94.

Taylor, Anna, and John Seaman. 2004. *Targeting Food Aid in Emergencies.* Special Supplement 1. Oxford, UK: Emergency Nutrition Network.

Tcherneva, Pavlina, and L. Randall Wray. 2005. "Gender and the Job Guarantee: The Impact of Argentina's *Jefes* Program on Female Heads of Poor Households." Working Paper 48. Kansas City, MO: University of Missouri, Center for Full Employment and Price Stability.

Teklu, Tesfaye. 1994. "Labor-Intensive Rural Roads in Kenya, Tanzania and Botswana: Some Evidence on Design and Practice." *Ethiopian Journal of Economics* 3 (2).

Ter-Minassian, Teresa. 1997. *Fiscal Federalism in Theory and Practice.* Washington, DC: International Monetary Fund.

Ter Rele, Harry, and Ed Westerhout. 2003. *Does an Increase of Public Expenditure Justify Slower Debt Reduction?* Report 1. The Hague: Central Planning Bureau.

Teruel, Graciela, and Benjamin Davis. 2000. "An Evaluation of the Impact of PROGRESA Cash Transfers on Private Inter-household Transfers." Washington, DC: International Food Policy Research Institute.

Tesliuc, Cornelia Mihaela. 2004. "Poverty Trends in Bulgaria: 2001–2003." Unpublished report. Washington, DC: World Bank.

Tesliuc, Cornelia Mihaela, Lucian Pop, and Emil Daniel Tesliuc. 2001. *Saracia si sistemul de protectie sociala.* Iasi, Romania: Polirom.

Tesliuc, Emil. 2004. "Mitigating Social Risks in Kyrgyz Republic." Social Protection Discussion Paper 0408. Washington, DC: World Bank.

Tesliuc, Emil, David Coady, Margaret Grosh, and Lucian Pop. Forthcoming. *Program Implementation Matters for Targeting Performance: Evidence and Lessons from Eastern and Central Europe.* Washington, DC: World Bank.

Tesliuc, Emil, and Kathy Lindert. 2004. "Risk and Vulnerability in Guatemala: A Quantitative and Qualitative Assessment." Social Protection Discussion Paper 0404. Washington, DC: World Bank.

Thompson, Alan. 2004. "Russia: Administrative Data System for Targeted Allowances." Draft. Washington, DC: World Bank.

Tibble, Mike. 2005. "Review of Existing Research on the Extra Costs of Disability." Working Paper 21, Corporate Document Series. London: Department of Work and Pensions.

Tien, Marie, and Grace Chee. 2002. *Literature Review and Findings: Implementation of Waiver Policies.* Technical Report 009. Bethesda, MD: Abt Associates, Inc., Partners for Health Reformplus Project.

Tietjen, Karen. 2003. *The Bangladesh Primary Education Stipend Project: A Descriptive Analysis.* Dhaka: The Partnership for Sustainable Strategies for Girls' Education.

Timmer, Peter. 1991. "Food Price Stabilization: Rationale, Design, and Implementation." In Dwight Perkins and Michael Roemer, eds., *Reforming Economic Systems*, pp. 219–48. Cambridge, MA: Harvard University Press.

———. 1996. "Does BULOG Stabilize Rice Prices in Indonesia? Should It Try?" *Indonesian Economic Studies* 32 (2): 45–74.

———. 2004. "Food Security in Indonesia: Current Challenges and the Long-Run Outlook." Working Paper 48. Washington, DC: Center for Global Development.

Trairatvorakul, Prasarn. 1984. "The Effects on Income Distribution and Nutrition of Alternative Rice Price Policies in Thailand." Research Report 46. Washington, DC: International Food Policy Research Institute.

Tritah, Ahmed. 2003. "The Public Distribution System in India: Counting the Poor from Making the Poor Count." Toulouse, France: Universite des Sciences Sociales, Groupe de Recherche en Economie Mathématique et Quantitative.

Tuck, Laura, and Kathy Lindert. 1996. "From Universal Food Subsidies to a Self-Targeted Program: A Case Study of Tunisian Reform." Discussion Paper 351. Washington, DC: World Bank.

Uauy, Ricardo, Cecilia Albala, and Juliana Kain. 2001. *Obesity Trends in Latin America: Transiting from Under- to Overweight.* Santiago: Universidad de Chile, Instituto de Nutricion y Tecnologia de los Alimentos.

UN (United Nations). 1948. "Universal Declaration of Human Rights." www.un.org/Overview/rights.html.

———. 2002. *Population Ageing Report 2002.* New York: UN, Economic and Social Affairs Department, Population Division.

UNAIDS (Joint United Nations Programme on HIV/AIDS), UNICEF (United Nations Children's Fund), and USAID (U.S. Agency for International Development). 2004. *Children on the Brink 2004: A Joint Report of New Orphan Estimates and a Framework for Action.* New York: UNICEF.

UNHCR (United Nations High Commissioner for Refugees). 2003. *Refugees by Numbers.* Geneva: UNHCR.

UNHCR (United Nations High Commissioner for Refugees) and WFP (World Food Programme). 1999. *Guidelines for Selective Feeding Programmes in Emergencies.* Geneva: UNHCR.

UNICEF (United Nations Childrens Fund), Innocenti Research Centre. 2003a. *Changing Minds, Policies and Lives—Improving Protection of Children in Eastern Europe and Central Asia: Gatekeeping Services for Vulnerable Children and Families.* Florence: UNICEF and World Bank.

———. 2003b. *Changing Minds, Policies and Lives—Improving Protection of Children in Eastern Europe and Central Asia: Improving Standards of Child Protection Services.* Florence: UNICEF and World Bank.

———. 2003c. *Changing Minds, Policies and Lives—Improving Protection of Children in Eastern Europe and Central Asia: Redirecting Resources to Community-Based Services.* Florence: UNICEF and World Bank, Florence.

USAID (U.S. Agency for International Development). 1999. *Improving Girl's Education in Guatemala.* Impact Evaluation. Washington, DC: Center for Development Information and Evaluation.

U.S. Census Bureau. 2005. *Alternative Poverty Estimates in the United States: 2003.* Washington, DC: U.S. Department of Commerce, Economics and Statistics Administration. www.census.gov/prod/2005pubs/p60-227.pdf.

USDA (U.S. Department of Agriculture). 2005. *Making America Stronger: A Profile of the Food Stamp Program.* Alexandria, VA: Food and Nutrition Service Office of Analysis, Nutrition, and Evaluation.

———. 2008. "A Short History of the Food Stamp Program." www.fns.usda.gov/fsp/rules/Legislation/about_fsp.htm.

U.S. House of Representatives, Committee on Ways and Means. 2000. "Child Support Enforcement Program." In *2000 Green Book,* Section 8, 463–570. Washington, DC: U.S. Government Printing Office.

Vaitsman, Jeni, Roberto W. S. Rodrigues, and Rômulo Paes-Sousa. 2006. *The System for Evaluating and Monitoring Social Development Programs and Policies: The Case of the Ministry of Social Development and the Fight against Hunger in Brazil.* Policy Papers /17. Brasilia: United Nations Educational, Scientific, and Cultural Organization.

Valdés-Prieto, Salvador. 2004. "Social Security Coverage in Chile, 1990-2001." Background paper for *Keeping the Promise of Old-Age Income Security in Latin America.* Washington, DC: World Bank, Latin America and the Caribbean Region.

van Berkel, Rik. 2006. "The Decentralisation of Social Assistance in the Netherlands." *International Journal of Sociology and Social Policy* 26 (1–2): 20–31.

van der Berg, S. 1997. "South African Social Security under Apartheid and Beyond." *Development Southern Africa* 14 (4): 481–503.

———. 2002. "Devising Social Security Interventions for Maximum Poverty Impact." *Social Dynamics* 28 (2): 39–68.

van de Walle, Dominique. 2002a. "Poverty and Transfers in Yemen." Middle East and North Africa Working Paper Series 30. World Bank, Washington, DC.

———. 2002b. "The Static and Dynamic Incidence of Vietnam's Public Safety Net." Policy Research Working Paper 2791. Washington, DC: World Bank.

———. 2003. "Behavioral Incidence Analysis of Public Spending and Social Programs." In François Bourguignon and Luiz. A. Pereira da Silva, eds., *The Impact of Economic Policies on Poverty and Income Distribution. Evaluation Techniques and Tools*, pp. 69–83. Washington, DC: World Bank.

Vodopivec, Milan. 2004. *Income Support for the Unemployed: Issues and Options.* Regional and Sectoral Studies. Washington, DC: World Bank.

Vodopivec, Milan, Andreas Wörgötter, and Dhushyanth Raju. 2003. "Unemployment Benefit Systems in Central and Eastern Europe: A Review of the 1990s." Social Protection Discussion Paper 0310. Washington, DC: World Bank.

von Braun, Joachim, Tesfaye Teklu, and Patrick Webb. 1992. "Labor-Intensive Public Works for Food Security in Africa: Past Experience and Future Potential." *International Labor Review* 131 (1): 19–33.

———. 1999. *Famine in Africa: Causes, Responses and Prevention*. Baltimore: Johns Hopkins University Press.

Wagstaff, Adam, and Naoko Watanabe. 2000. "Socioeconomic Inequalities in Child Malnutrition in the Developing World." Policy Research Working Paper 2434. Washington, DC: World Bank.

Wahlberg, Katarina. 2008. *Food Aid for the Hungry?* New York: Global Policy Forum.

Walker, T. S., R. P. Singh, and M. Asokan. 1986. "Risk Benefits, Crop Insurance and Dryland Agriculture." *Economic and Political Weekly* 21 (June): A81–88.

Warlters, Michael, and Emmanuelle Auriol. 2005 "The Marginal Cost of Funds in Africa." Policy Research Working Paper 3679. Washington, DC: World Bank.

Warren, David. 2003. "Coping with a Natural Disaster: Hurricane Mitch and the Honduran Social Investment Fund." *Spectrum Magazine* (fall): 20–21.

Washington Post. 2005. "La. To Cut Jobless Benefits, Raise Taxes." October 7, p. A8.

Webb, Patrick. 2002. "Emergency Relief during Europe's Famine of 1817. Anticipated Responses to Today's Humanitarian Disasters." Tufts Discussion Paper No. 14. Boston: Tufts University, Friedman School of Nutrition Science and Policy.

Webb, Patrick, and Beatrice Rogers. 2003. *Addressing the "In" in Food Insecurity*. Occasional Paper No. 1. Washington, DC: U.S. Agency for International Development, Office of Food for Peace.

Weigand, Christine, and Margaret Grosh. 2008. "Levels and Patterns of Safety Net Spending in Developing and Transition Countries." Social Protection Discussion Paper. Washington, DC: World Bank.

WFP (World Food Programme). 2005. *Global School Feeding Report 2005*. Rome: WFP.

———. 2006a. *Food for Education Works: A Review of WFP Programme Monitoring and Evaluation 2002–2006*. Rome: WFP.

———. 2006b. *Global School Feeding Report 2006*. Rome: WFP.

WHO (World Health Organization). 2001. *The International Classification of Functioning, Disability and Health (ICF)*. Geneva: WHO.

———. 2008. *An Update of the Global Burden of Disease in 2004*. Geneva: WHO.

Wietler, Katharina. 2007. *The Impact of Social Cash Transfers on Informal Safety Nets in Kalomo District, Zambia: A Qualitative Study*. Social Safety Net Project. Berlin: Ministry of Community Development and Social Services and German Agency for Technical Cooperation.

Werner, Alain. 2004. *A Guide to Implementation Research*. Washington, DC: Urban Institute Press.

Willibald, Sigrid. 2006. "Does Money Work? Cash Transfers to Ex-Combatants in Disarmament, Demobilisation and Reintegration Processes." *Disasters* 30 (3): 316–39.

Wilson, Michael. 2006. *Moving Toward Free Basic Education: Policy Issues and Implementation Challenges*. Washington, DC: United Nations Educational, Scientific, and Cultural Organization and the World Bank.

Witter, Sophie. 2005. *An Unnecessary Evil? User Fees for Healthcare in Low-Income Countries*. London: Save the Children UK.

World Bank. 1999a. *Bulgaria: Poverty during Transition*. Report 18411. Washington, DC: World Bank.

———. 1999b. *Cambodia Poverty Assessment*. Report 19858-KH. Washington, DC: World Bank.

———. 1999c. *Consumer Food Subsidy Programs in the MENA Region*. Report 19561-MNA. Washington, DC: World Bank, Middle East and North Africa Region, Human Development Group.

———. 1999d. "Improving Social Assistance in Armenia" Report 19385-AM. Washington, DC: World Bank.

———. 2000a. *Bangladesh: National Nutrition Project*, vol. 1, *Project Appraisal Document*. Washington, DC: World Bank.

———. 2000b. "Maintaining Utility Services for the Poor: Policies and Practices in Central and Eastern Europe and the Former Soviet Union." Report 20874. Washington, DC: World Bank.

———. 2000c. *Panama Poverty Assessment: Priorities and Strategies for Poverty Reduction*. Report 20307. Washington, DC: World Bank.

———. 2000d. *Republic of Yemen: Comprehensive Development Review, Phase I Poverty and Social Safety Nets Building Block*. Washington, DC: Middle East and North Africa Region, Social and Economic Development Unit.

———. 2000e. *World Development Indicators 2000*. Washington, DC: World Bank.

———. 2000f. *World Development Report 2000/2001: Attacking Poverty*. New York: Oxford University Press.

———. 2001a. *Brazil: An Assessment of the Bolsa Escola Program*. Report 20208-BR. Washington, DC: World Bank.

———. 2001b. *Brazil: Attacking Brazil's Poverty*. Report No. 20475-BR. Washington, DC: World Bank.

———. 2001c. *Brazil: Eradicating Child Labor*. Report 21858-BR. Washington, DC: World Bank.

———. 2001d. *Hungary Long-Term Poverty, Social Protection, and the Labor Market*. Report 20645-HU. Washington, DC: World Bank, Europe and Central Asia Region, Poverty Reduction and Economic Management.

———. 2001e. *India—Improving Household Food and Nutrition Security: Achievements and the Challenges Ahead*, 2 vols. Report 20300-IN. Washington, DC: World Bank, South Asia Region, Rural Development Sector Unit.

———. 2001f. *Jamaica: Social Safety Net Assessment*. Washington, DC: World Bank, Latin America and Caribbean Region.

———. 2001g. *Kingdom of Morocco Poverty Update*, 2 vols. Report 21506-MOR. Washington, DC: World Bank.

———. 2001h. *Social Protection Sector Strategy: From Safety Nets to Springboards*. Washington, DC: World Bank.

———. 2001i. *World Development Indicators 2001*. Washington, DC: World Bank.

————. 2002a. *Armenia Poverty Update 2002*. Report 24339-AM. Washington, DC: World Bank.

————. 2002b. *Bulgaria: Poverty Assessment*. Report 24516-BUL. Washington, DC: World Bank.

————. 2002c. *Bulgaria: Public Expenditure Issues and Directions for Reform*. Report 23979-BUL. Washington, DC: World Bank.

————. 2002d. *Colombia Social Safety Net Assessment*. Report 22255-CO Washington, DC: World Bank.

————. 2002e. *Costa Rica Social Spending and the Poor*. Report 24300-CR. Washington, DC: World Bank.

————. 2002f. *Poverty in Bangladesh: Building on Progress*. Report 24299-BD. Washington, DC: World Bank, South Asia Region, Poverty Reduction and Economic Management Sector Unit.

————. 2002g. *A Sourcebook for Poverty Reduction Strategies*. Washington, DC: World Bank.

————. 2003a. *Argentina Crisis and Poverty 2003. A Poverty Assessment: Main Report*. Report 26127-AR. Washington, DC: World Bank.

————. 2003b. *Armenia: Poverty Assessment: Main Report*. Report 27192-AM. Washington, DC: World Bank.

————. 2003c. *Armenia Public Expenditure Review*. Washington DC: World Bank, Europe and Central Asia Region, Poverty Reduction and Economic Management Unit.

————. 2003d. *Bangladesh Female Secondary School Assistance Project: Project Performance Assessment Report*. Report 26226. Washington, DC: World Bank.

————. 2003e. *Caribbean Youth Development: Issues and Policy Directions*. World Bank Country Study. Washington, DC: World Bank.

————. 2003f. *Guatemala: Poverty in Guatemala*. Report 24221-GU. Washington, DC: World Bank.

————. 2003g. *Kyrgyz Republic Poverty Assessment*. Report 24638-KG. Washington, DC: World Bank.

————. 2003h. *Romania: Poverty Assessment*. Report 26169-RO. Washington, DC: World Bank.

————. 2003i. *A User's Guide to Poverty and Social Impact Analysis*. Washington, DC: World Bank.

————. 2003j. *Workshop on Conditional Cash Transfer Programs: Operational Experiences*. By Ayala Consulting. Quito.

————. 2003k. *Yemen, Republic of: Second Public Works Project*. Implementation Completion Report. Washington, DC: World Bank.

————. 2004a. *Ethiopia Public Expenditure Review: The Emerging Challenge*. Report 29338-ET. Washington, DC: World Bank.

————. 2004b. *Good Practice Note: Using Poverty and Social Impact Analysis to Support Development Policy Operations*. Washington, DC: World Bank.

————. 2004c. *Malawi Second Social Action Fund Project: Implementation Completion Report*. Report 28608-MAI. Washington, DC: World Bank.

———. 2004d. "Private Sector Assessment for Health, Nutrition and Population (HNP) in Bangladesh." Draft. Washington, DC: World Bank.

———. 2004e. *World Development Report 2005: A Better Investment Climate for Everyone.* Washington, DC: World Bank.

———. 2004f. *Yemen, Republic of: Third Public Works Project.* Project Appraisal Document. Washington, DC: World Bank.

———. 2005a. *Bangladesh: Social Safety Nets in Bangladesh: An Assessment.* Report 33411-BD. Washington, DC: World Bank, South Asia Region, Human Development Unit.

———. 2005b. *Conditional Cash Transfers on Trial: A Debate on Conditional Cash Transfer Programs.* Washington, DC: World Bank.

———. 2005c. "Egypt—Toward a More Effective Social Policy: Subsidies and Social Safety Nets." Draft Report 33550-EG. Washington, DC: World Bank.

———. 2005d. *Ethiopia: Risk and Vulnerability Assessment.* Report 26275-ET. Washington, DC: World Bank.

———. 2005e. *Global Monitoring Report 2005—Millennium Development Goals: From Consensus to Momentum.* Washington, DC: World Bank.

———. 2005f. *Household Energy Supply and Use in Yemen*, vol. I, *Main Report.* Report 315/05. Washington, DC: World Bank.

———. 2005g. *Household Risk Management and Social Protection in Chile.* Country Study. Washington, DC: World Bank.

———. 2005h. *Managing Food Price Risks and Instability in an Environment of Market Liberalization.* Report 32727-GLB. Washington, DC: World Bank, Agriculture And Rural Development Department.

———. 2005i. *The OVC Toolkit for SSA: A Toolkit on How to Support Orphans and Vulnerable Children (OVC) in Sub-Saharan Africa (SSA)*, 2nd ed. Washington, DC: World Bank, Africa Region, and World Bank Institute.

———. 2005j. "Peru—Social Safety Nets in Peru: Background Paper for RECURSO Study." Washington, DC: World Bank, Latin America and the Caribbean Region, Human Development Department, Bolivia, Ecuador, Peru, and Venezuela Country Management Unit.

———. 2005k. *Project Performance Assessment Report: Bangladesh Integrated Nutrition Project (CREDIT 2735-BD).* Washington, DC: Operations Evaluation Department.

———. 2005l. *Russian Federation: Reducing Poverty through Growth and Social Policy Reform.* Report 28923-RU. Washington, DC: World Bank.

———. 2005m. *Shocks and Social Protection: Lessons from the Central American Coffee Crisis*, vol. I, *Synthesis of Findings and Implications for Policy.* Report 31857-CA. Washington, DC: World Bank.

———. 2005n. *World Development Report 2006: Equity and Development.* Washington, DC: World Bank.

———. 2006a. "Country Program Profiles." Report prepared for the Third International Conference on Conditional Cash Transfers, Istanbul, June 26–30, 2006.

————. 2006b. *Heads of Household Transition Project: Project Appraisal Document.* Report 32463-AR. Washington, DC: World Bank.

————. 2006c. "Implementing Free Primary Education: Achievements and Challenges." Draft. Washington, DC: World Bank, Education Department.

————. 2006d. *India's Employment Challenge.* Report 35772-IN. Washington, DC: World Bank.

————. 2006e. *India: Rural Governments and Service Delivery,* vol. III, *Main Report.* Report 38901-IN. Washington, DC: World Bank.

————. 2006f. *Indonesia: Making the New Indonesia Work for the Poor.* Report 37349-ID. Washington, DC: World Bank.

————. 2006g. *Mongolia Poverty Assessment.* Report 35660-MN. Washington, DC: World Bank.

————. 2006h. *People with Disabilities in India: From Commitments to Outcomes.* Washington, DC: World Bank, South Asia Region, Human Development Unit.

————. 2006i. *Productive Safety Net Project APL II for the Federal Democratic Republic of Ethiopia. Project Appraisal Document.* Report 37224. Washington, DC: World Bank.

————. 2006j. *Reducing Poverty through Growth and Social Policy: Reform in Russia.* Washington, DC: World Bank.

————. 2006k. *Social Protection in Pakistan: Managing Household Risks and Vulnerability.* Report 35472-PK. Washington, DC: World Bank.

————. 2006l. *Support to Reform the Bono de Desarrollo Humano.* Project Appraisal Document. Report 35064-EC. Washington, DC: World Bank.

————. 2006m. *World Development Indicators 2006.* Washington, DC: World Bank.

————. 2007a. *Argentina Jefes de Hogar (Heads of Household) Program: Implementation Completion and Results Report.* Washington, DC: World Bank.

————. 2007b. *Bangladesh National Nutrition Projects, Implementation Completion and Results Report.* Washington, DC: World Bank.

————. 2007c. *Control and Accountability Mechanisms in Conditional Cash Transfer Programs: A Review of Programs in Latin America and the Caribbean,* vol. 1, *Operational Innovations in Latin America and the Caribbean.* Washington, DC: World Bank, Latin America and the Caribbean Region.

————. 2007d. *Development Results in Middle Income Countries: An Evaluation of the World Bank's Support to Middle Income Countries.* Washington, DC: World Bank, Independent Evaluation Group.

————. 2007e. *Fiscal Policy for Growth and Development Further Analysis and Lessons from Country Case Studies.* Washington, DC: World Bank.

————. 2007f. *Implementing Free Primary Education: Achievements and Challenges.* Washington, DC: World Bank, Education Sector, Human Development Network.

————. 2007g. *Income Transfer Policies in Uruguay: Closing the Gaps to Increase Welfare.* Report No. 40084-UY. Washington, DC: World Bank.

————. 2007h. *Indonesia Public Expenditure Review 2007—Spending for Development: Making the Most of Indonesia's New Opportunities.* Report 38772. Washington, DC: World Bank.

———. 2007i. *Latvia—Sharing the High Growth Dividend: A Living Standards Assessment.* Report 38437-LV, Washington, DC: World Bank.

———. 2007j. *Pakistan: Promoting Rural Growth and Poverty Reduction.* Report 39303-PK. Washington, DC: World Bank.

———. 2007k. *Pakistan—Social Protection in Pakistan: Managing Household Risks and Vulnerability.* Report 35472-PK. Washington, DC: World Bank.

———. 2007l. *Panama: Support to the "Red de Oportunidades" Project.* Appraisal Document, Report 39193-PA. Washington, DC: World Bank.

———. 2007m. *Peru: Social Safety Nets in Peru.* Report 42093-Pe. Washington, DC: World Bank.

———. 2007n. *Productive Safety Nets Project (APL 1): Implementation Completion and Results Report.* Washington, DC: World Bank.

———. 2007o. *Social Assistance in Central Europe and the Baltic States.* Washington, DC: World Bank.

———. 2007p. "Social Protection for a Changing India." Draft. Washington, DC: World Bank.

———. 2007q. *Urban di Bao in China: Building on Success.* Washington, DC: World Bank.

———. 2007r. *World Development Indicators.* Washington, DC: World Bank.

———. 2008a. "Addressing the Food Crisis: The Need for Rapid and Coordinated Action." Background paper for the Group of Seven Ministers of Finance Meeting. Washington, DC: World Bank.

———. 2008b. *Beating the Odds: Sustaining Inclusion in a Growing Economy: A Mozambique Poverty, Gender, and Social Assessment,* 2 vols. Report 40048-MZ. Washington, DC: World Bank.

———. 2008c. "Guidance for Responses from the Human Development Sectors to Rising Food Prices." Social Protection Discussion Paper. Washington, DC: World Bank.

———. 2008d. "Rising Food Prices: Policy Options and World Bank Response." Background note for the Development Committee. Washington, DC: World Bank.

———. 2008e. *World Development Indicators 2008.* Washington, DC: World Bank.

———. Forthcoming. *Conditional Cash Transfers for Attacking Present and Future Poverty.* Washington, DC: World Bank.

Xu, K., David B. Evans, Patrick Kadama, Juliet Nabyonga, Peter Ogwang Ogwal, and Ana Mylena Aguilar. 2005. *The Elimination of User Fees in Uganda: Impact on Utilization and Catastrophic Health Expenditures.* Geneva: World Health Organization.

Yamano, Takashi. 2007. "The Long-Term Impacts of Orphanhood on Education Attainment and Land Inheritance among Adults in Rural Kenya." *Agricultural Economics* 37 (2–3): 141–49.

Yap, Yoon-Tien, Guilherme Sedlacek, and Peter Orazem. 2001. *Limiting Child Labor through Behavior-Based Income Transfers: An Experimental Evaluation of the PETI Program in Rural Brazil.* Washington, DC: World Bank.

Yapa, Lakshman. 1998. "The Poverty Discourse and the Poor in Sri Lanka." *Transactions of the Institute of British Geographers,* New Series, 23 (1): 95–115.

Yates, Jenny, Ros Cooper, and Jeremy Holland. 2006. "Social Protection and Health: Experiences in Uganda." *Development Policy Review* 24 (3): 339–56.

Yonekura, Hitoshi. 2005. "Institutional Reform in Indonesia's Food Security Sector: The Transformation of BULOG into a Public Corporation." *Developing Economies* 43-1 (March): 121–48.

Younger, Stephen D. 2003. "Benefits on the Margin: Observations on Marginal Benefit Incidence." *World Bank Economic Review* 17 (1): 89–106.

Zalimiene, Laimute. Forthcoming. *Program Implementation Matters for Targeting Performance—Evidence and Lessons from Eastern and Central Europe. Country Study: Lithuania.* Social Protection Discussion Paper. Washington, DC: World Bank.

Zaman, Hassan, Chris Delgado, Don Mitchell, and Ana Revenga. Forthcoming. "Rising Food Prices: Are There Right Policy Choices?" Development Outreach. Washington, DC: World Bank.

Zeidan, Abdu, Zakariya Mohammed, Ilham Bashier, and Bo Eriksson. 2004. "The Impact of User Fee Exemption on Service Utilization and Treatment Seeking Behaviour: The Case of Malaria in Sudan." *International Journal of Health Planning and Management.* 19 (S1): S95–S106.

Index

Page numbers followed by n. and a number refer to numbered notes. Page numbers followed by t or f refer to tables or figures, respectively. Page numbers in *italic* refer to boxed text.

Safety Nets Primer Papers and Other Resources

The World Bank Social Safety Nets Primer series is intended to provide practical resources for those engaged in the design and implementation of safety net programs around the world. New papers and translations are added regularly. All the papers and notes can be found at www.worldbank.org/safetynets.

Topic	Author	SPDP #	Translation	Note	Translation
Program Interventions					
Social Safety Nets in World Bank Lending and Analytic Work: FY2002 – 2007	Milazzo & Grosh	0810			
Social Safety Nets in World Bank Lending and Analytic Work: FY2002 – 2006	Milazzo & Grosh	0705			
Uninsured Risk and Asset Protection: Can Conditional Cash Transfer Programs Serve as Safety Nets?	de Janvry, Sadoulet, Solomon & Vakis	0604			
Examining Conditional Cash Transfer Programs: A Role for Increased Social Inclusion?	de la Brière & Rawlings	0603			
Community-Based Health Insurance and Social Protection Policy	Tabor	0503		✓	Rus, Sp
A New Approach to Social Assistance: Latin America's Experience with Conditional Cash Transfer Programs	Rawlings	0416		✓	Bah, Rus, Sp
Community-Based Social Services: Practical Advice Based upon Lessons from Outside the World Bank	McLeod	0327			
Redirecting Resources to Community Based Services: A Concept Paper	Fox & Götestam	0311			
Waivers and Exemptions for Health Services in Developing Countries	Bitrán & Giedion	0308	Fr, Sp	✓	Bah, Rus, Sp
Systemic Shocks and Social Protection: Role and Effectiveness of Public Works Programs	Subbarao	0302	Fr, Rus, Sp	✓	Bah, Rus, Sp
Evaluating the Impact of Conditional Cash Transfer Programs: Lessons from Latin America	Rawlings & Rubio	WB PR 3119			
Workshop on Conditional Cash Transfer Programs: Operational Experiences	Ayala	Final report on Web	Sp		
Ensuring Access to Essential Services: Demand-side Housing Subsidies	Katsura & Romanik	0232	Fr, Rus	✓	Bah, Rus, Sp
Food-based Safety Nets and Related Programs	Rogers & Coates	0225	Fr, Rus, Sp	✓	Bah, Rus, Sp
Subsidies as a Social Safety Net: Effectiveness and Challenges	Alderman	0224	Fr, Rus, Sp	✓	Bah, Rus, Sp
Assisting the Poor with Cash: Design and Implementation of Social Transfer Programs	Tabor	0223	Fr, Rus, Sp	✓	Bah, Rus, Sp
Social Services Delivery through Community-Based Projects	McLeod & Tovo	0118	Sp		

Topic	Author	SPDP #	Translation	Note	Translation
Themes					
Targeting					
Redistributing Income to the Poor and the Rich: Public Transfers in Latin America and the Caribbean	Lindert, Skoufias & Shapiro	0605			
Designing and Implementing Household Targeting Systems: Lessons from Latin America and the United States (an overview) Country Studies: Brazil, Chile, Colombia, Costa Rica, Mexico, and USA	Lindert & Castañeda with de la Brière, Fernandez, Hubert, Larrañaga, Orozco & Viquez	0526	Latin America & U.S. – Pr, Rus	✓	Rus, Sp
		0527	Brazil – Pr		
		0528	Chile – Sp*		
		0529	Colombia		
		0530	Costa Rica – Sp*		
		0531	Mexico – Sp*		
		0532	U.S. – Rus		
Targeting of Transfers in Developing Countries: Review of Lessons and Experience	Coady, Hoddinott & Grosh	Book	Rus, Sp	✓	Bah, Rus, Sp
Targeted Transfers in Poor Countries: Revisiting the Trade-Offs and Policy Options	Ravallion	0314	Sp	✓	Bah, Rus, Sp
Community-Based Targeting Mechanisms for Social Safety Nets	Conning & Kevane	0102	Sp		
Payment Mechanisms					
A Technology White Paper on Improving the Efficiency of Social Safety Net Program Delivery in Low Income Countries: An Introduction to Available and Emerging Mobile Technologies	Gallaher	0522			
Delivery Mechanisms of Cash Transfer Programs to the Poor in Bangladesh	Ahmed	0520			
Transferring Cash Benefits Through the Banking Sector in Colombia	Lafaurie & Leiva	0409	Sp		
Political Economy and Institutions					
Brazil's Bolsa Escola Program: The Role of Local Governance in Decentralized Implementation	de Janvry, Finan, Sadoulet, Nelson, Lindert, de la Brière & Lanjouw	0542			
A Lecture on the Political Economy of Targeted Safety Nets	Pritchett	0501		✓	Rus, Sp
Institutional Analysis Toolkit for Safety Net Interventions	Mathauer	0418		✓	Sp
Public Attitudes Matter:: A Conceptual Frame for Accounting for Political Economy in Safety Nets and Social Assistance Policies	Graham	0233	Fr, Rus	✓	Bah, Rus, Sp
Incentives and the Role of Institutions in the Provision of Social Safety Nets	de Neubourg	0226	Fr, Rus	✓	Bah, Rus, Sp

Topic	Author	SPDP #	Translation	Note	Translation
Miscellaneous					
Management Information Systems in Social Safety Net Programs: A Look at Accountability and Control Mechanisms	Baldeon & Arribas-Baños	0819			
Levels and Patterns of Safety Net Spending in Developing and Transition Countries	Weigand & Grosh	0817			
The Nuts and Bolts of Brazil's Bolsa Família Program: Implementing Conditional Cash Transfers in a Decentralized Context	Lindert, Linder, Hobbs & de la Brière	0709			
Reducing Error, Fraud and Corruption (EFC) in Social Protection Programs	Tesliuc & Milazzo	on Web**		✓	Rus
Benchmarking Government Provision of Social Safety Nets	Besley, Burgess & Rasul	0315	Rus		
Gender and Risk in the Design of Social Protection Interventions	Ezemenari, Chaudhury & Owens	0231	Fr		
Vulnerability and Poverty Measurement Issues for Public Policy	Duclos	0230	Fr, Sp		
Strengthening Public Safety Nets from the Bottom Up	Morduch & Sharma	0227	Fr, Rus, Sp	✓	Bah, Rus, Sp
Country Context					
Low Income					
Performance of Social Safety Net Programs in Uttar Pradesh	Ajwad	0714			
Food Aid and Food Security in the Short- and Long Run: Country Experience from Asia and sub-Saharan Africa	del Ninno, Dorosh & Subbarao	0538			
Household's Vulnerability to Shocks in Zambia	Del Ninno & Marini	0536			
Mitigating Social Risks in Kyrgyz Republic	Tesliuc	0408			
Testing Vietnam's Public Safety Net	van de Walle	0319			
What Role for Safety Net Transfers in Very Low Income Countries?	Subbarao & Smith	0301	Fr, Rus, Sp	✓	Bah, Rus, Sp
Transition					
Safety Nets in Transition Economies: A Primer	Fox	0306	Fr	✓	Bah, Rus, Sp
Safety Nets in Transition Economies: Toward a Reform Strategy	Andrews & Ringold	9914			
OECD					
Social Safety Nets and Targeted Social Assistance: Lessons from the European Experience	de Neubourg, Castonguay & Roelen	0718			
Social Safety Nets in OECD Countries	Tesliuc	On Web**		✓	
Crisis					
Guidance for Responses from the Human Development Sectors to Rising Food Prices	Grosh, del Ninno & Tesliuc	0818			

Topic	Author	SPDP #	Translation	Note	Translation
Social Safety Nets in Response to Crisis: Lessons and Guidelines from Asia and Latin America	Blomquist, Verhoeven, Cordoba, Bouillon & Moser	Draft on Web	Sp		

Post-conflict

Topic	Author	SPDP #	Translation	Note	Translation
Living in Limbo: Conflict Induced Displacement in Europe and Central Asia	Holtzman & Nezam	Book			
Emerging from Ethnic Conflict: Challenges for Social Protection Design in Transition Countries	Bodewig	0229	Rus		

Special Vulnerable Groups

Topic	Author	SPDP #	Translation	Note	Translation
Aging and Poverty in Africa and the Role of Social Pensions	Subbarao & Kakwani	0521		✓	Rus, Sp
Disability and Social Safety Nets in Developing Countries	Mitra	0509		✓	Rus, Sp
The OVC Toolkit for SSA: A Toolkit on How to Support Orphans and Other Vulnerable Children (OVC) in Sub-Saharan Africa	Tovo, Prywes, Kielland, Gibbons & Saito	On Web**		✓	Rus, Sp
Costs of Projects for Orphans and Other Vulnerable Children: Case Studies in Eritrea and Benin	Prywes, Coury, Fesseha, Hounsounou & Kielland	0414		✓	Bah, Rus, Sp
Supporting and Expanding Community-Based HIV/AIDS Prevention and Care Responses: A Report on Save the Children (US) Malawi COPE Project	Hunter	0211			
World Vision's Experience Working with HIV/AIDS Orphans in Uganda 1990-1995	Muwonge	0210			
Long-Term Welfare and Investment Impact of AIDS-Related Changes in Family Composition: Evidence from Uganda	Deininger, Crommelynck & Kempaka	0207			
Orphans and Other Vulnerable Children: What Role for Social Protection?	Levine (ed)	0126			
Reaching Out to Africa's Orphans: A Framework for Public Action	Subbarao & Coury	Book		✓	Rus, Sp
Social Protection of Africa's Orphans and Vulnerable Children Issues and Good Practice Program Options	Subbarao, Mattimore & Plangemann	AFR WP 22909			

NOTE: SPDP # refers to the Social Protection Discussion Paper number, and the first two digits indicate the year of publication. Translations available where indicated: Sp (Spanish), Fr (French), Pr (Portuguese), Rus (Russian), Bah (Bahasa – Indonesian).

*Only available in language indicated.

**Only a primer note is available.

www.ingramcontent.com/pod-product-compliance
Lightning Source LLC
Chambersburg PA
CBHW081425270326
41932CB00019B/3097